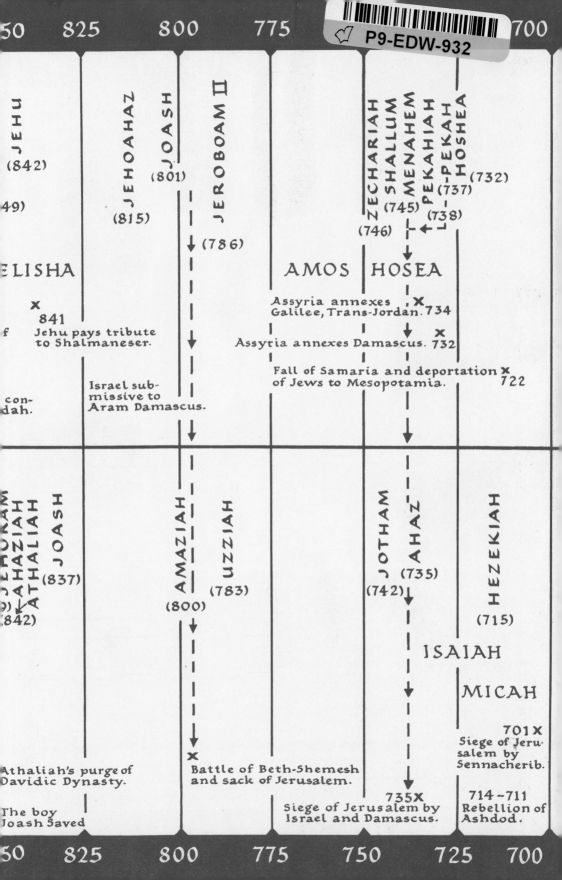

JEHU
(842)

49)

JEHOAHAZ
(815)

JOASH
(801)

JEROBOAM II
(786)

ZECHARIAH
(746)

SHALLUM
(745)

MENAHEM
(745)

PEKAHIAH
(738)

L-PEKAH
(737)

HOSHEA
(732)

ELISHA

AMOS | HOSEA

x
841
Jehu pays tribute
to Shalmaneser.

Assyria annexes
Galilee, Trans-Jordan. 734 x

con-
dah.

Israel sub-
missive to
Aram Damascus.

Assyria annexes Damascus. 732 x

Fall of Samaria and deportation x
of Jews to Mesopotamia.   722

JEHORAM
AHAZIAH
ATHALIAH
JOASH
(837)

9)
842)

AMAZIAH
(800)

UZZIAH
(783)

JOTHAM
(742)

AHAZ
(735)

HEZEKIAH
(715)

ISAIAH

MICAH

701 x
Siege of Jeru-
salem by
Sennacherib.

Athaliah's purge of
Davidic Dynasty.

Battle of Beth-Shemesh
and sack of Jerusalem.

735 x

714~711
Rebellion of
Ashdod.

The boy
Joash Saved

Siege of Jerusalem by
Israel and Damascus.

A LIGHT TO THE NATIONS

HARPER & ROW, PUBLISHERS
NEW YORK, EVANSTON, AND LONDON

A LIGHT TO
THE NATIONS

AN INTRODUCTION TO THE OLD TESTAMENT

NORMAN K. GOTTWALD

PROFESSOR OF OLD TESTAMENT

ANDOVER NEWTON THEOLOGICAL SCHOOL

It is too light a thing that you should be my servant
  to raise up the tribes of Jacob
  and to restore the preserved of Israel;
I will give you as a light to the nations,
  that my salvation may reach to the end of the earth
                                                    —Isaiah 49:6

TO BARBARA

TO BARBARA

CONTENTS

X.   THE DECLINE OF JUDAH

XI.   THE PEOPLE IN EXILE

XII. RECONSTRUCTION UNDER THE PERSIANS

XIII. RECONSTRUCTION UNDER THE HELLENISTS

MAPS

CHARTS

ILLUSTRATIONS

ABBREVIATIONS

ANET   *Ancient Near Eastern Texts Relating to the Old Testament* (J. B. Pritchard, ed.), Princeton University Press, 2nd rev. ed., 1955

ASV   American Standard Version of the Bible

CB   The Cambridge Bible

DOTT   *Documents from Old Testament Times* (D. Winton Thomas, ed.), Thomas Nelson and Sons, 1958

ERV   English Revised Version of the Bible

IB   The Interpreter's Bible

ICC   The International Critical Commentary

KJV   King James or Authorized Version of the Bible

LXX   Septuagint

MT   Masoretic Text of the Old Testament

NCB   The New Century Bible

RSV   Revised Standard Version of the Bible

SBT   Studies in Biblical Theology

WC   Westminster Commentaries

PREFACE

This book presents the Hebrew-Jewish faith in its historical continuity, with special attention to the literature of the Old Testament. It is neither a technical introduction to the books of the Hebrew Bible, nor a history of Israel, nor a theology of the Old Testament. It is rather a synthesis of the interests and values of all three. In form it is nearest to a literary history, but its aim is broadly cultural and specifically theological. Throughout there has been an attempt to integrate the literature, history, and religion, and to point up connections between the faith of Israel and that of the later synagogue and church.

In a work of this scope, no scholar is able to study in detail each of the subjects treated. He must rely on the work of his predecessors and contemporaries. On several issues, such as the route of the Exodus, the marriage of the prophet Hosea, the Immanuel sign of Isaiah, and the authorship and purpose of Lamentations—to name but a few —I have followed minority viewpoints. In every case, however, personal opinion has been placed within the context of wider scholarly judgment.

In addition to incalculable indebtedness to Old Testament scholars the world over, I am particularly grateful to Professor James Muilenburg of Union Theological Seminary, New York City, whose guidance in the linguistic, historical, and theological maze of Old Testament study I have come to appreciate increasingly with the passage of years. His gifts in communicating his enthusiasm for the Hebrew Bible and his sense of sound method, without creating rigid disciples, are as remarkable as they are rare. His insights will be found on the following pages; of some I am pointedly aware, while others have doubtless become a part of my larger thought. His reading of parts of the manuscript is acknowledged with appreciation. To Professor Samuel Terrien of Union Theological Seminary I am indebted for stimulating lectures on Jeremiah and Job, and to Professor Arthur Jeffery of Columbia University for his direction amid the intricacies of the canon and text of the Old Testament. Professor James F. Ross of Dartmouth College read the entire manuscript and made a number of suggestions as to style, organization, and content. His comments on canon and text were especially valuable. Professor Cyrus H. Gordon of Brandeis University gave gracious advice concerning editions of the nonbiblical texts that appear in the appendix.

If adequate concern has been shown for the larger cultural and sociological setting of the religion of Israel, it is in large measure due to the stimulus of Professor Horace L. Friess and Mrs. Marguerite Block of Columbia University, whose course on the history of religions—submitted to originally as a requirement—has proven one of the lasting influences in my thought. It was from them that I learned the intellectual discipline of taking pains to understand religious institutions and ideas alien to my own experience and preference.

My wife's contributions to the book go far beyond her many hours of secretarial labor; her sharp eye and questioning mind have greatly improved the organization, logic, and style. I am appreciative of the same service performed by my students at Columbia University and Andover Newton Theological School who have heard many of these chapters in lecture form. In particular I am indebted to Mr. J. Wright Williamson for his assistance in preparing the indexes.

Acknowledgment is due to the publishers of *Interpretation; A Journal of Bible and Theology* for permission to reproduce portions of my article "Studia Biblica: Lamentations," IX, No. 3 (1955), and to the Clarendon Press, Oxford, for permission to reproduce the chart on Pentateuchal authorship from H. H. Rowley, ed., *The Old Testament and Modern Study*, 1950. To my former colleague Paul S. Minear goes credit for the title of Chapter I which appears as the heading of Part I in his *Eyes of Faith*, Westminster, 1946. Individuals and museums have coöperated in providing photographs. Credits will be found in the list of illustrations. Similarly, I am grateful to publishers for permission to reprint the nonbiblical texts. Proper acknowledgments are given with each translation.

Biblical quotations are for the most part taken from the Revised Standard Version of the Bible, but I have not hesitated to make my own translation whenever a specific purpose is better served. Footnoting has been held to a minimum. The annotated bibliography at the end of the book, organized by chapters and concluding with a list of commentaries and special studies on biblical books, not only provides students with material for independent inquiry, but indicates the nature and extent of my dependence on biblical scholarship recorded in the English language. Specialists will be aware of my debt to foreign research, even beyond that indicated in the footnotes; but it did not seem wise to burden the bibliography with titles unintelligible to a majority of the users of this text.

Near Eastern dates before 1500 B.C. are given according to the so-called lower chronology. For the monarchy of Israel I have followed the chronology of W. F. Albright, primarily because it is the one most widely referred to in recent reference works, but I am not unmindful of the problems or of the reputable alternative schemes of men such as Joachim Begrich and Edwin H. Thiele. The names of the kings of Judah and Israel constitute a special problem. Not only do five of the names appear in both kingdoms, but as many as twelve of the rulers have variant names. Frequently it is a matter of variant spellings of the same name in abbreviated and full forms. In other cases, however, when a king ascended the throne he adopted or was given a new name. The variant spellings and names are used rather indiscriminately in the Hebrew text and consequently also in the English translations. In order to avoid cluttering the endpaper charts, I have confined the variants to the list of kings of the divided monarchy which appears as Chart 8, p. 538.

It is my conviction from experience that the Old Testament can only be understood in an overarching historical framework. Accordingly, I have provided charts of the historical periods in the ancient Near East and of the kings and prophets of Israel, as well as a series of period maps of the Near East and Palestine. Through the united kingdom the history is interspersed with treatment of the literature and religion, but beginning with the divided monarchy each chapter is prefaced with a historical sketch. By reading these sections continuously, with close reference to the maps, the student will gain a panoramic view of biblical history from 922 to 63 B.C.

As with all scientific disciplines, biblical study has developed its own jargon. To have avoided the technical terms in every case or to have attempted to explain them at length in the text would have inflated the work unduly. In the glossary, therefore, I have made a point of including the technical terminology of Old Testament study, as well as words likely to be confused because of their several meanings or because of their similarity in sound.

I shall be more than satisfied with the results of this volume if its readers come to a fuller appreciation of their biblical heritage, and if, from among their company, a significant few are inspired to dedicate their lives to biblical science.

N. K. G.

Newton Centre, Massachusetts
February, 1959

✤ 1 ✤

ANGLE OF VISION

Adequate understanding of the Old Testament is achieved only by imaginative and disciplined study. Many a teacher has learned how fruitless it is to place in the hands of a novice a copy of the Old Testament, accompanied only by vague admonitions to read. Piecemeal clarification of difficult passages, while temporarily helpful, fails for lack of a larger context. What is needed is a unitary approach, a reasonably systematic and inclusive preparation that lays foundations of the sort indispensable to progress in any field of human knowledge. We have too long allowed ourselves to think that the student can gain a working knowledge of the Old Testament through sermons and random sampling of popular passages. It is regrettably true that the very religions that prize the Old Testament as Scripture are largely failing to teach their adherents its contents, to say nothing of its over-all meanings. The deficiency cannot be made up by gimmicks and platitudes, nor even by the good intentions of reading through the Bible. Insatiable curiosity must be accompanied by sound literary and historical method and crowned by theological insight.

OBSTACLES

At the start let us frankly consider the major obstacles to an understanding of the Old Testament. On even slight acquaintance with the Hebrew Bible we are impressed by its *vastness and diversity*. To be sure, in comparison with some of the Far Eastern scriptures its bulk is negligible. But in our own literary milieu the thousand tightly packed

1

pages of the typical Old Testament translation loom as a sizable chore in reading. Yet the vastness cannot be registered by pagination or format alone. It is the variety of the separate books: their chronological span, their motley literary types, and their fluctuating viewpoints that create the most bewildering barriers to the inexperienced. Unless the student can be led through this maze one step at a time, supplied with signposts and shown techniques of study applicable at once, in however limited a degree, he is likely to be permanently thwarted in his desire to unlock the Old Testament. Even the strongest motivation cannot persist in the face of repeated frustrations.

We can more fully appreciate the sheer sweep of the Old Testament if we realize that the component materials were written over a period from about 1200 to 100 B.C. If we momentarily transpose that time span into our own culture it would compare with the period from Charlemagne to the First World War, and would embrace English literature from Beowulf to G. B. Shaw! Similarly, the Old Testament is an anthology of writings to which many men have contributed during a thousand-year span. The typical college student presented with a volume of English literature well stocked with Chaucer, Spenser, Donne, Milton, Thackeray, Browning, and with no other help, is in no worse plight than the student of the Old Testament left to his own devices. Indeed the latter is at a greater loss, for the Old Testament is not in his native language and it speaks to him out of a greater antiquity and from a stranger culture. Try though we may to find some short cut, we are continually thrown back upon the fascinating but baffling kaleidoscope of literary, historical, and religious diversity with which we must come to terms before the true unity of the Old Testament can be appreciated.

We have hinted at a second factor of great importance in our study and that is the *remoteness* of the biblical world-view. Not only does a chasm in time separate us from the Old Testament, but equally a great chasm in viewpoint. The world-view, composed of the implicit and often unconscious presuppositions that underlie cultures, is for us widely different from that of the Hebrews. It would not be fair to overstate the contrast. We are after all debtors to the Hebrew tradition in a way not true, for example, of Hindu or Buddhist strains of thought. Nevertheless the line of descent from our Hebrew forebears to ourselves is not direct but devious and subtle. Without previous acquaintance and orientation, we cannot expect to have the same facility with

Hebrew categories and terminology that we might have in approaching a modern novel. The Old Testament inevitably challenges our world-view because it presents us with another.

Can we be more precise in defining the remoteness of the Old Testament? What basic attitudes separate us from its writers? On the one side there is our modern attachment to *philosophical* and *scientific* pursuits. It cannot be too vigorously asserted that, in common with all ancient Oriental culture, the Old Testament is strictly speaking prescientific and nonphilosophical. In anything like their limited and proper senses, science and philosophy simply do not appear in the Bible. There is no endeavor to relate the phenomena of the natural and human worlds to one another immanently (as in the natural and social sciences), nor is ultimate reality sought through the exercise of reason or the categories of logic (as in philosophy). It would be tempting on such grounds to relegate the Old Testament to the realm of antiquarian interest and to concede its irrelevance for us. Actually it is only when a rather sharp distinction is drawn between the realm of discourse in which the Old Testament moves and modern philosophical and scientific realms that one can read the ancient literature with an approach to objectivity, i.e., in terms of the intention of the original writers. In other words, it is in the interest of true scientific method to acknowledge the absence of science and philosophy as formative factors in the Old Testament world. Of course the Old Testament is concerned about final questions, but the perspective of the ancient Jews cannot be called "philosophical."

But the most incisive evidence of the remoteness of the Hebrew Bible is not in what it lacks but in what it contains: a thoroughly *theocentric view of life.* It has been said that the subject of the Old Testament is God—and so it is. But we must know what such a proposition means. The God of the Old Testament is not mainly an object of human reason, though it is assumed that the will of God can be known by man. He does not figure as the subject of religious and philosophical debate, for rather than being argued, he is assumed The Old Testament regards God as the unconditioned reality who is thoroughly personal, the source of all natural and human life. But the term "source" and even such words as "Creator" and "Sustainer" are too static to express the Hebrew sense of God's activity among men. Above all, that which distinguishes the Hebrew deity is his *entering into relation with man,* who as a created being is subordinate to God. All "meaning" and "value" (neither term has a Hebrew equivalent) attached to human life is derivative meaning and dependent value.

To say that the Old Testament is theocentric is not, however, to pose a sharp antithesis to anthropocentric thought as though God and man are exclusive alternatives. God and man are neither confused in identity nor separated by essential hostility. The Old Testament insists that in finding God (or in being found by him) man finds himself. The wholeness of human life is possible only in fellowship with its ground and source. The Old Testament displays both a vertical dimension (the affirmation of the divine) and a horizontal dimension (the affirmation of the world). At the same time, these are not truths deducible from nature or the self. They are "given" and are therefore inescapable elements of the human environment—in fact the decisive elements. Our initial response to this attitude may be little more than amused condescension or amazed curiosity, but unless we seek to understand the Old Testament on its own conditions we will either dismiss it as irrational nonsense, venerate it as divinely approved mystification, or simply read our own ideas into it.

Another obstacle to overcome in serious study of the Old Testament is its *sacredness*. The scriptural status of the Old Testament for Jew and Christian is likely to make critical discrimination difficult at first, if not actually prevent it altogether for some students. Moreover, its sanctity is a stumbling block for believer and unbeliever alike through the illusion that acquaintance is knowledge. Too many of the devoutly religious and the devoutly irreligious overestimate their biblical knowledge. Familiar wording and sketchily remembered stories are offered as the equivalent of basic understanding. If what we have attempted to say is true, the Old Testament is a much more complex book than most people realize.

Let us be clear. It is not suggested that in order to understand the Old Testament without prejudice ideally one must surrender allegiance to Judaism or Christianity. Such a notion is to be rejected as an instance of false objectivity. No one asks that the sociologist withdraw from society or that the historian of American life be an alien. What we do ask is the development of a critical faculty, the willingness to raise questions, to make discriminations, to reëvaluate tradition.

In the end, the student's religious appreciation of the Old Testament stands to benefit by careful critical study but in the process there may be growing pains. For those who have developed emotional and psychological aversions to traditional religion, there will be similar adjustments. Negativism will have to give way to a sympathetic attitude. It is in just such inner tensions, in the constant formulation and reformulation of concepts and attitudes, that true learning takes place. We thus recapitulate in our own study what the ancient Hebrew knew well: that all knowledge becomes significant precisely at that point where it calls for responsible decision. In the Hebrew world religious poses have no place; the elemental realities of life are boldly treated. Since the whole of life is perceived religiously, there is no separate sphere labeled "religion." With unerring acumen the Old Testament invites us to penetrate the form of religion to its substance.

PERSPECTIVES

It is well to review a number of approaches to the Old Testament, to examine the strengths and weaknesses of each, and to sketch in broad outline the paths to be followed in this study. It will readily be seen that the writer is more sympathetic toward some approaches than toward others, yet he would concede at once that from each he has learned something of lasting value.

We may approach the Old Testament as *literature*. The emphasis will likely be upon the aesthetic excellence of classic passages: the patriarchal narratives of Genesis, the poetry of Psalms and Job. We may speedily agree that close and accurate analysis of the literary genius of the Old Testament is an indispensable part of critical study. In actual practice, however, literary studies of the Old Testament have too frequently drawn superficial lines of connection between Hebrew and English literature to the virtual exclusion of the unique history, culture, and religious perspective of the former. One of the abler exponents of the literary method is Mary Ellen Chase. Yet when she compares Amos to Milton, Hosea to A. E. Housman, and Second Isaiah to Shelley, we question the weight placed upon technical and temperamental similarities at the expense of the radically different "world-views" entertained by the Hebrews and the British men of letters. The position of the Hebrew prophet in his own cultural and religious context was so unlike even that of the ecclesiastical Milton that little seems to be gained by the parallels and much can be obscured.

It is not our intent to deny the greatness of the Hebrew literature, but recognition of its beauty and grandeur is best served by wariness of literary dilettantism. The ablest literary critics of the Bible are those who relate the written materials to the mind set and culture of the author and his age. The Hebrew artistic forms were fashioned in the service of rigorous religious proclamation. There is a severity and naked simplicity in poetry and narrative that reflect the iconoclasm of the first commandment: "Thou shalt have no other gods before me!" The literary vehicle could never become an end in itself. The Old Testament is true to the canons of art in that it shares with all great creative works of man a convincing self-forgetfulness, a triumph of content over form. It was, for the most part, not sullied by the fabrication and straining after effect typical of decadent periods of culture. The Hebrew seldom has to search for something to say, for an occasion or opportunity to display his art. The ensuing study will give full attention to the literary forms and the relation between form and content, but the literary approach must be subordinate if we are to realize the aims of the writers who, unlike classical authors, were not greatly concerned with rhetoric.

We may approach the Old Testament as a *cultural tradition*. In so doing we turn our attention to the nature and extent of the Old Testament contribution to our own civilization. Although everyone agrees that the influence is enormous, there are surprisingly few studies and all fall short of the exhaustive, nearly encyclopedic scope such treatments would have to approximate if justice were to be done to the subject.

It is axiomatic that no educated person can understand his own world who does not have at least a speaking acquaintance with the Old Testament. Yet we face a special danger at this point: the temptation to engage in analysis of Western culture instead of study of the Bible. It may be assumed that courses in history and sociology and literature have given us a reasonably comprehensive picture of the Western way of life. This is no place to analyze it once again, even in summary fashion. We must strike at the heart of the matter: the Hebrew literature itself, how it arose, the history it reflects, the faith it enshrines. Nevertheless, the great value of a cultural perspective is its constant reminder that Old Testament study can never be strictly "academic," any more than study of the Greco-Roman world can proceed on purely antiquarian grounds. When we read Genesis and

Isaiah, as when we ponder Plato and Sophocles, we are contemplating our own history—and no one reviews his ancestry with total detachment. The reader of the Hebrew Bible will often be happily surprised to discover the origin of turns of phrase or figures of speech that have become common coinage in his own language: Job's "as the sparks fly upward" (5:7), "you are the people" (12:2), "when the morning stars sang together" (38:7); or Daniel's god with feet of clay (2:33–45), the handwriting on the wall (5:5), and "the Law of the Medes and Persians" (6:8,12). Such discoveries rival the delight and astonishment of meeting old friends far from home. It is well then that the remoteness of the Old Testament should not be overstated; it is still our heritage and therein is an immediate basis for our interest.

We may approach the Old Testament as *inerrant Scripture*. When the Bible is so regarded it is thought of as a divinely inspired oracular utterance, of equal authority and importance in all its parts and representing a transcript of the will of God. The usual image pictures God as one who dictates while the various writers function as his scribes. While the "secretaries" may be allowed considerable freedom in the choice of words, their authentic individuality and their organic connection with a history and culture are usually forgotten, if not in effect denied. Although formulated in the interest of a vital religious faith, this conceptual framework is really static and rationalistic. It makes of the Old Testament a book of dogma, independent of circumstance and only accidentally related to a particular people.

It may be pointed out that the theory of verbal inspiration is seldom followed rigorously by its adherents, and that there is much "picking and choosing" motivated for the Jew by the reinterpretations of the Talmud and for the Christian by the norm of Christ, and also for both by a tacit recognition of what is practical and impractical. Still it persists as the conceptual framework for piety. Such a view, abandoned by innumerable Jews and Christians, continues to be advocated by conservative spokesmen. Its supporters are firm in maintaining that the Bible contains no errors, moral blemishes, or trivialities. On the surface such an attitude would seem to honor the Bible but it is a special pleading that depreciates the human elements in order to exalt its divine origin. Those who categorically reject the premises and conclusions of verbal inspiration must not be cast in the role of the devil's advocate, for rather than disparaging the Bible they seek the overthrow of a theory about the Bible that is historically untenable and religiously deceptive. This last point must be amplified.

The most telling objection to the view of biblical inerrancy is not so much its seeming backwardness and incredibility. The main defect in verbal inspiration is that it does not understand the nature of the faith it is trying so desperately to preserve. When the vivid literary, historical, and religious flux of the Old Testament is obscured by a static doctrine of dictation, for which the writings themselves offer little or no evidence, then the true nature of the religion is changed into something quite unrecognizable. The living religious experience of the Hebrew is stultified into dogma. Faith is no longer a relation to God but a subscribing to doctrine and ritual. And finally, this position verges on bibliolatry, worship of the Bible itself, which is so at variance with the condemnation of idolatry intrinsic to Judaism and Christianity. It ought to be insisted that a view of verbal inspiration, insofar as it refuses to acknowledge the true humanity of the Old Testament (including its relativity in time and space), sets up a deity alongside the one true God who, according to the whole biblical tradition, cannot be equated with or confined to holy writings.

We may approach the Old Testament as a *historical and cultural deposit*. This manner of studying the Hebrew Bible waxed in our culture in proportion to the waning of the dogmatic attitude. The basic tool of this approach is the so-called critical method. The term "critical" should be understood in accord with its root meaning: "to divide, to make distinctions, to discriminate." Our language has witnessed the debasing of the word "critical" until it is often equated with destructive negativism. At the start the record should be set straight: the critical method does not aim to destroy but to understand. In the course of investigation, some cherished beliefs may be toppled and others may be confirmed. The results can never be assured in advance since genuine critical method is not interested either in proving or disproving tradition but only in evaluating it. Naturally, as with all attempts at objectivity, this is an ideal. We often suspect that particular critics have been overly prejudiced either by their radicalism or their conservatism. Yet the continuing course of critical study may in the end cancel out the extremes of individual critics. As one examines the great critics of the past he notes their differences in temperament and background, in philosophical and religious viewpoint. In particular eras biblical criticism has been powerfully influenced by prevailing philosophies (e.g., rationalism in the eighteenth century and Hegelianism in the nineteenth), but the critical movement as a whole cannot be stigmatized as the product of one school of thought.

It can be argued that the only presupposition common to all Old Testament critics is the necessity of questioning tradition, of examining a religious literature as we would examine any other writings in order to determine authorship, date, sources, and historical background. This at once sounds the death knell for verbal inspiration, but beyond that it does not dictate conclusions as to the basic philosophical or religious framework through which the Old Testament should be viewed. The framework is important, but at the level of critical study it is possible for men operating from different worldviews to agree on problems such as the sections of the book of Isaiah written by the eighth-century prophet or the date to be ascribed to the earliest strand of the Pentateuch. It must be emphasized at the same time that critical study is not a substitute for the kind of total valuations provided by philosophy and religion.

The emphasis upon the biblical literature in its own context led inescapably to a corresponding scrutiny of Hebrew history and culture. The Hebrews were not simply passive instruments of deity, but their tumultuous history and their unique spirit were expressed in all they wrote. Criticism of the Old Testament, awakened by the Renaissance, is sometimes said to have begun in 1753 when Jean Astruc, French court physician, supplied the clue to unraveling the sources of the Pentateuch. We may accept this date as marking the beginning of a rapidly accumulating body of knowledge. The real results appear from that date onward. They were presented systematically in the *Introduction to the Old Testament* (1780–1783) by J. G. Eichhorn. His was the first of a long line of introductions to the Old Testament that presented the summary results of intensive studies into separate books and sources. For a century and more the Old Testament books were analyzed in detail and exhaustive theories of authorship and source were developed. The literature was spotted along a time line and a majority of the Old Testament books were dated with confidence. The climax of this process was the brilliant work of Julius Wellhausen who in his *Prolegomena to the History of Israel* (1883) gave lucid and compelling expression to the "assured results" of a century of study. The great gain of this critical scrutiny was not only that it analyzed the literature with precision but that it showed how the writings of the Old Testament issued out of the peculiar history of the Jewish people.

The cultural aspect has received its due only in the twentieth century. There was an understandable tendency in the first flush of critical study to regard the Old Testament in a somewhat bookish and academic way, to think of the Hebrew writers as we would regard modern authors, especially professors or graduate students engaged in research. When the critics discovered that books were composite (written by more than one person) they tended to think of composition as editorial patchwork, a process that has been dubbed the "scissors and paste" method. The relation of the literature to the history was not taken quite seriously enough, perhaps because the ancient Semitic world was not as fully unveiled to the nineteenth century as it is to the twentieth. Although Wellhausen and his predecessors saw in principle the connection of Israel with its neighbors, it was not until the phenomenal recoveries of Sumerian, Hittite, Hurrian, and Canaanite civilizations—as well as the further elucidation of the Egyptian and Assyro-Babylonian cultures—that the impact of the relation was fully felt.

If for convenience we think of Astruc as the initiator of the first phase of critical Old Testament study, we should perhaps consider Hermann Gunkel the stimulant in the second. At the opening of this century, Gunkel's studies in the early epics pointed out the formative influence of oral tradition and the folk imagination of Israel. He made it clear that it was insufficient to think solely in terms of literary methods or the historical life of Israel. One must take into account the cultural situation in its broadest sense, including the psychology and sociology of a people: the modes of their thinking and the forms of their social existence. Gunkel opened up a whole area of study, but the aspect in which he excelled was the description of the literary types and their "situation in life." He made tenable the theory of "community authorship." Gunkel applied his theories with particular brilliance to the narratives of Genesis and to the Psalms. Now for the first time the psychological realism and the anonymity of Israelite literature forced their way through the academic rigidity of earlier criticism. Subsequently his insights have been elaborated and applied throughout the Old Testament.

Typical of the new phase of Old Testament study is Johannes Pedersen whose two-volume *Israel: Its Life and Culture* (1926, 1940) is an engrossing study of the Hebrew mentality both in its concreteness and its vividness. Accompanying this greater emphasis upon the cultural has been a renewal of the debate over the extent to which the Hebrews borrowed from their neighbors. The discussion is not so much with respect to particular elements as it was in the nineteenth century (e.g., the creation story, the flood story, etc.). Now it centers on the fundamental pattern of Hebrew life and faith. The so-called Myth and Ritual School, British in origin but most ardently supported by Scandinavians, contends that the cyclical scheme of the Near East at large was adopted by the Hebrews and that what the earlier Wellhausian criticism saw as "lay religion" or prophetic judgment on priestly religion must now be thought of as ritualistic in its origin and function. The revival of interest in the cultic life of Israel has been one notable concomitant of the new emphases.

So the study of the Old Testament has entered upon exciting days. At mid-century the situation is in flux. There are convinced literary critics who hew to the line of Wellhausen, admitting little or no validity to the more recent trends. There are equally convinced "tradition-historians" (a term for those who emphasize the oral tradition and question the overprecise dating of Wellhausen). The great bulk of scholars fall somewhere in between. They are unimpressed by the either/or struggle of the fanatical elements in both wings. They accept with gratitude the work of the earlier historical and literary stages of investigation, but they do not canonize any critic, including Wellhausen. The criticisms based upon the social and psychological disciplines are acknowledged as justified at many points. Few thoughtful students of the Old Testament are willing to renounce the hard-won gains of nineteenth-century criticism, but they gladly welcome correction. Oral tradition and cultic recitation, folk psychology and sociology, all have their places as supplements to the older canons of literary and historical criticism. But of course a synthesis is more easily held as an ideal than worked out in practice. The truth is that constructive scholarship, which must have time to reflect and assimilate, has not been able to keep pace with the great mass of data that analytical scholarship has placed at our disposal. We see the parts and the several aspects of the Old Testament far better than we see the whole. In these formative and crucial days it is perhaps the better part of wisdom not to force a synthesis, but it is equally important not to impede advance through timidity or scholarly dogmatism.

We may approach the Old Testament as the *record of a religious encounter*. We have earlier observed that the basic presupposition of the Hebrew Bible is theocentric. God is at the center and human life is derivative in existence and value. If the woof of the Old Testament writings is the sturdy virile historical life of the Hebrew people, then its warp is the experience of a history-creating and a history-controlling God who brought the Israelite people into existence to serve his purposes. The decisive ethos of the Old Testament is not religious in some vague or sentimental fashion, but it is radically religious in that all self-understanding begins with knowledge of God. The assertion of the Calvinist catechism that "the chief end of man is to glorify God and to enjoy him forever" is a page from the Hebrew book, with the provision that the dimension "forever" developed rather late in Old Testament times.

How are we to distinguish this religious approach to the Old Testament from what we have earlier described as belief in its inerrancy? Once having set aside the notion of a God who speaks oracular words to passive recorders, would it not be wise to set aside entirely the religious dimension and rest content with the historical and cultural? This problem really has two aspects, and they must be sharply distinguished.

First, the religious dimension may be understood simply as belonging to the historical and cultural plane. The story of the Hebrews and their faith in God is a phenomenon in the history of religion. Indeed, it is the cardinal feature of the Hebrews, without which they possess little distinction. It would be an instance of gross injustice to treat the Old Testament without reference to its religious convictions. One might just as well essay to evaluate the Greeks without considering philosophy and art or the Romans without regard for law and engineering. So far it is a matter of logic.

But objectivity must be balanced by empathy. The reader of the Old Testament must seek to project himself into the world of the Hebrews and think their thoughts after them. In this role he is not the critic but the sympathetic observer who in his identification with his material becomes well-nigh a participant. Often this will involve reckoning with attitudes and ideas foreign and obnoxious to himself (e.g., holy war, animal sacrifice, oracles by lot). Insofar as possible he must suspend judgment in order to see the religion as it was experienced by its devotees. As historian, there are no value judgments passed and the selfhood of the observer does not feel called into decision or action by what he reads. Thus one might study the religion of the Hebrews, the Babylonians, the Hindus, the Aztecs and appreciate them all (which in this context means to see how they function and what they meant to their adherents) without believing in any of them as a viable contemporary faith. This is why we may properly summon any serious student of the Old Testament to examine the religion of which it speaks without intruding upon that person's freedom to believe what he will. Historical study of religion does not necessarily lead to religious commitment nor does it necessarily lead away from it. Religious faith belongs to another realm; it may be clarified by historical study of religion but it rises elsewhere: from the experience of the responsible self as to the meaning of history.

In spite of all that has been said about objectivity and detachment in studying the Old Testament (and the fight for such openness must never cease, both against totalitarian forces without and prejudice within), the fact is that value judgments are inescapable. We all come to the Old Testament with some ultimate perspective, even if it is to deny the ultimacy of the Hebrew claim. It is not only the student who belongs to one of the traditional religions who possesses presuppositions. His may be more obvious and, because the Old Testament is Scripture to him, he may have greater initial difficulty in striking off the shackles of tradition. But the agnostic, the naturalist, the humanist, the pantheist (and these terms may be taken to refer not so much to clearly distinguished, hard and fast groups as to the various options to traditional religion)—each has his own conceptual framework within which he views the common subject matter.

Why is so much being made of what might be called man's inveterate disposition to commitment? It is neither to heap unreserved praise upon objectivity or commitment but to realize that we each live in a tension between the two factors as they contend and strike a balance of power. In actual practice we sometimes read our Old Testament solely to revel in the sheer variety and grandeur of its experience of life. We read the bloodthirsty cries of the Song of Deborah not because they express anything native to our own belief but because we are thrust emphatically into the experience of a fellow human. Objectivity thus construed does not mean cold detachment but willingness and ability to appreciate a quality of experience that remains in the last analysis alien to us.

But it is to be doubted that anyone has ever read the Hebrew Bible for any length of time—be he critic, poet, or ordinary student—without being confronted by the ultimate questions that leap out of the ancient history to address present history. It is only our sophistication that leads us to think we can ever dispense with the decisive question of faith and unfaith. How does this differ from the dogmatic approach? The latter calls us to a closed tradition and flirts perilously with intellectual annihilation. The former, in keeping with the Old Testament's viewpoint, calls us to give ourselves wholly to God in trust that involves assent but is focused on present responsibility rather than on fidelity to a document literally interpreted. Verbalisms and concepts must be united with commitment in life: acting as though God were the Lord. For faith so understood is not merely or even mainly the belief that God *is* ("isness" here stated as a metaphysical postulate) but the resolve to act in each moment of life with the knowledge that God *is Lord* ("isness" here becomes transitive and refers to God's sovereignty over human life). The Hebrew idea of faith was essentially a "walking before God."

The critical method and analysis employed in this book do not require that the reader adopt any particular position with respect to the validity of the Old Testament faith, or of its daughter religions Judaism and Christianity. To do so would seriously confuse the categories of the historical (What does the Old Testament say?) and the theological (What does it mean? Is it true?), but the two categories are contiguous and they impinge upon the same person. It is specious reasoning to ignore the issues of validity. In the course of our analysis of the Old Testament there may come those moments when, like Moses, we remove our shoes because we stand on holy ground. At other times, we may with the psalmist be forced to cry, "Where art thou, O Lord?" The Old Testament speaks of a deity who comes and goes at his pleasure and not at our conjuring. Sometimes, in the emptiness of his departure, we may say with the cynic, "Vanity of vanities, all is vanity." Yet even such despair yearns for the lost God and is often the prelude to faith. The biblical witness to God the Lord is profoundly conceived and ought to be pondered earnestly, whatever the reader's standpoint.

✢ 2 ✢

THE ANCESTRY OF THE OLD TESTAMENT

Every literary product has a history and the older that product the more complex the history. When literature has passed from one language into scores of others and has continued to wield an immense influence through the authoritative place it occupies in two religions, the history becomes uncommonly complex—and fascinating. Naturally the tracing of literary origins and the analysis of canonical and textual developments require special linguistic and historical skills coupled with phenomenal patience. Exacting labor and painstaking detail are the price that must be paid for an ever-increasing fund of knowledge about biblical origins. The clarity and accuracy of modern translations depend upon those who give their lives to minute study of the texts and versions, and the realism and depth of our interpretation is constantly indebted to those who have placed the Old Testament books in their historical context. In the end the hard-earned results, while not always world-shaking, illuminate the Old Testament and in addition form a running commentary on three thousand years of the history of thought and culture.

In this phase of our study we intend to discover how the Old Testament came into existence and eventually reached us in the versions we know. Rather than examine content or interpretation, we are to trace the history of the Old Testament, first in its separate units and finally as a totality. Approximately when and under what circumstances were its parts written? What literary forms were employed? When and how did the books receive their status as Scripture? How was the text of the Old Testament preserved and transmitted? Into what languages was it translated? What motivations and methods controlled the translators?

The answers to most of these questions cannot be supplied merely by examining the biblical writings. The student will find thirty-nine books in the English translation of the Old Testament, but he will not know why these thirty-nine were chosen, and there are no hints as to why the Hebrew Old Testament has fewer books and the Greek version more. Reasoning from his general knowledge of anthologies the reader may assume that the thirty-nine books are in their approximate order of composition, but he will be altogether wrong in this assumption. He may even take it for granted that the division of the books into chapters and verses was a feature of the original manuscripts but again he will have misjudged. As a matter of fact mere scrutiny of the external form of the Old Testament can be grossly misleading. Only a study of the literary history can supply us with the data we need.

EMERGENCE OF THE WRITINGS

The chief value of historical and literary criticism of the Old Testament is the success of that method in revealing the organic relation between the history of Israel and the literature proper. Axiomatic for critical study is the realization that every Old Testament writing arose in a particular milieu as the result of the blending of unrepeatable circumstances.

Though such a judgment is broadly applicable to any literature, owing to the lack of abstraction and generalization in the Hebrew mentality it is uniquely true of the Old Testament. For the Hebrew everything must be stated concretely, and not only with spatial concreteness (the colors and forms of the visible world) but also with temporal concreteness (the flux, the clash and impact of historical event and encounter). This does not mean that the Hebrew was unable to see relationships and totalities. He did not see them with a philosophically analytic or synthetic mind. His grasp upon reality was intuitional and spontaneous. Even in his profoundest assertions about God and human life, he never forsook the specific. The result is that the Old Testament literature, both in form and content, bears the unmistakable stamp of circumstantiality. It is indicative that the cornerstone of Hebrew religion, the revelation at Sinai, is couched in narrative form. Furthermore, the quality of stark historicity permeating the Old Testament makes for perplexity whenever the history of particular portions is lost to our view. Often, when we cannot understand a prophet, it is not because his message is esoteric but because we are not aware of the maelstrom of thought and event that engulfed him and those to whom he spoke.

For centuries men were almost entirely content to regard the Hebrew Bible as the statement of timeless truth. Even rationalism, which had no sympathy for the religious claims of the Old Testament, continued to treat Hebrew literature as though it were basically concerned with principles and ideals. It was only when men began to take the history seriously that strides were made in genuine understanding. Thus the phenomenal success of the critical method is directly traceable to the concreteness of its approach. Far from being a modernization of the Old Testament, it has really amounted to an unveiling of the biblical world. At the same time this approach opened a way for solutions to the myriad literary problems hitherto obscured by traditional theories.

By applying questions to each of the Old Testament books, as well as to their component sources, critics began to get answers. Simple in principle, these questions are essentially those that mark any analytic study of literature: Was there more than one author? In what form did he (or they) express himself (themselves)? Where did he get his material? To whom did he write? When did he write? What motivated him? In the light of all these conditioning factors, what is the meaning and import of his words? The final step is the most difficult. It is usually possible to work out a literal translation of an Old Testament passage, but the interpretation of the words in their total context calls for the utmost in informed historical imagination. Since the Old Testament is not the work of men who consulted one another or sought uniformity, the result of critical cross-examination can never be determined in advance. There are constant surprises and revelations for the patient student. First impressions to the contrary, the Bible is not a dull and stereotyped book.

The following chronological sequence of Old Testament literature is intended to prepare the student for an examination of the individual books. While not entirely self-explanatory, it will provide a sense of the relation of the parts to the whole. By such a sequence we do not mean the times to which the books of the Old Testament *refer* but

Chart 1. Chronology of Hebrew Literature

1300–1200   *The Mosaic Age*
    *Decalogue of Exodus 20 (The Ten Commandments)
    Poetic Fragments of the Pentateuch:
        Song of Lamech, Gen. 4:23–24
        Song of the Ark, Num. 10:35–36
        Song of the Well, Num. 21:17–18
        Song of Miriam, Exod. 15:21

1200–1000   *The Settlement in Canaan*
    Poetic Portions of the Pentateuch:
        Curse of Canaan, Gen. 9:25–27
        Joshua's Address to Sun and Moon, Josh. 10:12–13
    Song of Deborah, Judg. 5
    Decalogue of Exodus 34
    Book of the Covenant or "Canaanite" Code, Exod. 20:23–
    23:19

1000–900   *The United Monarchy*
    David's Lament over Saul and Jonathan, II Sam. 1:17–27
    Stories of the Judges (as distinguished from the frame-
    work of the book)
    Court History of David, II Sam. 9–20; I Kings 1–2
    "J" Source of the Pentateuch (one of four anonymous
    strata in the first five books of the Old Testament)

900–800   *The Divided Monarchy*
    "E" Source of the Pentateuch (second of the four anony-
    mous strata in the first five books)
    The Prophetic Stories of Elijah and Elisha, I Kings 17–
    II Kings 13

800–700   *Fall of the Northern Kingdom*
    Amos
    Hosea
    Isaiah 1–12; 28–31
    Micah 1–3

700–600   *Decline of the Southern Kingdom*
    "D" Source of the Pentateuch (third of four strata, "D"
    consisting substantially of Deuteronomy)
    Zephaniah

Chart 1 (*Continued*)

Habakkuk
Nahum
First Edition of the Book of Kings
Jeremiah (in part)

600–500   *Exile and Return*

Jeremiah (in part)
Ezekiel
Judges (final compilation)
Final Edition of Kings
Lamentations
Isaiah 40–55
Haggai
Zechariah 1–8

500–400   *Persian Domination*

Malachi
Micah 4–7
Isaiah 56–66
"P" Source of the Pentateuch (the last of the four strata comprising the five "Books of Moses")
*Job
*Song of Songs

400–300   *Greek Domination*

Jonah
Ruth
*Joel
Chronicles
Ezra-Nehemiah
*Proverbs (final compilation)

300–200   *Ptolemaic Domination*

*Psalms (final compilation)
Ecclesiastes
*Zechariah 9–14

200–100   *Seleucid Domination and Maccabean Revolt*

Daniel
Esther

rather the times when they *originated*. Occasionally the two periods are not identical. Deuteronomy, while purporting to be the work of Moses, was probably written in the eighth and seventh centuries B.C., from five to six hundred years after Moses. A further caution is in order: frequently a single Old Testament book is a compilation. Thus in arranging the literary materials on a date line, it is often necessary to split books. Isaiah 1–12 belongs to the eighth century, whereas Isaiah 40–55 belongs to the sixth. The entries marked with an asterisk are those whose dates of composition are most unsettled. Detailed discussion of the dating of particular books or sources will be found at appropriate points in this text.

This sketch is useful only if it is not taken too pedantically. For one thing it does not register the role played by oral tradition. Behind each of the four Pentateuchal sources (indicated by the critical short-hand J, E, D, P) there is no doubt an extensive oral tradition. The same may also be true of many of the preëxilic prophets. When it is said that the book of Amos dates from the eighth century B.C., that may not be strictly true. His striking oracles, delivered as sermons, may have been preserved by his disciples and written down decades later. And yet, if they were so memorable in form that they impressed themselves upon the minds of his followers, then for all practical purposes they had achieved a fixity that nearly rivals that of the written page.

It must be further emphasized that much of the Old Testament literature defies dating. Nearly all the writings outside the prophets are anonymous to begin with. When internal criteria are lacking or extremely vague, as is often the case in the devotional and wisdom genre, even the desire of the critic cannot supply anything more than an informed guess, give or take a few centuries! As one instance, the poetry now compiled in the Psalms represents most periods of Israelite history. Though genuine experiences lie behind many of the poems, the absence of name and historical allusion typical of prayer has made it well-nigh impossible to know to what centuries most of the Psalms belong. Under such circumstances, it seems best to list them as products of the third century only because that may be regarded as the likely time of final compilation.

All in all, we are now witnessing a tendency in Old Testament study, typical of the "tradition-historical" phase of study, in the direction of earlier dating and of less dogmatism concerning chronology.

This is not all due to the rediscovery of the preliterary stages of development. It may be attributed partly to an uneasiness about nineteenth-century evolutionary views. Wellhausen was not only a great Old Testament scholar, he was also a Hegelian who traced in history an inevitable upward advance. In the development of the Hebrews from animism through the levels of polytheism and monolatry to monotheism he saw an illustration of the gradual progress of mankind. Because the stages were rather clearly marked off, being characterized by certain ideas, Wellhausen was able to assign dates to the literature with greater definiteness than we now feel to be justified. It may still be correct to speak of progress in the Old Testament (one hears often of "progressive revelation"), but it is accompanied by troughs and periods of retrogression. The advance is not uniform; the creative insights of the great leaders often take centuries to be accepted and earlier crudities have an uncanny survival capacity. In the nontechnological realms, especially religion, knowledge does not accumulate as rapidly or consistently as in the tangible aspects of man's culture.

Yet when allowance has been made for uncertainties, we still possess a generally clear picture of the origins of Hebrew canonical literature. Nineteenth-century criticism, though handicapped by the rigid threefold Hegelian scheme of thesis, antithesis, and synthesis, nevertheless made good its promise of demonstrating how the literature emerged out of the viable history of the Israelite people. Even when they must perforce remain anonymous, the spokesmen of the Hebrew spirit have become for us living and persuasive figures. Whatever the future may hold for Old Testament study, the fundamental work of the older criticism—from Astruc to Wellhausen—in clarifying the roles of those ancient poets, historians, and prophets is certain to stand as one of the great achievements of modern learning.

LITERARY TYPES

We now have some notion both of the *times* when the Hebrew literature was written and of the real *units of composition* which in some cases, especially in the Pentateuch, are not the same as the biblical books (cf. J, E, P, which extend through several books, so that our present Genesis, Exodus, Numbers were formed by an interweaving of the previously separate sources). But what of the constituent types of literature? One does not read very far into the Old

Testament before its uneven character becomes apparent. Not only is there abrupt transition from poetry to prose and vice versa, but the poetry and prose in turn resolve into subtypes. From the standpoint of literary forms, the Old Testament is clearly a composite, although its basically anthological character is constantly forgotten.

Conditioned as they were by certain formal types, Israelite writers yet succeeded to an astonishing degree in transcending the strictures of form. This can be appreciated only by comparing the Old Testament material with its Near Eastern counterparts: Egyptian, Babylonian, Hittite, and Canaanite. The freedom and expressiveness of the former is consistently superior to the rather stilted and monotonously reiterative features of the latter. To say this is not to depreciate the literature of Israel's neighbors nor to overlook the Israelite debt to them, a debt that was enormous, especially since the Hebrews were late arrivals on the stage of ancient history. Individual works, notably *The Gilgamesh Epic* in Babylonia and *The Story of Sinuhe* in Egypt are worthy prototypes of Old Testament prose.[1] The basic poetic forms of the Old Testament are amply illustrated outside Israel. Wide reading in the contemporary writings demonstrates beyond a shadow of a doubt that the various literary forms to which Israel fell heir were shaped in a wide cultural setting and already had a venerable history and usage when the Hebrews took them over. How like and yet how different were the literatures of Israel and the surrounding peoples!

Biblical scholars are not of one mind in their classification of the literary types, for no one system has proved both inclusive enough to deal accurately with the variety of types and detailed enough to make convincing distinctions. There are too many borderline literary units, and the incidence of mixed genre in the Old Testament is in proportion to the Hebrew genius for improvising on borrowed elements. Extensive editing has also contributed its share of confusion. Still more fundamental is the lack of agreed-upon criteria for determining literary type. Sometimes content is stressed, sometimes form, and on occasion judgments about the historicity of the narratives heighten the subjectivity of the analysis. Finally, the nomenclature is

---

[1] See Appendix 2, pp. 575–580, for *Gilgamesh Epic.* James B. Pritchard, ed., *Ancient Near Eastern Texts Relating to the Old Testament,* 2d rev. ed., Princeton University Press, 1955 (abridged as *The Ancient Near East,* Princeton, 1958) provides readable translations and critical introductions for these and many other ancient nonbiblical documents. A comparable selection with fuller notes is available in D. Winton Thomas, ed., *Documents from Old Testament Times,* Nelson, 1958.

woefully inconsistent; Old Testament science still awaits a Linnaeus who will standardize the terminology. The classification below was made after careful study of the proposals in several Old Testament Introductions.[2] The three major categories (songs, sayings or oracles, prose) and their subdivisions will each be followed by appropriate commentary.

SONGS

"Profane" or secular songs:
   Work songs, Num. 21:17–18
   Drinking songs, Isa. 22:13
   Wedding songs, Ps. 45
   Funeral songs, II Sam. 1:17–27
   War songs, Judg. 5
   Mocking songs, Num. 21:27–30

"Sacred" or cultic songs:
   Hymns, Exod. 15:21; Pss. 48; 84; 103
   Laments, individual, Pss. 6; 22; 69, and collective, Joel 2:17; II Chron.
      20:1–13; Pss. 44; 74; 137
   Thanksgiving songs, individual, Jonah 2, and collective, Pss. 67; 124

The distinction between "profane" and "sacred" is a dubious one in this context. Religion reached into all aspects of Hebrew life, at least potentially. The separation of spheres, common to our thinking since the breakup of the Medieval Synthesis of religion and culture, was certainly foreign to the ethos of ancient Israel. Perhaps the subdivisions may best stand as descriptive categories, distinguishing between those songs in which the relation to God is the central feature and others in which it is peripheral. Even so it is scarcely true to say that the relation to God is peripheral in the war song of Judges 5, for it is the concept of Israel under the God Yahweh that permeates the poem and rouses the speaker to lyrical ecstasy. But in defense of the distinction of spheres we may cite the Lament over Saul and Jonathan, which never mentions God but simply pours forth the grief that overcame David at the loss of those whom he loved and honored.

---

[2] Aage Bentzen, *Introduction to the Old Testament*, 2d ed., vol. 1, Gad, 1952, pp. 102–264; Otto Eissfeldt, *Einleitung in das Alte Testament*, 2. Auflage, J. C. Mohr, 1956, pp. 8–168; R. H. Pfeiffer, *Introduction to the Old Testament*, Harper, 1941, pp. 20–40; Ernst Sellin and Leonhard Rost, *Einleitung in das Alte Testament*, 8. Auflage, Quelle & Meyer, 1950, pp. 5–20; Artur Weiser, *Einleitung in das Alte Testament*, 2. neubearb. Auflage, Vandenhoeck & Ruprecht, 1949, pp. 24–57.

The criteria for the "profane" categories are obvious enough; they are named by the life functions or activities with which they are connected: work, marriages, funerals, war. The "sacred" types are less apparent and in singling out their fundamental characteristics all subsequent interpreters acknowledge dependence upon the epochal work of Gunkel.[3] *Hymns* are cast in direct address to the deity and extol his attributes and works. Generally they do not seek any end other than praise and adoration. The *laments* are occasioned by threats to the worshiper or the community at large. In the one case, sickness and unjust accusation seem to be the most frequent complaints and, in the other, famine and military defeat. The plight of the complainant is frequently catalogued in gruesome detail and God is entreated to take action. Often the lament closes with an affirmation of confidence that God will hear. Now and then one finds laments that decry the sin of the suppliant; they are in effect personal confessions and entreaties for forgiveness (the most notable is Psalm 51). *Thanksgiving songs* stand on the other side of the disaster that provoked the lament. They are often close to the hymn form but are more precise in their praise, usually naming the original threat and always focusing upon specific deliverance.

But the novice must not imagine that he can categorize every Hebrew song. Gunkel distinguished certain categories on the basis of content rather than form (e.g., royal and wisdom psalms) and he also emphasized that a large number of psalms are actually mixed, no doubt through their repeated use in the cult or occasional editorial accident or ineptness. There are many instances of fusion of types, but two will suffice for illustration. Psalm 89 is composed of a hymn (vss. 1–18), a prophetic oracle (vss. 19–37), and a lament (vss. 38–52). The deeply introspective individual thanksgiving song of Psalm 139 (vss. 1–18), is followed without warning by an invective against wicked men (vss. 19–24). In the Psalter, so-called "purity of type" is the exception rather than the rule. The greatest Hebrew poems are those in which the poet bends the forms to his purposes. The Near Eastern songs adhere much more rigidly to formal types and are by that same token extremely stereotyped and repetitive, whereas the greater casualness of the Hebrews toward exactitude of

---

[3] Hermann Gunkel, *Einleitung in die Psalmen,* Vandenhoeck & Ruprecht, 1933 (finished by his pupil J. Begrich). A fuller analysis of the sacred poetic types will be found in the discussion of the Psalms, Chap. XIII of this text.

form is the measure of their literary brilliance and the secret of their power of communication. Finally, with respect to the songs, some of the illustrations given above, e.g., Judges 5 and Jonah 2 (scores could be cited in addition), were intended to show that by no means all examples are to be found in the book of Psalms. Scattered through the Old Testament are a number of songs, many the literary and religious equal of the Psalter, which together would form a fair-sized collection.

SAYINGS OR ORACLES

Prophetic oracles, Amos 1–2; Jer. 2
Wisdom sayings:
    Maxims, the Book of Proverbs
    Riddles, Judg. 14:14
Priestly sayings:
    Oracles, Gen. 25:23
    Blessings and Cursings, Num. 6:24–27; Deut. 27:15–28:6

The "situation in life" for this type of literature is the functioning of the religious leaders of Israel as interpreters of the divine will. Prophet, priest, and wise man were consulted by kings and commoners. At times their oracles were unsolicited, particularly the scathing messages of certain of the prophets. Jeremiah 18:18 contains explicit reference to the parallel but separate roles of these three, not unlike the way in which we speak of the minister, the doctor, and the teacher: ". . . the law shall not perish from the priest, nor counsel from the wise, nor the word from the prophet."

Originally such oracular pronouncements must have been short, and commonly marked by rhythmic cadence. But as literary interest developed the brief oracles became nuclei for whole corpora of law and prophecy and wisdom. Here and there in the prophets, notably in the well-preserved books such as Amos, we observe the smaller units that are no doubt independent oracles delivered by the prophet on various occasions. While it is an oversimplification, leaving out as it does the crucial contributions of Israel's epic writers and historians, we may say that the three parts of the Hebrew canon are roughly the products of the three groups named above: the Law being by the priests, the Prophets by the prophets, and the Writings by the wise men.

PROSE

Speeches and Sermons, Josh. 24; Ezek. 18
Prayers, I Kings 8:22–53; Neh. 9:6–37
Documents:
    Lists, Gen. 5; Josh. 12–21
    Edicts, Ezra 1:1–4
    Letters, Jer. 29:1–23
Apocalypses, Dan. 7–12
Laws, Exod. 20–23; Leviticus; Deut. 12–26; Ezek. 40–48
Myths, Gen. 1–3; Gen. 6:1–4
Legends:
    Aetiological, Gen. 19
    Heroic, Gen. 12–15; Exod. 1–14; Judg. 13–16
History, II Sam. 9–20; Jer. 26–45 *passim*
Fables, Judg. 9:7–15
Parables, Isa. 5:1–7

In the prose genre more than in the previous two we encounter difficulty of classification, especially in those elusive categories of myth, legend, and history. We may dismiss at once that view of *myth* which regards it as pure fiction or fantasy. Myth may be more accurately defined as a story in which gods or divine beings are the chief characters. In this sense there is almost no myth in the Old Testament, for only here and there do we note traces of that polytheistic framework from which the Hebrews radically departed. The few instances are exceptions that prove the rule. In Genesis 6:1–4 are summarized the escapades of "the sons of God" (or "the gods") with "the daughters of men," their offspring being the Nephilim or giants who once inhabited the earth as "mighty men . . . the men of renown." With only minor changes this story would be perfectly at home in Greek mythology, but there are no other equally blatant Hebrew examples of myth in this sense. The narratives of Genesis 18 and 19, while referring to the divine visitation in the person of three angels, are in fact legends, concentrating as they do upon the promise to Abraham and the deliverance of Lot from Sodom. Isaiah 14:3–21, while presupposing a myth about a rebellious angel (see especially vs. 12), is really a poetic imitation employing the myth for symbolic and artistic purposes.

But the term myth may be used in a more inclusive sense. It may refer to ancient man's poetic and imaginative efforts to interpret the world he lived in. As such it was the ancient equivalent of philosophy and science. It stood apart from those disciplines in its failure to distinguish sharply between man and nature, subject and object, and in its loose conception of causality.[4] The ancient Egyptians and Mesopotamians viewed their world in terms of the way it directly and personally affected them, the "I-Thou" framework rather than the "I-It" of modern man. The Hebrews shared with their neighbors many of these basic thought modes. As an example, anthropomorphism (by which we mean the ascription to God of human features and qualities, e.g., God talks, walks, is angry, changes his mind), in which Hebrew literature abounds, may be regarded as essentially mythical. By means of the anthropomorphisms the effective action of God upon his world is recorded. If this line is pursued to its end, myth may simply become another term for pictorial language, i.e., for the perpetual necessity of religion to talk about the unseen by means of analogy with the seen.

While "myth" in such a broadly figurative way is present everywhere in the Old Testament, the term is best restricted to those narrative portions, written in the grand style, in which the origins of the world and mankind are recounted. This provides a definition for myth midway between the polytheistic "story of the gods" and the much too ambiguous notion of "picture language." For purposes of literary exactitude, myth seems to be concerned either with the interrelations of the divine (polytheism) or the origins of the world (cosmology). Since the first is rare, the cosmological themes of the opening chapters of Genesis constitute the only parts of the Old Testament properly called myths. The primary reason for the scarcity of myth as a literary form in the Old Testament is the fact that Hebrew religion disagreed violently with the ideological basis of mythology. Israel either replaced mythology with historiography or else retained it for merely symbolic purposes.

Legend is distinguished from myth by the fact that its protagonist is man rather than God or gods. Legend is set off from history in that the element of credibility cannot be established. The line between legend and history is frequently nebulous. Most scholars will agree that the stories of Genesis 4–11 are legends, but not all will relinquish

[4] One of the most illuminating expositions of myth in this sense has been given by Henri Frankfort, ed., *The Intellectual Adventure of Ancient Man,* University of Chicago Press, 1946, chap. I; also appearing as *Before Philosophy,* Penguin Books, 1951 (Pelican A198).

a substantial core of historicity in the patriarchal accounts. The story of David's reign contained in II Samuel 9–20 has long been held up as the model of Hebrew historiography, while the materials of Kings (edited no doubt by the same circle responsible for Samuel) are of an exceedingly uneven character, ranging from court annals to folk legends.

Most recent studies in the meaning of history, biblical and otherwise, have emphasized that all history has its share of legend, i.e., of images and notions that cannot be strictly validated by the ordinary criteria of historiography. It is suspected, likewise, that legends survive because they retain a kernel of historicity. *Aetiological legends* have for their *raison d'être* an explanation of the origins of names, places, sanctuaries, cult practices, social customs, and geographical features. Genesis, and Joshua to a lesser extent, abound in such legends. So-called *hero legends,* often designated *sagas,* recount the exploits of the great leaders of Israel, which for the Old Testament means their struggles with God. It is doubtful whether any other of the world's legends and epics are peopled with heroes who are as pacifistic as the patriarchs and prophets. Even the mighty Moses is no military figure and must rely upon Caleb and Joshua for the success of Hebrew arms.

Fable, as here employed, refers to a story in which plants or animals act and speak as humans for the purpose of pointing a moral. The *parable* is a simile extended into a story; its function, like that of the fable, is patently didactic and hortatory. The occurrence of fable and parable in the Old Testament is infrequent.

The one literary type noticeably absent from the Old Testament, and almost the only one, is drama. Contrary to the view of several literary analysts, Job is not a drama and was never intended for staging. It may be conjectured that this seeming disregard for an actor-audience situation is partly attributable to the Hebrew sense of personal involvement. Drama as a form is still bound to ritual. The objectification and projection essential to the dramatic form was something the Hebrew never achieved. Another prohibitory factor was the intense Hebrew animus against representing God with idols. The same distaste was felt toward miming deity. Paradoxically, however, the Hebrew sense of participation in history has impressed a dramatic quality upon much of the literature. Plot, characterization, conflict, and resolution—the very stuff of drama—are boldly employed by Old

Testament writers; the dramatic elements remain, however, within the narrative and ritual forms.

CANON

We have seen that the Old Testament is regarded by Judaism and Christianity as Scripture, i.e., a written religious authority. Canon, from the Greek form of an Old Babylonian term for "reed" or "measure," refers to a collection of books invested with sanctity and accepted as authoritative. The canon thus becomes the standard by which the views of adherents may be tested and a guide for all subsequent interpretation. Canonization refers to the process by which sacred books are selected, imbued with authority, and thus set apart from other religious writings that are either heretical or simply of devotional value.

Inspiration and canonical status must be distinguished, even though the former is the precondition of the latter. Many sermons are preached in the conviction that they are inspired, but neither pastor nor people would elevate them to the level of absolute authority. We have every reason to believe that a number of the Old Testament books were written under the compulsion of a divine mission, especially in the case of the prophets. They were regarded as inspired, breathing a message from God. But nowhere do we see evidence of either the writers or the community of faith treating them as canonical until a long while after their composition, with the possible exception of the book of Deuteronomy. This accords with what we know of the process of canonization in other scriptural religions. Time is the indispensable element in turning inspired religious writings into canonical authorities.

It is evident, therefore, that the Old Testament is not an anthology of belles-lettres. The decision to include or exclude was not based on literary merit but on religious usage. Moreover, probably the great majority of the Old Testament books were received through common consent, so that a "decision" by the canonizing council did little more than formalize an authority already acknowledged. Most of the selections had been made long before the rabbis met to seal them.

We can be certain that the Old Testament as we know it is only a part (and probably a small part) of the Hebrew literature extant in pre-Christian times. The accepted books make numerous references to works now lost, except as they are quoted or material embodied in the canonical writings. We hear of *poetic anthologies* that must have been among the earliest Israelite creations: the Book of Jashar (Josh. 10:13; II Sam. 1:18) and the Book of the Wars of Yahweh (Num. 21:14). Our extant books refer to *histories:* the Book of the Acts of Solomon (I Kings 11:41), the Chronicles of the Kings of Judah (I Kings 14:29, etc.), and the Chronicles of the Kings of Israel (I Kings 14:19, etc.). Biblical Chronicles refer to a number of sources, the majority of which are *prophetic chronicles or histories* attributed to men such as Samuel, Nathan, Gad, Ahijah, Iddo, Shemaiah, Jehu, and Isaiah (I Chron. 29:29; II Chron. 9:29; 12:15; 13:22; 20:34; 32:32). Unequivocal proof of the complexity of the literary sources behind the surviving history is the remark in the last two citations that the works mentioned were preserved in the books of the Kings of Judah and Israel, which were employed in turn by the author of the Old Testament Chronicles.

More than this, the Hebrew Bible as we know it is the limited collection of Palestinian Judaism. The Greek version, whose nature and significance remain to be considered, included books not found in the Hebrew and English versions. That any gathering of rabbis had formally delimited the extent of this Greek version is unsupportable, but there is evidence that many Hellenistic Jews and early Christians treated the additional books of the Greek Old Testament (since called apocryphal) as on a par with portions later adjudged canonical.

There were two events in early Israelite history that initiated the canonical process. The promulgation of the book of Deuteronomy as the law of Judah by Josiah in 621 B.C. marked the first time in Hebrew history that a particular book became authoritative. What precipitated the process begun by Deuteronomy was the destruction of the Judean state in 587 B.C. and the long Exile, during which an understandable thirst for authority led to a careful study and preservation of the surviving literature. Lacking a significant present, Judaism began to live in its past. It is this sense of a classical, normative age in a people's past that alone makes the canonization of ancient literature possible. Vivid awareness of the creative past as against the stagnant present is seen in the Jewish notion that all prophecy ceased with Ezra. It is henceforth the function of the community to guard and cherish the authentic records of God's revelation, and from this it is an easy step to the position that the writings themselves are the revelation. Postexilic Jews in direct ratio to their national and historical impotence and their need for stanch authority became the people of the Book.

Complicating this drive toward canonization, but all the time furthering it, was the rise of apocalyptic literature. One of the distinctive marks of apocalyptic was the habit of cloaking its message in the guise of an utterance by some ancient figure, an Enoch or Moses, an Abraham or Ezra. In the presence of a flood of marginal literature, it was necessary to define the limits of Scripture by distinguishing the books that spoke for the community of faith from those that either spoke contrary to it or simply increased the flood of apocalyptic writings (since any one who wanted his work to be taken seriously would find it convenient to allege that it was written by one of the leaders before Ezra).

What finally conspired to "close" the canon was the rise of a Christian literature claiming to interpret the Old Testament correctly. Much of the Christian literature was apocalyptic in nature and thus forced Judaism to renounce apocalyptic almost entirely. The rabbinic assembly which in A.D. 90 pronounced upon the canon was convened in the shadow of two momentous events: the destruction of Jerusalem and the temple in A.D. 70 and the aggressive growth of Christianity from a sect within Judaism to an independent faith.

The stages in the canonization of the Old Testament writings correspond roughly to the threefold division of its contents: the Law, the Prophets, and the Writings. The Law, containing the basic revelation to Moses, was given full authority around 400–350 B.C., between 150 and 200 years after the restoration of the Jews to Palestine. Ezra, the priest and scribe, seems to have played the dominant role, for it was he who impressed upon the struggling theocratic community that only through fidelity to the written law could the faith survive. No council was convened; rather there was a public ceremony in which part or all of the five books of Moses were read and the people solemnly reasserted the primacy of the Law (Neh. 8:8; 9:3). But as far as Ezra and his contemporaries were concerned, they were not investing the Law with authority but simply recognizing and obeying its inherent authority, which means that the canonical halo surrounding it had been gathering for a long time. The Samaritan sect that broke away from the main body of Judaism in the postexilic period regarded only the Law as its scripture. This fact strongly suggests that at the time of the breach only the Law had sufficient sanctity to make it a written religious authority. Traditionally dated in 397 B.C., the Samaritan separation may have been as much as two hundred years later. Unfortunately the date of the schism is uncertain.

At some time around 200 B.C. the Prophets, gradually growing in sanctity, were regarded as fully canonical. The Law, thought to have been written by Moses, with its centuries of literary history, could appropriately be canonized in the fourth century B.C. The Prophets took another two hundred years to attain the requisite dignity, for it had only been at the time of Ezra (c. 400 B.C.) that prophecy had ceased. Two hundred years of sifting and mellowing were yet needed. The date for this second stage is indicated by the Prologue to the Greek translation of the Wisdom of Ben Sira by the author's grandson, written not many years after 132 B.C. The prologue speaks of the Prophets as though they are on a level with the Law and the body of the text shows that by 180 B.C. the prophetic collection was in substantially the present form.

The final stage was the rabbinic assembly—hardly a council or synod in the strict sense—in A.D. 90, which met in the small Palestinian town of Jamnia located on the coastal plain. Rabbi Johanan ben Zakkai was the leading figure. So far as the Law and the Prophets were concerned there was little to be done except "rubber-stamp" the collective conviction of Judaism. Ezekiel, the one exception, was questioned because of its weird visionary character and the discrepancies between its ritual requirements and those of the Law.

But a third group of books, known by the eclectic and nondescript title of "The Writings," and which Ben Sira designated by the loose expression, "the other books of our fathers," had been serving as a catchall for highly regarded works not included in the Law or the Prophets. Most of these had established themselves so firmly in the usage of Palestinian synagogues that there was no question about their acceptance, but strong objections were offered to others: notably Song of Songs, Ecclesiastes, and Esther. While to some the love poetry of the first seemed profane and vulgar, the skepticism of the second shocking and irreverent, and the lack of reference to God in the third disconcerting, all three were rescued for the canon. The Song of Songs and Ecclesiastes were accepted as the work of Solomon; Esther was approved because it had become a symbol of Jewish survival in the face of overwhelming odds. At Jamnia the fringe books of the Greek canon used by Hellenistic Jews and Christians never had a chance for approval because they bore the onus of compromise with heathen culture and were already stigmatized as the special possession of the Christian movement with its dangerous and erroneous messianic interpretations.

Recent study of the Old Testament canon has emphasized two points easily overlooked. One is that the dates for the first two stages, 400 and 200 B.C., are an approximation and perhaps the former should be revised downward by as much as a century. There were no formal pronouncements of canonization at those times; in fact, the only canonical judgment was that arrived at by consensus in discussion at Jamnia and covering the entire canon in its three parts. No edict was ever released by the rabbis. When we accept the three gradations represented by the dates 400 and 200 B.C. and A.D. 90, we do not deny that by 400 most of the Prophets had been written and were commonly used or that by 200 nearly all the Writings had been completed. Thus the idea of three stages hermetically sealed off from one another is fallacious and, lacking canonical decrees, the time at which Law and Prophets had reached the level of scriptural authority must remain somewhat obscure. Even after the rabbinic decisions at Jamnia we hear of controversy concerning some of the books, such as Esther, and the rumblings of discontent do not subside until the end of the second century. To summarize: there were three stages of collection and veneration, with the Law first gaining authority, then the Prophets, and finally the Writings; but the three stages overlapped and there was only one official act of canonization, and even that act was not formalized by official edict.

Another essential point to be kept in mind is that the canon was never an edition of the text, but always a judgment about authority. Since books were written separately on scrolls, it would have been unwieldy and impracticable to include more than one good-sized book such as Isaiah in a single scroll. Thus what we mean by a canonical collection is simply the bringing together in the synagogues of several books regarded as equal in value and authority but as yet copied on separate scrolls. In the case of the Prophets and Writings, certain shorter books would be grouped on a single scroll, but this does not affect the principle that at no time in the pre-Christian era were all the books of the Law edited on a single scroll, much less the entire three categories of Scripture. The canon was a controlling idea of the utmost importance for it insured the careful preservation of the text and determined the survival of the books, but it was never an edition of the text until the codex form was adopted by Jews, probably not before the third or fourth century A.D. Because the scroll form prevented a single edition for many centuries, the order of the books in the later Hebrew editions often differs. There are also differences between the Hebrew order and the sequence of books in the Greek and English versions. The English versions of the Old Testament contain thirty-nine books while the Hebrew generally reckons them at twenty-four. Chiefly responsible for the difference is the Jewish custom of incorporating the shorter prophets in the single "Book of the Twelve," whereas they are treated separately in the English. A comparison of the sequences in the Hebrew and English will sharpen the similarities and variations.

Explanations of the divergences between the Hebrew and English arrangements are not easily arrived at. We recognize that the English order is drawn essentially from the Greek version. It is also clear that the grouping of the books in the Hebrew Old Testament follows the three main canonical divisions. There are no subgroupings in the English Old Testament corresponding to the Law, Prophets, and Writings in Hebrew. Sometimes the books Genesis to Deuteronomy are called law, Joshua to Esther history, Job through Song of Songs poetry, and Isaiah through Malachi prophecy; but these divisions are not made in the text and are thus purely descriptive. So far as the respective sequences of the books are concerned, it looks as though several factors have been at work, their varying combinations resulting in the Hebrew and English orders.

Sometimes the order is a matter of *simple historical sequence*. Genesis through Kings tell a continuous story from the creation of the world to the fall of Jerusalem in 587 B.C. With the exception of Leviticus (which lacks narrative), these books can be placed logically in only one order. But the English versions have been a little more rigorous in inserting Ruth after Judges, to which general period it belongs, and in placing Chronicles, Ezra, Nehemiah, and Esther after Kings to round out the history.

Authorship is another element. The English versions place Lamentations after Jeremiah because of the claim that the prophet was its author. An uneasiness about the traditional authorship of Daniel is preserved in the Hebrew order. Ordinarily one would expect to find Daniel among the Latter Prophets but its inclusion with the Writings,

Chart 2. Hebrew and English Old Testament Canons

Hebrew	*English*
The Law: (*Torah*)	Genesis
Genesis	Exodus
Exodus	Leviticus
Leviticus	Numbers
Numbers	Deuteronomy
Deuteronomy	
	Joshua
	Judges
	Ruth
	I Samuel
	II Samuel
	I Kings
The Prophets: (*Nebi'im*)	II Kings
Former:	I Chronicles
Joshua	II Chronicles
Judges	Ezra
Samuel	Nehemiah
Kings	Esther
Latter:	
Isaiah	Job
Jeremiah	Psalms
Ezekiel	Proverbs
The Book of the Twelve (Hosea	Ecclesiastes
to Malachi)	Song of Songs
	Isaiah
	Jeremiah
	Lamentations
	Ezekiel
	Daniel
The Writings: (*Kethubim*)	Hosea
Psalms	Joel
Proverbs	Amos
Job	Obadiah
Song of Songs	Jonah
Ruth	Micah
Lamentations	Nahum
Ecclesiastes	Habakkuk
Esther	Zephaniah
Daniel	Haggai
Ezra–Nehemiah	Zechariah
Chronicles	Malachi

the final section of the Hebrew Bible, supports the view of modern scholarship that Daniel was not written until the second century B.C., by which time the prophetic canon was fixed.

Public religious usage sometimes determined the grouping. The five short books between Job and Daniel in the Hebrew order are known as Megilloth (scrolls), because in Judaism they are employed at the important annual festivals. The common order of the Hebrew manuscripts is in the calendar order of the celebrations when the books were recited: Song of Songs (Passover), Ruth (Feast of Weeks), Lamentations (Ninth of Ab), Ecclesiastes (Tabernacles), and Esther (Purim). It is interesting, however, that some Hebrew manuscripts prefer to arrange them in accordance with their supposed order of writing: Ruth, Song of Songs, Ecclesiastes, Lamentations, Esther.

Editorial convenience accounts for the English habit of dividing Samuel, Kings, and Chronicles into two volumes each. The practice stems from the Greek version inasmuch as that language, unlike early Hebrew, was always written with vowels. This meant that, on the average, a Greek translation of any Hebrew book would be considerably longer than the original. Scrolls get unwieldy beyond a certain size and the Greek translators of the historical books solved the problem by copying the longer books on two scrolls each. What they called the Book of Kingdoms, with parts I, II, III, and IV became I and II Samuel, I and II Kings in English. Something of the same factor may be seen in the practice of lumping together all the shorter prophetic books (called the Twelve in Hebrew and the Minor Prophets in English parlance) and including them after the so-called Major Prophets. If historical order had been followed Amos and Hosea would have preceded Isaiah and other prophetic books would have been placed earlier. Micah would appear nearer Isaiah, his contemporary; and Habakkuk, Nahum, and Zephaniah would be close to Jeremiah.

In one instance the *desire for a happy ending* may have determined the Hebrew order. Ezra and Nehemiah obviously continue the story of Chronicles, but in the Hebrew Bible Chronicles is regarded as the last book. Presumably this is because both Ezra and Nehemiah end on rather dark notes, whereas Chronicles closes with the prospect of hope: the Edict of Cyrus permitting the return of the Jews to Palestine.

TEXT

It remains for us to inquire into the transmission of the Old Testament writings to our own day and to examine the various translations that have arisen. Our study divides logically into two parts: before and after the invention of printing. The printed Bible is an intriguing subject, particularly the story of the English versions from Tyndale to the present Revised Standard Version. However, beyond a few remarks intended to help the student evaluate the English versions available to him, the modern phase will not be considered. The rationale for this concentration on the earlier history of the text and versions is precisely our unfamiliarity with the conditions of handwritten texts. Our use of print is too prodigal to appreciate the sacrifice that went into handwritten books, and also the peculiar difficulties inevitably associated with their production.

All the original copies of the biblical writings have perished or eluded the excavator. Palestine, damper through half of the year than Egypt, has failed to preserve rich manuscript treasures similar to those of the Nile Valley. The scrolls found along the Dead Sea are a special case, for some of the manuscripts were protected by storage in jars and the majority were written on more durable material than papyrus. Judging by internal evidence and our knowledge of ancient Near Eastern scribal techniques, the biblical originals were written on papyrus, made from the sliced stem of a fibrous Egyptian plant. As the writings became more valued and won canonical status, there was a preference for copying them on leather, usually from the skin of sheep or goats. When made from skins of high quality and prepared by special treatment the leather was known as parchment or vellum. Throughout the entire pre-Christian period, the manuscripts (whether on papyrus or leather) were in scroll form. The book or codex form first appears in the Christian manuscripts of the third and fourth centuries. The codex format, with its ease of reference and capacity for indefinite enlargement through the addition of pages, soon replaced the awkward scroll for most purposes. Synagogues continued to employ the archaic scroll form for copies of the Pentateuch.

Just as the Babylonian exile in the sixth century B.C. led to a renewed interest in the religious documents of Israel, so it gave rise to

Inkwells and writing table from Qumran. The shallow depressions in the table may have held water for ritual washing by the copyists.

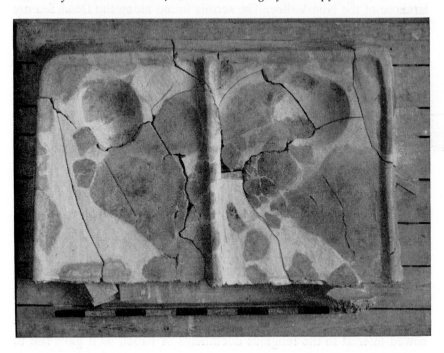

a class of scribes known as Sopherim ("bookmen") who became the guardians of the received text and in time its official interpreters. As the center of gravity in postexilic Judaism shifted from the role of the spoken word (the prophet) to the role of the written word (the sacred writings), the position of the Sopherim became primary. As in every ancient society where only a few men were literate, Israel had long possessed scribes to minister in court and temple. The post-exilic Jewish scribe, however, was not simply a technician but a student and interpreter of the writings he copied. The Pharisees (arising in the second century B.C.) continued the scribal tradition of interpretation by developing Oral Law as a supplement to the written Law. Although most of the Pharisees were no longer secretaries, the technical expression "scribes and Pharisees" attests to the original close relation between the art of writing and knowledge of Scripture.

During the centuries between the canonization of the Law in 400–350 B.C. and the Christian era the Hebrew script changed from the older so-called Phoenician script to the Aramaic or square script. The latter is a bold angular form of writing in which the letters are more sharply distinguished than in the previous cruder form. A number of Palestinian inscriptions such as the Moabite Stone of King Mesha and the record of Hezekiah's workmen in the Siloam Tunnel at Jerusalem (dated about 842 and 700 B.C. respectively), retain the more primitive script.[5] Some of the Dead Sea fragments are in the Phoenician script, in most cases probably owing to a revival of archaism typical of the Maccabean age. The climax of the work of the Sopherim was in the standardizing of the consonantal text in the time of Rabbi Akiba (about A.D. 100).

In the centuries following the destruction of Jerusalem in A.D. 70 the Jews turned with renewed devotion to the Scriptures. It was during the period A.D. 600–1000 that the Masoretes[6] brought the Old Testament to its finished form. The Masoretes were the heirs of the Sopherim. Masora means simply "tradition" and the Masoretes were those scholars who preserved the most valuable Hebrew tradition, the canonical writings. Like the Sopherim, they were scribes constantly engaged in the task of replacing outworn scrolls with new

---

[5] See Appendixes 8 and 9, pp. 590–591.
[6] The variation in spelling, whether Masoretes or Massoretes, reflects uncertainty as to the Hebrew form of the word. Most scholars prefer the short form.

ones whose accuracy and beauty would be assured. No easy task! Something of the care with which they discharged their duties is indicated in the rabbinic requirement that all new manuscripts were to be proofread and defective copies discarded at once. The Jewish reverence for the Scriptures is seen, furthermore, in the fact that no copy, whether old or defective, could be burned or otherwise destroyed. They were to be withdrawn and placed in a special chamber in the synagogue, known as the geniza ("treasury, storehouse"). Periodically the contents were buried. In a few instances, as at the Old Cairo synagogue, the geniza was walled off and its valuable manuscripts were preserved for posterity.

But the Masoretes made contributions of their own. One was the provision for vowel pointing in the text. In Hebrew there is a basic consonantal text represented by a generally large and bold script. With few exceptions, the vowels are not included in the consonantal formation but gather around the consonants, mostly below but sometimes above them. The vowel symbols are smaller than the consonants and thus give the appearance of planetary satellites clustered around their parent bodies. The appearance of written Hebrew suggests that the vowels are dispensable or at least late arrivals in the formation of the text, and this first impression is quite accurate. The Hebrew text of the Old Testament was not supplied with vowels until early medieval times. Tradition provided correct interpretation. In most cases the context would clarify the meaning, but there are instances where the text would be ambiguous as long as the vowels were not actually placed in the manuscript. The Masoretes, motivated by a desire to preserve the tradition of interpretation accurately, began the practice of supplying vowel pointing. The result was the standard Hebrew text, known as the Masoretic Text (abbreviated MT).

Beyond this scrupulous concern for the vowels, the Masoretes extended their interests into the field of grammatical and statistical data. They noted the occurrence of peculiar words or forms, the number of times the divine name appeared in a given book, variations in spelling, etc. Total numbers of letters and words and verses were computed. Middle verses and letters were specified. It is reported that two Masoretes arguing over the identity of the middle letter of the Old Testament finally solved it by making an on-the-spot recount! The observations resulting from such minute statistical study were at first preserved orally. Gradually they were noted in the text, sometimes along the margin and sometimes at the end of manuscripts. Eventually these notes, known as Masora, became so bulky that they were compiled in separate tracts. The basic motive for the compilation of statistical information was to insure the correct copying of the text—and in this aim the Masoretes were eminently successful.

Other contributions of the Masoretic scholars were the systematizing of the liturgical units into which the text was divided for reading in the synagogue services and the marking of the text with accentuation. The elaborate accents served both as punctuation and guidance for cantillation (the chanting of the Scripture).

In many of these areas the Sopherim had made beginnings but the Masoretes carried through with systematic resolve. Until the discovery of the Dead Sea Scrolls, virtually all that we knew of the Hebrew text came to us from Masoretic manu-

A ninth-century masoretic manuscript of Gen. 50: 23–26 and Exod. 1:1–13 with marginal notes.

scripts. Our scrutiny of the latest finds only serves to enhance our admiration for the exactitude and thoroughness of those scholars. While their fanatical love of detail at times bordered on the ludicrous, it was the acuteness of the Masoretes' observations that made possible accurate copying and recopying of the Old Testament text.

It used to be felt that the Masoretic tradition was uniform but Paul Kahle's study of the manuscripts uncovered in the Cairo Geniza has shown not only that there were Masoretic schools in Babylon and Palestine, but that the Palestinian Masoretic notes and vowel systems do not always agree. The School of Tiberias prevailed and other types of manuscripts tended to disappear. The two embodiments of the Tiberian Masora were the codices of Moses ben David *ben*

Naphtali and of Aaron ben Moses *ben Asher,* both of the tenth century. It is widely felt that the ben Asher text is a more accurate one than the printed text of Jacob *ben Chayyim* based on relatively late ben Naphtali manuscripts from the thirteenth and fourteenth centuries. Ben Chayyim's text has been the basic received text (Textus Receptus) reproduced in the various printed Bibles and employed by the translators of the chief English versions, including the King James.

Until 1947 none of our complete Hebrew manuscripts dated from a time earlier than A.D. 1008, although there were substantial portions from A.D. 850–900 and a few fragments from earlier periods, e.g., verses from Exodus 20 and Deuteronomy 5 and 6 in a probable first century A.D. text for liturgical or educational purposes (the Nash Papyrus). But in 1947 a new chapter in the history of the Old Testament text was opened dramatically by the discovery of scrolls in a cave on the precipitous slopes overlooking the western shore of the Dead Sea. These scrolls had been meticulously secured in large jars and had escaped plundering by intruders through two millennia. Among the scrolls was a copy of the book of Isaiah in its entirety. Competent scholarship has narrowed the range within which this manuscript was written to the first two centuries B.C. (most likely) and the first Christian century (possibly). In subsequent years additional discoveries have been made in caves in the same general area. In Cave IV portions of almost one hundred biblical manuscripts were found. Of the canonical books, only Esther has not appeared. The scrolls were deposited in the caves by a sect of ascetic Jews (probably Essenes) whose communal headquarters at the foot of the cliffs, known today as Khirbet Qumran, has been excavated extensively. The central place that the Scriptures—notably the Prophets—occupied in the Qumran sect is vividly illustrated in the biblical commentaries and in the so-called Manual of Discipline, which gives the ideals and rules of the community. Among the interesting finds at Qumran was a long writing bench on which the inkwells of the copyists were still to be seen.

It will be many years before the full meaning of these finds can be assessed, for there is an inevitable time lag in publication and new materials are constantly appearing. Especially exciting is the discovery of additional relatively complete scrolls from Cave XI, including copies of Leviticus and Psalms. Exhaustive study of the

Cave IV Qumran. Entrance is through the upper opening.

Cave XI Qumran. Here the first complete manuscripts have been found since Cave I.

Isaiah manuscript shows that the text in this one instance did not suffer essential change during the nine hundred to one thousand years elapsing between Qumran Isaiah and the earliest Masoretic copy of the prophet. The proto-Masoretic text certainly goes back well into the pre-Christian period. Nevertheless the textual tradition was far from static. There are occasional differences in the proto-Masoretic text, as represented by the intact Isaiah scroll, which appear to be improvements on obscurities or corruptions in the Masoretic text (the RSV of Isaiah adopts thirteen Qumran readings, identifying them with the marginal note "One ancient MS"). Variants in spelling indicate that the Hebrew of this period was in transition. But most striking is the fact that at Qumran three or more text types were in circulation, and while the prototype of MT was already in the ascendancy, it was not the sole or necessarily superior witness to the original text.

Our discussion to date has emphasized the relative accuracy of the scribes in transmitting the Hebrew text. Now and then one hears the irresponsible charge that the Old Testament text has undergone such change, intentional and accidental, that it scarcely corresponds with the original at any point. No reasonable student of literature doubts that he has substantially the words of Sophocles when he turns to *Oedipus Rex* or of Plato in *The Dialogues*. And yet the Hebrew manuscripts are on the whole older and more reliable than those we possess for most of the classics. Having said this, we must qualify by reminding the student that, while the Jewish scribes were phenomenal in their discipline and fidelity to the text, they were only human. If occasional errors still slip through in printing, even after innumerable proofreadings, we must not think that they were wholly eliminated from the work of men who had to copy everything by hand.

The majority of textual alterations were inadvertent, the sort of secretarial lapses familiar to any writer or typist. Similar letters were frequently confused. Consonants were reversed, often because the eye anticipated the hand. For centuries the Hebrew text was written continuously with only dots or strokes to indicate how words should be divided. Inevitably this led to occasional incorrect word divisions. Letters, words, or phrases were sometimes erroneously repeated. Recurring words, phrases, or passages gave rise to omission of material. When two successive or proximate sentences begin or end with identical terms the possibility of the deletion of the intervening text is especially great. Not all errors can be so readily explained. Some were doubtless due to the copyist misunderstanding the meaning. Fatigue probably took its toll. One error sometimes induced others, so that the disorder in certain passages may be due to a chain of mistakes that can no longer be reconstructed. The alterations can easily be detected when they are confined to particular manuscripts or manuscript families, and uncontaminated texts can be used to correct those in error. When, however, the changes occurred in the prototypes of all existing manuscripts, and when they do not fall into the recognized categories of scribal error, it is much more difficult to restore the original. In such circumstances our main help has been the Greek or other versions of the Old Testament. Recent discoveries of pre-Christian Hebrew manuscripts at Qumran have pushed back considerably the frontiers of textual knowledge, although we are barely beginning to reap the benefits.

Some of the variations in the textual tradition are due to deliberate change. This may be suspected more often than can be proved, but the evidence of alteration in some cases is compelling. In the prologue of Job the euphemism "bless" is used consistently in contexts where the sense requires "curse" (1:5,11; 2:5,9). Israelites bearing the name of the pagan deity *baal* are sometimes stigmatized with the substitute *bosheth,* meaning "shame" (thus Eshbaal, "man of Baal," becomes Ishbosheth, "man of shame"; cf. II Sam. 2:8 with I Chron. 8:33; 9:39).

Masoretic tradition identifies eighteen passages in the Old Testament as "emendations of the Sopherim," and various rabbinic works give lists. Nearly all the modifications have as their purpose the safeguarding of the holiness of God. Genesis 18:22 read originally "But the Lord stood yet before Abraham"; it was changed to "But Abraham stood yet before the Lord." Even the thought of deity dying is dismissed in Habakkuk 1:12 by altering "art thou not from everlasting . . . thou diest not" to "we shall not die." The denial of the ugly presence of polytheism in Israel is accomplished in II Samuel 20:1 by substituting "every man to his tents!" for the original "every man to his gods!" Since these changes are not indicated in the text, there is a difference among scholars as to the reliability of the tradition that reports them. And yet the very existence of a tradition of change among those who had such reverence for the text may be taken as ample proof that modifications in the interests of piety have occurred. Such deliberate changes may be acknowledged at the same time that the general trustworthiness of the textual tradition is maintained. Had wholesale correction of the text taken place, we can see literally hundreds and thousands of points at which a later age would have re-written the tradition but failed to do so.

One further word about the text. The chapter and verse divisions of the Old Testament were not original. The Hebrew authors and poets were as unconcerned about the problem of locating passages in their works as are modern novelists and poets. It was only with canonization and continuous religious usage that the need for some common system of reference was felt. Consequently verse divisions were introduced by the Jews in the period of the later Sopherim, prob-ably A.D. 200–400. Different systems were employed in Palestine and Babylon. The verses as we know them were first numbered in six-teenth-century printed Bibles. To mark divisions larger than verses the Jews, during the early Christian era, blocked off the text into paragraphs. The chapter divisions currently employed are generally attributed to Stephen Langton of Canterbury in 1205. These Chris-tian chapter divisions first appeared in a Jewish manuscript in 1448 and in the Rabbinic Bible of 1516 were marked in the margins. Later Jewish editions adopted the Christian chapter and verse divi-sions. The student is thus in a position to see that the chapter and verse divisions are relatively late in the history of the text. More-over it is disturbing to note how poorly they sometimes correspond with the real units of composition. One of the most telling instances of violence done to an author is in Isaiah where chapter 52 is severed from 53. It does not take much acumen to see that 52:13 through chapter 53 is a single theme and that no purpose can be served by dismemberment.

TRANSLATIONS

Prior to the discovery of the Dead Sea Scrolls our only witnesses to the pre-Masoretic text were translations of the Hebrew Old Testa-ment into other languages: Greek, Syriac, Latin, and Aramaic. The most important versions were translated before the time of the Masoretes and, in the case of the first Greek version, even before the Christian era. From the way the versions render particular passages we often get an insight into the Hebrew text used by the translator. Sometimes the original Hebrew text, corrupt in MT, can be restored by a judicious use of the versions.[7]

Textual critics have sometimes solved difficulties by highly conjectural reconstructions of the text. Until recent decades there was a fad of textual emendation with the intent of restoring the Hebrew "original." While many cautious critics deplored such speculation, it was only with the discovery of the Dead Sea Scrolls that we were in a position to see what the Hebrew text looked like prior to the versions. In the main the accuracy of the Masoretic Text has been vindicated. Nevertheless MT is but one form of the Hebrew text; there are significant instances of Qumran fragments agreeing with the Greek version or the Samaritan Pentateuch against the Masoretic Text. It now appears certain that several Hebrew text types or recensions, perhaps regional in origin, existed in pre-Christian times. Only as the hundreds of Dead Sea manuscripts are published, studied, and the text types delineated, can we undertake the arduous task of determining which is closest to the original. Values will doubtless be seen in each so that future Hebrew editions of the Old Testament will be eclectic, drawing readings from proto-Masoretic, proto-Greek, and proto-Samaritan manuscripts in order to correct and supplement the Textus Receptus.

The value of the versions is not confined to textual criticism. In a real sense they are episodes in the history and thought of Judaism and Christianity. The Jewish dispersion and the Christian missionary movement gave birth to the versions, for the multilingual demands of these two world-wide faiths made it imperative that the Scriptures be set forth in the language of the people. None of the translations of the Old Testament into other languages was a strictly academic undertaking. Great learning often went into the work, as in the case of the scholar Jerome, but the pressure for translation always came from the religious needs of communities of Jews and Christians. We have reason to believe that versions once thought to have been translated at one time and by one man (or group of men), were actually created piecemeal by scattered synagogues and churches who needed

---

[7] By textual "corruption" is meant alteration of the original, intentionally or unintentionally. The term has no moral connotation and does not imply any judgment as to the motive or occasion of alteration.

Pre-Christian biblical fragments from Qumran. Above: Exodus in archaic Hebrew script. Below: Samuel in the Hebrew text underlying the Septuagint.

portions of the Old Testament in the vernacular. Only somewhat later were the various books collected and edited, or more often simply left with telltale evidences of the numerous translators.

ANCIENT VERSIONS

The first and most momentous of the versions was Greek. It is known familiarly as the Septuagint ("The Seventy") because of the tradition that seventy (actually seventy-two) men translated it. Commonly it is represented by the Roman numerals LXX. The story of its creation has been preserved in the legendary Letter of Aristeas. Aristeas would have us believe that the Septuagint was an official project of the Ptolemaic government of Egypt. Ptolemy II Philadelphus (285–246 B.C.) in his zeal for learning desired that the venerable Hebrew Law be made available in Greek and placed in the magnificent library of Alexandria. Accordingly seventy-two learned Jews from Palestine were secured, who, working on the island of Pharos in the harbor, completed their task in seventy-two days. Later tradition elaborated this account by reporting that the scholars, working in pairs in individual cells, produced thirty-six copies of the entire Old Testament at the identical moment and without a variation in the Greek!

Probing behind the obvious schematic character of the Letter of Aristeas, scholars have concluded that the Septuagint was probably due less to the initiative of Greek culture than it was to the demands of the Jewish population in Egypt. Forced exile, the poverty of Palestine, and the proximity of Egypt had contributed to a steady movement of Jews into the Nile Delta ever since the prophet Jeremiah had been carried there by a group of his compatriots, and perhaps even earlier. By the third century B.C. it is estimated that about a million Jews were living in Alexandria. No longer able to understand Hebrew, if they were to know anything of their sacred writings, the books would have to be cast into the vernacular Greek, known as the "koine." The Law was translated about 250 B.C. and the remaining books completed by about 75 B.C. Far from being the product of united endeavor, there is ample evidence of many hands at work in the Septuagint. The Law is a relatively uniform and accurate translation but the Prophets and Writings are rendered more loosely.

The importance of the Septuagint is manifold. While the first result of the Dead Sea discoveries was to eclipse temporarily the significance of the Greek, that version has since risen to new importance as a result of the discovery of Qumran manuscripts preserving the Hebrew text used by the Septuagint translators. It is especially evident that the Septuagint of Samuel is based on a Hebrew text superior to the often garbled Masoretic Text. Fragments of Exodus, Deuteronomy, and Jeremiah also support the fact that the Greek version was based on a faithfully rendered Hebrew text. The worth of this proto-Septuagint Hebrew tradition, and its relation to the proto-Masoretic, will be the subject of intense inquiry as the Qumran materials are published and evaluated.

The way in which the Septuagint reflects the encounter of Greek and Hebrew ideas and their interpenetration is especially intriguing to the student of philosophy and culture. In the Alexandrian Jewish community the Greco-Roman culture could not be ignored. Philo, the gifted Jewish philosopher and allegorist, who sought to integrate the revelation of Moses with the vision of Plato, was one notable instance of an attempted rapprochement of Judaism with the Greek world. But the Septuagint was a precondition for Philo's work. Although the translation is hardly missionary or polemical in intent, it nonetheless amply illustrates the impingement of Hellenism on the thought and life of dispersion Judaism. The evidences of the influence are everywhere. The peculiar Old Testament name for God, usually understood as YAHWEH (comparable with any specific divine name such as Egyptian Re or Greek Zeus), was entirely eliminated in the Septuagint, being replaced by a more comprehensive and universal designation: LORD (in Greek: *Kurios*). It was far more appropriate to a cosmopolitan and monotheistic age. Innumerable anthropomorphisms are dismissed as symbolism, e.g., "the hand of God" becomes "the power of God" and "his robe" becomes "his glory."

A wider range of books was permitted in the Septuagint than in the Palestinian canon. Such fringe books are known by the confusing terms Apocrypha and Pseudepigrapha. Technically, *apocrypha* ("hidden, concealed things") are writings that purport to reveal coming events previously sealed away by divine commandment, and technically *pseudepigrapha* ("false, spurious writings") are books attributed erroneously to ancient figures of renown, such as Enoch, Moses, Daniel, and Ezra. The literal meanings, however, apply to only a few of the books included in the collections called Apocrypha and Pseudepigrapha. Furthermore, in the Septuagint manuscripts these books are not distinguished from the writings eventually accepted in the Palestinian canon, nor do all the books of the Apocrypha appear in any one manuscript. For that matter most of the Pseudepigrapha do not appear in Septuagint manuscripts at all.

Accordingly the terms are best understood as follows: the Apocrypha are books in the Alexandrian Jewish community that were excluded from the Palestinian Jewish canon altogether and given a secondary rank in Protestant canons, but have been fully accepted in the Roman Catholic and Eastern canons. The Pseudepigrapha are marginal books that eventually found acceptance in the Eastern Churches. Some critical editions of the Pseudepigrapha have included works never taken into any Christian canon, such as the Letter of Aristeas and the Aramaic book of Ahiqar. Roman Catholics title the Apocrypha "deuterocanonical," thus reserving "apocryphal" for the Pseudepigrapha. In an effort to escape the terminological morass some students of intertestamental literature have recommended that all noncanonical books simply be called "apocryphal."

Among the important Apocrypha are the Wisdom of Ben Sira or Ecclesiasticus (not to be confused with the biblical Ecclesiastes and the Wisdom of Solomon), the historical I and II Maccabees, and the short stories Tobit, Judith, and Bel and the Dragon. The Apocrypha also includes additions to the canonical books of Esther and Daniel. Among the more noted Pseudepigrapha are the Psalms of Solomon, the Testaments of the Twelve Patriarchs, and the apocalyptic writings of Baruch, Enoch, and the Assumption of Moses. It is to the advantage of every student of the Old Testament—and of the New Testament as well—to read the major apocryphal books.

The Bible of the first Christians was the Septuagint, at least insofar as the bulk of converts were Greek-speaking. In fact the codices of the Septuagint we possess are all Christian, since the Jews renounced the Greek version because of its wholesale appropriation by the daughter religion. Many of the distinctive terms and ideas of the New Testament receive their orientation and flavor from their usage in the Greek Old Testament, among the most striking cases being "covenant," "Lord" as applied to Jesus, and "virgin" with reference to Mary. A majority of the New Testament quotations of the Old are based on the Greek version rather than the original Hebrew. It is owing to the early dominance of the Greek Old Testament that the

Latin and English versions have often been influenced by the Septuagint, even to the names of books (e.g., Genesis, Exodus, Deuteronomy).

In time other Greek versions appeared. Aquila, close friend of Rabbi Akiba, made an exceedingly literal Greek translation about A.D. 100 to replace the Septuagint. The translation was careful to exclude Christian interpretations; evidence of its conservatism may be seen in Aquila's habit of representing the Hebrew God by a Greek transliteration of YAHWEH. The Greek translations of Theodotion and Symmachus were probably also made in the second century A.D. It is not certain whether they were under Christian or Jewish auspices. Symmachus at any rate gives a free and idiomatic translation, probably to counteract the clumsiness of Aquila. We possess a few Aquila manuscripts from the Cairo Geniza but all that we know of the others comes to us from the few fragments of Origen's great compilation of the Greek translations. In six parallel columns Origen included (1) the Hebrew text, (2) a Greek transliteration of the Hebrew, (3) Aquila, (4) Symmachus, (5) Septuagint, and (6) Theodotion. Not merely a compilation, the *Hexapla* ("six columns") became in the hands of Origen a critical edition of the first importance with textual variations specified by diacritical marks. A century and a half later while working on his Vulgate, Jerome consulted the Hexapla in the library at Caesarea of Palestine. It is one of the great losses of antiquity that the Hexapla, except for fragments, has perished.

The other versions may be introduced more quickly. The notable expansion of the Christian church westward from Palestine to Rome should not blind us to its successes in the Near East. The Syriac Old Testament, known as the Peshitta ("common, vernacular"), was a product of the Christian mission in the Syrian interior, where Greek was not spoken. Probably the translation was made in the late first or second century. As a witness to the original Hebrew text it is generally less reliable than the Septuagint. This Syriac version was doubtless carried by the first Christian missionaries to India and China.

Most of the urban inhabitants of the western Roman Empire were able to speak Greek. It was not until the end of the second century that we find evidence of Latin as a church language. It was then that Tertullian began to employ it and it is from about 200 that we have evidence of the first rendering of Old Testament books into Latin.

These early translations are generally called the Old Latin version, but it is no more a unity than the Septuagint, in fact less so. We can account for the roughness and numerous shifts in style only on the supposition that it was not a single official translation but rather the result of independent and widely separated efforts to supply the needs of local congregations.

So unsatisfactory were these translations from both the literary and religious points of view (Augustine comments on his disgust at the barbarisms of the Old Latin) that in A.D. 382 Pope Damasus commissioned Jerome to produce an official revision. Originally he worked only from the Greek but, having studied several years with Palestinian rabbis, before long he realized the necessity of dealing directly with the Hebrew. The resulting revision was known as the Vulgate, a term in Latin meaning almost the same as Peshitta in Syriac ("common, vernacular"). It was a long while before the Vulgate supplanted its predecessors and in some of the remoter areas, as in northern Europe, the Old Latin lasted well into

The Jerome window in the Latin chapel in Bethlehem.

the Middle Ages. But the uniform style and the sonorous cadences of the Vulgate eventually secured it a place of undying affection in the liturgical usage of the church.

Hebrew ceased to be spoken by the Jews sometime after the first Exile (587–538 B.C.). In the dispersion it was replaced by Greek, thus giving rise to the Septuagint and other Greek versions. In Palestine, however, Aramaic became the language of the people. Hebrew Scriptures continued to be read in the synagogue services but, in addition, an Aramaic paraphrase (*targum*) by an interpreter (*meturgeman*) was introduced for the understanding of the congregation. What we know as the Targum is the eventual written form in which these oral renderings were cast beginning early in the Christian era. Even more than with the other versions, the Targums are characterized by free interpretations that do not hesitate to expand or change the original in order to expound a message. For this reason it must be used with more than the usual amount of caution whenever it departs from the Masoretic Text. The most important of the Targums are Targum Onkelos (Pentateuch) and Targum Jonathan (Prophets).

ENGLISH VERSIONS

The early versions from the Anglo-Saxon through Wyclif were all based on the Vulgate. With the invention of printing and the rediscovery of Greek and Hebrew occasioned by the Renaissance, William Tyndale produced the first English version to be based on the original languages, although his translation of the Old Testament was confined chiefly to the Pentateuch (1529). Throughout the sixteenth century a series of versions appeared, all in some measure dependent on their predecessors, and yet each contributing something to the tradition eventually to mingle in the King James translation. Worthy of singling out are Coverdale's Bible (1535), "Matthew's" Bible (1537), the Great Bible (1539), and the Geneva Bible (1560). Pressure for uniformity in the English versions led to the summoning of the Hampton Court Conference by James I in 1604. For the following seven years approximately fifty scholars labored in committees to produce the Authorized Version of 1611, commonly known since as the King James Version (KJV). Coming in the midst of the Elizabethan Age, when the English language had flowered, and capitalizing on the brilliant work of Tyndale and others, the King James has continued, in the words of John Livingston Lowes, as "The Noblest Monument of English Prose."[8] After three and a half centuries its beauty and felicity of style still elicit admiration. Yet, as with most new versions, its superiority was not at once apparent and for a matter of years the Geneva Bible continued to offer the King James stiff competition.

Increasing uneasiness with the insecure textual foundations of the Authorized Version, plus the inevitable changes in the English language, led to the Revised Version of 1885 in England and the Amer-

[8] John Livingston Lowes, *Essays in Appreciation,* Houghton Mifflin, 1936, pp. 1–31.

ican Revised in 1901. Both of these revisions, while more accurate, are far from being the literary equal of the King James. They are characterized by literal constructions and at times by an almost pedantic style. In subsequent decades they have been widely used as study Bibles but have failed to replace the King James in general usage.

The most recent development in the engrossing story of the English Old Testament was the publication in 1952 of the Revised Standard Version. The work of a committee of American scholars, the translation stands in the King James–Revised tradition but makes use of more reliable manuscripts and especially of the work of Paul Kahle in uncovering the ben Asher text. It is apparent that the RSV is far closer to the literary excellence of the King James than was either the English or American Revised, especially in familiar passages. In fact the King James was changed by the revision committee only when necessary to discard outmoded English or to correct inaccuracies based on poor Hebrew manuscripts. Time alone can tell whether this version will replace the King James, but it seems already to have made greater strides than either of the previous Revised Versions.

There are other valuable English translations. James Moffatt, who produced *A New Translation of the Bible* (1926; Revised 1935), was a highly literate and broadly educated New Testament scholar. In spite of the fact that he did not bring quite the same resources to the Old Testament section as he did to the New, it is nevertheless a brilliant idiomatic rendering. A popular translation is *The Complete Bible, An American Translation* (1939), commonly called the Chicago Bible. The Old Testament was prepared by Alexander R. Gordon, T. J. Meek, J. M. P. Smith, and Leroy Waterman (New Testament and Apocrypha by Edgar J. Goodspeed). In 1917 the Jewish Publication Society of America released *The Holy Scriptures according to the Massoretic Text* (reissued 1955); this is a translation that takes into account the existing English versions but draws heavily on Jewish tradition in the Talmud and the medieval commentaries. In America, scholars of the Catholic Biblical Association have prepared the so-called Confraternity Bible. British Protestant scholars are at work on an official translation. Broadly similar to the RSV project, it is a more ambitious undertaking in that it is a completely fresh translation, without reference to previous English versions. Since language is in constant development, the need for fresh renderings of the Bible is a never-ending one.

Our cursory survey of the history of the Old Testament from the inception of the separate writings to the present day versions has retraced a story unexcelled in drama and human interest. At every point the history of canon and text impinges upon general historical and cultural movements, and the chief actors in the drama have seldom been recluses or pedants but rather men of action and religious concern who sought to keep the writings before the people in their native tongue and to preserve the original text. The modern reader will approach the Old Testament more intelligently and appreciatively once he has glimpsed its history through thirty centuries.

✦ 3 ✦

THE OLD TESTAMENT WORLD

Geography and history are profoundly and intimately connected. Geography is the womb within which history and culture grow. To say this is not to deny the mystery of personal and group distinctiveness, which can never be wholly explained by heredity or environment. But neither a man nor a culture is understandable without reference to what has gone before and the setting in which maturation takes place. Any student of classical civilization knows that the city-state experiment of Greece is not understandable apart from the broken mountain ranges and islands of the Aegean. And who can deny that American history has been deeply affected by the expansion of the nation to the Pacific, so that we have been forced to think not only in terms of Europe but of the Orient as well?

THE NEAR EAST

When we reconstruct the stage on which Israel acted out her part in world history, it proves to be far larger than Palestine alone. "From Dan to Beersheba" (the biblical expression for designating the far limits of the promised land) does not begin to encompass the true extent of the biblical setting. Any accurate analysis of the Old Testament world will have to take into account not merely the region where the Hebrews lived, but the lands of their origin and the people with whom they had repeated and significant contact. This immediately brings into the student's survey a large area of land at the meeting place of the three continents of Europe, Asia, and Africa.

57

It is commonly called the Near East and embraces territory in the present states of Turkey, Iran, Iraq, Syria, Lebanon, Jordan, Israel, Saudi-Arabia, and Egypt.

The Egyptologist James Henry Breasted referred to the curving zone of arable soil from Mesopotamia to Egypt as "the Fertile Crescent."[1] The term has persisted in spite of the fact that much of the region is far from fertile by normal standards. Another weakness in the term is that the Crescent does not take into account the mountains or desert, which were of great significance in the historical geography of the Near East. A more accurate setting was given by Stanley Cook in the Cambridge Ancient History.[2] The uneven rectangular area that he blocked out had for its boundaries (1) the mountains of Iran (Zagros range) and the Persian Gulf on the northeast, (2) the Armenian and Anatolian highlands (Taurus range) and the Mediterranean coast on the northwest, (3) the Red Sea on the southwest, and (4) the Gulf of Aden and Indian Ocean on the southeast. This Semitic quadrilateral has the merit of including much of the plateau and mountain region and also the great land mass of Arabia. Unfortunately it does not embrace Egypt because Cook was thinking in ethnic terms and the Egyptians were not Semites.

[1] J. H. Breasted, *Ancient Times, A History of the Early World*, Ginn, 1916, p. 100.
[2] Stanley Cook, *The Cambridge Ancient History*, Macmillan, 1924, 2nd ed., vol 1, chap. 5.

MOUNTAINS

Broadly speaking there are three zones in the Near East. The most northerly is the series of mountain ranges and plateaus extending in a semicircle parallel to the Fertile Crescent, from the Persian Gulf on the southeast to the Mediterranean on the west. At points rising to towering peaks as in Armenia (site of Mt. Ararat), they are elsewhere a tangled network of hills as in Palestine. Here and there they are pierced by passes permitting traders and conquerors to move from the less hospitable highlands into the plains. The Gate of Zagros or Median Gate, a pass along the Diyala River, connected Babylonia and Persia; on the magnificent Behistun Rock the Persian

monarch Darius I inscribed his accomplishments. On the northwest, the Cilician Gates cut through the Taurus range from Syria into Asia Minor, a route traversed by Hittite, Persian, and Macedonian armies, as well as by the Apostle Paul.

This mountain region produced a hardy people. The center of the Hittite Empire was located in Asia Minor and the Medes and Persians came to power in Iran. These "uplanders" were major forces in

THE ANCIENT NEAR EAST 3000~500 B.C.

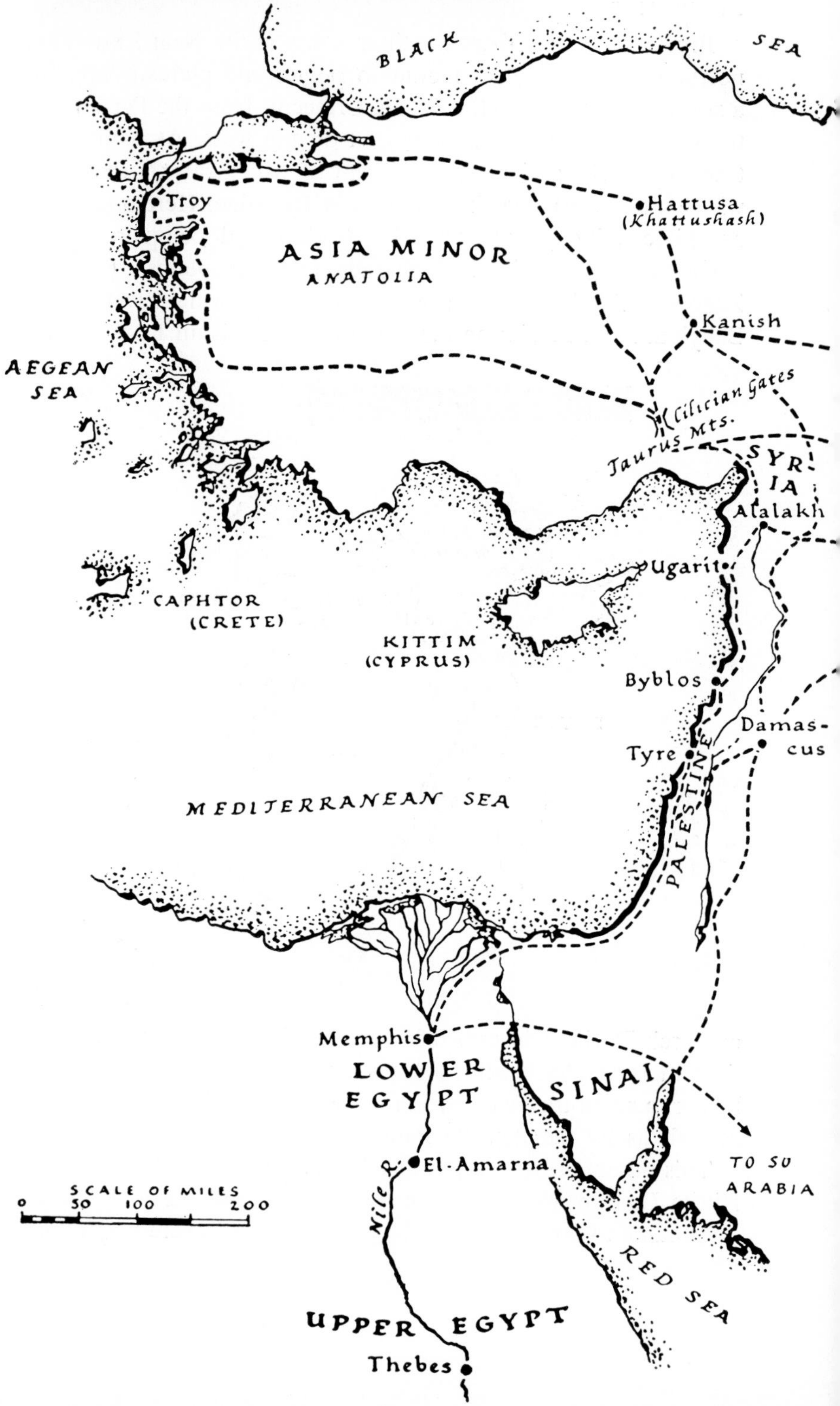

BLACK SEA

Troy

ASIA MINOR
ANATOLIA

Hattusa
(Khattushash)

Kanish

AEGEAN
SEA

Cilician Gates

Taurus Mts.

SYR-
IA

Alalakh

CAPHTOR
(CRETE)

Ugarit

KITTIM
(CYPRUS)

Byblos

Damas-
cus

Tyre

PALESTINE

MEDITERRANEAN SEA

Memphis

LOWER
EGYPT

SINAI

SCALE OF MILES
0   50   100   200

El-Amarna

Nile R.

TO S.
ARABIA

RED SEA

UPPER EGYPT

Thebes

CASPIAN SEA

Carchemish
Haran
ASSYRIA
Nineveh
Euphrates R.
Ashur
Tigris R.
Nuzi
Diyala R.
Ecbatana
Median Gates
PERSIA
Mari
BABYLONIA
Babylon
Nippur
SUMERIA
Susa
TO INDIA
Erech
ur
PERSIAN GULF

ARABIA

---------- MAJOR ROUTES

ancient Near Eastern history. Less familiar inhabitants of the mountains were the Guti (meaning "highlanders") and the Kassites, whose
military prowess enabled them to conquer and hold southern Mesopotamia for centuries. In the Armenian mountains around Lake Van
lived the Urartu. The Assyrians had all they could do to keep these
tough fighters from their doorstep and they never really succeeded in
subjugating them. It should be clear from these examples that the

*The Royal Gate at the Hittite capital of Hattusa. The 7-foot figure of a
god adorns the left jamb.*

highlands provided many of the eventual inhabitants of the Fertile
Crescent. Sometimes the invaders were culturally inferior (the Guti
and Kassites) but often they were equal or superior to those already
dwelling in the plains (the Hittites; the Persians). The first inhabitants
of Mesopotamia in historic times were the Sumerians (not to be confused with Samaria or Samaritans), whose origins are still problematic, although they likely originated in the mountain region that
rims the Crescent. Should this prove to be the case then the first high
civilization in the Tigris-Euphrates valley may be regarded as at
least partially derived from the mountain peoples.

FERTILE CRESCENT

The Fertile Crescent proper extends in a great curve between the two termini of the lower Mesopotamian valley (Babylonia or Sumeria) and Egypt. The distance from the head of the Persian Gulf to the Nile Delta is roughly twelve hundred miles. The Crescent grows progressively less fertile as one moves away from the two extremities. Upper Mesopotamia and interior Syria are in effect a desert. For that matter the entire region would be a desert had the populace to depend upon rainfall. Babylonian economy and civilization were dependent on the maintenance of the canals that distributed the silt-laden waters fed into the two great rivers by the mountain run-off. The present desolation of much of lower Mesopotamia can be attributed to failure to maintain the irrigation canals. One of the first steps in the rehabilitation of modern Iraq has been the development of water resources. Egypt likewise was without appreciable rainfall but the annual inundation of the Nile, flooding down out of the Ethiopian highlands, produced a five-to-ten-mile-wide green ribbon along the Nile that extended over five hundred miles from the first cataract (modern Aswan) to the sea. The Crescent in its north-south course through Syria and Palestine is a jumble of contrasts, steep mountains abutting the sea, with appreciable rainfall on the seaward slopes but meager amounts in the interior valleys. The mountains and desert have pressed so close together that there is neither soil nor water to produce the agricultural abundance typical of the terminal river valleys. Exceptions are found in the plains such as the Philistine and Esdraelon in Palestine.

The two extremes of the Crescent are unequal in their degree of exposure to outside influence, and thus in the homogeneity of the cultures they produced. Since the Mesopotamian plains were open to the incursions of uplanders, Babylonia was repeatedly invaded. Not only was this so from the one side, but also from the other, that is from the desert flank. Two of the greatest Mesopotamian empires, the Akkadian of Sargon I and the Amorite of Hammurabi, probably had their origin in migrations of nomads from the Arabian desert who conquered the Sumerians and, benefiting from their culture, developed far-flung empires. The powerful Assyrians were likewise at least partially the offspring of one of the innumerable infiltrations of Semitic people from the desert into the plain. The history and geography of the ancient Near East are thus crucially conjoined: the history of the Crescent, from Mesopotamia to Palestine, is the history of high civilizations developed in the valleys but continually fed by fresh sources of strength from the mountains and deserts. While the culture developed a uniform character, with newcomers adapting many elements of the old, the ethnic and political fortunes of the Crescent were extremely checkered.

Egypt offers a striking contrast to the remainder of the Crescent. For most of its length it is sealed off from Asia by the Red Sea. Near the Delta, at its one point of contact with Asia, a string of marshes, lakes, and military outposts effectively isolated the land of the Nile (through this region the Suez Canal was eventually dug). On the west the desert formed a bleak barrier and southward the cataracts of the Nile prevented extensive contact with the interior of Africa. Furthermore, the people west and south of Egypt were without the political development and military technology necessary to pose a serious threat to the Egyptians. When Libyan and Ethiopian usurpers did take the throne, it was due to internal weakness and the "conquerors" were thoroughly Egyptianized.

There were invasions, to be sure. The Hyksos, a vigorous warlike people who introduced the horse-drawn chariot into Near Eastern warfare (the Kassites used horses for transport and battle but did not have chariots), conquered Egypt and ruled for 200 years. Assyrians, Persians, and Macedonians briefly possessed the Nile. But the latter conquests significantly all took place after Egypt was in decline and, even then, they were remarkably brief. Only Greek culture, coming at the twilight of Egyptian glory, was able to make inroads. There were ups and downs in the dynastic affairs of Egypt, alternating strong and weak rulers, periods of feudal regression and civil chaos. But through it all there is an essential continuity well expressed in the fact that when the Egyptian historian-priest Manetho (writing in the third century B.C.) recorded the dynasties of Egypt he numbered them consecutively from I to XXX. Allowing for gaps, since known as Intermediate Periods, he felt no incongruity in adhering to the numbered sequence as an expression of the unity of Egyptian history through 2,500 years. We speak of Sumerian city-states, Akkadian Empire, Old Babylonian Empire, Assyrian Empire; but there was only one Egypt. There might be Old Kingdom, Middle Kingdom, and New Kingdom, but through all its phases Egypt bore a fundamental identity.

Typical ancient Near Easterners. These Egyptian captives are, from left to right, a Libyan, a Semite, a Hittite, a Philistine, a Semite.

DESERT

The third zone in the ancient Near East is the desert that hugs the inside of the Crescent and extends for hundreds of miles southward into Arabia. Desert in this context is not necessarily sandy and un-inhabited wasteland, but rather land that will not support settled life. Some stretches are much more hospitable to man than others, the winter rains bringing enough green shoots to allow the pastoral nomad to range widely with his flocks, whereas in the summer he clings to the water available at the oases. This rhythm of living half the year in one place and wandering the other half constitutes the life of the seminomad. Job was just such a seminomad, although a notably prosperous one.

Out of the desert vortex bands of nomads passed into the Fertile Crescent, seeking a less marginal form of life. It is really from the viewpoint of the nomads that we may speak of the Crescent's fertility. It offered opportunity for a settled life, for the growing of grain and the enjoyment of succulent fruit and stimulating wine. As with their counterparts in the mountainous north, the nomads entered the Crescent as conquerors or would-be conquerors, sometimes veiled in the merchant's garb. The opening wedge for others was their engagement as mercenaries. They brought with them the vitality and hardihood of those who have been forced to pit themselves against nature in order to survive. They stayed as settlers, adopting the culture of the vanquished at the same time they modified it, in turn succumbing to the influx of other nomads. It is a process described by one Orientalist as "the conflict between the Sown and the Unsown."[3] To this general pattern of movement from the desert zone into the Crescent the Hebrews belong. Entering as nomads they turned to agriculture and eventually were called upon to resist the entrance of other nomads.

Our characterization of the wider Near Eastern world demonstrates that Palestine was a vital segment of it, not in terms of resources or political power, but in terms of strategic location. Its position on the trade routes between the two great centers of river valley civilization made it inevitable that Palestine would be much traveled and often fought over, a center of commerce and the exchange of culture, a

[3] James Montgomery, *Arabia and the Bible,* University of Pennsylvania Press, 1934, p. 18.

prize of war. Between Egypt and Mesopotamia ran a series of roads arching northward around the Crescent, keeping to the main concentrations of population and avoiding the great desert that lay between. Palestine was astride these routes and was therefore a kind of land bridge or corridor that every great power needed to control if it were to protect its flank and tip the balance of power in its favor. Since only rarely was there strong political and military power centered in Palestine, the periods of Hebrew independence were in reality merely interludes in the centuries-long subservience of Palestine first to Egypt, then to Assyria, Neo-Babylonia, Persia, Macedonia, Rome, and the Arabs.

Taking into account Palestine's location in the Fertile Crescent and its close proximity to the desert, we can see two historical pressures operating in the Old Testament period, sometimes one and sometimes the other being more influential: (1) the fight for independence (or at least choice of overlord) in the face of the constant power struggle between the great empires that needed to control the corridor between the Nile and the Tigris-Euphrates in order to hold the balance of power; (2) the fight for local security owing to the threat of nomadic tribes pressing in from the desert. As a result, it is no surprise that Palestine was affected by nearly every major political, cultural, and religious movement in the ancient world. The Hebrews, in spite of the fact that they did not originate any strong political or cultural forces (other than in religion), were nevertheless always near to the center of Near Eastern political and cultural contention. We shall see how decisively this has contributed to Israel's faith.

We have indicated briefly the scope of the biblical world, its various inhabitants, as well as something of their natural and historical environment. Our procedure has been random in the sense that the observations have been determined by historical geography, or geopolitics as it is called currently, rather than chronology or cultural unity. The justification for the neglect of culture and history per se is that later chapters will call our attention to specific features of Sumero-Akkadian, Egyptian, and Canaanite culture. We shall keep our eye on Near Eastern history in the large, sensitive to Israel's involvement, for it is surprising how often Israel was affected by the crucial events.

The present introduction concludes with a simplified chart of the historical periods synchronized with the archaeological ages. The political eras are indicated with dates and important rulers or ruling peoples specified. The first two columns represent Egypt and Meso-potamia respectively; the third column is reserved for peoples or rulers whose center of government was outside the Fertile Crescent proper. The accompanying period maps of the ancient Near East visualize these historical periods from the dawn of history to the rise of Rome. It is hoped that in the course of study the reader will return often to the chart and maps with a view to relating the details of history to an overall scheme.

Chart 3. Historical Periods of the Ancient Near East, 3000–63 B.C.

EGYPT		MESOPOTAMIA	
	EARLY BRONZE AGE	3000–2000 B.C.	
Protodynastic Period Dynasties I–II (*Menes*)	2900–2700	Sumerian City-States	2800–2400

Old Kingdom or Pyramid Age
      2700–2200
Dynasties III–VI
  (*Khufu; Khaf-Re*)
		Akkadian Empire
		  (*Sargon I; Naram-Sin*)
			2400–2200

First Intermediate Period Dynasties VII–XI	2200–2000	The Guti or Highlanders	2200–2100

		Sumerian Renascence
		  (*Gudea* of Lagash
		  Ur-Nammu of Ur)
			2100–1950

	MIDDLE BRONZE AGE	2000–1500 B.C.	
Middle Kingdom Dynasty XII (*Amen-em-het III*)	2000–1780	Elamites	1950–1830

Second Intermediate Period
Dynasties XIII–XVII
  (*Hyksos*)
	1780–1550	Old Babylonian Kingdom
		  Amorite Dynasties
		  (*Zimri-Lim; Hammurabi*)
			1830–1550

	LATE BRONZE AGE	1500–1200 B.C.	

New Kingdom 1550–1085
Dynasties XVIII–XX
  (*Thut-mose III*
  Akh-en-Aton
  Seti
  Ramses II
  Mer-ne-ptah)
	Assyrian Kingdom
	      1700–1100
	(in northern Mesopota-mia; *Ashur-uballit I*)
	Kingdom of Mitanni
	      1500–1370
	(*Hurrians* in northern Mesopotamia)
	Kassite Kingdom
	      1500–1200
	(in southern Mesopo-tamia)
		ANATOLIA
		Hittite Kingdom
		      1700–1200
		(*Suppiluliumas I*
		Hattusilis III)	

Chart 3 (*Continued*)

IRON AGE	1200 B.C.—

The Decline   1085–332
Dynasties XXI–XXX
  (*Shishak*
  Psamtik I
  Necho)
	Assyrian Empire 1100–612
	  (*Tiglath-pileser I*
	  Shalmaneser III
	  Tiglath-pileser III
	  Shalmaneser V
	  Sargon II
	  Sennacherib
	  Esarhaddon
	  Ashurbanipal)
	Neo-Babylonian Empire
	          612–538
	  Chaldean Dynasty
	    (*Nebuchadnezzar*
	    Nabonidus)

IRAN

Persian Empire   538–333
  (*Cyrus*
  Darius I
  Xerxes I)

MACEDONIA

Macedonian Empire
          333–323
  (*Alexander the Great*)

The Diadochi (Successors)

Ptolemaic Kingdom in Egypt 323–30 (*Ptolemy Philadelphus*)		Seleucid Kingdom in Syria 312–63 (*Antiochus Epiphanes*)

PALESTINE

Historical geographers have long described the topography of Palestine in terms of longitudinal strips extending, more or less unbroken, throughout the 150-mile length of the land. They have not always been clear enough in emphasizing that topographically Palestine is simply an extension of Syria. The same four zones can be traced northward to a point where Asia Minor begins, and are thus characteristic of that whole region lying between the Sinai Peninsula and the upper reaches of the Euphrates River. The zones of Palestinian geography will be discussed in sequence from west to east.

COASTAL PLAIN

For its entire length Palestine is flanked on the west by the Mediterranean, but two things prevented the Hebrews from becoming a maritime people. One was the lack of any all-weather harbor between Egypt and Tyre. The larger coastal cities were not ports: Gaza, Gath, Ashdod, and Ekron. To this natural bulwark against com-

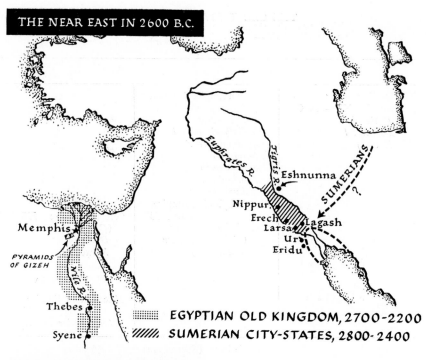

THE NEAR EAST IN 2600 B.C.

Euphrates R.
Tigris R.
Eshnunna
SUMERIANS ?
Nippur
Erech
Larsa
Lagash
Ur
Eridu
Memphis
PYRAMIDS OF GIZEH
Nile R.
Thebes
Syene

▦ EGYPTIAN OLD KINGDOM, 2700-2200
▨ SUMERIAN CITY-STATES, 2800-2400

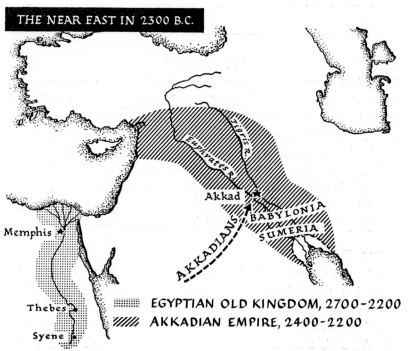

THE NEAR EAST IN 2300 B.C.

Tigris R.
Euphrates R.
Akkad
BABYLONIA
SUMERIA
AKKADIANS
Memphis
Thebes
Syene

▦ EGYPTIAN OLD KINGDOM, 2700-2200
▨ AKKADIAN EMPIRE, 2400-2200

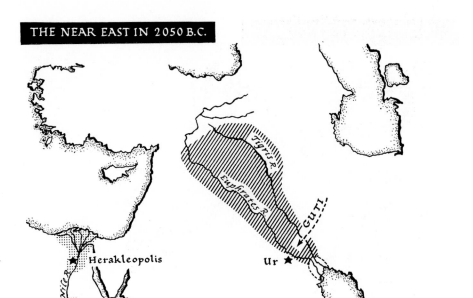

THE NEAR EAST IN 2050 B.C.

Herakleopolis

Thebes

Tigris R.

Euphrates R.

GUTI

Ur

EGYPTIAN FIRST INTERMEDIATE PERIOD, 2200~2000
THIRD DYNASTY OF UR, 2100~1950

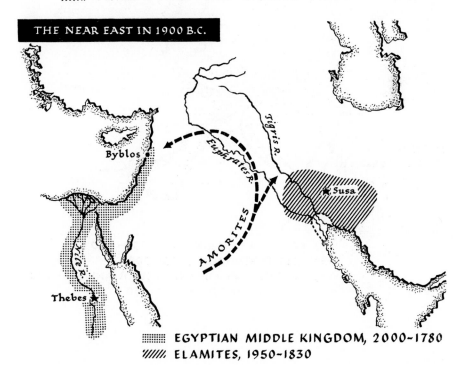

THE NEAR EAST IN 1900 B.C.

Byblos

Nile R.

Thebes

Tigris R.

Euphrates R.

Susa

AMORITES

EGYPTIAN MIDDLE KINGDOM, 2000~1780
ELAMITES, 1950~1830

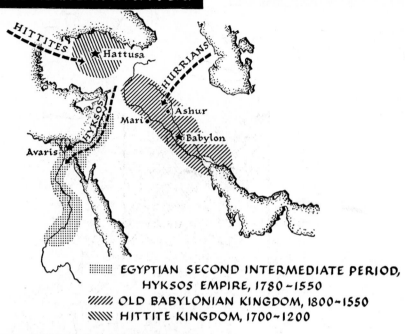

THE NEAR EAST IN 1700 B.C.

HITTITES
Hattusa
HURRIANS
HYKSOS
Ashur
Mari
Babylon
Avaris

::::: EGYPTIAN SECOND INTERMEDIATE PERIOD,
HYKSOS EMPIRE, 1780~1550
///// OLD BABYLONIAN KINGDOM, 1800~1550
\\\\\ HITTITE KINGDOM, 1700~1200

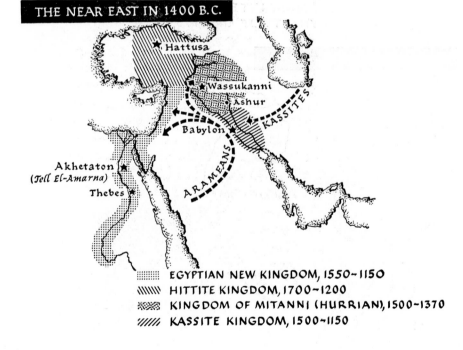

THE NEAR EAST IN 1400 B.C.

Hattusa
Wassukanni
Ashur
KASSITES
Babylon
Akhetaton
(Tell El-Amarna)
ARAMEANS
Thebes

::::: EGYPTIAN NEW KINGDOM, 1550~1150
\\\\\ HITTITE KINGDOM, 1700~1200
▨▨▨ KINGDOM OF MITANNI (HURRIAN), 1500~1370
///// KASSITE KINGDOM, 1500~1150

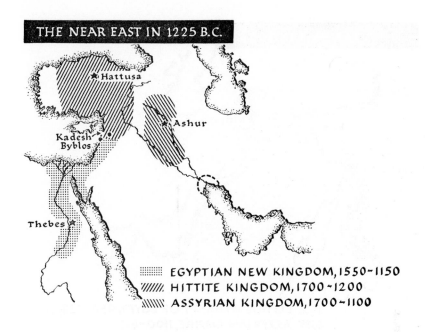

THE NEAR EAST IN 1225 B.C.

★ Hattusa

★ Ashur

Kadesh
Byblos

Thebes ★

▦ EGYPTIAN NEW KINGDOM, 1550~1150
▨ HITTITE KINGDOM, 1700~1200
▧ ASSYRIAN KINGDOM, 1700~1100

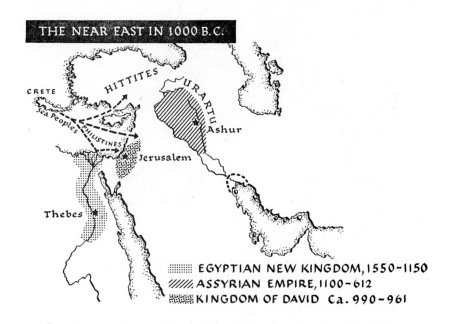

THE NEAR EAST IN 1000 B.C.

CRETE

HITTITES

URARTU

Sea Peoples

PHILISTINES

★ Ashur

★ Jerusalem

Thebes ★

▦ EGYPTIAN NEW KINGDOM, 1550~1150
▨ ASSYRIAN EMPIRE, 1100~612
▩ KINGDOM OF DAVID Ca. 990~961

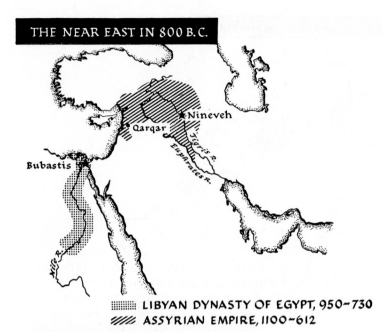

THE NEAR EAST IN 800 B.C.

Nineveh

Qarqar

Tigris R.

Euphrates R.

Bubastis

Nile R.

▓▓▓ LIBYAN DYNASTY OF EGYPT, 950~730
/// ASSYRIAN EMPIRE, 1100~612

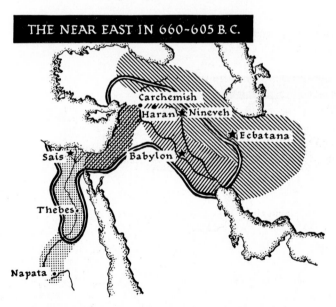

THE NEAR EAST IN 660~605 B.C.

Carchemish
Haran Nineveh
Ecbatana
Sais
Babylon
Thebes
Napata

〰 ASSYRIAN EMPIRE AT ITS ZENITH, Ca. 650
▒▒▒ SAITE DYNASTY OF EGYPT, 663~525
▓▓▓ HELD BY EGYPT, 609~605
\\\\\ MEDIAN EMPIRE, 612~550
/// CHALDEAN OR NEO~BABYLONIAN EMPIRE, 612~539

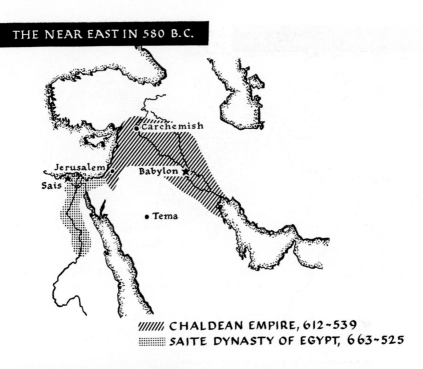

THE NEAR EAST IN 580 B.C.

Carchemish

Jerusalem
Sais

Babylon ★

• Tema

////// CHALDEAN EMPIRE, 612~539
SAITE DYNASTY OF EGYPT, 663~525

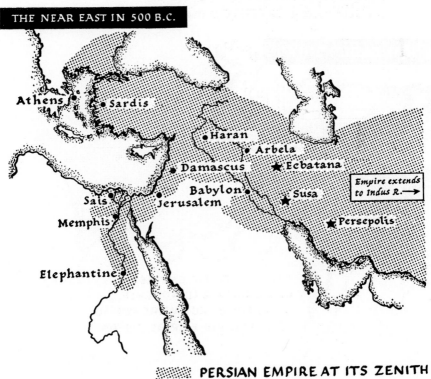

THE NEAR EAST IN 500 B.C.

Athens
• Sardis

• Haran
• Arbela

Damascus   ★ Ecbatana

Babylon •

Empire extends
to Indus R.→

Sais
Jerusalem   ★ Susa

Memphis

★ Persepolis

Elephantine •

PERSIAN EMPIRE AT ITS ZENITH

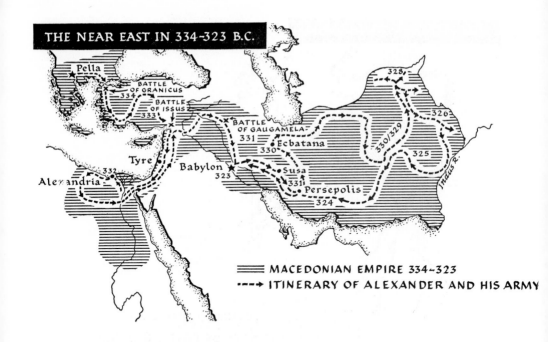

THE NEAR EAST IN 334~323 B.C.

Pella
BATTLE OF GRANICUS
334
BATTLE OF ISSUS
333
BATTLE OF GAUGAMELA
331
Ecbatana
330
Tyre
Babylon
323
Susa
331
Alexandria
332
Persepolis
324
330/329
328
326
325
Indus R.

≡≡≡ MACEDONIAN EMPIRE 334~323
---→ ITINERARY OF ALEXANDER AND HIS ARMY

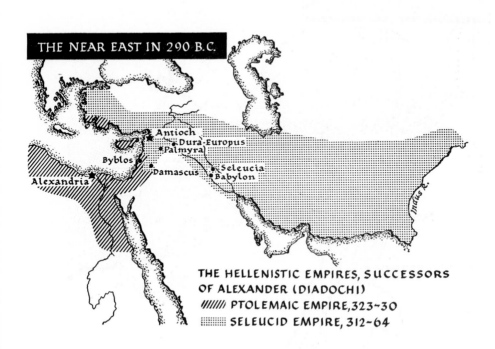

THE NEAR EAST IN 290 B.C.

Antioch
Dura-Europus
Palmyra
Byblos
Damascus
Seleucia
Babylon
Alexandria
Indus R.

THE HELLENISTIC EMPIRES, SUCCESSORS
OF ALEXANDER (DIADOCHI)
/////// PTOLEMAIC EMPIRE, 323~30
▒▒▒ SELEUCID EMPIRE, 312~64

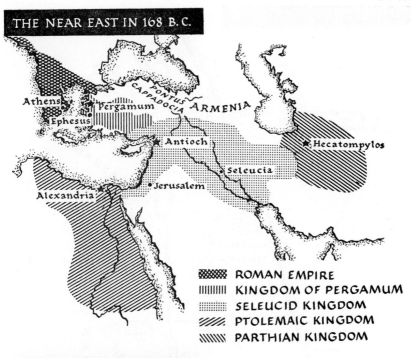

THE NEAR EAST IN 168 B.C.

Athens
Pergamum
Ephesus
PONTUS
CAPPADOCIA ARMENIA
Antioch
Hecatompylos
Seleucia
Alexandria
Jerusalem

▨▨ ROMAN EMPIRE
|||||| KINGDOM OF PERGAMUM
⠿ SELEUCID KINGDOM
▨ PTOLEMAIC KINGDOM
⦚ PARTHIAN KINGDOM

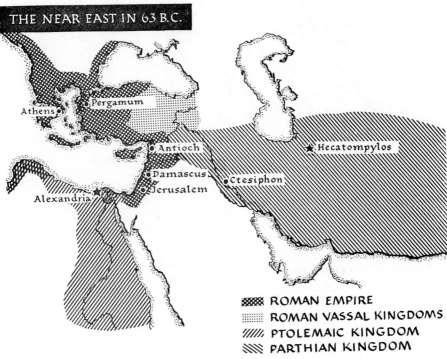

THE NEAR EAST IN 63 B.C.

Athens
Pergamum
Antioch
Hecatompylos
Damascus
Ctesiphon
Jerusalem
Alexandria

▨▨ ROMAN EMPIRE
⠿ ROMAN VASSAL KINGDOMS
▨ PTOLEMAIC KINGDOM
⦚ PARTHIAN KINGDOM

77

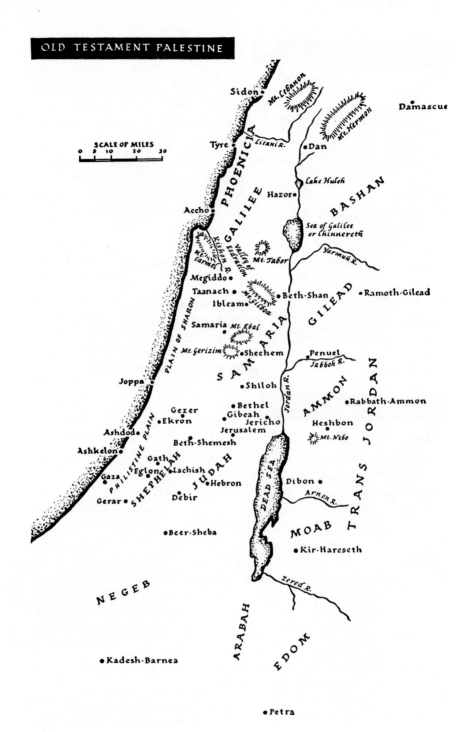

OLD TESTAMENT PALESTINE

SCALE OF MILES
0 5 10   20   30

Sidon

Mt. Lebanon

Damascus

Mt. Hermon

Tyre

Litani R.

Dan

PHOENICIA

Lake Huleh

Hazor

BASHAN

Accho

Sea of Galilee
or Chinnereth

GALILEE

Kishon R.

Valley of
Esdraelon

Mt. Tabor

Yarmuk R.

Mt. Carmel

Megiddo

Taanach

Mt. Gilboa

Beth-Shan

Ramoth-Gilead

Ibleam

GILEAD

Plain of Sharon

Samaria

Mt. Ebal

SAMARIA

Mt. Gerizim

Shechem

Penuel

Jabbok R.

AMMON

Joppa

Shiloh

Jordan R.

Rabbath-Ammon

Gezer

Bethel

Gibeah

Heshbon

Ekron

Jericho

Jerusalem

Ashdod

Mt. Nebo

Beth-Shemesh

TRANS JORDAN

Ashkelon

Gath

PHILISTINE PLAIN

Eglon

Lachish

JUDAH

DEAD SEA

Dibon

Gaza

SHEPHELAH

Debir

Hebron

Arnon R.

Gerar

Beer-Sheba

MOAB

Kir-Hareseth

NEGEB

ARABAH

Zered R.

Kadesh-Barnea

EDOM

Petra

78

mercial exploitation of the sea, add the long period during which the Philistines controlled the seacoast and at once the land-oriented rather than sea-oriented character of Israel's life becomes understandable. The sea, while frequently visible from the Hebrew highlands, remained a mystery. In Psalm 107 "those who go down to the sea in ships" are spoken of with a note of awe and when Jonah wants to flee to the very ends of the earth he boards a Mediterranean freighter sailing for Spain. It was quite otherwise with the Phoenicians who inhabited the coastal strip north of Acre. With their backs against the mountains and their faces to the sea, they made of Tyre and Sidon the mercantile centers of the eastern Mediterranean. The more northerly coastal cities of Byblos and Ugarit were important centers of trade long before the full flower of Phoenician civilization.

From north to south the major areas of the coastal strip were (1) the Plain of Acre (or Accho), with the most adequate port available to the Hebrews, though they held it only sporadically, (2) Mt. Carmel, (3) the Plain of Sharon, and (4) the Plain of Philistia (its Latinized form became the eventual name of the whole area: Palestine). Sharon was marshy and not thickly settled, whereas Philistia was a fertile agricultural plain, deriving its name from the sea raiders who settled there from about 1100 B.C. onward. The main road between Egypt and Babylonia passed through the Plains of Philistia and Sharon, cutting inland across the saddle between Mt. Carmel and the central ridge. Only rarely, as in the reign of David and Solomon (and later under Jeroboam II and Uzziah), did the Hebrews control this route and derive rich revenues from its busy traffic.

WESTERN HIGHLANDS

This was the backbone of Palestine, an almost continuous chain of hills and mountains, never lofty (high point near Hebron is 3,370 ft.) but frequently rugged, with a western slope exposed to the winter rains and thus suitable for farming, especially viticulture. This ridge with its innumerable lateral projections and precipitous ravines was the center of Hebrew history and civilization.

The central range, forming a southern spur of the Lebanon Mountains in Syria, divides into Galilee in the north, Samaria in the center, and Judea (or Judah) in the south. An important east-west rift through the highlands, separating Galilee and Samaria, was known as the Plain of Esdraelon or Jezreel. Mt. Tabor (1,843 ft.) in Galilee and Mt. Gilboa (1,698 ft.) in Samaria face one another across the plain. The main trade route entered the plain through a pass between Mt. Carmel and the hills of Samaria, and continued northeasterly toward Damascus, passing west of the Sea of Galilee. Esdraelon was the most fertile grain-growing region in Palestine. It was also the scene of some of the most significant battles in biblical history. Here Deborah defeated the Canaanites and Gideon routed the Midianites; Saul fell on the slopes of Gilboa; Josiah was put to death by Pharaoh Necho at Megiddo. Across the southern portion of the plain and in the foothills overlooking it was a belt of Canaanite fortified cities (Jokneam, Megiddo, Taanach, Ibleam, Beth-shan), which the Israelites were unable to capture until the time of David. As with the coastal plain, Esdraelon and Galilee were never regarded as Israelite strongholds.

The middle portion of the mountain range falls in Samaria and merges imperceptibly into the territory of Judea. The high points are Mt. Ebal (3,085 ft.) and Mt. Gerizim (2,849 ft.), twin peaks overlooking Shechem. Important cities in Israelite history were Samaria, Shiloh, and Bethel. The Judean hill country, after reaching its height around Hebron, begins to flatten out into a vast broken plateau known as the Negeb (Southland) reaching on into the Sinai Peninsula. The major Judean settlements were Jerusalem and Hebron. Westward from the main Judean spur extend the lateral ridges and valleys of the Shephelah (or Lowlands). Here were located the fortified cities of Lachish, Debir, and Beth-shemesh. Grain, figs, grapes, and olives thrived. Several passes into the Judean heartland were the scenes of conflict between invader and defender. Joshua, David, and Judas Maccabaeus proved their mettle as guerrilla fighters in these steep defiles.

JORDAN RIFT

Throughout Syria and Palestine extends a great geological fault. In Syria it forms the valleys of the Orontes and Litani rivers, the former flowing northward to enter the Mediterranean near Antioch and the latter flowing southward into the sea at a point near Tyre. On either side of these river valleys extended the Lebanon and Anti-Lebanon mountains. In Palestine the Jordan River traverses the gorge. One of the strangest rivers in the world, it begins in the foothills of Mt.

Hermon, flowing through Lake Huleh and then the Sea of Galilee (Old Testament Chinnereth). At the Sea of Galilee the river is already 685

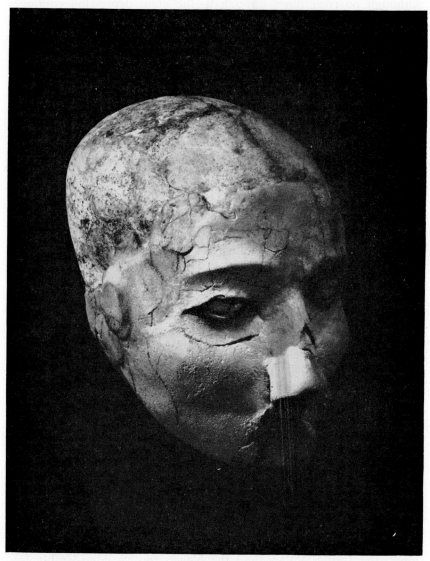

A plastered skull from Neolithic Jericho, packed with clay and the eyes inset with shells. The practice may reflect ancestor worship.

feet below sea level and continues on to empty into the Dead Sea at 1,290 feet below sea level. The Dead Sea has no outlet and, owing to the high percentage of chemical deposits in the water, no life. Jericho in the Jordan Rift is the world's lowest and oldest inhabited site. Although no river flows through it, the great depression continues southward from the Dead Sea to the Gulf of Aqabah, another hundred miles. The gorge, from Galilee to Aqabah, was known to the Hebrews as the Arabah ("dry or desert place"), and to the Arabs as the Ghor ("depression").

EASTERN HIGHLANDS

The area east of the Jordan, called Trans-Jordan, is a continuation of the Anti-Lebanon range of Syria dominated by Mt. Hermon (9,100 ft.). The sheer cliffs of the Trans-Jordan mountains rise abruptly and imposingly out of the Jordan gorge. The highest point in the eastern range is Mt. Nebo or Pisgah (2,644 ft.), from which Moses surveyed the land (Deut. 34:1–4). On the east, however, the mountains trail off toward the desert interior where a major trade route ran a north-south course from the Gulf of Aqabah to Damascus ("the King's highway"); it was to Israel's advantage to be strong enough to control Trans-Jordan commerce.

The eastern highlands are divided into five more or less definite areas separated from one another by east-west tributaries of the Jordan and the Dead Sea. *Bashan,* the most northerly, located east of the Sea of Galilee, was set apart from *Gilead* by the River Yarmuk. The River Jabbok, entering the Jordan about halfway between the Sea of Galilee and the Dead Sea, formed the boundary between Gilead and *Ammon.* South of the River Arnon lay *Moab,* roughly east of the Dead Sea, and beyond the River Zered was *Edom.* Both Moab and Edom were occupied in biblical times by people ethnically related to the Hebrews, with whom they were in frequent warfare.

The climate of Palestine is semiarid and is dominated, like many parts of the American Southwest, by two seasons, the rainy and the dry. Rain falls normally from late October into April, when the winds prevail from off the Mediterranean. The coastal plains and seaward slopes of the ranges receive the bulk of the precipitation. The eastward slopes, the Jordan Valley, and the Negeb receive considerably less rainfall. It is difficult for a person unacquainted with the climatic "freaks" of semiarid regions, where there is so much diversity depending on altitude and exposure, to realize that areas only a few miles apart may have radically different amounts of rain, dissimilar temperatures, and be suitable for quite varied crops: grain in the coastal plains; grapes and figs on the slopes; dates in the Jordan Valley. From May to October when the winds blow from the northwest, and less frequently from the east and south, no rain falls.

Vineyard and watchtower in the Judean hill country.

Palestine was a land marked by a great variety of terrain and climate within a relatively small compass. It is customary to liken its size to the state of Vermont and, like that area, because of the mountains its distances seem greater than they are. To the ancient, traveling on foot or by beast, it was an ample land. There were many parts of it that the average or even privileged Israelite had never seen. The land was modestly endowed with the good things of life. It was neither rich nor poor. In contrast to Egypt and Mesopotamia it left much to be desired, but compared with the desert to the south and east it was a paradise "flowing with milk and honey." To the industrious farmer and shepherd it could yield an adequate substance, although, especially in the highlands, it could never hope to support a large population. Finally, the combination of plains and trade routes, together with broken mountain ranges and plateaus, affords the geographical clue to the strange mixture of historical involvement and isolation that typified the Hebrews at different periods in their history. By and large it was a history of involvement, but the central range around Jerusalem offered a place of retreat when later Judaism, in the struggle for survival, withdrew from much of its earlier historical activism.

✤ 4 ✤

THE FATHERS OF ISRAEL

. . . offspring of Abraham his servant . . .
Ps. 105:6

According to biblical tradition the first Hebrew was Abraham, son of Terah. We have no direct information other than that contained in Genesis. All else is background material that seems to bring the world of Abraham into sharper focus but not Abraham himself. The background knowledge is nevertheless considerable and helps to narrow the range of the speculation about the origins of the Hebrew people. The patriarchal age is a puzzle with enough pieces now supplied so that the outline is clear even while the details remain incomplete.

THE ERA OF ABRAHAM

The problem of dating Abraham begins with the Old Testament chronology. Solomon initiated construction of the temple 480 years after the Exodus (I Kings 6:1). A date for the building of the temple somewhere in the period 973–958 B.C. seems assured. Reasoning backward we come to a fifteenth-century date for the Exodus. Exodus 12:40 states that the sojourn in Egypt totaled 430 years, which would place the descent of Jacob into Egypt in the nineteenth century B.C. When miscellaneous chronological notes in Genesis are computed (47:9; 25:26; 21:5; 12:4) they yield a date for Abraham's departure from Ur of 2098–2083 B.C. Older scholars found a possible verification of this framework in the equation of Amraphel in Genesis 14:1 with Hammurabi, who according to the accepted chronology also lived around the dawn of the second millenium B.C.

More recent study, based in large measure on the discovery of the

Assyrian king list with its welcome chronological detail, has tended to lower or telescope ancient Near Eastern dating. In the case of Hammurabi it has had the result of lowering him to the eighteenth century or even early seventeenth century B.C. To be sure it is now doubtful whether Amraphel and Hammurabi are the same king, so that Hammurabi and Abraham could easily be dissociated as contemporaries. If ancient history as a whole must be chronologically lowered, there are additional reasons for dating Abraham in the eighteenth century, as there is also increasing support for the view that the Exodus occurred in the thirteenth century B.C. Such a shift in dating would obviously fly in the face of the biblical chronology but the net result of the modification is to preserve elements of the Old Testament account that would have to be discredited if the Old Testament chronology were accepted. Without going into intricate analysis, and reserving the fuller consideration of dating for the discussion of the Exodus and conquest, we may emphasize that the majority of scholars today place Abraham in the Middle Bronze Age, generally in the period 1750–1650 B.C.

What do we know of the Middle Bronze Age? It was the era of Amorite power in Mesopotamia and of the overthrow of the Egyptian Middle Kingdom by the Hyksos. Civilization in both river valleys already had known more than a thousand years of recorded history and had reached impressive material, social, and religious heights. In fact both Egypt and Mesopotamia had seen their greatest cultural flowering in previous ages, the former under the Old Kingdom when the massive pyramids were built (2700–2200 B.C.) and the latter during the Sumerian city-state era (2800–2400 B.C.). Abraham appeared not among primitives or in a dark age of cultural eclipse but in a populated, prosperous, and self-assured age in Near Eastern history.

It is with the Babylonian development that we are most concerned for our knowledge of Hebrew origins, since biblical tradition explicitly identifies Abraham with the cities of Ur and Haran, located respectively in the far south and north of Mesopotamia. At the opening of the Middle Bronze Age we find an elaborate agricultural and commercial society centered in city-states scattered over the alluvial plain of middle and lower Mesopotamia. From time to time strong rulers, such as Hammurabi of Babylon, were able to assert control over other city-states but these Mesopotamian empires were always singularly insecure until the Persians introduced more effective administration.

The economy was based on the constant repair of the canal system, the breakdown of which would admit the inexorable return of the desert. The strength of the city, either on its own (Ur under the leadership of Ur-Nammu) or as the center of an empire (Babylon under Hammurabi), was evident in commercial enterprises extending around the Crescent and into Elam, Anatolia, and Egypt. A silver weight system and methods of credit and exchange facilitated trade. The cities, confined behind towering walls, were medieval-like with their narrow winding streets and the temple tower (called a ziggurat or "peak") dominant above the squat, closely packed houses. The prevailing theory is that the ziggurat, rising in terraced stages, was an artificial mountain, reflecting the original mountain home of the Sumerians.

The pantheon formed a bureaucratic hierarchy. Each god or goddess functioned in one or more realms of nature and society, often overlapping in duties and yet associated with particular cities as patrons. The high father god Anu was the patron deity of Erech; Enlil, the storm god, of Nippur; Enki, god of the sweet irrigation water, of Eridu; Inanna or Ishtar, goddess of fertility, of Ur; Utu, moon god, of Larsa and Sippar. These Sumerian gods were taken over, sometimes in transformed guise and with new names, by later invaders of Mesopotamia. The Amorites, as can plainly be seen in the epilogue of Hammurabi's Code, magnified Marduk as lord of Babylon and the characteristics and powers of the other divinities were attributed to him. Such absorption of one deity by another was only a gesture toward monotheism and quite different from the eventual monotheism of the Hebrews. Even the Egyptian monotheism of Pharaoh Akh-en-Aton was more thoroughgoing.

A method of writing on clay tablets with a tapered stylus produced cuneiform ("wedge-shaped") script. Introduced by the Sumerians, this script was continued by subsequent peoples who occupied Babylonia, especially the Akkadians who adapted it to their own Semitic tongue. It was also employed by the Assyrians. In its Akkadian-Assyrian form, cuneiform was widely circulated in the Near East as the international language of diplomacy and commerce. Elamites, Hittites, and Persians also adopted cuneiform scripts. Even as late as the fourteenth century, letters written from Palestinian vassals of Egypt to the Pharaoh's court were prepared in the Akkadian language.

The literary remains of the Sumero-Akkadian age are largely economic and social in character, consisting of contracts, receipts, inventories, etc. Some of the most significant discoveries have been the law codes, not only the widely publicized compilation of Hammurabi, but also some of the shorter Sumerian prototypes as much as two hundred

A tablet of the Babylonian flood story inscribed in cuneiform script.

years older, which offer clear proof of what Hammurabi himself indicated—that his laws were gathered from many sources. Magic and ritual texts have been found in great number. The most engrossing of the texts are the lengthy *Enuma Elish,* an account of creation, and *The Gilgamesh Epic,* the story of a demigod's search for immortality.[1] However naïve the form of the stories, they deal with some of the basic questions of human existence and show how far ancient man had progressed in attempting to unify the reality that confronted him in nature and society and to come to terms with it.

The Middle Bronze Age was not only one of manifest cultural attainment but also an era of internationalism, in the sense that the various parts of the Near Eastern world were aware of one another and in frequent commercial, diplomatic, and military contact. Sargon of Akkad had instituted a pattern of imperial expansion that was imitated by the revived Sumerian dynasties, especially under Gudea of Lagash and Ur-Nammu of Ur. The aggressive cosmopolitanism of Hammurabi is perhaps better known than that of his contemporary and rival, Zimri-Lim of Mari on the middle Euphrates. Mari's palace of 250 rooms and archives of 20,000 tablets were uncovered by French excavators in 1936–39. Among them are diplomatic and intelligence reports from far and wide aimed at insuring Mari's control of the trade routes leading to such distant lands as Asia Minor and Elam, and even to the islands of Crete and Cyprus. Zimri-Lim was eventually defeated by Hammurabi, who annexed his territory and trade. Another instance of the internationalism of this age was Alalakh, excavated by Sir Leonard Woolley, who had set out in deliberate search of the point of maximum intercommunication in the ancient Near East. He found it on a plain in northern Syria that formed a natural crossroads for traffic moving in all direction, not only around the Fertile Crescent, but to and from Asia Minor and the Mediterranean islands. The little kingdom of Alalakh was at its height from about 1800 to 1400 B.C. As he had hoped, Woolley found the Hittites, Egyptians, and Mesopotamians in frequent contact with Alalakh, chiefly through commerce.[2] Throughout the Crescent cultural interchange on many levels was far advanced, as can be seen *materially* not only by the business documents but by the discovery of artifacts in Palestine from all over the Near East, and *socially* as is evidenced in the many similarities among the Hittite, Assyrian, Old Babylonian, and Hebrew law codes.

The natural accompaniment of cultural interchange is ethnic inter-

---

[1] See Appendixes 1 and 2, pp. 565–580.
[2] Leonard Woolley, *A Forgotten Kingdom,* Penguin, 1953.

mingling and, from what we can determine on the basis of our still limited knowledge of the age, it was astonishingly prevalent. The various migrations and invasions did not destroy or displace the old inhabitants en masse. Rather the old and new populations lived side by side, intermarrying and assimilating physical and cultural features. We must keep this fluid state of affairs in mind when we ask: Who was Abraham? What was his race or ethnic group and manner of life?

Broadly speaking, there were three great waves of Semitic folk movement into the Fertile Crescent in the second and third millenia B.C. The earliest, about 3000–2500 B.C., for want of a more precise name may be termed *Akkadian* because it was in part due to this influx that the Sargonid dynasty of Akkad was founded and the first great empire of antiquity was fashioned. The invaders mingled with and gave new strength to Semitic elements that had occupied the north and middle regions of the river valley for centuries. It is also believed that the Assyrians who settled northern Mesopotamia along the upper Tigris were offshoots of this group.

The second wave, about 2200–1800 B.C., has been called *Amorite,* which means simply "The Westerner," apparently applied by the river dwellers to these Semitic intruders at the time of their invasion from the desert. From them sprang the Amorite dynasties of Zimri-Lim and Hammurabi; others of their number spread into Syria and Palestine, in the latter case forming the Canaanite population that the Hebrews encountered when they sought to occupy Palestine.

The final wave was the *Aramean* of 1500–1000 B.C., which led to the establishment of a large number of relatively small states in Syria and Palestine: Damascus, Hamath, Zobah, Edom, and Moab. The first three states and other smaller ones in the area are sometimes designated as the Syrians because Syria was the geographical locale in which they took root. The Arameans were remarkably adept as commercial middlemen and their language spread rapidly over the Near East, eventually replacing Akkadian as the international tongue. Under the Assyrian and Persian empires Aramean was the official language of the western provinces (Isa. 36:11). Known as Aramaic in the Bible, it replaced Hebrew in ordinary use among the Jews sometime after the Exile. Two sizable portions of the Old Testament are written in Aramaic, Ezra 4:8–6:18 and Daniel 2:4–7:28. It is generally believed that Jesus and his disciples spoke Aramaic, the common tongue of their day.

Had we simply to identify Abraham with one of these three Semitic folk movements our choice might be reasonably narrowed to the second or Amorite wave. But other ethnic groups and fragments of tradition complicate the picture. In the Middle Bronze Age there were also *Hittites* of Asia Minor who exerted influence on Syria and Mesopotamia and the partially Semitic *Hyksos,* conquerors of Egypt. Most baffling of all are the Hurrians and the Habiru.

The *Hurrians* have been recognized only since about 1925. They are unquestionably the people referred to rather casually in the Old Testament as Horites. They are sometimes called Subarians (Semitic name for them) or Mitanni (a major northern Mesopotamian state largely populated by Hurrians). Like the Sumerians before them, their origins are mysterious and many of their cultural features are neither clearly Semitic nor Indo-European. Seldom the political masters, they possessed distinctive customs of which we have considerable knowledge from excavations at Nuzi in Assyria and from Hittite reports. Evidence of their cultural influence has been found throughout the Fertile Crescent.

Similarly widely distributed in the Crescent were the *Habiru* who first came to the attention of the modern world with the discovery of the Tell el-Amarna letters written in the fourteenth century B.C. from Palestinian city-state rulers to their Egyptian overlords. Many of the letters speak of hostile invaders called "Habiru" who have captured strongholds and are threatening others.[3] In the first flush of discovery it was assumed that Habiru and Hebrew were linguistically equatable terms and that here was extrabiblical confirmation of the Hebrew conquest of Canaan. Additional occurrences of the term Habiru, however, have pointed to the more cautious conclusion that they were actually a social class of outcasts and freebooters, operating in some areas as organized brigands and elsewhere as mercenaries. When captured they often became slaves. They appear, among other places, at Hurrian Nuzi but their relation to the Hurrians is not clear, other than that both groups were mobile and contained diverse ethnic elements.

A population analysis of the Near East in the Middle Bronze Age underscores the absence of hard and fast ethnic lines. There was considerable migration and intermingling due to seminomadic life, marginal survival conditions, commerce, predatory raids and invasions, intermarriage, and alliances. Internationalism was apparent not only in

[3] See Appendix 3, pp. 580–581.

the exchange of culture but in ethnic cosmopolitanism. T. J. Meek, who has examined the question of Hebrew origins with exacting detail, concludes that "it was amid this welter of diverse nationalities, rapidly commingling, that the Hebrew people were born."[4]

The idea, entertained off and on by a minority of Jews and Gentiles, that the Jews are a people of physically distinct origin is utterly negated by the present evidence. The distinctiveness of the Jew is in his religion and the cultural traditions built up over centuries. The biblical Hebrew was not markedly distinguished from his neighbor in appearance or general culture. His bodily equipment and way of life were demonstrably hybrid. Even his unique religious faith was under constant threat of collapse in the face of enticing cults that never lacked Israelite devotees. The ethnic and cultural ingredients of the first Hebrews apparently included Hittite, Hurrian, Amorite, Aramean, and Sumero-Akkadian elements, but the era is still too imperfectly known to warrant complex reconstructions. The heterogeneous origins of the Jews were not forgotten in biblical tradition. The Exodus was thought to have included non-Hebrews, "a mixed multitude" (Exod. 12:38), and Ezekiel says to the daughter Jerusalem "your father was an Amorite, and your mother a Hittite" (16:3). The notion of Jewish "purity of race" (either as a basis for self-glorification or anti-Semitism) is a fantasy as surely as the Nazi myth of Aryan racial purity. Neither anthropology nor Near Eastern history support such nonsense. The Old Testament concept of "a chosen people" is not only indifferent to but actually antagonistic toward "purity of race."

THE PATRIARCHAL TRADITIONS

With the cultural and ethnic situation of the Middle Bronze Age in mind, we shall now turn to the patriarchal traditions of Genesis 12–50. The attempt to correlate the historical background and the textual data, however tentative, permits some instructive conclusions. Fifty years ago these questions were generally answered negatively: Were there actual men by the names of Abraham, Isaac, and Jacob? Can . we know anything of them as historical figures? A more cautious mood is upon us and no doubt a far wiser one. Scholars are constrained to believe that there are more authentic memories in Genesis than they once thought. Indeed some have jumped to the opposite extreme, affirming that all sorts of details in Genesis have now been "proved" ac-

[4] T. J. Meek, *Hebrew Origins*, Harper, rev. ed., 1950, p. 6.

curate. More valuable than tracing the controversy is a knowledge of the factors on which the biblical student must base his judgment.

ORAL TRANSMISSION

The major new evidence comes from the discovery of the remarkable accuracy of Genesis in picturing social customs. The fifteenth-century documents from Hurrian Nuzi describe a number of practices that tally repeatedly with the Genesis reports. They speak of the widespread custom of adoption (cf. Gen. 15:2–4), although at Nuzi many of the transactions were legal fictions for personal gain. Since land must be held inalienable by the family, those who wished to sell property would simply "adopt" the prospective buyer, thereby making him technically a part of the owner's household. The sale was then legal! We read also that it was customary for sterile wives to give handmaidens to the husband (cf. Gen. 16:2) in the hope of obtaining children. Nuzi law explicitly protected the rights of the handmaiden, who could not be peremptorily dismissed after her usefulness was over. This may be the background for Abraham's uneasiness about expelling Hagar, even at the insistence of Sarah and after a divine command (cf. Gen. 21:8–14). There is a report of the sale of birthright by one brother to another (cf. Gen. 25). One Nuzi tablet indicates that the possession of the family idols was a sign of the right of inheritance. This may explain the feverish dismay of Laban when Rachel made off with the household gods ("teraphim" in KJV; cf. Gen. 31:30). The deathbed blessing, familiar to all readers of Genesis (cf. chap. 49), is likewise illustrated at Nuzi.

What do these affinities mean? Apparently they signify that the early Hebrews derived some of their way of life from Hurrian culture as illustrated at Nuzi. Here was a pattern of social life peculiar to the second millenium B.C. Though its elements disappear in following centuries, many of them are faithfully retained in the narratives of Genesis. It is hardly possible and certainly not probable that those who centuries later put Genesis in writing could have invented so many details. This points toward the conclusion that oral tradition preserved these elements correctly through many centuries, although we are not able to determine from this fact alone how extensively the traditions were revised and enlarged by those who handed them on and by the historians who gave them their final shape. At any rate what we have learned from Nuzi correlates acceptably with the general picture of

Chart 4. The Lineage of the Patriarchs
(Tribal eponyms capitalized)

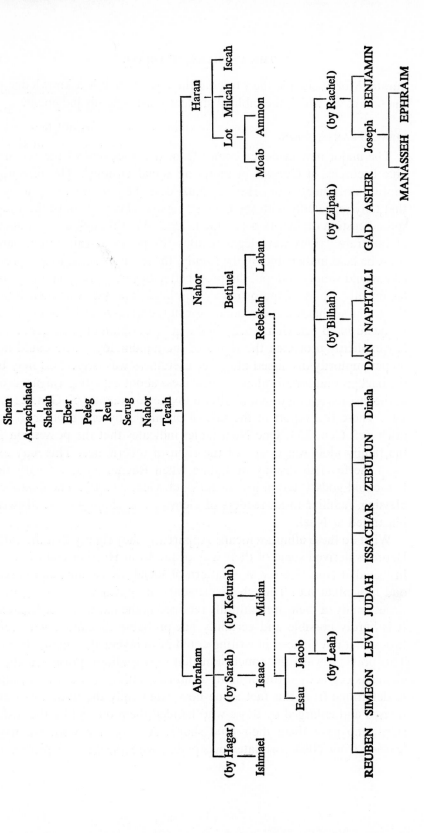

Genesis according to which Abraham migrated from Ur in lower Mesopotamia to Haran in the far north. Around Haran the Hurrian culture was no doubt strong. Further confirmation of the overall features of the tradition is seen in the various patriarchal names that are similar to place names in the Haran area, e.g., Peleg, Serug, and Nahor (cf. Gen. 11:16,20,22). Recent study of the background of Genesis enhances the probability of the narratives in their broad outlines if not in details. Other factors, however, make it plain that such corroboration of the traditions is not the same thing as "proving" the Bible to be literally accurate.

We have spoken of oral tradition preserving many of the characteristic features of Hurrian society that were also typical of the first Hebrews. But on what grounds are the stories of Genesis attributed to oral tradition? The form of the oral legend in Genesis was astutely analyzed by Gunkel.[5] He observed that Genesis tends to break up into separate units, each unit being reasonably brief, with few participants, simple descriptions, lack of introspection, laconic speech, and artful use of suspense. The big bold strokes of narration, colorful and memorable, would be especially suited to oral transmission. Another evidence of oral transmission is in the content of the stories. What, after all, does Genesis 12–50 tell us about if not the affairs of a few families? They are uniquely family traditions. In terms of their own time they were not truly public events that would interest people at large.

How much credence can be given to such an oral tradition? To that question there is no simple answer. It all depends on who tells the stories, how closely they are kept, and for what purposes they are recited. The same oral tradition may preserve some elements while it drops, introduces, or enlarges others. Simplification and the heightening of dramatic detail, especially by supplying exact conversations, would be almost inescapable and this process could well take place without endangering the essential features of the tradition. It is perhaps hard for us who are accustomed to copyrights and strict ideas of historical accuracy to appreciate the spiritual creativity of oral legend, which nevertheless is not mere fancy but attaches itself to solid historical kernels. Merely because a narrative was orally transmitted for centuries neither guarantees nor dismisses it as historically authentic.

Another factor that must be reckoned with frankly in determining the historical accuracy of Genesis is the extent to which the patriarchs

[5] Hermann Gunkel. *The Legends of Genesis,* Open Court, 1901.

as described are individuals and the extent to which they are tribal symbols. The technical term is *eponym,* a person whose name or actions represent a people, place, or institution. The view that in Genesis tribal history is veiled as personal experiences has sometimes been pressed beyond reason. The end result might easily be allegorical subjectivism. Still there are some stories where the theory is attractive. The rivalry of Jacob and Esau, as the story itself implies, is an account of the enmity between Israel and Edom, the blood brothers representing the two closely related Semitic peoples. In an approximate sort of way we can see that the rivalry of Jacob's wives with the two groups of sons produced by Leah and Rachel corresponds to the northern and southern tribes of Israel, who though related (common father Jacob), have separate and contending histories (rival mothers).

Many scholars believe that tribal history is reflected in the feigned covenant of Levi and Simeon with Shechem (Gen. 34) and in the affair of Judah and Tamar (Gen. 38). In the one case we may see, in legendary form, reference to an unsuccessful attempt to occupy Shechem by certain Israelite tribes (Simeon, Levi). In the other case we may conjecture that the incident verifies the impression that Judah was a Canaanite or partially Canaanite tribe (note his relations with Tamar). Obviously there is a highly subjective element in eponymous interpretations, since what appears symbolic to some readers conveys no such meaning to others. But this kind of double meaning cannot be dismissed altogether, inasmuch as it is clearly resorted to in the text (e.g., the open identity of Esau as Edom and Jacob as Israel), and is also typical of Hebrew thought patterns, which often conceive the group as a corporate personality. There is also ample precedent in epic literature (e.g., in the German *Nibelungenlied,* the fifth-century slaughter of the Burgundians and the violent death of Attila are represented under the guise of a dynastic feud). Only the interpreter's good sense can keep him from going to unwarranted extremes.

In fact the eponymous motif with its veiled tribal history fits into the whole tendency of Genesis to deal with origins, not in any scientific sense, but in the sense that the Hebrews had traditions about how certain peoples and places came into being. The national curiosity was satisfied through the recital of the stories. Generally the etymologies offered for names and the explanations of customs are fanciful in the extreme and cannot be supported linguistically or anthropologically. But the content of many of the traditions is historically valuable.

In the accounts of how various holy places were established, as for example at Bethel or Beer-lahai-roi or Moriah, mention is made of stones and trees, either in natural position or placed as pillars. It used to be assumed that the patriarchs were animistic, believing in spirits who inhabited these sacred objects. By the time Genesis was written this polytheistic view of the ancestors was supposedly forgotten and thus the present form of the book does not show the more primitive attitude very clearly. Recent study of religion in the ancient Near East, however, suggests that from the historic period onward there is little evidence of true animism in the Fertile Crescent. Rather than believing in amorphous spirits resident in natural objects the citizens of that world looked to high gods, beings who dwelt in the heavens and had distinct personalities.

Of course this is still polytheism but it is a much more precise and definite kind of belief than the rather nebulous stage of animism. The general Semitic names for deity, El and Baal, which mean something like "power" and "lordship," would thus be associated with specific holy places and the god of that place would have a particular character and worship. Genesis may well contain allusions to a pre-Mosaic stage of religion in Canaan when deities such as El Elyon, "El Most High" (Gen. 14:18–20); El Olam, "El Eternal" (Gen. 21:33), and El Roi, "El Who Sees" (Gen. 16:13–14) were in vogue. The traditions about these gods were encountered by the Hebrews as they entered Palestine. Eventually the Hebrew God displaced all the others and the traditions about them, no doubt sharply curtailed and transformed, became part of Hebrew literature. While this does not guarantee the tradition in detail, at least an authentic recollection of religious practices in pre-Hebrew days has been passed on in Genesis.

What deduction is possible at this stage? It ought to be evident from the types of evidence just surveyed that wholesale rejection or wholesale endorsement of the historical accuracy of Genesis 12–50 would be erroneous. This much appears likely: There were actual persons Abraham, Isaac, and Jacob who lived a seminomadic life and whose ethnic roots were in the Amorite migration and possibly also in the Aramean. The social and religious tradition was partially Hurrian but the excitement over Nuzi should not blind us to the Amorite and Sumero-Akkadian elements. The Hebrew language is Northwest Semitic, closely allied to Canaanite, thus pointing toward a predominance of Amorite ingredients, both ethnic and cultural.

Whether the patriarchs were father (Abraham), son (Isaac), and grandson (Jacob), as Genesis conceives them, is not as certain. It is well known that the ancients often conflated generations, dropping out unimportant individuals who appear between significant ancestors. For another thing it is conceivable that these men were the heads of separate groups who eventually merged to form the biblical Hebrews, and tradition has tended inevitably to bring them into the same family and to project the later unity into the earlier days. The traditions and heroes of each group would thereby become the common possession. For instance, Abraham may have been the leader of the primary Amorite element, whereas Jacob seems to have his affinities with the Aramean movement. If Abraham were the father of the Hebrews and Jacob his grandson it seems strange that it was the latter who gave his name to the people Israel (Gen. 32:28). On the other hand, if they were originally separate groups we can conjecture that in joining together they chose the name of the more numerous or influential group, which happened to be the Jacob-Israel clans. But they did not renounce the figure of Abraham and the oral tradition about him. Abraham's conversion into the grandfather of Jacob may express the sense of the traditionists and later writers that Abraham was a more ancient figure and that in a real sense it was with him, and not with the more immediate ancestor Jacob, that Hebrew faith began.

Conjectural and tentative though this reconstruction may be, it is not far-fetched for it is precisely in such ways that great bodies of national literature reflect the history of the people who have created them. Against those who would give a uniformly negative or positive answer to the trustworthiness of Genesis for determining the origins of the Hebrew people, it must be maintained that we are faced with remarkably vivid material whose historicity exists in varying depths and degrees. Genesis contains a genuine but not absolute value for historians and thus for the student who wants to get a glimpse of the beginnings of the Hebrews.

THE RELIGION OF THE FATHERS

Genesis is not mainly concerned, however, with the patriarchs as the physical fathers of Israel. They are celebrated in the tradition as men of faith and their significance is above all else a religious significance. With what confidence can we identify in the legends some knowledge of the religion of the historical Abraham, Isaac, and Jacob? Such a question anticipates and involves the extent to which Moses was the true founder of Hebraism and the extent to which the prophets were responsible for its eventual form. Change and growth will be abundantly demonstrated in our study, but can the seminal stirrings of Hebrew faith be pushed back beyond Moses to the seminomadic clansmen who lie behind the Genesis stories?

Sir Leonard Woolley, who excavated Ur and studied the religious complexion of the city in the patriarchal age, concluded that Abraham carried with him to Canaan one of the domestic cults commonly practiced in Sumeria. Abraham contributed the crucial factor of delocalization of the god who henceforth could travel with his client. In some way not clear to Woolley or his readers, this was the germ of the personal, moral, and universal God of Judaism.[6] Aside from glaring gaps and fuzzy reasoning, it should be noted that Woolley assumed Abraham to have been an urban dweller whereas the likelihood is great that he was a tentsman who lived within the jurisdiction of the city of Ur. Also, the household gods of the ancient Mesopotamians were crude and magical and the steps in their transformation are not even guessed at by Woolley.

A more attractive hypothesis was proposed by Albrecht Alt, who believed that the patriarchs were the founders of originally separate cults, in which the deities were given distinctive names compounded with the personal names of the founders. He points to the following proper names for the respective patriarchal gods: Shield of Abraham (15:1); Fear of Isaac (31:42,53); Strong One of Jacob (49:24). Alt cites analogies from the Palmyrene and Nabataean Arabs, although the closeness of the parallels is open to question. Later the originally separate patriarchal gods were fused and equated with Yahweh.[7] This process would accord well with the probability, arrived at on other grounds, that Abraham, Isaac, and Jacob were the leaders of distinct Semitic clans that later merged to form the Hebrews.

Not widely held but vigorously propounded by those who favor it is the notion of a primitive monotheism, either world-wide (as advocated by the Roman Catholic anthropologist Wilhelm Schmidt) or among the Semites (as argued by Stephen Langdon the Assyriologist). The basic tenet is that, contrary to the evolutionary scheme, monothe-

---

[6] Leonard Woolley, *Abraham*, Scribner's, 1936, chap. 6.
[7] Albrecht Alt, "Der Gott der Väter," *Kleine Schriften zur Geschichte des Volkes Israel*, 1953, Vol. 1, Beck, pp. 1–78.

ism preceded polytheism. Man's slow return from polytheism to monotheism represents a return to the true light. This view easily accords with the concept of an original harmony between God and man, broken by sin and expulsion from Paradise, and leading to idolatry and polytheism. The belief of various ancients and modern primitives in a high father god, who has faded behind the many lesser deities who take over urgent mundane matters, is adduced as a surviving trace of original monotheism. Langdon in particular called attention to Anu who, even though a remote father god, was in some sense superior to all the other deities.

Anthropologically the idea has gained little headway because the father god in any pantheon may be better understood as an integrating development within polytheism than as a vestige of monotheism. The phenomenon certainly does witness to a clamant urge within man to see his world and the power behind it as a whole. It may reasonably be used by the monotheist as an argument for the validity of his faith, but that is a different matter from proving there was an explicit monotheism prior to the Hebrews. The argument for an older Semitic monotheism breaks down for lack of evidence, being built on dogmatic presuppositions or shaky linguistic foundations. Furthermore, if the patriarchs were simply reintroducing a monotheism known of old, why is Moses granted such prominence in the tradition? In large parts of the Old Testament the patriarchs are completely overlooked and the uniqueness of Israel is located in the Exodus rather than in the migration of Abraham.

Is there then any reason at all for believing that the patriarchs differed religiously from their neighbors, especially since we have seen how little they differed ethnically? The one clue we possess is in the Moses narratives, where emphasis is placed on the fact that the God of Moses is also the God of the fathers. One source in Exodus, and probably the oldest, identifies the deity by the name also known in the patriarchal age—Yahweh. Owing to the verification of Genesis in a number of historical and social details, it seems unlikely that the tradition of patriarchal religious uniqueness—so deeply ingrained in Genesis-Exodus—is wholly without foundation in fact. Perhaps of all the theories Alt's description of the deity who takes the very name of the founder is the most appealing, but even so it is little more than an informed guess. All we can really say is that Abraham, Isaac, and Jacob must have practiced a form of religion in which clan loyalties were cemented and exalted (common to Semitic seminomads everywhere) but bearing within it the seeds of Mosaic faith: the dynamic of the divine-human relationship, ethical demand, divine concern for men (the uncommon contributions of Hebrew faith). These qualities are dramatically recollected by means of stories of extraordinary simplicity and grandeur. Historically, however, we are not yet in a position to discern the inception or structure of patriarchal religion. For firmer historical foundations we must turn to Moses.

✛ 5 ✛

THE PEOPLE OF THE COVENANT

When Israel was a child . . .
Hos. 11:1

How is the reader to appraise the undoubted difference between the patriarchal and Mosaic traditions? For one thing there is a clearer *dramatic unity* in Exodus. The patriarchs move without historical motivation; they are pilgrims. It is the divine promise that supplies what unity the rather enigmatic figures of the patriarchs and their random actions possess. Moses begins with the same tentativeness, fleeing to Midian in order to save his life but, from the moment of his call, a purposeful direction enters the narrative. Moses and the people of Israel are escapees from Egypt and incipient conquerors en route to Canaan. The promise to the patriarchs is implemented through Moses. It is by no means an effortless fulfillment. There are outward hardships and inner apostasies, but the goal and the means of accomplishment are clear.

A second difference is in the contrast between family and *tribal traditions*. The family traditions of Genesis function in a double role. They relate an exciting story and they also symbolize the later destiny of Israel. The symbolism is generally restrained and subtle while the story moves ostensibly on an interfamily plane. In Exodus, however, the traditions are explicitly tribal and national. There is a great difference between the sons of Israel in Genesis, the direct offspring of the father Jacob-Israel, and the people of Israel who meet us on the first pages of Exodus. Unlike Abraham or Jacob, Moses is not susceptible to treatment as an eponym or symbolic ancestor. Moses is a far more historically plausible figure than any of the patriarchs.

But before proceeding with the story of Moses we must evaluate the tradition that assigns to Moses the authorship of the first five books of the Bible.

THE PENTATEUCH

One of the certain results of modern Bible study has been the discovery that the first five books of the Old Testament were not written by Moses. The present Pentateuch ("five scrolls") was constructed from anonymous sources (commonly designated J, E, D, and P) only at a relatively late date. Since many scholars believe that the same sources continue into Joshua, they sometimes speak of the Hexateuch or "six scrolls." On the other hand, recent proponents of oral tradition have insisted that the characteristic J, E, and P sources are not found after Numbers, that Deuteronomy is actually the introduction to a lengthy history of Israel from Moses to the fall of Judah (Deuteronomy through Kings) and thus entirely separable in composition from Genesis–Numbers, which may for convenience be termed a Tetrateuch ("four scrolls"). Two contemporary European scholars, Ivan Engnell and Martin Noth, have independently favored such a Tetrateuch. But whether one accepts a Pentateuch, a Hexateuch, or a Tetrateuch the basic fact that there are anonymous strata edited or compiled to form the historical books of the Old Testament is accepted by virtually all Hebraists.

On what evidence has the Mosaic authorship of the Pentateuch been set aside and what is the alternative? As far as technical possibilities go, Moses could have written the books. Writing had been known for at least fifteen hundred years prior to Moses and the evidence of his court connections and his facility in tribal law point strongly in the direction of scribal skill. It is internal evidence, however, which suggests that the books were not composed by any one person and that, in their present form at any rate, they are much later than the age of Moses. The evidence falls roughly into six categories.

1. *Textual References to Moses*

Although tradition has credited these books to Moses since the time of Ezra, an objective reading uncovers data to the contrary. Moses is spoken of everywhere in the third person. In itself this might be accounted for by modesty and professional scribal etiquette (as when the contemporary writer is advised not to use the personal pronoun "I" except in an essay). More relevant is the habit of specifying the

portions written by Moses. He is said to have written a curse against
Amalek (Exod. 17:14), the laws at Sinai (Exod. 24:4), and an itinerary of the wilderness wanderings (Num. 33:2). The implication is
clear that the writer does not think of Moses as the author of extended
books such as the history he himself is writing. He knows of traditions
about Moses writing but in each case the tradition has to do with some
specific record of public moment that the writer makes use of in his
own way.

2. *Chronological Lapses or Anachronisms*

Here and there in the Pentateuch are indications that the standpoint
of the writer was later than the age of Moses. (A modern example of
the sort of unconscious slips that disclose a later age was noted in an
early Hollywood film of Christians being thrown to the lions in the
Roman arena. One of the actors was wearing a wrist watch!) There are
a number of anachronisms or time confusions in the Pentateuch. Philistines (Gen. 21:32; 26:1,8,14–15,18) did not come into Palestine until
after the time of Moses. Camels (Gen. 24:10–14; 31:17) were apparently not domesticated until about 1000 B.C. A deliberate blunder of
this type was made in a movie that showed domesticated camels in
Egypt at the time of Pharaoh Cheops about 2500 B.C. The producer
decided that he simply could not have a movie about Egypt without
camels; historical accuracy must bow to atmosphere! The notation
"before any king reigned over the Israelites" (Gen. 36:31) points to
the days of the monarchy, and "the Canaanites were then in the land"
(Gen. 12:6; 13:7) betrays a period in which the Canaanites and Israelites had merged in the kingdom of David. Such inadvertencies indicate the point of view of Hebrews living *after* and not before the occupation of Canaan—and probably some centuries afterward.

3. *The Differences in the Divine Name*

Sometimes the general term Elohim, a cognate of the widespread
Semitic El, is used (translated in the RSV as God). At other times
the specific Hebrew name for the deity appears, Yahweh (RSV—
Lord). Less frequently El Shaddai occurs (RSV—God Almighty).
Although it does not figure in the distinction of sources, there is yet a
further divine appellation, Adonai (RSV—Lord). By themselves such
variations would mean little more than the right of an author to use
synonymous terms. Many opponents of the critical view of the Penta-

teuch concentrate on the weaknesses in this argument as though the theory stood solely on the differences in the divine name. It is true that Astruc first discovered the clue for dissection of sources in the alternation of names, but the analysis into sources has progressed far beyond the elementary stage and now includes additional and interlocking criteria.

4. *Differences in Language and Style*

This category is actually an extension of the differentia in the divine names. Eichhorn, following up the pioneer work of Astruc, observed that certain words tend to appear in passages where one or the other of the divine names predominates. The result is that there are certain "constants" or invariables in the vocabulary that regularly appear together and are related to the occurrences of the names for deity. That this is something more than mere employment of synonyms for literary effect is apparent in the different proper names for the same person or place. In sections of the Pentateuch, for example, where the name *Yahweh* (LORD) is employed the mountain of the covenant is called *Sinai,* the original inhabitants of Palestine are *Canaanites,* and Moses' father-in-law is named *Reuel* or *Hobab.* But in contexts where the principal divine name is *Elohim* (God) the covenant mountain is *Horeb,* the pre-Israelite populace of Canaan are *Amorites,* and Moses' father-in-law is *Jethro.* As to style, some portions of the Pentateuch are vivid and pictorial, while others are dull and make for tedious reading. The vocabulary and style typical of the various sources will be discussed in more detail when the sources are treated separately in later chapters.

5. *Differences in Conceptions of God and Man*

In some parts of the five books God is presented in nearly human form, physically and emotionally. Anthropomorphisms abound. Elsewhere he is more removed from man and reveals himself in dreams and by angelic messengers. At times men approach him through prayer and moral decision and in other cases they come to him through ritual. The attitude of the Pentateuch toward the leaders of Israel is interesting. Sometimes their faults are presented frankly, as when Abraham is depicted as a liar and Jacob as a cheat. But in other instances the same weaknesses are toned down or passed over (compare Gen. 12:10–20 and 20). The moral sensitivity of parts of the Pentateuch is much greater than others. Students of the Pentateuch have noted that there is a definite correlation between various religious and ethical conceptions and the linguistic differentia noted above.

6. *Duplicate Narratives or Doublets*

Frequently two or even three accounts of the same incident appear. Occasionally these versions are placed side by side (as in the two stories of Creation, Genesis 1–2:4a and 2:4b–24). At times they are woven together to form a continuous story (as in the flood account of Gen. 6–9). Now and then they are distributed in different contexts, apparently because they were understood as separate incidents by the writers or editors (the three episodes of Abraham and Isaac passing off their wives as sisters, Gen. 12:10–20; 20; 26:1–11). The parallel accounts strongly corroborate the impression derived from other internal evidence that we are dealing with diverse sources in the Pentateuch, each of which has had its own history.

This helps to account for a lack of smooth connection between the parts. Readers of the Bible have always sensed the disorder and confusion of the Old Testament. It is expressed in the conundrum that every teacher of the Bible has heard at least a half-dozen times: Where did Cain get his wife? Once we see that the stories of Genesis often had separate origins, then such questions can be dealt with intelligibly. It seems clear, for example, that the Cain and Abel legend assumed the presence of other people in the world besides the family of Adam. When it was brought into connection with the story of the Garden, the author of the source or editor of the book either did not see the problem or else was untroubled by it. Again we must remind ourselves that the kind of rational and scientific interests that mark our age in history were remote from the interests of the ancients, especially when they were tracing their ancestral roots. If the Hebrew stories are superior to all other such accounts in antiquity, it is not because they are more logical and more neatly edited but because a more profound sense of the divine-human relation and the meaning of man's life pervades them.

On the basis of the above types of evidence, scholars have concluded that at least four different authors or groups of authors (often called "schools," although what is implied is not a formal academic institution but a circle of scribal activity in which several men developed similar styles and interests) have had a part in writing the books of the

Law. They worked anonymously. We do not have copies of their separate documents. Thus the solution proposed is of necessity a hypothesis that is not objectively demonstrable but a majority of biblical scholars believe that this theory, in some form or other, is more adequate than the theory that Moses or indeed any one individual was the author.

The first contributor to the Pentateuch is thought to have lived in the period 950 to 850 B.C., roughly between the time of Solomon and Elijah. He was a citizen of the Southern Kingdom or Judah and because he preferred the divine name Yahweh (German Jahweh; English corruption Jehovah) is called the Yahwist or J writer. Making use of oral tradition he wrote down the story of his people as it was current in Judah. He excelled in narratives; the bulk of his work is in Genesis and the first half of Exodus. He wrote with an unusual brilliance of style and was in many ways the greatest storyteller Israel ever produced. His work ranks with and many would say exceeds that of Homer in literary excellence (see detailed discussion of J, pp. 214–233).

The second writer is generally placed about a century later, 850 to 750 B.C. He probably finished his work by the time of Amos and Hosea and, like those prophets, labored in the Northern Kingdom or Israel. Because of his preference for the divine name Elohim he is called the Elohist or E writer. His treatment is close in subject matter to the J document but he gives the northern version and both omits and includes elements found in the Yahwist. The E account of Hebrew beginnings has not come down to us in anything like the wholeness of the J account. While his style is generally inferior to the Yahwist's, the Elohist has fashioned some gems of unforgettable beauty and power such as the story of Abraham's barely averted sacrifice of Isaac in Genesis 22. E, like J, is mainly confined to Genesis and Exodus but it has no material for the pre-Abrahamic period (see discussion of E, pp. 246–254).

Thirdly, in the seventh century B.C. an unknown writer (or writers) compiled the law code of Deuteronomy, which formed the basis for King Josiah's Reformation in 621 B.C. (cf. II Kings 22–23). Nineteenth-century criticism tended to regard the law code as an original work given the name of Moses to commend it to Israel. Today the trend is to recognize older elements that run back into northern Israel before the fall of that kingdom a century prior to Josiah's revival of Yahweh religion. The compiler may have had substantial reasons for believing that at least the essential spirit, if not some of the provisions, went back to the founder Moses. As late as 550 B.C. others who shared his style and thought edited the history of Israel from Judges to Kings (Engnell and Noth would say from Joshua to Kings). The compiler of the law code and the several editors are known as the D writer(s), because they have a relatively homogeneous view of Israel's history that is stated most explicitly in the book of Deuteronomy. Scarcely any D elements are detectable in the first four books of the Pentateuch (see discussion of D, pp. 334–346).

Finally, during and after the Exile, from 550 to 450 B.C., an immense work was written describing the origin and history of the religious institutions of Israel. It is called the P source because of its priestly interests. The P writer(s) traced the revelation of God to Israel against the backdrop of creation and world humanity. They understood that the basic provisions of that revelation were institutional, insuring the perpetual celebration of the Mosaic Law through festival and sacrifice, circumcision and food laws. While a number of its provisions have been outdated (sacrifice, for example) the majority have persisted as the structural bulwarks of Judaism. Much of the latter part of Exodus, as well as Numbers and Leviticus (entire) are from the P source. It is also represented in Genesis, notably in the magnificent account of creation in the first chapter (see discussion of P, pp. 448–463).

By about 400 B.C. all these sources had been brought together, probably in gradual stages, to produce the monumental history of Hebrew beginnings. This finished work was for the Jews what it would have been for the Christians had the four Gospels been compiled as one and the individual Gospels eventually lost. The documents or strands, designated J, E, D, and P, run through the five books of the Pentateuch, either parallel (as in Genesis and Exodus) or in successive blocks (Leviticus, Numbers, Deuteronomy).

It is the conviction of many informed and thoughtful believers, both Jewish and Christian, that a frank and full acceptance of the genuinely human origins of the biblical books is not modern prejudice but the modern discovery of an ancient reality. As such it was the means by which God made himself known to men. Surely the Jew, with his fearless tradition of iconoclasm, cannot be hurt by the realization that the Old Testament is not infallible or inerrant. And the Christian who takes seriously the humanity of Jesus Christ cannot very well balk at the humanity of the Bible. Pentateuchal authorship, as it now appears to the student of the Bible, only more forcefully thrusts upon the synagogue and the church the import of the worship of a Person rather than a Book. In the last analysis it has always been the Spirit speaking through the human heart that has created faith. Only insecure and immature faith can prevent our looking honestly at the biblical writings in their original setting. The time has long since passed when we can neglect to do so. A faith that has something to hide or that has not taken account of its own origin and history is no match for the crises of our age.

Chart 5.

A. THE OLDER DOCUMENTARY HYPOTHESIS:

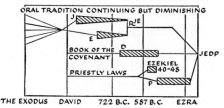

B. THE PRESENT TENTATIVE POSITION:

THE MOSAIC TRADITIONS

The overarching unity of the traditions from the Exodus to the settlement in Canaan would be much plainer except for the present form of the Pentateuch. Into the narratives of Exodus and Numbers the Pentateuchal writers and editors have introduced a large body of legal prescriptions. There is a definite increase in the legal materials as we move from earlier to later Pentateuchal strata: J had hardly any; E somewhat more; D and P large amounts. What does this mean for an understanding of the Moses traditions?

Exodus through Deuteronomy contains a huge collection of traditions as complex as any in the literature of the world. The Mosaic age has attracted successive interpretations of the meaning of Israel's birth and commission. Here are the focal events, the real beginnings, whatever may be made of the preceding patriarchal promises. And the crux of it all is not inept editorial fabrication but the enlarging meaning of Moses, the increase of understanding in Israel, the perpetual necessity of tying later developments to the original intentions. The Pentateuch is not merely a heterogeneous mass, with elements thrown together haphazardly, although to our literary and logical instincts it appears so. We would have collected the laws properly organized in an appendix, but there is a Hebrew logic in it all.

The growth of the traditions has occurred at two points: (1) the deliverance from Egypt and guidance to Canaan; (2) the covenant between Yahweh, the delivering God, and the delivered people. The former bulks the largest in the J writer's account. It is also interesting that many of the later summaries of the Mosaic age omit all mention of a covenant or law and emphasize rather the rescue from Egypt and the gift of the land (e.g., Deut. 26; Josh. 24). The prophets, with few exceptions, do not speak of a covenant in the Mosaic age. It is too simple, however, to delete the notion of covenant from the Mosaic period altogether. Both of the early Pentateuchal sources describe the sealing of a covenant with legal directives, although the E writer gives more of the compact than the J writer. Many later summaries of the Mosaic age, while they do not explicitly discuss the Sinai pact, regard a Mosaic covenant as one of the fundamental features of Israel's desert experience (e.g., Pss. 78; 105). The insistent collective witness of all the Pentateuchal strata to a Mosaic covenant requires some basis in reality. Nevertheless not all of the recollections of the covenant connect it with Mt. Sinai nor do they agree as to the stipulations. The extent of variation in the four Pentateuchal strata may be judged by schematic analysis of the covenant traditions.

It is rightly stressed that the complexity of the Pentateuch is due in part to Israel's habit of attributing all law to Moses and in part to the disinterest or unwillingness of the final editors to organize the legal materials consistently. This means that the great blocks of legal data which constitute so large a part of the Exodus-Deuteronomy traditions are secondary and often ill-fitted to the flow of the story. But the astounding regularity of later Israelites in regarding Moses as a lawgiver strongly urges some element of truth in the tradition. This is especially so because no law is ever presented in the Old Testament as promulgated by a king—in contrast to the legal codes of all other ancient Near Eastern peoples. Although no law in the Pentateuch in its present form is unequivocally derivable from the Mosaic age, the resolute connecting of Israel's order of life with the desert can come ultimately only from the figure of Moses.

The other great theme in the Moses traditions is that of deliverance from Egyptian bondage and the journey to Canaan. When the complex and uncertain legal corpora are removed from the Pentateuch, the Moses traditions assume much more manageable proportions. They are found in Exodus and Numbers alone, since Leviticus is entirely Priestly law and Deuteronomy is largely Deuteronomic law,

Chart 6. The Mosaic Covenant Traditions

Source	Location	Act of Establishment	Stipulations
J	Mt. Sinai	Exod. 24:1–2, 9–11 34:1–10	Ritual Decalogue Exod. 34:11–26
E	Mt. Horeb	Exod. 24:3–8	Ethical Decalogue Exod. 20:1–17 Covenant Code or Canaanite Civil Code Exod. 20:22–23:19
D	Mt. Horeb	Deut. 4:9–14 5:1–5, 22–27	D Decalogue Deut. 5:6–21
	Moab	Deut. 29	Book of the Covenant Deut. 12–28
P	Mt. Sinai	Exod. 19:1–2 24:15–18 34:29–35 40:34–38	Exod. 25–31; 35–40:33 Holiness Code Lev. 17–26 (27) Priestly Code Lev. 1–16 Num. 1–10:10
	Kadesh?		Num. 15; 18–19
	Moab		Num. 28–30; 35–36

their setting in narrative offering little information not already found in earlier books (except for Deut. 34, which tells of Moses' death). The narrative traditions about Moses may be briefly outlined:

The Oppression of Israel	Exod.	1–2:10
The Flight of Moses to Midian		2:11–25
The Call of Moses		3–4
Futile Attempts at Deliverance		5–7:3
The Plagues and Passover		7:4–13:16
The Flight and Exodus		13:17–15:21
From Reed Sea to the Mountain		15:22–18
The Covenant		19; 24
The Golden Calf and Covenant Renewal		32–34
From the Mountain to Kadesh	Num.	10:11–12:16
Rebellion at Kadesh		13–14; 16–17; 20:1–21
From Kadesh to Moab		20:22–25:18; 27; 31–32
Death of Moses	Deut.	34

Simply by passing from legal to narrative sections we do not, however, escape complications. The narratives have inconsistencies, repetitions, and gaps that no convenience of outline can hide from the puzzled reader. Quite as much as the law codes, the legends of Moses have had a long history. We observe at least two, if not three, accounts of the call of Moses in Exodus 3–7. The Passover celebration is twice described (12; 13). The covenant is sealed by blood sacrifice and the common meal (24), only to be reinstituted after the golden calf incident (34). Sometimes the law written by the hand of God is in view and then again it is the law written down by Moses (24:12; 34:1 cf. 24:4; 34:27–28). The narratives assume some written terms for the covenant but not necessarily the precise provisions now appearing nor can we be entirely sure of the tradition of Moses writing. Moses passes up and down the covenant mountain at will with herculean disregard of the climb and little explanation of the reason for his repeated trips. Some fairly large poetic pieces have been inserted into the story, notably the Song of Moses (Exod. 15) and the Oracles of Balaam (Num. 23–24). Certainly the latter and probably the former are not earlier than the monarchy. And so we could continue. It is a waste of time and good sense to try to harmonize all these conflicting details. On the other hand, there are enough difficulties without the interpreter manufacturing discrepancies owing to his failure to appreciate the Hebrew mind. That is the wise caveat of the oral traditionists.

If anyone comes to the Moses stories bent on getting unobscured history he can only deceive himself or turn away in dismay. History here is transformed and recast through centuries of experience. Instead of a biography of Moses we have a biography of Israel, an aetiology of the covenant, in which of course Moses figures in a powerful way as the instrument of God's action. He is called often "Moses, the Servant of Yahweh" and that is the only guise in which he is ever presented. Weaving in and out through the narratives are at least three different sources that tell of Moses in their own characteristic ways. But even they have not related events with the kind of motivations that govern the writing of contemporary history, as though our only problem is the harmonizing of three separate historical accounts.

The nature of the writings owes much to the oral recitation in the sacral life of Israel. The reader senses this especially in Exodus 1–15, which functions as a Passover legend, accounting for the feast and picturing the struggle of Yahweh with the gods of Egypt as embodied in the Pharaoh.[1] The plagues are the signs and demonstrations of the superiority of Israel's God over all gods. The deliverance from Egypt is not presented as a chapter in the development of democratic institutions or an uprising of slaves in protest against intolerable tyranny. It is solely the will of Israel's God and his desire to release a people for his service that account for the escape of Israel.

The whole slant of the material is entirely other than we normally expect in history. There is no probing of secondary causes. The tissue of circumstantial relationships is not explored at all. This leads to glaring omissions that would not be tolerated in documented history; for example, we are not even given the name of the Pharaoh "who knew not Joseph" (Exod. 1:8) or of the Pharaoh of the Exodus!

Nor can we solve the problem by saying that a series of awesome events is later interpreted as due to God. It is rather that from first to last the stories know nothing of events that stand in causal relation apart from the direct purpose and power of the living God. History is not an independent self-contained sequence that runs its course with miraculous interventions here and there. History is rather the quality and order of events created by the God who enters into the life of man. We shall have many occasions to see that Israel's concept of history, one of her greatest gifts to mankind, arose in and never departed from an indelible sense of the purpose and power of God in

[1] Johannes Pedersen, *Israel, Its Life and Culture,* Oxford University Press, 1940, vols. 3–4, pp. 728–737.

his world. It is not that the one way of writing history is wrong and the other right but only that we make no serious approach to the issues until we see that they are *different* in presupposition and purpose, and thus in method.

THE ERA OF MOSES

No matter how sympathetically we view the biblical reading of events, and even if we regard it as ultimately the most important way of understanding history, we cannot but raise questions from the standpoint of our method of looking at history. In what sort of age did Moses live? Who were the Israelites? What was the religion of Moses? Whence his God? What happened at the Reed Sea? Where was the mountain of revelation? Which of the narrative elements are most likely grounded in the historical Moses and which are born of pious imagination? Owing to the increasing recovery of the biblical environment, though not of the actual biblical events, some of these questions can be more satisfactorily answered than others. Some remain basically unanswerable, and over all, the answered and the unanswered, there broods a sense of momentous and mysterious stirrings at the depths of history.

The following picture of Moses emerges from the traditions: He was a Hebrew born in Egypt, brought up as an Egyptian (the name Moses probably means "son" or "child"), who in manhood identified himself with his people. Having killed one of the chiefs of the labor battalions and fearing for his life, he fled to the desert for asylum. He married into and lived for some years with a nomadic tribe of Midianites (or Kenites); his father-in-law was Jethro. Moses was confronted with a revelation from the God Yahweh (two of the sources, E and P, emphasize that this was a new name for the deity) who was nevertheless the God of the fathers. He commissioned Moses to deliver the people Israel from Pharaoh's iron grip. Reluctantly Moses accepted the task and, with his brother Aaron, attempted, at first unsuccessfully, to convince both Israel and the Pharaoh that Yahweh wished his people to be released so that "they might serve him." A host of severe catastrophes struck Egypt and Moses led the people through one of the lakes or marshes that formed the eastern frontier, narrowly escaping disaster at the hands of the Egyptian troops. The people were formed into a religious community by a covenant with the delivering God Yahweh, pledging faithfulness to him while he promised his presence and pledged the possession of a land. The exact terms of the covenant are not known but that there was detailed community order based upon the covenant is clear from Moses' function as a judge. Moses gathered capable leadership around him in the persons of Aaron and Jethro, Caleb and Joshua. He led the covenant people through the wilderness region between Egypt and Canaan and directed the assault on the Trans-Jordan region but did not live to enter Canaan.

Is there any time in ancient history when a career of the sort described in Exodus can be located? The biblical chronology places Moses in the fifteenth century B.C., thereby making the probable Pharaoh of the Exodus Thutmose III (1504–1450). If the descent of Jacob is also pinpointed according to the biblical chronology it would fall in the nineteenth century—about a century before the time of the invasion of Egypt by the Hyksos, who were at least partially Semitic. The cordial reception of Joseph and his people in Egypt could then be understood since the Hyksos rulers of the period would have had a special fondness for fellow-Asiatics. The Pharaoh "who knew not Joseph" would be Ahmose I (1570–1545), the founder of the XVIIIth dynasty who expelled the Hyksos. Additional support for this viewpoint appeared with the discovery of the Tell el-Amarna letters with their repeated warnings that people called Habiru (possibly Hebrews?) were penetrating Palestine and capturing cities in the period 1400–1350 B.C. This would allow for the Hebrews, leaving Egypt late in the reign of Thutmose III (ca. 1450 B.C.), to spend forty years in the wilderness and enter Palestine shortly before 1400, the Tell el-Amarna letters telling of their continuing struggles to occupy Canaan. When Garstang, the excavator of Jericho, came to the conclusion that the city fell to the Israelites shortly before 1400 and certainly not later than 1380, the case for a fifteenth-century Exodus in keeping with the biblical dates seemed wholly defensible.

But there are difficulties with the fifteenth-century hypothesis. For one thing, the genealogical data of the Old Testament are at variance with the explicit chronology. The great-grandson of Joseph is regarded as contemporary with Moses, a suspiciously small number of generations to cover 430 years (Num. 32:40). Also, the grandson of Moses is mentioned in Canaan not earlier than about 1150, which allows only two generations for three hundred years (Judg. 18:30). Furthermore, the Edomite list of royalty in Genesis 36 gives only eight kings for the period from Moses to David, four hundred years on the biblical chronology. An average reign of fifty years for a king is highly improbable. The list suggests that the period in question was not more than two hundred years and likely less.

Ancient Jericho. This 50-foot-deep trench exposes the levels of occupation dating from prehistoric through patriarchal times.

The description of Egyptian conditions in the Pentateuchal accounts also points in another direction. The argument that the nearness of Joseph's residence to Jacob in Goshen (Gen. 45:10) necessarily points to the Hyksos delta capital of Avaris is extremely flimsy. According to Genesis, the Pharaoh gave a daughter of the priest of Heliopolis or On to Joseph as wife (41:45), but in Hyksos times the worship of Heliopolis was in disrepute and this gesture could hardly have been a royal favor. It is far from demonstrated that the Hyksos age *must* have been the age of Jacob's migration to Egypt. Egyptian records tell of other periods when Semites rose to positions of high leadership and when Semitic tribes were permitted to live along the frontier.

The crux of the objection to a fifteenth-century Exodus is found, however, in the record that the Pharaoh "who did not know Joseph" enlisted the Israelites in building the store cities of Pithom and Ramses. The erection of cities of that name occurred only in the reign of Ramses II (1301–1234) or possibly his father Seti I (1313–1301). While the exact sites of these cities are still in dispute, the proposed identifications are all in the Goshen region. There are Egyptian texts from the period of Seti I–Ramses II that speak of Asiatic Apiru (Habiru? Hebrews?) who were put to work on public building projects. In addition, in Exodus the Pharaoh's capital is near the land of Goshen, which was not true in the XVIIIth dynasty. Only with Ramses II was a capital built in the eastern Delta region for the explicit purpose of controlling the revived Asiatic empire. His capital, also identifiable with the store city of the same name, was called Ramses and is generally placed at the site of the old Hyksos capital of Avaris (also known as Tanis and Zoan).

There are archaeological data relating to the conquest that also suggest a thirteenth-century Exodus. One is the surface explorations throughout Trans-Jordan carried out by Nelson Glueck. He discovered that there was no settled occupation in the region from 2000 to 1300 B.C. Therefore, if the biblical accounts of the struggles between the migrating Israelites and the already urbanized Moabites and Ammonites are to be accepted as at all accurate, they must be dated in the thirteenth century. There would have been no city dwellers in Trans-Jordan a century before. Excavations at a number of Palestinian cities indicate that they fell to violent attack between 1250 and 1200 B.C. and not earlier. This would apply especially to Bethel, Lachish, and Debir. Continued diggings at Jericho have revealed that Garstang's Joshua wall was actually centuries older. It is now almost certain that the badly eroded mound has few, if any, remains of the city destroyed by the Israelites.

Today the majority of scholars regard either Seti I or Ramses II as the oppressing Pharaoh and Ramses II or Mer-ne-ptah (1234–1222)

The Amon Temple at Karnak near Thebes built by Seti I and Ramses II.

as the Pharaoh of the Exodus. In the one case the Exodus would be about 1290–1280 with the entrance into Palestine about 1250. In the other case the departure would be about 1230 and the entry into Canaan about 1200 or before. Those who favor the latter tend to dismiss the forty-year wilderness tradition as an approximation for a generation that could well be only a matter of a decade or two or even less. Those who favor the early thirteenth-century date are motivated by the evidence that southern Palestinian cities were destroyed 1250–1200 B.C., and also by the victory report of Mer-ne-ptah who, about 1230 B.C., stated that along with other Syrian and Palestinian cities, "Israel is no more, her seed is not."[2] If Mer-ne-ptah speaks of Israelites who took part in the Exodus, they had to leave Egypt long enough beforehand to be in Palestine about 1230 B.C. This, incidentally, is the first nonbiblical reference to Israel.

Such a view of the thirteenth-century Exodus is usually accompanied by the assumption that not all the tribes were in Egypt and involved in the Exodus. The Tell el-Amarna references to Habiru entering Canaan in the fourteenth century most likely refer to some of the early penetrations of Arameans, among whom were some who later broke away and entered Egypt. Depending on how much we dare to compress the chronology, we may even regard these Habiru penetrations as corresponding to the biblical patriarchal accounts, although Genesis pictures generally amiable relations between Hebrews and natives. The tribes in Egypt, led out by Moses, rejoined their fellows in Canaan. The covenant at Shechem in Joshua 24 refers to the covenantal binding together of the Exodus tribes and those who never were in Egypt but recognized their kinship. Thus a whole series of historical issues from the patriarchs down to the occupation of the land are involved in deciding the date of the Exodus. Furthermore, most scholars now regard the occupation of Canaan as a gradual process involving many tribes who did not participate in the Exodus and wilderness covenant. A reconstruction of the settlement of the land and a discussion of the implications appear in the next chapter.

THE EXODUS

We have sketched a setting for the biblical account of deliverance corresponding to some of its salient features: namely, Semitic laborers recruited forcibly for the lavish building programs of the Pharaohs

[2] See Appendix 7, pp. 588–590.

Ramses II, portion of a colossal statue from Memphis. The height of the original was 42 feet.

of the XIXth dynasty and the proximity of the laborers of Goshen to the capital at Ramses. Beyond this we find little to assist us. The plagues in their cumulative power can hardly be explained as merely natural phenomena, although most of them are identifiable as recurrent or occasional blights in Egypt. To rationalize them grossly is to cut out the heart of the story: the power of Yahweh. We have no means of isolating one or two of the plagues as historical, from which the others grew by legendary accretion, although something of the sort may be suspected since not more than four of the ten plagues are included in any two of the Pentateuchal sources. The attempt to treat the plagues as causatively related to one another (e.g., the organic discoloration of the Nile attracting frogs which bred flies and led to plague, etc.) is intriguing but ill-advised.[3] The minimum that must be said is this: natural disasters struck Egypt, disasters in which Moses and the people saw the power of their God and which finally gave them occasion to flee from Pharaoh.

What happened at the sea? In the first place, the Hebrew name is "Sea of Reeds" or "Papyrus Marsh" (*not* the Red Sea!) and could apply to any of the lake and marsh region along the eastern frontier of Egypt, roughly in the vicinity of the present Suez Canal and stretching some sixty-five miles from the Mediterranean to the Red Sea. The place names cited in the biblical account after the store city Ramses are vague and impossible of sure identification (Exod. 12:37; 13:20; 14:1–2). At some point along that frontier the Hebrews were hemmed in, with water before them and the Egyptians at their heels. We may set aside the fantastic numbers of the P source (603,-550 males eligible for military service! Num. 2:32) and, on the evidence of two midwives being sufficient to deliver their children (Exod. 1:15), estimate that the Hebrew escapees were not more than two to five thousand in number. The Egyptians pursuing them, as the record shows, were no army but a police force (Exod. 14:6–7).

Suddenly a way through the sea was opened for the Israelites. The Egyptian chariotry was drowned in the same waters that Israel had crossed. The "cloudy pillar" that had led the Hebrews suddenly shifted and stood behind them, indicating perhaps a stormy darkness separating the pursuer and the pursued, preventing the Egyptians from swift dispatch of their duty. With the shield of the "cloudy pillar"

[3] A. H. McNeile, *The Book of Exodus* (WC), Methuen, 2d rev. ed., 1917, pp. 42–46.

TRADITIONAL (SOUTHERN) ROUTE OF THE EXODUS

⟶ ROUTE OF THE EXODUS
┈┈▶ ALTERNATIVE CROSSINGS
OF "THE SEA OF REEDS"
┄┄▶ MAJOR TRADE ROUTES

came "a strong east wind" that blew back the water throughout the
night. The J description of the actual crossing, if it ever existed, has
been deleted in the present story. The morning courage of the Egyptians was overcome by "Yahweh in the pillar of fire and of cloud" as
he "looked down" and frustrated the enemy by bogging down his chariots and drowning his soldiers in the sea.

We may interpret the cryptic phenomenon as a violent storm, but
even so it does not provide a completely rational explanation: How
could Israel cross in the face of such a wind? If the water were so
shallow as to be blown back appreciably by the wind, could the people not have waded across unaided anyway? And, while the chariots
might have been immobile in the muddy bottom, why would the men
have been drowned by the resurging water? The elements of nature
were certainly involved in the delivery, perhaps in the form of a tidal
wave. We should not rule out the possibility that the rout was completed by the Hebrews turning on the survivors with their own weapons. The Israelites were at one moment trapped against the sea, facing
watery death, annihilation, or recapture; at the next moment they
were across the waters and the Egyptians were dead. The J writer puts

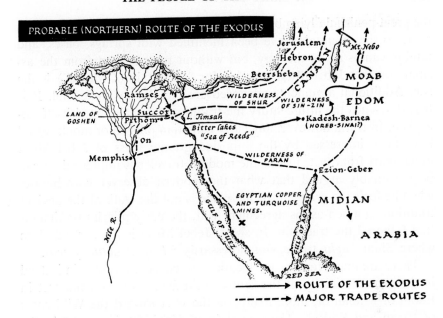

PROBABLE (NORTHERN) ROUTE OF THE EXODUS

ROUTE OF THE EXODUS

MAJOR TRADE ROUTES

it this way: "Thus Yahweh saved Israel that day from the hand of the Egyptians; and Israel saw the Egyptians dead upon the seashore" (14:30). Much as we should like to know more precisely the historical means of deliverance, whatever it was would not alter the basic datum that for those Israelites who lived through the experience Yahweh was perceived as the redeemer of his people. That this is no mere theologizing of later sources may be seen in the poetic couplet preserved by the E writer and containing the initial response of Israel. Following the first stunned silence and as the women began to dance and make music, Miriam took up a spontaneous refrain, never to be forgotten among her people:

Sing to Yahweh, for he has triumphed gloriously;
the horse and his rider he has thrown into the sea (15:21).

THE HOLY MOUNTAIN

The wilderness itinerary of the Hebrews is understandably obscure. Archaeology is at a loss to identify oases and temporary campsites. All that one can go by is the survival of place names in tradition and the general geographical configurations suggested by the biblical account. Tradition has located Mt. Sinai near the southern extremity of the great peninsula lying between Egypt and Arabia, and the stops en route to the mountain have been identified with springs, oases, and mining camps along the way, but without reason apart from the assumption that Jebel Musa (Arabic for "Mountain of Moses") is the site. Additional arguments advanced are circular or ineffectual. It is true that since the fifth century the tradition has maintained itself unbroken. In truth, however, any early Christian pilgrim or monk would have been impressed by the imposing granite mass of Jebel Musa quite apart from fact, just as the modern traveler is impressed. It can be reasonably argued that what the modern observer corroborates when he feels the grandeur of the place is not the truth of the ancient tradition so much as his agreement with the early pilgrim sentiments that fathered the tradition. In short, Jebel Musa is the sort of place where Sinai *ought* to be, not necessarily *where it actually was*.

There are many reasons for locating the covenant mountain instead in the general vicinity of the southern Arabah, either on the east in Edom or Midian or, more likely, on the west toward the Wilderness of Paran and Kadesh. The mountain of Sinai-Horeb, except in the schematic itinerary of P (Exod. 33), seems much closer both to Kadesh and to Midian than is Jebel Musa. Midian is the region at the head of the Gulf of Aqabah and eastward in Arabia. Kadesh is the one wilderness site (apart from Ezion-Geber at the head of Aqabah) that is reliably identified. Its name is retained in the spring 'Ain Qedeis, located about 140 miles due east of Goshen, 50 miles southwest of Beersheba (southern limit of Canaan), and 80 miles northwest of Midian. In the area, within a few hours of one another, are two other springs, which together could have supported several thousand fugitives for the thirty-eight years tradition assigns them. It was while tending the flocks of Jethro the Midianite that Moses was called of Yahweh at the mountain. It is doubtful whether Moses would have been ranging as far from Midian as the southern part of the peninsula. After the Exodus it is improbable that Moses would have led his people toward Jebel Musa since he would have had to pass the Egyptian copper mines around Serabit el-Khadim and thus run the danger of meeting troops.

Consider also that Jethro, coming forth to the mountain to meet Moses (Num. 10:29–32), is implored not to return home but to accompany Israel as a scout. If the mountain were Jebel Musa, Moses and Jethro could have proceeded together for some distance before parting, since Midian is between Jebel Musa and Canaan. But if Sinai-Horeb was in the region of the Arabah, then when they left the mountain it would be a parting of ways for the two men, since Moses would head north to Canaan and Jethro south to Midian. The most convincing of all arguments for the location of Sinai-Horeb in the vicinity of the Arabah is found in the several poetic compositions of Israel that picture the movement of Yahweh from his holy desert abode into the land of Canaan to fight for his people or to bring them rain. These representations are consistent in identifying the desert cradle of Israel's religion with Paran and Seir, the regions on either side of the Arabah (Deut. 33:2; Judg. 5:4–5; Hab. 3:3). What slight information we have seems to favor a site in the Wilderness of Paran and probably not far from Kadesh.

The role of Kadesh in the wilderness experience of the Israelites was probably greater than the present narrative suggests on the surface. As conceived in biblical tradition it was from Kadesh that the spies went forth only to bring back a discouraging report. In punishment for their faintheartedness the generation delivered from Egypt had to remain in the wilderness. Thus the many years of sojourn at Kadesh are wasted and unhappy ones. Nevertheless as historians of religion we must ask: What does it mean that so large a part of the time spent in the wilderness, indeed thirty-eight out of forty years in terms of the tradition, was passed at Kadesh? If we bring the mountain of revelation close to Kadesh, the answer is apparent. Actually all the wilderness events —the reunion with Jethro, Moses' judging of the people, the covenant, the abortive attack upon southern Canaan—were located in the Kadesh region. There is no need to postulate extensive wanderings and to separate Sinai from Kadesh as the P source has done.

The escaped Israelites made straight for Kadesh, avoiding the trade routes to the north and south. In the call of Moses, Yahweh commands him and the elders of Israel to go to the Pharaoh and say, "Yahweh, the God of the Hebrews, has met with us; and now, we pray you, let us go a three days' journey into the wilderness, that we may sacrifice to Yahweh our God" (Exod. 3:18). Most interpreters regard this simply as a general figure, meaning "some distance," but the definite number recurs (Exod. 5:3; 8:27). What it probably signifies is the distance from Goshen to Kadesh, in that a pilgrim following the Way of the Wilderness of Shur could make the journey in about three days. The goal of the "three days' journey" for the purpose of "sacrifice to

Yahweh" is thus not *any* wilderness site, although Moses may keep the place purposely obscure to confuse Pharaoh. It is the mountain where God revealed himself and it is no surprise that as the fugitives reach the mountain they are met by Jethro, who presides as priest over a sacrificial meal.

After heading three days into the Wilderness of Shur, the slow-moving column without benefit of familiar highways had not come to the waters of Kadesh and rebellion began to stir (Exod. 15:24). As they straggled on, one of the stopping places is called Meribah ("Contention") because of the revolt of the people (Exod. 17:7); a similar occasion at Kadesh furnishes reason for calling it "the waters of Meribah" (Num. 20:13). Is this a doublet further indicating that the line of flight from Egypt led, not to the traditional site of Sinai in the far south, but due east toward Kadesh and the holy mountain nearby? We may observe also that a note in Genesis 14:7 identifies Kadesh as En-Mishpat ("The Well of Judgment"), which may point to the place where Moses, under Jethro's leadership, obtained skill in judging the people.

THE ORIGINALITY OF MOSES

The question of the location of the mountain Horeb-Sinai and the route of the wandering has brought us to the crucial related question of the nature of the religion which tradition connects initially with a dramatic call to Moses at the sacred mountain. While the form of the legends, and especially the contexts in which the law codes have been set, give the impression that Moses' religion was a direct supernatural gift, there are indications that some of its features were influenced by environmental factors. This need in no way diminish the greatness of Moses. It simply recognizes the principle that no matter how unique his view of God, the form in which it was expressed was that of his age. Moreover, we do not deny anything essential to a proper view of revelation if we insist that all revelation must be received and expressed in the structures of contemporary human life. The question now is whether such structures are observable in the case of Moses.

For the peculiar thrust and impact of the religion of Moses we look in vain to the historical patriarchs. Even the formal contents and appointments of Mosaic religion do not appear in Genesis. Genesis *in its spirit* shows patriarchal religion as Mosaic: belief in the one God who has given his promise to make of Israel a great nation and to give him a land. But in the *actual practice* of religion, so far as it can be discerned, the forms are not identical and often are dissimilar in Genesis and Exodus: in the former there is no ark, few sacrifices, but rather a simple family cult with household idols in some cases. It is not surprising then that any historical estimate of the patriarchal contribution to Moses is hazardous. The continuity between patriarchs and Moses is best explained as a general ethnic and religious connection more or less vaguely remembered by the Israelites in Egypt but reactivated by Moses following his call. Where and how then did Moses remember "the God of (his) fathers Abraham, Isaac, and Jacob"?

ATONISM

It is frequently argued that the monotheistic revolution of Pharaoh Akh-en-Aton was the prototype and source of Mosaic religion. Amenhotep IV, a physically weak but intellectually vigorous ruler, attempted to replace the effete and sterile Egyptian religion with worship of the life-sustaining sun disk (the Aton). He changed his name from Amenhotep ("Amon is satisfied") to Akh-en-Aton ("He who is serviceable to the Aton") and, breaking away from the ecclesiastical hold of Thebes, shifted his capital to a specially erected site, Akhet-Aton ("Place of the Horizon of the Aton," modern Tell el-Amarna). He provided the precincts of his palace with garden estates and open-air temples. The names of other deities, especially Amon, were obliterated from temples and monuments, and such names as were retained were absorbed by the solar disk. Accompanying the revolution was a new artistic style, naturalistic and humanizing. The representations of Akh-en-Aton and his queen Nefertiti are powerfully realistic, showing the ill-proportioned, womanish body of the king and the graceful features of his wife. At his death the capital was deserted and the Theban priesthood of the god Amon regained the upper hand, utterly suppressing the work of Akh-en-Aton.

The Amarna Revolution of Akh-en-Aton is difficult to evaluate. The clearest expressions of the nature of the religion are found in the hymns addressed to the Aton. They are marked by a spacious cosmic perspective; all nature, lands, and races of men are spread beneath the lordly reign of the sun. There is emphasis upon the right rule of the king and the right conduct of the subject who acknowledges Aton. Atonism appears to have been infused by an uplifting sense of the unity of mankind within the beneficent unity of nature. Its ethics insofar as they can be judged were high-minded. Akh-en-Aton has no doubt been overidealized. Breasted called him "a lonely idealist . . .

Akh-en-Aton, from a pillar statue in the Temple of Amon at Karnak. The names of the sun god Aton are enclosed in royal rings on the Pharaoh's arms.

the first individual in history."[4] The pendulum has returned so far that some have dismissed him altogether as an adolescent weakling who was actually the "front" for some unknown genius. Others believe that the "revolution" was not startling since its roots were in earlier forms of sun worship and his father seems to have introduced the initial reforms.

One thing does seem indisputable: the only direct worshipers of the Aton were the Pharaoh and his family; all others approached the sun through them. This had the effect of strengthening the royal institutions and thus in its basic ideology Atonism did not depart from the age-old concept of the king as the god incarnate. Foreigners were related to Aton through submission to the rule of Egypt. While more like Stoicism than any other Near Eastern faith except Christianity, Atonism lacked the truly personal and universal character of the teachings of Epictetus and Seneca. The Amarna Revolution was a brilliant development, whether solely the work of the king or not. It failed at the crucial point: it had no contagion among the people at large. It was perhaps too abstruse and theoretical; then again the king may not have been personable or impressive as a popular leader; or the short period of his labor may not have been a match for the deeply entrenched priesthoods of the older gods.

If Moses is dated in the thirteenth century, he followed Akh-en-Aton by about a century. There is no hint of his indebtedness to Akh-en-Aton in Egyptian or Hebrew sources, but that alone is no adequate rebuttal of the theory. Atonism was so ruthlessly suppressed at the Pharaoh's death that the means by which his revolution might have become known to Moses is highly problematic, but that is not the controlling factor either. The only course open is to compare the beliefs of the two men.

The religion of the Egyptian was oriented around the sun and conferred largely natural benefits. It was based on royal ideology. Atonism was characterized by a rich iconography, the Aton represented by a many-armed sun disk, each arm ending in a hand outstretched in soothing benediction. It possessed a cosmic view of the Aton as the creator of all men and a typically Egyptian concern with the preparation of men for life after death.

On the other hand, the religion of the Hebrew was not oriented toward any particular natural object. If any were singled out it would be

[4] J. H. Breasted, *Development of Religion and Thought in Ancient Egypt*, Scribner's, 1912, pp. 335, 339.

the electric or volcanic storm rather than the sun; but Yahweh was detachable from the storm theophanies on his holy mountain, for he could rescue his own from Egypt and fight for them in Canaan. The covenant ideology of Yahwism made for a more democratic leveling that put Moses essentially on a par with his fellows before Yahweh. This is not merely a theological differentiation, of course, since it is connected with the more equalitarian attitudes of nomads. The basic boon of Yahwism is social order, although physical good is not divorced from this concern. The iconoclasm of Moses is in sharp contrast to Atonism, although again this must not be credited solely to theological factors. Nomads are bound to be much less skilled artistically than people with a fifteen-hundred year history in the plastic and graphic arts. The interest in creation and cosmology was underdeveloped in the religion of Moses. It may have been implicit ("Who has made man's mouth? Who makes him dumb, or deaf, or seeing, or blind? Is it not I, Yahweh?" Exod. 4:11), but nowhere in the Moses traditions is there anything approaching the wide cosmic view of the Hymn to Aton. As to life after death, Yahwism rigorously eschewed all interest in it, in part a reaction against Egyptian religion and in part an attempt to root out the necromancy and ancestor worship that must have been constant temptations to the Hebrews.

All in all a close comparison of the two men shows little reason to believe that Akh-en-Aton was a decisive influence upon Moses, or vice versa for that matter. In many dimensions the religion of Moses was far less sophisticated and developed than that of Akh-en-Aton; but in its historical activism, its consuming sense of the holiness of God, its powerful communal conscience, the religion of Moses far outstripped Atonism in its appeal and vitality. Compared to the God of the Hebrews, Aton seems curiously placid and unexciting; it is of course the difference between nature religions and religions of history.

For one who wishes to grasp the different ethos of the two religions, a comparison of the Hymn to Aton and Psalm 104 is instructive.[5] At many points alike, the psalm possibly even formally dependent on the hymn, there is a world of difference in the spirit of the two compositions. Aton *is* the sun. The divine reality *is* the harmonious perfection of nature. But Yahweh is *not* the sun, nor is he any part of nature, nor the sum of it. Behind all the orderly phenomena of nature stands

[5] See Appendix 6, pp. 585–588.

Yahweh in his inexhaustible creative power. While Yahwism developed its fullest cosmic reflection under the influence of Egyptian and Babylonian thought, in the fundamental point of Yahweh's transcendence, his personal uniqueness, his inner withdrawnness from nature and mankind and yet his manifestation as holy presence, there is a yawning gulf between the religion of Moses and Atonism.

KENITE YAHWISM

The most likely immediate source of Mosaic religion was the Midianite tribe (possible the Kenite clan thereof) to which Moses fled, and particularly Jethro, his father-in-law, the priest. Two of the Pentateuchal sources emphasize that the name Yahweh was not used before Moses, even though they concede that he was the God of the fathers. The P source goes out of its way to say this explicitly: "I am Yahweh. I appeared to Abraham, to Isaac, and to Jacob, as God Almighty (El Shaddai), but by my name Yahweh I did not make myself known to them" (Exod. 6:2–3). The E source, by using the divine name Elohim until the revelation to Moses, concurs in this view. If the patriarchal forerunners of Moses did not call their deity Yahweh, where did Moses get the name if not among the people in whose company he sought refuge? Is it not likely that the mountain of God was a Midianite holy place?

The priest Jethro is pictured in Exodus 18 as greeting Moses and the people in a joyous family reunion at which Jethro himself officiates over the sacrifice and common meal. Many would interpret this gathering as clear evidence that Moses derived the name and cultic and judicial features of his religion from the Midianites. It is known as the Kenite or Midianite Hypothesis of the origin of Mosaic Yahwism. It is further supported by the traces of Midianite (or Kenite) fidelity to Yahwism in the following centuries. Some of these people actually accompanied Israel into Canaan (Judg. 1:16; 4:11,17; I Sam. 15:6). Among the most fanatical Yahweh worshipers were the Kenite Rechabites who refused to adopt Canaanite civilization, despising wine and settled dwellings (II Kings 10:15–17,23; I Chron. 2:55; Jer. 35:1–19).

The Kenite Hypothesis fits well into the prominence of Kadesh in the wilderness experience of the Israelites, for once the great mass of law is removed and the glorification of Sinai as a remote ethereal place is corrected by bringing it into conjunction with Kadesh, it can be seen that the longstanding Midianite holy places at the sacred springs (Kadesh) and the sacred mountain (Sinai-Horeb) have given to Moses a number of the features of his faith. Those who have adopted this view, rather than regarding it as an embarrassment to the significance of Moses, find it an enhancement of his stature. What becomes important is the factor of choice. In an age when gods were the natural patrons of their respective lands, Moses brought to Israel word about a god who had chosen those who were not his own by nature. Yahweh's choice of Israel and Israel's choice of Yahweh impart to Mosaic religion its distinctively ethical elements. Though every individual element was paralleled in Midianite religion, the transformation wrought by ethical choice has given to Israel's religion a distinctive quality from its very inception in the vision of Moses. Karl Budde, one of the first advocates of the Kenite theory, gave pointed expression to its significance: "Israel's religion became ethical because it was a religion of choice and not of nature, because it rested on voluntary decision which established an ethical relation between the people and its God for all time."[6]

The theory is an appealing one but it has its problems and many able scholars have been unwilling to accept it. To begin with, the third Pentateuchal source in Genesis-Exodus, namely the Yahwist, regards Yahweh worship as pre-Mosaic, being practiced not only by the patriarchs but also by men in general as far back as the time of Enosh (Gen. 4:26). Whence this tradition if Israel knew nothing of Yahweh before Moses? Then again Exodus 18 need be regarded as nothing more than Jethro's acclamation of the god whose power he now acknowledges. It is pointed out by some that the Hebrew expression in 18:12 states only that Jethro "procured" or "brought" the sacrifice, not that he offered it. In addition he is called "priest of Midian" and not "priest of Yahweh." Others contend that there is nothing exalting or ethical per se in the choice of another God. History affords many instances of switching from one god to another and none produced anything like Israelite monotheism. It appears, however, that the crux of the objection to the Kenite Hypothesis is the fear that in some way it undercuts or destroys the significance of Moses or that it imparts a false simplicity to a complex problem. Such, however, is a misunderstanding.

When properly understood, the Kenite Hypothesis does not pretend

[6] K. Budde, *Religion of Israel to the Exile*, Putnam, 1899, p. 38.

to a *theoretical explanation* of Mosaic Yahwism, unambiguously accounting for its separateness by its ethical character or subtly dismissing it by cutting it down to the level of a seminomadic tribal cult. Admittedly some of the proponents of the hypothesis have veered dangerously one way or the other. Essentially, however, it simply presents *a description of attendant circumstances,* of influences that operated upon Moses. It is beyond the province of the hypothesis and the limited evidence on which it is based to say that the religion of Moses was wholly contained in its Midianite prototype. It is also beyond the scope of the theory, and even counter to some of the evidence, to make Yahwism so radically new a thing in Israel that the uniqueness of Moses becomes his salesmanship in convincing his people to risk the new deity.

The Kenite Hypothesis is correct in its fundamental insistence upon the strong religious influence that Jethro and the Midianites exerted upon Moses. The theory puts Kadesh in its rightful place and brings the covenant mountain into the orbit of previous Midianite religious veneration. It gives Moses a convincing environment and it explains the prominence of Jethro as priest, legal advisor, and wilderness guide. It accounts for the conviction of two of the Pentateuchal sources that Yahweh was a new name with Moses. But it must be enlarged or modified to allow for the continuity of Israelite tradition. How may this best be done? It is a widely held theory that not all the Israelite tribes were in Egypt, that by the fourteenth century or earlier Hebrews were entering Palestine, probably in scattered groups (cf. the Tell el-Amarna Habiru). There is evidence that the tribe of Judah was one of those that did not share in the bondage and Exodus but rather, moving into Canaan from the south, emerged in league with the other Israelite tribes only in the time of David. It is also likely that into the make-up of the tribe of "Judah" went groups such as Simeonites, Calebites, Jerahmeelites, and Kenites.

The relation then between Israelites and Midianites–Kenites was apparently not confined to the single contact of Moses and Jethro. Let us suppose that the god Yahweh had been worshiped in the general region of Kadesh by proto-Judean Kenites who, by the time of Moses, had already left the region and had begun to occupy southern Canaan. This would leave open the question of whether Yahwism in its pre-Mosaic form had reached Kadesh from Arabia via the Midianites or from Mesopotamia via the Amorites. When Moses found Yahweh among the Midianites he was among a people closely related to the Hebrews. Although for his group the name Yahweh was new, Moses could rightly connect Yahweh with the god of his fathers. The one great advantage of some such thesis is that it would explain why the J source of the Pentateuch, written by Judeans, regards Yahweh worship as very ancient, while both E and P begin the name Yahweh only with Moses. Judean tribal memories would carry back to times and situations quite apart from Moses when Yahweh was worshiped. In this way the values of the Midianite Hypothesis and the biblical traditions about pre-Mosaic Yahwism may be retained with a measure of harmony. (See the reconstruction of the settlement, pp. 160–165.)

THE RELIGION OF MOSES

COVENANT AND DECALOGUE

The question of Yahweh's nature is far more than a matter of names. To seek the uniqueness of the Mosaic religion is to turn instinctively to the notion of covenant. Deeply wrought in the tradition is the memory that Moses brought his people into compact with the God by whose power they had been delivered. Whatever Hebrew religion may have been in patriarchal times, the covenant opens the recognizably Yahwistic phase of Hebrew religion. The faith of Israel as recorded in the Old Testament is firmly rooted in the covenant that followed deliverance.

The notion of covenant is fundamental to the closely knit Semitic societies. A covenant is a compact or agreement whose most apparent aspect—its contractual character—is not the most profound. The binding force of covenant is psychic community. It may be between equals or near equals, as in the case of David and Jonathan (I Sam. 20) or the Shechemites and Israelites (Gen. 34). One party may be dominant, as when a king covenants with his people (II Sam. 5:1–5). This is still clearer when a treaty imposed by Ahab upon the subject Syrians is called a covenant (I Kings 20:33–34). The stronger party may not hope to receive in proportion to what he gives: the covenant becomes virtually a promise or gift, in which the superior strength of the leading member is pledged to the support of the weaker one. To be sure, when covenant is taken advantage of it may be used as a cunning trick for wronging the other, for getting without giving, for insuring special privileges. But this feigning of covenant as a "shrewd deal" is a debasement of its real meaning: covenant arises when men assent to their social dependence and when they actualize their personal responsibility by public promise and performance. It is the recognition and support of the interrelations that form the very basis of human life, and which are only incidentally a matter of sentiment. Covenant is one of the finest examples of Hebrew realism.

The Hebrews sealed their covenants by various solemn acts. Originally it seems to have been a cutting of the wrists, with the intermingling of the blood of the two parties. Sometimes animal sacrifice was offered instead; "to cut a covenant" remained a common idiom. An apparent extension of the mixing of blood was the handshake. Sometimes an altar or pillar was set up as a third party to witness to the sincerity of those compacting; the inanimate object is naïvely thought to "oversee" the covenant (cf. Gen. 31:44–50). Especially impressive was a meal in which the solemn covenant act was confirmed. In eating and drinking the common life finds its perfect symbol. The most ordinary function gains the most profound religious connotations. Here is the root of the Jewish and Christian practice of grace before meals, for eating is the epitome of man's dependence upon God and other men. It is not surprising that the central ceremonies of Judaism (the Passover) and Christianity (the Eucharist) are meals.

The covenant is at the basis of Hebrew life in more than a sociological sense. The Hebrew apprehension of God and man was covenantal through and through. One interpreter of Judaism has described its cornerstone as "the awareness of the *reciprocity* of God and man, of man's *togetherness* with Him who abides in eternal otherness."[7] The covenant is no mere *entente cordiale;* it demands engagement of will, definition of group goals, participation in a common life. The covenant traditions, insofar as they are associated with Moses, are preserved in Exodus 19–24 by the J and E sources. The summons to the mountain (19), portentous in its promise, is followed by the so-called Ten Commandments (20:1–17). In Deuteronomy 5 they are given in somewhat different form, and a third version is found in Exodus 34. The name "Ten Commandments" (Hebrew "ten words"; Greek, *Decalogue*) does not appear in Exodus 20 but is used for the two

[7] A. J. Heschel, *Man Is Not Alone,* Farrar, Straus & Young, 1951, p. 242.

variant catalogues (Exod. 34:28; Deut. 4:13; 10:4). The stipulations of the Decalogue as enumerated by the majority of Protestants are as follows:

1. Exclusive allegiance to Yahweh (vs. 3)
2. Imageless worship (vss. 4–6)
3. Holy regard for the divine name (vs. 7)
4. Sabbath observance (vss. 8–11)
5. Honoring of parents (vs. 12)
6. Proscription against murder (vs. 13)
7. Proscription against adultery (vs. 14)
8. Proscription against stealing (vs. 15)
9. Proscription against false witness (vs. 16)
10. Proscription against covetousness (vs. 17)

Lutherans and Roman Catholics regard vss. 3–6 as the first commandment and the prohibition of covetousness (vs. 17) is divided to form the ninth (against covetousness of a man's house) and the tenth commandments (against covetousness of his wife, servants, or animals). Jews treat the introduction "I am Yahweh your God, who brought you out of the land of Egypt, out of the house of bondage" as the first commandment and join vss. 3–6 to form the second.

Objections to the Mosaic origin of the Decalogue are twofold: (1) the general and compendious character of the list is indicative of a late stage in religious development when a "catechetical" interest in Yahwism has arisen; (2) certain conditions of life are presupposed that were not in effect during the lifetime of Moses.

The first is a rather nebulous point, depending in great measure on exactly how abstract the Decalogue is and how much abstraction one can imagine in a "practical" leader like Moses. It is quite clear that the commandments are not strictly legal in character, since the key terms are not specified but depend upon the law codes for their definition. What is it to take Yahweh's name "in vain"? How does one "honor" his parents? What is murder, adultery, stealing, false witness? As bold prophetic statements these are understandable, but for a wandering people they would need very careful definition and implementation. Such a dramatic epitome of the law might not be inconsistent with the kind of prudential skill familiar to Moses the judge, but it is clear that the Ten Commandments could not in themselves govern a group.

It is a loose and naïve way of speaking when a man or community says that its rule of life is to follow the Ten Commandments, for they are capable of many interpretations. For example, neither Moses nor any Jew in biblical times seems to apply "You shall not kill!" to warfare, but the contemporary pacifist feels that his reading of the commandment is the only one that does justice to its deepest dimensions. Although Jewish family morality was the highest in antiquity, adultery was never a crime against the woman but only against her husband. Thus fornication was excluded from the prohibition. Christian and Jewish monogamists insist that the true implications of the command "You shall not commit adultery!" are not observed until it is applied equally to women and men. If Moses was able to start a moral and religious revolution that led eventually to his people summarizing the impact of his teaching in the Decalogue then his significance is no less great than if he actually wrote the words.

As for the second objection, the present form of the commandments concerning the Sabbath and covetousness are said to assume an agricultural mode of life. According to them the Hebrews own houses, lands, domestic servants, and beasts. To have any meaning legal prescriptions must grow out of need and present circumstance. Even though he may have hoped that his people would regain Canaan, it is not probable that Moses would enjoin observances upon the people that could not be fulfilled until years later. Nevertheless many scholars believe the nucleus or "short form" of the Decalogue to derive from Moses. By excluding the decrees about Sabbath and covetousness, as well as the expanded form of the prohibition of images, eight brief pithy statements remain, the essence of Mosaic religion preserved from the lips of Moses if not from his pen. While significant, the issue here can be exaggerated. If we should grant the "short form" of the E Decalogue to Moses, central questions about his religion are still unanswered: Who is the Mosaic God? What are the forms and institutions of Yahweh worship and piety? When we begin to ask such questions, the whole corpus of traditions, ranging far beyond the Ten Commandments, must be taken into account.

THE DIVINE NAME

The name of the God Yahweh is an obscure one. Affinities produced from around the ancient Near East all fail of demonstration. The key passage is the E account of the divine self-disclosure. When asked his name, God says to Moses, "I am who I am" or "I will be that which

I will be" or "I will bring to pass what I choose" (*'ehyeh 'asher 'ehyeh*) Exod. 3:14, cf. also 6:2). This story seems to regard *Yahweh* as derived from the common Hebrew verb *hayah,* "to be." Yahweh may thus mean, "He who is," which is the understanding of the Septuagint. James Moffatt renders Yahweh by "The Eternal." This is somewhat abstract and metaphysical for the Hebrew mind. Others regard "to be" in a more active, phenomenological sense, pointing to 3:12 (E), "But I will be with you" and 4:15 (J), "I will be with your mouth. . . ." Accordingly, Yahweh could mean "He who is present."

The more likely source is the Semitic verb *hawah,* "to blow," or "to cause to fall." In its most primitive usage Yahweh might have been regarded as "the Blower" or "the Feller," God of the storm. In Mosaic religion this element persists in the fire, smoke, and clouds (lightning? volcano?) surrounding the mountain of revelation. But the name might also mean, "He who causes to be." This is understood either as a belief in Yahweh as Creator, the one who causes things to exist (again quite abstract for early Hebrew thought), or Yahweh as the executor of his promises, the one who causes his word to be fulfilled.

Further complicating the problem of the divine name is the appearance of the short form "Yah" in parts of the Old Testament (e.g., Exod. 15:2; Isa. 12:2; Ps. 68:18). Is Yah a contraction or the original? Yah is a form nearly always found in poetic and liturgical compositions. It is equally arguable, on the one hand, that it represents archaic survival in ritual tradition and, on the other, that for poetic purposes the name was shortened. Some who believe that Yah was the original name of Moses' God find its origin in the involuntary emission of wonder in the presence of the mysterious deity: "Yah!" ("O!").

To be preferred among the theories cited are those that stress Hebrew dynamism, e.g., "He who is present" in each crisis and confrontation or better still, "He who executes his promises." At best, however, these etymologies are rationalizations after the event. From the name alone, we have no clear notion of the religious understanding of Moses.

The name Yahweh taken in context is more instructive. All three of the sources present the crucial conversations between Moses and Yahweh (*J:* Exod. 3:5,7–8,16–18; *E:* Exod. 3:6,9–15; *P:* Exod. 6:2–7), in which two themes recur: Yahweh is God of the fathers Abraham, Isaac, and Jacob; and Yahweh is God of the Hebrews, whom he continuously describes as "my people." In the summons to the mountain, there is a soaring passage: "You have seen what I did to the Egyptians, and how I bore you on eagles' wings and brought you to myself. Now therefore, if you will obey my voice and keep my covenant, you shall be my own possession among all peoples; for all the earth is mine, and you shall be to me a kingdom of priests and a holy nation" (Exod. 19:4–6). The heart of Moses' faith is Yahweh, the living God, who calls his people into responsible relation with himself and with one another.

Relationship to Yahweh creates a community that is set against all other communities. This means radical separation from the Egyptians, even at the cost of their lives and against the seemingly insuperable odds of a great power with its invincible armies and its mighty gods. But "nationalistic" as this religion is, the sense of responsibility to Yahweh creates a disciplined community obligated to emulate the divine character. This was the dynamic impulse that Moses released into the mainstream of his people's life: the overpowering sense of Yahweh who cared and was strong to save, and the corollary obligation of Israel to her Lord. Yahweh and Israel; God and people—these are the poles between which the religious experience of Moses moved with elemental power.

Mosaic Theology

The nature of the divine-human polarity and its implications invite exploration. Yahweh is *the terribly holy God*. Holiness (*qodesh*) is to be understood primarily in its religious rather than ethical aspect. It is the quality of Yahweh's Godhood: awesome, overpowering, attracting and repelling the worshiper, holding him entranced. Holiness is that which separates God from man; it is his withdrawn, utterly distant selfhood. This is brilliantly depicted in the so-called theophanies or appearances of God to Moses and the people. Fire serves to express this reality of God, whether in burning bush (3:2) or smoking mountain (19:16,18; 24:15–18). Yahweh is also described as the jealous God, making total demands upon his people (20:5). Thus holiness has a peculiar double aspect. It is God's apartness from man, but at the same time it is his nearness.

The bipolar experience of God is magnificently expressed in the impassioned prayer of Moses, who has grown weary with leading an unresponsive people, as he begs a fuller disclosure of divine favor.

Boldly he asks to see the glory (*kabodh*) of Yahweh, his holiness made visible. But holiness conceals at the instant it reveals: "Behold, there is a place by me where you shall stand upon the rock; and while my glory passes by I will put you in a cleft of the rock, and I will cover you with my hand until I have passed by; then I will take away my hand, and you shall see my back; but my face shall not be seen" (Exod. 33:21–23). Yahweh insists on drawing close to his people and impressing upon them a life patterned after his own being. The holy God demands a holy people (Exod. 19:6; Lev. 19:2). Inescapably, holiness implies both otherness and nearness, separation and dedication, vision and presence. The central paradox of Moses' faith is that the God who in the most radical sense is not man nevertheless deigns to be near man. In fact it is legitimate to regard the paradoxical experience of the distance and the nearness of God as the interpretative key to Old Testament piety.

Yahweh is *the only God for Israel*. It is doubtful that Moses was a monotheist in the full sense. Whether framed by himself or at a later period, the first commandment seems to take the existence of other gods for granted, "you shall have no other gods before (or besides) me!" There are "gods many and lords many" for the nations, but for Israel there is a single undivided loyalty. Central to the question of monotheism is the fact that the theology of Moses was not so much a theology of existence as a theology of potency. For a god to exist was to have power; efficacy *was* existence for the Semitic mind. Of basic importance in analyzing the religion of Moses is not so much giving him the correct name, monotheist or otherwise, as it is discovering the extent and nature of the power of his God, and thus the relation of Yahweh to the other gods.

Yahweh is shown as victorious against all other powers. The plague stories demonstrate his superiority to the gods of Egypt and his striking of the first-born son of Pharaoh, his power over a god incarnate. The theme of the contesting gods has no doubt been elaborated by later tradition, but at the heart of Moses' persuasion of his people to follow him must have been an "ordeal" in which the power of his God against the gods of the captors was proved to the Israelites' satisfaction. This experience of a God whose demand upon his worshipers was total and whose power over other gods was decisive at every test is not entirely what later Jews and Christians have meant by monotheism. With Moses there is little if any reflection on God's role as

Creator or his relation to other tribes and nations, except in a punitive sense. In anything like the later understanding of Israel and the Christian Church, monotheism is a misleading term for the religion of Moses. If we must adopt a label, *henotheism* is perhaps the best, the belief in one God for a people without denying the existence of other gods; or a practically identical term *monolatry,* the worship of one God without excluding the right of other peoples to worship different gods.

More basic than the name is the recognition that Moses unleashed a religious dynamic and called for an exclusive loyalty whose inner logic drove toward a culmination in monotheistic conviction. Thus some would speak of "incipient monotheism" or "implicit monotheism." This belief could not be a once-for-all doctrinal formulation. It is a long way from the thirteenth-century Moses to the sixth-century prophet of Isaiah 40–55. The prophet brought the founder's faith to a glorious climax; but while the two men in their vital effect cannot be understood apart from each other, no historical or religious purpose is served by trying to equate Moses' understanding of God with Deutero-Isaiah's. Moses was no monotheist but the quality of his henotheism made Jewish and Christian monotheism possible.

One of the most astounding things about the God of Moses is his *resistance to human representation.* There are many vivid anthropomorphisms that enrich the stories of the Pentateuch, but the poetic and theological necessities for expressing the living character of God are offset by the maintenance of "distance" between God and man. In sharp contrast to other theologies, Moses presents no story of the birth of Yahweh. He is underived. This is partly due to the undeveloped myth-making mind of the seminomadic Hebrews. But that Moses' mind was a key factor is apparent in the complete absence of a consort or female counterpart to Yahweh. His self-distinction, his underived nature is uncompromised by the anthropomorphism of sex, widespread in the surrounding religions. The exclusion of sexual duality in deity is not due to a supposed Israelite distaste for sex—a distaste that they in fact never had. Such reticence serves rather to protect the otherness and isolation of God in his inmost self; when he relates himself to man it is not by any natural mode but on his own terms, for which human experience is only the palest analogy. In fact so resistant were the Hebrews to admitting sexual symbolism, lest it debase Yahweh to one of the fertility gods, that it was relatively late before the husband-wife analogy was permitted to describe the divine-human relation. Only the impact of a convinced leader could account for this unfailing Israelite conviction, in spite of the severest tests and the apostasy of many Israelites. Naturalistic polytheism was not something slowly sloughed off by later Jews; it was excluded radically by Moses, although the battle to exclude it had to be fought on shifting lines in each new generation. Infidelity to God found novel forms and fidelity called for new commitments to Yahwism. Moses was the innovator, yet his innovation of loyalty to the "unnatural" God was one that needed constant rediscovery and ever-new appropriation.

The crowning proof that for Moses Yahweh was not to be equated with anything on this earth is seen in the founder's *prohibition of images*. This has been attacked as much too rarefied a concept for an unsophisticated leader like Moses. But it accords with all that we can gather of his belief about a God who transcends man and nature. He did not have abstract ways of stating this conviction; early Hebraism remained a philosophically inarticulate religion, but at the decisive point Moses asserted his conviction: man cannot represent Yahweh. Yahweh is not identifiable with any thing or person or any class of things or persons. Yahweh is behind all reality that bears upon Israel but he himself is apart from it. Theological affirmations of the first order are implied in Yahwism, but they are set forth in a specific prohibition whose terms are unmistakable. The force of the command has persisted without abatement to this very day, so powerful that no rationalizations can destroy it, so emphatic that no Jew or Christian has been able to escape its clear demand, yet so germinal that its meaning must be rethought in each age. Many Jews apostatized and turned to idolatry, frankly forsaking Yahweh or trying to court a number of deities at once, but every bit of evidence thus far assembled from written sources and from excavations bears out the fact that Yahweh could not be "imaged."

MOSAIC CULT

As to the formal structure of Mosaic Yahwism, there are many perplexing problems. The basic difficulty is that the traditions reflect later situations and practices that have been cast back into the Mosaic period, always with the feeling that what was true and worthy had its origins in Moses. The fullest accounts of Mosaic rites are in the D and P sources, which show quite an elaborate system of sacrifices and festivals. We should not assume uncritically that all these dicta were in effect in the time of Moses. In fact the provisions often betray settled life in Palestine. Some scholars deny that the seminomadic Hebrews had any sacrificial system, but the oldest stipulations of the J and E sources, while reducing the ritual element, do not exclude it altogether. Several features stand out as integral to the Mosaic cultus.

The *ark* was a portable box, probably representing an imageless throne. It accompanied the Hebrews in their wanderings and went with them into battle. A short poem addressed to the ark evokes something of the aura of holy power surrounding it:

> Arise, O Yahweh, and let thy enemies be scattered;
>> and let them that hate thee flee before thee.
> Return, O Yahweh, to the ten thousand thousands of Israel
>> (Num. 10:35–36).

There have been countless conjectures as to the contents of the ark, all of them fruitless (including the late Pentateuchal statement that the tablets of the law were kept in it, Exod. 25:16; and the tradition of Heb. 9:4 that the rod of Moses and a jar of manna were with the law). But the ark, which finally found its way into the Temple of Solomon, was simply a sign of the God who accompanied his wandering people. If it had any other meaning for Moses that meaning has been lost.

The ark was placed within a *tent,* called by the E source "Tent of Meeting," located outside the camp; and by the P source "Tabernacle," located inside the camp. The discrepancies of name and position and the respective descriptions cannot be easily harmonized. With this apparatus went a *priesthood*. When the traditions speak of worshiping Yahweh three days' journey in the wilderness (Exod. 5:3; 10:25–26), we are probably to think of a mode of worship known to the Israelites in Egypt but supplemented by Moses' contact with Midian. The priests had charge of the tent and ark and at least a minimum of sacrificial rites. They also supervised the *sacred lots,* known as Urim and Thummim (Exod. 28:30; Lev. 8:8), by which Yahweh's will was consulted. The story of the bronze serpent intended to counteract snake bites is apparently a recollection of sympathetic magic (Num. 21:4–9). A chance note in II Kings 18:4 shows that the Israelites had preserved this object and were venerating it as late as the eighth century B.C., when a reforming king destroyed it. It is problematic as to whether the story arose to explain the object or whether Moses actually had such an object cast.

A portable divine throne, oracular lots, and sympathetic magic may seem inconsistent with the Mosaic faith previously described, but they are only so if we try to make of him a founder who embodied the fullness of the faith he started. He was of his age and many of his beliefs would no doubt have appeared incredible to the prophets, not to mention present-day Jews and Christians. One cannot resist the impression, however, that the real thrust of Moses was religious and ethical, that he took over forms already existing, destroyed only those utterly inconsistent with his insight, notably images. It was the content he poured into the forms, the dynamic that infused them, the experience of the God who required them—but who was ethic-demanding as well!—that mark his uniqueness. A discarnate, noninstitutional Mosaism did not exist; his genius falls nevertheless in the sphere of ethos, of a vision of God and people so tremendous that it gave life to Israel long after the specific institutional forms were outworn and new ones had to be created. A wise interpreter of Moses has insisted that his faith was not anticultic but supracultic: "The sacral principle remained; but the sacral assurance, the sacral power of utilizing the God, was uprooted; as was demanded by His character and essence. This sacral power was replaced by the consecration of men and things, of times and places, to the One who vouchsafes His presence. . . ."[8]

Behind all the historical uncertainties, the fine questions of interpretation, stands a figure towering above his people, abased before his God. Something new has entered Israel's life and is resolutely bent on fulfillment: God's togetherness with man, Yahweh and his people, holiness—revealed and responding. It is marvelously captured in the almost liturgical exclamation: "Yahweh, Yahweh, a God merciful and gracious, slow to anger, and abounding in steadfast love and faithfulness, keeping steadfast love for thousands, forgiving iniquity and transgression and sin, but who will by no means clear the guilty, visiting the iniquity of the fathers upon the children and the children's children, to the third and fourth generations" (Exod. 34:6–7).

[8] Martin Buber, *Moses,* East and West Library, 1946, p. 129.

THE SETTLEMENT OF THE LAND

. . . they went after other gods . . .
Judg. 2:12

The settlement of the wandering Israelites in the land of Canaan is described directly in the book of Joshua and obliquely in the book of Judges. Joshua implies that it was a speedy and total occupation. Judges gives a more candid account of the long struggle for possession of the land, a conflict whose most decisive phases were not military but cultural and religious.

THE CANAANITES

The land the Israelites chose to occupy was not unsettled. Canaan, "land of purple," was named for the valued dyes extracted from the murex shellfish (popular among royalty, hence "wearing of the purple"). The inhabitants were known as Canaanites, "dealers in purple dyes, merchants." The Canaanites formed a part of the Amorite movement, the second great Semitic migration in the Fertile Crescent, and were thus closely related to the Old Babylonians. Insofar as the earliest Hebrews were a part of that Amorite movement, they were akin to the Canaanites. Although they were at times bitter contestants for the land, the Canaanites and Hebrews had no basic difficulty in assimilating one another biologically and culturally.

Many Canaanites lived in strongly fortified cities that were generally set on commanding sites overlooking the trade routes. The major cities were concentrated in the lowlands along the Mediterranean coast, across the plain of Esdraelon, and at a few key points in the Jordan valley. The density of population was not great in the plains and it fell off sharply in the mountainous interior; it was thus easier for Israel to gain a toehold in the highlands where less opposition would be faced and her guerrilla-like forces could be deployed to advantage. Utensils and pottery excavated from Canaanite cities reveal a thriving artisan class not technologically creative itself but making able use of the forms typical of surrounding civilizations; Aegean influence on ceramic styles is especially striking. Canaan was suited by its position to produce cultural middlemen rather than political experts. After the rise of Assyrian power, the Canaanites who lived along the coast north of Mt. Carmel became known as Phoenicians; their mercantile empire extended to Carthage, Sicily, and Spain. No cultural break separates the Canaanites from the Phoenicians.

Commercial enterprise made possible the development of strong urban centers on the trade routes traversing Palestine and Syria. The majority of Canaanites were farmers, however. The land provided a modest living for its inhabitants, but seldom any agricultural surplus. The main crops were grain in the lowlands; figs, olives, and wine in the mountains. Sheep, goats, and cattle were kept, sometimes in great number, especially in the more pastoral regions of Judah and the Negeb.

The basic unit of social and political life was the city-state, patterned roughly on the lines of the Babylonian system. As with the Greek city-states, rivalry among these units, often flaring into open warfare, was a constant drain on manpower and a continuous depletion of the economy. Down to about 1500 B.C. the dominant influence in Canaan was exerted by Babylon, though at such a distance as to represent little internal interference. For the next three centuries the expansion of the Egyptian empire brought it within the sphere of the Nile, but even Egyptian suzerainty was a sporadic and often nominal matter. Garrisons were established at points such as Gezer and Bethshan; local potentates served as vassals of Pharaoh. Rather than creating harmony, however, this policy led to charges and countercharges of disloyalty to Egypt. The Tell el-Amarna correspondence is marked by mock suppliance before the Pharaoh, bitter accusations and vigorous denials of disloyalty, and panicky reports of hostile neighbors and nomadic intruders. In these documents the Habiru appear as threats to the established order.

Literary evidence and archaeological finds point to the virtual absence of a strong middle class. Between the ample homes of the nobility and the cramped hovels of the poor, there are no other quarters in most of the cities excavated. Wealth fell into the hands of the rulers, merchants, and landlords; the good fortune of the few was built on a broad base of virtual serfdom. At any moment enervating wars could bring devastation to the structures of wealth and prestige reared at great human cost. This situation was roughly similar to society in most of the Near East, but the precarious political security and exposed position of Canaan made for more uncertainty and turmoil than was characteristic of Egypt or even of Babylonia.

In the midst of such struggle, little cultural contribution would seem likely, and in most respects the Canaanites were mere imitators of their neighbors in Egypt, Babylonia, and Asia Minor. Yet in one instance they were innovators of the first rank, for it is to the Canaanites that we owe the alphabetic system. Several gropings in the direction of the twenty-two letter Hebrew and twenty-four letter Greek alphabets have been found in the area; the most primitive was carved in rock by mine workers in the Sinai peninsula. Essentially what happened was that about 1500 B.C. the picture language of Egyptian hieroglyphs was stylized and certain signs were given arbitrary letter values. The Phoenicians then disseminated the system among the Greeks, whence all Western languages have received it. The Canaanite language was adopted by the Hebrews, with only a normal amount of dialectical modification. That borrowing is in itself impressive evidence of the tremendous cultural debt of the Hebrews to the Canaanites. A facile reading of the Old Testament gives the impression that Hebrews and Canaanites were such mortal enemies that they had little in common; actually it was their great similarity and the powerful allure of Canaanite religion that made it necessary for Yahwists among the Hebrews to wage ideological and cultural war against the natives.

Canaanite religion was naturalistic polytheism, similar to that of Babylonia, but more eclectic, drawing upon Egyptian sources as well. Agricultural and human fertility were the basic concerns of religious myth and ritual. *Ba'al,* "lord, master" (pl. *baalim*) was the generic name for the male fertility deity, whose manifestations were as numerous as the city-states or localities with their peculiar natural features: trees, springs, rocks, etc. Baal Berith, "lord of the covenant," was the god of Shechem (Judg. 9:4,27). Baal Melkart was the patron deity of Jezebel, wife of Ahab (I Kings 16:31–32). The female counterpart of the *ba'al* was the *'asherah.* The divinities were worshiped not only in temples but also in open-air sanctuaries or "high places." The *ba'al* was generally represented by a large standing stone or *massebah*, the *'asherah* by a wooden pole known by the same name (Asherim, pl.; a variant form for the goddess is Ashtoreth, sing., and Ashtaroth, pl.).

Canaanite cult objects from eleventh-century Megiddo: altars, incense burners, offering bowls, jugs.

Orgiastic revelries and ritual prostitution made Canaanite religion crude and vitalistic. A Saturnalian spirit seized the revelers at the harvest festivals, especially grape-gathering (Judg. 9:27; 21:19–21). One purpose of ritual prostitution was to induce fertility in the land through sympathetic magic. Corps of male and female temple personnel were recruited. Even with the best of intentions it is easy to see how such a practice would pander to lust and immaturity. Women cherished figurines and amulets of the mother goddess as stimulants to pregnancy. A sacrificial cultus provided many types of offering by which the unseen but all-too-human powers could be approached and won to man's favor. Human sacrifice developed in at least two forms: sacrifice of the first-born son as the due of the gods and foundation sacrifice as the means of prospering building operations. The extent of human sacrifice is debatable, since by no means all excavations of Canaanite cities have uncovered tiny skeletons of children such as are laid out in jars at Gezer. Even this evidence is disputed since some scholars find no proof of infant sacrifice but only demonstration of a high infant mortality rate. In foundation sacrifice the victim was sealed in the cornerstone.

It was once thought that Canaanite religion had practically no mythology. This impression, drawn from the meager Old Testament data, has been corrected by the discovery of religious texts at the north Syrian seacoast town of ancient Ugarit (modern Ras esh-Shamra). Substantial portions of three fourteenth-century mythological and ritual texts have appeared. The *Baal and Anath* "epic" is a mosaic of fragments whose precise order must frequently be inferred.[1] It tells of Aliyan Baal (Baal most high) who seeks a house from El (the father God) but is murdered by Mot (god of Death) and returned to life with the aid of his bloodthirsty sister Anath. Among the several deities mentioned in the epic are Lady Asherah of the Sea, wife of El; Kothar wa-Khosis, artificer god and Canaanite equivalent of Vulcan; Prince Yam (Sea) and Judge Nahar (River), represented as warring with Baal and exemplifying the ancient Semitic view that the powers of chaos stem from the primordial waters that the gods must control in order to create the cosmos. The other religious texts, *Keret* and *Aqhat,* are chiefly valuable for the standards of royal rule and customs of family life they portray. There are a number of strong statements about the responsibility of leaders to execute justice and to uphold the weak, a theme that was to become central in Israelite belief.

*A Canaanite stone pillar (*massebah*) from fourteenth-century Beth-shan.*

Jews and Christians have been extreme, even scurrilous, in their estimate of Canaanite religion. Sometimes, as a means of justifying the Jewish possession of the land and the command to destroy its inhabitants, the religion of Canaan has been pictured as an unending orgy of sex and blood, so that the Jews were doing mankind a favor in

[1] See Appendix 4, pp. 581–584.

rooting out this social cancer. As long as the only source of our knowledge was the Old Testament, such a judgment was defensible. With a larger view now available, it is clear that Canaanite religion was only a little more violent and orgiastic than Mesopotamian religion and that it rested on fundamentally the same principles and prac-

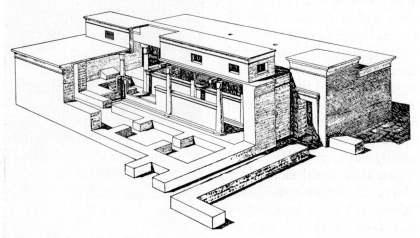

Reconstruction of a Canaanite temple at fourteenth-century Beth-shan. Indirect entrance prevents outsiders from looking at the altar.

tices: naturalistic polytheism with rites by which man's rapport with his world was enacted and secured. The almost total lack of morality among the gods is shocking to moderns; but such, after all, was typical of gods the world over, the Greek pantheon included. The sexual element prominent in religious practice was capable of corruption and in actual fact was frequently a morally debilitating factor. Ritual prostitution was not promiscuity, however, for it was hedged about by protective devices. Furthermore, human sacrifice was probably not as common as some have implied.

Indeed, the attempt to render theological justification to the Hebrew claim upon the land by depreciating the Canaanites is a thankless and misguided task. Israel claimed the land and fought for it, but the lines of the struggle were not as clearly drawn as the present form of the Old Testament suggests. The Hebrews and Canaanites were closely related Semitic peoples, whose basic difference was in the clash of nomadic and sedentary life. The essence of the nomadic life for Israel was, moreover, her Yahwistic religion. By all the rules of the ancient game of religion, her belief in Yahweh ought to have given way to the Baals or at least have been so submerged as to become only one among many religious cults. Both of these perils were real; it was not a mock struggle. The superiority of Israel's faith was not something patent at

A north Syrian fertility goddess. Ivory plaque from Ugarit (Ras esh-Shamra).

the start by which she rejected the Canaanites and obliterated them; her faith was as much something that only became "superior" in the course of conflict with Canaanite religion. A greater depth and expansion of vision, an emotional warmth and color entered Yahwism because of the Canaanites. This is seen most clearly in the prophet Hosea. The Canaanite religion perished but lived on in its victor, both as vanquished opponent and needed corrective. Men often learn much from that which they most bitterly oppose.

THE TRADITIONS OF JOSHUA

The Israelite occupation of Canaan is described in Joshua, whose first twelve chapters are patently composite. Two or more strands appear in the stories of the crossing of the Jordan River (chaps. 3–4), the seizure of Jericho (chap. 6), the Battle of Ai (chap. 8), and the defeat of the Amorite league of cities at Beth-horon (chap. 10). According to one strand, for example, the memorial stones were piled as a cairn on the western bank of the Jordan, whereas in the other they were placed in the river bed. The famous command of Joshua to the sun and moon at Aijalon was no doubt originally in poetic form:

"Sun, stand thou still at Gibeon,
   and thou Moon in the valley of Aijalon."
And the sun stood still, and the moon stayed,
   until the nation took vengeance on their enemies (10:12b–13a).

Taking the poetic apostrophe from the anthology known as the Book of Jashar, the prose author of the story interpreted it with flat literalism: "The sun stayed in the midst of heaven, and did not hasten to go down for about a whole day," or at least he provided the opening chink for those who have since read the account with an air of solemn factuality. What army, when the battle has been going its way, has not prayed for a lease on daylight!

The older Documentary Hypothesis found that the Pentateuchal strata E and P continued into Joshua. Chapters 1–12 present an idealized account of the total conquest of the land by a united Israel under the leadership of the Ephraimite Joshua, and chapters 22–24 a pair of farewell speeches and an account of a covenant at Shechem. This is E material extensively edited by D, the latter being largely responsible for chapters 1, 11, and 23. In the E and D portions of the book there is a manifest interest in northern sites, especially Benjamin and Ephraim (cf. 4:7,20; 5:3,9; 7:26; 8:30; 24:1,25). The geographical data in chapters 13–21 (which usually prove formidable for even the most doughty Bible reader) were regarded by critics as inaccurate for the period of the conquest but valuable for the seventh through the fifth centuries. The lists of tribal boundaries and cities were attributed to the P writer, who therein gives us the most ancient extended geographical description of Palestine.

The situation today is less distinct. The arguments of Martin Noth and Ivan Engnell to the effect that Genesis–Numbers is a history separate from Deuteronomy–Kings have been influential even among those who cannot accept their detailed conclusions. The weightiest objection to this separation is the fact that without some account of the occupation of the land, Genesis–Numbers is a truncated epic. No one is prepared to argue that this history was compiled *before* the entrance into the land. It is difficult to believe that traditionists would have developed the stories of the origins of the Hebrew people and failed to carry through to the stage at which they themselves stood, especially since Genesis through Numbers are liberally supplied with references to a land yet to be inherited.

This objection can be allowed for if we assume that the D historians assimilated the closing portions of the J and E sources into their own history. Thus J and E, insofar as they exist in Deuteronomy–Kings, are not easily recognizable because they have been largely rewritten. The reason for the radical reworking of this portion of the JE traditions may have been the D historians' dissatisfaction with the current accounts of the taking of the land that were too realistic in their appraisal of the limited gains made under Joshua. It is equally likely that the D writers arbitrarily chose to begin with the entrance to the land, since the burden of their writing is the theology of the land, the terms on which it is to be occupied, and the special temptations and blessings it offers. It is barely possible that the ending of JE, telling of the occupation, had already been lost by the time of the D writers, who then supplied the deficiencies with such materials, written and oral, as could be assembled.

Be that as it may, present critics are rather skeptical of finding materials in Joshua that can be tied directly to the sources of Genesis–Numbers. Older critics were unable to find any J at all; what looks like E is really northern tradition recast by D; and as for P, at the very most we see only editorial touches in chapters 13–21. Once the geographical data are cut loose from P, Albrecht Alt and his pupils tend to locate them at an earlier preëxilic period, as boundary lists and city inventories—some dating back to pre-Solomonic times. A cursory

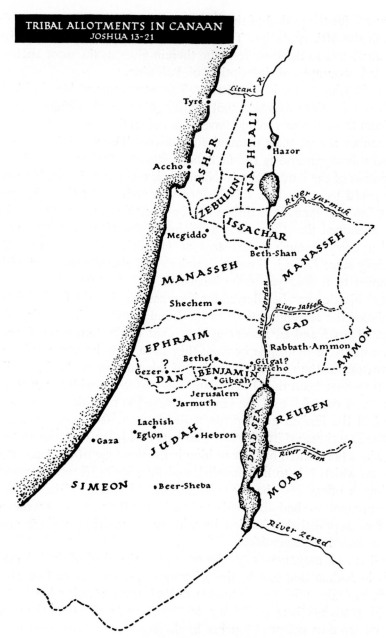

TRIBAL ALLOTMENTS IN CANAAN
JOSHUA 13-21

Litani R.

Tyre

ASHER

NAPHTALI

Hazor

Accho

ZEBULUN

River Yarmuk

ISSACHAR

Megiddo

Beth-Shan

MANASSEH

MANASSEH

Shechem

River Jabbok

River Jordan

GAD

EPHRAIM

Rabbath-Ammon

AMMON

? Bethel

Gilgal?

Gezer

Jericho

?

DAN

BENJAMIN

Gibeah

Jerusalem

Jarmuth

REUBEN

DEAD SEA

Lachish

Eglon

JUDAH

Hebron

?

River Arnon

Gaza

SIMEON

Beer-Sheba

MOAB

River Zered

---- TRIBAL BOUNDARIES
? UNCERTAIN BOUNDARIES

glance at the work of the Alt school might imply that it treats the historical material of the Old Testament with greater credence than the documentary critics. But this is largely illusory. The other aspect of its method is a rigorous use of the *aetiological* principle. Wherever a story shows signs of explaining some natural or historical feature, its historicity is well-nigh dismissed. Aetiology is given a large role as the fabricator of tradition.

The way this works in Joshua is that the conquest narratives are explained as elaborations of an original stratum in which "Joshua" was the hero of Benjamin alone and concerned only with the limited region around Gilgal and Bethel, cities that figure prominently in chapters 1–11. The aetiological motif, accented by the recurring phrase, "as it is unto this day" or "so it remains unto this day," explains a cairn of rocks in the bed of the Jordan River, a circle of monoliths at Gilgal, a stone heap at the valley of Achor, a deserted ruin near Bethel, the subject position of the Gibeonites in Israel, and five trees and a blocked-off cave at Makkedah (cf. 4:8–9,20; 7:26; 8:28–29; 9:27; 10:27). In none of these stories, except for chapter 10, is Joshua supposedly germane to the plot. Ephraimites revamped the Benjaminite traditions to make the northern conquest look like a campaign master-minded by one of their tribesmen. Finally, Judah took over the traditions and in a second editing made Joshua the successor to Moses (who according to Alt was a southerner) and thus minimized the northern element.[2]

This analysis does great service by stressing the fact that Joshua cannot be taken at face value. The stress upon the aetiological elements is a welcome one, for it reminds us that tribal and local history are seldom dispassionately objective. Any effort to get behind the façade of a complete conquest by united Israel should be encouraged, even if it has weaknesses—and the weaknesses of the Alt approach are conspicuous. Aetiology is given far too creative a role; it is not sufficiently recognized that the explanatory instinct of the storyteller is not his only concern and that interpretative details often attach themselves secondarily to a story that has arisen on other grounds. John Bright, whose commentary on Joshua shows indebtedness to Alt's viewpoint, is rightly critical of the overuse of the aetiological theory to dismiss the historicity of Joshua. He notes whimsically that

---

[2] Albrecht Alt, "Josua," *Kleine Schriften zur Geschichte des Volkes Israel,* Beck, 1953, vol. 1, pp. 176–192.

while it is possible to explain the tale of the landing of the Pilgrims at Plymouth as a device to account for the presence of a large rock, it is also faintly possible that Pilgrims did land at Plymouth harbor, quite apart from the question as to just where on the shoreline they set foot![3] In other words, one may be rightly suspicious of details in stories, the main lines of which hold up under scrutiny.

Another objection to Alt is that he overstates the separateness of the tribes. His own pupil Martin Noth has overcome this deficiency by positing the existence of a tribal league early in Israel's life in Palestine.[4] Granted that the conquest of the land was more piecemeal than the book of Joshua implies, it is still possible to contend that two or more tribes acted in concert under the leadership of a forceful leader such as Joshua. Of course the unity of these tribes may have been a tenuous one. With their fierce nomadic independence, even a common worship of Yahweh might fail to rally all the tribes to concerted action at every crisis. In short, there is no good reason why Joshua could not have led Benjamin, Ephraim, Levi, and such other northern elements as had been in Egypt, in their attack on the land. It may also be seriously doubted that Moses was a Judean who had to be grafted onto the northern traditions and converted into a forerunner and superior of Joshua. Without doubt there were separate groups of Hebrews involved in taking the land, but Alt's reconstruction is much too arbitrary.

Thanks to the careful work of recent scholars such as Alt, Noth, and Albright, the complexity of the conquest traditions is not likely to be underestimated in future study. To give one striking example of the nature of the problems, the student of Joshua's life cannot fail to be impressed by the many similarities to the life of Moses. Moses crossed the Reed Sea, Joshua the Jordan. Moses sent spies ahead to Hebron, Joshua dispatched spies to Jericho. Moses instituted circumcision at Sinai, and Joshua at Gilgal. Moses celebrated the Passover in Egypt, and Joshua at Gilgal. Moses gave the Law at Sinai, and Joshua at Ebal. Moses officiated at the covenant at Sinai, and Joshua enjoined the covenant at Shechem. Moses appointed cities of refuge for the inadvertent murderer (Num. 35) and Joshua named them anew (Josh. 20). Moses "took off his shoes" before the burning bush, and Joshua removed his sandals in the presence of the sword-bearing messenger

---

[3] John Bright, *Introduction to Joshua* (IB, vol. 2), Abingdon, 1953, p. 547.
[4] Martin Noth, *The History of Israel*, Harper, 1958, pp. 85–108.

of God. Joshua is a veritable Second Moses. The similarity does not in itself discredit the traditions. As a close follower of the lawgiver, Joshua would imitate many of his predecessor's patterns. The ritual forms could be reënactments, as the book of Joshua indeed interprets them. But the large number of affinities, coupled with the idealization of the conquest, create the presumption that the narrators have cast the traditions with a view to emphasizing Joshua as the counterpart of Moses. This factor of accommodation in the traditions must be taken into account, even though it does not throw any serious doubt upon the actuality of Joshua.

TOTAL CONQUEST

The traditional account of the conquest pictures it as an immediate and total defeat of the Canaanites, followed by their swift extermina-tion. Only when the Israelites are disobedient to Yahweh are they vulnerable; otherwise they are invincible, striking terror among the native princes who either join them by artifice, as in the case of the Gibeonites (9:3–15), or oppose them, sometimes in confederacies, as in the case of the five Amorite cities of Jerusalem, Hebron, Jarmuth, Lachish, and Eglon (10:1–5).

Joshua's plan of attack is presented as a threefold strategy. Operating from Gilgal in the Jordan valley, he struck first at the central highlands, taking Ai and joining with the Gibeonites through their own clever stratagem. (Observe that a covenant once contracted, even with deceivers, cannot be revoked.) The

Potter's wheel and cultic mask from the probable level of Israelite destruction at thirteenth-century Hazor.

second phase of the war of occupation was the defeat of the Amorite league and the destruction of four of their cities, Jerusalem alone being unscathed. The final action was in the far north at Hazor, where a confederacy of northern kings was roundly defeated. The account breaks off with a sweeping summary from the hand of the Deuteronomist: "So Joshua took all that land, the hill country and all the Negeb . . . and the lowland and the Arabah and the hill country of Israel and its lowland from Mount Halak, that rises toward Seir, as far as Baal-gad in the valley of Lebanon below Mount Hermon. And he took all their kings, and smote them, and put them to death" (11:16–17). So thoroughly were the Canaanites trounced that the Israelites were able at once to apportion the land among the tribes.

Now it is apparent that this summary schema is born of the theological disposition of the Deuteronomists who see the struggle less in the light of military action than in the light of religious conflict. It is not a social-military-political contest between two peoples that engages the interest of the D writers. It is the possession of the land as a gift from Yahweh that concerns them. The Canaanites figure as no more than foils to the people of God or instruments of Yahweh's punishment upon his faithless people. The struggle as D sees it is from first to last a matter of "holy war." He thus slips into generalizations that the stories he has related do not bear out.

The practice of "devoting to destruction," namely, the slaughter of war captives (including civilians) and the burning of spoils in honor of the tribal god, was typical of seminomadic peoples. An illuminating parallel is found in the memorial stone of an eighth-century Moabite king who speaks of "devoting to Chemosh" (the Moabite god) Israelites captured in battle.[5] While this was ideologically acceptable, there is no evidence that any ancient people was exterminated systematically; "devotion to destruction" was applicable in times of special excitement but was not carried through methodically. The D account of Israelite behavior in this respect is grossly misleading. One might think that the whole of Canaan had been devastated and its population slaughtered. In a sense the D writer is saying: it is too bad we didn't slay them all as we were commanded, for it is our long history of compromise with Canaanite ways of life that has brought us to our present plight! It is a case of reading history after the event, finding a contemporary meaning in it, and then virtually rewriting the prior history. That is not a habit that people have outgrown or ever will. We look back upon the stirrings of National Socialism in Germany or of

[5] See Appendix 8, pp. 590–591.

communism in China and wonder how men could have mistaken their first insidious portents. Since they ought to have been recognized and renounced at the start, those who opposed them are heroes and those who did not are morally culpable. The D writers were following an intensely human trait when they read history morally and fell into the error of foreclosing the evidence.

So the dramatic portrayal of sweeping victory accomplished within the lifetime of Joshua has determined the thinking of Bible students through all the centuries. Yet the Deuteronomic history is checkered with obvious contradictions of that view. Not all the nations were destroyed at once, so that the land might not return to wilderness (Deut. 7:22); we read of "the nations that Joshua left when he died" which are to continue as a means of testing Israel's fidelity to Yahweh (Judg. 2:21), or to teach later generations of Israelites the arts of war (Judg. 3:2). When all the exceptions to the theory of a total conquest expressly stated in Joshua are tallied up, the theory is exposed as a blatant overstatement. One exemption alone states that the coastal region from Egypt to Sidon was not taken (Josh. 13:2–6). Of the great walled cities of the north, only Hazor was captured by Joshua (11:13). The Jebusite stronghold of Jerusalem remained impregnable (15:63). Manasseh was unable to reduce the string of Canaanite fortresses guarding the Valley of Esdraelon: Beth-shan, Ibleam, Dor, Endor, Taanach, Megiddo (17:11).

Serious qualifications must therefore be applied to the exuberance of the D writers; their own sources do not tolerate the constructions they put upon them and, in fact, their constructions vary considerably. Their intention was not to deceive by distorting a past chapter of history; if it had been they would have been much more meticulous in deleting counterevidence. Rather the disparate evidence out of the past was brought together and the interpretation of the history prevailing in their circles was applied to the material, the two being only partly congenial to one another. One critic summarizes a careful study of the D view of the conquest by saying, "All we can charge him with is overschematization of his material."[6] In historical writing, of course, this is no mean charge but religious and antireligious historians through the centuries have been prone to overschematize, and not all have been

---

[6] G. E. Wright, "The Literary and Historical Problem of Joshua 10 and Judges 1," *Journal of Near Eastern Studies* 5 (1946), p. 107.

so generous as to permit the corrective of their bias to remain conspicuously displayed in their writings!

THE SETTLEMENT RECONSTRUCTED

If the general impression of the book of Joshua gives an inadequate framework for conceiving the occupation of Canaan, whāt is a proper one? The first step is to replace the common term Conquest with Settlement (cf. the German *Landnahme*). To speak of Conquest fails to do justice to the many ways in which the Canaanites culturally conquered the Hebrews. It ignores the gradual merging of the two peoples so that the Canaanites became Israelites under the kingdom of David. It underplays the nonmilitary factors involved in the entrance of the Hebrews: their occupation of pastoral land unused by the Canaanites and their alliance and intermarriage with closely related groups in the land. Recalling our discussion of the patriarchs, the traditions in Genesis may be seen as reflecting the first penetrations of Canaan by the Hebrew tribesmen. The evidence indicates that there was a relatively peaceful coexistence of the newcomers and the natives. Probably there were several such movements, Abraham and Jacob representing the two primary groups. Some of these groups entered from the north, while others came up from the south. Abraham was the hero of the southern group that found its center at Hebron. Jacob was the hero of the northern clans whose centers were at Bethel and Shechem.

But these two groups tend to break down into other units with histories of their own. The southern group was composed of the "Abraham" element that migrated from Mesopotamia and the "Judean" element that was partly of Midianite-Kenite origin. This group probably pressed into Canaan from the desert regions of Arabia and in the Negeb joined with the "Abraham" element, absorbing native Canaanites at the same time, the result being an amalgam of migratory Amorite and Arabian groups on Canaanite soil. They were the source of the tribe of Judah. The northern group was made up of a "Jacob" faction from Mesopotamia, probably Aramean, and a splinter party that broke away and went into Egypt, no doubt because of economic pressure. The memory of their affinity with the Palestinian Jacob tribes was retained. Moses was the leader of these clans at the time of their liberation. Through his contact with Jethro the Midianite, Moses learned of the southern Hebrews and their worship of Yahweh. It is possible that he was the first Hebrew to see the potential unity of these several groups, owing to his connections with the northern and southern tribes. The memories of distant tribal worship were suddenly activated by the dynamic Midianite worship of Yahweh, the holy God.

We are hampered in our reconstruction by the very hazy evidence from the pre-Mosaic period. We cannot dogmatically say how pronounced were the ties among these various groups. If they had no common worship then how could Moses have had a vision of their unity? And yet if their commonness was as explicit as the present state of the tradition indicates by putting the tribes together from the start, how then do we explain the relative silence about the patriarchs in most of the Old Testament and the historical evidence for widely scattered infiltrations of Canaan? We are balancing elements, either of which if pressed unduly obscures the other. About all that we can say is that sufficient unity of culture and religion bound the northern and southern Hebrews together for Moses to seize upon it and actualize it in a covenant relationship that was accepted by all subsequent Hebrews. Yet the unity must have been diffuse and inarticulate and the patriarchal worship of Yahweh far less virile than the faith of Moses.

The settlement of Canaan was not an easily described occurrence of a decade or so, but was a matter of centuries of history prior to, concurrent with, and subsequent to the Egyptian sojourn and Exodus. Joshua's dramatic attack was one important phase of the occupation, but the patriarchs had begun the process and throughout the period of the Judges and until the time of David the Settlement proceeded. Moses and Joshua, members of the northern tribes, congealed the latent unity and were the first Hebrews to elicit the veneration of all or most of the tribes. Later that veneration was extended to the heroes of the separate groups, Abraham, Isaac, and Jacob.

The several phases of the Settlement may be reconstructed as follows:[7]

1. The first movement of Hebrews into Canaan occurred *ca.* 1750–1650 B.C., consisting of clans headed by Abraham (Gen. 12:1–3). As a small part of the Amorite migration, they entered from the north but settled around Hebron in the south (Gen. 13:18; 14:13; 18:1). Their relations with the inhabitants were mainly peaceable.

2. Aramean Hebrews entered Canaan under Jacob *ca.* 1500–1350 and settled in the north around Bethel and Shechem (Gen. 28:18–19; 33:18–20; 35:1–20) and in Trans-Jordan (Gen. 31:25; 32:1,22).

[7] The paragraph numbers coincide with the map numbers on p. 162.

Their relations with the natives were more hostile, as reflected in the greater pugnacity of Jacob and his aggressive sons Simeon and Levi (Gen. 34). The latter phases of this movement probably coincide with the Habiru invasions described in the Tell el-Amarna documents.

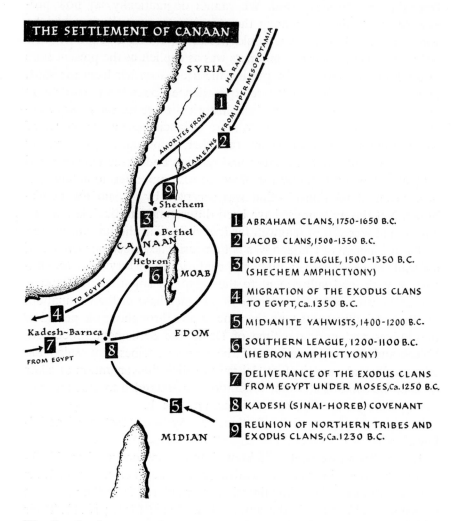

THE SETTLEMENT OF CANAAN

1 ABRAHAM CLANS, 1750-1650 B.C.

2 JACOB CLANS, 1500-1350 B.C.

3 NORTHERN LEAGUE, 1500-1350 B.C. (SHECHEM AMPHICTYONY)

4 MIGRATION OF THE EXODUS CLANS TO EGYPT, Ca. 1350 B.C.

5 MIDIANITE YAHWISTS, 1400-1200 B.C.

6 SOUTHERN LEAGUE, 1200-1100 B.C. (HEBRON AMPHICTYONY)

7 DELIVERANCE OF THE EXODUS CLANS FROM EGYPT UNDER MOSES, Ca. 1250 B.C.

8 KADESH (SINAI-HOREB) COVENANT

9 REUNION OF NORTHERN TRIBES AND EXODUS CLANS, Ca. 1230 B.C.

The Jacob clans were however no more than a small fraction of the Near Eastern social drifters loosely labeled Habiru.

3. The Jacob clans, augmented by other Hebrews, developed a tribal league, nowadays called an amphictyony—derived from the Greek

term for a religious confederacy bound by common worship at a central sanctuary defended by the tribal members. Shechem was the amphictyonic center (Gen. 33:18–20; a few scholars prefer Shiloh, cf. I Sam. 4:3). The nucleus of the league was formed by the so-called Rachel tribes: Joseph (Manasseh and Ephraim) and Benjamin. Probably all the twelve tribes of Genesis 29:31–30:24; 35:16–21, except Judah and possibly Reuben, were included in the league. That some of the tribal ancestors are credited to Jacob's concubines (often called "concubine tribes"), probably expresses the conviction that Gad, Asher, Dan, and Naphtali were native Canaanite tribes who joined the amphictyony later (Gen. 30:3–12). It should be noted, however, that such status did not prejudice the great praise given to Naphtali in the Song of Deborah (Judg. 5:18).

4. Part of the northern Hebrews—whether whole tribes or clans is difficult to determine, but at least the Levites and probably also Ephraim—left the region of Shechem and went into Egypt where semi-nomadic tribes were in the habit of living on the frontier (Gen. 47:1–12). They probably entered because of economic compulsion during a famine; later as conscripted labor their lot grew onerous (Gen. 47:4; Exod. 1:8–14). These Hebrews retained the memory of their connection with the Jacob tribes (Exod. 3:6).

5. The Midianites (or Kenites) who lived in the area around the Gulf of Aqabah south of Palestine were Yahweh-worshipers who may have been previously introduced to the cult by some of the migrating Hebrew groups. From the Midianites Moses learned of Yahweh, whom he was convinced was also the God of his ancestral tribes in northern Palestine (Exod. 3:13–15). Yahwism was probably not as dominant or developed a faith among the Jacob clans as it was among the Midianites, but the dormant faith of Moses was aroused when he dedicated himself to Yahweh, the God of Israel, whom he fully trusted as the God of his fathers.

6. The Midianite Yahwists moved on into the Negeb, perhaps some of them having made contact with the Abraham clans before the time of Moses. The Abraham Hebrews and the Midianite Yahwists formed a league at Hebron that later emerged under David as the tribe of Judah.

7. Moses, with his faith composed of aspects new and old, returned to his people in Egypt and persuaded them that the ancient tribal God

had an unexpected power and concern for Israel (Exod. 4:29–31). Moses led them out in the name of Yahweh (Exod. 5:1–2; 14:13–14).

8. At Kadesh, the religious center of the Midianites, the Moses group was organized in a covenant community built around social law and religious cultus (Exod. 18–24). Jethro was the medium for the transmission to the Exodus tribes of the institutional facets of Yahwism (Exod. 18:8–24). Although the Shechemite amphictyony possessed a cultus, the distinctive ritual features of the Pentateuch came from the Midianites via Moses. After a lengthy stay at Kadesh, Moses sought to return to Canaan and reunite with the Jacob tribes but did not live to consummate his hope.

9. Joshua, the successor of Moses, brought the Exodus Hebrews and the Jacob Hebrews together in a covenant at the old amphictyonic center in Shechem (Josh. 24). The rather diffuse ethnic and religious bonds were now strengthened by the powerful impulse of the Mosaic faith. Shechemite cultic elements were absorbed into Mosaic religion, providing a more elaborate sacrificial system and opening the way for Canaanite influence. This means that while military action was needed to take parts of Canaan not all the inhabitants were hostile to the invaders. It is frequently noted by scholars that there is no description of Joshua's battles in the center of the land and it is precisely there, at Shechem, that we hear of the covenant between the invaders and the natives.

We see then how futile it is to draw a sharp cleavage between "Hebrew" and "Canaanite." In a sense all those who had not been in Egypt and thus lacked the Mosaic experience of Yahweh were "Canaanites," even the earlier Abraham and Jacob clans, for they had settled down to varying stages of accommodation to Canaanite civilization. But some of these groups could be won to Yahwism because of their keen nomadic memories and their affinity for the faith of Moses against the softness of civilization. At the same time these earliest Hebrew immigrants exerted a reflex Canaanite cultural and religious influence on the nomadic core of Yahwism.

In the above analysis the ambiguity of "Hebrew" and "Yahweh" creates an unavoidable looseness and imprecision owing to the gaps in our knowledge; any reconstruction is hypothetical and at best says far too little. "Hebrew" without the Yahwism of the Old Testament in effect denotes little more than nomadic Semites of the Amorite and Aramean migrations who settled in the vicinity of Palestine.

In this connection it is of interest that Hebrew is reserved in the Old Testament almost exclusively as a name employed by outsiders (or by Israelites when addressing foreigners). Furthermore, if Genesis intends to connect it with the patronym Eber (10:25; 11:14–16), then all the Semitic tribes of his line would be Hebrews: Arabs, Ammonites, Moabites, Edomites as well as Israelites. If "Hebrew" is only a tepidly Yahwistic designation, then apart from the novel religious factor the Abraham Hebrews, stemming from the same Amorite migration as the Canaanites, are scarcely distinguishable from them. Linguistically Hebrew is simply a dialectic variation of Canaanite. The language of the invaders was presumably Aramaic or Akkadian; they adopted "Hebrew."

THE TRADITIONS OF THE JUDGES

Since the Hebrews were not the only contenders for control of Palestine, an urgent historical question arises: Why should Israel, of the many invaders, prove successful in establishing rule over Canaan? The answer is partly discoverable in Israel's nomadic élan. But the same élan might be expected of nomadic groups closely related to Israel: Moabites, Edomites, Ammonites. A fuller answer is in the drive of Mosaic Yahwism, which produced a remarkable unity in spite of strong countercurrents making for division and fragmentation. W. F. Albright, in discussing the Settlement, comments on the centripetal and centrifugal forces operating in this era. There existed "an unusually powerful centripetal force in the Mosaic tradition. . . . The religion of Moses was a missionary faith with dynamic appeal to the nomadic and seminomadic tribes of that time."[8] But there were threatening disintegrative forces: the geographical disunity of Canaan, which always discouraged political unification, and the weakening of the missionary impulse of Yahwism as it came in contact with the agricultural ethos of the sown land. It seemed for a time that the exclusive and demanding faith of Moses might succumb to the more aesthetically appealing and sensual Baal worship. We shall have much to say of this struggle as a perennial concern of the prophets. But the long and mortal strife

[8] W. F. Albright, *The Biblical Period*, reprinted in 1950 from *The Jews: Their History, Culture and Religion* (ed. Louis Finkelstein), Harper, 1949, pp. 17, 19.

between the two religions is already apparent in the book of Judges.

Such was the balance of competing powers: on the one side driving the Hebrews to success (their nomadism and Yahweh religion) and on the other frustrating their efforts by decentralization and cultural assimilation (the geographical disunity and religious compromise and decline). What resolved this "tug of war" so that Israel was able to consolidate her hold in Palestine and rise to political mastery? Something was needed to bring all the inhabitants of Canaan together against a common enemy. Historians agree that the factor tipping the scales in Israel's favor was the entrance of the non-Semitic Philistines, the sea peoples who were castoffs of the Aegean world and bearers of a proto-Greek civilization. It was their superiority in arms and organization that alerted the latent unity of the Israelite tribes and hastened the coöperation of the Canaanite and Hebrew populations who had lived side by side for a century or more. The threat from the Philistines appeared already in the time of Samson and eventually set the stage for the monarchy of Saul and David.

It is important to see that contrary to the explicit view of the D source, Canaanite and Hebrew were not sharply opposed realities. In truth they held so much in common, were in effect becoming so much a single people, that the religious distinctiveness of Mosaic religion, uncongenial to toleration and syncretism, was under constant pressure to relax its demands. Israel triumphed in Canaan by making common cause with the Canaanite people, so that their mutual fortunes against the Philistines became one, and yet Israel's culturally "inferior" religion was maintained and developed. It is surprising to note that of all the military deliverers named in the book of Judges, only one waged war against Canaanites; all the others *defended Canaanites and Israelites* against intruders seeking to repeat the pattern formerly followed by Hebrew invaders. T. H. Robinson has put it in a stark but not inaccurate way: "It is true that the military prowess of Israel was a prominent factor in achieving the final result, but the book of Judges makes it clear that it was not by defeating the Canaanites, but by defending them, that Israel attained a dominant position in Palestine."[9]

The period of history treated in the book of Judges extends from the entrance of the Exodus tribes about 1200 to the founding of the

[9] T. H. Robinson, *A History of Israel,* Oxford University Press, 1932, Vol. 1, p. 140.

monarchy about 1020 B.C. The basic unit of social life continued to be the tribe, ruled by elders who had charge of judicial functions and made all the important tribal decisions (treaties, warfare, provision for famine). Beyond this, the amphictyonic structure possessed no delegated authority over the tribes. The Israelite government of this period has been likened to the brief experiment in American history when the sovereign states tried to coöperate under the unwieldy Articles of Confederation. It is easy to see why concerted action by the Israelites was almost always reserved for urgent external threats against the community. The anarchic tendencies inherent in such a loose structure are well expressed in the notation with which Judges ends: "In those days there was no king in Israel; every man did what was right in his own eyes" (21:25).

As inappropriate as Conquest is the English term "judge." Hebrew *shophet* means "one who brings vindication, who sets things right"; it as readily applies to a military deliverer as to a magistrate. With the exception of Deborah, the biblical judges are not credited with exercising judicial skill; that was the function of the elders. But the special significance of the judge was that his gifts were religiously endowed. He was the beneficiary of divine power that suddenly seized him and made him irresistible, even impervious in battle. The nearest analogies in our Western history are Joan of Arc and Oliver Cromwell, both of whom we would be inclined to call fanatics or at any rate extremists. Max Weber, the sociologist of religion, has dubbed leaders of this type "charismatic" (from the Greek word *charisma*, meaning "gift").[10] The charismatic does not reign by heredity or election; he is a "bearer of the spirit" whose right to the support of the community is self-authenticating. The niche of the charismatic in our bureaucratic society is filled by the political or religious demagogue who is able to enlist popular sentiment in his cause. It was no doubt among charismatic patriots that the first stirrings of Hebrew prophecy arose.

The primary feature of the book of Judges is the framework binding the originally separate narratives. It is stamped with the same philosophy of history that predominates from Deuteronomy through Kings. This so-called Deuteronomic philosophy of history is set forth fully in the tedious verbiage of Judges 2:11–23. There is a sober and far-reaching actuality to Israel's life under the covenant: apostasy from Yahweh

[10] H. H. Garth and C. W. Mills, eds., *From Max Weber: Essays in Sociology,* Oxford University Press, 1946, pp. 51–55, 245–252.

leads to historical reversal for Israel. Change of heart, return to Yahweh, leads to deliverance from oppression. The enemy in each case is the instrument of divine chastisement. The judge is the instrument of divine deliverance. History has no accidents or imponderables; it is perfectly transparent to Yahweh's will. An almost mathematically precise formula emerges: APOSTASY→OPPRESSION→REPENTANCE→ DELIVERANCE.

But the contents of the stories are for the most part blithely ignorant of this full-blown Deuteronomic theory. Many of them have no sense of apostasy and are not notably aware of the covenant demands of Yahweh. The utter social and religious separation of Israel from the Canaanites is not only absent in practice but is scarcely enjoined as an ideal. The impact of the stories with which the Deuteronomic theory is illustrated is thus inimical to the latter's highly theological stance. This discrepancy is of tremendous importance to the historian. We can see that the D editor, for whatever reason, has chosen to preserve the individual stories largely as he found them, instead of attempting a rewriting as in Joshua. Because of his deference, our knowledge of the period of the judges is fascinatingly first-hand. We may conclude with some confidence that the substance of the book of Judges antedates the D framework by several centuries. A number of the stories may have arisen orally at a time nearly contemporary with the events recorded, although chapters 17–21 have the appearance of an appendix later in origin than the rest of the book. The Song of Deborah is probably an eyewitness account.

Many critics believe that the stories were already assembled before the D writers compiled their history, but there is no decisive basis for demonstrating or refuting the hypothesis of a pre-D book of Judges. On their own terms, the stories are far from homogeneous. The exploits of Gideon are interrupted by the recital of the treacherous designs of Abimelech. For the D editors the pretensions of Abimelech to kingship are condemnable but in its original form the tale may have intended to memorialize the cunning of its hero. Samson, with only a thin veneer of Yahwism, emerges as a prankster not unlike Jacob, possessed by prodigious strength. The milieu of the tales is patently folkloristic.

Literary problems similar to those in the earlier biblical books appear in Judges. There are double traditions, as in the prose and poetic accounts of Deborah's and Barak's battle with the Canaanites (chaps.

4 and 5). The call of Gideon can be reduced to two sources with features similar to J and E; one source has the angel of Yahweh who appears to Gideon at the altar of Baal (J), and the other has a theophany
that instructs Gideon to destroy the altar and supplies the sign of the
fleece, which has the effect of a proof for the doubting Gideon as did
the rod for Moses (E). But attempts to carry through the Pentateuchal
analysis of J and E in Judges are very unsatisfactory. Scholars have

*A 5-ton Canaanite altar from Hazor, partly removed from its base, possi-
bly by Israelites.*

professed to see in the first chapter a surviving portion of the lost J
account of the occupation of Canaan. The narrative is less schematic
than Joshua, for it shows the tribes going up separately to possess their
domains, and indicates how fragmentary the victories actually were.
But its historicity is open to question, for it has details less trustworthy than their equivalents in Joshua (Joshua's Adonizedek as the
name of the king of Jerusalem is certainly preferable to Judges' Adoni-

bezek; and the claim of Judges 1:8 that Jerusalem was captured by Judah at this early date runs counter to all other biblical evidence, including that in Joshua). Whether composed of portions of J and E, the bulk of the narratives of the judges do come from early sources that have been pressed into service by the Deuteronomic historians.

Each of the episodes of the judges is prefaced by the Deuteronomic formula: "and the people of Israel did what was evil in the sight of Yahweh and Yahweh gave them into the hand of (the oppressing enemy) and the people cried unto Yahweh and Yahweh raised up a deliverer for the people of Israel who delivered them." Following the story of the judge, the statement is appended, ". . . and the land had rest (forty) years." Forty years in biblical tradition is a loose expression for "generation," "lifetime," or "a long time."

Twelve judges are named but some receive no more than a passing reference. Six are "major judges": Othniel (3:7–11), Ehud (3:15–30), Deborah (4–5), Gideon (6–9), Jephthah (10:6–12:7), and Samson (13–16). Of the "minor judges" the enemy is mentioned only in the case of Shamgar, whose prodigious single-handed victory against the Philistines reminds the reader of Samson. The framework takes for granted that the judges were rulers of all Israel but the stories themselves sometimes name only one or two tribes and, in the case of the Song of Deborah, it took a serious emergency for even a majority of the tribes to rally. The amphictyony was by no means a secure and unshakeable concept; its fortunes were dependent on the rise or fall of loyalty to the covenant God Yahweh. The present order of the episodes is arbitrary, and we have only a few hints for offering a reliable sequence. Shamgar and Samson seem to belong to a time early in the struggle with the Philistines, for the border raids are carried on sporadically, Israelite relations with the invaders are for the most part friendly, and the Danites are still living in the Shephelah between Ephraim and Judah. Later they moved to the headwaters of the Jordan River, as described in the legendary appendix of Judges (chaps. 17–18).

The battle commemorated in the Song of Deborah has been dated by some scholars at about 1125 B.C., because the nearby city of Megiddo was deserted at that time, and they argue that only under such circumstances would the Hebrews have ventured into the Plain of Esdraelon. There are several indications that Deborah lived in the twelfth century, e.g., the Shamgar who fought the Philistines with Samson-like tactics is mentioned (5:6) and the Danites are still living in their southern homeland (5:17). Then too the furious battle with the Canaanites does not seem as likely at a time in the eleventh century when the Philistines were exerting mounting pressure on the Palestinian hinterland. The fascinating account of the renegade Abimelech, on the other hand, looks like one of the latest episodes in Judges for we see plainly what great inroads Canaanite ways of thinking about kingship and religion were making upon the Israelite newcomers. But attempts to be more precise about the relative order, much less the chronology of the judges, are unavailing. When all the years given in the book are totaled the sum figure of 410 is greater than will harmonize with the Deuteronomists' note in I Kings 6:1 to the effect that 480 years elapsed from the Exodus to the building of Solomon's temple. Only 70 years are left for the wandering in the wilderness, Joshua, Eli, Samuel, David, and three years of Solomon's reign. But of the preceding for whom D gives dates, 123 years are indicated, thus exceeding the 480-year summary by a minimum of 43 years. Harmonizations have been sought by deleting some or all of the "minor judges" on the assumption that they did not belong to the original D edition. We are probably wisest in regarding the chronological schema of D as a relatively late feature which, even as it stands, gives little more than a show of accuracy owing to the complicated editing, the omission of data for some of the leaders, and the loose use of "forty years" for any considerable period of time.

SONG OF DEBORAH

The poetic recital of the victory of Deborah and Barak over the Canaanites in the Valley of Esdraelon appearing as chapter 5 of the book of Judges is of immense significance for the student of the Old Testament. For its size it is the most ancient writing preserved in the Hebrew Bible; its literary, historical, and religious import call for careful appraisal.

The poem is a lyric celebration of a public event, but it lacks the continuity and orderly description of most victory odes. Highly episodic, the action consists of a number of brilliant vignettes pictured in a sort of "impressionistic, atomistic" technique. The poem may be divided into fourteen subsections:

Invocation and Exordium	vss. 2–3
Yahweh's March	4–5
The Former Impotence of Israel	6–7
Praise of the Volunteers	8–9

The basic poetic type is a psalm of praise to Yahweh for his victory over the Canaanites, but several formal poetic types are woven together, e.g., hymn, blessing and cursing, mocking song. The poet fixes upon those facets of the event that dramatize Yahweh's power and the loyalty of his people. We see the victory through the eyes of a Yahweh enthusiast who does not take time to set the scene of the battle or to describe the opposing forces except in an incidental manner. More is said about the circumstances of Sisera's death than about the actual battle! The primitive force of Hebrew poetry invigorates the work, heating it to an almost incandescent fury. As in most Hebrew literature, the verbs bear a special weight; in the Song they forcefully underscore the action, decision, and violence.

Poetic devices of repetition and contrast are employed with telling but unconscious artistry. The basic feature of Hebrew poetry is known as parallelism of members (see chap. IX under Hebrew Prophecy), which may be described as the repetition of ideas in successive poetic verse members. The typical poetic line or unit of thought states the same thing in two ways, and the Song of Deborah teems with such parallelisms:

Yahweh, when thou didst go forth from Seir,
  when thou didst march from the region of Edom (5:4*a*).

She put her hand to the tent peg
  and her right hand to the workmen's mallet (5:26*a*).

Out of the window she peered,
  the mother of Sisera gazed through the lattice (5:28).

The examples given are clear-cut cases of direct parallelism, but the Hebrew poet was capable of seemingly endless variations in his development of the repeated idea: through contrast, the shortening or lengthening of lines, the increase of parallel verses to three, the inversion of parallel members, etc. In the hands of able poets the net effect of parallelism is aesthetically pleasing. It introduces pictorial fullness, a rhythm and tempo that can be sharply hastened or retarded, giving an effect startlingly close to the dissonance and syncopation of modern music. The types of par-allelism in the Song of Deborah are similar to those in the Ugaritic poetry of *Baal and Anath* and find their closest biblical parallels in poems such as Deuteronomy 33, Habakkuk 3, and Psalm 68.

Close scrutiny of the structure of the Song will show how it depends for its order on the principle of contrast. One scene tends to call forth its opposite. The strength of Yahweh (4–5) suggests the weakness of Israel (6–7). The ready response of the loyal tribes (13–15*a*) is in glowing contrast to the hesitancy and refusal of the faithless tribes (15*b*). The curse of Meroz (23)

A noble woman or goddess looks through a recessed window (Judges 5:28; II Kings 9:30).

balances the blessing of Jael (24), and the known fate of Sisera (25–27) clashes ironically with the naïve expectation of his mother (28–30).

The antiquity of the poem is argued by the archaic grammar and style, elements of which are unfamiliar to Hebraists; the poor state of the text, indicating that the poem was copied and recopied long after some words and idioms had dropped out of usage; the vividness of the account, still vibrating with the thrill of the participants; and the absence of anachronisms that would betray the viewpoint of a later age. Because of its antiquity, some lines are barely translatable or are capable of several reasonably intelligible meanings. The parallel prose account of chapter 4 has some extensive departures from the Song, but in no respect does its variation appear preferable. In the prose Sisera is a general of Jabin, king of Canaan, rather than the ruler at the head of his own armies (a probable confusion with Joshua 11); only Zebulun and Naphtali are involved rather than six tribes; and Sisera is killed as he sleeps within the tent rather than as he drinks at its entryway. An ambiguity exists as to whether the Song is *by* Deborah or addressed *to* Deborah. The introduction to the poem and the Hebrew of vs. 7, "until *I* Deborah arose," argue for the former; but the versions read "until *you* Deborah arose," and verses 12 and 15 refer to the prophetess in the third person. Originally written about Deborah, tradition tended to transfer the Song to her as one more instance of her charismatic powers.

Among the major historical values of the composition is the light it casts on the methods of the conquest. The arduous struggle was far from completed at the death of Joshua. The Canaanites held the plains, their walled cities and chariotry making them virtual masters of the trade routes. Communication among the Israelite tribal centers was in jeopardy, and only a courageous and dynamic leader could dispel the faintheartedness of Israel and call forth her latent loyalty to Yahweh. The Hebrews had to make up in ferocity and dedication what they lacked in weapons and manpower. The distribution and names of the tribes are particularly illuminating, since we possess in the Song by far the oldest enumeration of the members of the amphictyony. The list is similar to that given in the later sources of the Pentateuch, but there are enough differences to show that the Song has not been given a harmonistic revision.

The members of the league who do battle against Sisera are Ephraim, Benjamin, Machir, Zebulun, Issachar, Naphtali. Condemned for failing to take part are Reuben, Gilead, Dan, and Asher; the implication is obvious that they stood under an obligation which they scorned. Machir is probably another name for Manasseh and Gilead a variation of Gad. Of the four inactive tribes, Dan, Gilead, and Reuben were remote enough from the Plain of Esdraelon to feel that their welfare was not directly affected. Asher's reluctance is harder to account for, since its position contiguous to the valley would make it a tribe with one of the greatest stakes in the outcome. Perhaps Asher's exposed position, close to the northern coastal cities, was leading to advanced Canaanization so that there was little disposition to heed the imperatives of the tribal league.

Only three of the tribes known from other sources are not mentioned: Judah, Simeon, and Levi. Judah's absence is best explained by the virtual separation of the northern and southern Hebrews until the time of David. The Song of Deborah does not hold Judah blame-worthy because Judah was not a member of the Shechemite am-phictyony but rather of a southern league of Hebrews at Hebron. Sim-eon is lacking probably for the same reason. Many scholars also regard Levi as a southern tribe. Such an identification would indeed suit the evidence of the Song, but that would make Moses a southerner, since he was clearly of the tribe of Levi. Less biblical data seem to call for juggling by regarding Moses as a northerner. Then why is Levi omitted in the Song of Deborah? As one of the northern tribes should it not have been summoned to battle? Perhaps its transformation into a priestly tribe was already far advanced and its males thus exempted from military service. But how are the association of Simeon and Levi in Genesis 34 to be explained? After the ill-fated attack on Shechem, they probably parted company, the Simeonites retiring to the Negeb where they joined with the "Abraham" Hebrews and Midianites, while the Levites went into Egypt.

The religious spirit of the Song of Deborah is simple and ardent. Its single insistent theme is praise of Yahweh, the deliverer. The God of the desert and the Exodus strides into Canaan at the head of his vic-torious army, dispersing the enemy before the storm that showers destruction. Although Moses is not named, the poem is an indirect validation of the Mosaic origins of Yahwism. The theophany of Yah-weh (vss. 3–5) shows that the desert southland is the proper home of Israel's God ("Sinai" in vs. 5 is generally regarded as a gloss); the region of Edom and Seir (Kadesh) is the place of Yahweh's origin. The Pentateuchal accounts of Moses as the organizer of an intertribal covenant are necessary to explain the religious cohesion of the invad-ing Hebrews, who continued to look outside of Canaan for their stand-ards and impetus.

Nearest analogies to the Song of Deborah are the triumphal odes of the Assyrian Tikulti-Ninurta I and the Egyptian Ramses II (both thir-teenth century B.C.), but as literature they are wooden and, in their praise of the gods, perfunctory and formalistic alongside of the diony-sian power of the Hebrew ode. Yahweh's doings are accomplished with the instrumentality of the leaders and peasantry (vss. 2,9,11) who come to the help of Yahweh (vs. 23). The translation "locks were worn loose in Israel" is preferred by many scholars to "the people of-fered themselves willingly" (vs. 1); this would refer to the vows of the soldiery not to cut their hair until victory, also calculated to strike terror among the smooth-shaven Canaanites. The concept of "holy war" is parallel to the Song of Moses in Exodus 15:3 where Yahweh is called "a man of war" (see also address to the ark in Num. 10:35). One of the earliest anthologies of Hebrew poetry is cited in the Old Testament as the Book of the Wars of Yahweh, and it is likely that the Song of Deborah was extracted from that collection by the editor of Judges.

Complementary to the notion of fidelity to the tribal God Yahweh is the élan of pan-Israel. This was not primarily a political concept, although it finds minimal political expression in the tribal amphictyony. The summons to come "to the help of Yahweh" ought to have enlisted all the tribes. The Song knows nothing of apostasy and repentance in the strict Deuteronomic sense, but its abhorrence at breach of covenant through failure to defend Yahweh's cause in war is strongly stated. Furthermore, an overdrawing of the contrast between the sense of sin in the D framework and the Song proper is perilous. The theology of any religious group is not likely to appear in toto in a victory hymn. Subsequent interpreters of twentieth-century American religion would get a rather jaundiced view if chance should leave them only a few songs such as "Praise the Lord and Pass the Ammunition!" or "God Bless America."

A point usually taken for granted in the battle is that the Kishon River, temporarily swollen to overflowing by a cloudburst, bogged down and swept away the Canaanite chariots. Interpreters have written imaginative reconstructions of the battle between the vastly superior troops of Sisera and the guerrilla fighters of Israel aided by the torrent Kishon.[11] But all the theorizing as to what took place rests on a brief stanza in the Song:

> The kings came, they fought;
>> then fought the kings of Canaan,
> at Taanach, by the waters of Megiddo;
>> they got no spoils of silver.
> From heaven fought the stars,
>> from their courses they fought against Sisera.
> The torrent Kishon swept them away,
>> the onrushing torrent, the torrent Kishon (vss. 19–22).

[11] G. A. Smith, *The Historical Geography of the Holy Land,* Hodder and Stoughton, 1894, pp. 391–397, and John Garstang, *The Foundations of Bible History; Joshua, Judges,* R. R. Smith, 1931, pp. 289–306.

This strophe is commonly coupled with the opening theophany, replete with the storm phenomena of the Sinai-Kadesh stories, "the heavens dropped, yea, the clouds dropped water." It is concluded that exactly as the Hebrews of the Exodus saw Yahweh in the cloudy pillar and the engulfing waters of the Reed Sea, so the Hebrews of the Conquest perceived Yahweh in the storm over Esdraelon and the onrushing waters of Kishon.

Even if this view of events remains provisionally the best, some cautions must be urged. The theophany at the opening of the Song also implies earthquake or volcanic activity ("the earth trembled," "the mountains quaked") and if the phrase "the clouds dropped waters" is taken literally, by what logic does one interpret the other expressions as merely figurative? The prose version of the battle says nothing about downpour or flood. Similar terms from ancient Near Eastern battle hymns raise the probability that idioms of this sort should not be pressed unduly. A victory of Ramses III is celebrated, for example, with the exclamation, "The stars of the *seshed*-constellation were frightful in pursuit of them" and Ashur-uballit's defeat of the Kassites is attributed to the storm god Adad (another name for Baal) who "drove down a flood against their fighting line."[12] The context in neither instance points to storm or flood. We must not overstate the uniqueness of the Song of Deborah, which is sufficient when all allowances are made, nor draw hasty inferences from rather doubtful bases. Yahweh as the God of Israel and Israel as the people of Yahweh—that is the Song's fundamental motif, bearing out the Mosaic origins of Yahwism. It is shaky exegesis, however, to rest a whole view of Israel's historically oriented religion upon a few verses in an impressionistic piece of poetry. It would be very difficult to guess the ethical dynamic of the religion of Moses and the prophets from the Song of Deborah.

RELIGION DURING THE SETTLEMENT

The value of the happenings related in the book of Judges is simply inestimable for the portrayal of Israelite life and customs in the twelfth and eleventh centuries B.C. Methods of agriculture and trade, marriage mores, family relations, petty strife among cities and chieftains, guerrilla warfare, and the exaltation of physical strength and prowess

---

[12] Quoted in Jacob M. Myers, *Exegesis of Judges* (IB, vol. 2), Abingdon, 1953, p. 726.

in war pass before our eyes in fascinating array. The religion and morality described are of a dismally low order: Ehud's deceptive murder
of Eglon, Jael's violation of the law of hospitality in killing Sisera,
the Baal altar built by Gideon's father, the torturing of the seventy-
seven elders of Succoth, the idol cast by Gideon, the fealty of Israelites
to Baal-berith (Baal of the Covenant, the Shechemite deity), Abimelech's murder of Gideon's other sons, the burning of the tower of
Shechem, Jephthah's harlot parentage and his vow of child sacrifice,
civil war between Gilead and Ephraim, Samson's "affair" with the
Philistine harlot, the treachery of Delilah, the Danite theft of Micah's
idol, and the rape of the Levite's concubine. There are few more
sordid and unabashed tales in literature.

Here was plainly an age of barbarism and crude disregard of life,
for which many parallels could be found in Western civilization: the
Thirty Years' War in Germany and the Roaring Twenties in the United
States, to mention only two. As our estimate of those eras tends to be
based largely on the most extreme and shocking incidents, so the D
writers have culled out the more appalling aspects of the period of the
judges to enforce their lessons. It is evident that the vitality of the religion of Moses had flagged dangerously, that in many respects the Hebrews were becoming identical with the Canaanites, not merely in
farming and social customs, but in ethical standards and fertility worship.

While the book of Judges has the avowed purpose of relentlessly
reciting such grisly scenes, the age is not without its idyllic representations of happy family life and deep piety. For, though its present form
is postexilic, the book of Ruth manifestly refers to the same period.
It tells of the loyalty and charm of the heroine and of the large-heartedness of Boaz, even though its sexual mores are not ours and Ruth's
night on the threshing floor has had to be explained delicately to generations of church school children! The early chapters of I Samuel,
which relate the closing phases of the period of the judges, tell of the
saintly priest Eli and the devotion of Hannah to Yahweh, her solicitude
and careful upbringing of the boy Samuel.

Even in their unvarnished frankness, the narratives of Judges tell of
Yahweh enthusiasts, charismatics who kept alive the consciousness of
a separate people under a unique God. Imperfect as their insight was
in comparison with Moses or the prophets, they yet clung to the simple
amphictyonic convictions. Gideon, when asked to rule as king, said

curtly, "I will not rule over you, and my son will not rule over you; Yahweh will rule over you" (8:23). The summary comment of a narrator of the Abimelech story (probably not D) speaks of a war in which neither side fulfills God's will; the wrongs of both Abimelech and the Canaanites are noted (9:56–57). The gripping story of Gideon's triumph over the Midianites (note that not all of them were Yahweh-worshipers, but possibly only the Kenite clan) by a hand-picked corps of three hundred is introduced with the trenchant observation, "The people with you are too many for me to give the Midianites into their hand, lest Israel vaunt themselves against me, saying 'My own hand has delivered me.'" (7:2). The thin line of Yahwism may have been ragged but it did not fail even in the sorriest days. The two hundred years from Moses to Samuel were times of severe testing, as the nascent faith of the Hebrews sought adjustment to a whole new order of life. The wonder is not how barbaric were the times; the marvel is rather that the nomadic religion of Moses could survive the charms and corruptions of Canaan. The prophets were later to deepen and purify the tradition which all the temptations of a more advanced civilization had not overwhelmed but only fructified.

+ 7 +

THE GREAT KINGDOM

. . . a king to govern us like all the nations . . .
I Sam. 8:5

The four-hundred year Israelite monarchy is an epoch to be seen from many perspectives. It is the account of Israel's final "Conquest" of Canaan, her political mastery of Canaanite and Philistine, and of the reflex assimilation of Israel by the culture of the conquered. It is the tale of bitter struggle between Baalism and Yahwism for the allegiance of the Hebrew people. It is the story of international crisis and of the failure of Israel's political experiment, the split into two kingdoms, and their eventual extinction—ground to pieces between the world powers. It is the recital of conflict between prophet and king, of contest between autonomous political rule and theocracy, between the right of self-determination and the obligation of covenant faith. It is the drama of men caught between the instinct to self-preservation and the imperious call of the word of God for self-sacrifice. To read attentively the books of Samuel and Kings and the corresponding prophetic writings is to sense how realistically they pose the challenge of living by the promise and the covenant in the midst of a hostile world, a world whose insecurities and apostasies penetrate to the heart of Israel and to the very soul of the prophet. The monarchy was the era of Israel's coming of age in that dimension which was her greatest gift to humanity: her understanding of man vis-à-vis God.

THE PHILISTINES

Kingship was a relatively late institution in Israel, in contrast to the higher civilizations of the Near East. From their emergence on the scene of history, the Egyptians and Sumerians possessed dynastic government. The Hebrews resorted to royal rule only after the pressure of historic events compelled them and with grave misgivings. The continuous rivalry of Canaanites and Hebrews was broken by the abrupt entrance of the Philistines into Canaan. A part of the larger migration of sea peoples, the Philistines had moved from the Aegean islands because of the pressure of other Aryans who displaced them. After a savage sea battle in the Nile delta, the sea peoples were repelled by Ramses III, and a group of them settled along the Canaanite coast south of Mt. Carmel. Shortly after their arrival (1190–1175 B.C.) the Philistines were Semitized to the extent that they adopted Canaanite names and worshiped Canaanite deities such as Dagon, Atargatis, and Baal-zebub. There were five principal cities, each ruled by a Seren (Gr. *tyrannos,* "tyrant") and bound in a league. Contemporary sources speak of "the five lords of the Philistines," who formed a formidable military alliance. The Greek form of their name became the Roman term for Canaan: Palaestina, and in English: Palestine.

From the start the Philistines were a major threat to all Canaan, for they occupied some of the most fertile land along the Mediterranean littoral and controlled the coastal trade route. Being men of large stature and well armed with iron weapons, they were fierce combatants. The initial phase of their engagement with Israel was hit and run border fighting as described in the Samson stories. Increasing pressure on the Shephelah led to the expulsion of the Danites, who relocated north of Galilee. The central highlands of Ephraim and Benjamin were seriously threatened. A turning point was reached at the Battle of Ebenezer; Israel was routed, the ark captured, and its resting place at Shiloh destroyed (I Sam. 4). Symbolic of Philistine supremacy was the garrison stationed in the heart of Benjamin at Gibeath-elohim. It became the first object of attack when Saul began in earnest to expel the invaders (I Sam. 10:5; 13:3–4). In an effort to counter the alarming successes of the Philistines Saul was called as the first king of Israel.

THE BOOKS OF SAMUEL

The books of Samuel recount the stories of three men whose lives and destinies were intimately joined. Unlike the isolated narratives of Judges, the fabric of Samuel is more closely knit. The books may in fact be divided according to the respective predominance and interplay of the principals: Samuel (I Sam. 1–7), Samuel and Saul (I Sam.

8–15), Saul and David (I Sam. 16–31), and David (II Samuel). The books trace the transition from charismatic to dynastic leadership, Samuel standing for the one and David for the other. In between is the ill-fitting figure of Saul, both judge and king and yet not effectively either, tormented and expendable.

First impressions of a tightly composed narrative must be revised when the text is examined closely. The trait of duplicate narratives— seemingly omnipresent in Israelite historical writing—is conspicuous in I Samuel. A striking example occurs in the account of the founding of the monarchy. One source shows Samuel as a local Benjaminite seer who takes the initiative in anointing Saul as king at the instigation of Yahweh. Saul is acclaimed king at Gilgal after delivering Jabesh Gilead from Ammonite attack. This is *the early promonarchic source* (9:1–10:16; 11:1–11, 15; vss. 12–14 redactional?). A second source depicts Samuel as judge of all Israel who travelled a circuit (although its extent was limited to the Benjaminite cities of Bethel, Gilgal, and Mizpah, 7:16). The elders of Israel brought the request for a monarch, to which Samuel objected vehemently, acceding only after the reluctant permission of God. Saul is selected by lot and acclaimed king at Mizpah. This is *the late antimonarchic source* (8; 10:17–25; 12).

While there are several variations in these accounts, the outstanding difference is that the early source is favorable to the monarchy and the late source is antagonistic. The one probably reflects the initial enthusiasm following the destruction of the Philistine threat and the expansion of the Davidic Empire. The other source stems from the oppressive policies of later kings, especially Solomon, and expresses the independent spirit of Israel. While the present form of the sources depends upon this later experience, it is very likely that Samuel himself was ambivalent toward the advisability of kingship. Israel remained double-minded in its estimate of the monarchy, even though friend and foe of the office were alike committed to it by historical necessity.

Other signs of doublets are abundant. Two settings for the origin of the proverb "Is Saul also among the prophets?" are provided at widely separated points in Saul's life (I Sam. 10:10–12; 19:18–24). David's entry into Saul's court is first accounted for by his appointment as armorbearer and musician to quiet the fevered mind of the king with his lyre (I Sam. 16:14–23). But immediately afterward David, unfamiliar to Saul, comes from Bethlehem to the battlesite at the valley of Elah and joins issue with the Philistine giant (I Sam. 17:12–58).

There can be little doubt that the two versions were originally separate. It is interesting also that II Samuel 21:19 attributes the slaying of Goliath to Elhanan son of Jaareoregim the Bethlehemite. This discrepancy was noted by the Chronicler who explained that Elhanan actually killed Goliath's brother, Lahmi (I Chron. 20:5). An ingenious theory is that David was the regnal name of the Bethlehemite Elhanan, a fact lost sight of everywhere else in tradition except the note in II Samuel 21:19 (at Mari *dawidum* is a title, perhaps meaning "leader" and similar to Pharaoh, Sultan, or Czar). It is more likely, however, that one of the exploits of David's heroes has been transferred to the king. The giant who opposed David may have been anonymous in the first recital, the name Goliath creeping into the text in I Samuel 17:4; 21:9; 22:10 from the comment about Elhanan. Other instances of variant traditions are the two reports of the flight of David from Saul, of David's sparing the life of Saul, of Saul's death at Gilboa, and the lists of David's officials.

Some critics trace the JE sources of the Pentateuch through the historical books and into Kings. Others are very skeptical about the presence of "constants" that would give controlled evidence of the continuation of sources. More likely the stories of Samuel took shape among narrators who lived in the same era and were under the influence of the Pentateuchal historians. The indefiniteness of the J and E strata, whether the work of individual authors or editors or schools of traditionists, does not permit sharp comparison with other bodies of material. If "JE" simply refers to the narrative styles of the tenth to the eighth centuries, as expressed in the Pentateuchal sources, then we may label the sources of Samuel JE. But that is not to say anything very precise or informative. If the symbols "JE" have greater exactitude, referring to particular authors with peculiar style and viewpoint, then the JE character of the sources after Deuteronomy is extremely dubious. But many scholars agree that an early, more trustworthy source and a later, more legendary one are present in Samuel.[1] Others

---

[1] L. Rost, *Ueberlieferung von der Thronnachfolge Davids,* Kohlhammer, 1926, distinguishes: (1) the Story of the Succession in II Samuel 13–20; I Kings 1–2, with an introduction in the ark stories of I Samuel 4–6 and the account of the establishment of David's dynasty in Jerusalem, II Samuel 6–7; 9–12; (2) the Story of David's Triumph over Saul, mainly in I Samuel 23–30 and II Samuel 1–5, possibly also II Samuel 8. These were not woven together as literary critics assume but placed one after the other as blocks, the D editor being responsible for the present order.

Aage Bentzen, *Introduction to the Old Testament,* Gad, 2d ed., 1952, vol. 2, pp. 93–96, finds the essence of the books of Samuel to be a cultic aetiology of the

contend for the necessity of a three-source analysis, with two strands in the early source.[2]

All critics recognize in II Samuel 9–20 and I Kings 1–2 an especially valuable source for the reign of David. Its significance as a prose eye-witness account ranks it with the Song of Deborah as a first-rate historical document. This so-called Court History of David or Succession Story has been lauded as the first genuine historiography in antiquity. Herodotus, the Greek historian and supposed "father of history," wrote some five hundred years later. The author, unswayed by royal fear or favor, has certainly shown a surprising degree of detachment in his assessment of the reign of David. The author of the Court History was likely one of the priestly participants in the events of David's time, Abiathar or Ahimaaz.

SAUL

Saul was the last of the judges as well as the first of the kings. Kingship to him and to his subjects was an emergency measure, chieftainship writ large. The king was *primus inter pares*. Saul was a charismatic military figure whose continuity of leadership matched the continuity of the Philistine onslaught. The core of his army was drawn from Benjamin, but he gathered to him the forces of all the tribes and was recognized as the undisputed leader. The organization ordinarily associated with a kingdom was lacking. Saul retained his headquarters at his provincial home of Gibeah, where he erected a fortress but no palace. We hear nothing of court officials of the sort who became frequent under David. There is no evidence of taxation or labor corvée. All supertribal authority was directed toward a single purpose: the expulsion of the Philistines. Public works projects and the pomp of court life that drain the economy of Oriental monarchies were absent during Saul's reign. He was a rustic with simple tastes, devoid of ostentation. Saul began as the popular choice of the people; the tragedy that lengthened over his life was mainly due to forces beyond his control.

Saul produced immediate results. He and his equally valiant and adept son Jonathan, by a series of spectacular exploits, drove the

---

Davidic Dynasty. The Succession Story of II Samuel 9–20; I Kings 1–2 is prefaced with two strands, each containing early and late elements. These two "strands" are roughly identical with the usual literary-critical early and late sources, but Bentzen doubts that they are J and E.

[2] Adolphe Lods, *Israel from its Beginnings to the Middle of the Eighth Century*, Routledge & Paul, 1932, pp. 352–356.

Philistines out of the highlands. They did so with a fierce brand of militant Yahwism, for Saul was a wholehearted Yahwist. His religious practice was in accord with accepted tradition. As king he played an active role in promoting Yahwism and officiating in the cult. He declared a food taboo during a battle, punishable by death, and was prepared to carry it out even when his own son unknowingly violated it (cf. Jephthah's sacrifice of his daughter in fulfillment of a hasty vow,

Ruins of Saul's headquarters at Gibeah in Benjamin.

Judg. 11:29–40). Sorcerers and mediums were banished from Israel in a purge of the always-appealing cult of the dead with its promise of communication with the spirit world. The will of Yahweh was sought through the priestly oracle, which required a casting of lots to determine a simple yes or no answer. A new moon meal was observed with ritual cleansings.

This record of devoted if simple-minded Yahwism has been defaced by the theologizing of the late source of Samuel. Saul is severely rebuked by Samuel for presiding at the sacrifice of burnt offerings before a battle. Saul's commendable desire to sacrifice before entering

the fray and his willingness to wait for Samuel until his army was beginning to desert him—these extenuating circumstances are brushed
aside by the narrator. That priestly-lay divisions of duty were not
rigidly kept in the early monarchy is apparent from the way that David
led the procession of the ark and offered burnt offerings (II Sam. 6).

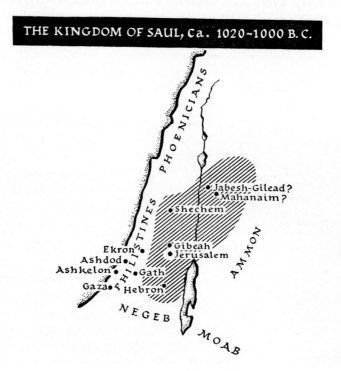

THE KINGDOM OF SAUL, Ca. 1020–1000 B. C.

The very action scathingly denounced by Samuel (and Yahweh) in
the case of Saul is praised in the case of David!

The final break between Samuel and Saul is depicted in the classic
story of I Samuel 15, one that has had great significance as a support
for the temporal authority of the Church and its right to dethrone
kings. Saul, whose religious duty it was to commit all captives and
booty to the ban ("devote to destruction"), saved the life of the Amalekite king Agag and some of his beasts. The rage of Samuel and his
anathema upon Saul are unmitigated by any show of understanding or
mercy. Saul's confession and contrition are ignored. The king is
doomed, for Yahweh has rejected him. Again the manifest unfairness
of the judgment is apparent when only a little later we read of David's

raids in the Negeb and of the spoil that he took from the same Amalekites (I Sam. 27:8–9; 30). The Yahwistic ban that Saul was required
to adhere to faultlessly was ignored by the outlaw David and later also
by David the king. The late source thus pictures Samuel as a pompous
ecclesiastic and Saul as a stubborn blunderer. Neither of these is a true
estimate of the men; the breach between them was real enough—the
late source has not invented it—but the reasons offered are unconvincing.

The fundamental cause of the rift between Samuel and Saul seems
to have lain in the failure of the judge's confidence in the king's leadership. Just what form the disillusion and uncertainty took is not easily
discoverable. But the root of the problem was Saul's disordered mind.
Men of antiquity, unprepared to understand mental illness, turned
Saul's darkness of mind into stubborn disobedience. Samuel may have
read the jealousy and vacillation of Saul as a sign that he was bereft of
Yahweh's favor, but the pro-David bias of the Judean editors of the
historical books was disposed to emphasize everything critical of Saul.
They played upon the downfall of Saul, his rejection by Samuel, and
his impotence before David for maximum effect, in order to vindicate
David's right to be king. All in all, Saul has fared unjustly at the
hands of later generations.

It is fruitless to try to diagnose the precise psychological disorder of
Saul, although it may have been some form of schizophrenia (his
spells alternate with periods of clarity and composure). His intensely
ecstatic nature is shown in his associations with the wandering prophets. Their spirit of wild prophesying seized Saul and he lay naked for a
day and night after one such orgy (I Sam. 19:24). We ought not exag-
gerate this factor as proof of mental imbalance, for the ecstatic prophets were socially approved in their age. Excitability of nature, which in
our culture might find release in the arts or sports, in early Israel
found an outlet in ecstatic prophecy.

But behind the theologizing summaries of the text, the reader sees in
the irrational moodiness of Saul a demonic darkness that was *not* approved by his social peers. This is described as "an evil spirit from
Yahweh" whose descent upon Saul was coincident with the rise of
David as a captivating young courtier and skillful warrior. David's
popularity and ability became a fixation with the king. The dramatic
irony of the fall of Saul and the rise of David is underscored at every
turn. David first comes to Saul in order to exorcise the evil spirit with

music, but his own success at court reawakens and feeds the evil spirit. With every move David is attended by good fortune, while Saul is driven into deeper frustration. When this dimension of tragic necessity is laid bare the story takes on the quality of unrelenting doom typical of Greek tragedy. The events move with grim inevitability; all Saul's efforts at escape are futile gestures. The absence of a sense of moral responsibility is only feebly supplied by the doctoring of the late source.

Only one explanation of the unhebraic atmosphere of doom that hovers around Saul is adequate and that is mental illness, for which the deeply religious narrator could find no accounting other than Saul's reprobation by Yahweh for heinous disregard of divine commands. But Saul's life was too upright to find a really convincing basis for reprobation. The best reason would have been Saul's senseless slaughter of the priests of Nob but even the late historian recognized that this occurred too long after the beginning of Saul's decline; it was a sign of advanced disintegration rather than an underlying cause. In his madness, the king sought David's life by any means. After several close scrapes David fled into Philistine jurisdiction where he gathered a band of social and political malcontents and cleverly joined the service of Achish of Gath, living off the countryside while feigning attacks on Hebrew communities.

Confusion has been doubly confounded by the anti-Benjaminite bias of the stories. The D editors of Deuteronomy through Kings were Judeans who compiled their account after the northern kingdom had collapsed. Benjamin and Saul were of the north and thus not of the same political stock as David the southerner. The undoubted increase of David's fortunes has been legitimated by showing Saul as a tyrannical foil who deserved to be relieved of his rule. David in exile was the Robin Hood of the Hebrews, dashingly at home in the no man's land between Philistia and Judah, making men everywhere beholden to him. In his rocky strongholds he was virtually untouchable by the frantic Saul, for he had won the confidence of the local populace who gave warning whenever Saul was in the vicinity. In contrast to Saul's dark obsession is David's large-heartedness in twice refusing to take his life. The motive of David is presented as respect for Yahweh's anointed; but David gained much by his largesse as he publicly belittled and degraded Saul, protesting his own innocence and insisting "it's all in your mind" (I Sam. 24:9–15; 26:18–20).

The guilelessness of David has been so winningly presented that

Bible readers are as quickly persuaded by it as his contemporaries. But it stands to reason that a man of David's ambitions and abilities was not unaware of the means by which he could become king; we are not advised as to how much the conniving of David, his using of Michal and Jonathan, actually precipitated the downfall of Saul. It is naturally a moot question how much David pressed his advantages and how much he simply let circumstances play into his hands. His adeptness at assuming innocence but designing guile is displayed in his treatment of Nabal, the wealthy herdsman of the Negeb, who was tactlessly independent and uncoöperative when David insisted on "protection money" (I Sam. 25). His beautiful wife Abigail placated David with gifts and, following a midnight party which doubtless ended in a violent argument, Nabal dropped dead. David wasted no time in wooing and winning Abigail as his own. David must be judged by then current standards and he does not come off badly when compared with other Near Eastern monarchs. Perhaps if he had not been so ridiculously idealized and built up as a paragon of virtue, historians would not be so impishly tempted to show up his cunning and knavery. When they pick flaws it is in full cognizance of David's tremendous gifts and contributions to Israel.

Seemingly at a point where his playing of Philistines against Israelites was about to reap a harvest of disaster, David was miraculously rescued from a hard decision. When his master Achish of Gath mustered his troops to join in an all-out thrust against Saul, David must have had some harrowing moments. He could not afford to appear less than enthusiastic about fighting Israel; yet his revulsion at the prospect would naturally be great, not to mention the undoing of all the careful cultivation of Israelite loyalty to his cause. As it turned out, Achish relieved David of the necessity of choice by excusing him from the engagement because of the suspicions of the other Philistine lords that David under the circumstances would be a "security risk."

In his last hours Saul is a pitiable but regal figure. In final desperation he consults a medium at Endor, one of the class whom he had driven from Israel. If divine resources cannot be granted him on Yahwistic grounds, he will turn to the realm of necromancy. The shade of Samuel, conjured by the medium and recognizable to Saul, rises to pronounce a final curse upon the doomed hero. Saul's pathetic cry is his epitaph: "I am in great distress; for the Philistines are warring against me, and God has turned away from me and answers me no more, either by prophets or by dreams; therefore I have summoned you to tell me what I shall do" (28:15). Samuel's reply maintains the expected moralizing of the late source: "Why then do you ask me, since Yahweh has turned from you and become your enemy?"; the most that he can promise Saul is that he and his sons will join him in Sheol on the morrow.

The tale is a moving one, for the spiritualistic powers of the woman are taken seriously and Saul in disguise has to swear immunity for the medium against his own royal ban on necromancy. Such is the decline of the king that the last rites of Saul are attended by a necromancer and a handful of servants. The battle on the slopes of Mt. Gilboa is an anticlimax. Saul bears himself with pride and dignity to the end. Refusing to die at the hand of the enemy, he falls on his own sword. Jonathan and two other of his sons were struck down in the battle that eclipsed the great gains of Saul against the Philistines.

The shock of Israel at the loss of her great leader is expressed in the Lament which tradition ascribes to David, an ascription no critics are prepared to quarrel with. Lacking any explicit religious reference—perhaps because death was not yet Yahweh's realm—it nevertheless is infused by a deep love and respect for the fallen heroes:

> Thy glory, O Israel, is slain upon thy high places!
>   How are the mighty fallen!
>
> . . . .
> Saul and Jonathan, beloved and lovely!
>   In life and in death they were not divided;
> they were swifter than eagles,
>   they were stronger than lions.
>
> . . . .
> How are the mighty fallen,
>   and the weapons of war perished! (II Sam. 1:19,23,27).

Saul was a worthy founder of the Hebrew monarchy, a man to whom the words of Hamlet about his father are well suited: ". . . he was a man; take him for all in all, I shall not look upon his like again" (Act I, scene 2). He towered head and shoulders above other men, not only physically but in sheer leadership abilities. As a ruler he seems to have been as loved and trusted as David, even more so. The men of Jabesh-gilead risked their lives to remove Saul's exposed body from the ramparts of Beth-shan that it might be given burial. The northern tribes remained loyal to his dynasty for years after David had won over Judah. The grief of David in the Lament was more than mere duplicity.

It must have lain heavily on the conscience of David that the one who stood in his way to the kingship was the man he most revered. He could find many valid excuses for his desertion to the Philistines but he could not easily forget that the presence of his seasoned fighting men on Saul's side at Gilboa might have turned the tide of battle in Israel's favor. Saul was essentially guileless; in his deepest emotional and mental distress there was a grand integrity about him. In our time we have learned to praise the great qualities of men who were sullied by dark despair and mental agony, the Robert Schumanns and the Vincent van Goghs. Biblical tradition, the synagogue, and the church have been far too niggardly in giving credit to one of the noblest of their progenitors, great in his inception to the kingship and regal in his downfall, victim not alone or even primarily of Philistine arms but prey to a demented mind and an ambitious subordinate.

DAVID

The pathway had been well prepared for David to step into the vacancy created by the deaths of Saul and Jonathan. Thereafter the tide of events worked to David's benefit, for he proved to be a master of the waiting game. After slaying the Amalekite who claimed to have taken Saul's life and publicly mourning the leader's death, David returned from exile and established his headquarters at the southern tribal center of Hebron where he was proclaimed king over Judah. He thereupon set about to strengthen every possible tie with the northern tribes, preparatory to the day when they too would acknowledge him as king. He sent congratulations to Jabesh-gilead for the heroic rescue of Saul's body, tactfully bidding for support.

Particularly shrewd were his maneuvers toward the house of Saul. Ishbaal, sole surviving son of Saul, ruled the northern tribes from the Trans-Jordan city of Mahanaim, safe from the marauding Philistines who now controlled virtually the whole of the western highlands north of Judah. But dissension arose between Ishbaal and Saul's general, Abner. In a jealous rage and hoping to gain a high place in the new regime, Abner sent to David saying, "To whom does the land belong? Make your covenant with me, and behold, my hand shall be with you to bring over all Israel to you" (II Sam. 3:12). Abner rallied the pro-David sentiment among the northern elders who regarded David as a charismatic worthy of succession to Saul.

Two last-minute developments cleared the way for David to become king of united Israel, with no serious contenders and no costly political indebtedness. Joab, David's general and "hatchet man," coldly killed Abner, presumably in blood revenge for the murder of his brother Asahel. Two of Ishbaal's captains, hoping to win David's favor, assassinated the northern king and took his head to Hebron; their only reward was execution as murderers. The removal of Abner and Ishbaal without stain on David's honor (note the effect of the king's public lament over Abner which "pleased the people," II Sam. 3:36–37) and the righteous retribution of David upon the murderers of Ishbaal meant that those most likely to have been obstacles to the free exercise of David's power were eliminated with no aspersions on the king. David had waited seven and a half years for this propitious moment—and it proved more propitious than his wildest hopes.

The ten northern tribes came to Hebron to make a covenant with David and the house of Judah. The royal office was still regarded as large-scale chieftainship, for the covenant was arranged by the elders who thus placed definite ideological limits upon the king. We have no evidence of any written terms but the Yahwistic ethos of the Israelite brotherhood was clearly antiabsolutist and the agreement was in effect a sharply limited monarchy. Later, when David's role was thought to be too arbitrary, his show of favor to Judah too flagrant, the northerners were to remind Judah, "We have ten shares in the king, and in David also we have more than you" (II Sam. 19:43). Even the second king of Israel was still a charismatic whose forceful leadership welded a personal union resting its ultimate authority in the consent of the tribal elders and in fealty to the assumptions of the old amphictyonies.

The emergence of Judah under David is one of the striking phenomena of Israelite history. The choice of Hebron as capital was not accidental. Hebron housed the sacred shrine at which the Abraham traditions had developed—the oaks of Mamre; it was the cultic center of the southern tribes. Years after Jerusalem had replaced Hebron as the avowed religious center of Judah, it seemed natural for Absalom to request permission to fulfill a vow to Yahweh by going to Hebron (II Sam. 15:7–9). The two amphictyonies, having grown separately in the north and in the south, had been forced together in support of

Saul against the Philistines and now under David's steady leadership they were finding a more secure unity—but that unity was still fragile and untried.

With the support of all the Israelite tribes, David moved rapidly to cement the kingdom. While the ethos of the people remained amphictyonic, David's drive was toward the shaping of a powerful kingdom built on the dynastic principle. In a bold stroke, David captured the strategically located Jebusite fortress of Jerusalem and transferred the capital there. The political ingenuity of the move to Jerusalem is almost incalculable. It was a neutral site that had no previous connection with any of the tribes; the loyalties of Israel could be fastened upon David and the new political order, bypassing all the old allegiances, associations, and vested interests. This radical attempt to suppress sectional jealousies and prerogatives before they could gain headway has been likened to the decision of the youthful government of the United States to put its capital in the District of Columbia and the locating of the Australian capital at Canberra in the Australian Capital Territory.

Joab led a select force in a surprise seizure of the city, the precise method being obscured by the brief and cryptic biblical description of the operation (II Sam. 5:8). Many historians believe that David's men gained entrance to the city through a watershaft, enabling them to take the Jebusites unaware. We can be certain that the sudden capture of the city, whose precipitous slopes made it one of the military strongholds of Palestine, was a tactical victory of no small proportions in enlisting the amazed confidence of the tribes in David. The Jebusite city, occupying about twelve acres, was located on the southeastern ridge known as Ophel or Zion, separated by the Millo from the main eminence on which the temple was eventually built. The Millo was either a fortress guarding the northern approach to Ophel or a fill of rocks and dirt to shore up the wall at its most vulnerable point. A crude system of watershafts and conduits provided the city with ample water. It is no wonder that the Jebusites taunted David from the city wall, "You will not come in here, but the blind and the lame will ward you off." After further Israelite building operations Jerusalem became a difficult city to capture, even for the armies of Assyria and Babylonia.

David launched a building program to fortify the city and to outfit it as his royal seat. He erected a palace and assembled wives and concubines in a fashion that would have been abhorrent to Saul. Religious loyalties were centralized. With fanfare and pageantry David officiated at the bringing up of the ark to Jerusalem from its confinement in the house of Abinadab in Kiriath-jearim where it had been left because of its harmful effects on Philistines and Israelites. The Benjaminite ephod, the oracle for consulting Yahweh's will that Abiathar had brought from Nob into the custody of David, was likewise brought to the capital. Nehushtan, the Levite sacred serpent, probably was

Ancient fortifications of Jerusalem on the southeast hill (Ophel), possibly Jebusite or Davidic.

taken there at the same time. Whether sincere or merely politically shrewd, David was certainly not ignorant of the need to forge strong political and religious ties that would bind him to his people. The question of David's own conviction is about as fruitlessly argued as the motive of Constantine in accepting Christianity as a state religion.

The likelihood is, however, that David was as sincere in his Yahwism as Saul, that they were both avid believers, although by no means original thinkers or pioneers in religious reform. David's priestly func-

tions are even more in evidence than Saul's, as befitted his more ceremonial conception of royal office. David "danced before the ark"
and officiated at the sacrifice attending the housing of the ark in a tent
at Jerusalem. He referred repeatedly to the oracular lots to guide him
in military campaigns and key political decisions.

David also seemed anxious to build a house for Yahweh to replace
the tent but was discouraged by the prophet Nathan. The conversation
between king and prophet is preserved in II Samuel 7, a chapter usually dismissed by earlier criticism as historically worthless. Its status is
still problematic, since its present form is late. The intense theological
interest in the temple and Davidic dynasty has led to considerable rewriting of the content; it is not difficult, however, to believe that a
kernel of historicity lies beneath all the subsequent "overlays."

It is altogether plausible that David, with his cultural aspirations,
saw the incongruity of the national god remaining in a tent when the
king had a palace. Anyone with status had his own house! (Note in
the Ras esh-Shamra texts the ambition of Aliyan Baal to erect a temple.) It is also reasonable that Nathan would advise against it, if not
because of his own firm nomadic instinct that Yahweh was a migrating God, at least because he saw that it was not the wise moment to
initiate too revolutionary a change in the old Yahwism. More ques-
tionable is the promise of Nathan that David would have an enduring
dynasty (the passage has a play on the double meaning of Hebrew
bayith, "house" and "dynasty"; David will not build a "house" for
Yahweh but Yahweh will build a "house" for David). Such a firm
belief in the enduring dynasty of David is more likely after his line was
long established, some would insist after its decease in 587 B.C.

David apparently continued his spellbinding effect on the Philistines. The only explanation for the freedom they allowed him in Hebron is that they still thought of David as a vassal. His control in the
south was regarded as a check on the House of Saul. As long as the Israelites were divided, the Philistines did not object to able leaders like
David strutting about as petty princes. Too late, when north and south
had united and Jerusalem was in David's hands, they realized that he
had tricked them. The sources are practically silent about David's wars
with the Philistines, but his success was such that thereafter they were
never a serious threat to Israel. Prominent in the few engagements reported are the exploits of "the mighty men" of David (II Sam. 21). It
is quite likely that some of the Philistines deserted to their former ally

David and, after a few impressive victories over them, the Philistine opposition may have become only nominal. With the fullest respect for their military prowess, David apparently enlisted Pelethites and Cherethites (Philistines and Cretans!) as a part of the foreign mercenaries who under Benaiah constituted the core of his army. Although the Philistine cities retained independence, they ceased from their forays into the hill country. The name "Philistine" survived as a synonym for "pagan" (as also the epithet "uncircumcised") and in English as a derisive term for those who oppose culture and progress.

With the elimination of the archenemy Philistia, Israelite dominion expanded rapidly. Moab and Edom were defeated and made subject to tribute. The Ammonites were conquered and numbers of their people pressed into slavery. The Aramean kingdoms of Syria (Damascus and Zobah) poured tribute into Jerusalem's coffers. David worked out advantageous diplomatic relations with the Phoenician Hiram of Tyre. The economies of the two countries supplemented one another admirably: Phoenicia mercantile and rich in timber, Israel agricultural and rich in human resources. Tyre supplied building materials and the skilled craftsmen to erect David's palace. There must have been some return offered by David. No doubt his willingness to keep the trade routes open so that caravans would flow freely to the trading centers of Phoenicia was one recompense. Another may have been shipments of grain and even labor gangs such as we hear of in Solomon's time; while the sources do not speak of Israelites being pressed into royal servitude during David's reign, an Adoram is named as "in charge of forced labor" (II Sam. 20:24; LXX has Adoniram, cf. MT of I Kings 4:6; 5:14).

Under David, Israel was at the pinnacle of political greatness. On all sides the major powers were quiescent. The Hittites were destroyed as a force outside of Asia Minor, while Assyrians and Egyptians were occupied with internal affairs and without strong rulers. The era 1200–900 B.C. in Palestinian history is well described as "the Era of the Little Peoples." Among the smaller powers, the Israelites under David emerged as the dominant force, ruling either by direct conquest (as in Edom, Moab, Ammon, the Aramean states) or by hegemony (as over Philistia and Phoenician cities). The Pentateuchal description of the ideal extent of the promised land, "from the river of Egypt to the great river, the river Euphrates," was surely formulated during the kingdom of David.

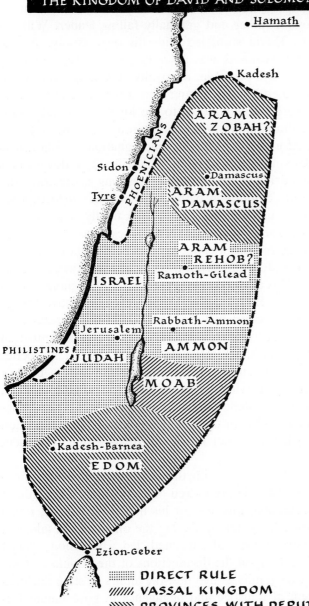

THE KINGDOM OF DAVID AND SOLOMON, 1000~922 B.C.

Hamath

Kadesh

ARAM ZOBAH?

Sidon

PHOENICIANS

Tyre

Damascus

ARAM DAMASCUS

ARAM REHOB?

ISRAEL

Ramoth-Gilead

Rabbath-Ammon

Jerusalem

PHILISTINES

AMMON

JUDAH

MOAB

Kadesh-Barnea

EDOM

Ezion-Geber

DIRECT RULE
VASSAL KINGDOM
PROVINCES WITH DEPUTY GOVERNORS
(REVOLTED UNDER SOLOMON)

CITIES UNDERLINED WERE IN
COMMERCIAL ALLIANCE WITH ISRAEL

Such is the account of David the statesman par excellence, the political father of his people. The Court History presents in contrast David the unsuccessful father and gradually failing leader. With all his political talents, David stumbled with his own family. At the heart of his domestic weakness was an indulgent nature, seemingly spoiled by the luxuries and privileges of royalty. The king's sin in taking Bathsheba is narrated less as a matter of lust than of callous absolutism, posed in unforgettable contrast to the loyalty of Uriah to his lord. In one of the most telling instances of irony in Hebrew prose, David's desperate effort to disguise his impregnation of Bathsheba runs against the adamant fidelity of Uriah who will not go down to his own house to eat and drink or lie with his wife as long as the army and the ark of Yahweh are camped in battle array. Uriah's incorruptible integrity costs him his life, for the frantic king finally sends him to Joab with a letter that seals the unsuspecting messenger's doom. To any Israelite reader the real sin was not against Bathsheba but against her husband. David could be forgiven a moment's weakness, but the cold murder of one of his devoted men is a devastating comment upon the monarch's character. In fairness to David, few rulers have had so candid a reporter as the court historian; probably more brutal tales could be recounted about his contemporaries. David felt compunction and acknowledged to Nathan that he had sinned against his better knowledge of God's commands. By devising parabolically a case of injustice of the sort that David was in the habit of judging, Nathan forced the king to pass sentence upon himself (II Sam. 12). Yahweh's forgiveness of David is in unexplained contrast to his rejection of Saul for wrongs that were not nearly so great—even by ancient standards.

Rather than the story ending with the death of Bathsheba's first-born, the weaknesses of David are passed on to his sons. They inherit his indulgent vices. Amnon, lovesick for his half-sister Tamar, raped her; Absalom requited his sister by slaying the offender. Absalom, a handsome young man, brash and conceited, led a rebellion against his father, playing freely upon the disaffections of the populace. During the years of David's family difficulties, the affairs of state declined badly and resentment at injustice and negligence in government festered in the land. Absalom, with the twin gifts of the demagogue, a winsome personality and a glib tongue, won the hearts of the people.

Forced to flee Jerusalem with his faithful followers, David slowly

climbed the Mount of Olives en route to Trans-Jordan, the perennial
political asylum of Israel. This trek, garnished with legend, presents
him in strangely mixed hues: on the one hand, a tired old man, fum-
bling and inept, his tears unavailing against his son's designs on his
kingdom; on the other hand, the David of old, taking care to leave
spies behind who will send him information, and withal a pride of
bearing that remains unruffled by the gibes of his enemies, toward
whom he displays a marvelous magnanimity. But the image of David
as the invincible warrior determined the tactics of Absalom who decided to wait in Jerusalem until his forces were fully assembled rather
than strike David before he could cross the Jordan. This was the rebel's
fatal mistake, for the regrouped troops of the king, dispersed in the
wilderness of Gilead and led by Joab, proved too much for him. Although instructed by David to spare his son's life, the heartless Joab,
coming upon Absalom caught by the hair in the branches of a tree,
thrust three darts into his heart.

With the death of Absalom the two failures of David's life come to a
crushing climax: his failure as a father and his failure as "a man of
blood." It is Joab who embodies this latter flaw in his role as executor
of the evil by which David attained and held his kingdom. Joab sym-
bolizes the wantonness and bloodguilt of David; his trusty general is
the king's alter ego, the personification of all that is worst in himself.
But David knows only too well that he cannot absolve himself of the
wrongs of Joab when he has been content to profit by them. That
point is firmly urged in Joab's rebuke of the unnerved king: "You
have today covered with shame the faces of all your servants, who have
this day saved your life, . . . because you love those who hate you
and hate those who love you. For you have made it clear today that
commanders and servants are nothing to you; for today I perceive that
if Absalom were alive and all of us were dead today, then you would
be pleased. Now therefore arise, go out and speak kindly to your servants; for I swear by Yahweh, if you do not go, not a man will stay with
you this night; and this will be worse for you than all the evil that has
come upon you from your youth until now" (II Sam. 19:5–7). Thus
Joab holds David to the code under which they have operated. With
biting logic he reminds the king that it is too late now "to call the game
quits." At great cost to himself, and expecting nothing more than second place, Joab had carved out a kingdom for his master. Indulgent
and sentimental love for a rebellious son could not stand in the way of

the empire that belonged to the strong-willed and the nimble-witted.

It is impossible to judge how explicitly David gave voice to his deep misgivings over the morally ruinous tactics by which his throne had been held secure. Many scholars doubt that David's deathbed speech, in which he unburdens himself and asks Solomon to visit vengeance on Joab (I Kings 2:5–6), is true to the facts. They regard it as the D writer's attempt to purge David of guilt, which of course it does not, but rather shows him as a vacillating coward who asks his son to settle the father's accounts. The fact that shortly after Absalom's death David replaced Joab with Amasa as the head of the militia argues that he made some effort to alleviate his pangs of conscience. But it was too late; when Joab killed Amasa and regained his position, David had no answer. The king had gone in too deeply ever to pull himself out. Toynbee comments on David and Solomon: "The man of violence cannot both genuinely repent of his violence and permanently profit by it."[3] Troubled though he was David chose to profit rather than to repent.

While the Court History is objective in that it portrays the many-sidedness of situations, it is by no means lacking in a point of view. Moralizing and theologizing are kept to a minimum by the writer who intrudes himself far less than many modern historians. There is nonetheless a frankly prophetic outlook about the moral nature of human life. Considering the emotional impact of the events, the few theological judgments are restrained. After David's adultery and the murder of Uriah, and before Nathan's audience with the king, the narrator says: "But the thing that David had done displeased Yahweh" (II Sam. 11:27b). When Absalom disregarded Ahithophel's advice to pursue David before he could recover his defensive stance, the historian notes: "For Yahweh had ordained to defeat the good counsel of Ahithophel, so that Yahweh might bring evil upon Absalom" (II Sam. 17:14b). Indeed the reader is so moved by indignation at David and wonderment at the providential turn of events that these statements seem entirely apt and necessary.

The historian has a mature view of the relation of God to human life. His attitude is not mechanistic, treating men as the pawns of deity, nor is it interventionist, regarding God as a manlike being who occasionally takes part in events at the crucial points. Yahweh is the

---

[3] Arnold J. Toynbee, *A Study of History*, Oxford University Press, 1935, vol. 6, p. 180.

Lord of mankind, sovereign "above" the world, active "within" it. The historian takes care to preserve human freedom. He also seeks to work out the interrelation of human actions, along the lines of the general conviction that men reap as they sow. But the loose ends of events that do not fit the preconceived designs of reward and punishment are left for all to see. There is serious concern with freedom and destiny, truth and falsehood—joined to an honest respect for the uniqueness of persons and events. The writer has no interest in types, but is absorbed by people under tension.

The major question raised by the historian is not David's sexual sin, but his ruthlessness in the exercise of power that allowed him to treat persons as expendable: Bathsheba, Uriah, Abner, and even his own sons toward whom he displayed a doting but loveless sentimentality. The portrait of David is nevertheless warmly drawn; the author is not set on proving a point but on dramatizing a life in its fateful impact upon others. David is neither mocked nor patronized. Whatever the court history may be, it is no partisan polemic. With all his faults candidly exposed, we are impressed by the epic proportions of the hero, his great capacity for love and grief, generosity and personal charm. The man David seems very like the man Saul, a fact which might be more apparent had the Saul narratives been written with the empathy granted David. The one all-controlling difference, aside from Saul's mental derangement, was the shrewd and calculating element in David so at variance with the naïveté and straightforwardness of Saul. As a result the sins of Saul were open and clumsily executed, while David's lapses were covert and suave.

Like other spirited and influential leaders of history, David was strangely paradoxical. The same sources can be read in utterly opposing ways, and it is an illusion to think that had we been alive in his day the one truly "objective" view could have been gained. He struck his contemporaries in the same way; men were likely to be passionately pro-David or equally ardently anti-David. We may still make him out as a Machiavellian strategist, full of guile in politics but incredibly feeble in the domestic sphere; or we can construe him as the mighty fashioner of Israelite statecraft, devoutly religious and sincerely dedicated to the advance of his people. In short, the Court History refuses to give us a David who is a mere ideal or stereotype; he is real because he is complex. If David was far worse than orthodox thinking has rated him, he was surely better than the cynics and debunkers realize.

David was a Yahweh devotee who took the power struggle seriously, a man of blood, ruthless and aspiring, determined to win, yet conscience-stricken and devout, loving and hating, loved and hated. He was the one man who could have succeeded in his task: to secure the international corridor for Israel. In the court historian's frank appraisal David's career poses the tormenting question that Israel never escapes and never really answers: How is Israel to be the people of God and yet hold her own in history? Can there be theocracy without autocracy, covenant theology without royal authority, religious vitality without political power?

SOLOMON

Solomon is probably the most overrated figure in the Old Testament. It is difficult to reconcile the tradition of his wisdom with his almost total disdain of sound government. His accession shows him as the pampered son of David, not technically in line for the throne but skillfully promoted by his mother Bathsheba and the prophet Nathan —whose Yahwistic sixth sense failed him in this choice. Crucial for understanding the outlook and policies of Solomon is the fact that he was the offspring of an Oriental harem, a man who enjoyed the fruits of his father's labors with little thought of the cost of replenishment. He inherited the sins of his father without David's virtues. He lived in another world from that of the Israelite citizenry. It is small wonder that the house he built was founded on sand. Had the genius he displayed in amassing and dispensing wealth been applied to the long-range improvement of Israel's economy he could have made a lasting contribution to his people.

The written sources on his reign are a mixture of court annals, temple chronicles, and legends extolling the king's wealth and wisdom. The material is uneven in historical value. In general the more trustworthy passages expose the ineptness of Solomon's rule and the shallowness of his character. The more legendary passages place a halo around his head and never tire of recounting his greatness. The Deuteronomic compiler was faced with the problem of doing justice to the two lines of evidence. He hit upon the idea of grouping the laudatory data in Solomon's youth and early reign, presenting him as a model king who prospered at Yahweh's hand; whereas the condemnatory sources are placed later in his reign, following his apostasy to the foreign gods of his many wives. The chipping away of the vast Davidic domain by the revolt of Edom and Aram was explained as punishment by Yahweh for Solomon's senile defection.

Solomon was bent on entering the circle of the great nations and putting Israel on an equal footing with the most advanced civilizations. To that end he encouraged ostentation and luxury. He overtaxed the economic capacity of his people by squandering their resources of wealth and manpower. Solomon's sanest effort was to continue David's policy of making Israel a commercial middleman. Tolls were exacted from the caravans that crisscrossed his domain. Particularly lucrative was his selling of horses in Egypt that he had acquired in Asia Minor.

The relatively modest construction of David was exceeded by the lavish projects of his son. Several public buildings, including a palace and temple, were modeled on Canaanite-Phoenician lines. Tyre again provided craftsmen. Solomon's diplomatic alliances were sealed by marriages to foreign princesses, the harem being less a symbol of lust than of pretension to power. For the first time the Israelite army developed cavalry and chariotry. Jerusalem's fortifications were buttressed and several defensive citadels enlarged or rebuilt: Hazor and Megiddo in the north; Gezer, lower Beth-horon, Baalath, and Tamir in the south. At Ezion-geber on the Gulf of Aqabah he built a port city from which a fleet sailed every three years to Ophir (south Arabia, Abyssinia, India?). Landlocked Israel for a brief season even tried seafaring—thus did Solomon hunger to ape the nations! More basic to the economy were the copper smelting furnaces at Ezion-geber, situated so that the prevailing winds down the Arabah served as natural bellows.

The king also had his eye on administrative improvements; he divided the realm into twelve regions and required that they take turns in supplying sumptuous fare for the court. A study of the brief description of the regions and officers (I Kings 4:7–19) has led most scholars to the conclusion that Solomon devised his administrative districts to cut across the old tribal boundaries, thus hastening centralization of power in Jerusalem and a corresponding breakdown of tribal loyalties and outlying centers of power. The crowning insult of this clever bit of gerrymandering seems to have been Solomon's exemption of the tribe of Judah from the onerous provisions asked of

Solomon's stables at Megiddo. (Above) Remains of a unit for about 24 horses, with tie-posts still standing. (Below) Reconstruction of a 5-unit compound.

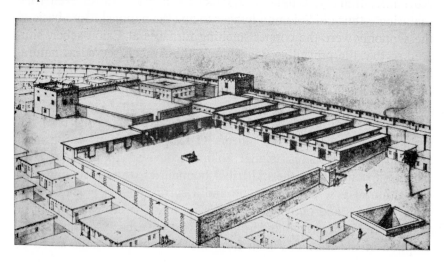

the districts; only Alt among recent scholars feels that the administrative list does not indicate favoritism toward Judah.[4] The king's taxation was exorbitant and to make matters worse for the independent peasantry, he requisitioned crops and drafted labor battalions as he saw fit. Not only did Israelite laborers serve on public works projects, but they were sent to the help of manpower-scarce Phoenicia in fulfillment of treaty obligations with Tyre.

Although great wealth had passed through Solomon's hands, it was spent largely on lavish buildings and court luxury. As a result the destitute king was finally driven to cede twenty Galilean towns to Hiram in return for gold. Only Gezer was added to his dominion —as dowry from his marriage to the Egyptian princess. On the debit side, Edom and Aram revolted. Their loss meant a drastic curtailment of caravan revenue, for it put the Trans-Jordan King's Highway beyond the secure hold of Solomon. Superficially opulent, the boom prosperity of

THE TEMPLE OF SOLOMON

Drawing of the Temple of Solomon as reconstructed from biblical data and from similar nonbiblical temples. Note the threefold division: from right to left, the porch with free-standing pillars; the "holy place"; and the innermost "holy of holies." Rows of chambers extend around three sides.

Solomon was short-lived and shared in only by the Jerusalem nobility and the upper classes of the larger cities. The agricultural base of the

[4] Albrecht Alt, "Israels Gaue unter Salomo," *Kleine Schriften zur Geschichte des Volkes Israel,* Beck, 1953, vol. 2, pp. 76–89.

land was depleted through the shipment of crops to Phoenicia, the requisitioning of supplies for the court, and the draining off of farm manpower for the labor corvée. Although Solomon seemingly brought Israel to the pinnacle of political greatness, it was an abortive achievement; surrounding the plenty of the court was the want of the populace.

In the light of his short-sighted rule what is the historian to make of

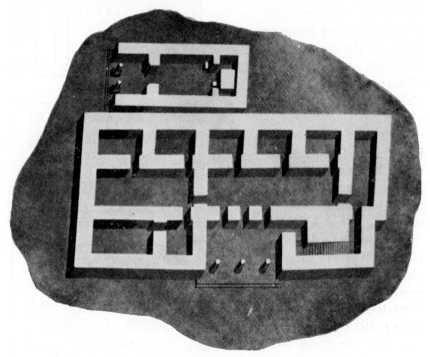

The royal chapel and palace at Tell-Tainat in north Syria. In size and lay-out the chapel is similar to Solomon's.

the venerable tradition of Solomon's wisdom? It is perplexing that one so lacking in statesmanship and so devoid of the Yahweh devotion of Saul and David should have been exalted by subsequent tradition. There seem to have been two reasons for the glorification of Solomon: he built the temple and he sponsored the wisdom movement in Israel.

In the total program of the ambitious monarch the temple was only one rather secondary item. Its dimensions (90 feet by 30 feet), smaller than his palace (exact figures not given but it took thirteen years to build in contrast to seven years for the temple), indicate that it was merely a royal chapel where the national religion could be celebrated with appropriate pageantry. Contrary to the impression of the D source, the Jerusalem temple was never intended by Solomon, or any king before Josiah, to be the sole center of worship. It did not replace the sanctuaries at Hebron, Bethel, etc., nor was its erection accompanied by suppression of the Canaanite high places that dotted the countryside.

Modest in proportions, the temple was nevertheless exquisitely wrought in the finest traditions of Phoenician architecture. Temples of similar style have been unearthed in Syria and most recently at Hazor in Galilee. The threefold division of the temple into open porch, main sanctuary or holy place, and inner chamber or holy of holies is analogous to ancient Near Eastern practice and corresponds roughly to the narthex, nave, and chancel in a Christian church. The *décor* was thoroughly Canaanite, from the cedar paneling and gold leaf to the fertility motifs of lilies, palms, and pomegranates. Two freestanding pillars in front of the porch—given the cryptic names Jachin and Boaz—may have been representative of the mountain supports of the cosmos. A great brass basin, fifteen feet in diameter and resting on the backs of twelve oxen, was filled with water, doubtless to represent the cosmic ocean so central to ancient Near Eastern mythology. Like all ancient places of worship, the sanctuary was without seats, for there were no stated times of indoor worship. The great national festivals were observed in the homes or in the temple courtyard.

The offering of sacrifice was the one functional purpose of the temple and yet, despite the show of detail in Kings, the altars are not clearly described. We read of an altar for burnt offerings placed in the forecourt (I Kings 8:64; II Chron. 4:1; Ezek. 43:13–27) and of an altar of incense in the holy place (I Kings 6:22; 7:48). The site chosen by Solomon for his temple was the ancient holy place of Zion connected by tradition with the threshing floor of Araunah (II Sam. 24:15–25). Its natural rock altar made it a holy place; the exposed limestone ridge is venerated even today as a sacred rock by Moslems who have built the Dome of the Rock directly over it. Whether the sacred rock was in the floor of the holy place or in front of the porch is not known. A short stairway led into the innermost chamber where the ark was kept, adorned by half-human and half-animal mythological creatures, the winged cherubim. This was doubtless the imageless throne of Yahweh, filling as it did the niche where other peoples placed their idols. The chamber was shrouded in darkness and no man—except for the high priest once a year—dared enter it.

The Deuteronomic account of the building of the temple draws on reliable but sketchy material. Although the Hebrews had tremendous gifts of pictorial writing, they had no exact insight or vocabulary for technical subjects, so that while Kings intends to give a sufficient description of the temple, the resulting picture is lacking in many details and blurred in others. To this day it is almost impossible to picture the rows of chambers around three sides of the temple (apparently used for storage). Embedded, however, in the prayer of dedication is a poetic couplet regarded by many scholars as expressive of the belief of the temple builders:

> Then Solomon said,
> "Yahweh has set the sun in the heavens,
>   but has said that he would dwell in thick darkness.
> I have built thee an exalted house,
>   a place for thee to dwell in for ever" (I Kings 8:12–13).

This hint of the motivation of Solomon in building a temple confirms the importance of the dark inner chamber. In spite of all the Canaanite aspects of the temple, in respect of Yahweh's being (his connection with the desert storm clouds and his prohibition of images), the essence of Yahwism was retained. The result is that the temple was a Canaanite-Yahwistic hybrid.

To the great majority of Israelites, the building of the sanctuary at Jerusalem did not require any revolution in their religious belief and practice. Of the three kings of united Israel, Solomon was the most opportunistic, so that it is unlikely that the temple came from any very profound faith on his part. But as the temple grew in importance and became the sole center of worship under the Deuteronomists, Solomon loomed correspondingly large as the designer and builder. Religious fancy dwelt upon the question: What sort of man would create so splendorous a place of worship for Yahweh? The answer is given in the beautiful dedicatory prayer of I Kings 8 which combines a strong sense of Yahweh's love for Israel with a keen awareness of his surpassing greatness, uncontainable in human forms. "But will God indeed dwell on the earth? Behold, heaven and the highest heaven cannot contain thee; how much less this house which I have built! Yet have regard to the prayer of thy servant and to his supplication, O

A Canaanite temple at Hazor (1400–1200 B.C.) clearly shows its three-chamber construction. At the left, two pillar bases are set on either side of the doorway leading from the porch to the central chamber. The innermost chamber is lined with one course of dressed rock slabs.

Yahweh my God . . . that thy eyes may be open night and day toward this house, the place of which thou hast said, 'My name shall be there,' " (vss. 27–29). In good faith but with obvious naïveté Solomon was decked out in the religious garb of a seventh-century Deueronomist.

Solomon's highly touted wisdom also has some basis in fact. His clever ruling that the child disputed by two women should be cut in two and a half given to each has numerous parallels in folklore. The

Close-up of the Hazor temple's "holy of holies." Cult furnishings include an incense altar on its side.

clearest glimpse of the king's wisdom is in the statement that "he also uttered three thousand proverbs; and his songs were a thousand and five. He spoke of trees, from the cedar that is in Lebanon to the hyssop that grows out of the wall; he spoke also of beasts, and of birds, and of reptiles, and of fish" (I Kings 4:32–33). We may judge then that Solomon's acumen lay chiefly in formulating gnomic sayings of the sort that appear in the book of Proverbs; it is possible that many of the epigrams in the older parts of that book come from the Solomonic age. The subjects of his epigrammatic art were apparently botanical and zoological, perhaps in the style of Aesop's Fables, the nonhuman world being used to moralize about human nature. While instances of this type of wisdom are relatively rare in the Old Testament, a few specimens have survived; e.g., Jotham's Fable (Judg. 9:7–21, in which trees represent men) and certain of the Proverbs (30:24–31, where the traits of insects and wild animals are likened to human qualities). Solomon may have contributed some of the several thousand epigrams attributed to him, but primarily he was patron of the scribes who spent their time in collecting the sayings. He was more the sponsor of wisdom than its practitioner. It is hard to believe that the spendthrift and gaudy king could have written the whole of Proverbs, which lauds the life of sobriety and the golden mean, and includes admonitions against royal tyranny.

The fabulous attainments of Solomon awed his people but also developed a deep resentment, especially among the northern tribes who suffered the brunt of the abuse of his power. The tribal covenant into which David had entered at Hebron was virtually ignored by Solomon; in fact, it may be more than accident that no mention is made of Solomon confirming it at his accession. So while he was remembered for "all his glory" and for his supposed piety, already in his lifetime there was a smoldering hatred for the heavy hand that he laid upon his subjects. It would have been one thing had severe measures been necessitated by a national crisis to which the whole people lent their sacrificial energies, but they were so patently for the enhancement of the king's pleasures that it did not take long for the people to "see through" Solomon. The dislike of his people was more than distaste felt for a strong personality; it was rather an intuitive recognition that the welfare of his subjects never really lay close to the heart of Solomon as it did with Saul and the younger David. Outwardly magnificent, his rule was inwardly weak and no small part of the political decay of Israel must be charged to Solomon.

THE SECESSION OF THE NORTH

At the king's death, the scene was a dramatic one. His son Rehoboam journeyed to Shechem, bent on fulfilling the formal requirements of covenant renewal with the northern tribes. The visit was staged as a brief propaganda excursion to placate the people by a ceremonious show of deference to tribal feelings. Instead he met the stern demands of the aroused citizenry that the burdens of his father be lifted. After consultation with his advisors, Rehoboam chose a repressive policy, replying to the northerners with a stinging rebuff that has

become an adage, "My little finger is thicker than my father's loins.
. . . My father chastised you with whips, but I will chastise you with
scorpions" (I Kings 12:10–11). Rehoboam was hardly prepared for
the spontaneous uprising of the people who put him to flight and declared their independence under Jeroboam, son of Nebat. Jeroboam
had been a seditious leader of one of Solomon's labor battalions.
Forced into Egyptian asylum, he returned at word of the king's death.
The discontent among the drafted laborers of the north was capitalized
upon by the able leader, aided by the Yahwistic prophet Ahijah the
Shilonite, who announced symbolically with a garment torn into
twelve pieces that ten of the tribes would follow Jeroboam (I Kings
11:26–40).

Immediate cause of the breakup of the united monarchy was the
heavy-handed reign of the despotic Solomon, with its spawning materialism, economic depletion, suspension of tribal and personal freedoms, favoritism toward the south, sensuality, and religious syncretism—all capped by the prospect that Rehoboam would outdo his
reckless father.

Although Solomon hastened the crisis, the schism had deeper underlying causes. The disintegrating forces that had obstructed the
tribal amphictyonies continued to impede the political aspirations of
united Israel: (1) the hilly terrain that encouraged sectional insularity
and hampered communication; (2) the different geographical and
economic orientations, with north Israel faced toward the plains and
thus toward agriculture and commerce, while Judah faced toward the
desert with its pastoral life and nomadic ideals; (3) the original separation of the northern or Jacob Hebrews and the southern or Abraham
Hebrews, and their grouping in two confederacies that did not come
together significantly until the time of Saul and David. All these were
deep-rooted hindrances that could not be swept aside in a generation.
A series of able rulers would be needed to steer the Israelites from
tribal confederacy to monarchy. David's skilled beginning was halted
and even reversed by Solomon's disregard of the older tribal sensitivities. With external threats at a minimum and internal affairs running
against the people's grain, it is no wonder that the union could dissolve so quickly. To be sure Jeroboam had ambitions of his own, and
the north was not long in falling into the despotism it had shaken loose.
Nevertheless, the constant reassertion of tribal sympathies was to be
one of the formative factors in Old Testament history, a force com-

pounded of pride of clan, independence of spirit, and covenantal loyalty to Yahweh. The king who vaunted himself above his people was bound to meet resistance from a citizenry whose memories were still alive with the stern beliefs of nomadic Yahwism.

The discontent of the northerners came to the surface in the appointment of new religious centers. The present form of the stories treats the action of Jeroboam in setting up sanctuaries at Dan and Bethel as blasphemous and apostate: first, because he used golden calf images; second, because he did not worship at the one and only center, Jerusalem. The second is a gross anachronism, for no contemporary of Jeroboam—not even Jerusalemites—would have shared the later Deuteronomic opinion that worship outside of Zion was contrary to God's will. As to the first objection, it may be noted that we know little about the temples at Dan and Bethel. Granted that they did house golden bulls, a critic of Solomon's temple could have caviled at the fertility objects there, including the twelve bronze oxen supporting the molten sea. Albright's contention that the bulls of Jeroboam were the throne attendants or supports of the invisible Yahweh has been too summarily dismissed.[5] When we consider the hostile and biased attitude of the southern Deuteronomists toward the founder of the northern kingdom (Jeroboam became ever afterward the incarnation of royal evil, as David was the incarnation of royal piety), we ought to be wary of the intent of D to downgrade Jeroboam and stigmatize his religion as pagan. It is more likely that Jeroboam introduced Yahwism at sanctuaries in his own domain and that his cultic appointments, like Solomon's, were a mixture of Yahwistic and Canaanite features. Northern Yahwists were saying in effect that their religion was not dependent on the regime at Jerusalem.

That is not to deny that the aim of some northerners was simply to build a monarchy along the lines of David and Solomon in which they could exercise power. As Brutus from high-minded motives and Cassius for personal gain conspired to strike Caesar, so men of many stripes joined in the secession of Israel from Judah. The future of the religion of Israel was now a doubtful one. In both north and south there were progressive elements that verged on assimilation with Canaanite religion, under royal persuasion and the drift of culture. There were reactionary conservative elements that clung tenaciously

[5] W. F. Albright, *From the Stone Age to Christianity*, Doubleday, 2d ed., 1957, pp. 299–301.

to the values of the past and were likely to be anticultural. Yahwism had reached an impasse; it appeared in danger of demise or of petrification. The future growth of the faith of Israel depended upon those who were neither simply purveyors of the Canaanite way of life nor simply idolaters of the old nomadic order. A combination of conviction and largeness of vision was requisite. In men like the prophets and the unknown author of the earliest source of the Pentateuch we find such forward-looking leaders. To the latter we must give particular attention, since in some respects he was a forerunner of the great prophets.

THE YAHWIST

Among the consequences of the united monarchy was an extraordinary literary flowering. The native gifts of the Hebrew for observation and narration, which had shaped the oral tradition, suddenly found fluent written expression. The cultural sophistication of the monarchy and a scribal class possessed of the leisure and ability to write provided optimum conditions for good literature. The Court History of David is a signal example of the prose art of the time. The consolidation of political and religious loyalties under the monarchy created the climate for a national epic. The earliest stratum in the Pentateuch, known as J because of the source's preference for the divine name Yahweh (German Jahveh), was brought together by an anonymous writer who was probably contemporary with Solomon. He was a citizen of Judah, so that the abbreviation "J" also refers conveniently to the place of origin.

The criteria for dating the J writer or Yahwist in the time of Solomon are somewhat nebulous. The style of the J source is in the best tradition of Israelite narration as found in the early materials of Judges and Samuel, dating from 1100 to 800 B.C. The Yahwist cannot be earlier than the latest events he recounts, but we can only be certain that he carried his story as far as the Exodus and wandering of the Moses tribes. The latest possible date would seem to be about the middle of the eighth century, for the writing prophets of that period, Amos and Hosea, allude to the J tradition, although the possibility of dependence on an oral form of the stories cannot be ruled out.

But there is more specific evidence. A body of references in the Yahwist's work alludes to Israel's political ascendancy. The conquest of Edom (Gen. 27:40) and the preëminence of Judah (Gen. 49) are presupposed; both of these were actualities only under David. The way in which J incorporates the traditions of the various tribes into a single history of Israel suggests a time after the monarchy succeeded in bringing all Israel together under a central government. Furthermore, the programmatic conception of the extent of the promised land from the River of Egypt (Gen. 15:18, possibly E) to the Euphrates points to the only time when Israel was the near master of that entire region: namely, under David and Solomon. The older Documentary Hypothesis dated the J writer about 850 B.C. but this choice was never convincingly defended against the stronger evidence for a date during the united monarchy. The Yahwist's insistent declaration of the promise of Israel's greatness, the multitude of offspring, and the possession of the land are best understood against the backdrop of national expansion and optimism. The reign of Jehoshaphat, the Judean king of the early ninth century, is not so likely a period for J as the early reign of Solomon, before his thoughtless policies had begun to take a toll of morale.

The several strata or sources of the Pentateuch do not exist as separate documents in any of the manuscripts we possess, since all copies of the first five biblical books come from some centuries after the final editing. The J, E, D, and P strata are intertwined, sometimes so closely that critics have had to dissect half-verses, on the assumption that sentences were sometimes pieced together by editors out of phrases from two or more sources. To set forth the niceties of Pentateuchal criticism demands a knowledge of the Hebrew language and calls for painstaking study. It is sufficient for our purposes to note that when the J material is isolated, a more or less continuous story results, from the creation of the world to the entrance into Canaan. Without attempting to include every verse or half-verse regarded as J, the following broad outlines of the Yahwist's epic may be distinguished:

1. *The Traditions of the Beginnings: Genesis 1–11*
   The Creation and Fall of Man   2:4b*–3:24
   The First Murderer (Cain and
      Abel)   4:1–16
   The Origins of Nomadic Society 4:17–26

* Source divisions *within* verses, indicated by symbols *a* and *b,* are specified by phrase only when they do not obviously coincide with the indentation or punctuation of the RSV.

The Fall of the Divine Beings   6:1–8
The Flood (Noah and his Sons)   7:1–10,12,22–23;
                                       8:2b–3a,6–12,13b,20–22
The First Drunkard (Noah)   9:18–27
The Descendants of Noah   10:8–19,21,24–30
The Tower of Babel   11:1–9

2. *The Traditions of the Fathers* (*Patriarchs*): *Genesis 12–50*
The Call and Journey of Abra-
   ham to Canaan   12:1–4a
Abraham in Egypt   12:10–20
Abraham and Lot Separate   13:1–18
The Birth of Ishmael to Hagar   16:1–2,4–14
The Destruction of Sodom and
   Gomorrah   18:1–19:28, 30–38
The Birth of Isaac   21:1a,2a (. . . in his old age)
The Renewal of the Promise to
   Abraham   22:15–18,20–24
Rebekah Obtained for Isaac   24:1–67
Later Sons of Abraham   25:1–6
The Birth of Esau and Jacob   25:21–34
Isaac's Relations with Abimelech
   of Gerar   26:1–33
Jacob Obtains Isaac's Blessing   27:1–45
Yahweh Appears to Jacob at
   Bethel   28:13–16
Jacob Meets Rachel and Laban   29:2–14
The Birth of Jacob's Sons   29:31–35;
                                       30:4–5,9–16,24
Jacob's Trickery and Flight from
   Laban   30:25–43;
                                       31:1,3,46,48–50
Jacob's Struggle at the Jabbok
   and his Reunion with Esau   32:3–12,22,24–32;
                                       33:1–17
Dinah and the Shechemites   34:3,5,7,11–12,18,25–26,30
Joseph Sold to Ishmaelites by
   his Brothers   37:12–18,21,25–27,28b,31–35
Judah and Tamar   38:1–30
Joseph and Potiphar's Wife   39:1–23
Joseph's Detention of Benjamin
   and the Plea of Judah   42:38–44:34
Jacob Reunited with Joseph   46:28–47:4

Joseph's Economic Statecraft	47:13–26
Jacob's Deathbed Blessing	49:1–28a
Jacob's Death and Burial in Canaan	50:1–11,14

3. *The Traditions of Bondage and Exodus: Exodus 1–14*

Oppression of Israel After the Death of Joseph	1:6,8–12
Moses' Flight to Midian	2:15–23a
The Call of Moses to Deliver Israel	3:2–3,5,7–8,16–18; 4:1–16, 19–20a, 22
The "Bridegroom of Blood"	4:24–26
Moses' Demand to Pharaoh, Persecution and Discontent of Israel	4:30–31; 5:3,5–6:1
The Plague Stories	
Nile Turned to Blood	7:14–18,21,23–25
Frogs	8:1–4,8–15
Swarms of Flies	8:20–32
Cattle Disease	9:1–7,13–21
Hail	9:23b,25b–34
Locusts	10:1–11,13b (and Yahweh brought an east wind . . .), 15–19, 24–26,28–29
Death of Egyptian First-born	11:4–8 12:29–30
Festival of Passover and Unleavened Bread	12:21–27 13:3–16
Flight of Israel and the Crossing of the Reed Sea	13:21–22; 14:5–7,10–14,19b–20, 21b (from "and Yahweh drove the sea" through "made the sea dry land"), 24–25,27b,30–31

4. *The Traditions of the Wilderness Wanderings (Sinai-Kadesh): Exodus 15–Numbers 34*

From the Sea to the Mountain	15:22–27; 16:4,5,25–30; 17:1b–2,7
The Revelation at Sinai	19:3b–9 (and Yahweh called him out of the mountain . . .)

The Covenant Feast	24:1–2,9–11
Moses Prays for Israel and Purges the Apostates	32:9–14,25–34
Yahweh Reveals His Glory to Moses	33:1–4,12–23
Tablets Reinscribed with "Ritual" Decalogue	34:1–28

(In Numbers it becomes difficult to disentangle J and E so that many scholars treat them as a unity, JE)

Departure from Sinai with Hobab	10:29–33,35–36
Provision of Quails	11:1–35
Miriam and Aaron Criticize Moses	12:1–16
Spies Sent to Canaan	13:17b–20 (Go up into the Negeb . . .), 22–24, 26b–33
Forty Year Wandering Decreed	14:3–4,8–9,11–25,31–33,39–45
Revolt of Dathan and Abiram	16:12–15,25–34 (omit Korah)
Moses Excluded from Canaan	20:1–13
Edom Refuses Israel Passage	20:14–21
Defeat of Sihon and Og	21:1–35
Balaam's Oracles	22:2–24:25
Israelite Apostasy to Baal Peor	25:1–6
Reuben and Gad Settled in Trans-Jordan	32:1–17,20–27,34–42

THE CHARACTERISTICS AND PURPOSE OF J

The Yahwist has fashioned a work of truly epic proportions that could arise only on the frontier between the naïve and the sophisticated. Pfeiffer rightly praises it as a creation that "combines nobility with simplicity."[6] Commentators are unanimous in their acclaim of the literary craftsmanship of J, the untutored artistry, the wonderful transparency of the narratives, attained by compactness and pungency of style. Economy of expression and emotional restraint hold the plot in sharp relief and yet no vital detail seems lacking. The Yahwist highlights the divine-human relationship in bold and vivid strokes, allowing the myriad surroundings of the physical and human environments to recede into the background, in a way quite contrary to the careful descriptions of Greek writers. Thus the Yahwist is impression-

[6] R. H. Pfeiffer, *Introduction to the Old Testament,* Harper, 1941, p. 156.

istic, while Homer is photographic. The Yahwist is turbulent and portentous, even though the scope of his narrative in Genesis is largely domestic; Homer is placid and prosaic by contrast, although his stories concern the clash of armies and heroes.[7]

The J writer has a distinctive vocabulary and style: "to know" as a euphemism for sexual intercourse; "to call upon the name of Yahweh" as the worshipful approach of man to God; "to hearken to the voice of Yahweh" for obedience to God; "to bless" as the beneficent action of deity toward the people; "to find favor or grace" in the sense of "to please someone"; "according to these things," i.e., "in this way, after this manner" (a common narrative transition); Canaanite for the aborigines of Palestine (Amorite in E); Hobab or Reuel for the father-in-law of Moses (Jethro in E); Sinai for the holy mountain (as in P, but Horeb in E); Israel for the third patriarch (Jacob in E). Also, J favors the pronominal periphrasis "my lord" for "you" and "your servant" for "I"; and has a liking for verbal hendiadys in order to emphasize an action, e.g., "look and behold." Many of his peculiarities are accessible only to the student of Hebrew. He prefers, for example, Hebrew *shiphhah* for "maidservant" (*'amah* for the same in E) and *'adhamah* for "ground" or "soil" (elsewhere as "land" or "country"). Other favorite expressions are: "to hasten," "it may be" ("peradventure" in the older English versions), "there was none left," and "behold now."

The Yahwist discloses a wide-ranging interest in aetiology. He is far more intrigued by names, places, and customs than he is by chronology. He revels, for example, in popular etymologies of the names of persons and places, often cast in the form of puns: Eve, "the mother of all living" (Heb. *hawwah* resembles *hay,* "living," Gen. 3:20); Babel, where the tongues were confused (Bab. *Babel,* which really means "gate of god," resembles Heb. *balal,* "to confuse," Gen. 11:9); Edom, the other name for Esau (resembles Heb. *'adhom* "red," Gen. 25:30); Israel, "he who strives with God" (replaces the name Jacob, "the supplanter" or "heel-grabber," Gen. 25:26; 32:27); Marah, "bitterness" (because of the acrid waters, Exod. 15:23); Meribah, "contention" (where Israel rebelled against Yahweh, Num. 20:13). These etymologies are generally among the most

[7] See especially Erich Auerbach, *Mimesis; the Representation of Reality in Western Literature,* Princeton University Press, 1953, chap. 1; also Mary Ellen Chase, *Life and Language in the Old Testament,* Norton, 1955, pp. 95–118.

untrustworthy features of Hebrew tradition, since they almost invariably arise from the association of words that have similar sounds but whose affinities are largely fanciful.

This associative linguistic habit is typical of the folk mind the world over. An example from the St. John River Valley of New Brunswick, Canada, will illustrate. A legend about the naming of the Tobique River (a Micmac Indian word) recounts that the devil attempted to pass Indian Point where the Tobique joins the St. John, but the chief challenged him. They agreed to a test of strength. Each would hurl a rock and if the devil threw farther he could continue on his way; if not, he would have to turn back. They threw two huge rocks (still observable in the St. John River about six miles below Indian Point) and the devil's went slightly farther. In throwing, however, the devil's foot had crossed the line; the chief saw it and shouted: "Toe back!" (Tobique!) And so the river has ever been named. This aptly parallels many of the Hebrew aetiology legends since word associations that naïvely confuse two languages and explanations of natural phenomena are involved. But this continuous Hebrew concern with names provides not only an often whimsical touch but reflects the importance attached to names as bearing the content of a man's being or embodying the true spirit of a locale.

The land and its sacred sites is one of the main motifs in the patriarchal stories. Many of the Abraham, Isaac, and Jacob accounts are in reality "sanctuary stories." They tell why Bethel, Shechem, Hebron, Penuel, Beer-lahai-roi, etc., are sacred places; the rationale is regularly found in the personal histories of the fathers. These are sacred places, Israel declares, because our fathers sojourned in this land and met Yahweh here. A radical process of transformation has made the old Canaanite holy places into Yahwistic shrines. One scholar comments that in J there is "no open fight against these paraphernalia of Canaanite worship but a quiet reinterpretation, which displaced their old meaning and made them harmless."[8] The reinterpretation was not to remain "quiet" nor was the Canaanite ethos entirely "harmless," but the Yahwist at any rate sought to defeat Canaanite religion on home ground by making over its traditions in the likeness of Yahweh.

Of course the accomplishment was not the J writer's alone. During the two or more centuries since the reunion of the northern and

[8] Julius Bewer, *The Literature of the Old Testament*, Columbia University Press, rev. ed., 1933, p. 72.

Exodus tribes (and thus of the Jacob and Moses factions) and during the half-century or more since the northern and southern (Judean) groups had been closely associated, a unification of their respective traditions had been going on apace. The God of the Hebrews received his basic character from the Mosaic and thus strictly Yahwistic mainstream, but into that current flowed the many tributaries fed by previous Hebrew experience in Canaan. The God of the older Hebrews (of Abraham and Jacob) had been worshiped at the Canaanite holy places, and from the point of view of Mosaic Yahwism this Palestinian practice may have been indistinguishable from Canaanite religion. But the marvelous thing about the Yahwist is that he absorbs the pre-Mosaic traditions of the land, naturalizes the older "Canaanite" cultus to the newer Mosaic faith, and at the same time maintains a very high degree of Yahwistic conviction and an ethical vision that make him a worthy precursor of the prophets. J thus typifies the facility of the Hebrews for making use of the Canaanite religion in order to broaden and deepen their basic faith, without diluting it unduly. The Canaanite sanctuaries taken over by Israel are "baptized" into Yahwism, being no longer understood as baal centers but as memorials of the meeting of Yahweh with the fathers and of his promises to them.

Without a tenacious integrating center for Yahwism, the desert faith would either have been swamped or else left behind at a stunted level of growth, appealing only to the more reactionary-minded. But Yahwism kept pace and the J writer shows us the breadth of insight and the constructive genius that could range widely over tradition and marshal it in the service of a progressive faith. His balanced perspective, employing yet not capitulating to Canaanite religion, was not easily grasped by Israelites in general. It was to be some years before the prophets furthered the earnest beginning of the Yahwist in the reinterpretation of their faith.

Among the most striking features of the J source is its broad interest in all that is Israelite in contrast to the more restricted "religious" concern of some of the later Pentateuchal sources. It preserves and relates with gusto the feats of the fathers; it does not flinch at the lie of Abraham (Gen. 12:10–20), the deceit and conniving of Jacob against Esau and Laban (Gen. 27; 30:25–31:1), Simeon's and Levi's ruse against the Shechemites (Gen. 34), or the rashness of Moses (Num. 20:10–13). While he does not necessarily approve of the conduct, the Yahwist does not feel it incumbent to rationalize these actions as do other Israelite writers, especially the Elohist.

Furthermore, the Yahwist retains traditions that seem curiously unassimilated to his own viewpoint. He is the least censorial of the Pentateuchal writers toward his materials. The story of the divine beings who lay with women is the most frankly mythological fragment in the Old Testament (Gen. 6:1–8). Its presence as an explanation for the human sin that precipitated the flood shows that the Yahwist does not regard the story of Adam and Eve as a theoretical account of the origin of all human wrongdoing. The story of Jacob's struggle with a night demon at the ford of the Jabbok was probably rewritten in the tradition before J, but its primitive elements show through without embarrassment to him (Gen. 32:24–32). The "bridegroom of blood" story, in which Yahweh irrationally accosts Moses but is appeased when Zipporah circumcises their son (Exod. 4:24–26), is cryptic to begin with (possibly an attempt to explain the origin of circumcision) but, on any interpretation, is utterly foreign to the religious insight displayed elsewhere in J's epic.

In some respects then the Yahwist is an editor who surveys with hearty delight and enthusiasm the prior traditions of his people and brings them together in a single composition. His sources are various, from the briefest scraps of isolated traditions to the medium-sized cycles such as the Abraham-Lot sequence or the Jacob-Laban account, and finally to the good-sized and tightly woven novelistic story of Joseph. But his contribution is great, for in the process of writing down he has placed his own stamp upon the material. The sequence he gives to the isolated stories and larger cycles and the way in which he sees a connected and sweeping movement of divine purpose elevate him also to the rank of a creative author. Over the whole of his material, the high and the low, the eloquent and the banal, he has cast a dominating presence—the presence of Yahweh who purposes and performs his will.

The J stratum presents an intensely realistic conception of God, replete with anthropomorphisms and anthropopathisms. Without abashment the Yahwist pictures God coming down to stroll in the Garden in the cool of the day (Gen. 3:8), sealing the door of Noah's ark because no sympathetic humans remain to perform the necessary courtesy (Gen. 7:15c), visiting and dining with Abraham before the tent (Gen. 18:1–22), going down to see if the sin of Sodom and

Gomorrah is as bad as he has heard "via the grapevine" (Gen. 18:21), and taking the wheels off (or clogging?) the Egyptian chariots in the sea (Exod. 14:25). He thinks of Yahweh in well-nigh corporeal terms. Even as man cannot be conceived except as a body-soul, and thus there is no disembodied "spirit," so God, while "spiritual," also has embodiment. Yahweh does not possess omniscience and fore-knowledge, but has an experimental openness toward his creation, be-ing quite willing to forsake one line of action for another. On more than one occasion he is perturbed by man, his ingenuity taxed for new ways of coping with human waywardness. The Yahwist's God is a living being, indeed the chief member of the cast without whom there would be no story to tell.

Yet withal there is no easy familiarity toward deity. Yahweh is a "high god" who dwells in the heavens and is not to be confused with the animistic spirits infesting the trees and rocks and wells of the countryside. He is an awesome transcendent being not to be trifled with; his ways are high above the ways of man. The anthropomor-phisms are actually an advance over the theriomorphisms (representa-tions of the gods in animal forms) which were common in the Egyp-tian religion (Amon the ram, Horus the falcon, Hathor the cow, Sekhmet the cat, Thoth the ibis and baboon). For depicting his God the Yahwist finds the most suitable imagery in the human realm. Yahweh is not an abstraction or feeling but a personal living reality who cannot be less than the personal reality of man whom he has created and for whom he has high purposes. Without being a philos-opher of religion the Yahwist was nevertheless the first to give ex-tended and graphic literary expression to a conception of God that has prevailed in Judaism and Christianity ever since. Before the great writing prophets, at least some in Israel (no doubt the direct heirs of Moses) experienced their God as a personality but not a mere man, as one concerned for his creation without being sentimental, respect-ing the freedom of man without being impotent, moral without being moralistic, holy but not capricious.

The divine will, central to the Yahwist's whole conception, does not flatten or annul the human element. If anything, the emphasis upon Yahweh seems to enhance the humanity of the heroes; they are in this respect literally "in the image" of their Maker. The personalities of the great leaders are thrown into sharp relief: the faithful Abra-ham, the crafty Jacob, the forgiving Joseph, the titanic Moses.

The realistic appraisal of divine will and human freedom, of the determined and the open, a sense of their interplay, and sensitiveness to the ultimate mystery behind them make of the J narrative not only first-class literature but also the exponent of a religion whose essential features the human spirit has not outgrown. Life's urgent issues are given confident and engrossing answers, not in generalities but in stories that never cease to compel attention and awaken the imagination.

The J Writer in Genesis

Some of the central episodes in the Yahwist's epic deserve closer scrutiny. Genesis 1–11 show a large interest in the world-wide setting of Yahwism. Von Rad regards the inclusion of this primeval history as one of the daring innovations of the author.[9] Yahweh is the creator God from whom stem all the races of the earth. He is concerned with foreigners; in fact, the entire primeval history deals with pre-Israelite history. Later sections of J bear out this concern. Yahweh and the patriarchs display genuine cordiality toward non-Israelites. The Arab progeny of Ishmael are blessed. The reprehensible conduct of Israelites toward outsiders is discountenanced even when recounted. Pharaoh's innocence in taking Sarah is upheld and the breach of faith by Levi and Simeon against the Shechemites is disapproved in spite of the Shechemite rape of Dinah. The appearance of a more intense nationalism in the Moses traditions was doubtless dictated by the circumstances of the Egyptian bondage and Exodus, which accented the opposition of in-group and out-group. But also oral tradition probably accurately reflected the fact that the Abraham and Jacob clans on the whole lived peaceably with the people of the land.

The J story of creation (Gen. 2:4b–3:24) is a movingly ingenuous tale, profound in the issues it plumbs. Here the far-reaching questions about human origin and destiny are clothed in a form intelligible to the simplest mind, yet tantalizing to the wisest. The viewpoint of the tale is that of a Palestinian peasant, for Adam is none other than the tiller of the soil. All life depends upon the fickle rains rather than on the irrigation waters of the great river valleys. Chaos is a waterless waste, and aridity the bane of the farmer. The J view is highly anthropocentric. Man is created before plants or animals. He is shaped di-

---

[9] Gerhard von Rad, *Das erste Buch Mose: Genesis Kapitel 1–25,* Vandenhoeck, 1952, pp. 15 f.

rectly from the dust and becomes "a living being" (not "soul" as the older versions had it), a body-spirit totality, dust and divinity. When plants and animals appear they are provided as an afterthought for man's use. The garden of bliss is called Eden (cognate of Babylonian *edinu,* "plain" or "desert," translated by LXX *paradeisos,* English Paradise). The formal elements in the story may be north Canaanite; Ezekiel 28:12–19 contains the more original form of the myth. There is evidence of composite sources: the antiquarian interest in the rivers and precious metals (Gen. 2:10–14) and the tree of life (2:9*b*). The presence of two trees is ignored until the end of the story (3:22) and the reader wonders why the man and woman did not eat of the tree of life immediately after tasting of the tree of the knowledge of good and evil, thereby securing everlasting life. The tree of life is best explained as an unassimilated detail in the Yahwist's sources or a later addition.

The man (Adam, "groundling, peasant") is placed in Eden "to till and keep it," an important detail overlooked by interpreters who assume that work is a part of the curse for man's sin; actually the curse is in the fruitlessness of his labor and the niggardliness of the soil (3:17–19). When animals fail to satisfy man's hunger for fellowship, the human species is sexually bifurcated. The inextricable union of male and female is epitomized in the charming aetiology of woman's creation from the man's rib. "Bone of my bone, flesh of my flesh; she shall be called *'ishsha,* because she was taken out of *'ish,*" a word play happily preserved in English "Man" and "Woman." Human freedom is limited, however, to certain spheres. The meaning of the tree of the knowledge of good and evil has been endlessly discussed. Like all profound myth, it is likely to have several legitimate meanings, according as different men see truths in it. It is probable, however, that the Yahwist was not thinking mainly of moral discretion but of the knowledge of good and evil destinies, of the secrets of the divine being, which can never be the possession of man.[10]

The entrance of sin is personified in the serpent who is not diabolical and malicious as much as cunning, crafty, and artful. He is certainly not equated with Satan, a much later figure in Hebrew thought. Far more significant than the exact origin of the serpent image is the unusually penetrating psychological analysis of temptation. Sin is defiance of known standards; man is a moral being who

[10] S. H. Hooke, *In the Beginning* (The Clarendon Bible, vol. 6), Oxford University Press, 1947, pp. 28–32.

inwardly understands his own status. Thus sin masquerades as some wiser understanding of the divine intent. Doubt is created ("Did God say, 'You shall not eat of any tree of the garden'?"); the senses are appealed to as a sufficient guide (" . . . the woman saw that the tree was good for food, and that it was a delight to the eyes"); and human pride and thirst for knowledge are stimulated ("For God knows when you eat of it your eyes will be opened, and you will be like God, knowing good and evil.") In keeping with our previous interpretation, the meaning here is not that man passes from innocence to moral discretion, but rather that he aspires to be the arbiter of destiny on a par with God. Sin cannot enter except by rationalization. It must be rendered into an apparent good, and the passing of responsibility from Adam to Eve to the serpent touches upon the inveterate self-justifying instinct of humankind.

What did the Yahwist signify by the eating of the fruit? (Note that it is *not* an apple!) A common theory is that he meant the sexual act, plausible enough because of the sudden recognition of nakedness after the eating and the curse of pain at childbirth. Some have found in this story a desired justification for suspicion of sex, including Augustine whose youthful promiscuities affected his feelings on the subject. But there are several weighty objections to believing that the Yahwist held such a negative attitude. We have already shown that the fall story introduces sexuality as a natural and desirable thing, the means of man's true contentment and self-completion. The emphasis upon man's satisfaction with woman, unprovided by the animals, may be a deliberate rebuff of bestiality, one of the crudest sexual practices of agricultural society (cf. Exod. 22:19; Lev. 20:15–16; Deut. 27:21). Furthermore, the prohibitory command concerning the tree is given to the man before woman's creation. When the Yahwist wants to speak of the sexual act he does not resort to symbolic contortion but says simply, "Now Adam knew Eve his wife, and she conceived and bore Cain" (Gen. 4:1). The curse upon the woman is not intercourse or childbearing, but the *pain* of birth (3:16). To be sure, a sense of sexual self-consciousness and shame arises after the act of disobedience (which may be partially explained by an anti-Canaanite bias), but this is one of several disruptive results. Man may sin sexually but sex is not the root of sin.

While the metaphysical or didactic import of the story was probably only partly articulate in the Yahwist's mind, if any "point" is to be established the one most expressive of the story's meaning is that the crux of the "fall" is not to be located in some particular wrong act but in man's attempt to exceed his divinely appointed limitations. Overweening pride and distrust of God, which could take almost any conceivable form, are at the base of the downfall of man. If such a formulation comes closest to what the Yahwist intended, then the metaphysical and theological implications of the story are considerable. It is rather surprising that before intertestamental times Judaism did not theorize about the relation between the sin of the first man and the sin of all men. But Christianity has since made up for the slow start. Perhaps there has never been a story so combed for meaning, its overtones and implications studied so intently. Such is the compelling power of the great archetypal images of primeval bliss and woe, whether psychologized or theologized.

The prehistory of the remaining legends of Genesis 1–11 had to do with such aetiological questions as these: Who was the first murderer? Why is the offering of the shepherd preferable to that of the farmer? Whence arose the classes of nomadic society? How did the destructive flood of ancient times come about? Who was the first drunkard? Why are the Canaanites so morally degraded? Who built the great Mesopotamian temple towers? Why do men speak different languages? Gunkel has rightly shown that these aetiological legends were shaped in diverse situations.[11] Recent students of the Pentateuch are also correct in stressing the architectural unity of the traditions as linked by the Yahwist. The J writer sketches the gradual deterioration of man. There is an increase of sin parallel to the increase of man's knowledge and skill. The more clever and adaptive man becomes the more he turns against his Creator. Man was set in the garden to live under the divine will in contented productivity but, exceeding his proper limits, all his inventiveness is now corrupted. It does not gain him unalloyed blessings but leads rather to social anarchy. Since the Yahwist goes on to describe the patriarchal experience in Canaan and brings Israel to the verge of the land under Moses, he probably did not intend an unqualified depreciation of civilization but rather a sharp warning against its insidious dangers. When the terms of Yahweh's lordship are ignored, no matter what man may have accomplished, it is all in vain. The Yahwist may have been speaking to the kings and nobility

[11] Hermann Gunkel, *The Legends of Genesis,* Open Court, 1901.

of his own day. Was he one of the first to discern the follies of Solomon?

In the main the Yahwist introduces into each of these stories the same moral emphasis as in the story of the garden. Man is responsible before Yahweh but he seeks to bolt this responsibility in favor of his own designs. Cain murders Abel because of resentment and envy (the probable meaning of the very difficult vs. 4:7). The increase of sin and the casual disdain of those warned by Noah's building of the ark issues in a catastrophic flood. The base of the flood story is Mesopotamian and appears in Babylonian form in the Gilgamesh Epic where the counterpart of Noah is Utnapishtim, and in an older Sumerian version where he is called Ziusudra. Various legends arose to account for the severe inundations that at times struck the Tigris-Euphrates Valley. According to excavations, however, no flood affected the whole valley, much less the entire inhabited world. The J account of the flood is interwoven complexly with the P account; among its distinctive features are the seven pairs of clean animals and two pairs of unclean taken into the ark, and the rain that lasted for forty days and receded in two (or three) seven-day periods. The Mesopotamian versions explain the flood by divine caprice and regard the sparing of one man as a necessity for feeding the gods who were hard-pressed for provisions because of the slaughter of mankind. By contrast the J version shows the flood as divine punishment, and Noah is spared because of the divine purpose to begin anew the human experiment. The J account closes with a pledge by Yahweh that henceforth man may depend upon the regularity of nature, "While the earth remains, seedtime and harvest, cold and heat, summer and winter, day and night, shall not cease" (8:22).

The Yahwist's contempt for the Canaanites is expressed in the story of Noah's drunkenness (9:20–27). Canaan inadvertently sees his grandfather exposed. Because of this, Canaan's servitude to his brethren is justified, the moral enervation of the Canaanites being traced to their eponym. The passage has been used more than once as the excuse for treating racial minorities as inferiors. However, the story is not more supercilious than the traditions of men the world over who have tended to read the status quo of contemporary group hostilities into the past and to excuse their own particular prejudice on "objective" grounds. We can be sure that drunkenness was a special problem for Israel as a newcomer to the grape-growing economy of Canaan. Only a few strict parties, such as Nazirites and Rechabites, seem to have prohibited wine altogether, but its excesses and associations with pagan worship were attacked by prophets and sages. The Yahwist sounds the warning that even the righteous Noah was reduced to a senseless fool by the orgiastic lure of drink. From this point of view the episode is as severe on Noah as on Canaan.

The Promethean stress upon the divine jealousy appears stronger in the Tower of Babel story than elsewhere. Yahweh, in consultation with the lesser divinities in his heavenly court, grows fearful of the coöperative evil that men may contrive by means of their common speech. When he sees the sky-scaling tower that they have reared, he decides to strike the race with a multiplicity of tongues. Not only is this a gibe at the haughty spirit of those who build cities such as Babylon, but it traces the division of languages to a moral basis. In this day of anthropological inquiry into the origin and diffusion of the languages of mankind, the account impresses us as hopelessly childish. The Yahwist's story, however, lays bare a truth behind all scientific linguistic inquiry, namely, that the problem of communication among men is not merely a matter of defining words or even of variant cultural complexes, but also a moral problem. In truth, man often does not understand his fellows because he does not want to, and the community of man breaks down into a multiplicity of competing centers.

Difficult as it is to discern the configurations of meaning in the cryptic stories of the beginnings, the Yahwist seems to have intended them as an account of man's significance as a creature answerable to Yahweh, a creature who has broken his relation with God. But this is not the end, for the "fall" or the "break" is not complete. Man is still in bond with God, not only because of the necessity for man to seek godliness on some terms, but because of the continuous magnanimity of God's mercy. All the while Yahweh God seeks to reëstablish the strained and shattered relationship, even though the stories end in an impasse between the adamant will of God and the adamant resistance of man. It is in the light of the primeval history of mankind's broken ties with Yahweh that the traditions of the Yahwist first speak of the calling of the Hebrews as the answer to the general human situation.

The patriarchal legends are thematically clearer than the primeval history. The call of Abraham is a call to create a people. The divine purpose is released in history; his commands and blessings determine the communal life of Israel, for Israel is present by promise in the tiny clan of Abraham. Genesis 12–50 is the aetiology of Israel, called into existence to live as a people responsive to Yahweh's will, but not to greatness of any sort except greatness in community with God. Abraham is to separate from the nations, journeying in faith from Ur to a land as yet unknown. The command to separate is total and unqualified: "Go from your country and your kindred and your father's house to the land that I will show you" (12:1). The promise is equally categoric. Abraham will become a *great nation* (a people and only secondarily a political entity): "And I will make of you a great nation, and I will bless you, and make your name great, so that you will be a blessing" (12:2, repeated in essence throughout the patriarchal history, 13:6; 15:5; 17:2–4; 18:17; 22:17; 26:4,24; 28:3–4,14; 32:12; 35:11; 46:3; 48:16,19).

Abraham will also be a *blessing to the nations:* "I will bless those who bless you, and him who curses you I will curse; and by you all the families of the earth will be blessed (or will bless themselves)," (12:3, cf. also 22:18; 26:4; 28:14). Von Rad in particular regards this promise as the Yahwist's solution to the tragic impasse of the primeval history; Abraham is called to create a saving community in which the sin of mankind can be overcome.[12] It is easy to overtheologize a point like this and to infer much more than was ever in the author's mind. Nevertheless, the sharp juxtaposition of the non-Israelite traditions with the call and promise to Abraham certainly argues for a large measure of truth in the theory, especially when the "families of the earth" are specifically referred to in the call of the patriarch. Finally, Abraham is to *possess the land*. As Abraham wanders through Canaan, Yahweh appears to him at Shechem with the promise, "To your descendants I will give this land" (12:7, cf. 13:15; 15:7,17–19; 17:8; 24:7; 26:3; 28:4,13; 35:12).

And so the drama of the fathers begins. The Yahwist discerns the full destiny of the people of the promise in their modest inception. The inner history of Israel's struggle to realize her relation with God is cast against the seminomadic backdrop of her historic beginnings. The inner and the outer histories are entwined but the enduring facet is the inner history and, above all, the divine purpose for human life. The ways of God are germane to human life at a thousand points but

[12] G. von Rad, *op. cit.,* pp. 137–139.

they cannot be simply identified with human good. Morality is not irrelevant to his will but the ethical life is one dimension of the divine concern rather than the whole of it. In particular, man's notions of justice are no final arbiter or measure of God's ways. In all literature there is no more sublime combination of the ethical and the shuddering sense of holiness than the intercession of Abraham on behalf of Sodom: "Wilt thou indeed destroy the righteous with the wicked? . . . Far be it from thee to do such a thing, to slay the righteous with the wicked, so that the righteous fare as the wicked! Far be it from thee! Shall not the Judge of all the earth do right?" Abraham trembles before the deity whose very presence is abounding holiness, "Behold, I have taken upon myself to speak to the Lord, I who am but dust and ashes. . . . Oh let not the Lord be angry, and I will speak again but this once." The keen Hebrew sense of righteousness is engulfed in the mystery of a holiness that is righteous—and yet more than righteous.

The humanity of men before God is fully lived out, even when distasteful both to the Yahwist's standards and ours. The patriarchs sin boldly even as they taste boldly of the covenant promises. They are impulsive and contrite by turns. Judah says of Tamar whom he had hypocritically judged because she practiced the prostitution he had patronized, "She is more righteous than I." On the verge of facing Esau again, Jacob confesses, "I am not worthy of the least of all the steadfast love and all the faithfulness which thou hast shown to thy servant." The Yahwist not only tells the robust tales of the sinner-saints of Israel because he relishes them and because primitive tradition has preserved them; he tells them because his own vision is of a God beyond human deserving. Yahweh, God of the promise, does not draw nigh because of man's desert but often in spite of man's unworthiness. The Yahwist does not regard the patriarchs as somehow more religious people than their contemporaries; they are normally religious for their day and the call of Yahweh to them is a call to live the whole of life under his sway. Not religion as some distinct province of life but life accepted in trust and lived in promise, life perceived as Yahweh-oriented throughout, that is the burden of Israel's existence.

Thus the purposes of God seek fruition in the common life of man and yet they encounter obstacles not merely extrinsic but intrinsic to Israel. Abraham is by turns doubter and coercer of the promise. He forsakes the one wife who might give him a son in order to save his life. He takes a youthful concubine in a desperate attempt to secure a male heir, and Sarah herself laughs within the tent when she hears that she is to bear a son. And what shall we say of the knavery of Jacob, the snobbishness of Joseph, and the envy of his brothers? Resistance to God's purposes is not alone a quality of mankind in the large, or of the enemies of Israel, it is also the behavior of the chosen ones. The promise nevertheless endures. The blessing laid upon the fathers cannot be destroyed by their faithlessness and repeatedly that blessing summons them to almost superhuman commitment: Abraham's surrender of his son, Jacob's wrestling with the night visitor until he limps, Joseph's forgiving love for his brethren. The power of the blessing is seen both in its precedence over human merit and in its capacity to call forth a deeply moral response in Israel.

It is obvious that the Yahwist did not create Israelite religion. The undisputed twelfth-century Song of Deborah is already deeply ingrained with Israelite devotion to Yahweh. We can only account for this faith by tracing it back to Moses and the covenant with Yahweh at the holy mountain. But the J writer articulates the conviction with tremendous power and lucidity. While not the only people in the patriarchal lineage (Arabs, Edomites, Ammonites, and Moabites are all sons of Terah), Israel alone has been given the blessing. Something of nationalistic pride lurks in this notion but it is astonishingly free from the idea of inherent superiority. Israel's position is not only a privilege but a responsibility in subservience to the higher ends of Yahweh, however dimly perceived. The solemn words with which Yahweh summons Israel to the mount express the obligation, not of being "choice" but of being "chosen": "if you obey my voice and keep my covenant, you shall be my own possession among all peoples; . . ." (Exod. 19:5).

The Yahwist's epic could be similarly analyzed in the traditions of the Exodus and wandering. Although less connected, especially owing to the apparent dislocation and deletion of parts of the Sinai-Kadesh section—including a virtual absence of Mosaic legislation, except for the "ritual" decalogue of Exodus 34—the essential themes of the earlier portions are continued. The center of interest is in the deliverance from Egypt and the passover celebration, the covenant and Moses' candid conversations with God. In the plague cycle Moses brings the plagues through direct command without help of the rod and Aaron hardly figures at all in the narrative (in contrast with the P source). Great emphasis is placed upon Israel's believing response to Yahweh and his servant Moses (Exod. 4:1,31; 14:31; 19:9). Faith as such was not to become a central Israelite theme until the prophet Isaiah.

The fundamental thesis of J in Exodus–Numbers as in Genesis is the sovereign freedom and unplumbed mystery of God who relates himself to man in an ordered history held by the continuity of the generations and the power of the blessing. It is the first philosophy of history in human experience, woven of the fabric of Israel's unique faith in Yahweh, based upon a frank religious personalism, and grounded in man's communal nature. Israel never produced another narrator with the literary gifts of the anonymous Yahwist, but the faith he so ardently advocated was cherished, deepened, and given equally vital and noble expression by later Israelites.

✤ 8 ✤

THE KINGDOM DISRUPTED

They made kings, but not through me . . .
Hos. 8:4

Our primary sources of information about the kingdoms of Israel and Judah are the books of Kings, which form the finale of the Deuteronomic history from the covenant at Horeb to the fall of Jerusalem in 587 B.C. The same history is paralleled in the books of Chronicles but in the monarchy the Chronicler follows the plan of Kings, quoting liberal extracts therefrom, and offering only a minimum of additional trustworthy data. The reigns of some of the eighth-, seventh-, and sixth-century kings are generously documented by the prophetic books. The Assyrian and Neo-Babylonian records bear vitally upon the history of the monarchy at key points. In fact Jehu, Hezekiah, and Jehoiachin are specifically named in foreign sources.

THE D THEOLOGY OF THE MONARCHY

As with the Deuteronomic history in general, Kings are uneven in bulk and value. The episodes of Judges were fitted into a framework that lent to the finished history a distinctive point of view calculated to impress upon the reader the dangers of apostasy and the glories of faithfulness to Yahweh. Kings also have a scaffolding. Each of the kings of the north (Israel) is introduced with a notice of the date of accession expressed in relation to the year of the contemporary southern king, a statement of length of reign, and a judgment upon the king passed from the standard of seventh-century religion. For the rulers of the south (Judah) these minimal details are supplemented by the age of the monarch at his accession and the name of the queen mother. Jeroboam II of Israel and Hezekiah of Judah will serve to illustrate the introductory formulas:

> In the fifteenth year of Amaziah the son of Joash, king of Judah, Jeroboam the son of Joash, king of Israel, began to reign in Samaria, and he reigned forty-one years. And he did what was evil in the sight of Yahweh; he did not depart from all the sins of Jeroboam the son of Nebat, which he made Israel to sin (II Kings 14:23–24).

> In the third year of Hoshea son of Elah, king of Israel, Hezekiah the son of Ahaz, king of Judah, began to reign. He was twenty-five years old when he began to reign, and he reigned twenty-nine years in Jerusalem. His mother's name was Abi the daughter of Zechariah. And he did what was right in the eyes of Yahweh, according to all that David his father had done (II Kings 18:1–3).

In the pre-Roman history of antiquity there was no absolute chronology. The Christian system of dating before and after the birth of Jesus Christ was developed by Dionysius Exiguus in the sixth century. Judaism had no generally agreed-upon absolute chronology until the middle ages, when the supposed date of creation became the common era (the year one being equivalent to 3760 B.C.). Even when the sequence and length of Egyptian and Mesopotamian reigns could be reconstructed, there was no fixed beginning date. Years were sometimes remembered by natural happenings such as earthquakes or eclipses. More often the basis of dating was memorable events such as military campaigns, the siege and fall of cities, the accession and death of kings, and building operations. In Assyria each year was designated by the name of some official (an eponym), as if Americans should call a year by the incumbent Secretary of State or Chief Justice of the Supreme Court.

The means for translating the ancient chronological systems into our terms was provided by mention of an eclipse that could be dated in 763 B.C. Since Assyrian history impinges on Hebrew affairs repeatedly, particularly with the Battle of Qarqar in 853 B.C., a correlation was found for dating the Israelite and Judean monarchies. The biblical data are very carefully worked out by a scheme of synchronization, the kings of the south and north being constantly related to one another. In practice this means that the order of treatment of the kings is a rather confusing one, without consideration of organic development. The account switches back and forth from one kingdom to the other in this fashion: after a king's reign is recounted, all rulers in the other state who came to power before his death are then taken up. As soon as a king is reached whose death was later than the last figure treated in the other kingdom, the story reverts to the next monarch of the original state. To illustrate, the north's Jeroboam (922–901) gives way to the south's Rehoboam (922–915), Abijah (915–913), and Asa (913–873). Since Asa came to the throne before Jeroboam's demise but ruled long afterward, the narrative turns to Israel with the rules of Nadab (901–900), Baasha (900–877), Elah (877–876), Zimri (876), Omri (876–869), and Ahab (869–850), before taking up Jehoshaphat of Judah (the biblical dating of his accession in "the fourth year of Ahab" is generally regarded as erroneous; his actual dates were 873–849).

This rather ingenious technique was used in synchronizing Assyrian and Babylonian king lists, but the biblical system is marred by corruptions in the text and inaccuracies in the computation of figures. A further problem is our ignorance of the methods for reckoning coregencies and the first year of a monarch's rule (was the first year of a king the year in which he ascended the throne or the first *full* year of office?) In spite of the difficulties the Deuteronomist carried through the chosen chronological device with regularity and the content of the historical survey is a monumental achievement in a world accustomed only to chronicles, annals, and royal panegyrics.

The standards of judgment applied to the kings are annoyingly simple and one-sided. Where we might expect political, social, and economic analysis there are only theological verdicts. Touchstone of the evaluation is the dogma of the centralization of worship at Jerusalem which the D historians applied from the date of the temple's building. This meant that Jeroboam's break with Solomon could only be interpreted by them as apostasy. Jeroboam son of Nebat is the archsinner of Israel. Correspondingly, David, who made Jerusalem central and longed to build the temple, is the chief saint. The regular stereotype for describing the reprobation of the northern leaders is: "He walked in (all) the way of Jeroboam (the son of Nebat) and in his sin(s) which he made Israel to sin." Since none of the northern kings encouraged worship at the Judean capital, it is not surprising that not a single Israelite king is wholeheartedly praised by the D historians. Jehu received favor because he purged Israel of the baalistic Omri dynasty but "Jehu did not turn aside from the sins of Jeroboam the son of Nebat, which he made Israel to sin, the golden calves that were in Bethel, and in Dan" (II Kings 10:29). The lukewarm approval of Jehu concludes with the promise that his dynasty will rule for four generations, longer than that of any other Israelite monarch—but not perpetually like the Davidic dynasty.

The model for the south is David, whose role as the ideal king is praised with as much fervor as the renegade action of Jeroboam is denounced. But very few southern kings measure up to the standards of David. Only Asa, Hezekiah, and Josiah are praised for their loyalty to Yahweh. While we may be rather chary of such sweeping religious dispositions of history, the D account is more than a chauvinistic propaganda sheet of the Judean court. The record of Judah is almost as disappointing as that of Israel, for it too has been a history of apostasy. In this alone the larger perspective of D becomes apparent. He shows that the Canaanite high places continued to be patronized even by the Judeans and that the syncretistic worship in Jerusalem under Manasseh became so alluring that Yahwism was mortally threatened. In other words, for D the religion of Israel is not simply a matter of *place* of worship—vital as that is—but of *quality* of worship and morality. When the historians failed to see the fruits of Yahwism they were vocally critical not only of the more remote kingdom but of their own land.

The conclusion to each of the regnal summaries underscores the peculiar aim of the Deuteronomist's "history." In addition to a notice of the death and burial of the king and the accession of his son or usurper, the summation records the source of information. It is one of the earliest instances of documentary historiography. A résumé for a king from each of the kingdoms will clarify the form:

> Now the rest of the acts of Jeroboam, and all that he did, and his might, how he fought, and how he recovered for Israel Damascus and Hamath, which had belonged to Judah, are they not written in the Book of the Chronicles of the Kings of Israel? And Jeroboam slept with his fathers, the kings of Israel, and Zechariah his son reigned in his stead (II Kings 14:28–29).

> The rest of the deeds of Hezekiah, and all his might, and how he made the pool and the conduit and brought water into the city, are they not written in the Book of the Chronicles of the Kings of Judah? And Hezekiah slept with his fathers; and Manasseh his son reigned in his stead (II Kings 20:20–21).

Aside from portions quoted or paraphrased in Kings, we know nothing of these Chronicles of the Kings of Israel and Judah. (They are not the much later biblical books of Chronicles.) The repeated reference to these sources means that the Deuteronomic writers were not intending to fill a gap in the readers' knowledge, in any factual or purely informative sense. They knew that accounts of the fundamental information already existed, and the wise reader either had already consulted them (note the repeated rhetorical question: "As for the rest of the deeds . . . are they not written?") or else would be gently prodded into doing so after he had read about the Chronicles 37 times!

In this context the religious and moral bias of the history is more understandable. It is similar to studies from some special point of view produced by men in public office, educators, news commentators, or critical analysts. They focus upon some movement or period in history that they have neither the time nor inclination to repeat in detail, but to which they bend all their energies in highlighting an aspect: the tracing of a political notion such as the rise of constitutionalism, or in urging a case: the call to the defense of civil liberties or the cessation of the nuclear arms race. We get nowhere by railing at them for not providing historical compendia, which they and we know already exist aplenty. The only question is: How adequate an analysis have they given and how worthy is their plea? Do they distort the history or represent it with general fidelity?

So too the Deuteronomic historian is a philosopher or theologian of history arguing his case that infidelity to the God Yahweh has destroyed both states, Israel and Judah. In his view Israel failed in her outer history because she betrayed the terms of her inner history, her reason for being: her covenant with God. It is a grandiose conception, the truth of which, like all great convictions, is contestable. It is a conception not necessarily inconsistent with the premises of political, social, and economic history, all of which have their just claims upon the story of Israel. Oversimplified though it certainly is —and what philosophy of history is not?—this Deuteronomic theology of the covenant is not unconversant with the "facts." It makes clear the rationale by which Yahweh worshipers after the fall of the state retained their faith and read the sad story of their past.[1]

[1] Although a first edition of Kings probably was produced before 587, the present form of the books is exilic; see, e.g., Norman Snaith, *Introduction to the First and Second Books of Kings* (IB, vol. 3), Abingdon, 1954, pp. 10–12.

There may be a large measure of naïveté in the moral portraiture, but the observations are far from puerile, being strikingly broad and incisive, made possible only against the backdrop of a maturing prophetic witness.

THE RIVAL KINGDOMS, 922–800 B.C.

The divided monarchy in the ninth century is largely a story of its northern branch. Israel was the stronger of the two kingdoms, both in population and economic resources. The initial growth of Israel in the wake of the cultural and economic initiative of the united monarchy was much more rapid than that of Judah. The more fertile lands fell to the northern state and the trading potential was vaster since the control of the Plain of Esdraelon meant that the international highway was in Israelite hands. Correspondingly Judah was more isolated in the highlands and needed to expand all the way to the Mediterranean or far into Trans-Jordan in order to dominate trade. Urbanization of the populace was more rapid in Israel and the growth of a wealthy class, with consequent abuses, was greatly accelerated over the more pedestrian pace of the south.

By the middle of the century a strong dynasty ruled in the north, the Omrids, who were involved in extensive foreign relations by compact with Phoenicia and by war with Damascus. The Omrids made one of the key contributions to an alliance that momentarily checked the westward advance of Assyria. During the same century Judah was quiescent; her connections with the other powers were generally as victim or suppliant, as when Pharaoh Shishak raided Jerusalem and other Palestinian cities, including some in Israel, during Rehoboam's reign, and when Asa appealed to Damascus for aid against Israel. For the last half of the century Judah was merely the unwilling ally of the Omrids.

Jeroboam's vigorous establishment of Israel as an independent state was challenged by the campaign of Shishak, who intended to revive the old Asiatic Empire of Egypt. He crippled the war potential of south and north so that neither held a distinct advantage. Postponement of southern recapture of Israel naturally worked to the advantage of the secession policy of the north. While the two kingdoms skirmished often over the frontier, and the north at one point nearly eliminated the Davidic dynasty, the south never again had the strength to challenge Israel. Jeroboam shifted his capital from Shechem to Tirzah. His weaker son was assassinated and the usurper's son met the same

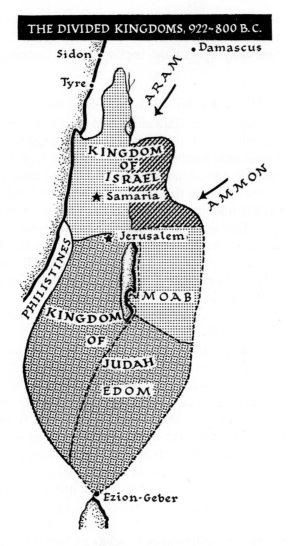

THE DIVIDED KINGDOMS, 922~800 B.C.

Sidon •
• Damascus

Tyre •

ARAM

KINGDOM
OF
ISRAEL

★ Samaria

AMMON

★ Jerusalem

PHILISTINES

MOAB

KINGDOM
OF
JUDAH

EDOM

• Ezion-Geber

REVOLTED FROM JUDAH
AFTER 850 B.C.
REVOLTED FROM ISRAEL
AFTER 850 B.C.
TRANS-JORDAN TERRITORY
LOST TO ARAM AND AMMON
AFTER 838 B.C.

fate. During one of the border struggles, Asa of Judah paid Damascus to relieve his situation by bringing pressure to bear on Israel; Damascus gladly obliged. This was the beginning of the long and enervating wars between Aram (Damascus) and Israel that were a constant drain upon the human and material resources of the north. It was also typical of the political enmity between Israel and Judah that they did not hesitate to appeal to outsiders in their internecine rivalry.

While for the first fifty years of the schism the two kingdoms were roughly balanced in power, the north forged rapidly ahead under Omri, who founded the virile dynasty that earned for Israel the Assyrian name, "House of Omri." He is also termed "David of the North," principally because he forged a political unity out of the northern tribes and founded a new capital at Samaria. With its impregnable position, double wall, and imposing architecture, Samaria was indeed a worthy northern counterpart to Jerusalem. The capital lay west of the divide at the head of a valley descending toward the coastal plains; its position signalized Omri's determination to place Israel in the commercial forefront of the Syro-Palestinian states. Trans-Jordan territory lost to Aram and Moab was regained. (One of the first moves of any strong preëxilic ruler, whether of Israel or Judah, was to assert sovereignty over the regions beyond the Jordan and to exact tribute from the trade routes.) Omri's affinities with David are further evidenced by his diplomatic ties with Phoenicia. An alliance with Ethbaal ("man of Baal"?) was sealed by the fateful marriage of Omri's son, Ahab, to the Tyrian princess, Jezebel. This introduced into Israel Baal Melkart, patron deity of Tyre; the new queen wasted no time in showing herself a zealous devotee of the god.

Under Omri the situation in the north had become disturbingly like that under Solomon. A strong leader was impressing his will upon the people, pushing the small state to its economic limits and securing friends through alliance or vassals through conquest. With the centralization of power went a distressing foreign religious factor, now even more perilous than the syncretism of Solomon. Jezebel, not merely an ardent member of the Melkart cult, was possessed of a fanatical exclusive claim for her deity. There was room for only one state cult. Whether this was the usual Phoenician attitude or a personal trait of the queen is not easily judged. But we can judge the effect of her enormous energy in furthering the cause of her god. When such enthusiastic Baalism met equally enthusiastic Yahwism a tremendous conflict was precipitated. This mortal struggle is recounted in the Elijah stories. The Yahwism of Elijah was as thoroughly nationalistic as Jezebel's Baalism; the religion of the state of Israel was the religion of Yahweh, and Israel as a people must choose him or reject him. There was no "halting between two opinions." Presumably Ahab and the courtiers would rather have patronized both cults, but the tempera-

The hill of Samaria. The palace of Omri and Ahab stood on the summit. The outermost of three walls encircled the base of the hill.

ments of Jezebel and Elijah made such "peaceful coexistence" unthinkable.

Ahab is to this day overshadowed by his more illustrious and diabolical wife, but in his own right he was a leader worthy of his father's mantle. His crowning achievement was participation in a coalition of states that successfully checked the Assyrian penetration of Syria. With the accessions of Ashurnasirpal II (883–859) and Shalmaneser III (858–824) to the throne of Assyria, the Syro-Palestinian "Era of the Little People" rapidly drew toward a close. The titan of the Tigris, long the major power of Mesopotamia, was now reasserting her authority over the international corridor. Suddenly shaken by the threat to their independence, several of the small kingdoms joined forces: primarily Israel, Damascus, and Hamath. At Qarqar on the Orontes the battle was joined. The Assyrian report is the only one we have and, as usual, it claims victory; but Shalmaneser's numerical claims—fourteen thousand slain—are modest compared to the usual boasting. Furthermore, Shalmaneser failed to follow up his "victory." For a decade or so the coalition managed to hang together whenever Assyria appeared, although this did not keep the members, especially Israel and Damascus, from fighting among themselves whenever the Assyrians did not have an army in the field. Indicative of the commanding position of Israel among the smaller states is the fact that Ahab provided two thousand chariots for the Battle of Qarqar, eight hundred more than Hadadezer of Damascus and nearly three times as many as Hamath.

An uneasy alliance with Judah was arranged and sealed by the marriage of Jehoshaphat's son Jehoram to Ahab's daughter Athaliah, who shared the implacable will and adept wiles of her mother. Jehoshaphat, obviously the weaker member of the pact, was an unwilling ally in the wars against Damascus. In one of these battles Ahab perished. Meanwhile Moab had been lost; the event, in itself no more important than other such revolts, has been memorialized in the famous Moabite Stone that gives the version of Mesha the Moabite king.[3] The ancient interpenetration of religion and politics is blandly assumed. In Mesha's henotheistic understanding, Yahweh holds the same position in Israel as Chemosh in Moab. He does not doubt the reality of either deity; the power of each is shown by the test of arms. Many of the presuppositions of the older Yahwism of Israel are illuminated by the parallel assumptions of the Moabites. We see that holy war in the Deuteronomic sense was not a novel idea and we do not need to find some theological excuse for a practice that was well attested and thoroughly recognized in that day. With necessary change of names, the Moabite inscription reads like a leaf out of Joshua, Judges, or Samuel. Insofar as the early religion of Israel was nationalistic Yahwism, its fundamental similarity with surrounding religions cannot be denied. The wonder of that early faith is that it had

[2] See Appendix 10, pp. 591–592.
[3] See Appendix 8, pp. 590–591.

the potency to transcend itself and to correct the nationalistic henotheism with self-critical insight, and to define the scope of the divine nature and human response to it in ever larger and more exacting terms.

The Moabite Stone is a 3-foot high stele recounting the victory of Mesha over Ahab.

The grim battle between Baalism and Yahwism came to its head with the Yahwists victorious. In a bloody purge, Jezebel and all the followers of Melkart were liquidated by Jehu, the hand-picked instrument of Elisha, who was himself successor to Elijah. Jehu was a fanatical Yahwist, less interested in enforcing the social equalitarian terms of the faith than he was in exterminating Baalism. Among those who fell in his *coup d'état* was Ahaziah, Judean king and son of Athaliah. The horrible bloodletting by which Jehu swept into power was never forgotten. For some it was not a glorious triumph but a heavy burden on the conscience, and a later prophet insisted that because of this violence the dynasty of Jehu and the state of Israel would be cut off (Hos. 1:4). One measure of the growth of Israel's insight is that the acts approved and instigated by earlier prophets were condemned by later ones.

Jehu's foreign relations were a dismal failure. He had doomed any positive developments by alienating Phoenicia and Judah with his murders of Jezebel and Ahaziah. Trans-Jordan was surrendered to Aram and in 841 Jehu was one of the statesmen who paid tribute to Shalmaneser III. He was the first and only Hebrew king represented in Near Eastern art. His prostrate figure appears on the memorial stele known as the Black Obelisk of Shalmaneser.[4] The Syrian coalition was not resolute enough to repeat the joint action at Qarqar.

[4] See Appendix 10, p. 592.

Jezebel wreaked posthumous revenge on Yahwism in the person of her daughter Athaliah, who led an anti-Yahwistic purge in Judah. But for the pious priest Jehoiada who saved the infant Joash, the proud dynasty of the son of Jesse would have been obliterated. Ruthlessly successful for a season, the tide turned against Athaliah and at the instant of her assassination the rightful heir to the throne was proclaimed king. Joash, a lad of seven at his accession, had a long and seemingly effective reign. He is remembered by the D writer for his restitution of the Jerusalem temple. In truth, however, the two kingdoms were weaker in the last third of the ninth century than at any time since the schism. Under Jehoahaz, Jehu's son, Israel was a virtual vassal of Aram. Joash of Judah was likewise subject to Damascus, averting siege or pillage only by paying a heavy tribute. With the passing of Shalmaneser III the kingdoms of the Syro-Palestinian corridor earned a reprieve. Assyrian advance westward was abruptly halted for the following kings were less forceful men who had their hands full with disorders at home.

The net impression of the ninth-century monarchies is that, in spite of promising periods under Asa in the south and Omri–Ahab in the north, the schism had led to the political depletion of the Hebrew people. Still, it is senseless to overplay the significance of the parting of the ways between north and south. Even with all the tribes united, it

The Black Obelisk of Shalmaneser III. Jehu appears in the second panel. Approximate height is 7 feet.

would have taken an uncommonly able succession of leaders to have built up a kingdom with any commanding political power. From the perspective of that period of history, the breach of Israel and Judah was just another instance of the fiercely independent spirit and internecine rivalry of the small Syro-Palestinian states. They could cooperate briefly in alliance but never consistently and they would turn upon one another whenever some advantage seemed immediately attainable. The kings in any of these lands who could see beyond the opportunistic present were rare indeed. As in all periods of human history, political vision was at a premium. It does not appear as any-

The Jehu panel from the Black Obelisk. Two Assyrian officers stand behind the Israelite king who is prostrate before Shalmaneser.

thing more than idle theorizing to conceive a Hebrew nation of political magnitude; should such have arisen and grasped control of the Crescent it might have been at the cost of religious distinction. That nomadic Yahwism could accommodate itself to political expediency was grimly apparent in the revolt of Jehu. The heights of Israelite faith were yet to be reached in the prophets, and they often denounced a political power that had to be asserted at such cost to the covenant obligations. Realistically appraised, the divided monarchy went in the only possible direction: downward.

THE ELOHIST

J and E are the twins among the Pentateuchal sources, although far from identical. When all that is typical of the Yahwist is isolated, there remains a stratum of traditions that cannot be identified as the later sources D and P. Biblical scholars have called this the work of the Elohist, owing to the writer's habit of using the divine name Elohim prior to the revelation of Yahweh to Moses. E also conveniently represents the provenance of the source, Ephraim. As chief tribe of the north Ephraim was the poetical equivalent of the political entity, Israel.

Several features of the E material argue for a northern origin. The Abraham-Lot cycle of stories centering at Hebron and the Cities of the Plain is omitted; the key cities and locales are northern, with particular attention to Bethel and Shechem (Gen. 28:17; 31:13; 33:19–20). Joseph, progenitor of the tribes Ephraim and Manasseh, and his mother Rachel, are given a central place. The polemic against calf worship in Exodus 32 may reflect firsthand and unfavorable reaction to the golden bull cult at Dan and Bethel. If the Elohist continues into Joshua, the prominence of the Ephraimite Joshua also supports the northern origin. The name Horeb for the holy mountain is also found in the northern stories about Elijah. Some scholars feel that the E traditions were deliberately circulated as a refutation of the Judean ideology of the Davidic dynasty and temple. The oral traditions of the Hebrews had been circulating among the tribes and under the united monarchy were given voice by the southern Yahwist. After the disruption, a northern version was compiled to offset the southern.

The E traditions seem less amenable to monarchy than the J account. This less-than-enthusiastic attitude toward royalty probably derived from the bitter experience with Solomon and the realization that the new line of kings in the north was little better. The baalistic reign of Ahab may have led to the final disillusion. The Elohist was probably a sympathizer with the Elijah revolution, but he seems to have been a more perceptive and far-ranging thinker on religious matters. He did not find the golden bull cult of Dan and Bethel a solution to the religious waywardness of the time. He was thus the first northerner to unmask the dangers of idolatry in the name of Yahwism and to begin, with Elijah, to criticize the excesses of monarchy. Yet he was no friend of the south, for he believed that the way to renewal of faith in Yahweh was not through submission to Jerusalem and the line of David but through the recovery of covenant theology springing directly from the faith of Moses. Like the Yahwist, the Elohist was a creative mind who used the traditional stories to set forth a point of view.

The present state of the E source is much more fragmentary than

J. The probable reason for this is that the editors of the Pentateuch were more generous in their inclusion of the southern J and P than of the northern E. While all the strata have been pared down to fit the present Pentateuchal scheme, the most truncated is E. It does not begin before the story of Abraham in Genesis 15 and thus lacks the world-wide setting of J. At only two points is its account fuller than the corresponding sections of the Yahwist, namely, in the Joseph cycle and in the covenant of the Exodus tribes. In fact so skimpy is the E narrative at times that some critics have questioned whether an independent source E ever existed; rather they regard it as a series of disconnected supplements to the J document. This notion has found no wide support; all the critical Introductions to the Old Testament in recent years continue to adhere to E as a distinct source with a history of its own and a definite tendency, in spite of its curtailment by editors. The surviving contents of the Elohist's work are outlined through the book of Exodus. The separation of JE in Numbers is very difficult (see J analysis).

1. *The Traditions of the Fathers: Genesis 12–50*

Abraham's Night Vision	15:1–21 (mixed with J)
Abraham in Gerar	20:1–17
The Expulsion of Hagar and Ishmael	21:6–21
Abraham's Covenant with Abimelech	21:22–32,34
God Tests Abraham's Faith	22:1–14,19
Jacob's Vision and Vow at Bethel	28:11–12,17–18,20–22
Jacob Takes Leah and Rachel as Wives, the Birth of Their Sons	29:1,15–23,25–28,30 30:1–3,6,8,17–23
Jacob's Flight and Covenant with Laban	31:2,4–45,47,51; 32:1
Gifts for Esau	32:13–21,23
Purchase of Shechem	33:19–20
Return to Bethel and Birth of Benjamin	35:1–8,16–20
Joseph Left in a Pit by his Brothers	37:1–11,19–20,22–24,28a, 29–30,36
Joseph Interprets the Officials' Dreams	40:1–23
Joseph Interprets Pharaoh's Dream	41:1–36
Joseph as Administrator	41:37–45,47–57
Joseph's Brothers Seek Grain in Egypt	42:1–37
Joseph Reveals Himself, Reunion with Jacob	45:1–46:5
Jacob Blesses Ephraim and Manasseh	48:1–2,8–22
Joseph Reiterates his Forgiveness	50:15–22
Death and Mummification of Joseph	50:23–26

2. *The Traditions of Bondage and Exodus: Exodus 1–15*

Birth of Moses and Introduction to Court	1:15–2:10
Moses Kills an Egyptian	2:11–14
"I AM" Calls Moses to Deliver Israel	3:1,4,6,9–15,19–22
Moses Enlists Aid of Jethro and Aaron	4:17–18,21,27–28
Pharaoh Refuses to Free Hebrews	5:1–2,4
The Plagues	
Nile Turned to Blood	7:15b,17,20b (. . . he lifted)
Hail	9:22–25 (except for 23b and 25b which are J),35
Locusts	10:12–13a,14a,20
Darkness	10:21–23,27
The "Expulsion" from Egypt	11:1–3; 12:31–39,42a; 13:17–19
The Songs of Moses and Miriam	15:1–18,20–21

3. *The Traditions of the Wilderness Wanderings (Horeb-Kadesh): Exodus 17–Numbers 34*

Water from the Rock at Horeb	17:3–6
Israel Wars with Amalek	17:8–16
Moses Reunited with Jethro, the Covenant Meal	18:1–27
Israel Consecrated for the Covenant	19:2b–3a (from "and there Israel encamped" through "went up to God"), 10–11a,14–17,19
Ethical Decalogue	20:1–20
The Covenant Code (Canaanite Civil Code)	20:23–23:19
Covenant Sealed with Blood Ceremony	24:3–8
Moses Receives the Tables of Stone	24:12–14,18b; 31:18b (the tables of stone . . .)
The Golden Calf	32:1–8,15–24,35
The People Discard their Amulets	33:4–6
Moses and the Tent of Meeting	33:7–11

Taken as a whole the Elohist does not display so spontaneous and brilliant a style as the Yahwist, but his standards are high enough; occasionally, as in the story of the sacrifice of Isaac, his touch is as deft as any in Hebrew prose. One notes a tendency toward verbosity in the speeches and the descriptions are somewhat more prolix and less graphic than in J. The great beauty and vividness of the oral tradition has assured that both writers would be agile and pungent in expression, but the independence of the two as writers asserts itself in the stylistic edge that the Yahwist shows over the Elohist. Such a judgment must be made, of course, with the full realization that we cannot determine the extent to which editors have altered the original accounts; some stylistic defacing has occurred (as when sentences or phrases have been torn out of their original setting and given a context from one of the other sources), but the crisp prose of JE argues that the literary garbling of the sources has been kept to a minimum.

In style and vocabulary E has identifying traits sharply at variance with J: Amorites for the inhabitants of Canaan (Canaanites in J); Jacob for the third patriarch (Israel in J); Horeb for the holy mountain (Sinai in J); Jethro for Moses' father-in-law (Hobab or Reuel in J); *'amah* for maidservant (*shiphhah* in J); the temporal use of "after these things" in narration, i.e., "after the aforementioned" (instrumental in J, "after this manner"). "The River" designates the Euphrates; *baal* is used of man as "master" or "husband"; the common Hebrew verb "to give" is frequently used with the special sense of "to allow, give leave" (KJV "to suffer"). Stylistically the Elohist has a fondness for repetition, especially in direct address: "Abraham, Abraham!" (Gen. 22:11) and "Moses, Moses!" (Exod. 3:4). "Here am I!" is a favored expression on the lips of one replying to his divine or human superior.

The slackening of literary accomplishment is accompanied by an increase of moral and religious sophistication. The moral imperfections of the patriarchs, which J did not blush to tell, are glossed over or explained. Abraham's lie is mitigated by the notation that Sarah was after all his half-sister, a permissible kinship marriage. The callous expulsion of Hagar from Abraham's household is explained as a direct divine command. Jacob's theft of Laban's flocks is attributed to the blessing of God; E rather innocently misses the mutual skulduggery of uncle and nephew. The cruder anthropomorphisms of the Yahwist are omitted and in their place the Elohist customarily supplies dream visions or angels as the media of revelation. Jacob's vision at Bethel happily combines a dream with heavenly messengers. Not only to Israelites, but to Egyptians as well, Elohim discloses his will and reveals the future in dreams. The gift of interpretation is confined, however, to the Hebrew Joseph. The Elohist has the effect of removing God from a too familiar intimacy with man, but at the same time such obliqueness deprives his stories of some of the imaginative and pictorial power of the J version.

The ritual interest is more pronounced in E than in J. In the latter the various altars raised at the sanctuaries are memorial in nature and are never described as places of sacrifice, but in E they are frankly used for offerings. Among the abundant instances of ritual are the call of Abraham to sacrifice his son, Jacob pouring oil on the stone pillar at Bethel, his promise of a tenth to God, Moses' consecration of the people at Horeb by the washing of garments and abstinence from sexual intercourse, the sealing of the covenant with blood, and the making of the golden calf. Pfeiffer believes that the Elohist was a priest at the Bethel temple.[5] Yet the E writer draws a distinction between past and present ritual. He acknowledges the polytheism of the forefathers: Rachel's household gods are buried by Jacob under the oak at Shechem (Gen. 31:19,33–34; 35:4), and in his farewell speech Joshua reminds the covenanting tribes of their ancestral paganism, "Your fathers lived of old beyond the Euphrates, Terah, the father of Abraham and of Nahor; and they served other gods . . . put away the gods which your fathers served beyond the River, and in Egypt, and serve Yahweh" (Josh. 24:2,14b).

In the Mosaic age, Aaron is prominent as colaborer with Moses, and the rod wielded by Moses is the agent in producing the plagues instead of the word of Moses (as in J) or the rod brandished by Aaron (as in P). The rod parts the waters at the Sea, induces water from a rock, and achieves victory over the Amalekites. Only shreds of the E account of the plagues survive, but it is to E that we owe the preservation of the shorter and longer versions of the song of victory on the seashore (Exod. 15). The Covenant Code, which gives the earliest body of Hebrew law, is presented as the basis of the covenant (20:23–23:19); it is the keeping of these "ordinances" to which Israel agrees in the covenant ceremony (21:1 cf. 24:3). In preparation Moses is said to have written the words of Yahweh in "the book of the covenant" (24:4–6), which appears also to have included the "words" of the Ethical Decalogue (20:1 cf. 24:3). This book is to be distinguished from the "two tables of stone" inscribed by God with "the law and commandment" (24:12). In the J source the

[5] R. H. Pfeiffer, *Introduction to the Old Testament*, Harper, 1941, p. 173.

Ritual Decalogue of Exodus 34 is written down by Moses on a second set of tablets, after the first were smashed by the irate leader when he saw the golden calf (34:27–28). The P source speaks of the "tables of the testimony . . . written with the finger of God" (31:18). Thus the traditions about the covenant terms and their written form are very poorly related to one another. It may be that the E Decalogue takes us closest to the words of Moses but even that is a moot point.

The classical Documentary Hypothesis regarded E as later than J, by as much as a century. Among the factors are the refinement of moral and theological attitudes; the influence of the prophetic movement on the narration of early events (Abraham is called "prophet" and Miriam "prophetess"); the admonitions to put away foreign gods, presumed to have as background the idolatries common in the reigns of Solomon, Omri, and Ahab; the jaundiced view of a total conquest (assuming the Joshua account to be mainly E) which men living prior to the united monarchy could not have held. These are admittedly precarious criteria. Noth argues, for example, that E's formulation of the basic oral tradition has features often more primitive than J,[6] and Pfeiffer singles out a number of details more accurately transmitted in E than in the older Pentateuchal source (e.g., E correctly identifies Abimelech as king of Gerar and not of the Philistines, a J anachronism).[7]

All in all, the strongest argument for the priority of J is the assumption that no E tradition would have been written down had the monarchy remained united; the political disruption was the *sine qua non* for a parallel written epic of Israel's beginnings. Also the generally more antiquarian spirit of J is unmistakable. Both J and E, however, embrace early and late features; considering the nature of oral tradition, neither can be precisely dated. Since they reflect two regional treatments of the traditions, the presence of varying reliability, abundance or lack of anthropomorphisms and ethical concern, etc., may simply reflect the group interests and not constitute grounds for chronological judgments. There is much truth to the exaggerated statement of Bentzen that "the sources of the Pentateuch are as much parallel as they are successive."[8]

[6] Martin Noth, *Ueberlieferungsgeschichte des Pentateuchs,* Kohlhammer, 1948, pp. 248 f.

[7] Pfeiffer, *op. cit.,* p. 171.

[8] Aage Bentzen, *Introduction to the Old Testament,* Gad, rev. ed., 1952, vol. 2, p. 64.

The didactic purpose of E is salient; the writer tends to draw morals and to exhort copiously. There is more explicit religious teaching and less inclination to let the narrative have the upper hand. But his "lessons" are not usually obnoxious nor disruptive of the continuity of the story, for often he skillfully introduces his insights by putting them on the lips of the chief participants. So Joseph discloses his deep awareness of the purposes of Yahweh that have shaped the course of his life, when at the reunion with his brothers he says to them, "God sent me before you to preserve for you a remnant on earth, and to keep alive for you many survivors" (Gen. 45:7), and later he quiets their fears by insisting, "As for you, you meant evil against me; but God meant it for good, to bring it about that many people should be kept alive, as they are today" (Gen. 50:20). Yahweh himself offers the only explanation of the divine name found in the Old Testament, the cryptic "I AM WHO I AM" (Exod. 3:14).

Most impressive of all the Elohist's narratives is the story of the barely averted sacrifice of Isaac by his father Abraham. It is a literary masterpiece, ironic in its disparity between intensity of emotion and paucity of words. There is no analysis of the psychological states of father and son, but only the agonizing pathos inferred in the terse conversation between them. In monumental starkness, the form perfectly masters and expresses the spirit. Equally it is a religious highpoint. Often readers have been repulsed by the crudity of the concept of human sacrifice. A little knowledge of Canaanite practice shows that it was not a rare occurrence for children to be sacrificed. Any devout soul in that time could have understood the divine will as requiring of him the sacrifice of his dearest possession. The outcome of the story gives a most emphatic rejection of child sacrifice while it respects and retains the intention of sacrifice: the giving of everything to God. Elohim accepts the intention in place of the act.

The story is redolent with the life of faith and devotion, with the conflict of interests inherent in two great loves, the most powerful that move the human race: love of family and love of God. It is not unduly subjective to see in this tale a parable of God's continual testing of his people to discover if they will live by faith. There is a terrifying irrevocability about the binding of the boy to the altar; Abraham has chosen his course, bitter as it is, and he will not renege. Soren Kierkegaard, the nineteenth-century philosopher of religion and critic of the institutional church, built a treatise around this biblical event as the quintessence of the radical meaning of faith. When the value of everything we have treasured is questioned and in jeopardy, only then does religion take on its true depth. It is a commitment against insuperable odds and in the spiritual life the rewards are in proportion to faith, for "only he who draws the knife gets Isaac."[9] While Kierkegaard obviously ranges far beyond the original story and does not pretend that Genesis 22 is a prooftext for his views, there has seldom been a more acute interpreter of the root idea of the Hebrew narrator.

THE ORIGINS OF HEBREW PROPHECY

In the narratives of Kings a large section is devoted to the prophets Elijah, Micaiah ben Imlah, Elisha, and anonymous "men of God." They are not the first mentioned prophets in the Hebrew Bible. There are a few Pentateuchal references to prophetic personalities, such as Abraham (Gen. 20:7) and Miriam (Exod. 15:20). Moses is represented as exceeding the prophets in his direct rapport with Yahweh (Num. 12:6–8). These passages are generally regarded as E source and reflect ideas about prophecy current in Israel in the time of Elijah, rather than the views of the patriarchal and Mosaic eras. Especially characteristic is the connection drawn between prophecy and dream communications. Moses is distinguished because he spoke with Yahweh "face to face." It is doubtful that later prophets such as Jeremiah would have accepted this distinction.

One particularly valuable Pentateuchal commentary on prophecy is found in the Balaam Oracles of Numbers 22–24. To be sure the present form, an interweaving of J and E, presents a matured teaching of the providence of God in overruling men's devices. Balaam is the prototype of the later prophets in that he speaks what is true and not what is popular or lucrative. But the description of the seer Balaam is in the manner of a primitive enthusiast. Balaam, being a professionalist, is paid for his divination (22:7). He is susceptible to direction by omens (24:1), and his directives come ordinarily in the trance state (24:3–4). His word is received as a thing of unalterable power (22:6). The priestly element is apparent in the offering of sacrifices in order to induce trance revelations (23:1–6).

That Balaam's traits were shared by Israelite prophets is proved by descriptions of "the sons of the prophets" as traveling guilds in the time of Samuel. We are on solid historical ground with this first lucid picture of the early Hebrew ecstatic (1 Sam. 10:5–13). "Prophesying"

[9] Soren Kierkegaard, *Fear and Trembling,* Doubleday, 1954, p. 38.

in Samuel means speaking ecstatically, engaging in wild dance. It does not seem to have had any necessary teaching aspect. The prophets roved in bands and were associated with the Canaanite high places. Their behavior was musically induced; when the seizure occurred the prophet was said to be "another man" or to possess "another heart." Raving and bodily agitation as the essence of prophetic activity are epitomized in the epithet for the prophet, "madman" (II Kings 9:11; Jer. 29:26). It was in the company of such prophets that Saul received the charismatic endowment to become a military deliverer. No doubt these "firebrands of war" (II Kings 2:12; 13:14) were of the same ilk as all the prophets before Amos, namely, ardent nationalists who advocated "holy war" in the name of Yahweh.

Among the court prophets of the united monarchy there was deviation from the earlier pattern in one significant feature: they were interpreters of the covenant standards of Israel. When Nathan brings David to boot for his callous murder of Uriah, we have in germ the great moral denunciations of Hebrew prophecy; but this element is not sustained, for the same Nathan appears as one of the advocates of Solomon in the son's schemes to succeed David. Ahijah the Shilonite embodies the protests of the people against Solomon when he promises Jeroboam a kingdom. During the united monarchy prophecy gained somewhat in critical power but its relation to political instrumentalities was still quite unreflective and naïve.

Prophetic inspiration was not uniquely Israelite. This is evident in the Old Testament itself. Witness Balaam and the 450 prophets of Baal and the 400 prophets of Asherah (I Kings 18:19). Additional glimpses of non-Israelite prophecy come from eighteenth-century Mari and eleventh-century Byblos. At Mari "a man of the god Dagan" delivers unsolicited oracles to the king; he is under the compulsion of a divine directive, "Go . . . thou shalt say, . . ." The contents of the few Mari oracles are cultic and political in that they instruct concerning building a sanctuary, making offerings to a dead king, or promise victory in battle. While the greatest achievements of Hebrew prophecy far exceed the Amorite institution at Mari, the formal parallels are striking. The Old Testament contains many such cultic and political imperatives in the name of prophecy.[10] The Egyptian story of Wen-Amon tells of a diplomatic mission to the Phoeni-

[10] Martin Noth, "History and the Word of God in the Old Testament," *Bulletin of the John Rylands Library*, 32 (1950), 194–206.

cian port of Byblos where the Pharaohs habitually obtained cedar for their large buildings and ceremonial sun barques. Pharaoh's emissary Wen-Amon is snubbed (indicative of the decline of Egyptian influence after 1200) and is about to return to his homeland when an unnamed Phoenician courtier is "seized by the god" and advises the king of Byblos to receive Wen-Amon.[11] It was in such a milieu two centuries later that the prophets of Baal Melkart won the devotion of the resourceful Jezebel.

A number of Egyptian models of prophecy have been proposed, but they are less apparent parallels than the Syrian and Babylonian examples just examined. We know of no prophets in Egypt. Some writings have a prophetic tone in that they sound a note of social protest. The fascinating story of *The Protests of the Eloquent Peasant* tells of a countryman, wronged by a social superior, who carries his case to the Chief Steward and though at first rebuffed persists in his demands until justice is granted him. The peasant is indeed eloquent; he becomes the sounding board for lofty ideals of the state's function to dispatch justice without respect of person.[12] The literary form of the prophetic books of Israel often follows the pattern of threat and promise, denunciations of the people giving way to pledges of a brighter day. This twofold structure of threat and promise has been found in several Egyptian court writings from the Old Kingdom. The aims of this Egyptian "prophecy," as of all non-Israelite examples, are pronouncedly political and dynastic. Hebrew prophecy transcended this simple identification of religion and politics, but in its origins the two were closely connected.

Every evidence at our disposal suggests that one of the borrowings of Israel from her Canaanite environment was the institution of prophecy, which had been ultimately derived from Babylonia. In its written form, Egyptian models probably played a part. The Egyptian influence came chiefly through Canaan and not during the sojourn in Egypt when the cultural contact of the overlords and subjects was inconsiderable.

THE PROPHETIC NARRATIVES OF KINGS

Among the sources of Kings were narratives about northern prophets vitally connected with the dynasties of Omri and Jehu. Possibly

[11] Pritchard, ANET, pp. 25–29.
[12] *Ibid.*, pp. 407–410.

these stories existed in separate cycles before their incorporation into Kings. We can make out roughly the lineaments of an *Elijah cycle* (I Kings 17–19, 21 and II Kings 1–2) and of an *Elisha cycle* (II Kings 2–9:3; 13:14–21). The suture between the two complexes of tradition is the story of Elijah's conferring of authority upon Elisha (II Kings 2:1–14), but Elisha already appears in the Elijah stories (I Kings 19:19–21). The Elijah legends are broken by the story of the siege of Samaria by Damascus (I Kings 20) and the tale of Micaiah ben Imlah (I Kings 22), while the Elisha legends are interrupted by the story of Jehu's purge (II Kings 9:4–10:35) and the accounts of Athaliah (II Kings 11) and Joash (II Kings 12).

These prophetic narratives may have been drawn from the Chronicles of Israel so often referred to in Kings, but it is more likely that they came from a separate source, possibly still in oral form when the D historian decided to use them. The point at which the prophetic narratives shade off into the more strictly political sources of Kings is hard to determine. The story of the siege of Samaria, for example, has no dominating prophet as its hero, but at least three anonymous prophets are central to the action and are closely involved in the final outcome. Then too the purge of Jehu might be read as a purely "secular" account, but it is instigated by Elisha and may have been an integral part of the Elisha cycle from the beginning. The prehistory of the D historian's sources was complex and there are not enough surviving clues to reconstruct it.

One thing that impresses the reader in the prophetic narratives is their indelibly graphic style. Here is legend in the grand manner, its epic proportions rendering the action bold, titanic, and portentous. Mendelssohn's oratorio *Elijah* capitalizes on the dramatic potentialities of the story. The narration of the Elijah stories, in particular, is unexcelled in Hebrew prose. A master storyteller has preserved the sense of elemental wonder evoked by the prophet among the populace loyal to Yahweh, also the supine fear that Jezebel struck in their hearts, and the rather pitiable spectacle of Ahab, not strong-willed enough to understand either his wife or his critic. The action moves swiftly with effective use of conversation and abrupt change of scene. All in all, the narratives provide an authentic picture of the Yahwistic folk religion of north Israel and of the leadership of the undaunted Yahweh-partisan Elijah and his disciple Elisha.

Elijah of Tishbe in Gilead is thrust into the narrative of Ahab's reign without mention of his parentage or prophetic calling. This fits his ethereal habit of appearing and disappearing without warning. His impulsive moves, propelled by the word, the Spirit, the hand, or the angel of Yahweh, are a source of amazement, bringing consolation to the faithful and consternation to the foe. When Obadiah was asked to announce the prophet's presence to Ahab, he replied, "As soon as I am gone from you, the Spirit of Yahweh will carry you whither I know not; . . ." (I Kings 18:12), for the steward feared that Ahab, regarding it as a mocking jest, might put him to death.

Phenomenal endurance and agility characterize Elijah. He thrives on the food supplied by ravens while others languish from famine, and he races the eighteen miles from Carmel to Jezreel in front of the chariot of Ahab. His mantle transfers his power. The aura of the superhuman reaches its peak in the legend of the prophet's departure into heaven in a chariot of fire. Some factually minded onlookers insist on searching in nearby valleys for the vanished prophet, but Elisha knows better; Elijah his master was not wholly of this earth. To this day Elijah holds a central place in Jewish tradition. One of the late prophets declares that he is to be the forerunner of the last things (Mal. 4:5), and the Passover celebration still provides an empty chair and a cup of wine for the absent Elijah—on the chance that he might manifest himself during the meal. The New Testament reinterprets the prophecy to apply to John the Baptist as the messianic forerunner of Jesus Christ.

Crux of the Elijah stories is the contest for control of the Sown Land: is it Yahweh's or Baal's? The proof of power is in the giving and withholding of rain. During the time of famine, Yahweh feeds his prophet by the ravens (I Kings 17:3–7) and then by a foreign woman (17:8–16). He keeps alive prophet-witnesses by the good offices of the steward Obadiah who conceals them in a cave (18:4), and at last he feeds all of his people with the return of the great rains (18:41–46). The widow's willingness to give up some of her meager store of bread and oil becomes a testing of her faith. "For thus says Yahweh God of Israel, 'The jar of meal shall not be spent, and the cruse of oil shall not fail, until the day that Yahweh sends rain upon the earth'" (17:14). It is the story of the hidden and manifest power of God; when it is manifest even the dullest Israelite believes, but the strength of the prophet is in his power to see the truth while it is still hidden and to direct his whole life toward it.

In the contest on Mt. Carmel the prophetic imperative is seen at its best. The stakes are high and the exclusive claims of Yahweh will not allow easy tolerance or syncretism. "How long will you go limping with two different opinions? If Yahweh is God, follow him; but if Baal, then follow him" (18:21). "And you call on the name of your God and I will call on the name of Yahweh; and the God who answers by fire, he is God" (18:24). The futility of Baal worship is commended by the silence following the appeal of his priests, for "there was no voice; no one answered . . ." (18:26, 29). At the critical moment, Elijah prays: "O Yahweh, God of Abraham, Isaac, and Israel, let it be known this day that thou art God in Israel, and that I am thy servant, and that I have done all these things at thy word. Answer me, O Yahweh, answer me, that this people may know that thou, O LORD, art God, and that thou hast turned their hearts back" (18:36–37). What contrast to the frenzied shrieks and self-mutilations of the Baal prophets! Elijah asks that Yahweh reveal his love for his people and that their allegiance to him be manifest. He is utterly confident that God will be true to himself. And the fire fell, consuming the offerings of Elijah. The people in chorus cry, "Yahweh, he is God; Yahweh, he is God."

So there flow together in this account the simple faith of the people who are swayed by external signs, as quickly won as they are lost, and the more deeply rooted trust of the prophet who lays hold of the old Mosaic heritage and trusts a God of mighty doing. But what shall we say of the fire? There is nothing we can say that does not destroy the impact of the story. Let us admit that it is legend, but could the terms of the struggle between Yahweh and Baal have been more truthfully told? Something happened that demonstrated to the satisfaction of many Israelites who had been half-hearted in their faith that Yahweh was a God to be worshiped alone, without any admixture of Baal. That reversal of the course of religious affairs was real enough.

We are still inclined to ask: what "really happened"? Was the liquid that soaked the offerings actually naphtha, known to exist in deposits on the slopes of Carmel? Such conjectures are mistaken if they are used to dismiss the incident as an *accident* (as if the fire were a sheer coincidence, since the lightning happened to strike when Elijah prayed; or the "water," unknown to the prophet, was combustible and ignited owing to a chance spark) or as *collusion* (as if Elijah waited until the electric storm was approaching in the hope that the exposed summit of Carmel would draw a bolt, or intentionally drenched the offerings with naphtha and then secretly ignited it). Dishonesty of motive is a poor match for the evident sincerity of Elijah; the dismissal of religious claims by charging deception is generally a feeble last resort. As to the possibility of coincidence, let us concede that if we knew all the circumstances some "natural" instrumentality could be constructed to "explain" the fire. Yet that would still leave untouched the fact that what gives the fire its meaning is *the context of religious ordeal*. The "objective" events were read meaningfully as "signs" and "proofs" of divine working. No matter how sophisticated our understanding, no explanation of the contest on Carmel is in the least recognizable that does not allow for the personal will of God behind the event. We must preserve the integrity of Elijah's faith, both in the sincerity of his motive and the reality of the God whom he worshiped. We may reserve the right to question the form and content of the legend, but the faith of Elijah and his converts that created the legend is too authentic to tamper with, even though we cannot hold their faith in the same way.

Soon after his hour of vindication, Elijah fled before Jezebel. With profound psychological insight the legend reveals the sudden revulsion in the prophet's soul. Indomitable and fearless one day, he melts in terror the next. Headlong he flees for his life. One day he is in Jezreel drenched by the downpour of rain, the next he lies parched beneath a juniper tree in the scorching waterless waste. Once again Yahweh feeds his servant who, invincible before men, is but a human after all. Strengthened by the angel's provision, Elijah goes on to Horeb where he lodges in a cave. Most scholars believe that the cave is intended as "the cleft in the rock" where Moses beheld the glory of Yahweh (Exod. 33:22). Elijah returns to the source of revelation by visiting the holy place where the mighty Moses met God. But Yahweh cannot be found in flight from duty, least of all in the mere physical surroundings in which men of old received power. The story warns against the reliquary instinct of pious people and nostalgia for "the good old days." Only in "a light whisper" or "a gentle stillness" is Elijah able to hear the one question that can have meaning for him: "What are you doing here, Elijah?" (I Kings 19:13). His petulant sense of self-importance and nicely nourished martyr complex are shattered by the discovery that there are still many thousands who have not bowed to Baal, though they have not shared the limelight with the prophet.

Then comes the command to return and establish new dynasties. Interpreters have tended to treat the command to anoint Hazael king in Syria and Jehu in Israel as unrelated to the story. The major problem is that if it were a command laid on Elijah he did nothing about it but let it lapse until Elisha executed it. The argument is well advised; the present form of the command is doubtless an example of later editorializing, another means of linking the two prophets. But the spirit of the command is authentic: Elijah, get back into action, secure new victories for Yahweh in the state of Israel! The mystic retirement of Elijah ends in renewed political action, springing from the ardor of his trust in Yahweh as the God of his people and of the Sown Land.

The attempt of Ahab to expropriate the property of Naboth, a small landowner who had an attractive piece of ground adjacent to the royal precincts, was a perfectly logical royal decision. After all, monarchy had rights taking precedence over the common citizenry. The fierce sense of family ownership, a legacy from the nomadic heritage, had not, however, been lost in Israel. Elijah was a savage partisan for the maintenance of the conservative rights of the little man. Yahweh who waters the land is also its defender and proprietor; he opposes the right of eminent domain that Jezebel takes for granted and that Ahab is easily prompted to exercise. The plan of the monarchs is to charge Naboth with blasphemy and to bribe witnesses. Almost precisely as in David's treatment of Bathsheba and Uriah, the original sin is covered by one more heinous: murder. Ahab's dismay at seeing Elijah is given voice in his impatient protest, "Have you found me, O my enemy?" to which the prophet replies, "I have found you, because you have sold yourself to do what is evil in the sight of Yahweh" (I Kings 21:20). The sharp-edged exchange is reminiscent of the earlier meeting of the two, when the king accosted Elijah, "Is it you, you troubler of Israel?" and the prophet retorted, "I have not troubled Israel; but you have, and your father's house, because you have forsaken the commandments of Yahweh and followed the Baals" (I Kings 18:17–18). In these confrontations, as in Nathan's incisive accusation of David, the unwavering covenant norm to which even kings are answerable is upheld by the prophetic voice.

Elijah's impact was immense. The tenacious purpose of a monarch to introduce a new state cult and to abolish Yahwism was thwarted by his decisive turning of the people's allegiance. It was a crude victory in many respects. Elijah did not hesitate to oppose violence with violence, killing the discredited prophets of Baal as ruthlessly as Jezebel executed Yahweh priests and as he would have died had he lost the ordeal on Mt. Carmel. The burden of his attack was not upon idolatry in the strict sense of image worship, for he seems never to have objected to the bull worship of the north (the only verse in the prophetic narratives that speaks of idols is probably a D gloss, I Kings 21:26). That he approved of iconic representation of Yahweh cannot be proved one way or another, but the essence of his warfare was the very survival of Yahwism. It remained for prophets a century later to show how readily a religion nominally claiming to be Yahwism could absorb the idolatrous forms and spirit of Baalism. Elijah's task was a singularly unsophisticated one. His was neither the temperament nor the time in history to make subtle distinctions. He stood his ground against a frontal attack and fought with the weapons of the opponent. For him the name and the tradition of Yahweh meant everything. His grasp of Yahweh's claim and Israel's duty was as profound as any Hebrew's between Moses and the writing prophets.

Micaiah ben Imlah in I Kings 22 displays the trait of Balaam in prophesying the unpopular truth. Like Elijah against the prophets of Baal, Micaiah stands against the four hundred parrotlike prophets of Yahweh. Speaking in a chorus the four hundred advise Ahab and Jehoshaphat to go up in battle and prosper in a campaign against Syria. When Micaiah at first repeats their auspicious word (he had wearied of ever being heeded!), Ahab rebukes him since he had already told his Judean ally about Micaiah's predilections for doom. In earnest Micaiah then describes a vision of Yahweh on his throne, calling for a volunteer spirit to go forth and deceive Ahab by being "a lying spirit in the mouth of all his prophets." On behalf of the prophets, Zedekiah their spokesman bitterly mocks Micaiah with a blow on the cheek and the contemptuous question, "How did the Spirit of Yahweh go from me to speak to you?"—an ironic jest, meaning "how did *my* 'lying' spirit possess *you* so quickly?" The prophet insists that Israel will be routed in battle; left behind in prison, Micaiah avers: "If you return in peace, Yahweh has not spoken by me."

In a frantic effort to frustrate the prophet's foreboding, Ahab disguises himself as a common soldier, hoping that Jehoshaphat arrayed in royal garb will draw the Aramean attack. Instead, "a certain man drew his bow at a venture, and struck the king of Israel between the scale armor and the breastplate." Though propped in his chariot by his warriors, who hoped to rally the last strength of the Israelites, Ahab died at evening and the battle turned into a debacle. So the word of Yahweh by the one true prophet confounded the four hundred and all the schemes of the king himself, for that divine word directed an unaimed arrow to a chink in the disguised king's armor. Ahab embraces the destiny that he knew in advance but could not avoid. The story is magnificently expressive of the Israelite view of prophecy and providence, of the efficacy of the divine word and the divine nemesis that will find a man, evade them though he try. Yahweh rules and overrules.

Elisha in many respects looks like a double of Elijah, and some scholars have urged that the two cycles refer to a single prophet. Similar experiences are attributed to each (the revival of the widow's son, the parting of the Jordan with a mantle, and the calling down of punitive fire), and it is not beyond possibility that in instances the action of one has been credited by tradition to the other. But on the whole Elisha emerges as a prophet with a character all his own. The primary distinction is that Elijah was a solitary champion of Yahweh, while Elisha was at the head of bands of prophets. Comparing prophetic origins to monastic beginnings, the one was like the anchorite monastic Anthony and the other like the cenobitic Pachomius. Elisha, a veritable spiritual father, was attentive to the practical needs of the prophetic orders, wisely providing their food and shelter.

The miraculous element in the Elisha cycle is extensive and as fantastic as the Old Testament affords. Miracle in the Old Testament is generally in the service of moral and religious purpose; the intrinsic meaning of the miracle is in its witness to God's purpose with his people. Miracle is not the merely erratic but the discharge of divine purpose which, to be sure, has a wonderful character arousing awe and compelling devotion. But in the Elisha stories miracle is adventitious. It is used to enhance the skill and cunning of Elisha. We rather feel ourselves in the midst of a medieval saint's company. In fact, Elisha is the only figure in the Old Testament of whom miracles are related mainly to enhance the man; of all others, the miracle is the action of God—as often amazing to the Hebrew leaders as to the people. But we read of Elisha purifying the water supply of Jericho with salt, of his cursing the boys who playfully mock him by calling the bears to kill forty-two of them, of the antidote for the poisoned pottage, of the axhead floating, and of the corpse revived instantaneously when it contacts the bones of the prophet. A slight check upon the lush growth of miracle appears in the story of the Shunammite's son who would not respond to treatment by remote control (the rod of Elisha placed upon him) but only to the outstretched body of the prophet (perhaps the earliest recorded instance of artificial resuscitation).

Of particular beauty is the account of the Syrian Naaman who humbled himself in search of an Israelite prophet to cure his dread leprosy and who was not disdained for being a foreigner. Both this story and the tale of the faithful Phoenician widow of Zarephath greatly impressed Jesus; he spoke of them as typical of the awakened Gentile world that would listen to the good news of Israel's God (Luke 4:25–27). The narrative stands also as one of the classic rebukes of venality. Elisha refuses payment from the grateful Naaman, but the prophet's servant Gehazi overtakes the journeying nobleman and feigns a change of mind on his master's part. The knowing Elisha asks his servant, "Where have you been, Gehazi?" And he said, "Your servant went nowhere." But Elisha counters, "Did I not go with you in spirit when the man turned from his chariot to meet you? Was it a time to accept money and garments, olive orchards and vineyards, sheep and oxen, menservants and maidservants?" (II Kings 5:26). The leprosy of Naaman falls upon the greedy Gehazi.

The ministry of Jesus owed much to the work of Elijah and Elisha. They shared the same itinerant labor among the people, including the rhythm of withdrawal into solitude (Elijah) and ministry to the crowds (Elisha). Healing miracles and the raising of the dead were similarly prominent. Jesus also went to a Phoenician woman and praised her great faith. Peter, like Elisha, would not leave his master even in the last hours of his life. One of the rumors about the identity of Jesus was that he was Elijah returned. His teaching mentions the two prophets as signs of the present faithless generation. Some critics believe that the Gospel form of writing, an early Christian literary invention, owed more to the biographical narratives in Kings than to any other source, biblical or classical.

Our survey of the ninth century B.C. bears out the conclusion that the political and religious virility of the Hebrews was greatest in the north, in spite of the derogatory evaluation of Israel by the Deuteronomists. Omri and Ahab find only weak equivalents in Asa and Jehoshaphat. More significantly, we hear of no one to equal Elijah, the rugged champion of Yahweh, or the pastoral Elisha, or the integrative thinker known to us as the Elohist. The nearest is the saintly priest Jehoiada. We can be sure that had memories existed concerning prophets who were as influential in the south as in the north, the D historians would have told us of them. As it was, Israel —point of maximum political, social, and economic maturation— became the point of maximum religious maturation. Only as like crises encroached more slowly on Judah did southern Yahwism distinguish itself.

9

THE COLLAPSE OF ISRAEL

. . . Assyria, the rod of my anger . . .
Isa. 10:5

ASSYRIA AND THE FALL OF ISRAEL, 800–700 B.C.

In the eighth century B.C. the mounting power of Assyria finally came to bear with full force upon the divided Hebrew kingdoms; the north was swallowed up and the south reduced to vassalage. But the political course was not steadily downhill. The grim outcome was preceded in both countries by a vigorous if short-lived reawakening of strength. It was in this unnatural period of prosperity and expansion masking the impending doom that the first great prophets Amos and Hosea arose to sound a warning and to interpret the times by means of the religious call and destiny of Israel. Their message was not sufficient to turn the tide of affairs and their counterparts in the south, Isaiah and Micah, were only a little more successful in influencing state leadership. In general the prophets seem to have been dismissed as minority pessimists, whereas the majority of Yahweh prophets (dubbed "false" by the canonical prophets) preached peace and prosperity. The Hebrew prophets spoke resolutely of the total situation of Israel, and not of a limited sphere of life tagged "religion." They insisted on the political, economic, and social implications of Israel's trust in God. While they always saw much deeper than political instrumentalism, they were vitally concerned with the state policy of the Hebrew people and in constant contact with the leaders of state, often to the irritation and discomfort of both. To understand the prophetic figures of Israel one must understand the times in which they lived and relive the tensions of historical life in the Fertile Crescent—tensions that have a perennial and universal quality about them.

The unreal "boom" period in both kingdoms was made possible by the fact that Assyria had advanced into Syria far enough to neutralize the power of the Aramean states (in 805 B.C. Adad-nirari III exacted tribute from Damascus) but not quite far enough similarly to affect Israel and Judah, since Assyria was frustrated by a succession of comparatively weak rulers. Beginning with Joash in the north and Amaziah in the south, the Hebrew states were momentarily freed from the harassment of Assyria and Damascus. Trans-Jordan was again occupied by Israel. Israel's highwater point was reached by Jeroboam II, whose rule rivaled the heyday of Omri. The historian says sweepingly that "he restored the border of Israel from the entrance of Hamath as far as the Sea of the Arabah" (II Kings 14:25). In the middleman's role that David, Solomon, Omri, and Ahab had played so skilfully, Jeroboam guarded the overland trade routes to the Phoenician port cities; with Phoenicia he worked in economic symbiosis.

The growing social and economic inequalities of Jeroboam's reign are immortally catalogued in the prophecy of Amos. Abuses of wealth without social conscience, to which Oriental countries seem to have been particularly prone, were a terrible price to pay for the renewal of Israel's status as a nation. The fantastic growth of the urban upper class was attended by commercial "killings" and the curse of absentee landlordism. The lower classes began to lose their pride of independence in the inflationary economy, slipping first into debt and then tenant farming. Their end was little better than serfdom. To cap it off the court system was thoroughly corrupted by the sudden wealth, so that the weak had no redress against the strong. The increased religiosity of the people drew the whiplash of scorn from the prophets, who spared nothing in their derisive attacks upon those who worshiped Yahweh in name but denied him in spirit and in fact.

Uzziah's forty-year reign in Judah, contemporaneous with Jeroboam's rule, was likewise outwardly magnificent. Edom was recaptured and trade with Arabia encouraged. Unfortunately we have no detailed reports of the south in Uzziah's time, for no prophet analogous to Amos has left his impressions. But it is probable that during this time much of the economic and social backwardness of Judah was overcome because, shortly after the death of Uzziah, Isaiah the Judean prophet was lambasting his people for the kinds of evil that Amos had scored in the north. The base of leadership and wealth in both kingdoms was shifting from the landed aristocracy to the *nouveaux riches,* who were little restrained by the old cultural and religious mores.

With the demise of Jeroboam the northern kingdom disintegrated with unbelievable rapidity. Assyrian imperialism was renewed with the

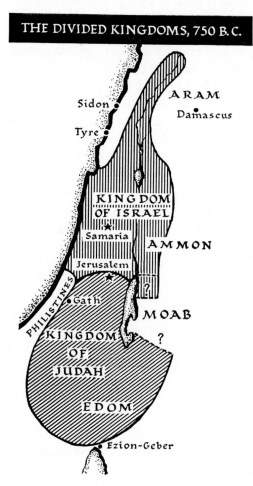

THE DIVIDED KINGDOMS, 750 B.C.

indefatigable Tiglath-pileser III (biblical Pul). In the unsettled atmosphere surrounding the awakening of the slumbering Assyrian giant, no stable leadership appeared in Israel. In twenty-odd years four kings were assassinated and none gained the trust of the people. Waves of pro-Egyptian and pro-Assyrian sentiment swept the capital, and royal aspirants rode to power on their crests. Hosea's prophecies plaintively bemoan the decay of statesmanship and the shifting course of the state, aimless and futile as the flight of doves or the wandering of wild asses. While Israel spent her last years in frenzied clutching at survival, Assyria advanced relentlessly westward and southward.

There was a brief hope that the glorious alliance that had stopped Assyria a century earlier at Qarqar might be reconstituted. Damascus and Israel formed the core of the coalition. They invited Judean participation, since it was especially important that the country to their rear be in active sympathy with the anti-Assyrian movement. When Ahaz did not appear coöperative, Pekah of Israel and Rezin of Damascus advanced threateningly toward Jerusalem. Ahaz probably did not feel the As-

syrian pinch as acutely as his northern neighbors and he may have
objected that the alliance smacked too much of north Israelite hegemony. Isaiah tells of the crisis and reports his counsel to resist
Pekah and Rezin, but Ahaz went beyond Isaiah's advice in inviting Assyria to come to his aid. The craven political motives of the time did
not respond to the prophetic preachments; men living in the shadow
of great visions were as small-souled as men have so often been in their
exercise of authority. Ahaz became in effect a subject prince of Assyria
and while Judah remained technically independent in contrast to the
fate of the north, it was at the cost of cultural and religious as well as
political subjection to Assyria.

Tiglath-pileser exploited the opening wedge in Palestine created by
Ahaz' appeal to Assyria. By 734 B.C. Galilee and Trans-Jordan, the
northern and eastern segments of Israel, were annexed as Assyrian
provinces. Two years later Damascus fell. The violently anti-Assyrian
revolt of Hoshea, spurred on by the futile hope of intervention from
Egypt, led to quick subjugation of the whole country outside Samaria.
The stanchly fortified capital held out for three years and when it fell
in 722, the supporting forces of Egypt and Gaza were also trounced.
Sargon falsely claimed for himself the capture of Samaria and the
deportation of its populace,[1] whereas they were actually completed by
Shalmaneser V shortly before his death. He transported thousands of
Israelites to parts of Mesopotamia and introduced possible dissidents
from those regions into Israel; his logic was that potential trouble-
makers would be less dangerous in countries where they were less at
home. The deported northerners (not more than one-fifth of the population), have since been called "the ten lost tribes of Israel," although
that is not a biblical expression. The mixture of native Israelites and
foreign transplants produced the later Samaritans, whom the Judeans
regarded as a bastard breed. But the Jews of the north were no more
mixed than those of the south, since the whole course of Hebrew and
Jewish history is the story of a religion and way of life persisting in the
face of ethnic and cultural commingling. The occasional flare-up of
excitement over finding "the ten lost tribes" is a ridiculous bit of
sensation-mongering. The deported Israelites did not form tribal en-
tities in the first place and, if they have any descendants today, they
would be the surviving Jews of the Babylonian dispersion that flourished in the early middle ages but withered before the advance of
Islam.

[1] See Appendix 10, p. 592.

For the last quarter of the century Judah stood alone, but merely as a petty kingdom tributary to Assyria. Among the paraphernalia brought into Judah by the compact of Ahaz with Tiglath-pileser was an Assyrian altar given priority over the Yahweh altar on the temple esplanade. Hezekiah, who succeeded Ahaz, was a more ardent Yahwist than his father; he spearheaded a reform intended to suppress the high places. Some scholars believe that the core of the present book of Deuteronomy, originating in Israel and passing into Judean hands after 722, formed the basis for Hezekiah's purge of Canaanite religious practices. Naturally coupled with such a program were stirrings of armed rebellion. Rumors of revolt periodically swept the western provinces. Hezekiah was dissuaded by Isaiah from joining in the insurrection of 714, but his efforts did not avail in 705 when a major rebellion was instigated by the amazingly active and persuasive Babylonian prince Marduk-apal-iddin (biblical Merodach-baladan), a constant thorn in Assyria's side.

Hezekiah made careful preparations for the revolt by strengthening Jerusalem's defenses and water supply. A lasting monument to his engineering ability is the Siloam Tunnel.[2] Water was brought for a distance of 1,700 feet from the Pool Gihon, outside the wall, through a winding aqueduct cut in the solid rock of Ophel, into the Pool of Siloam. When the uprising broke loose, Padi of Ekron, who remained loyal to Assyria, was imprisoned as a hostage in Jerusalem. Sennacherib was not long in initiating his accession by a stunning reprisal campaign against the west. He quickly quelled the coastal rebels, overthrew Lachish, and advanced on Jerusalem. The city was left alone, as the prophet Isaiah says, "like a lodge in a cucumber field," and Hezekiah, as the Assyrian annals describe it, was "shut up like a bird in a cage."

The Hebrew account of the siege of the city (II Kings 18:13–20:21, paralleled in Isaiah 36–39) and the Annals of Sennacherib (the so-called Taylor Prism)[3] agree that Jerusalem was *not* captured, but the reasons offered are somewhat at odds. The biblical report states that 185,000 Assyrians were slain in a single night "by the angel of Yahweh" (a plague?). Sennacherib tells of an immense tribute paid by Hezekiah (cf. II Kings 18:13–16). No doubt both reports have settled for aspects of the campaign most flattering to their side. Some tribute

[2] See Appendix 9, p. 591.
[3] See Appendix 10, p. 593.

*Marduk-apal-iddin (biblical Merodach-baladan, Isa. 39:1–8) makes a
land grant to an official.*

Sennacherib receives the surrender of Lachish during the Judean campaign of 703–701 B.C.

was likely paid by Hezekiah when his plight became severe enough to exhaust the food supply after months of siege, but it may not have been all that Assyria demanded. At the same time a plague of serious proportions may have ravaged the ranks of the invaders who had already turned the countryside into a charnel house by plundering and living off the land. Difficulties at home are hinted at in the Assyrian records and these may have prompted Sennacherib to settle for what he could get from Hezekiah. By that time he had reduced Jerusalem to an isolated garrison that would think twice before joining any more insurrections.

And so the century ended with the collapse of the northern kingdom and the near extinction of the southern. Yet the Davidic dynasty clung to its slim hold on the throne of Judah and the city was spared the ravages visited on the countryside.

HEBREW PROPHECY

The peculiarities of the prophets' mind and style make their writings among the most forbidding and puzzling in the Old Testament. Reading them is rewarding or frustrating in the extreme, according to one's expectations of a prophet. If the prophet's context in Israel's history and religion is ignored, then the modern reader may expect either too much or too little. If the unique character of a prophetic writing is overlooked, the student may exhaust his energies and interest looking vainly for a structure more familiar to his western mind. Orientation is clearly advisable before approaching any individual prophet.

MISCONCEPTIONS

Unfortunately the prophets labor under some damaging misconceptions. Two shortcuts to understanding them are widespread and equally erroneous, although each contains a substantial measure of truth. The first is the orthodox Christian view that the prophets foretell future events. Often the predictions are thought to forecast the coming of Jesus Christ and to specify events of his life, death, and resurrection. Other predictions are applied to events still future, especially those preceding the end of the world. The exegetical principles by which the predictions are allocated, some to Jesus of Nazareth (the first coming of Christ) and some to the last days (the second coming of Christ) are not clear and the classification of the prophecies varies considerably among interpreters.

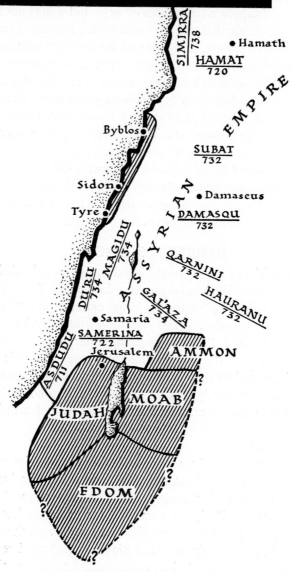

JUDAH UNDER HEZEKIAH, 711~700 B.C.

SIMIRRA
738

• Hamath

HAMAT
720

EMPIRE

Byblos•

SUBAT
732

Sidon•

• Damascus

Tyre•

DAMASQU
732

SYRIAN

QARNINI
732

DURU
734

MAGIDU
734

ASSYRIAN

HAURANU
732

GAL'AZA
734

• Samaria

SAMERINA
722

Jerusalem

AMMON

ASDUDU
711

JUDAH

MOAB

?

?

EDOM

?

?

UNDERLINED ASSYRIAN PROVINCES
WITH DATES OF INCORPORATION

TRIBUTARY BUT INDEPENDENT KINGDOMS
AND CITY-STATES

In evaluating this view we must grant that prediction is a significant feature in the prophets but it is uniformly connected with the moral and spiritual present. The future described by the prophet is one toward which men now living have a responsible relation by the choices they make; it is not a fated future that holds men transfixed as they peer from afar. It is a future they have helped to shape. The extent to which future happenings could be seen in advance (second sight or clairvoyance) is a matter open for constant examination. Psychological data have been amassed suggesting that the powers of the human mind are greater than the rationalistic image of man has normally allowed. But whatever the supernormal capacities of these prophets, they would all insist that what concerned them most was the morally conditioned present. They were not soothsayers or diviners but spokesmen for the crucial issues of the divine-human relationship and thus protectors of human freedom, however much circumstance hedged it about.

What does this imply for the supposed Christian predictions in the prophets? It means that so far as we can determine, when studied in their contexts apart from dogmatic preconviction, no prophet leaped across the centuries and foresaw the specific person Jesus of Nazareth. It is a plain violation of historical context to think that they did so and in practice those who interpret the prophets as predictors of Jesus obscure the settings in which the prophets functioned. They are treated as shadowy unrealities whose connection with their own day was virtually nil. History before Christ becomes practically without a meaning of its own, since early ages and men existed mainly if not exclusively to foresee later events.

The truth in the position is retained by recognizing that the prophets were in a line of development culminating in Jesus of Nazareth. Some of their deepest convictions were his and the spirit of his ministry was that of prophecy reincarnate. More than that, the prophets discerned the modes and aims of God's purpose for his world; they looked deeply into the sacrificial grace and firm righteousness which found their fullest embodiment in the one man Jesus Christ. The Christian who believes that "God moves in mysterious ways his wonders to perform" will have no difficulty in thinking that the Father of Jesus Christ prepared the prophets as precursors of his more perfect revelation. Such valid religious-historical and theological connections between the prophets and Jesus can be given their full weight without obscuring the careers of the prophets in their own day by reducing them to fore-casting automata.

In reaction to the traditional Christian estimate, which tended to deprive the prophets of their distinction as historical individuals, nine-teenth-century biblical scholarship gave birth to the image of the prophet as social reformer. With the supernatural element lopped off, this seemed a perfectly tailored substitute, especially amenable to the spirit of the times in which men were striving for their rights against vested economic, political, and social wrong. The truth is that the church had long hidden the lamp of prophetic criticism of institutional evil, and so it was that movements such as Christian Socialism in Brit-ain and the Social Gospel in America were eager to lay claim to the courageous communal conscience of the Hebrew prophets.

Sometimes in their enthusiasm those social champions of Christi-anity unknowingly transposed the motivations and presuppositions of the prophets into those of liberal humanitarian reformers. While the prophets' affinities with modern reformers are significant the two are often far apart in the form their insights take. While reformers talk of "the rights of man," the prophets spoke of "the Word of Yahweh." While some reformers think largely of individuals cushioned against mass social shocks, the Hebrew prophets had an implacable blend of the personal and communal. They saw the whole people of Israel stamped with a purpose and destiny that demanded the expression of the divine nature in its total life. The prophets thought not of mass forces of social, economic, and political disintegration or integration, of security and welfare measures, of rehabilitation and reform, but only and always of the realm of personal responsibility before God, of the relentlessly personal and, by that very token, the communal de-mands of covenant. Everything in their outlook was grounded in Is-rael's relation to Yahweh, in the persistent pushing of religious mean-ing into every facet of life, in the ultimate personalizing of even the most abstract and casual of human relations.

Theirs was a daring vision, some might say utopian and impossibly idealistic. It is certain that their hope has never been fully realized and that they serve even today as a sharp warning to religious smugness and "culture religion" that simply identifies popular sentiments as the will of God and restricts religion to "safe" topics. Hebrew prophets were realists and pragmatists whose high vision of God never be-trayed them into slick answers or self-deceptions. Their words blow through the organized religion of every generation with an arresting freshness and sometimes with a cataclysmic fury.

The Meaning of Prophecy

The most frequent word for prophet is *nabi'*, generally connected with the Akkadian word *nabū*, "to call or to speak forth" and thus "to speak forth, declare," and as a noun form, "spokesman." It may have had its origin in the agitated behavior of the ecstatic prophet who appeared "to boil" as the inspirational frenzy overtook him. Two less common words for the prophet are *hozeh* and *ro'eh*, "seer," both from verbs meaning "to see, gaze, stare, behold visions" and emphasizing the dream mechanism of inspiration. A note in I Samuel 9:9 advises us that "he who is now called a *nabi'* was formerly called a *ro'eh*," which shows that after Samuel the term "seer" fell into disuse and was replaced by "spokesman"; but it is hard to date the notation with precision. In general, *ro'eh* and *hozeh* are the more primitive terms and only in Amos 7:12 is the latter applied to a writing prophet (and only then by a critic, the priest Amaziah), but the verb *ra'ah*, "to see, behold visions" is used in Ezekiel 1:1 and the more technical verb *hazah* and its derivative *hazon*, "vision," are applied to the inspiration of several of the prophets (cf. Isa. 1:1; Obad. 1:1; Mic. 1:1; Nah. 1:1; Hab. 1:1; note that the occurrences are all in the superscriptions, indicating that the terminology belongs to editors). No really fruitful results from the study of the terms alone are possible. We should note, however, that the LXX translation of *nabi'* by the Greek *prophetes*, "one who speaks for another," is the source of English "prophet."

In the Priestly source's explanation of the relation between Moses and Aaron as collaborating deliverers of Israel, there is a lucid though inadvertent clarification of the term *nabi'*. "And Yahweh said to Moses, 'See, I make you as God to Pharaoh; and Aaron your brother shall be your *nabi'* ' " (Exod. 7:1). The prophet is the mouthpiece or spokesman of God. The pith of Hebrew prophecy is not prediction or social reform but the declaration of divine will. The prophets were first of all religious figures, "mystics" in the sense that their experience of God was the center out of which radiated their preaching and teaching, but "realists" in the sense that the God they experienced was the covenant Lord of Israel who had a purpose for his people and for his world. To an astounding degree otherworldly and thisworldly elements were fused in the blazing heat of their experience. The reader must, therefore, be prepared for the sharpest juxtapositions of visionary flight with mundane detail. It did not seem to them incongruous to pass from a vision of God in the temple (Isa. 6) to the story of a city's fear before a foreign alliance (Isa. 7); from the stentorian declaration of justice's high demands (Amos 5:21–24) to a threat against the popular idols Sakkuth and Kaiwan (Amos 5:25–27). They were observers of the times who managed to maintain a generally elevated literary style and a point of view that transcends moralism and banality. A knowledge of their paradoxical theism, otherworldly and thisworldly, austere but compassionate, despairing and yet sinewy with hope, is indispensable to understanding the prophets.

LITERARY FORMS

A typical prophetic writing is not an essay or a sermon or a poem but an anthology of materials both *by* the prophet and *about* him, in mixed poetry and prose. The contents may be classified roughly as:

1. *Short sayings* addressed to Israel (or persons or groups in Israel, e.g., king, nobility, merchants, women) spoken either by the prophet or Yahweh. These oracles are most often poetic in form and are generally from two to ten lines in length.

2. *Longer speeches* of the prophet, ordinarily in prose. These tend to be less effective in style and probably represent the work of editors. Although presumably oral in form, these "speeches" often have a pedantry and verbosity that betray their written origins. Some prophetic writings are remarkably free of these prose additions (Amos) and others have very sizable portions (Jeremiah and Ezekiel).

3. *Biographical or autobiographical narratives* that report selected incidents in the lives of the prophets. Some prophets give little or no such accounts and others, especially the more voluminous writings (Isaiah, Jeremiah, and Ezekiel), have substantial narrative passages.

The nub of the reader's difficulty with the composition of a prophetic book is that these three types of material are lumped together rather indiscriminately with only the barest attention to topical or chronological arrangement. The poetic oracles with their oral contexts appear side by side with the more bookish prose of the "speeches" and narratives. Furthermore, in only a few instances are the units introduced by explanatory notes as to time and place. Internal evidence shows, however, that these units often come from widely separated occasions in a prophet's ministry. We have oracles from Isaiah dating over at least forty years. Also the function of the followers of the prophets in collecting their masters' words must not be overlooked. In the case of Jeremiah there is explicit reference to his friend Baruch the scribe who made a compilation of the prophet's sayings (Jer. 36), and there is an allusion to the probable collecting activity of Isaiah's disciples: "Bind up the testimony, seal the teaching among my disciples" (Isa. 8:16). Finally, we must reckon with prophetic "schools" or "circles" who perpetuated the memories of their "founder" and in succeeding centuries added their own oracles to those of their master with as much sincerity of conviction as moved Plato to attribute many of his own views to his teacher Socrates.

The prophetic books are thus composite, not created at a single sitting nor within a single lifetime. It is as if portions of someone's notebook, including key passages from speeches and diary notations, were assembled without explanatory comments and enlarged with additions by those who claimed him as their leader. This may seem a most haphazard process but we must recall that no prophet was aware of writing Scripture, that in most cases the oral word was more important than the written and that, in spite of the lack of logical order and a good many missing gaps in our knowledge, the prophetic books display a rare power and brilliance of mind.

Prophetic oracles are of two kinds, either of doom or salvation. But the "oracle" in the strict sense of the declaration of a *fait accompli* is qualified in Israel by the moral and spiritual nature of the prophetic faith. The reasons for the impending doom are frequently set forth in so-called *reproaches* (often prefaced with the sharp warning cry, "Woe!"), the consequences of disobedience in *threats* (introduced often by "therefore"), and the conditions for salvation in *admonitions* (introduced by terms such as "Turn!" and "Seek!"). As one interpreter has summed it up: "In short, they are not only oracle-givers, but preachers and spiritual guides."[4] Thus the very forms of the prophetic speech visibly embody the nature of the message: repentance based upon man's knowledge of the divine covenant and hope based upon man's experience of the divine grace. The prophets speak only "of *what will be* because of *what is,* because Yahweh and no other God is *Lord.*"[5]

The diction of the prophetic books is unforgettably vivid. Their idiom had its roots in the priestly oracles delivered at the sanctuaries.

---

[4] Aage Bentzen, *Introduction to the Old Testament,* Gad, rev. ed., 1952, vol. 1, p. 198.

[5] R. B. Y. Scott, *The Relevance of the Prophets,* Macmillan, 1954, p. 14.

The earliest prophets were probably sanctuary personnel who in time became dissociated from the cult, at least to the extent that they could bring scathing criticism to bear upon the priestly apparatus. Nevertheless some of the great prophets were of priestly lineage (Jeremiah and Ezekiel) and they do not seem to have believed that priests and sacrifice were intrinsically evil but only subject to corruption; certainly they never proposed a religion of "free spirit." The imagery of the prophets is a constant delight; it is seldom florid or bombastic (except among the latest prophets), but with a chasteness and simplicity like that of a Grecian vase or a play of Aeschylus, they convey the utmost in emotional and spiritual power.

The poetic gifts of the prophets were to a preëminent degree sensuous, imbuing spiritual realities with a color and texture and warmth. Often the substance of an oracle is a single word that has burned itself into the inspired prophetic mind and may evoke a whole range of visionary and auditory associations. No one has so dignified the lowly and despised pun as the prophets of Israel (e.g., Amos 8:1–3, *qayits,* "basket of summer fruit" and *qets,* "end"; Isa. 5:7, *mishpat,* "justice" and *mishpah,* "spilling of blood"; *sedhaqah,* "righteousness" and *se'aqah,* "outcry"). The poetic oracles must be read aloud for maximum effect, for only then do their rolling cadences and sublime imagery receive their due. It is a pity that they are so often poorly read from the pulpit, if read at all.

Parallelism of members, the basic element of all Hebrew poetry, already noted in the Song of Deborah, is also present in the prophetic books. Without detailed discussion of the nomenclature of Hebrew poetry, which is rather technical and still scientifically imprecise, an example will suffice to point out the instinctive parallelism of the prophetic style:

> 1. a. Hear, O heavens,
>   b.   and give ear, O earth;
>   c.   for Yahweh has spoken:
>
> 2. a. Sons have I reared and brought up,
>   b.   but they have rebelled against me.
>
> 3. a. The ox knows its owner,
>   b.   and the ass its master's crib;
>
> 4. a. but Israel does not know,
>   b.   my people does not understand.

This opening oracle of the book of Isaiah consists of four verses or lines of thought, which in turn break down into verse members—each of which is a meaningful phrase in itself. Ordinarily there are two verse members or distichs in a verse, but sometimes there are three members or tristichs. In the example above only 1 is a tristich (consisting of stichs a, b, and c), while all the others are the more common distich pattern (consisting of stichs a and b). In each case the second stich parallels the thought of the first, ordinarily by repetition (synonymous parallelism), but often by contrast (antithetic parallelism) or by extension (synthetic parallelism). One of the variant possibilities is to parallel two verses: in 3 and 4 above not only does 3b parallel 3a and 4b parallel 4a synonymously, but 4 in its entirety parallels 3 antithetically. The Hebrews did not have a science of prosody, though they had the art. They had no terms for "parallelism of members" and for the loose meters they employed. Theirs was rather an intuitive mode of expression, typical of ancient Near Eastern poetry in the large, but carried to perfection. While it is true that Israel never excelled in the plastic arts, it is noteworthy that her greatest religious spokesmen were gifted with literary genius.

Yet this literary beauty and power were subservient to their great hope of preserving a people from folly and disaster by turning Israel to its ancient covenant responsibilities. With all their genius they did not succeed in the short run but the existence of the Old Testament, of the Jewish people, of the Christian Church, are posthumous monuments to their greatness. The greatest of prophets said sadly, ". . . you build the tombs of the prophets and adorn the monuments of the righteous, saying 'If we had lived in the days of our fathers, we would not have taken part with them in shedding the blood of the prophets.' Thus you witness against yourselves, that you are sons of those who murdered the prophets. Fill up, then, the measure of your fathers" (Matt. 23:29–31).

AMOS

The first prophet to leave written records was Amos, of whom we know only what is reported in his small book appearing third in the Hebrew Book of the Twelve (English Minor Prophets). We can sketch only the very haziest picture of the man. He was from Tekoa, south of Jerusalem, in the Wilderness of Judea. According to the editorial introduction he was from "among the shepherds," and he says of himself: "Yahweh took me from following the flock" (7:15). Generally he is conceived as a shepherd and migrant laborer who during the harvest season was "a dresser of sycamore trees," probably one who punctured the fruit so that it could ripen.

There is nothing to prohibit the view, however, that Amos was a man of some means, like the sheep owners Nabal and Job. Since sycamores do not grow at the altitude of Tekoa, Amos may have owned another home at a lower altitude in the Shephelah. Many feel that his animus against the rich indicates his own poverty, but his attack is never against wealth per se but rather against the soft luxury and the social abuses it encourages. If we allow the possibility that he was a person of property, then he was a prophet who saw the dangers in a way of life in which he was implicated. His economic position is uncertain one way or the other, but it is unsound to predicate his radical criticism upon his own deprived state or to make too much of the fact that he was a southerner preaching in the north. In short, Amos cannot be reduced to a proletarian reformer or a chauvinistic outsider.

Amos disavows membership in the prophetic orders, "I am not a *nabi'*" (7:14), apparently in renunciation of mercenary motives. Elsewhere, however, he speaks favorably of the long line of prophets that God had sent his people (2:11; 3:7–8). He lived during the affluent age of Uzziah and Jeroboam II and is dated in the period 760–745 B.C., generally close to 750—after Jeroboam had brought Israel to its peak of power and before the threatening advances of Tiglath-pileser. The superscription says that he prophesied "two years before the earthquake" (or "during two years"); unfortunately this trembler, recalled also in Zechariah 14:4, cannot be dated satisfactorily.

Contributing factors to the prophetic call of Amos are obscure. His pastoral pursuits in "an environment abounding in emptiness and stillness" may have sharpened his intellect and power of observation and inculcated a dislike for city softness and moral decay. Here also was the source of his cogent style, stripped to the bone, cutting and stark. It has been conjectured that in selling his wool he made frequent visits to the northern trading centers of Bethel and Samaria, perhaps also to the Philistine cities and Damascus. In all these journeys he did more than tend to personal business; he was an acute observer whose eye detected the moral rot. His astuteness served him well in sensing the rise of the Assyrian menace when it was still no larger than a cloud the size of a man's hand. While these factors by themselves fall far short of explaining the prophetic fire that raged in Amos' soul, they were at any rate the materials ignited by his call.

The introductory note, perhaps by a disciple-editor, says: "The words of Amos, . . . which he saw concerning Israel. . . ." Such a hackneyed prophetic formula does not prove that Amos had a specific call vision, as some of the prophets clearly did (Isaiah, Jeremiah, Ezekiel). Some commentators believe that one or all of the visions recounted in chapters 7 and 8 are "call visions," that in watching the objects and events described he heard Yahweh's summons. While the present form of the book puts no emphasis upon a call *vision,* the imperious nature of Amos' *call* is voiced in his insistence that "Yahweh said to me, 'Go, prophesy to my people Israel'" (7:15). It is seen also in the vivid rationale of prophecy, regarded by many scholars as a later editorial generalization·

Surely Adonai Elohim does nothing
  without revealing his secret
  to his servants the prophets.
The lion has roared;
  who will not fear?
Adonai Elohim has spoken;
  who can but prophesy? (3:7–8).

Apart from the superscription, the only explicit biography in the book is the description of the climactic moment when Amos, having spoken against the rule of Jeroboam, was rebuked by Amaziah, priest of the national shrine of Bethel. It is widely theorized that the prophet chose a holy day when the temple environs were thronged to deliver his excoriating attacks. Amaziah and Amos, sharply set against one another in mutual distrust and antipathy, are the classic examples of the age-long tension between priest and prophet. The clash was seldom so sharply drawn, since later prophecy tended to modify in a priestly direction and the priesthood itself was permeated by prophetic ideas. Because he was so savagely rebuked and told to return to Judea, it is often assumed that Amos immediately "turned tail" and sought retirement from a public ministry. Presumably at this time he put his oracles in writing to secure them a hearing. The brevity of his book apparently argues for a short ministry, but we do not know that even a majority of his public words have been preserved and it would be surprising if so fearless a Yahwist were deterred by official opposition.

Indeed it is hard to think that a voice so dauntless and caustic could be silenced by a government directive!

THE STRUCTURE OF THE BOOK

A semblance of organization can be made out in the book. The editors have collected the separate units into several divisions: (1) Oracles against Foreign Nations, chapters 1–2; (2) Oracles of Doom against Israel, chapters 3–6; (3) Vision Sequence with Biographical Insert, chapters 7–8:3; (4) Mixed Oracles of Doom and Promise, chapters 8:4–9:15.

1. The oracles against foreign nations are a forcefully articulated series of indictments against neighbors of Israel, climaxed by a stinging attack upon the people of Israel. The groups he scores and the charges brought against them are:

Damascus	barbarity in war (1:3–5)
Philistia	slave-raiding (1:6–8)
Tyre	slave-raiding (1:9–10)
Edom	warfare with Israel (1:11–12)
Ammonites	barbarity in war (1:13–15)
Moab	desecration of the dead (2:1–3)
Judah	disregard of the law (2:4–5)
Israel	social and religious default (2:6–16)

Four of the oracles are suspect as later additions: Philistia, because Gath is not mentioned and thus a time after the city's fall to Assyria in 712 is indicated; Tyre, because the indictment is a copy of that against Philistia, with the awkward expression "covenant of brotherhood"; Edom, because its hostility toward the Hebrews was strongest after 587; and Judah, because the accusation is cast in Deuteronomic terminology. The objections to Tyre and Judah seem more valid than those against Philistia (the omission of Gath may be pure inadvertence) and Edom (preëxilic enmity was strong enough for both J and E to register it in their national epics).

The literary structure of the oracles is impressively regular and gives to the series a mounting sense of foreboding:

For three transgressions of . . .
    and for four, I will not revoke the punishment;
   because. . . .
So I will send (or kindle) a fire upon . . .

Here is one of the purest examples of the reproach and threat forms: "because . . . therefore" signify the unerring moral causality of Yahweh's rule among men, not only toward his people Israel but toward alien nations as well. The graduated numbers device is intended to emphasize the multitude and seriousness of the sins, but the precise figures (three and four) have no esoteric meaning. The next stich in Hebrew reads literally, "I will not cause *it* to return," presumably the penalty or punishment for sin; it is best translated by some phrase such as "I will not avert or reverse the punishment." The image is a strong one, implying that sins involve consequences that cannot be ignored or placated. Only divine mercy can grant a reprieve and Amos does not believe that Yahweh is any longer disposed to forestall nemesis. The punishment by fire is probably a military image, for Amos thinks largely in terms of the punishment of one nation by another, although in a later passage the fire is drought, 7:4–6.

If the oracles of chapters 1 and 2 (or all the authentic ones) were spoken by Amos in a single address we can imagine the electrifying effect. Beginning with the foreigners whose denunciation his listeners would approve, he came finally to the most severe castigation of all— the dereliction of Israel's covenant responsibilities. The oracles exhibit the consummate art of repetition and suspense that would have made oral delivery overpowering. While the present structure of the series argues strongly for their original linkage, it is possible that written compilation is responsible for their grouping, whether by prophet or editor. At any rate, the focus of the indictment is shown to be upon Israel not only by its being placed last but also because the reproach against Israel is richer in detail than the other oracles; the charge against Israel includes bribery, greed, cult prostitution, and use of ill-gotten gain for religious purposes. The reproach is followed by a recollection of Israel's holy history, the redemption wrought for Yahweh in the Exodus and Settlement, and the revelatory presence of rejected prophets. Only Israel has such a sacred history to recount. Finally the crushing impact of the punishment is announced. It is arguable that Israel in the oracle does not refer exclusively to the northern kingdom as a political entity but to the covenant people who embraced Hebrews in both kingdoms. The unity of north and south is more fundamental than the political breach. All the prophets appear to share the same conviction and to cherish the hope of reunion for the two peoples.

2. The oracles of chapters 3–6 are grouped by introductory catchwords, the most obvious being "Hear this word!" (3:1; 4:1; 5:1). Note also the verses beginning "I gave . . . withheld . . . sent . . . smote . . . overthrew," each concluding "yet you did not return to me" (4:6–11); the three oracles opening with "Seek!" (5:4–7, 14–15); and the three woes of 5:18; 6:1,4.

Among the memorable oracles of this section is the enunciation of national responsibility based on privilege. The election of Israel involves judgment by more rigorous standards than apply to others:

> You only have I known
> of all the families of the earth;
> therefore I will punish you
> for all your iniquities (3:2).

Then there is the vituperative attack on the feminine nobility of Samaria who spur their husbands on to provide greater luxury (4:1–3); the ironic call to worship at the increasingly well-attended and well-financed sanctuaries (4:4–5); the dirgelike lament over the prostrate virgin Israel, disclosing a tenderer side of the prophet's nature:

> Fallen, no more to rise,
> is the virgin Israel;
> forsaken on her land,
> with none to raise her up (5:2).

Amos' attitude toward sacrifice is debatable, for when he speaks on the subject it is briefly and in a condemnatory mood. In the most forceful terms he gives vent to Yahweh's rejection of the proffered worship. Yahweh loathes the holy day services, sacrifices, and music, which can never substitute for justice and righteousness (5:21–24). With expectation of a negative answer, Yahweh asks "Did you bring me sacrifices and offerings the forty years in the wilderness, O house of Israel?" (5:25). Whether he intends to say that sacrifice was definitely no part of the Mosaic cult or rather that there was no opportunity for it in the wilderness and thus the Hebrews got along without it, Amos certainly stresses the irrelevance of sacrifice to the main concern of religion. For him it is peripheral at best and insidiously dangerous at worst, for ritual has the habit of putting people into moral slumber so that thinking themselves fastidiously religious they do not hear the voice of Yahweh in its far-reaching demands. "Does Amos go too far in his sweeping denunciations? We shall not think so if we remember how readily men seek some substitute for true conversion."[6]

Amos makes the first mention in Israelite literature of the Day of Yahweh; he rebukes those who earnestly desire the coming of that Day. Apparently the Day was a popular religious-patriotic conception of the time when Israel's God would manifest himself in the defeat of enemy nations and the exaltation of Israel. The fantastic Israelite growth under Jeroboam encouraged such facile expectations. Amos would have none of it, for he insisted that the Day would be a time of judgment upon Israel; it would be "darkness, and not light." He seeks to shake the self-assurance of the people, their superficial religious hopes that are as baseless as the frothy prosperity of the times. Judgment, the laying bare of the true condition of Israel, is the essence of the Day of Yahweh. Amos set in motion the concept of the Day of Judgment, which was to assume such great significance in Jewish views of the end times. He did so with only the barest idea of how the Day would come about (armed disaster?) and certainly without positing the otherworldly aspects of later eschatology.

3. The vision sequence includes locusts (7:1–3), drought (7:4–6), plumb line (7:7–9), and basket of summer fruit (8:1–3), each prefaced by the formula, "Adonai Elohim (or He) showed me: behold . . ." In the first two the impending judgment on Israel is averted through the prophet's intercession ("this shall not be") but in the latter two the judgment is irrevocable ("I will never again pass by them"). The vision of Yahweh beside the altar, executing his judgment on the sanctuary, is different in form from the others and probably does not belong to this sequence (9:1). The intrusion of the Amaziah incident in 7:10–17 is best explained by the catchword principle, since the third vision ends with mention of Jeroboam who also appears prominently in the biographical interruption. An editor has linked the two references to Jeroboam in verses 9 and 10. The visions bring into sharp relief the intolerable inequities about to be requited. Israel is a wall so askew that it must be leveled in order to permit rebuilding. Israel is overripened fruit gathered in a basket, fit only for spoiling. Wherever Amos looked he saw attested in natural and human experience the reality of divine judgment.

4. In the miscellaneous appendix there are several oracles possibly later than Amos of Tekoa. The spacious descriptions of God's cosmic

[6] E. A. Edghill, *Amos* (WC), Methuen, 1914, p. 40.

power found in 9:5–6 (and earlier in 4:13 and 5:8–9) are from a later time, for they resemble the cosmological doxologies of Deutero-Isaiah and Job who wrote during and after the Exile. The promissory ending of the book of Amos was added by editors who wanted to conclude on a positive note. Not that Amos could not have held forth hope for his people (there is a faint glimmer in the admonition of 5:15, "Hate evil and love good, and establish justice in the gate; it may be that Yahweh, God of hosts, will be gracious to the remnant of Joseph") but the abounding hope of 9:8b–15 (the addition begins ". . . except that I will not utterly destroy the House of Israel") is psychologically inconsistent with the sense of impending doom pervading the book. The reference to the stricken Davidic dynasty ("the fallen booth of David") is a certain postexilic Judean notion. The crowning argument against Amos as author of the passage is the agricultural abundance and political revival of the future, unaccompanied as they are by the moral renovation on which Amos based everything. Without the contingency of true spiritual conversion, the golden age of future happiness was for Amos the merest illusion, the bitterest of mirages, "peace when there is no peace."

JUSTICE AND PRACTICAL MONOTHEISM

The task of assessing the contributions of Amos to the religion of his people is a formidable one. At best we know little about him and yet his words speak with an authentic and compelling ring. In his train there sprang up a succession of prophets who were not interested in canonizing Amos but in calling Israel as he had done to the observance of her total covenant responsibility. In at least two respects his message was epochal.

Amos was the covenant conscience of an irresponsible social and religious order. It is significant that the first great prophet arose amid the distressing acceleration of class inequities, enervating luxury, absentee landlordism, and judicial corruption that attended the Israelite boom of the mid-eighth century. In a society where monetary status predominated, Amos set himself against the vulgarization of Israelite man, his disfigurement and depersonalization. The God of Amos was the fierce protector of what we today would call "human rights," for the firm corollary of the covenant faith in the one God was the brotherhood of all Israelites. That brotherhood was now threatened by the exchange of the covenant ideals for the mercantile values of the

Canaanite world. To Amos it was not, however, a matter of rejecting the advance of civilization, but of keeping the old ideals alive in the midst of new and more complex situations. He insisted that while his people gained the whole world of commercial and technological advantage, they must not lose their covenanted soul. Israel's essential significance as a people responsible before God (cast always in the covenant framework, even though the word is not used) must never be sacrificed to the behemoth of materialism.

A Canaanite ivory box (Amos 3:15; 6:4).

When he turned his gaze upon what passed for religion in his day, Amos' fury knew no bounds. What he saw was a cultic adjunct of the state and of the ruling social caste. Karl Marx was not more blistering in his assaults on contemporary religion than Amos, a point to be remembered by those who feel that all criticisms of the *status quo* are "communist-inspired." Religion was indeed "the opiate of the people," not of the depressed alone but also of the advantaged who by obeisance to the cult succeeded in avoiding any decisive relation with God and any change in their values and manner of living. It is worth pondering that Amos did not attack Baalism or idol worship or the departure of the north from Jerusalem. What he attacked rather was the irreligion of the religious, that coarse religious utilitarianism in which the greedy and frothy-minded simply see their own powers magnified and validated by the gods they worship. As one writer on prophetic religion has put it: "Indeed, it is precisely in Amos that what we have said in general summary becomes especially clear: namely, that the struggle of the prophets was not a struggle between piety and godlessness, but rather a struggle between God's demand and the highest human piety, between true and false faith."[7]

In every time of "religious revival," when it is popular and patriotic to be devout, when religion becomes scarcely separable from culture and a man's church affiliation is accepted as naturally as his birthright, the trenchant criticism of Amos is astoundingly relevant.

[7] Paul Volz, *Prophetengestalten des Alten Testaments,* Calwer, 1949, p. 145.

His was the healthy skepticism that calls easygoing religious assumptions into question and insists that religious profession be tested by works, that fine sentiments must be given substance in the way men govern and conduct their business, or else such sentiments are better not held at all.

Amos was the spokesman of a mature practical monotheism. Amos represents the halfway house between the henotheism of Moses (in which other gods were admitted but only in their own national spheres) and the explicit monotheism of Deutero-Isaiah (in which the existence of any other gods is categorically denied)—and it may be that Amos is much beyond halfway. What is this in-between position? W. R. Harper speaks of the "intermediate step" as the recognition of "unlimited power."[8] Essentially Amos pushed the sovereignty of God into all the provinces of life. Yahweh was supreme in realms previously denied him: in Sheol (9:2) and among non-Israelite peoples (1–2:3; 9:7). In at least one instance a nation is condemned for an action in which no Israelites were involved (the Moabite desecration of Edomite royal tombs). Implicit in the foreign oracles is the concept of "natural law" or "international order" not to be flouted even by the powerful.

Amos goes so far as to hint at a positive relation on Yahweh's part with Ethiopians, Philistines, and Syrians. In what must have been the closing words of the original book, the prophet speaks for deity:

Are you not like the Ethiopians to me,
  O people of Israel? says Yahweh.
Did I not bring up Israel from the land of Egypt,
  and the Philistines from Caphtor and the Syrians from Kir?
Behold, the eyes of Adonai Elohim are upon the sinful kingdom,
  and I will destroy it from the surface of the ground (9:7–8).

The nations were selected by Amos with barbed rhetorical intent, for the Ethiopians were on the very perimeter of the known world, while the Philistines and Syrians were two of the hated historic enemies of Israel. Yahweh's abiding concern for the nations far and near, shown by his guidance of their migratory beginnings, opens up tantalizing vistas of thought that the prophet does not pursue. He directed his energy toward the covenant default of Israel and did not develop a positive approach toward the nations nor an explicit monotheism as did the exilic poet of Isaiah 40–55.

[8] W. R. Harper, *Amos and Hosea* (ICC), Scribner's, 1905, p. cxv.

Yet how traumatically the international character of the times has affected the mind of Amos! He lived in just such a germinal era as our own, when the old mores and circumscribed thoughts of men were not large enough. While remaining fervently loyal to the covenant faith of his fathers, he saw intuitively the implications of Yahweh's lordship over the Fertile Crescent. A like attitude had been typical of the Yahwist in his marvelous stories of the beginnings, and somewhat less evident in the Elijah and Elisha stories where those prophets have favorable dealings with a Canaanite widow and the Syrian nobleman Naaman. On the threshold of the era of Assyrian imperialism, Amos proclaimed the mental and theological adjustment that Israel must undergo. He was not intentionally an innovator, but the novelty of his insight and the thunder of his speech made Amos the initiator of a new day in Israelite religion. The double standard based on Israel's election by God could never again be interpreted to mean that Israel's lot was morally easier or that the nations were no concern of the covenant God.

Sometimes it is said that Amos spoke with too sharp a tongue and too bitter feelings, but it is idle to reform him at this distance, to require of him a tempered message, to drain off his genius, to quench the blaze of his wrath. Admittedly he spoke with "a magnificent one-sidedness" but what he said needs to be held before humankind, especially religious man, with just that vehemence and starkness which were his hallmarks. After reading Amos, we feel how serious it was for Israel to cease to express God's character, and equally how firm was God's intention to extend his purpose—without faithless Israel if need be. Was there fire in the ashes? Amos' violent and provocative words would stir up the embers and prove him wrong to the extent that the very capacity of a people to produce such a searing prophet and the willingness of at least a few to listen to him showed that the Mosaic vision of Yahweh was not lost altogether and that there was yet a great mission for the people of God.

HOSEA

Hosea, son of Beeri, was a native northerner whose prophetic ministry followed close upon that of Amos. Although the superscription states that he began to preach in the time of Jeroboam II, the bulk of the oracles in his book have as their background the rapidly deteriorating political and religious situation after the extinction of the Jehu dynasty in 745. Since Hosea only foresees the fall of the north, it is widely assumed that he ceased to prophesy before Samaria was captured by the Assyrians in 722; but the editorial superscription states that he was still preaching in the time of Hezekiah and in support of this some scholars contend that there are authentic Hosean passages which presuppose northern captivity. Certainly the great majority of Hosea's oracles mirror the chaotic last days of the northern kingdom, the Pollyanna climate of Amos' era having suddenly turned into panicky search for the leader and policy that could "buy time."

The hypothesis that he was of priestly origins is based mainly on his knowledge of the Israelite leadership and his incisive attacks on religious corruption and default, but one might as well argue that he was a baker because he employs the image of the overheated oven with such effect! Although we lack information as to his home town or occupation, the domestic life of Hosea is divulged in some detail. Yet mention of his wife Gomer and the three children is only in integral connection with his teaching; they are presented, not to satisfy biographical curiosity, but to clarify the message. They are frankly enigmatic; without them the book would be easier to interpret though less appealing.

Hosea's literary production is as chaotic as Amos' is orderly. The text is woefully mutilated, at points meaningless unless emended from the ancient versions. This is in large measure due to poor compilation and transmission, but a share of the responsibility must rest upon the type of person the prophet was. His emotional and distraught nature is reflected in short sentences with frequent lack of syntactic connection. The classical cadences of Amos dissolve into shrieks and sobs in Hosea. It is not easy to decide when the words of Hosea have been lost because of textual confusion and when they are before us exactly as disordered as the prophet's emotions.

Oracles cannot be as clearly delineated in Hosea as in Amos. The complexes are less evident, if indeed we have any basis for distinguishing internal groupings. The one clear division is this: chapters 1–3 have a common rootage in Hosea's marriage, whereas chapters 4–14 deal with the general political and religious situation. The introductory and concluding formulas that ordinarily mark off prophetic oracles are often missing. Since Hosea was no less conscious of prophetic inspiration than Amos, absence of the expression "Thus saith Yahweh" argues for fragmentary preservation of the text. Favorite devices in Hosea's oracles are imperatives: "Plead!" 2:2, "Blow the horn!" 5:8, "Sow for yourselves!" 10:12, "Return, O Israel!" 14:1; and rhetorical questions: "What shall I do with you, O Ephraim?" 6:4, "How long will it be till they are pure in Israel?" 8:5, "Shall not war overtake them in Gibeah?" 10:9, "O Ephraim, what have I to do with idols?" 14:8.

There are later additions to the book, but not as numerous as radical critics have supposed. The primary themes inviting supplement have been Judah and the glorious future. Many of the passages in which Judah is named look like glosses intended either to exempt the south from Israel's fate or to warn Judah that "it can happen here." Judean editors, in possession of the book after 722, were concerned to emphasize its relevance for their situation. Some of the Judean glosses are:

But I will have pity on the house of Judah, and I will
    deliver them by Yahweh their God (1:7).

Though you play the harlot, O Israel
    let not Judah become guilty (4:15).

For you also, O Judah, a harvest is appointed (6:11).

Ephraim has encompassed me with lies,
    and the house of Israel with deceit;
but Judah is still known by God,
    and is faithful to the Holy One (11:12).

The Judah reference in 5:8–12 is defended, however, by Alt who convincingly demonstrates that it relates to the Syro-Ephraimite crisis of 735 when there was border friction between the two Hebrew kingdoms.[9]

The most glaring addition of a promissory nature occurs at the close of the first chapter where the reunion of the kingdoms is promised and the original symbolic names Lo' 'ammi ("not my people") and Jezreel are reinterpreted. The secondary hand betrays itself by the self-conscious literary remark: "and in the place where it was said to them, 'You are not my people,' it shall be said to them, 'Sons of the living God' " (1:10b). Other doubtful sections are the covenant with the animals (2:18) and the image of Israel as a luxuriant plant

[9] Albrecht Alt, "Hosea 5,8–6,6. Ein Krieg und seine Folgen in Prophetischen Beleuchtung," *Kleine Schriften zur Geschichte des Volkes Israel,* Beck, 1953, vol. 2, pp. 163–187.

(14:5–7). The last verse of the book is widely recognized as a post-script tagged on by a wisdom writer.

Two passages often denied to the prophet are not objectionable. The description of the renewal of marriage vows between Yahweh and Israel in the desert stresses recognized preëxilic prophetic themes: "And I will betroth you to me for ever; I will betroth you to me in righteousness and in justice, in steadfast love, and in mercy. I will betroth you to me in faithfulness; and you shall know Yahweh" (2:19–20). The redundant quality of the passage may indicate editorial revision, however, and the following play on the names Jezreel and "my people" is doubtless late (2:21–23). The climactic oracle of 14:1–4 with its pledge of the freely given and healing love of Yahweh is congruous with Hosea's previous insight into the redemptive power of divine love. If all notes of hope were deleted from the oracles, on the rigid prescription that preëxilic prophets spoke only threats, then the book would have little left and the domestic analogy would seem purposeless. But we are anticipating an analysis of the prophet's marriage.

The Prophet's Marriage

Information about the marriage of Hosea is confined to the first three chapters of the book. Chapter 1 is biographical prose (third person); it recounts the marriage of Hosea to Gomer and the birth of a son Jezreel, symbolizing vengeance on Jehu's dynasty (cf. II Kings 9:36–37), a daughter Lo'ruhama, "not pitied," and a son Lo"ammi, "not my people." (In this account, 1:7 should be deleted as a later Judean gloss and 1:10–2:1 excised as eschatological commentary on the original vs. 9.) Chapter 2 is a cluster of poetic oracles (with a prose oracle in vss. 16–20); it applies the marriage metaphor to Israel. The prose and concluding poetry are often denied to Hosea (2:16–23), but the evidence is not decisive. The chapter is indirectly helpful in elucidating the prophet's marriage since it permits us to reason backward from his religious analogy to the domestic experience. Chapter 3 is autobiographical prose (first person); it relates how the prophet "bought" a harlot and forced her to live in isolation as a witness to Yahweh's love of his adulterous people. The last verse tells of the return of Israel (3:5) and is undoubtedly a Judean addition for Hosea would hardly have referred to "David their king," but verse 4 is authentic-sounding with its threat of the suspension of religious practice during a punitive exile from the land (the same notion is expressed by Hosea in 8:10). There is no valid reason for doubting Hosea's belief in an exile that would have a purgative effect.

In an effort to fit the three chapters together, a great number of hypotheses have been advanced. A provisional reconstruction of the marriage experience of Hosea is best introduced by considering some basic questions:

Was the marriage an allegory or visionary experience? This suggests itself as a simple way to remove the moral difficulty of a man of Hosea's sensitivities marrying a harlot. Instead of relating events in his life, he constructed an allegorical tale or recounted a vision in which imagined happenings became vehicles of religious teaching. Supporters of this theory point to the prophetic habit of visualizing actions that could hardly have been carried out, such as Zechariah's murder of three shepherds (11:8). But the objections are decisive. The sense of offense in the story is based on modern sex morality and is thus a manufactured difficulty. To reduce the marriage to allegory or vision "takes the teeth" out of the analogy that the prophet develops in such an effective and original way. There are details in the report that have no conceivable allegorical sense: the name Gomer means nothing, nor are the weaning of the second child and the ransom price given any double significance. Symbolic actions that from our point of view are coarse (and probably from theirs also) seem to have been engaged in by other prophets, as when Isaiah walked naked through the streets of Jerusalem in the posture of a war captive (Isaiah 20) and Ezekiel cooked his rations on a fire of dried dung (Ezek. 4:9–17). Finally, anything obscene about the marriage to a harlot is not removed by the allegorical or visionary view, for we must still reckon with the fact that the prophet chose to write of the event in a way central to his whole message.

Was Gomer a harlot at all? Another and more serious effort to remove the difficulties insists on seeing two different women, in chapter 1 Gomer the chaste and faithful wife of the prophet and in chapter 3 a common prostitute. Once the subject of chapter 3 is recognized as another woman, the only aspersion on Gomer's character is the epithet "a wife of harlotry," which is amply explained by the apostate condition of the land, "For the land commits great harlotry by forsaking Yahweh" (1:2). The interpretation of chapter 3 assumes that if the wife of chapter 1 were meant then the text would have said,

"Go, love *the* woman (or Gomer)." It also takes the imprecise "again" as belonging outside the command, "Yahweh said *again* (a second time) to me, 'Go, love a woman. . . .'" Also the silences of the chapter are capitalized on: would so important a matter as Gomer's complete departure from her husband so that she had to be "bought" back be passed over in absolute silence? Why are there no references to the children if the woman is Gomer?

Opponents, however, have arguments not readily dismissed. Gomer is certainly the woman of chapter 3 since no other is named or implied. The adverb "again" belongs to the divine command, "And Yahweh said to me, 'Go *again* (once more), love a woman. . . .'" The increasing faithlessness of Gomer, implied in the names Hosea gave to his children and the analogy of chapter 2, which speaks of Israel going after the Baals but returning to her first husband, indicates that Gomer had deserted Hosea and fallen into slavery or complete control by the sanctuary priests. While the proposal exonerates Gomer of infidelity, it has the effect of putting Hosea in dishonor. It certainly shows little respect for his wife and children to parade them in harlotrous symbolism if there were no foundation for it in fact. And what significance has the arbitrary choice of a prostitute by Hosea? Does that really convey his message? Doesn't he intend to say that Israel and Yahweh were bound with enduring ties? Can that be symbolized with an indiscriminate public purchase? The net effect of the "two women theory" is to render the involvement of either one in the imagery obscure and to distort the religious analogy almost beyond recognition. This is seen supremely in the theory's destruction of the heart of the analogy: namely, Yahweh's love for his one wife Israel. As Buber rightly insists, Hosea could only be commanded to love the woman again if he had already loved her.[10]

Was Gomer a harlot at the time of marriage? The alternatives are somewhat narrowed once we agree with tradition that Gomer was a harlot, but the options are still multiple. That Gomer only turned to harlotry after her marriage is a suggestion popularized in English by the lucid pen of George Adam Smith.[11] It has much in its favor. Hosea's abhorrence of sexual immorality in the oracles of chapters 4–14 is hard to reconcile with his marriage to a known harlot. It is

[10] Martin Buber, *The Prophetic Faith,* Macmillan, 1949, p. 113.
[11] G. A. Smith, *The Book of the Twelve Prophets,* Doubleday, 1929, vol. 1, pp. 241–268.

possible to see in the names of the children a progressive discovery of Gomer's unfaithfulness, till at the end the prophet does not regard the third child as his own (in 1:9, however, the "you" is a plural form). Then also the prophets sometimes state the consequence or result of a chain of events as though it were the purpose. With their visual compression of reality they do not keep strict separation between result and purpose. Isaiah reads the unhappy results of his preaching to the people into the terms of his call to preach (Isa. 6:9–13). Hosea finds that he was directed by Yahweh to marry one who turned out to be a harlot; prophetic realism easily takes the next step of insisting that he was commanded to marry a harlot.

Now the whole scheme has an attractive aura in that it renders psychologically feasible the divided state of Hosea's mind and the growing realization that his wife is faithless, which then is projected into the divine-human relation. But that is precisely its vulnerability: it is too feasible, too modern, almost romantic in character. We must be careful not to sell short the possibility that in literal obedience to a divine summons Hosea married a harlot. Leviticus 21:7 forbids priests to marry prostitutes, implying that other men did, and Hosea's ardent blast at cult prostitution is not at all inconsistent with his marriage to one who had been a prostitute. His union with Gomer would not mean that he was patronizing or condoning prostitution, but rather that he was "raiding the enemy camp," in a way setting out to do what so many novelists' heroes attempt: to reform the fallen woman. The difference here is that from the start she was not merely a woman toward whom he felt erotic attraction but a symbol of a whole religious fabric of thought. Instead of discovering his message about Yahweh's love in his marriage, Hosea set out to illustrate that love by the type of marriage he chose. Only modern romanticism would object that this eliminates his true love for the woman. What it shows is that the illustration, the symbolic action itself reinforced and strengthened his conviction of God's love as Hosea came to see how momentous a thing it is to be bound in a relation where the conflicting claims of righteousness and grace cry out for resolution.

Was Gomer a religious harlot? Herein seems to lie the most satisfactory solution to the baffling enigma of the prophet's marriage. If Gomer were one of the temple prostitutes who staffed the Baal fertility cults, in her devotion to the cult lovers she recapitulated Israel's own apostasy. Her status in society would then be, if not an honored

one, at least widely accepted as proper. There is evidence that married
women continued to give their services to the cult. It is objected that
the words for harlot in chapters 1–3 are different from the technical
term for "holy woman" or cult prostitute whose patronizing he deplores. The linguistic evidence is indecisive, however, especially considering the garbled transmission of the book. Hosea was far from a
sexual prude; he would not have thought of a sacred harlot as con-
taminated and if it fitted his religious convictions he would not hesitate
to seek one for his wife.

Psychoanalytic approaches to Hosea have suggested that he suffered
from a sexual mania, that he was attracted to the type of woman his
higher nature abhorred, but once drawn to her his strong sex drive
was sublimated to a great religious vision.[12] If so, he would not be the
only religionist for whom sex was a major struggle in his life: for example, Augustine. But the obstacles to psychoanalyzing so dimly perceived a personality as Hosea are insurmountable, and when the
Freudian terminology is examined it is not really saying anything irreconcilable with Hosea's prophetic call. The admission of pronounced
sexual factors in the religious faith of Hosea would not discredit his
faith but only show how all the basic concerns of human life are
potentially allied with religion. The effect of the association of sex and
religion in the prophecy of Hosea was not to demean religion but to
elevate sex.

A tentative surmise as to the events underlying chapters 1–3 suggests that Gomer was a sacred harlot whom Hosea married in full
knowledge of her profession. His relation to her was a sign of Yahweh's choice of wayward Israel. He gave the children symbolic names.
Gomer continued to serve as a hierodule at the Baal sanctuary. Hosea
did not share the tolerance of this practice, which typified Canaanite
society. Hosea tried to win her to sole fidelity to himself. Finally she
left him altogether to live in the temple precincts. Hosea undiscouraged
went to the temple and gained the legal right to take her away ("I
bought her" doubtless has the meaning "I gained power over her,
formal legal possession") probably through the payment of an amount
to compensate for the loss of her services, since it was customary for
the client's fee to go into the temple treasury. This may have been a

---

[12] Adolf Allwohn, *Die Ehe des Propheten Hosea in psychoanalytischen Beleuchtung*, Töpelmann, 1926.

fee paid directly to the god, "the marriage price."[13] Now her husband in the full sense, Hosea put her in "quarantine" as it were, with the hope that from her experience of the futility of pursuing "her lovers" and his own persistent devotion, Gomer's reclamation might result. In all of this the realism of Hebrew marriage, the total union of two persons in every dimension of life as well as the superior position of the husband, must be taken into account if we are not to miss the force of the image.

GOD'S LOVE FOR ISRAEL

As far as we can judge, Hosea was the first to use the marriage symbol to describe the relation between Yahweh and Israel. It had been long avoided because of the dangers implicit in fertility worship with its obvious debasements of the sexual drive. But the emotional satisfactions of Baal religion appealed to something in human nature that could not forever be disregarded by Yahwism. Hosea took the bold step of modifying the austerity of the desert religion, not by wholesale importation of Baalism (as the official cult attempted), but by insistence upon love as the primary aspect of Yahweh. To the common attribute of Yahweh, *hesedh* or covenant love, with its stress upon mutual fidelity, Hosea added *'ahabhah* or election love, with the connotation of love's freedom to express itself unilaterally, with spontaneity and emotional warmth. Actually Hosea treated both as fundamental aspects of the relation of God and man, and the marriage bond expressed them admirably for it partook both of the contractual and the voluntaristic aspects of love. Hardly secondary in significance is the prophet's imagery of the father-son relationship as picturing Yahweh's redemption of his people from Israel.

When Israel was a child, I loved him,
and out of Egypt I called my son.
The more I called them,
the more they went from me;
they kept sacrificing to the Baals,
and burning incense to idols.
Yet it was I who taught Ephraim to walk,
I took them up in my arms;
but they did not know that I healed them.

[13] A. D. Tushingham, "A Reconsideration of Hosea, Chapters 1–3," *Journal of Near Eastern Studies,* 12 (1953), 150–159.

I led them with cords of compassion
  with the bands of love,
and I became to them as one
  who eases the yoke on their jaws,
  and I bent down to them and fed them (11:1–4).

In nearly every oracle of Hosea there is an anguished sense of spurned and outraged love that gives his work a bittersweetness matched only by Jeremiah.

This bent of Hosea for presenting the life of faith in the imagery of human relationships has been called appositely "the Higher Anthropomorphism."[14] In place of the merely physical anthropomorphisms (the hands, eyes, mouth of God) he employs social anthropomorphisms. The most intimate experiences of human life become signs of God's abiding relation with man. Yahweh is husband and father, Israel is wife and child. In Hebrew thought God remains explicitly transcendent and "other" but he is implicitly immanent, somehow joined personally and directly to Israel. As Amos expresses the one facet, so Hosea dwells upon the other. The inseparability of God and man is advanced by every assumption of the prophet; Israel's lord could never be merely an external onlooker but always a vitally concerned participant in human affairs. Only the freedom and spontaneity of interpersonal contact could serve to articulate this reality. Hosea thus fills a void in Amos; the external judge is now seen as the involved redeemer.

SIN AND THE KNOWLEDGE OF GOD

The roster of sins assailed by Hosea has entries similar to those of Amos; he decries ill-gotten wealth (12:7–9), drunkenness (4:11, 18), empty cult worship (6:6), and ritual prostitution (4:13–14). Unlike Amos, he does not have much to say about the poor. He turns his invective mainly into political and religious channels. He is the first prophet to attack idolatry in the strict sense of image worship (4:12,17; 8:4; 13:2; 14:8). In particular he condemns the calf-worship of Bethel, which he stigmatizes as Beth-aven (house of iniquity or trouble):

A workman made it; it is not God.
  The calf of Samaria shall be broken to pieces (8:5).

[14] H. W. Robinson, *The Cross of Hosea,* Westminster, 1949, p. 22.

and in 13:2 he jests derisively:

> Sacrifice to these, they say.
> Men kiss calves!

He objects to the baalization of Israel's religion. Elijah's battle to reject Baal was not a victory for all time, because the allurements of the Canaanite fertility religion were perpetual and syncretism with Yahwism an unending threat in every village with a high place or temple. Even the golden bull images, whatever they once signified, were objects of worship to the people at large.

Hosea rebukes the usurpation of political power and approaches an antimonarchic animus. It is evident that in Hosea's day the lack of any able ruler made of the office a tempting prize for those with ambition. Hosea deplores the assassinations and facile trust of the people in their weak and unprincipled rulers. More than this, he seems to say in accord with the later source of Samuel that kingship is an abomination and the present decay of the office an inevitability.

> I will destroy you, O Israel;
>   who can help you?
> Where now is your king, to save you;
>   where are all your princes, to defend you—
> those of whom you said,
>   "Give me a king and princes"?
> I have given you kings in my anger,
>   and I have taken them away in my wrath (13:9–10).

Probably the phrase "days of Gibeah" (9:9; 10:9) refers to the institution of the monarchy, for it will be remembered that Saul was of Gibeah; however it may be an allusion to the Benjaminite outrage (Judges 19–20). The prophet pointedly denounces foreign alliances. Israel flits back and forth from Assyria to Egypt like a silly dove, or wanders like a wild ass over the uplands frantically seeking sustenance. She cannot see that these foreign attachments only hasten her collapse. Since it is Yahweh who like a lion rends Israel, no foreign king can heal the wounds. Israel thinks she can purchase her safety but she "has sown the wind and will reap the whirlwind" (8:7). It is an interesting sidelight on prophetic knowledge of the future that Hosea seems to think of Egypt and Assyria as equal menaces, as though he were not certain which would bring about Israel's downfall.

The root of sin for Hosea is comprehended in his fondness for the term *knowledge*. "Knowledge of God" for this prophet is a theme with boundless implications. To know God is not a matter of correct dogmatic theorizing or of properly performed ritual but rather to understand his nature and emulate it. Israel did not know that it was Yahweh who gave her the good things of Canaan. "My people are destroyed for lack of knowledge" (4:6),

> for I desire steadfast love (*hesedh*) and not sacrifice,
>   the knowledge of God, rather than burnt offerings (6:6).

But this knowledge is not as easily attained as might appear, for ignorance of God is not merely misinformation but a perverse will and a binding and enslaving deception. When Israel assumes herself possessed of God's truth and favor, then is she most deceived.

> To me they cry,
>   My God, we Israel know thee.
> Israel has spurned the good (8:2,3*a*).

> Their deeds do not permit them
>   to return to their God.
> For the spirit of harlotry is within them,
>   and they know not the Lord (5:4).

The presumed knowledge that Israel has of God has proved so often to be impermanent and fleeting, "like a morning cloud . . . like the dew," which graces the Oriental countryside in the summer months but is burned off by the rising sun. So the sin of Israel is the enslaving and ever-deceiving pseudo-knowledge that confuses labels with realities, that mistakes acquaintance for understanding, that accepts lip loyalties for life commitments.

Israel's separation from God thus has a strangely paradoxical character: it is deep-seated, radical, springing not merely from occasional evil deeds but rooting in a spirit that possesses and blinds; at the same time it is wilful and perverse, a course for which the people are responsible and cannot plead extenuating circumstances as a sufficient excuse. Sin is a compulsive and erratic master, moving men they know not where and often against their better judgments—witness the folly of Gomer! Yet it is *they* who have been moved and the only solution to their plight is not in rationalization, in pretended innocence but in repentance and conversion. So far Hosea stands close in his insight to the view of Plato that to know the right is to do the right, for knowledge of the good has an intrinsically attractive and self-authenticating quality. Political chaos, social disintegration, moral laxity, and religious defection—all these have at their core the failure to see the nature of reality. Not to know God is not to know one's own welfare.

Hosea moves on, however, to an insight that was outside the pale of Platonic thought. He grasped the truth that a separation from God so deeply rooted and so cleverly rationalized could never be healed by anything short of an equally grand compulsion. Gomer could not be won by preachments but only by the tenacity of Hosea's love implemented in redemptive acts. So the vision of divine grace rises resplendent in the prophetic mind, foreshadowing its Christian development to the point that one writer can speak of "the cross of Hosea" as of the same texture as the cross of Jesus Christ, for both were instances of human suffering evidencing the divine redemptive power.[15] One need not look for verses that predict the coming of Jesus to see in the fabric of Hosea's thought the presuppositions of the Christian Incarnation: that God steps into the life of man to uplift it at the cost of self-sacrifice.

Hosea intimates that the wrath of God, so terrifyingly envisioned by Amos, is really the obverse of his love expressing itself against all that would blight the welfare of Israel. Judgment is redemptive rather than merely retributive.

> How can I give you up, O Ephraim!
>   How can I hand you over, O Israel!
> How can I make you like Admah!
>   How can I treat you like Zeboiim!
> My heart recoils within me,
>   my compassion grows warm and tender.
> I will not execute my fierce anger,
>   I will not again destroy Ephraim;
> for I am God and not man,
>   the Holy One in your midst,
>   and I will not come to destroy (11:8–9).

That this is not tantamount to the sentimental waiving of deserved judgment is apparent in the closing words of the original prophecy where repentance and redemptive love are indissolubly united:

[15] *Ibid.*

Return, O Israel, to Yahweh your God,
    for you have stumbled because of your iniquity.
    . . . .
I will heal their faithlessness;
    I will love them freely,
    for my anger has turned from them (14:1,4).

YAHWEH, LORD OF NATURE

Lastly, Hosea reasserts Yahweh's dominion over the sphere of nature and agriculture, thus preëmpting the rights of the Baals and rendering their placation needless. This was once asserted by Elijah, but a century later the battle needed to be launched anew. Hosea makes fertility and sterility contingent upon loyalty to Yahweh. One of the most difficult of all ancient ideas for the modern reader is precisely this attribution of psychic life to nature so that nature participates in human culpability and human felicity. It became a cardinal idea in subsequent Jewish eschatology: the transformation of nature to accompany the renewal of man. Mythopoetic as the idea may be, there is much in it that modern sophistication might ponder, to take only so patent a "rationalization" of the idea as the depletion of natural resources owing to the irresponsibility of man. Hosea attacks Baalism on home ground; the "favors" of oil, grain, and wine, which Israel supposes to have been granted by her "lovers," are really the gifts of Yahweh. When Israel is faithless to him, he withholds the rain and the land languishes and mourns. The bountiful fertility of Ephraim will atrophy, "No birth, no pregnancy, no conception"—of man or beast! Even the incensed prophet stumbles in pronouncing the terrible curse:

Give them, O Yahweh—what wilt thou give?
    Give them a miscarrying womb and dry breasts! (9:14).

Only when God is sought in true knowledge will the boons of the earth be returned to Israel. Hosea does not, however, hold out this prospect as a bribe, as a purely external sanction but as a heartfelt promise of the goodness of God and the bounty of his world when held in trust. He knows that no outside sanction will suffice to change the wilful heart of those snared by evil. Hosea's love of the good earth (he could readily be imagined as an aristocratic landowner) and his associations with the soil lead him to see Yahweh's hand in the proc-

esses formerly ascribed to the Baals. The life of nature has its legitimate place in the religious interests of man, but the clue to the meaning of the whole is not to be drawn from vitalistic forces but from the
covenant love of Yahweh. The prophets were not like the reactionary
Rechabites who renounced civilization as such. Amos was willing to
accept the necessities of commercial urbanization when pervaded by
the spirit of the covenant. Similarly Hosea regarded the life of agriculture as proper and essential when the land was accepted as a
stewardship from the covenant God.

By his conception of the knowledge of God, Hosea summoned Israel
away from form to substance, from the unreal pursuit of power and
security back to the reality of God and thus to a sane society founded
upon the covenant will of Yahweh. By his unique proclamation of the
love of God and by his attribution of the functions of the Baals to
Yahweh, Hosea tempered the harsher features of Yahwism by expressing its essential features in terms of family imagery. He was able
to accomplish this without compromising the moral demands of Amos,
without sentimentalizing God nor denuding him of his majesty and
otherness. If anything, the justice of God is the more severe in Hosea,
for it stems from wounded and rejected love (Yahweh is like an en-
raged she-bear, 13:8). The justice and love of God are welded into a
single experienced truth. In this respect Hosea set the pattern for
Jewish and Christian thinking that has not changed in any basic regard.

It is indicative of the richness of the prophetic tradition that the first
two of the great prophets, though men fundamentally at one, were
yet so diverse in temperament and insight. Their differences are not
reducible to any kind of ideological conflict. They could have known
one another and approved of each other's message with no difficulty.
But the uniqueness of their own persons and their intensely transforming experiences of God, their peculiar idioms—all these mark them as
men fully caught up in their religious roles, sacrificing all their remarkable gifts to the call in which they so deeply believed.

MICAH

The prophet Micah, from Moresheth-gath in the Philistine Plain, is
dated as a contemporary of Hosea in the north and Isaiah in the
south. His ministry to the Kingdom of Judah is independently corrob-

orated in Jeremiah where we read that his prophecies of doom in the days of Hezekiah were remembered a hundred years later (26:16–19). Micah 3:12, foretelling the destruction of Jerusalem, is quoted in Jeremiah as typical of his message. Only the repentance of Hezekiah averted the disaster. There is no such biographical information in the prophetic book of Micah, so that the contemporaries of Jeremiah must have been drawing on some other source, whether oral or written we cannot say.

If the tenor of Micah's prophecies was doom, then their distillation is found mainly in chapters 1–3 which consist of Amos-like pronouncements of disaster built upon sweeping arraignments of social injustice. His oracles are not mere imitations of the prophet of Tekoa, however, for they are cast in his own style and studded with peculiar nuances of thought. He singles out the rulers for more direct attack than had Amos. He has barbed words for the professionalism of the prophets

> who cry 'Peace'
>> when they have something to eat,
> but declare war against him
>> who puts nothing into their mouths (3:5).

By contrast he describes his inspiration as fortification to declare the hard and unpleasant word of judgment:

> But as for me, I am filled with power,
>> with the Spirit of Yahweh,
>> and with justice and might,
> to declare to Jacob his transgression
> and to Israel his sin (3:8).

Micah speaks plaintively of the divine regret that the prophetic message must be so saturnine:

> "Do not harp"—thus they harp—
>> "one should not harp on such things;
>> disgrace will not overtake us."
> . . . .
> Do not my words do good
>> to him who walks uprightly? (2:6–7).

Remorselessly he exposes the baseless confidence of the people. The prophet sees the sins of the Hebrews concentrated in the vices of city life. All the burning indignation of a provincial citizen at the abuses of the big city come to a head in his fierce indictment of Samaria and Jerusalem:

> What is the transgression of Jacob?
>   Is it not Samaria?
> And what is the sin of the house of Judah?
>   Is it not Jerusalem? (1:5).

His words of course had sober truth behind them, for it was precisely these urban centers that first felt the impact of social and political corruption.

The remaining chapters of the book of Micah fall into two groups: chapters 4 and 5 are oracles of hope; chapters 6 and 7 are mixed oracles of threat and promise. In the former there is a sudden reversal of mood, 4:1–4 presupposing conditions hardly typical of Micah's time (Jerusalem is the exclusive sanctuary to which all the nations flow in obedience to the law of God). The same oracle is found in Isaiah 2:1–4. Probably written by neither of the prophets, it nevertheless found eventual lodgment in the traditions of both. It is one of the most beautiful of biblical expressions about the golden age of peace among men and is doubtless postexilic. The oracles of this section are marked by pronounced inconsistencies that point to their miscellaneous character (e.g., the heathen are courted in 4:3 but annihilated in 4:13; a single deliverer appears in 5:2 but several in 5:5). The same may be said of the anthological assemblage of materials in the last two chapters. From 7:8 on the Exile is presupposed, including the demolition of the wall of Jerusalem.

Poetic oracles from the eighth-century Micah may appear among the later chapters (possibly we should credit him with 5:10–14; 6:9–16; 7:1–8) but it is likely that chapters 4–7 represent additions in at least two stages: (1) chapters 4–5 are a Zion collection offering hope as a balance to the condemnatory message of Micah and appended to the genuine oracles on the catchword principle (note "mountain of the house" in 3:12 and 4:1); (2) a separate collection of warnings in chapters 6–7:7 to which passages of promise were added. These were finally joined to chapters 1–5. As a result of the editorial activity of the Micah "school," the proportion of promise to threat is much greater in the book of Micah than in either Amos or Hosea. The best explanation for this development is that the centrality of Jerusalem in Micah's message has attracted the religious interest of subsequent generations, thus pulling into the book many oracles not belonging to the prophet in order to qualify his stringent words. It is certainly true that precisely the prophets closely connected with Jerusalem are those whose books have been most expanded by later writers (Isaiah, Jeremiah, Ezekiel).

To further underscore the fact that the anonymous prophecies are not necessarily inferior, it is noteworthy that 6:6–8 contains a fine epitome of the prophetic understanding of faith, of the precedence of justice (*mishpat*) and lovingkindness (*hesedh*) and humble obedience to God over the costliest offerings, even sacrifice of the first-born, "the fruit of my body for the sin of my soul." Any attempt to explain the threefold requirement as three distinct aspects of the religious life is precluded by the obvious fact that the utterance is a poetic tristich and that justice, lovingkindness, and humble walking with God are nearly synonymous ways of stating the whole response of man to God. The final oracle of the book is a wonderful proclamation of the mercy of Israel's God:

> Thou wilt cast all our sins
> into the depths of the sea.

While Micah is not the intellectual, literary, or theological equal of the other eighth-century prophets, it must be remembered that few writers or leaders could rival Amos, Hosea, and Isaiah. Because he stands in their shadow, Micah receives less than his due. That he was a potent force in his day is attested both by the memory of Jeremiah's contemporaries and the finished form of his book with its anthology of memorable oracles.

ISAIAH OF JERUSALEM

Isaiah of Jerusalem, who received his prophetic call in the year of Uzziah's death (742 B.C.) and who was still active during the siege of Jerusalem by Sennacherib (705–701 B.C.), had the longest and most influential career of any eighth-century prophet. Not that his guidance was always heeded, but he did have an audience with kings apparently not granted to his fellow prophets. He was in a sense the official court prophet of Ahaz and Hezekiah, although his message covered a broader front and struck more decisively at the root of political policy than the earlier court prophets, Gad and Nathan. The common belief that Isaiah was an aristocrat is rather subjectively based on his free access to kings and the regal grandeur of his literary style. His imagery, with Jerusalem and its surrounding fields, shows him to be city-bred and thus the first Hebrew prophet closely identified with urban culture. He displays a sense of the solemnity and significance of kingship and temple, and a respect for the structure of society, the state, and its religious forms that seem almost conservative compared to Amos and Hosea.

The long ministry of the prophet may explain some of the inconsistencies with which he has been charged. He began to prophesy when men were under the spell of the opulent reigns of Uzziah and Jeroboam II, but his last recorded words come from a period when the Assyrian menace had engulfed Israel and had trimmed Judah down to a mere city-state, tributary to the invader. His early message seems to have been as severely negative as Amos' but the changed era and new revelations mellowed and deepened it into one with a measure of hope akin to Hosea's intimations of redemption. The popular conception of Isaiah as the prophetic protector of Jerusalem during Sennacherib's siege is no doubt an oversimplified legend (Isaiah 36–39), but it must have had some foundation in fact: in spite of his dire warnings against the south, Isaiah remained an advisor of kings and worked tirelessly for the salvation of his native city. Later legend could easily overdraw his patriotism.[16]

Isaiah was preëminently the prophet of Assyrian imperialism. He read the faith of Israel in the larger frame of world politics. That meant an ineluctable reckoning with Assyria at the height of her power under a succession of robust rulers, Tiglath-pileser III, Sargon, and Sennacherib. The question never far from the minds of men in the Syro-Palestinian corridor in the last half of the eighth century was: how are we to cope with the Assyrian onslaught? The basic policy devised was military coalition, not based, however, on any farseeing community of interests but rather on fitful expediency. Isaiah set himself against these shifting and thoughtless coalitions not because he was a doctrinaire isolationist, but because he saw how little they were founded upon any deep wisdom, political or religious. His call to neutrality was not a call to disinterest in political affairs or to mystic withdrawal but to absolute trust in Yahweh's lordship of history. During one of the rebellions engineered by Egypt, which brought Sargon

[16] Sheldon H. Blank, *Prophetic Faith in Isaiah,* Harper, 1958, pp. 11–13, 28–30.

on the double to crush the uprising at Ashdod, Isaiah roamed the streets of Jerusalem for three years simulating a prisoner of war in order to symbolize the fate of Egypt and the rebels (chap. 20). He did not generalize his message to mean that men should not take political action but, as a typical Hebrew, he insisted that in the then pertaining situation the fevered alliances of the small states were pointless. Actually, from the total scope of his preaching it is apparent that he believed in the king as a strong and forceful leader whose task it was to uphold the covenant standards of righteousness in the collective order. He resolutely affirmed that all the actions of the Israelite state must be based on justice and even more fundamentally on faith: the faith that history is in God's hands.

THE COMPOSITION OF THE BOOK

Of all the prophetic books, Isaiah's is the most complex. It is a compilation of compilations, a whole library of prophetic books. The genuine oracles of the eighth-century prophet (generally called Isaiah of Jerusalem to distinguish him from the anonymous author of chaps. 40–55 or Deutero-Isaiah) are mainly in chapters 1–12 and 28–31, with some in chapters 13–23, the oracles against foreign nations. Evidence of the non-Isaianic nature of many of these oracles may be seen in the references to historical circumstances of a later date (e.g., the Chaldeans and the Medes in chap. 13 who did not rise to historical importance until a century later than Isaiah). The revolutionary universalism of 19:24–25 is unthinkable before the Exile: "In that day Israel will be the third with Egypt and Assyria, a blessing in the midst of the earth, whom Yahweh of hosts has blessed, saying, 'Blessed be Egypt my people, and Assyria the work of my hands, and Israel my heritage.' " Chapters 36–39 are biographical and follow II Kings 18–20 practically verbatim. The remaining portions of the book of Isaiah have nothing directly to do with Isaiah of Jerusalem. The complex structure of the anthology may be divided for convenience into nine sections:

1. *Oracles against Israel and Judah,* chapters 1–12, with superscriptions in 1:1 and 2:1. Here is the heart of the message of Isaiah of Jerusalem, although there are considerable additions by disciple-editors.

2. *Oracles against Foreign Nations,* chapters 13–23, with superscription. Isaiah was probably responsible for those against Assyria

(14:24–27), Philistia (14:28–32), Damascus (17:1–6), Arabia (21:13–15), and possibly for those against Egypt (18) and Tyre (23:1–12). The others are non-Isaianic. The Taunt Song against Babylon is especially dramatic in its picture of Sheol welcoming the downfallen oppressor who is conceived under the Canaanite mythological allusion "Day Star, son of Dawn" ("Helel son of Sahar," also mentioned in the Ugaritic texts; the Vulgate translation "Lucifer" became one of the names for Satan).

3. *The Little Apocalypse,* chapters 24–27, is a potpourri of descriptions of the end of the present order and hymnlike lyrics. There can be little doubt that the cosmic desolations and renovations contemplated are far beyond the simple view of the future found in pre-exilic prophecy. Notable is one of two Old Testament references to resurrection of the dead (26:19). The oracles are from the fourth or third century B.C. A variation on the theme of Isaiah's Vineyard Song (chap. 5) is apparent in 27:2–4a.

4. *Oracles against Israel and Judah,* chapters 28–31, contain many if not mostly genuine Isaianic passages. The oracles deal in the main with the last public crisis in the prophet's ministry, the siege of Jerusalem; but that traditional view is open to debate in the case of several of the oracles.

5. *Messianic Oracles,* chapters 32–33, magnify the king as the guarantor of covenant justice and righteousness. While beautifully composed, the poems have a generality of expression that argues strongly against Isaianic authorship. They are impressive developments of a theme dear to the prophet's heart: the obligation of kingship.

6. *Oracles of Doom and Salvation,* chapters 34–35, in which cosmic portents signal the destruction of "Edom," symbolic of godless nations, and the reblossoming of the desert, symbolic of the cessation of exile. The diction is similar to chapters 40–66 with which some scholars connect it as an introduction.

7. *Historical Narratives,* chapters 36–39, relate Sennacherib's siege of Jerusalem and are drawn from the Deuteronomic history (II Kings 18–20) with minor modifications and expansions. They date from after 621 B.C. and probably from the Exile. The urgent conversation between the Hebrew leaders and the Assyrian commander is not so much a report on actual events as it is a dramatization of the issues involved in Isaiah's theology of history. The searching queries of the Rabshakeh (Assyrian for "great leader") pose sharply the perils of

obeying the prophetic counsel: "Do you think that mere words are strategy and power for war? (36:5) . . . Has any of the gods of the nations delivered his land out of the hand of the king of Assyria?" (36:18). We can be sure that Isaiah was reproached with just such arguments by his fellow countrymen.

8. *Lyric Oracles of Deutero-Isaiah*, chapters 40–55, contain the consummate poetry of an anonymous prophet of the Babylonian exile. They are set off sharply from the work of Isaiah of Jerusalem in setting, style, and mood (see Chap. XI for detailed criteria of separation).

9. *Miscellaneous Oracles*, chapters 56–66, are by disciples of Deutero-Isaiah who returned to Palestine. Some of the prophet's original work may be embedded in the collection (see p. 445).

A lodge in a vineyard near Jerusalem built as shelter for the watchman who guards ripening grapes against robbers and wild beasts (see Isa. 1:8).

The eighth-century Isaiah expressed himself with a high literary endowment. He attains often the sublimity of Amos, but adds the garnish of an elegance and sensuousness probably resulting from his more cosmopolitan associations. One does not quickly forget his images of the city as a defenseless man, stricken with bruises and sores from head to foot, or as a lone watchtower in a vineyard, able to give but the faintest semblance of protection (1:5–9). The Song of the Vine-yard is the quintessence of prophecy, its sharp and cutting point augmented by the jewel-like symmetry of its literary form (5:1–7). Open to the simplest mind, its parable of Israel as an unproductive garden is edged with irony and sheathed in anguished wrath. The final strophe rises to a jarring dissonance in one of the most savage puns in the Hebrew Bible:

> For the vineyard of Yahweh of hosts
>   is the house of Israel,
> and the men of Judah
>   are his pleasant planting;
> and he looked for justice (*mishpat*),
>   but behold, bloodshed (*mishpah*);
> for righteousness (*sedhaqah*),
>   but behold, a cry (*se'aqah*)!

The temple vision of the prophet is related in language of chaste splendor, of sensuous evocation, as the reader *sees* the seraphim, *hears* their call, *feels* the thresholds shake and the hot coal burn against the lips (6:1–8). The electrifying station-by-station communiqué of the advance of an enemy on Jerusalem sets the pulse to racing and strikes fear even at our distance from the event:

> This very day he will halt at Nob,
>   he will shake his fist
>   at the mount of the daughter of Zion,
>   at the hill of Jerusalem (10:32).

And who can surpass the wry tribute paid to Assyria as the mighty battle-ax against the nations, the egg gatherer who plunders the inviting nests of the captive peoples? (10:14–15). A keen rapierlike mind appears behind the diction of the book, heightening the Hebraic powers of observation and expression to the nth degree.

THE THREEFOLD MINISTRY

Concentrated at three points in the finished book of Isaiah is sufficient biography to enable us to reconstruct roughly three phases in the prophet's career. The genuine oracles may be allocated with some confidence to these phases, although within the periods there can be little certainty of proper order. In general the earliest phase is represented in chapters 1–12, the middle period in the foreign oracles, and the last segment in chapters 28–31. Some scholars have built a theory of the composition of the book around the assumption that there were two nuclei representing the opening and concluding portions of Isaiah's ministry (roughly 1–12 and 28–31 respectively), around which the other materials of the book grew. The division between the two sections is, however, at best only an approximation; late oracles are apparent in the opening chapters and at least one oracle to Ephraim (prior to 722 B.C.) appears in 28–31.

The first phase of Isaiah's work is reported in the narrative complex of chapters 6–8, which tells of his call vision in 742 B.C., the critical audience with Ahaz at the time of the Syro-Ephraimite war, and the symbolic names of his sons Shear-jashub ("A remnant shall return") and Maher-shalal-hashbaz ("The spoil speeds, the prey hastes"). The chapters form a Book of Signs probably ending with 8:18. The prophet intended that his message, so curtly rejected by the king, should be preserved among his disciples. Several of the recorded oracles give evidence of belonging to this period:

Against Ritual	1:10–17
"If"	1:18–20
Purified Remnant	1:21–31
Day of Yahweh	2:5–17
Against the Leadership	3:1–15
Against Indulgent Women	3:16–23
Song of the Vineyard	5:1–7
Sixfold Woe against Evildoers	5:8–24; (29:15–16?)
Against Israel (note refrain)	9:8–10:4; 5:25–29
Against the Syro-Ephraimite League	⎰10:27b–32 (33–34?) ⎱17:1–6
Against Ephraimite Drunkards	28:1–4,7–8

The second phase of the ministry is connected with the uprising of Ashdod and other city-states against Sargon in 714–711 B.C. Hezekiah was on the verge of participating, but the all-out warnings of Isaiah apparently dissuaded him. While the siege of Ashdod lasted, the prophet carried his monition through the city streets by posing as a prisoner of war (chap. 20). Only a few oracles appear to belong to this period and they may equally belong to a somewhat later time:

Against Philistia	14:28–32
Against Arabia	21:13–15
Against Shebna, the Steward	22:15–24 (note that by 701 Eliakim seems to have replaced Shebna as steward, 36:3).

The closing phase of the recorded career of Isaiah was connected with the spectacular revolt against Assyria in 705–701 in which Hezekiah was at last persuaded to join. The narrative reports of chapters 36–39 are valuable sources of information but cannot be taken uncritically, since they have tended to overestimate the king's piety and to popularize the prophet as a defender of the state. While Isaiah's love of his country was vast, his deepest convictions held that the nation must be founded upon loyalty to the national God. The oracles of this period do not support the view that Isaiah gave an unqualified assurance of the city's rescue from Sennacherib. More likely than not his serious wrestlings with the king, who was a thoughtful Yahwist as well as a practical politician, have been objectified in legends that miss the contingencies of the prophetic word. Isaiah spoke in no uncertain terms of what would be needed in the way of repentance and renewal if the city were to be spared. In retrospect men saw that the city had been spared and they jumped too readily to the conclusion that Isaiah predicted and guaranteed the outcome. In fairness to the narrator of 36–39, however, it should be observed that he reports the repentance of the king who was then granted restoration from sickness. But the national dimension is overlooked. At any rate the incisive moral and spiritual tone of the prophet's final message is better seen in his own words than in the popular legends:

The Desolate City	1:4–9
Ho Assyria!	10:5–16 (17–19?)
This Is the Purpose	14:24–27
Against Egypt	18
Siege Preparations	22:(1–8a?), 8b–14
Against Tyre	23:1–12
The Offense of Faith	28:9–22
Yahweh, God of the Sown Land	28:23–29
Lip Service	29:13–14
"That Broken Reed"	30:1–7
Waiting in Faith	30:8–18
The Impotence of Egypt	31:1–4

A later tradition says that Isaiah was put to death by the wicked king Manasseh. If so, he continued to preach for at least another fifteen years after the siege, but there are no traces in his book of oracles peculiar to that period.

Composite animal and human figures: sphinxes, cherubim, seraphim (see Isa. 6:2).

THE HOLY ONE OF ISRAEL

Above all else Isaiah was the determined advocate of the *holiness* of Yahweh. The title he coined for deity was "the Holy One of Israel." Determinative of holiness was the exalted temple vision. That the vision of Yahweh could come through the temple is something the iconoclastic Amos would never have granted. Nevertheless Isaiah's vision transcends the rigamarole of ritual. The throne of Yahweh, truly exalted, towers above temple and nation and yet his visible holiness, his glory, fills the whole earth. The throne attendants or seraphim (compound human and animal figures) sound the keynote of Isaiah's profoundest belief. The *trisagion* (thrice holy) is still widely used in Jewish and Christian services of worship:

Holy, Holy, Holy is Yahweh of Hosts
The whole earth is full of his glory! (6:3).

Yahweh is no mere nationalistic cult deity. The earth is resplendent with his living presence, even above the hauteur and terror of the Assyrian. The internationalism of the prophet was not born of philosophical monism nor of diplomatic strategy but rather from a transforming vision of the living God. No wonder that he did not fear for the course of human events:

> This is the purpose that is purposed
>   concerning the whole earth;
> and this is the hand that is stretched out
>   over all the nations.
> For Yahweh of Hosts has purposed,
>   and who will annul it?
> His hand is stretched out,
>   and who will turn it back? (14:26–27).

Isaiah's first response in the presence of God is not to light incense or produce an offering. Rather he falls down in complete unworthiness, for "my eyes have seen the King, Yahweh of Hosts." It is customary to recognize in the prophetic call one of the classic examples of the modes and rhythms of worship. Adoration (Isa. 6:1–4) leads to confession (vs. 5) and forgiveness (vss. 6–7), which finally issue in dedication (vs. 8) and mission (vss. 9–10). Those who seek "to defend the non-rational core of the biblical conception of God from all excessive rationalization" will draw unending inspiration from this prophet whose forms of expression were eloquent with the divine majesty.[17] Such awe of God left no room for unwarranted awe of men:

> Do not call conspiracy all that this people call conspiracy, and do not fear what they fear, nor be in dread. But Yahweh of hosts, him you shall regard as holy; let him be your fear, and let him be your dread (8:11–12).

Isaiah had found full answer to opportunism and demagoguery, but he was no ascetic separatist. What hurt him most was that so few men seemed to share his vision of the holy God as anything more than a nice sentiment, properly confinable to spheres other than business pursuits and affairs of state.

Faith as Trust

Hand in hand with holiness went *faith*. Faith for Isaiah meant confidence that the holy will of Yahweh was ultimate in the world. Faith was foremost a commitment of life, naturally involving an ideational form in that Yahweh's revealed nature in the covenant bond was the

---

[17] Rudolph Otto, *The Idea of the Holy,* Oxford University Press, 1950, p. 77.

mainstay of man's trust in God. Faith thus had a fixed "object"; the covenant was an index of the kind of God men were to trust. But faith was such that its opposite was not intellectual reservation but rather distrust, breach of relationship, and finally haste and impetuous clutching at life. Faith gave Isaiah relaxation and freedom in the midst of change and decay, clear-headed thought and the capacity both to act and to refrain from acting—all in the saving context of a firm trust in Yahweh's ways.

Isaiah's most celebrated statement of this faith is in his word to Ahaz as the distressed king faced the pressure of Israel and Damascus to join in their anti-Assyrian alliance. Ahaz is told not to fear "those smoldering stumps of firebrands," throwing sparks but fed by no lasting flame, for

> It [their threatening design] shall not stand,
>   and it shall not come to pass.
> . . . .
> If you will not believe (*'im lo' tha'aminu*),
>   surely you shall not be established (*ki lo' the'amenu*) (7:7,9).

The pun has perhaps been preserved best in the Scots dialect of G. A. Smith: No Faith, No Staith![18] Men may seek all manner of securities, but without trust they never will "be established," possess staying power.

What does the prophet mean by "being established"? Dynastic permanence, victory over enemies, social well-being? All are feasible but the imprecision of his expression suggests that Isaiah was breaking loose from the common assumption that the rewards of religion were tangible material ones. Isaiah may be accused of fuzzy impractical thinking. His prophetic conviction probably did not embrace a clear idea of how Judah would be delivered. This much was clear to him: there was no deliverance in alliances born of prostrate fear and selfish grasping. Isaiah seems to say that in crisis men reveal faith or unfaith; the true mettle of nations is also tested. All that is of real value in human life will not be lost by courageous faith. The prophet resists the bifurcation of material and spiritual, but there is no doubt that for him something corresponding to "spiritual" permeates the "material" and has priority. The covenant demands are laid upon distracted and struggling men in the life of the world and those demands

[18] G. A. Smith, *The Book of Isaiah*, Doubleday, new and rev. ed., 1927, vol. 1, p. 104.

are the ultimate good that must not be falsified or betrayed. In obedience to them many advantages of political and social security seem to be surrendered, but life outside the covenant in merely "natural" terms is one of illusion and impermanence. The value of the world is that it is the setting for the covenant relation. Judah and Ahaz must not forget that even when they are confronted with Assyria.

So Isaiah sets forth the radical uncompromising character of faith. He offers no bag of tricks or easy rewards. Faith in the sovereign God and the good life that he requires of the covenant people never has ideal conditions. A close reading of the prophet sweeps away forever the unfounded nostalgia that it was easier to believe in God in Bible times. Faith always involves the possibility of loss. Isaiah betokens this in the metaphor of the rock; a rock may be either the firm foundation on which men build or the obstacle over which they stumble.

> And he [Yahweh] will become a sanctuary (or snare?) and a stone of offence, and a rock of stumbling to both houses of Israel, a trap and a snare to the inhabitants of Jerusalem. And many shall stumble thereon; they shall fall and be broken; they shall be snared and taken (8:14–15).

> Behold, I am laying in Zion for a foundation
>   a stone, a tested stone,
> a precious cornerstone, of a sure foundation:
>   "He who believes will not be in haste" (28:16).

Faith is not a formula but a relation, a new orientation toward the Holy God, a transformed outlook upon the world—including power politics. No human circumstance or historical condition "determines" Yahweh and yet he, though sublimely free, speaks to man through history. There is no special realm of faith that man may flee to; faith must be virile enough to face all the turmoil of life in this world and to resist the temptation to write off God's creation as a loss. Faith is patient waiting upon God, driven on by an unquenchable optimism about the divine purpose, rejoicing in the freedom of Israel to throw in her lot with his ways in the earth.

THE SIGN IMMANUEL

This quality of waiting—not to be confused with lethargic resignation—springs from intensely creative conviction and is seen vividly in the sign of the child Immanuel. Probably the sign was given to Ahaz after he had rejected the prophet's faith and capitulated to Assyria. In his disapproval of this action we see how far Isaiah's thought was from encouraging any action moved solely by self-preservation, whether pro-Assyrian or anti-Assyrian. The prophet declares that a child is shortly to be born or has been born (the Hebrew tenses are practically nonexistent in the Western sense) and before he is at the age of moral discernment Damascus and Ephraim will be swept away. The child is called symbolically Immanuel (God-with-us). Attempts to understand the cryptic symbolism are clouded by doctrinal factors since Isaiah 7:14 is quoted in the New Testament as predictive of the virgin birth of Jesus Christ (Matt. 1:23).

A spate of theories has poured forth to solve the Immanuel enigma. Some treat Immanuel as an indefinite expression, capable of auspicious use by any woman who might call her child "God with us!" or ironically expressive of the baseless popular hope that God would rescue his people come what may. Others find allusion to a historical individual, either the son of the king (Hezekiah?) or the son of the prophet. In the former case Immanuel is usually identified as a messianic deliverer of the sort described in chapters 9 and 11. In the latter Immanuel is on a par with the other symbolic names in chapters 6–8, which undeniably refer to the prophet's own sons. The orthodox Christian view sees a prediction of Jesus of Nazareth. Others find allusion to a mythological deliverer, analogous to the widespread ancient theme of a divine mother and redeemer child. Still others equate Immanuel with Isaiah's idea of a saving remnant. A few scholars despair of the whole issue by saying that the passage is so overlaid with legend as to make theorizing useless.

Stalemated as the discussion may be, a few things are clear enough to be stated with confidence. For one thing, the role of the Immanuel child is that of an attendant sign and not that of a deliverer. He is invoked as the means of measuring the imminence of God's judgment on Israel and Syria. Neither the circumstance of his birth, his parentage, nor his office are integral to his function as a sign. Whatever merit the Christian belief in the virgin birth of Jesus Christ possesses, it finds no support in the Isaiah passage. Its sphere is more properly theological than historical. Likewise, the equation of Immanuel with a royal deliverer and thus with a son of Ahaz militates against the context. The mythological messiah is fantastically groundless. Also, the Immanuel sign as it now stands has a double character as threat and promise: the short-range menace of Assyria to Ephraim and Damascus is also a long-range threat to Judah. Ahaz may think that his appeal to Assyria is saving the kingdom, but his short-sightedness obscures the ultimate outcome; the hired razor will shave his scalp (7:20). So the paradoxical fact results that God's presence among men leads both to hope and consternation, woe and weal, according as they react to the options he holds out to them.

For the sign to have its fullest force it must have applied to some-one known to the king so that in the maturation of the child he could see the marking off of time as a daily reminder of the prophet's words. The most likely candidate for Immanuel is a son of the prophet, and thus brother of the other symbolically named sons (note the similarity in the annunciation of Maher-shalal-hashbaz' birth, 8:1–4). Immanuel's affinity with the other sons of the prophet has been lost by editorial treatment of the passage and the failure to recognize that 'alma (translated "virgin" by KJV but actually "young woman, maiden") as a term for Isaiah's wife probably had a technical cultic meaning: temple singer and prophetess, cf. 8:3.[19] Faith has a vital meaning to one who will stake his family's good name and future upon its vindication.

THE SAVING REMNANT

The richness of the prophet's message is apparent in yet another of his seminal contributions to the religion of Israel. He advanced the notion of *the remnant*. Like Amos' Day of Yahweh, it was to have major bearing upon Israel's thoughts about the future. In short, Isaiah began to make distinctions within the collective body of Israel. Amos seems to have believed without question that the entire populace would perish or be exiled, the righteous poor with the wicked rich. At least he did not make provision for distinguishing in any sense between "Israel after the flesh" and "Israel after the spirit." Rebuffed by the state, Isaiah saw that if his message was to endure it must be cherished among the few who were sympathetic toward it and that they were the leaven, the saving factor in God's plans for the future.

It has been claimed that in articulating this belief Isaiah gave birth to the idea of the church. This is an arresting way of formulating his role in Jewish-Christian tradition, but it must be balanced by the

---

[19] Norman K. Gottwald, "Immanuel as the Prophet's Son," *Vetus Testamentum,* 8 (1958), 36–47.

reservation that the prophet never envisioned a sectarian Yahwism of which he was founder. It is significant that no prophet favored sectarianism, so bound were they by Yahwism as the religion of the people. Isaiah saw, however, that the true spirit of a people may be embodied only in a very few. His views were not quantitatively equalitarian as though every man, because he was a Hebrew, had just as much grasp of truth as every other. His collective thinking was highly aristocratic—as indeed was that of the prophets in the main. The masses unchecked, the people as a mere aggregate, were no solution to Israel's problems. Only the covenant with its structure of rights and obligations could provide the proper balance of freedom and responsibility. Insofar as they can be analyzed there are factors both decidedly liberal and starkly conservative in prophetic thought. They were not doctrinaire theorists.

In the book of Isaiah the imagery of judgment and survival grows more lurid and profuse through the elaboration of the remnant idea by later commentators. In those passages indisputably Isaiah's the hope is nevertheless clearly present. Especially instructive is his expectation that the city's judgment would be a purgative process, like the smelting away of dross from metal. Righteousness will be restored and repentance will lead men from destruction to new life. He called his first son Shear-jashub ("A remnant shall return"), although it is debatable which of its nuances should receive the greater stress: the foreboding that *only* a remnant would be spared or the hopeful note that *at least* some would survive to begin a new day in Jerusalem. It seems also that the command of 8:16 and the following references to Isaiah's patient waiting with his children show that the prophet made central in his ministry the disengaged nucleus of believers who were openly at odds with the official state policy. It is possible that Isaiah's notion of the remnant embraced both the faithful within Israel who heeded his message but had to bide their time and those who, under the duress of the coming catastrophe, would turn to Yahweh.

In this connection the inaugural mission of the prophet with its hopelessly pessimistic form has baffled interpreters. How is such a command of doom to be rendered psychologically intelligible or squared with the undoubted Isaianic doctrine of the remnant? What man could accept a mission knowing that it would end in failure? A common rationalization is that the prophet wrote of his call some years afterward and tended to read eventual failure into the initial call, as Hosea may have interpreted the command from Yahweh to marry a harlot. Closely related is the opinion that the imperative is steeped in the dramatic and hyperbolic speech of the Orient and that, when allowance for this is made, what is expressed is "the gradual hardening and ultimately fatal effect on character of continued disobedience to the voice of God."[20] The elements of truth in these theories need not be despised, but students of Isaiah must reckon with the likelihood that the transcript of chapter 6 faithfully represents the expectation of Isaiah at the time of his call.

We must remember that the prophetic word was believed to carry power to bring about the doom it announced. Without the revelatory interpretation of the prophet who reads the times in covenant terms there was no judgment. Though dismal in its results, Isaiah's ministry would not be useless; without his preaching men could not know what was befalling them. Indeed, so closely were the events of history and the prophetic word construed that Isaiah's preaching literally made judgment actual. Yet that preaching was not mechanical or arbitrary. It belonged in the context of covenant responsibility. As inexorable and superficially fatalistic as it looks, his summons was within the framework of covenant freedom: Israel had chosen and was choosing still "the covenant with death" (28:15,18) and thus the people listened to Isaiah but did not understand, looked at him but did not perceive. Then too Amos and Hosea had little responsive hearing in the north. Why should Isaiah expect better results? Thus the dark presentiment of the call vision was not a dour afterthought but a deep conviction only modified as the prophet stressed the redemptive action of God through an instrumentality other than the people at large. In this sense the remnant was the answer to the dimming hopes that Isaiah's call expresses as radically as Amos' thundering doom.

SIN AS PRIDE

Complementing its description as distrust and haste, Isaiah emphasizes sin as *pride*. The Day of Yahweh, seen by Amos as a time of darkness, is for Isaiah a moment for the destruction of all that is lifted high. Like the Yahwist the prophet saw sin in the imagery of height, as arrogance and pretension. He lashes out at the overweening aspirations of man:

[20] G. B. Gray, *The Book of Isaiah I–XXVII* (ICC), Scribner's, 1912, p. 109.

For Yahweh of hosts has a day
  against all that is proud and lofty,
  against all that is lifted up and high;

. . . .

And the haughtiness of man shall be humbled,
  and the pride of men shall be brought low;
  and Yahweh alone will be exalted in that day (2:12,17).

Against the King of the universe there could be no greater affront than self-exaltation. Indeed, it is the worst vice of Assyria that, while executing Yahweh's judgments in the earth, she has become proud and pre-

tentious. With masterly insight into the devious motivations of men (showing that the prophet was not fooled into thinking of any people as innocent and therefore perfect agents of Yahweh), he hurls his barbed words at the conqueror:

Ah, Assyria, the rod of my anger,
  the staff of my fury!
Against a godless nation I send
    him,
  and against the people of my
    wrath I command him,

. . . .

But he does not so intend,
  and his mind does not so think;
but it is in his mind to destroy,
  and to cut off nations not a few
    (10:5,7 cf. 37:22–29).

Sargon II—limestone relief from his palace at Khorsabad.

But the ax or saw, the rod or staff do not guide the hand of their wielder; likewise boastful Assyria will be broken when Yahweh is finished with his tool. Many questions about the relation of national actions to the divine will remain, but Isaiah broke ground of a most revolutionary sort, opening the way for the broadly international vision of Jeremiah, Ezekiel, and Deutero-Isaiah.

THE MESSIAH

There are cogent arguments against the authenticity of the great messianic oracles of 9:2–7 and 11:1–9. Isaiah's hope was invested in a nonpolitical remnant. For the state at large he seems to have expected only destruction. The oracles are said to presuppose the cessation of the Davidic dynasty (note "shoot from the stump" in 11:1). Certain words and ideas in the oracles were common only in the postexilic age, such as "the zeal of the Lord" and the apocalyptic vision of peace among the animals. The contexts of the oracles are shaky, the transitions from chapters 8 and 10 being awkward and arbitrary. Furthermore, it is difficult to connect the poems with known events or periods in the prophet's lifetime.

Counterarguments have gained ground in recent criticism. Isaiah's respect for royalty is apparent even when he felt compelled to upbraid contemporary kings. The future described is the sort Isaiah had in mind, for its essence was righteousness and peace. None of the blatantly postexilic features are present, such as the regathering of the exiles, the submission of the heathen, or centralization of temple worship. The Davidic dynasty need not have been at an end to awaken the hopes expressed. The contrast between Ahaz or Hezekiah and the ideal king would have been sufficient to evoke these magnificent prophecies of a new epoch. While Isaiah was content to work through the agency of the purified remnant, it is not impossible to relate that hope to the expectation of a righteous king. Some scholars even regard the messianic oracles as coronation recitations, perhaps partly traditional in character, to which the kings gave assent at their accession.[21] If so, Isaiah held them up to the kings as a reminder of their oath and a measure of their defection.

Whether the words of the prophet or a nameless follower, these poems have entered intimately into the thinking of the Christian world and for multitudes are forever associated with their musical setting in Handel's *Messiah*. In all literature there are no more lofty declarations of the model ruler of men and, of all the strictly messianic passages in the Old Testament, they are among the most appropriately referred to the ministry and message of Jesus Christ. While he never was a king as here detailed, righteousness and justice were major elements in his

---

[21] R. B. Y. Scott, *Exegesis of Isaiah 1–39* (IB, vol. 5), Abingdon, 1956, pp. 231–234, 247–250.

teaching and his scepter has done more to enforce those qualities than all kings combined.

Isaiah was a man overcome by the holiness of Yahweh, willing to place his utmost confidence in the power of holiness in human life, hopeful of God's high purposes for those who believe, and yet appalled at man's casual disregard of the divine rule; he was implacable critic and invincible optimist. The extent of his influence may be measured by the scope and range of his message, the magnitude of his following evidenced in the editorial elaborations that have enlarged his work beyond that of any other prophet. His book became the repository of many later words by those who counted themselves true to his fondest beliefs and hopes. His was the most used prophetic writing in the Dead Sea community at the opening of the Christian era and the most quoted prophetic book in the New Testament. He managed to embrace the eloquence of Amos and to enlarge the theological versatility of Hosea.

After Isaiah prophecy went into an eclipse for half a century or more. The mounting crescendo of the prophetic ax-blows laid at the root of the state was suddenly broken off by the anti-Yahwistic reign of terror under Manasseh. After the first impact of the great eighth-century spokesmen of Yahweh, prophecy required a period of self-evaluation before its final flowering in the late seventh and sixth centuries. Emerging under Amos, Hosea, Micah, and Isaiah the prophetic faith could not have asked for abler representation. If the arts of persuasion inherent in great speech and noble minds were all that man needed to change his course of life, surely the eighth century in Israel should have been among the halcyon eras of mankind. Baseness, however, flourished alongside courage and folly companied with high wisdom. Although we dare not say that these prophets failed without writing off their deepest convictions, the enormity of their task is apparent in the great indifference and outright opposition against which they labored. Fortunately prophecy had not delivered its last word.

10

THE DECLINE OF JUDAH

I bring evil from the north . . .
Jer. 4:6

NEO-BABYLONIA AND THE FALL OF JUDAH, 700–587 B.C.

For three-fourths of the seventh century B.C., Judah was in the throes of an acute political and religious recession. By whatever means Ahaz and Hezekiah rationalized their acts of submission to Assyria, the consequences were supreme in Judean policy for a century. Riding the crest of power under her last two kings of eminence, Esarhaddon (who captured Egypt) and Ashurbanipal (famous for his library), Assyria lorded it over the small states. Manasseh, whose reign of fifty-five years was the longest of any Hebrew king, did more than sullenly accept Assyrian sovereignty. He reveled in it and doubtless profited by servile adherence to his superiors.

Polytheism and syncretism regained ground lost during the reform of Hezekiah. On the admission of the Deuteronomist, whose report at this point should be carefully heeded, Manasseh's brand of paganism exceeded that of Ahab and the legendary evil of the Canaanites destroyed by Joshua. No prophetic names or books come to us from the dark period of Manasseh, but we hear of prophetic opposition and the vivid threat quoted by D is hardly typical of his own rather prosaic style: "and I will wipe Jerusalem as one wipes a dish, wiping it and turning it upside down" (II Kings 21:13). Subservience to Assyria meant the invasion of the temple precincts by the astrological and divinatory rites of the conqueror. With them came a revival of the indigenous cults: Baalism and the barbaric rites of the Ammonite god Molech to whom children were immolated. We are told that Manasseh burned his own son, and Chronicles reports the same of Ahaz. The political terrorism by which he held his grip is tersely summarized: "Moreover Manasseh shed very much innocent blood, till he had filled Jerusalem from one end to another, . . ." (21:16). Manasseh's policies were continued by his less impressive son Amon whose two-year reign ended with a court coup.

Josiah, son and successor of Amon, was caught up in the same current of Assyrian control. It was not until the eighteenth year of his reign (he was then only twenty-six years of age) that he wrenched Judah from its long-accustomed paths and moved toward independence. The only account of his reign stresses his religious reforms (II Kings 22–23), but we can be certain that when he wiped out the Assyrian ritual in Judah he also declared political independence. This was possible because, a decade earlier, Ashurbanipal's death had left Assyria without direction. The first-rate leadership that had supplied the Assyrian throne for over a century failed to perpetuate itself. Lacking the administrative structure of later empires, a want of talent at the top could not long be disguised in Nineveh. Alarms were sounded through the length and breadth of the Near East. Josiah's revolt is intelligible only in terms of restiveness portending great upheavals in a stable order.

Josiah's vigorous policy of the revival of Yahwism was occasioned by the adoption of "the Book of the Covenant," probably to be equated with some portion of the present book of Deuteronomy (likely chaps. 12–26). This document harked back to the Mosaic foundations of Israel's religion and summoned the nation to an unqualified Yahwistic allegiance that barred all compromise with foreign cults. It is probable that the neo-Yahwism of Josiah inspired him to revive the Davidic empire. His military forays in north Israel bespeak the hope of recovering territory lost to Assyria and reasserting the unity of the tribes (II Chron. 34:6–7). In 609 he rushed to the Plain of Esdraelon "to meet" Pharaoh Necho. The rapidly slackening grip of Assyria upon the ancient world had been struck loose altogether with the capture of Nineveh in 612 by Cyaxares of the Indo-European Medes and Nabopolassar of the Chaldean dynasty ascendant in Babylon. Remnants of the Assyrian army that fled to Haran were defeated in 610. Egypt, confirmed enemy of Assyria, suddenly shifted her alignment. She saw that unless an effete Assyria could be bolstered, the Fertile Crescent would shortly have new masters. To Necho it seemed wise to seek a balance of power by throwing his weight *with* Assyria. In a situation admittedly perilous for Egypt, the Pharaoh could think of no better course than to rescue Assyria and make her beholden to him. It was a

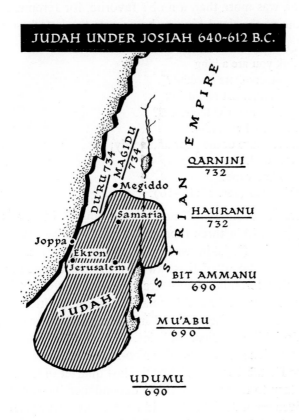

JUDAH UNDER JOSIAH 640-612 B.C.

▨▨▨ REVIVED KINGDOM OF JUDAH UNDER
JOSIAH, 640-609 B.C.
UNDERLINED ASSYRIAN PROVINCES
UNTIL 612 B.C.

gamble undertaken much too late, but not too late to prevent Necho from putting Josiah to death when the Judean king attempted to interfere with his troop movements toward Haran. By the time Egyptian troops were deployed at Carchemish there was no Assyrian militia to join them and in 605 the Chaldeans dealt a mortal blow to Necho's ambitions. That was the end of Egyptian dreams of Asiatic empire.

Josiah's death had profound repercussions on the reform he had instituted. Deuteronomy, the basis of his reform, never tires of enunciating the reward of the pious, but hopes were dashed and hearts grew heavy when the immensely popular and revered king met an untimely death. Josiah was more than a mob's favorite, for Jeremiah shows his high estimate of the dead king as he accosts the latter's son and successor:

> Do you think you are a king
>   because you compete in cedar?
> Did not your father eat and drink
>   and do justice and righteousness?
>   Then it was well with him.
> He judged the cause of the poor and needy;
>   then it was well.
> Is not this to know me?
>   says Yahweh (Jer. 22:15–16).

His son Jehoahaz (called Shallum by Jeremiah, 22:11) was chosen by the people, but within three months was deposed by Necho who appointed Jehoiakim (Eliakim was his nonregnal name) as an Egyptian puppet. The assessment of these two by the Deuteronomic historian and the prophet Jeremiah demonstrate beyond any doubt how unlike their father they were. The old social inequities, political supineness, and religious compromise returned in a backwash of revulsion at the failure of Josiah's grandiose policies. Within four years Jehoiakim transferred allegiance to Chaldea or Neo-Babylonia, now the dominant power in the Fertile Crescent. Thus the last quarter of the century saw Judea tributary to three peoples, her dependence broken only by the bold assertiveness of Josiah. The old landmarks of Assyrian imperialism had dissolved. The ascendancy of Babylon had been achieved only with the help of the Indo-European Medes, who were content to remain outside the Crescent (Cyaxares ruled over Asia Minor), but Babylonia was to be the last truly Semitic Empire.

Of the several prophets who spoke out in the latter half of the century, Jeremiah was by all odds the greatest. According to tradition his call was coincident with the death of Ashurbanipal, and his single unyielding word to Judah was astonishingly like Isaiah's a century before: desist from alliances, seek fidelity to the covenant God, lay the foundations of the new order beyond certain political disaster. The heft of Jeremiah's preserved message comes from the twilight of the southern kingdom as he brought all his influence to bear upon the despotic

Jehoiakim and the vacillating Zedekiah. Jingoist feelings were fanned with ever ready Egyptian encouragement, and in 598 a revolt of Judah was punished by a Babylonian expeditionary force aided by native forces of Syrians, Ammonites, and Moabites. Jehoiakim died before the siege began; his young son Jehoiachin capitulated to Nebuchadnezzar's troops not through considered deliberation of the prophet's advice but through abject fear. Officials, priests, and craftsmen were deported, for Nebuchadnezzar had learned well the Assyrian schemes for breaking opposition.

Zedekiah, the third and last son of Josiah to occupy the throne, was a spineless appointee of Babylon who could not stand up to the pro-Egyptian sentiments of his key advisors. His secret audiences with Jeremiah show a well-meaning but weak-willed young man who could do no more than gesture in the direction of the prophet's unflinching demands. Another revolt swept the capital and after a bitter siege lasting over a year and a half, the city was taken in the summer of 587. Walls were leveled and important buildings, including the temple, razed or gutted. Although the Exile is commonly dated in 587, fewer people were deported than in 598 (832 as against 3,023; Jer. 52:28–29) probably because there were not many actual or potential leaders remaining. Nebuchadnezzar directed the military operations from his encampment at Riblah and appointed Gedaliah as governor. Gedaliah was on the way to establishing a wise and temperate regime of reconstruction when he was assassinated by Ishmael the Ammonite, a fanatical aspirant to the throne. A large body of the Judeans, fearful of Babylonian reprisal, fled to Egypt, taking with them the unwilling prophet Jeremiah. Another deportation occurred in 582 (745; Jer. 52:30). The book of Kings ends the history of the Israelite and Judean monarchies with a note of modest hope. It tells of the favor accorded Jehoiachin by his admittance to the Babylonian royal table. As long as a Davidic shoot remained alive, and even longer, the hope of a restored kingdom did not die. Of a different sort was the hope of the prophet Jeremiah who foresaw the long exile of Jewry and anticipated the religious distinctiveness of his people detached from all certain political moorings.

The dynasty of David that had weathered crises more than once in its four-hundred-year history was not to earn another reprieve. Although the movement of events should have been apparent to any observant onlooker, and was clearly seen by the prophets, the end came upon an incredulous people. Organized temple worship ceased. The prestige of Jerusalem plummeted. Widespread disillusionment and despair set in. Only those prepared for the catastrophe by the steady witness of the prophets were laying the foundations of a new order.

ZEPHANIAH

Zephaniah was the harbinger of the renascence of prophecy after the barren half-century of Manasseh. He is the only prophet whose ancestry was traced back four generations, perhaps to emphasize his royal descent. But since Hezekiah is a rather common name we cannot be certain that his great-great-grandfather was the Judean king. Appearing during Josiah's reign, he was the first known prophet after Isaiah. He spoke prior to the fall of Assyria and doubtless before the reform of Josiah. His upbraiding of religious apostasy includes brief vignettes of astral worship, the Ammonite Milcom cult (variant of Molech), and the Philistine practice of "leaping over the threshold" (cf. I Sam. 5:5). His book is organized as a miniature Isaiah or Jeremiah; it begins with an indictment of the people of God (chaps. 1:1–2:3), goes on to a series of oracles against foreign nations: Cherethites (remnants of Philistines), Moab and Ammon, Ethiopia and Assyria (2:4–15), and concludes with mixed oracles (like Amos, Hosea, and Micah) that end with the promise of a bright future (3:1–20).

Zephaniah's major message is in the vein of Amos. He seizes upon the motif of the Day of Yahweh and amplifies it with unmitigated horror. True to his more distinguished predecessor, the prophet paints an awesome spectacle of divine wrath visited upon the indifferent and scoffing Israelites. Against the practical atheism of Judeans he sets the unfailing justice of his God:

> At that time I will search Jerusalem with lamps,
>   and I will punish the men
> who are thickening upon their lees,
>   those who say in their hearts,
> 'Yahweh will not do good,
>   nor will he do ill' (1:12).

Medieval artists customarily depict Zephaniah with a lantern. To the darkness imagery of Amos he adds a masterpiece of prophetic irony: the sacrifice motif. The guests summoned to a lavish banquet discover too late that they are the victims. It appears that Zephaniah thought of historical disaster, but the later development of the theme carried it into superhistorical realms where the sacrificial feast became part of the events at the end of the world. The Christian imagery of *Dies Irae* (Day of Wrath) owes much to this prophet, as evidenced in the Latin hymn:

> Day of wrath, O day of mourning!
> See fulfilled the prophet's warning,
> Heaven and earth in ashes burning!

Critics differ as to whether the sections prophesying universal disaster are from the prophet (notably 1:3,18; 3:8). It is possible that his disciples in collecting the oracles have enlarged upon the original scope of Zephaniah's message, but it is quite likely that the international crisis of Assyria's passing was awakening a cosmic vision in the prophets. A similar concern for the natural order appears in Zephaniah's younger contemporary Jeremiah.

The theme of humility sounds forth in Zephaniah with an urgency not noted before in Hebrew tradition. It probably had much to do with the approaching eclipse of the ancient Near East as the center of world history. As in the classical world after Alexander, a sense of cultural weariness overcame the Crescent. The impotence of the individual was coupled with the exaltation of humility, that state of receptive dependence in which man waits upon the powers beyond him. It is unwise to derive this accent upon humility solely from the tragic times. In a real sense the fundamental ethos already existed in the Hebrew understanding of God and the covenant relation, but the times intensified it and alongside of the demand of Amos for justice, Zephaniah inculcated an attitude of humility before God:

> Seek Yahweh, all you humble of the land,
> who do his commands;
> seek righteousness, seek humility;
> perhaps you may be hidden
> on the day of the wrath of Yahweh (2:3 cf. Amos 5:14–15).

Isaiah saw proud men "humbled and brought low"; Zephaniah saw men voluntarily humble themselves in hopeful meekness and expectant waiting:

> I will remove from your midst
> your proudly exultant ones,

and you shall no longer be haughty
　in my holy mountain.
For I will leave in the midst of you
　a people humble and lowly (3:11–12).

Judaism was to be thereafter more and more a waiting religion. It need hardly be added that this spirit is remote from the expansive mood that has dominated American history. For us humility is seldom a virtue. That it could be espoused as a basic spiritual orientation requires an act of imagination on our part that runs against our cultural grain. But in most cultures the time comes when humility can be understood.

Zephaniah was a curious blend of the austerity of Amos and the spirit of the new era. He thundered the wrath of God but he saw a purged and humbled remnant as the saving hope. He is chiefly significant as the first voice to break the religious silence of the seventh century, to call for the renewal of heart that Josiah was about to implement, and to anticipate the life of obedience beyond disaster envisaged by Jeremiah yet more daringly.

DEUTERONOMY

In Israel's long history there seems to have been only one Hebrew politician who wholeheartedly set out to make his reign the unqualified instrument of his faith in Yahweh. That is a sweeping statement, but Josiah was an extraordinary man. He reconstituted the nation on absolute obedience to God. He is the unexampled spectacle of a king willingly subjecting himself to Mosaic standards. All the peril of mixing politics and religion are seen in his undertaking; whatever failings his crusade involved were not due to lack of courage on his part.

JOSIAH'S REFORMATION

A cornerstone of biblical scholarship since De Wette's publication of the theory in 1805 has been the identity of Josiah's reform book with a part of the book of Deuteronomy. The hypothesis is built on the similarity between the provisions of reform attributed to Josiah by Kings and the injunctions of the law book. These are the key stipulations and their parallels in Deuteronomy:

1. Centralization of worship at Jerusalem
　　(II Kings 23:4–5,8,12–13,15–16,19 cf. Deut. 12:1–7)
2. Celebration of Passover in the Temple (previously at home)
　　(23:21–23 cf. Deut. 16:1–8)

3. Proscription of astral worship
(23:4–5,11 cf. Deut. 17:3)
4. Proscription of sacred poles and pillars
(23:4,6–7,14 cf. Deut. 12:3; 16:21–22)
5. Proscription of immolation of children to Molech
(23:10 cf. Deut. 18:10)
6. Proscription of magic and divination
(23:24 cf. Deut. 18:11)
7. Admittance of rural priests (Levites) to Jerusalem temple
(23:9 cf. Deut. 18:6–8)

It is of course possible that in order to idealize Josiah the Deuteronomic historian has cast him in the role of reformer and has pictured him as an ardent upholder of the law so dear to the heart of the writer. But the thesis does not survive a moment's reflection. Why would the historians of Kings, who have been so consistently depreciatory of other kings, suddenly turn to lauding Josiah if there were no sound basis? Perhaps some ancient monarch could have been dressed up in this manner but Josiah would have been remembered by many readers of the history. The account of his reform can be explained only as a reasonably faithful description of the initiation of the Deuteronomic movement in politics. One particularly revealing detail is the apologetic confession in Kings that the Levites did not come up to occupy posts at the Jerusalem sanctuary (II Kings 23:9). No explanation in Kings would have been necessary unless the writers were thinking of the injunction in Deuteronomy 18:6–8, which called for an expansion of the Jerusalem priesthood to make room for the rural priests unemployed by the destruction of the high places. Thus at the one point where Josiah's program diverges from Deuteronomy, the exception was deemed worthy of comment. The cumulative force of the evidence is such that only a few scholars have disputed the vital connection between the king's policies and the laws of Deuteronomy.

THE STRUCTURE OF THE BOOK

The title "Deuteronomy" is from the LXX translation of 17:18, "second law" (*deuteros nomos*) regarded as a second giving of the law—a misunderstanding of the verse since in Hebrew it means "a copy of this law," which the king was obligated to keep before him. Tradition has generally referred the title to Moses' second telling of the law on the plains of Moab before the people entered Canaan. The book falls into three parts: (1) *Historical Review* of the wilderness journey and recapitulation of the revelations and requirements of Yahweh disclosed at Horeb, chapters 1–11; (2) *Book of the Law,* containing the ethical and cultic dicta of the Deuteronomists, chapters 12–26; 28; (3) *Miscellaneous Addenda,* including the Blessings and Cursings (chap. 27), the Song of Moses (chap. 32), and the Blessing of Moses (chap. 33).

The book presents a deceiving impression of unity because of its stylistic uniformity. A sonorous and sometimes ponderous liturgical style characterizes everything produced by Deuteronomic writers and shows up in their editorial notes on the history of Israel from Joshua through Kings. To list some of the phrases distinctive of D is to recall familiar biblical clichés: "that your days may be long," "a people of special possession," "which I am commanding you this day," "take heed to yourself lest," "a mighty hand and an outstretched arm," "that the Lord thy God may bless thee," "the stranger, the fatherless, and the widow," "remember that you have been a slave in the land of Egypt," "to do that which is right in the eyes of Yahweh," "with all thy heart and with all thy soul," "abomination to Yahweh," "the land whither you are going over to possess it," and "to cause his name to dwell there."

Behind the linguistic façade, however, there is a glaring disjointedness in Deuteronomy. Annoying shifts in the persons of pronouns are explained in part by the fluidity of reference to Israel as an aggregation of individuals ("we") and as a corporate entity ("I"). Some of the confusion appears due to editing. Presented as a final address of Moses, the assumption is that he delivered it immediately before the entrance of Canaan; yet portions imply that they were given at Shechem, which dissociates them from Moses since there is no hint of his having entered the promised land. At times the original generation of wilderness wanderers is addressed but the second generation is implied elsewhere. In the main, henotheism is accepted (God made the stars for the nations to worship but not for Israel), yet in chapter 4 there is a magnificent statement of exclusive monotheism. The law code has two introductions (chaps. 1–4 and 5–11). Sections presuppose the Exile (28:47–57 and 32). The poems of chapters 32 and 33 are only loosely connected with context.

Most scholars agree that, initial appearances to the contrary, Deuteronomy is a composite work. Wellhausen suggested that the code in

12–26 had appeared in two editions, with 1–4 as the introduction to one edition, followed by 27; and 5–11 for the other edition, concluded with 28–30.[1] He assumed that the miscellaneous chapters were added after a single edition was worked out. Pfeiffer allows for four editions with redactions.[2] Noth advances the idea that 1–4 is the introduction to the whole Deuteronomic history of Deuteronomy–Kings and 5–11 is the preface to the law code.[3] Ingenious as the latter theory is, it is unconvincing, for if the twofold introduction was intentional it would have been more carefully devised. As it is the two sections are tediously repetitive and prolix. The Deuteronomists were no deft stylists but they could have done better than that. No theory proposed is conclusive, for the process of composition has been obscured by conflation and expansion. It is probable that the variant versions were developed for covenant renewal ceremonies such as are implied in chapters 27 and 31 (cf. also Joshua 24). Deuteronomy is a liturgical compendium lacking the rubrics we are accustomed to in books of public worship.

The Purpose of the Deuteronomists

Who were the enigmatic Deuteronomists and what did they intend to accomplish? The stock assumption of scholarship for many years was that they were mediators between the prophet and priest, seeking to institutionalize the prophetic teachings. This they did by writing cultic reforms that would embody the prophetic injunctions in a purified type of worship, and enjoining strict social righteousness upon the community. In the hostile reign of Manasseh they were forced to work underground. Attributing their work to the founder Moses, in 621 B.C. they managed to have their "pious fraud" discovered in the temple and Josiah was converted to its claims.

In judging this view it must be remembered that no act of dishonesty was implied in an Oriental attributing his own writings to a revered ancient. But if we consistently pursue that line of thought, it would also have been unnecessary to hide the law book in the temple. Actually the whole notion of deception is misplaced. The book was "found" in the temple because priests were studying it there. Josiah

---

[1] J. Wellhausen, *Die Komposition des Hexateuchs und der historischen Bücher des Alten Testaments,* Reimer, 3rd ed., 1899, pp. 193 ff.

[2] R. H. Pfeiffer, *Introduction to the Old Testament,* Harper, 1941, p. 187.

[3] Martin Noth, *Ueberlieferungsgeschichtliche Studien I,* Niemeyer, 1943, pp. 27 ff.; see discussion in G. E. Wright, *Introduction to Deuteronomy* (IB, vol. 2), Abingdon, 1953, p. 316.

had already begun refurbishing the temple when the law was brought to him. Its "discovery" does not mean that it was previously unknown but rather that Josiah was the first king to listen to its prescriptions and make them national law.

In truth the book that Josiah espoused in 621 was the heir of a long tradition; many scholars contend that it can be traced back to north Israel. The affinities of D with E and the prophet Hosea are striking. It is probable that the central sanctuary to which D originally referred was not Jerusalem at all but Shechem (at least so it seems in 11:26–32 and 27). With the fall of Samaria the document passed into the south and became the basis of the limited reforms of Hezekiah. It then went into retirement under Manasseh, probably all the while being enlarged in variant forms at different centers, as evidenced by the present diffuseness.

Gerhard von Rad has insisted that the book is not the product of a prophetic party nor of any specifically prophetic impulse.[4] His most telling argument is the interest of Deuteronomy in the revival of holy war to be prosecuted by free citizens in place of the mercenaries who by and large composed the armies of the monarchy. It may be doubted that the prophets would have had sympathy for this burst of neo-nationalism. Von Rad finds the source of the book among "the people of the land," a group of landed gentry and rural priests who remained Yahweh loyalists opposing the urban syncretists. A faction by that name appears behind several of the political uprisings in the southern kingdom, including Josiah's elevation to the throne (II Kings 11:17–20; 21:24; 23:30; 25:18–21). They wished to assert the national and religious independence of Israel against the domination of Assyria and the syncretism of the foreign cults. The difficulty with the theory is that the code was so soon accepted in Jerusalem. The merits in von Rad's position are not irreconcilable with the prophetic spirit of the book. Certainly the view that Deuteronomy was not a creation *de novo* in 621 is psychologically and historically more tenable than a spur of the moment composition. In no respect does this revision of view diminish the achievement of Josiah, who took a bold step in identifying himself with the minority Yahwist party.

[4] G. von Rad, *Studies in Deuteronomy* (SBT, No. 9), SCM, 1953, chaps. 4, 5; anticipated by J. C. Todd, *Politics and Religion in Ancient Israel*, Macmillan, 1904, chap. 19.

The spirit and purpose of Deuteronomy can best be approached by noting its sermonic admonitory character. If the Mosaic garb is taken literally the book becomes difficult to understand. When it is recognized as the application of Mosaic religion to the late monarchy its purpose is clear. In a real sense it is a second giving of the law, the opening of an opportunity for Moses to speak directly to the apostate age. The Deuteronomists seek to arrest the headlong plunge of the state into destruction. Much of the extremism and bombast of their utterance can be forgiven and even positively admired when the desperate urgency of the time is considered. The issue as they saw it was the life or death of Judah: to obey Yahweh is life, to forsake him is death. The greatest motivation for obedience was Yahweh's love and goodness in creating a people Israel. Deuteronomy serves to place the people once again at Mt. Horeb, canceling out six centuries of sin and failure and calling Israel to a new beginning.[5] The present decision rests on Yahweh's historic dealings with Israel. The note of judgment springs from a deep sense of the divine grace that has been spurned, but no longer with impunity.

The question of authorship is seen in a new light when we realize how realistically Israel thinks of herself as a totality through all time and space. The whole Israel was present at the mountain of revelation; seventh-century Judah, so remote from her origins in almost every mode of existence, holds within her grasp the possibility of restoring the pristine covenant relation. Deuteronomy insists that the old demands and the old mercies are still binding and relevant. Moses underscores the covenantal contemporaneity of all Israelites: "Yahweh our God cut a covenant with us in Horeb, not with our fathers did Yahweh cut this covenant but with us—we—these—here—this day—all of us who are alive!" (5:2–3). The passage of time, the complexity of new circumstances, the drift of evasion—none of these can revoke the essential covenantal nature of Israel's life. Judah, like her northern neighbor, must accept the full implications of being God's people. The terrible responsibility cannot be evaded.

CENTRALIZATION OF WORSHIP

The major cult reform of Deuteronomy was the centralization of worship at Jerusalem ("the place where Yahweh shall cause his name

[5] G. von Rad, *op. cit.*, pp. 70 f.

to dwell"). That is clearly the present purport of chapter 12, although in its inchoate form the central sanctuary was Shechem. Cult centralization was more than a jealous insistence on priestly prerogatives. To be sure such jealousy of rank prevented the dispossessed priests from outlying sanctuaries being accepted at Jerusalem. The primary motivation in the reform was theological: the unity of God must be mirrored in the unity of worship. As long as a multiplicity of sanctuaries was allowed, the nature of God would be corrupted by the associations and implications of paganism. Polytheism found its perfect mode of expression in the many high places and temples; monotheism must find its counterpart in a single place of worship. Theseus, legendary founder of the Attic state, is said to have centralized worship and government in Athens and celebrated the festival of Synoecia, "the Union of the Tribes"; the Greeks, however, remained polytheists.[6]

In what sense does Deuteronomy champion the oneness of God? The so-called Shema of 6:4–9, the nearest thing to a creed in Judaism, affirms God's sublime nature, man's undivided obligation, and the familial and memorial nature of Israelite religion: "Hear, O Israel: Yahweh our God is one Yahweh; and you shall love Yahweh your God with all your heart, and with all your soul, and with all your might. And these words which I command you this day shall be upon your heart; and you shall teach them diligently to your children. . . ." Clear as it seems, the very brevity of the Shema leaves much unanswered. Is the *oneness* of Yahweh intended in contrast to his multiplicity? Baalism was such a multiple religious manifestation, with as many forms of Baal as there were locales and moods of nature. Ingenious for preserving local customs and beliefs, the whole system was incompatible with the sternly Yahwistic mind of the Deuteronomists. Or does the Shema herald the *exclusiveness* of Yahweh? He alone is God, the one and only Yahweh! We are not forced to choose one or the other of these nuances, for they are corollary presuppositions of true Yahweh worship. Yahweh is one and for Israel the only One.

One of the latest strata (4:32–40), representing an exilic deepening of thought, scales the severe heights of monotheism, even to the point of denying the existence of other gods: "know therefore this day, and lay it to your heart, that Yahweh is God in heaven above and on the earth beneath; there is no other." Its author is the first explicit monotheist of whom we have record. He doubtless preceded the author of

[6] Thucydides, *History of the Peloponnesian War* (Loeb Classical Library), II.15.

Isaiah 40–55, to whom goes the honor of enlarging and developing the theme.

THE ENIGMA OF GOD'S LOVE

Central in the thought of Deuteronomy is the love of God for Israel and the reciprocating love of Israel for God. Only Hosea had plumbed the depths of the divine love with anything like the Deuteronomic insight into its unmotivated character. The Deuteronomists were fascinated by the question: why had he chosen Israel from among the nations? This question was possible only as the older nationalistic religion was encountering the cosmopolitanism of the end of the Semitic Age. Deuteronomy is in fact the only book in the Old Testament (as Romans is the only one in the New Testament) to face openly the deeply theological issue of God's choice of a small Near Eastern nation as his instrument, his holy people. The possibility that Israel was God's by direct quasi-physical descent is ruled out. The nearest the Deuteronomist comes to basing the choice on moral desert is his assertion that Israel was chosen because of the wickedness of the Canaanites, but the righteousness of Israel is disavowed ("you have been a stiff-necked people"). The fundamental mystery of the choice resides in the love of God and the oath that he swore to the fathers. None of the ordinary estimates of a people in terms of population and natural resources, political magnitude, or national virtue can account for Israel's election: "It was not because you were more in number than any other people that Yahweh set his love upon you and chose you, for you were the fewest of all peoples; but it is because Yahweh loves you, and is keeping the oath which he swore to your fathers, that Yahweh has brought you out with a mighty hand, and redeemed you from the house of bondage," (7:7–8). "Know therefore, that Yahweh your God is not giving you this good land to possess because of your righteousness; for you are a stubborn people" (9:6).

If the implications are not thought through or the consequent mission of Israel to the nations yet conceived (even in the Yahwist's rudimentary form), the Deuteronomist at least avoids the cheap answer of national self-righteousness and affirms the mysterious love of God in which Israel may not bask contentedly but that imposes heavier demands upon her. In this respect the prophets were mentors of the framers of the law book. In fact, it was Deuteronomy's imperative of love of God, coupled with the love of neighbor enjoined in Leviticus

19:18, that became the central commandment of Judaism. Jesus subscribed to it wholeheartedly, feeling that what he had to contribute as teacher fit within the framework of its requirements.

THE RETRIBUTIVE PHILOSOPHY OF HISTORY

Through the whole of the book runs the dominant philosophy of history by which Israel's past from Moses to Jehoiachin was surveyed in the corpus Joshua through Kings. It is a collective retributive view. Israel is an entity and her faithfulness leads to security in the land. One scholar speaks of "the theology of inheritance," the D code giving the terms on which Israel may hold the land.[7] Apostasy leads to natural and historical evil. Sin has an infectious contaminating power; it must be radically purged. Thus in the extirpation of the pagan cults natural feelings must be suppressed. Even the innate impulse of man to protect his family is disregarded; the loyal Yahwist must inform against his wife if she is flirting with pagan religion. The Deuteronomist devoutly believed that the trespass of any Israelite might bring disaster upon the whole people (cf. the story of Achan's withholding of spoil from Jericho and the consequent military debacle of Israel, Joshua 7). In such terms the unfeeling extermination of the non-Yahwist was defensible. The part must be sacrificed for the whole, although this was not quite the argument of the Inquisition that the body must be tortured in order to save the soul. There was no protection for the guilty dissident, for minority rights. Yet in fairness it should be noted that the dangers of hysteria or false accusation were restricted by the provision for at least two witnesses and the ruling that false accusers would suffer immediate death.

How could such a trim equation between morality and history be worked out and adhered to? The answer lies in the distinctive quality of Hebrew faith and the direction of its development. Fundamental to Hebraism was God's control of history. That passionate faith, with all the questions it raises, is integral to contemporary Judaism and Christianity. While strains of sectarian Christianity have sought salvation from evil in individual flight and heavenly retreat, the mainstream of Christendom continues to hold to the necessity for the renovation of this world.

The next step in the Deuteronomic formula was, however, a great and tragic oversimplification: history knows no exceptions to God's

[7] G. E. Wright, *op. cit.,* pp. 316, 327.

will. They were confident that if sought intently the moral significance of even the most random events could be grasped. But the attempt to spell out God's control in detail, to prescribe and predetermine his actions was one that verged on idolatry. It led to the treatment of worldly success as proof of righteousness and failure or illness as a sign of evil. The stage was set for the debasement of righteousness into a reckoning of merit and the contravening of the high sanctions of love and grace. It was against the blundering reduction of life's enigmatic experiences to rewards and punishments that some of the greatest Jewish minds spoke out: Deutero-Isaiah and the authors of Job and Ecclesiastes. Rounding out the Deuteronomic scheme was the absence in Israel of any morally relevant future life. Sheol was a dark and indeterminate existence. Reward and punishment had to be now. No matter what the realities of life might indicate, it would be natural to conclude that if this is God's world then every man is receiving his desert.

The theist who believes in God's providence in history finds so much admirable in the presuppositions of Deuteronomy that he may seem inconsistent in boggling at its application. But object he must, for the fact is that though little is left of Jewish-Christian faith if the fundamentals of historical religion are sacrificed, it is also true that little is worth keeping if it is debauched and prostituted so that the believer, however sincere his purpose, takes into his own hands the administration of the divine government.

LAW AND SOCIAL JUSTICE

Deuteronomy is the first Hebrew document to be chiefly a law code; the introduction and addenda are purely secondary features. The first step in the history of the canon was the promulgation of the book of Deuteronomy as the constitution of Judah, although the core of 621 is less scripturalistic than the exilic additions. There is for the first time in Israel an accent on the unalterable written word: nothing is to be added or detracted (4:2; 12:32). The consolation in having such a tangible rule of life is beautifully expressed: "the secret things belong to Yahweh our God; but the things that are revealed belong to us and to our children for ever, that we may do all the words of this law" (29:29). And in terms that express the genius of Judaism quite as much as does the Shema: "For this commandment which I command you this day is not too hard for you, neither is it far off. . . . the word is very near you; it is in your mouth and in your heart, so that you can do it" (30:11,14). Human nature cannot plead weakness as an excuse, for the law is fair and attainable. Deuteronomy thus revives basic beliefs of Moses: the practicability of torah and Israel's capacity to obey. Paul could not become a Christian until he had forever surrendered that conviction.

The law code demands a rigorous justice based on the broadly compassionate righteousness of Yahweh. The concern of Deuteronomy and of all the prophets is more than merely legal, for justice and righteousness are not abstractions but constituent elements of the divine nature and therefore of the covenant people. The code is impressively extralegal, for it goes beyond the statement of law to solemn appeals, theological sanctions, and humanitarian motivations. No bare instrument of jurisprudence ever read like this. Here is covenant law, law that describes what men owe to one another because they are brothers before God. The covenant experience is the warp and woof of the individual prescriptions, remote as they sometimes seem from specifically religious matters.

In insisting on provision for the poor, the code prods the conscience of the landowner: "Take heed lest there be a base thought in your heart, and you say, 'The seventh year, the year of release is near,' and your eye be hostile to your poor brother, and you give him nothing, and he cry to Yahweh against you, and it be sin in you" (15:9). Since every seven years debtors were released, this warns against assuming that the needy will be taken care of soon enough by somebody else. The command to release Hebrew slaves after six years of service is motivated with the reminder: "You shall remember that you were a slave in the land of Egypt, and Yahweh your God redeemed you; therefore I command you this today" (15:15). This combination of legal rigor and moral passion has breathed a vital spirit into the Jewish-Christian tradition. Josiah sought to revitalize the court system, to root out the perennial blight of bribery, to discern motive in murder and rape, to banish false weights, and to renew a concern in society for slaves, widows, and orphans.

Deuteronomy impresses us as a curiously dichotomous book: both attractive and repellent. Its model is a noble faith but it pays a heavy price in ignoring the fact that history is not as tidy as theories about it. It is sad to see how the deep faith of its authors contributed to the problem of religious externality. Its spirit of intolerance and harshness strikes us as woefully inconsistent with its vision of God's love and man's devotion. The double standard is frighteningly employed: foreigners and apostates do not deserve the same treatment as the covenant brother. The sanctions do not always soar on the lofty heights of the divine love but descend into bellicose threats of God's punitive action. The annihilation of the Canaanites, advanced as a religious dogma, is none the more attractive for being an artificial theory after the fact. The fanatical obsessive drive of religion, remorselessly destroying human feeling, is a hideous thing, even when held in check by moral and spiritual restraint as in medieval Christendom. Such tyranny over the body and soul of man does not seem more excusable in Deuteronomic Reform or in Spanish Inquisition than in its more damnable forms of outright exploitation. The revulsions following the great theocratic experiments of Protestantism—Calvin's Geneva, Cromwell's Commonwealth, and Puritan New England—have been born of human resistance to even the most worthy attempts at regimented goodness. The Deuteronomic spirit lived on in such Christian attempts to build a whole community around the Word of God. High-minded in intent, architectonic in structure, beneficent in many of their results, they all foundered in the end on the profound truth of the freely responding love of man for God and neighbor, regarded by biblical tradition as even more sacred than order and conformity.

But the weakness of Deuteronomy is a congenitally human weakness that should not blind us to its many excellencies. It calls for the implementation of religious faith in the common life. Modern Christians will be moved by its eloquence and sincerity, the absoluteness and scope of its call to love and obedience. They will understand why it is one of the three or four most quoted books in the New Testament and especially favored by Jesus Christ. The vividly sketched story of the Temptation of Jesus puts words of Deuteronomy upon his lips three times as his sole and indisputable answer to the Satan: "Man shall not live by bread alone. . . . You shall worship the Lord your God, and him only shall you serve. . . . You shall not tempt the Lord your God" (Luke 4:4,8,12). Yet Jesus repudiated its brutal measures for removing evil and found no refuge in its naïve interpretation of life as simply the working out of reward and punishment. Deuteronomy knows no halfway measures, no compromises, no evasions or deceits, either in its majesty or in its intemperance. George A.

Smith has rightly observed: "The *whole* Israel is here, as in no other book of the Old Testament—the whole Israel in its limitations as in its potentiality, in its sins as in its aspirations, in its narrow fanatic tempers as in its vision and passion for the Highest."[8]

NAHUM

Better than any other ancient source, the small prophetic book of Nahum shows the unrestrained joy of the subject peoples at the downfall of Assyria. It breathes the exhilaration of release from oppression and ignominy. But it does not acclaim accomplished fact; rather it declares in advance the impending collapse of Nineveh. Nahum ("comfort"), whose home of Elkosh is unknown, wrote his victory paean after the Assyrian sack of Thebes in 663 B.C. (3:8–10) but before the fall of Nineveh in 612 B.C. The nerve-tingling imagery, the rapidly paced lines, the emphatic expectation of the city's ruin—all speak for a date very close to the end, as the inexorable advance of Medes and Chaldeans closed a tightening ring around the Assyrian heartland.

The description of the siege, breach, plunder, demolition, and exile of Nineveh is sharply drawn with a wealth of impressionistic imagery. In her death throes Assyria the predatory lion (2:11–12) and seductive harlot (3:4) will find no helpers. She is like a drained-out reservoir (2:8), her fortresses ripe fig trees waiting to be shaken (3:12), her troops weak as women (3:13), and her upper classes like droves of locusts scattered before the winter cold (3:17). Poetry though it is, an impression of ancient methods of siege warfare can be derived from Nahum. The defenders are derisively advised to hasten their preparations:

Draw water for the siege,
   strengthen your forts;
go into the clay,
   tread the mortar,
   take hold of the brick mold! (3:14).

By contrast the first chapter of Nahum is a vapid composition preserving part of an original alphabetic poem, probably inserted as a liturgical introduction for the book. It is likely that, after Nineveh's

[8] G. A. Smith, *The Book of Deuteronomy* (CB), Cambridge University Press, 1918, p. xciv.

downfall, Nahum's work was used in the temple as a "de-historicized" account of God's destruction of all his enemies. Some would contend that it was written for the New Year's Festival and never referred specifically to Nineveh, but that is carrying a good idea too far. Nevertheless the contrast between the concreteness of the last two chapters and the diffusion and abstraction of the first chapter must be reckoned with. It is hard to believe that the poet of Nineveh's destruction intended such a weak preface, although it may have been an independent work of his that editors wished to preserve.

What estimate should be placed upon Nahum's prophecy? His message is bold and obvious, unclouded by editorial glosses and unmodified by subtlety of thought. With glee he preaches the destruction of a hated enemy. This is the kind of nationalistic prophecy that the majority of the biblical prophets oppose with all their strength, and Nahum may easily be ranked as a specimen of just such superficial prophetism. Yet we should hesitate to pass a total condemnation. If this is the whole of Nahum's thought we can be certain that he was no friend of Jeremiah and no deep student of the eighth-century masters. But suppose that only the foreign oracles of Amos had been preserved? We might stigmatize him as a pseudo-prophet who whipped up the passions of Israelites against neighboring peoples. Taken just as they are, the oracles of Amos and Nahum against the enemy are similarly severe. What relieves Amos of such objection is that the bulk of his book is addressed to his own people. Nahum to the contrary speaks no word of judgment on Judah, and draws no lesson of repentance or faith for his people.

But there is another side. While revenge is no worthy spirit, Nahum at least infuses it with a moral power that cannot be missed. Assyria is not merely a personal enemy with whom the Jews are piqued; she is the wronger of the nations. Nahum's protest is the instinctive outcry of the Fertile Crescent, the clamor of the outraged:

> Woe to the bloody city,
>   all full of lies and booty—
>   no end to the plunder!
>   . . . .
> All who hear the news of you
>   clap their hands over you.
> For upon whom has not come
>   your unceasing evil? (3:1,19).

Nahum thus sums up in spirited pictorial speech the nemesis long ago foreseen by Isaiah. His "behold I am against you, says Yahweh of hosts, . . ." echoes the calm conviction of a century earlier: "When the Lord has finished all his work on Mount Zion and on Jerusalem he will punish the arrogant boasting of the king of Assyria and his haughty pride" (Isa. 10:12). We cannot, on account of his severe words against Assyria, label Nahum a false prophet. On the other hand, merely because his work has been included in the Old Testament, we cannot assume that he applied the same critical insights to Judah. His book is the distillation of a mood aroused by the passing of a world power. When qualified by the larger vision and moral vigor of the greater prophets, Nahum's book is an acceptable supplement to their tradition.

HABAKKUK

One of the finest products of the international turmoil at the close of the seventh century is the prophecy of Habakkuk. We may conjecture that he was a "cult prophet" who, in the years following Carchemish and the swift advance of Neo-Babylonia through the whole Crescent, worked up a series of oracles consisting of dialogue (1:1–2:4) and woes (2:6–20) in which he conceded that Chaldea was an instrument of divine punishment but raised the question of Chaldean evil.

The prophet's name is not Hebrew (some derive it from an Assyrian word for an herb or plant) and the introductory formula provides no chronological information. The apocryphal story of Bel and the Dragon tells of the fanciful incident of Habakkuk the prophet being transported by his hair to Babylon where he fed the imprisoned Daniel. This tradition dating Habakkuk in the exilic period has no independent corroboration and is counterbalanced by the still later Jewish legend that makes him the son of the Shunammite woman revived by Elisha. In truth the only trustworthy clue as to date is the mention of Chaldeans in 1:6 of the prophecy, which would place Habakkuk in the period 626–587 B.C., i.e., after the rise of the Chaldean Nabopolassar and before the fall of Jerusalem.

There is no textual basis for questioning the authenticity of "Chaldeans" in 1:6 but Duhm changed it to "Kittim," the Hebrew term for Cyprus later applied to the Macedonians and Romans in a symbolic sense, since like the island of Cyprus those powers lay westward from Palestine. Duhm insisted that the descriptions of the marauding foe with its imperial ambitions best suited Alexander the Great.[9] Less radically, some critics have assumed that a second nation, Assyria, is referred to from 1:12 on, against whom the Chaldeans are sent as punishment. But there is no hint in support of the two-nation thesis. Another theory, that the work is cult prophecy intended for recitation in the Jerusalem temple, is thoroughly worked out by Paul Humbert.[10] In his view earlier oracles were incorporated by Habakkuk into a liturgical prophecy dated 602/601 and directed against the despotic Jehoiakim whose sins were to be requited by the Chaldeans. His view, shared by Mowinckel, that the prophet was a temple singer and liturgist, has much in its favor. The work has pronounced dramatic and liturgical qualities. Accordingly, it may not be necessary to delete the psalm of chapter 3; whether in its proper context now it is still conceivable as a composition of the prophet's, or at any rate drawn from a collection he used. The dialogue form of the early oracles also favors public recitation. These values in the liturgical approach do not extend to the view that the book can be precisely pinpointed as an attack on the king. While the callous impiety of Jehoiakim no doubt contributes to the mood of the prophecy, the crux of it is Israel's relation to the foreign conqueror. As to date, there is no reason why the book could not have been as late as 587, even parts of it later if the mention of temple (2:20) belongs to an earlier phase of the prophet's ministry. Apart from the prophet and the Chaldeans, no proper name occurs in the book (Shigionoth in the musical directions to the psalm is probably the name of a tune, 3:1).

At the center of Habakkuk's thought is the problem of theodicy— God's ways with man. Some critics date the book after the Exile because they think a preëxilic anxiety over the question of historical injustice would be abortive and unintelligible. That is not the case. Amos and Isaiah had set the stage for the issue of theodicy. They had unflinchingly decried the sins of Israel and Judah and preached retribution through foreign powers. Isaiah even named the power; the opening wedge for theodicy already appears in his astute discernment of the power ambitions of Assyria. Once it is conceded that even the instrument of Yahweh's chastisement is an imperfect one, with sins of

[9] B. Duhm, *Das Buch Habakuk,* Mohr, 1906, pp. 4 f., 19–30. His view is rendered even less tenable by the Dead Sea commentary on Habakkuk which reads "Chaldeans."

[10] P. Humbert, *Problèmes du livre d'Habacuc,* Neuchatel, 1944.

its own, the problem of inequitable retribution then rears its insistent head. Jeremiah, living in Jerusalem at the time of Habakkuk, was tormented by much the same problem, although he saw it in terms of the prosperous wicked among his own people. The naïve hopes of Judeans, that once Assyria was disposed of all would be well, were shattered by the realization that the successor Chaldea was not much better. (Shall we compare the baseless optimism of the Western world after the demise of Nazi Germany, dissipated almost at once by the postwar conduct of Soviet Russia?) As a matter of fact, the years immediately preceding the fall of Jerusalem, when anyone with the least capacity for objectivity could have seen its inevitable ruin, are perfectly suited to the probing queries of Habakkuk. It was the auspicious time for theodicy.

The questioning mind of the prophet breaks to the surface in the form of conversation with God. He poses his queries with passionate determination and their ardor is in striking contrast to his eventual submissive spirit. The first strophe (1:1–4) asks why and how long injustice is to go unpunished. The reply of God (1:5–11) is a sketch of the Chaldean army, terrorizing and seizing the inhabited earth, "whose own might is their god." It is prefaced by an Isaiah-like emphasis upon the truly wondrous international scope of God's action:

Look among the nations, and see;
  wonder and be astounded.
For I am doing a work in your days
  that you would not believe if told (1:5).

The retort of Habakkuk (1:12–17) is a poignant prayer for the dispatch of justice commensurate with the nature of the holy God. The words have an uncommon beauty and malaise, touching them with all the sad weight of wrong that can burden a sensitive heart:

Art thou not from everlasting,
  O Yahweh my God, my Holy One?
  We shall not die (probably originally: "Thou shalt not die").

O Yahweh, thou hast ordained them as a judgment;
  and thou, O Rock, hast established them for chastisement.

Thou who art of purer eyes than to behold evil
  and canst not look on wrong,

> why dost thou look on faithless men,
>   and art silent when the wicked swallows up
>   the man more righteous than he?

After the effective image of Chaldea as a fisherman who empties the sea with his nets and lives luxuriously on its cuisine, the prophet asks:

> Is he then to keep on emptying his net,
>   and mercilessly slaying nations for ever?

Then the prophet, delivered of his most burning protests and his most passionate hopes, retires to a watchtower where his sharp eye scans the horizon for some token of the divine answer (2:1). Like Job he is resolved to wait an eternity if necessary for his answer. The dialogue sequence comes to its climax in the short but textually obscure reply of God (2:2–4). While the nuances are problematic, its crux is not in doubt. The prophet is to emblazon on tablets the basic motto of the life of trust:

> Behold, he whose soul is not upright in him shall fail,
>   but the righteous shall live by his faith.

Fidelity to what is right will endure when wickedness has wasted and withered away. The Hebrew prophet found the only solution for injustice in the intrinsic worth of justice, in a way not unlike Socrates and Plato who insisted that the right is its own reward. But in a manner not characteristic of classical Athens, Habakkuk's conviction was tempered by patience and waiting. "The vision"[11] may be slow in coming; through long periods the life of faithfulness to God and his justice may seem but a farce—the veriest unreality! But its truth will surely dawn and will possess the innermost man with mighty conviction. Habakkuk apparently felt that such a vision was worth waiting for. As a matter of fact he could only write of it as he did because he had based his own life on faith in righteousness. He did not know any more clearly than before why the wicked Chaldeans were free to harass the earth; but he did know that the impulse to ask the question, to be shocked and affronted, was an impulse of righteousness more real than all the evil he could encompass in his imagination.

The great adage, "the righteous shall live by his faith," was a favorite

---

[11] No satisfactory antecedent of "the vision" can be found unless it is implied in the prophet's role as watchman.

with Paul who used it in key contexts in his discussion of justification
by faith (Gal. 3:11 and Rom. 1:17). It appears also in Hebrews
10:38. For Luther it became the rallying cry of the Protestant Reformation: not by dependence upon any human mediation but by faith
alone is man accepted before God. The Christian nuance is somewhat
different from the stress Habakkuk makes. For Paul and Luther the
accent is on faith: "The righteous shall live by his *faith*." For Habakkuk emphasis falls on righteousness and the last word might better be
rendered "faithfulness": "the *righteous* shall live by his faithfulness."
But the difference is far from irreconcilable. Paul and Luther may be
understood to spell out the implications of Habakkuk's insight that
in our relation to God and the good, to what is truly ultimate, there
are no "proofs" or demonstrations that in the last analysis justify our
faith. The Christian thinkers developed the same conviction with the
added dimension of God's grace in Christ. Isaiah's seed of faith had
fallen on good soil and was to grow from more to more.

The question had been asked in all its horrible cogency: Why? It
could never again be silenced. And the answers given to it would need
to be basic answers, not rationalizations or tricks, but insights into the
deeper ranges of the spiritual life: the intrinsic and unalterable worth
of knowing God and obeying his will.

JEREMIAH

The ominous and foreboding years of Judah's decease as a nation
produced one of the finest of Hebrews, a prophet whose distinction lay
in a rare blend of message and person. In no sense a popular leader,
his writings display an uncommon integrity and boundless love of
country that endeared him to later generations as a signal example of
the deep relevance and realism of prophecy—as well as Israel's tragic
rejection of her best leadership. As Hosea was the prophet of the collapse of the north, Jeremiah was the prophet of the dissolution of the
south. Yet in a manner beyond even the highest hope of Isaiah he saw
the continuing work of Yahweh emerge unscathed from Judean reversal. In quiet and serenity of spirit he held that the Exile was to be
the source of Israel's phoenixlike renewal. Often despairing, so that
jeremiad has become a byword for any mournful complaint, he demonstrated nevertheless a fundamentally invincible optimism. Those who
could see little relevance to the covenant and its high demands, who
scorned the rigors of trust and repentance, saw nothing in Jeremiah

but that dour intransigence that made the prophets from first to last as socially undesirable as they were intellectually disquieting. His sense of right would not pander to the heated chauvinist passions of his day, but equally his vision of the indestructible love of Yahweh would not surrender to the mass dejection of the same zealots turned defeatists.

THE PROPHET'S MINISTRY

We know of Jeremiah through the biographical passages of his book, which provide us with rich data for the period 608–587 B.C. The exciting account of his relations with kings and princes, his determined bid to save Judah, and the stout resistance of his opponents is somewhat disrupted by the present order of the incidents. When restored to proper sequence and read without interruption, the story of Jeremiah unfolds with dramatic impact and casts constant illumination on his recorded words. These memoirs of the prophet must have been composed by someone close to him. Most scholars believe that Jeremiah's scribal confidant Baruch wrote the recollections for posterity, perhaps when in Egyptian exile. While the exact limits of the memoirs are not agreed upon, they may be approximately reconstructed:

608 B.C.	Temple Sermon	Chap. 26 (cf. 7)
	Pashhur Puts Jeremiah in Stocks	19:14–20:6
605	Baruch's Scroll	36
	Jeremiah's Promise of Life to Baruch	45
598	Praise of the Rechabites	35
	Basket of Figs	24
595	Hananiah and the Iron Yoke	27–28
	Letter to the Exiles	29
589–587	Hypocritical Release of Slaves	34
	Jeremiah Imprisoned	37
	Purchase of Hanamel's Field	32
	Ebedmelech Rescues Jeremiah	38
	Siege and Fall of the City	39
	Interim Government of Gedaliah	40–41
	Flight to Egypt	42–44

It will be noted how heavily weighted the biography is toward describing the last days of Judean independence and the bitter opposition faced by the prophet. He was near death on at least two occasions. The memoirs have in fact been likened to the Passion Narrative of the Christian Gospels.[12] They share the same circumstantial description, interplay of contending personalities, and fateful consequences— sharply set off from the relative sketchiness of the earlier ministries of Jeremiah and Jesus. Students of the Bible have not been slow to observe the similarities between the two men. Both wept over heedless Jerusalem. Both insisted on the doom of the city for want of repentance. Both attacked the temple; Jesus actually employed the bitter words of the prophet (Mark 11:17 cf. Jer. 7:11). Both were reviled and buffeted, but Jesus had no influential friends to save him from death.

The crux of the memoirs is the clash between a prophetic covenantal reading of history's events and a narrow military-political appraisal. It is principle against expediency, but not that cold and abstract principle that is pompous and ineffectual (no prophet was this breed of moralist). Jeremiah's convictions are embodied in a life warm and tender, and above all, they are truths that he lived by. They placed continuing demands upon himself and were not high-sounding slogans for public consumption. He was hated and feared for this by the politicians of his day. Jehoiakim contemptuously sat before the palace brazier and as three or four columns of the collected sermons of the prophet were read to him, he cut them with a penknife and cast them into the fire. Zedekiah to the contrary wistfully clung to the good favor of Jeremiah, hoping that the prophet's virtue might somehow rub off on the city; but he would not change his own heart or lay a hand to the policies of state in order to stem or reverse the course of events. Against the war party, spurred on by the ubiquitous Egyptian conspirators, Zedekiah was paralyzed.

In these two kings we see the quintessence of social and political error: the cold malignity of the tyrant and the stumbling default of the weak-willed. The covenant demands of Yahweh fall with equal force upon those who overreach themselves in cruel ambition and those whose equivocations prevent them from acting responsibly. The prophet is as sharp with Zedekiah who thinks that good can come through taking no action at all as he is with Jehoiakim who makes his own rules and deliberately rejects the covenant norms.

If we are to believe the superscription to the book, Jeremiah began

[12] Paul Volz, *Der Prophet Jeremia,* Deichert, 1922, pp. xlvi f., 330–366.

to preach in 626 (the thirteenth year of Josiah), but the absence of biographical recollections and oracles from the years 626–609 has prompted second thoughts. Some would assume an error and correct the date to "the twenty-third year of Josiah," i.e., 616. A novel suggestion takes the year 626 as the date of Jeremiah's birth, since the prophet is unique in believing himself to be predestined from the womb as a mouthpiece of Yahweh (1:5).[13] Hyatt posits that the eighteen-year-old youth was called to a public ministry in 608 B.C. This also accords with the growing opinion that the oracles describing "the foe from the north" in chapters 4–6 do not apply to the barbarian Scythian hordes of 621 but to the Neo-Babylonians after 605. It is noted that the weapons and manner of warfare implied in these poems point to the technologically superior forces of Babylon rather than the guerrilla-like Scythians who were unable to take any of the walled cities of Syria and Palestine as they pillaged to the border of Egypt. The interpretation of Hyatt eliminates the silent period in Jeremiah's life; its major objection is that the superscription, which many attribute to Baruch, does not give any hint of such a subtlety.

If the traditional view of a call in 626 is retained, then also at stake is Jeremiah's attitude toward the Deuteronomic Reform of 621. It is widely assumed that he was at first sympathetic towards its aims and even its methods, perhaps itinerating as a priestly advocate of the reform. Later, however, he grew disgusted with the superficial results it obtained and saw increasingly that the root of Judah's trouble was an inward disposition untouchable by legal provisions. Portions of the book are written in a turgid Deuteronomic style and this might be adduced as evidence of his approval of the reforms, but the cogency of the argument is negated by the fact that the Deuteronomic passages do not belong to a single period in his life and are in sharp contrast to the poetic oracles dating from the same times. The most likely solution to the literary problem is the theory that a Deuteronomist has preserved some of the prophet's words and given them final form. It of course might be contended that if Deuteronomists were cordial toward Jeremiah he must at some time have been well disposed toward their efforts. But this need not be, for the exilic Deuteronomists showed a compiling mania toward the religious traditions of their people. They

[13] J. P. Hyatt, *Introduction and Exegesis of Jeremiah* (IB, vol. 5), Abingdon, 1956, pp. 779, 797 f.

revered the works of prophetic individualists such as Jeremiah, who themselves would have had many reasons for holding aloof from the Deuteronomic religious solution.

Perhaps the most interesting argument for some connection with the Deuteronomists is the fact that the clique of noblemen who were nearest to Jeremiah in the last years seem to have been sons of Shaphan, scribe under Josiah and chief figure in the reform of 621. These men were influential on Jeremiah's behalf: Ahikam spared his life in the face of the angry mob (26:24), from Gemariah's court Baruch read the prophet's scroll to the people (36:10), and Elasah was one of two messengers who delivered his letter to the exiles (29:3). Gedaliah, grandson of Shaphan, became the governor of Judah under Babylonian aegis and gave asylum to the prophet; prior to the governor's brutal assassination, Jeremiah was the power behind the throne. The prophet also praised Josiah. Certainly Jeremiah had no fixed ideological dislike of the reform, but he must have been deeply disturbed by its limited results and when its finest products, the noble family of Shaphan, could not swerve the course of the state from the disastrous shoals of pseudo-patriotism, he must have grown steadily doubtful of all measures that did not go to the heart of things.

THE COMPOSITION OF THE BOOK

The book of Jeremiah is baffling in its arrangement. A cursory breakdown shows three broad categories plus an appendix:

Oracles of the prophet in poetry and prose	Chaps. 1–25
Biographical Narratives	26–45
Oracles against Foreign Nations	46–51
Historical Appendix derived from II Kings 24:18–25:30	52

It is a difficult book to read; the chronological disarray and the alternation of crisp poetry and bombastic prose are distracting. That the book is far from being in its original form is apparent in the Septuagint's omission of about 2,700 words (one-eighth of MT) and its insertion of the foreign oracles after 25:13 in a more logical position (as in Isaiah and Ezekiel) and also in a different order.

One of the most helpful efforts to reduce the literary chaos to order is that of Mowinckel,[14] who distinguished three types of material in the

[14] Sigmund Mowinckel, *Zur Komposition des Buches Jeremia,* Dybwad, 1914; his position is slightly modified in *Prophecy and Tradition,* Oslo, 1946, pp. 61–65.

book: (A) Jeremianic poetic oracles, compiled mainly in chapters 1–25; (B) Historical narratives in chapters 26–45;[15] (C) Lengthy speeches with Jeremianic affinities but cast in Deuteronomic phraseology and thought. Like many scholars, Mowinckel takes chapter 36 with its account of Baruch's scroll as the starting point for unraveling the composition of the book. That scroll was basically composed of words of doom to Judah and predated 605 B.C. The contents of the original scroll are embedded in chapters 1–25 but cannot now be separated; they were combined with B by a redactor. In postexilic times a second editor added to AB a separate version of the prophet's words —C, written under Deuteronomic sponsorship. Instead of appending the contents of C *en bloc,* the editor distributed them throughout A and B according to what little chronological information he had. Anonymous words of promise and hope (chaps. 30–31), a collection of foreign oracles (46–51), and the historical appendix (52) were added still later.

MOWINCKEL'S THEORY OF AUTHORSHIP

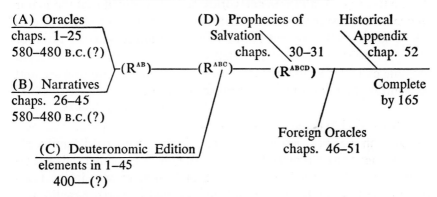

(A) Oracles
chaps. 1–25
580–480 B.C.(?)

(B) Narratives
chaps. 26–45
580–480 B.C.(?)

(C) Deuteronomic Edition
elements in 1–45
400—(?)

(D) Prophecies of
Salvation
chaps. 30–31

(R^{AB})———(R^{ABC})——— (R^{ABCD})

Foreign Oracles
chaps. 46–51

Historical
Appendix
chap. 52

Complete
by 165

Corresponding to Mowinckel's A and B, Hyatt[16] posits a Baruch scroll of 605, consisting of oracles in 1–25; in a second edition of 586 additional oracles, personal "confessions," and memoirs were supplied. In the Egyptian exile a Deuteronomic version of the prophet's message (Mowinckel's C) was prepared about 550 B.C., incorporating Baruch's edition. The Book of Comfort (chaps. 30–31) was appended

---

[15] Mowinckel discounts the biographical element and emphasizes that the only incidents related are those functioning as "occasions for memorable words" of the prophet.

[16] J. P. Hyatt, *op. cit.,* pp. 787–791.

in the period 538–450 B.C., and the oracles against foreign nations were inserted after the fall of Babylon in 538; a nucleus of these oracles may derive from the prophet.[17]

HYATT'S THEORY OF AUTHORSHIP

Baruch's Scroll 605 B.C.	2d Edition by Baruch? 586 B.C.	Deuteronomic Edition 550 B.C.	Book of Comfort
			538/–450 B.C.
Oracles	Oracles Confessions Memoirs		Oracles against the Nations

While there are pronounced differences in detail, most critics today seem agreed upon the three types of material (Mowinckel's symbols A, B, and C are widely used) and, unlike Duhm who believed that Jeremiah wrote only about sixty short poems (plus the letter of chap. 29) and Baruch only about 220 verses, they grant the presence of authentic tradition in all three categories. It is also agreed that the major source of confusion is the promiscuous distribution of the Deuteronomic speeches throughout the book and the unaccountable disorder of the memoirs. To acquaint oneself with the book it is best to begin with the call visions and memoirs, turn next to the poetic oracles, and concentrate finally on the prolix prose speeches.

THE CONFESSIONS

Jeremiah was of priestly lineage and from a propertied family. He had the means to purchase land from his cousin Hanamel. His hometown Anathoth, but a few miles north of Jerusalem, was in the territory of the tribe of Benjamin and thus steeped in north Israelite tradition. The prophet alludes to the northern tribal mother Rachel weeping for her children (31:15) and threatens that Jerusalem will become like Shiloh (7:12; 26:6,9). He seems never to have given up the hope that the northern tribes would be restored to life in the covenant.

His feelings for nature were keen; in his finest nature imagery lurks a disposition toward the romantic that is checked by the classical stricture of his Hebrew heritage. His observant eye discerned the hab-

---

[17] A majority of critics accept the graphic description of the destruction of Egyptian troops at Carchemish in 605 as the work of Jeremiah (chap. 46).

its of wild things, so that the migratory instincts of birds stood in inexplicable contrast to the stubborn waywardness of man (he did not share the sentiment of William Cullen Bryant's "To a Waterfowl" that the birds were a pattern of man's unerring homegoing), and the blind passion of a she-camel in heat typified the unreasoning and possessive power of Judah's evil ways. In one of the most effectively articulated of prophetic poems, Jeremiah visualizes the awful prospect of an earth deserted by the life he cherished:

I looked on the earth, and lo, it was waste and void;
    and to the heavens, and they had no light.
I looked on the mountains, and lo, they were quaking,
    and all the hills moved to an fro.
I looked, and lo, there was no man,
    and all the birds of the air had fled.
I looked, and lo, the fruitful land was a desert,
    and all its cities were laid in ruins,
        before Yahweh, before his fierce anger (4:23–26).

Only one thing he prized more than nature and that was nature's Creator. In thoroughly prophetic fashion the deeper sources of his faith were in the covenant bond and not in the sensory world. In another environment he might have been a lyric poet or a landscape artist. As it was his inmost privacy was invaded by a public calling. Yet there were occasional moments when he yearned for a life of retreat, "O that I had a wayfarers' lodge in the wilderness!" (9:2a). He would have been happy in the Dead Sea community at Qumran. Born to love a sheltered life, he was thrust into a career that abraded his contemporaries and left raw wounds in his own soul.

It is chiefly due to a series of individual laments that Jeremiah's psyche has been exposed. Since the Old Testament is so doggedly taciturn in giving up even the least psychological hints, these laments, often called the "confessions" of Jeremiah, are of incalculable worth. Compared to the usual breadth of the confessional genre, Jeremiah's laments are mere jottings. Unlike the Confessions of Augustine or Rousseau the prophet does not appear to have written for the public eye. They thus lack some of that special pleading which makes of even the best autobiography "a prolonged speech for the defense." At the same time they are limited to moods from which generalizations must be drawn with care.

It is certain that these poems were no part of Baruch's Scroll, not only because they are unlike the sort of thing a man would publish in his lifetime, but also because the command to the scribe does not embrace them: "Take a scroll and write on it all the words that I have spoken to you against Israel and Judah and all the nations . . ." (36:2). The Confessions are best regarded as private papers, leaves from the prophet's journal, published possibly through the devoted insight of Baruch, who would have been one of the first to perceive the immortal character of these prayers.

Although undated they are usually assigned to the reign of Jehoiakim, inasmuch as they presuppose a period when Jeremiah was mocked for the failure of his predictions, excluded from the temple, and his life threatened. John Skinner argues that the courage and fortitude of the prophet reported in the memoirs would be utterly incompatible with the despair and vacillation reflected in the prayers. Thus he contends that they derive from the days of Josiah and that under Jehoiakim the prophet emerged as the "fortified city, iron pillar and bronze wall."[18] Skinner seems to have missed the patent fact that the exterior and interior perspectives of a man are often very different. Outwardly Jeremiah may never have flinched but inwardly he knew torments unsuspected even by his biographer. There are analogies enough to crowd pages. Luther's bravery before prelates and princes was coupled with moods of dark anguish. Bismarck, who presented to the world the façade of a stern militarist, has revealed in his correspondence a startling tenderness and lightheartedness. One of the staple experiences of the ecstatic mystic has always been a lapse into that agonizing state known as "the dark night of the soul." It does not take unwarranted imagination to see the publicly fearless prophet cringing inwardly before the specters of doubt and loneliness. When we deny this clash of strength and weakness, of conviction and disbelief, of resolution and indecision, we cut the one nexus by which the traditions about the prophet can be held together meaningfully.

In this study we shall include the call visions in the "confessional" genre, since they disclose features indispensable to an understanding of the prophet's inner life. Alone of the prophets, Jeremiah reports a threefold call. In the present order the final two are visions of a budding almond tree (1:11–12) and a boiling pot tipped toward the south (1:13–19). The first is an audition rather than a vision and is of

[18] John Skinner, *Prophecy and Religion,* Cambridge University Press, 1922, p. 209.

crucial interest because of its sharp delineation of Jeremiah's retiring and deeply thoughtful nature (1:4–10). He has an overwhelming sense of divine foreordination. Known of God and consecrated to his calling before birth, the prophet understands his mission to be rooted in the deep and eternal counsels of God. Yet this surety does not prevent an instinctive diffidence from enveloping him: "I do not know how to speak, for I am only a youth" (1:6). He shies from the prophet's roll not because he lacks elocution but rather because he is no person to speak such a message; he does not know how to confront people with firmness. The divine assurance is simply the promise of God's presence, no more but no less; the promise "I am with you" was claimed more than once by the faltering prophet. The power of the divine word is further consolation, "Behold, I have put my words in your mouth." As he watches the gorgeously flowered almond tree (called in Hebrew "the watcher" or "awakener" because it is the floral harbinger of spring), Yahweh solemnly affirms that he is "watching" over his word to perform it.

The terms of Jeremiah's call to be "a prophet to the nations" (1:5) and the command that he was to be set "over nations and over kingdoms, to pluck up and to break down. . . . to build and to plant" (1:10; delete "to destroy and to overthrow" as redundant, cf. 24:6; 42:10; 45:4), have frequently been questioned on two counts: (1) that Jeremiah's real ministry was to Judah and his word to foreign nations was peripheral; (2) that he had no consciousness of a positive prophetic role, except perhaps at the end of his life. To the first objection, we need only recall that while Jeremiah read the historic times from the point of view of God's purposes for his people so that Judah was at the center, anything that happened in the known world of the Crescent was potentially relevant to Judah. He saw Judah's destiny as inseparably bound up with the nations. As for the second, it is true that the apparently earlier oracles of the prophet do not strike much of a note of hope but they are filled with the appeal to turn, to repent. Also, unlike Amos, Jeremiah was not left without resource when the political identity of his people was threatened. A man who could maintain a belief in the future of his people after the fall of the state and cultus, who could write the letter to the exiles, was one who had thought long about how "to build and to plant." On neither count is there justification for questioning the authenticity of the vocational command to the prophet.

The confessions in the more limited sense are struck off in a mood of protest and turmoil. The intimate relation of God and prophet is far from placid. At one point a desire to give up and flee from his task sweeps over Jeremiah in an almost monastic urge (9:1–3). His sensitivity to man's sin and weakness is not a mere doctrine but begins with his own self-consciousness, as he cries:

> Correct me, O Yahweh, but in just measure;
>   not in thy anger, lest thou bring me to nothing (10:24).

One of the cruelest wounds that the prophet endured was the hostility of his own townsmen ("A prophet has no honor in his own country," John 4:44). They went to the length of plotting against his life (according to the Deuteronomic version in Jer. 11:21–23). Some have attributed this antagonism to his support of the Deuteronomic reform that would have put the priests of Anathoth out of business owing to centralization of worship at Jerusalem. But the prophet's words give a better rationale; it was because of his warning of destruction unless Judah changed her ways that he was so despised (20:8,10). Jeremiah commits his cause to Yahweh and prays unabashedly for vengeance on his enemies (11:20).

In the first lament of substance Jeremiah raises the question of individual theodicy as Habakkuk had posed it for the nations:

> Righteous art thou, O Yahweh,
>   when I complain to thee;
> yet I would plead my case before thee.
> Why does the way of the wicked prosper?
>   Why do all who are treacherous thrive? (12:1).

Unjust suffering and unmerited prosperity stare at him out of the troubled city. If he is speaking Yahweh's word, why is his cause repeatedly rejected while the perverse go blandly on their way, successful and popular? The prophet asks that God again scrutinize his motives and then judge the wicked. The answer of Yahweh (most scholars omit vs. 4 as an intrusion) might be dubbed a magnificent irrelevance, for it side-steps the question of theodicy by summoning Jeremiah to face the yet stiffer opposition of the wicked. This is no hour for self-pity or for universalizing about the divine justice. It is the hour for strength in the dispatch of a heavy duty.

> If you have raced with men on foot, and they have wearied you,
>   how will you compete with horses?

And if in a safe land you fall down,
   how will you do in the jungle of the Jordan? (12:5).

He is not to trust the social amenities that men offer in place of change of heart (12:6).

Jeremiah gives expression to the sheer rapture of his prophetic vocation (15:16), even as his isolation from normal social ties lies heavily upon him. Not that he was ever an extrovert, but he wished for the joy of pursuing his faith in the company of good friends and in a sympathetic social environment. It is apparent both in the poetic confession and in adjacent Deuteronomic sections (Jer. 16:1–9) that Jeremiah felt an essential part of his mission to be social aloofness— to the extent of refusing to participate in feasts or funerals and even eschewing marriage (practically unheard-of among Jews). This was no denial of the flesh but a symbolically acted omen of the imminent cessation of all normal human activities: when the city meets its nemesis what will marriage and children and festivity amount to then? We see here with special clarity that Hebrew asceticism was always utilitarian and eschatological, dramatizing the relative unimportance of normal pursuits in the light of the huge crises of God's action. It is not doctrinaire asceticism built upon body-soul dualism that seeks to starve the emotions and root out offensive bodily pleasures. The daily round of life became for Jeremiah not an evil so much as a trivial thing. It was not wrong that men reveled and lived happily in the social world; what was wrong was their disposition to flee ignorantly from the realities by which the social fabric was kept strong and durable in favor of needful but anesthetizing daily duties. Nothing must shield Jeremiah and his people from the wrath and grace of God. In candor of soul they must face the shocking truth about themselves, their default and their allegiance, their doom and their hope.

In the same poem the prophet flirts with the possibility that he is wrong. The prophetic inspiration was not a monomania that left him unfeeling or unthinking. Scoffed at and rejected by so large a proportion of his people, he came to wonder about his own calling. Not for one moment did he doubt God's existence, but perhaps he had been deceived and misguided:

Wilt thou be to me like a deceitful brook,
   like waters that fail? (15:18).

As a desert traveler crazed with thirst beholds a mirage, has my mind so deluded me? Has God sent upon me "a lying spirit" such as infects the false prophet? Jeremiah is snatched from his reverie by the response of Yahweh. The answer is again firm and even rebuffing, charging the prophet with dereliction of duty, self-pity, doubt of his mission. But there is hope if the prophet will repent. Isaiah required cleansing before he felt worthy to accept the role of a prophet; for Jeremiah repentance and renewal of call were continuing needs. He had to convert not only his people but also himself. His own motives and spirit needed constant scrutiny lest he grow hard of heart, self-righteous, or self-consoling.

> If you return, I will restore you,
>   and you shall stand before me.
> If you utter what is precious, and not what is worthless,
>   you shall be as my mouth.
> They shall turn to you,
>   but you shall not turn to them. (15:19)

Commentators have rightly acclaimed this verse as a key to the processes of prophetic inspiration. It securely establishes the faculty of prophetic discernment. The dynamic compulsive word of Yahweh did not destroy the freedom of the prophet, the freedom not only to choose his words but to assent or object to the will of the God for whom he spoke. In stressing the realism of prophetic activity, we must not obliterate this dimension of freedom. Prophetic inspiration and activity were not monolithic. In fact it is the individuality, the uniqueness, the vitality of insight and thought that set off the great prophets from the automata of the bands of false prophets who were faceless because they were little more than the epitome of popular moods. Complain though he did, at his best the prophet heard the emphatic words that summoned him to reaffirm his belief in Yahweh's word for his people: "If you return. . . . If you utter what is precious. . . ."

Jeremiah develops the theme of alienation from those to whom he must preach and raises the far-reaching question of personal motivation (17:14–18; 18:20). Is he really the disinterested messenger of Yahweh he claims to be? Has he not rather on occasion desired the evil that he preaches? They mock him from year to year, as disaster delays, "Where is the word of Yahweh? Let it come!" (17:15). When the price of its delay is his own shame and mortification, how can he help but desire the day of disaster for private reasons rather than for the vindication of Yahweh and the covenant? We could ask for no

surer evidence of the remarkable self-objectivity of this prophet. Whatever morbid moods may have accosted him, he was able to look deeply
into his soul, to behold the dark stirring there, the unpurged hates and
the cherished revenges, and to admit to them and thus to be delivered
from them. His knowledge of God was the knowledge of utter grace;
his desperately wicked heart could not be reformed but he could
know the forgiveness of God and in that knowledge he could trust
against a thousand foes.

> I have not pressed thee to send evil,
>   nor have I desired the day of disaster,
>   thou knowest;
> that which came out of my lips
>   was before thy face (17:16).

In the confession now preserved as the last of the series (20:7–18),
Jeremiah pulls all stops and sounds forth every abasement and exaltation known to him. Deceived by God and forced into an unwanted
task (he talks as rashly to God as Moses, as only a friend can talk to
another), compelled to shout wearisomely, "Violence and destruction!," sometimes determined to renounce his call and preach no
more, denounced and schemed against by his friends; he nevertheless
goes on declaring the truths that are dearer than life and comfort,
trusting in the defense of Yahweh, certain that those conspiring
against him will stumble, rejoicing that he is known through and
through by the one whose knowledge supremely matters. His freedom
is to be fully what his call demands of him, to embrace the word of
God without remorse and to preach it as his only reason for being:

> If I say, "I will not mention him,
>   or speak any more in his name,"
> there is in my heart as it were a burning fire
>   shut up in my bones,
> and I am weary with holding it in,
>   and I cannot (20:9).

Jeremiah knows that in the last analysis his call is not a matter of
mood and feeling, but of the mandate of the divine word that is shaping history. "Is not my word like fire, says Yahweh, and like a hammer
which breaks the rock in pieces?" (23:29). The prophet, quite as
much as Assyria or Neo-Babylonia, was a scorching fire against the
pith of Judah, a sharp ax laid at the decayed root of the tree of evil

(5:14 cf. Hos. 6:5). And all this towering conviction beside the bleak depression with which the confession closes as he curses his birth, and thus by implication his parents and his God:

> Why did I come forth from the womb
>   to see toil and sorrow,
>   and spend my days in shame? (20:18).

We cannot date these prayers or be sure that verses 14–18 followed close upon verses 7–12; what we do see is a man continually under pressures almost inhuman, bearing himself with an equilibrium that did not come easily, repeatedly saved from the solipsism of despair to a career for which he received no thanks and hardly any understanding.

SIN AND REPENTANCE

We have dwelt at some length upon the rich devotional poetry of the prophet, partly because of its intrinsic merit and partly because for no other leader of Israel have we such personal reflections. But what of his public message? While he did not parade his inner states like an exhibitionist, the public declarations of the prophet notably accord with the spirit of the confessions. Basic to all his belief was the essential inwardness of faith, not in the sense of a merely personal matter, but in the sense that faith went to the root of the will where sin had its deepest entrenchment and grace its greatest opportunity. Sin and its solution had individual and collective aspects. That Jeremiah exerted a special influence in magnifying the individual aspect does not mean that he was any less a collectively minded prophet than the others before him. Yet he did behold the collectivity of Israel in a perspective that only his era and his personality could have grasped. The people of God were to find their distinctiveness by a rebirth of the old covenant convictions in the personal faith and repentance of Israelites. Jeremiah had no patience with religion by proxy, with innocence by association.

Continuing the tradition of Hosea he saw sin not as acts so much as a condition of the "heart" (in Hebrew psychology the heart is the seat of thought and will more often than of emotion). He speaks repeatedly of the "obdurate or stubborn heart." At times a gloomy pessimism about the prospect of change of heart sweeps over him:

Can the Ethiopian change his skin
　or the leopard his spots?
Then also you can do good
　who are accustomed to do evil (13:23).

Though "the heart is deceitful above all things, and desperately corrupt" (17:9), he calls upon his people to make a break with the past
order, not by means of self-reformation but through repentance and
the gift of a new heart:

Circumcise yourselves to Yahweh
　remove the foreskin of your hearts,
　O men of Judah and inhabitants of Jerusalem (4:4).

O Jerusalem, wash your heart from wickedness,
　that you may be saved.
How long shall your evil thoughts
　lodge within you? (4:14).

Ritual paraphernalia are no solution to sin, which is a matter of
will and the deepest dispositions of the mind. Jeremiah foresees the
day when the ark "shall not come to mind, or be remembered, or
missed; it shall not be made again" (3:16). In the holy precincts of
the temple the prophet denounced worship as blasphemous when it
companied with bland wrongdoing: "Behold, you trust in deceptive
words to no avail. Will you steal, murder, commit adultery, swear
falsely, burn incense to Baal, and go after other gods that you have
not known, and then come and stand before me in this house, which
is called by my name, and say, 'We are delivered!'—only to go on
doing all these abominations?" (7:8–10). Circumcision is no guarantee of acceptability to God since many Semitic peoples practice it
("they are circumcised but yet uncircumcised"); the supreme grief is
that "all the house of Israel is uncircumcised in heart" (9:25–26).
The call to scrupulous observance of the Sabbath in 17:19–27 is almost unanimously judged as non-Jeremianic. Its style and thought are
Deuteronomic and postexilic.

　For sin so far-reaching the only cure was inward repentance and
trust in the divine mercy. A word that rings through the prophecies
of Jeremiah (especially evident as a catchword linking oracles in
chaps. 2–4) is the summons: Turn! The whole will must be surrendered up to a new course, filled with a new affection, dedicated to a

new cause. But it is just this radical reorientation, with its exceptional demands, that raises the doubt of total national acceptance. Like Isaiah with his hope in the remnant, Jeremiah begins to discern that this is a course the masses will not follow but which must nevertheless be followed by some for the sake of all. Only in that respect is Jeremiah the father of personal religion. The believing individual does not desert the community or sever himself spiritually from it; that was impossible even for a man constitutionally as retiring as Jeremiah. The personal character of the prophet's faith has none of the marks of an otherworldly religion, though it has the signs of a religion of salvation. When Jeremiah's individualism is conceded, it must be sharply distinguished from humanistic independence and from rejection of the covenant responsibilities of the community. It is essentially the fulfillment of community through the faithful Jew resolving to bear his share of the covenant obligation no matter what others may do.

It is evident that the cast of piety typical of Jeremiah became immensely meaningful to Israelites of the Exile who but a few years before had despised him. His resolute pressing of the responsibility of each Israelite to saturate life with the covenant spirit was one of the chief means of stabilizing the tottering faith of the exiles. Devoid of sacrifice and temple pageantry, they turned to hearing the word of the prophets. This prepared them for synagogue worship, which was essentially a liturgy of obedience through hearing. Jeremiah with his contemporary Ezekiel was instrumental in Jewish weathering of the decease of political Yahwism as a religion of circumscribed cult acts; in its place grew a religion of life obedience, with minimal ritual observances to implement the Jew's trust in God.

The Future of Israel

As to the configuration of Jeremiah's hope for the future, it had at least four aspects. In the first place, he looked for the restoration of north Israel, purged of sin and in harmony with the south. The passages that speak most plainly of this belief are in the so-called Book of Comfort (chaps. 30–31). While there are undoubted glosses in this section, the style in the main is Jeremianic. The oracles of Israelite restoration (31:2–5, 12–22) are probably from the period of Gedaliah's interim reign when the remnants of all the tribes looked to a central government and agricultural reclamation was being pushed by the wise ruler.

Secondly, the letter of the prophet to the exiles of 598 B.C. shows that he anticipated a long period of enforced separation from the homeland and that faithfulness to Yahweh was only loosely connected with locale. The letter was part of an extensive correspondence exchanged between Babylon and Palestine. From the exiles came acrimonious accusations intended to silence the prophetic party in Jerusalem and especially Jeremiah (29:24–32). As is apparent in Ezekiel's book, the bulk of the exiles of 598 refused to accept the permanence of their state and from a distance continued to resist the prophet's message. In the midst of internal rifts of this sort, Jeremiah's document is sober, affirmative, and statesman-like: "Thus says Yahweh of hosts, the God of Israel, to all the exiles whom I have sent into exile from Jerusalem to Babylon: Build houses and live in them; plant gardens and eat their produce. Take wives and have sons and daughters; take wives for your sons, and give your daughters in marriage, that they may bear sons and daughters; multiply there and do not decrease. But seek the welfare of the city where I have sent you into exile, and pray to Yahweh on its behalf, for in its welfare you will find your welfare" (29:4–7). The program of Jeremiah's letter reads like a description of Jewish experience through the twenty-five hundred years since the prophet wrote. The single most distinctive feature of Judaism was that it succeeded in surviving political uprootedness and ritual alteration; it became thereby a religion in permanent exile.

Whether Jeremiah predicted a seventy-year Exile is disputed (25:11–12; 29:10), but the strongest proof that he did is the fact that the figure is an imprecise one that no postexilic writer would have been likely to concoct. If the Exile is dated from 598 it lasted at most sixty years, and if dated from 587 it was only forty-nine years. Jeremiah probably intended seventy as a round number (the maximum lifetime?) in contrast to the sanguine prediction of Hananiah ("within two years," 28:3). Some who deny the prophet's expectation of restoration to Palestine do so in the interest of preserving his universal outlook, assuming that he foresaw an indefinite exile apart from any taint of Zionism. But this is hardly fair to the prophet who himself preferred to stay in Palestine and retained a great love for his native land.

This leads to the third facet of his eschatology. In an action significant in its own right but also highly symbolic, Jeremiah purchased the field of a cousin from Anathoth. The contract transferring the property from Hanamel to the prophet was sealed during the final siege of the city. The prophet had been preaching unmitigated disaster, so that his action smacks of the same paradox as if a contemporary should forecast nuclear warfare and then proceed to buy a choice piece of real estate on Manhattan. Jeremiah took the occasion to show his confidence that God intended a future for the Judean people. In solemn ceremony before assembled witnesses, the prophet addressed Baruch: "Thus says Yahweh of hosts, the God of Israel: Take these deeds, both this sealed deed of purchase and this open deed, and put them in an earthenware vessel, that they may last for a long time. For thus says Yahweh of hosts, the God of Israel: Houses and fields and vineyards shall again be bought in this land" (32:14–15). Jeremiah's immediate expectation for the besieged city was dismal indeed, but he believed that there was yet another chapter to God's dealing with his people—not in a second life but here on earth, in his beloved country. Did he expect more? How was the infectious sin of the people to be overcome? Would punitive measures, the ravaging and plundering of the city and countryside, accomplish a conversion through terror? No, that was not the belief of any of the prophets; adversity was not inherently reformative. But he did hope that the stark events might turn people to thinking. Repentance might flower in their souls and they might receive new hearts.

Finally, Jeremiah advanced his notion of the new covenant, one of the high points in prophetic literature. In spite of stylistic inflation, there are no glaring signs of a later age and no thought inconsistent with the prophet's beliefs elsewhere expressed. We are justified in seeing the mind of the prophet in an oracle written down by a follower or enlarged by an editor (31:31–34). The genius of the new covenant is that it will be internally grounded and motivated ("I will put my law within them, and I will write it upon their hearts;"), yet it will be thoroughly communal and national ("I will make a new covenant with the house of Israel and the house of Judah"), and without the compulsive methods of state and church ("for they shall all know me"). The New Testament makes much of this expectation and proclaims that in Jesus Christ the reality Jeremiah envisaged was brought into being. It underlies the words of the Last Supper: "This cup . . . is the new covenant in my blood" (Luke 22:20; cf. also I Cor. 11:25) and recurs in Hebrews 8:8–13 and 10:16. It is the basis for the distinction between the Old Covenant in Moses and the New Covenant in Jesus Christ and, derivatively, the division of Christian Scripture into Old Testament and New Testament (*testamentum* is the Latin equivalent of covenant).

Any reader of the prophecy will instinctively agree with the judgment that "the book of Jeremiah does not so much teach religious truths as presents a religious personality. Prophecy had already taught its truths; its last effort was to reveal itself in a life."[19] The prophet was involved to the utmost in his teaching, and as in Hosea he reached after the Christian belief in Incarnation, though from afar. God through his saving presence accomplishes with men what he can never accomplish through adjuring them or their moralizing at one another. Out of the division and torment in his spirit, Jeremiah rose to a sympathy for his people which was never lost even when he cried out for vengeance. His faithfulness to his cause is breath-taking. The memoirs read like the roll call of Paul's hardships (II Cor. 11:23–29). His sense of the divine shaping of his life from its dim beginnings was shared also by the great Christian apostle (Gal. 1:15).

In Jewish tradition Jeremiah's influence was enormous. He was remembered as the author of the book of Lamentations where he is the model of the suffering nation in chapter 3, as he is surely in mind in the imagery of the Suffering Servant of Deutero-Isaiah. In Maccabean times he was a symbol of fidelity to the law and resistance to the pagan destroyer of Judaism (II Macc. 2:1–8; 15:13–16). He was spoken of with reverence by Ben Sira (49:4) and the Alexandrian philosopher Philo (*De. Cher.* 14). Jeremiah belongs among the worthy company of those who took Yahweh's call seriously, men who were in fact what they were because their character and message were created by their call. Jeremiah, against natural inclinations that would have left him at Anathoth living and dying with peace of mind, chose rather the hard path of faithful witness to the painful truth. The preponderance of memoirs in his book shows that many Jews must have asked themselves: If Yahweh could create a man like Jeremiah, could he not perform his promises to Israel? The greatest miracle of Hebrew faith was the quality of the men it produced.

[19] A. B. Davidson, "Jeremiah," Hastings, *A Dictionary of the Bible*, Scribner's, 1903, vol. 2, p. 576. This is also the implicit thesis of John Skinner's masterly study of Jeremiah, *op. cit.*

11

THE PEOPLE IN EXILE

Comfort, comfort my people . . .
Isa. 40:1

THE JEWS IN EXILE, 587–538 B.C.

Nebuchadnezzar's rule was long and prosperous (605–562 B.C.). He rebuilt and expanded Babylon until it was the most beautiful city in the known world. Temples, palaces, gardens, streets, walls, canals— nothing was spared in his vast dreams of expansion. While he lived it seemed that the Chaldean dynasty was invincible. For the Jews all hope of speedy return to Jerusalem was dashed; they settled down to make a home for themselves.

On the surface the lot of the exiled Jews was not difficult. Nebuchadnezzar's purpose in deportation was not so much punishment as prevention of further revolt. He had neither the intention nor the means to keep several thousand captives in prison, or even in detention centers. The exiles lived mainly in agricultural colonies where they had the privilege of local autonomy and economic freedom. By the time of Deutero-Isaiah, toward the end of the Exile, many had found their way into the capital and had entered commercial enterprises. Jewish prosperity in Exile is shown by the unwillingness of many to return to Jerusalem when they were finally permitted. Those for whom sentiment and faith counted for little could see no advantage in returning to a land where they would have to eke out an existence. There seems to have been no anti-Semitic feeling, although there may have been social disdain toward the small and insignificant body of Jewish provincials with their queer customs. The onus of the Exile was in a sphere other than the physical, economic, or social.

The temple area in Nebuchadnezzar's Babylon bordering the Euphrates River. The tower or ziggurat was known as Etemenanki ("the foundation platform of heaven and earth"). The Marduk temple or Esagila ("temple with uplifted head") is in the foreground.

We who thrive on the heritage of Judaism and experience it as a continuing faith can scarcely appreciate the precarious situation in which Israel stood in 587 B.C. No matter what view we take of the founder Moses, it is undeniable that for centuries the faith of Israel had been closely identified with the political life, first of the tribal leagues, then of the united monarchy, and finally of the twin kingdoms of Israel and Judah. As the territorial expanse and national influence of the Hebrews waned after Solomon, the prophets announced the transcendence of God above Israel and the persistence of the remnant within Israel. Still, in the main, as the pages of Jeremiah so tragically demonstrate, the people and leaders of Judah continued to cling to the shreds and tatters of Yahwism as a cloak of security and to lean upon the slender reed of nationalism buttressed by the state cult.

With the abrupt cessation of Judean statehood, certain pressing questions simply had to be answered and there could be no turning back from their fateful consequences. Some Israelites were not long in making the logical deduction that Yahweh had not proved the equal of the other gods. Either he was defeated by Marduk or, in default of his promises, had cast off his people. We can readily imagine the disaffected turning to the grim task of survival in a hostile world, seeking such religious aid as they could find among the gods that the Near East offered in profusion. Others, whose faith had probably been firmer to begin with, were stunned and gripped by the paralysis of indecision. They did not forsake Yahweh at once, but they could see no future. Israel had reached an impasse, for the fall of Judah implied the denial of everything that Yahwism had led its adherents to expect.

Some remembered the prophets whose declarations of doom now became strangely consoling. They remembered also the prophetic insistence, sometimes only an adumbration but occasionally articulate and luminous, that beyond disaster for the visible Israel there was hope for the purpose of God. These Israelites took heart, not as though they had any program for the future or any timetable of the divine plans, but as those who worship the sovereign Lord of history. They had come to the astounding conclusion that, far from perishing in the ruins of Jerusalem, Yahweh had brought about the reversal himself in order to vindicate his honor and to forward his purposes with Israel.

Stanch supporters of prophetic Yahwism were among those carried off to Babylon. This can be assumed by the ministries of Ezekiel and Deutero-Isaiah. Both prophets had hearers who formed the nucleus of the restored community. The same can be assumed in the final edition of the Deuteronomic history compiled in Exile as well as in the first collections of Priestly traditions. It is not as often realized that among Palestinian Jews there was like tenacity of faith. Sometimes it is assumed that since the flower of Judah was deported, no one of consequence was left in the demoralized land. It is the book of Lamentations that shows beyond dispute that a core of believing Israelites continued steadfast in the ruined homeland.

LAMENTATIONS

Lamentations consists of five alphabetic poems, four of which are true acrostics. Throughout every poem the 22 letters of the Hebrew alphabet appear in succession at the beginning of each verse or strophe. Poems 1 through 3 have three lines to each stanza (except for four lines in 1:7 and 2:19), whereas the fourth poem has but two lines to a strophe. The final poem is not acrostic, but is alphabetic in the sense that it contains 22 lines, the precise number of letters in the alphabet. Another variation is in chapter 3 where the acrostic device is used at the beginning of each line (thus there are three 'aleph lines, three beth lines, etc.).

It is somewhat of a surprise that a book as emotional as Lamentations should have such a strained and artificial style. By choosing the acrostic form, the writer deliberately limited himself, subjecting the vitality of feeling to the economy of form. The poems of Lamentations compare favorably with other laments in the Old Testament and the ancient Near East, although they lack the literary polish associated with the elegiac tradition in English literature. While one of the motivations for the acrostic form may have been to facilitate memory, another more cogent reason was to give expression to completeness of grief and despair, faith and hope. Parallels from later Jewish synagogue prayers, as well as Talmudic figures of speech, suggest the plausibility of such an inference.[1]

Reading the poems with an eye to literary qualities reveals that the style and imagery are similar to the Psalms and particularly to the laments of the Psalter. Numerous affinities may also be found in Jere-

[1] Norman K. Gottwald, *Studies in the Book of Lamentations* (SBT, No. 14), SCM, 1954, chap. 1.

miah, Deutero-Isaiah, and Job. Upon closer examination, the poems betray composite features. Chapters 1, 2, and 4 have traits of the funeral song of which the "purest" example is David's Lament over Saul and Jonathan (II Sam. 1:17–27). As Amos earlier applied a funeral lament to Israel (5:1–2), so does the author of Lamentations, although he does not picture the city as a corpse but as a despairing widow. The third poem, in individual lament genre, seemingly involves a lone sufferer. Given its context, however, it becomes clear that Israel is personified in the idiom of corporate personality. Any doubt about the communal interpretation of chapter 3 is erased by the explicit national reference of the individual imagery in 1:13–16. Thus funeral song and individual lament styles have been applied to the nation's downfall in order to lend poignancy and force to the laments.[2]

Tradition attributes the authorship of Lamentations to the prophet Jeremiah. His role in this regard has been classically pictured in the Sistine Chapel painting where he sits in the brooding and melancholy posture of lament. In the LXX the book is placed immediately after Jeremiah and specifically attributed to the prophet. The Vulgate follows the same tradition. Even the Talmud claims Jeremianic authorship. Apparent source of the tradition was II Chron. 35:25: "Jeremiah also uttered a lament for Josiah; and all the singing men and singing women have spoken of Josiah in their laments to this day. They made these an ordinance in Israel; behold, they are written in the Laments." The Chronicler did not refer to the canonical Lamentations, since it contains no lament over Josiah but only brief reference to Zedekiah. However, traditions have been set in motion with less justification; it is likely that the careful distinction of Chronicles was overlooked by later readers.

Internal evidence indicates not an iota of support for the traditional view. Jeremiah is never named or implied. There are as a matter of fact some fairly telling arguments against Jeremianic authorship. One wonders if the adamant prophet could have closely and sympathetically identified himself with the city's seeking of foreign help and undue trust in the king (4:16,19). Can we imagine the prophet, who remained in Palestine only a few weeks after the city's fall, writing the fifth poem with its ennui and lassitude induced by years of foreign

[2] *Ibid.,* chap. 2.

occupation? Is it probable that Jeremiah, who in the whole of his identified writings never resorts to extensive poetic formalities, should have undertaken the construction of alphabetic poems? Finally, if these poems are Jeremiah's, why were they omitted from the prophet's book, especially in the light of the many anonymous fragments and oracles that have been collected in his name?

With the surrender of the traditional theory of authorship most scholars have assumed the contribution of two or more poets to an anthology. It is true that differences among the poems are detectable; in particular the first and third chapters contrast with the second and fourth. Yet the affinities, linguistic and ideological, are considerable. Diversities *within* the same poem as great as those *between* poems can be singled out, but few would ignore the acrostic unity of each poem and argue for composite authorship within any given chapter. Diverse literary types and images have been freely appropriated and not wholly assimilated; still a single mood pervades the whole. Probably the first four poems, and possibly all five, come from the same poet. Some interpreters have suggested that nostalgia toward the king and enthusiasm for nobility (1:6; 4:7,20) point to an origin in court circles, perhaps the family of Shaphan that was so cordial to Jeremiah. One objection is that the ranks of the upper classes were severely decimated by execution and deportation.

The subtle differences between the poems, not to mention their repetitions, suggest that they were composed individually and not as parts of a whole. The fourfold repetition of the acrostic form makes this almost conclusive. There is no observable dramatic progress in the book. Lamentations is best thought of as a collection of liturgical laments to be sung on the annual fast days in remembrance of the fall of Jerusalem (cf. Zech. 7:1–5). Probably these poems represent the sifting of many seasons and even centuries. Out of a large number of compositions, long years of usage endeared these to the Jerusalem community as most expressive of the chastened mood of Judaism—both in its abysmal sorrow and its unshakeable faith. The fifth and final poem is a concluding summary appended to the four acrostics.

The process of compilation appears to have been more than haphazard. It follows a chiastic principle of arrangement. Chapters 1 and 5 are general summaries of the disaster; chapters 2 and 4 more detailed recitals of death and pillage; and chapter 3, with its intensified acrostic form and its exalted trust in the goodness of God, the pivot on which the collection turns. The central strophes from the standpoint of theology are the central strophes in the poem's structure (3:31–36). The effect of the compilation has been to build toward an emotional and theological climax in chapter 3 and then to recede from it by stages.

The nub of the book is the conflict between historical faith and historical actuality. Although this enigma may fairly be described as the age-old despair of religion, it took on peculiar urgency in Israel after 587. Lamentations asks pointedly: What is the meaning of the terrible calamities which have overtaken us between 609 and 587 B.C., from the death of Josiah, through vassalage and rebellion, siege and famine, to the city's humiliation and the extinction of the state? Can these events really be understood as expressing Yahweh's will? If so, what is our present role? Has Yahweh further plans? How are we to look upon God who has chastened his people without mercy? Lamentations reveals a deep sense of desertion by men and God; it confronts suffering as a threat to God's designs in history and thus inevitably to the very life of faith.[3]

In the poems of Lamentations, as perhaps nowhere else, we sense how vastly significant was the passing of the old order.[4] Before our eyes the impregnable and inviolable temple is sacked and desecrated, and the city walls demolished. The populace is decimated by plague and famine as well as by sword. Haughtily the enemy carries off captive leaders. Most of all one senses the anguish of disappointed aspirations. Israel had pinned her hopes upon the survival of the kingdom; in an instant it had been swept away. For over three centuries, nearly one hundred fifty years beyond the collapse of the north in 722 B.C., the Davidic dynasty had endured. In 621 Josiah had reëstablished the dynasty upon the sure rock of fidelity to the Mosaic covenant. But now, only a few decades later, the curtain falls decisively upon the brief play of Judean independence. In some ways the most poignant verses of Lamentations are those picturing the seizure of the fleeing Zedekiah:

Our pursuers were swifter than the eagles of the heavens,
Upon the mountains they chased us, in the wilderness they ambushed us.

[3] *Ibid.*, chap. 3.
[4] *Ibid.*, chap. 4.

The breath of our nostrils, the anointed of Yahweh, was captured in
   their pits,
Of whom we said, "In his shadow we shall live among the nations"
   (4:19–20).

Here was the mortal wound to the royal theology of Judah. No more
would Israel so naïvely put her trust in worldly might, in aping the
great ones of the earth. Later the Maccabees were to be supported
when they fought for the life of Judaism but deserted by many when
they sought sheer aggrandizement, and the subsequent rebellions of
A.D. 66 and 135 with their disastrous consequences only confirmed
the errors of Jewish nationalism in the minds of most leaders. This
was to be one of the basic inner tensions and contradictions of Judaism: How is God's will to be achieved in history when the human
instrumentalities are so imperfect? The messiah figure, though he was
expected to be a person in history with political impact, became increasingly a deliverer of extraordinary capacities, incorruptible and
perfectly obedient to Yahweh.

The reader of Lamentations is struck by its bitter realism. No efforts have been spared to portray the carnage and destruction. The
coarse and brutal enemy is shown gloating over his victim. The plight
of the emaciated and dying children is pictured in pathetic detail. Nor
is this mitigated by the fact that large parts of the text are in direct
prayer. Rather it seems to have been the boast of the writer to lift
before God the whole appalling scene and thus to lay the basis for
protest and plaintive appeal. In the candor and directness of his approach to deity is concentrated the questioning and assertive spirit of
Moses interceding for his people, Jeremiah interrogating his God or
cursing his birth, and Job calling for an accounting of the ways of
deity. The essence of biblical prayer in its vigor and honesty could
not be better illustrated.

This total expression of grief, wrung from hearts that have submitted reluctantly to the decisions of Yahweh, has the earmarks of a
liturgical catharsis. Greek drama was not the only such undertaking.
It can readily be seen that the public recital of the poems of Lamentations on the appropriate memorial days, perhaps with various readers
taking the parts of Zion, the citizens, the onlookers, etc., must have
been an effective outlet for the pent-up emotion of a people who had
lost practically everything that belonged to their former mode of life.
Catharsis is best achieved by full and savage expression of feelings

that have lain heavily upon a people's spirit. Who can deny, especially as he reads the text aloud, that Lamentations has been eminently successful in this?

The century-long heritage of Israel—the election of the fathers, the covenant of Moses, and the glory of David—all this now seemed at an irrevocable end, and a deserved one at that. Without exaggeration the sufferer can say:

> Thou hast rejected me from peace; I have forgotten good,
> So I say, "Gone is my endurance, my hope from Yahweh" (3:17–18).

And so it might have ended, with Israel henceforth obliterated from the mind of Yahweh. But God is not through with Israel; he stoops solicitously over his prostrate people: "Thou wilt surely remember and bow down to me!" (3:20).[5] The mood of the key passage (3:19–39) is a restrained and chastened confidence in the inscrutable but righteous God. It resounds with the spirit of Psalm 115: "Not to us, O Lord, not to us, but to thy name give glory, for the sake of thy steadfast love and thy faithfulness!" Chapter 3 expresses several of the dominant convictions of Judaism, which was to spring rejuvenated from the ashes and rubble of Yahwism: responsibility for sin, the disciplinary value of suffering, the absolute justice and abiding love of God, the inscrutability of his ways, the unconquerable trust of the believer, the necessity of patience.[6] With sobriety and persuasion Lamentations proclaims Israel's incredible faith and writes it indelibly into the liturgical practice of Judaism.

EZEKIEL

The uniqueness of each prophet is well illustrated in the contrast between Jeremiah and Ezekiel, contemporaries who strove equally to inculcate an attitude of individual responsibility by which the faith of their people could outlast political decline. Both preachers of nemesis on Jerusalem, both champions of a renewal of faith, they were yet men of dissimilar temperaments and styles of speech. In passing from one to the other, one moves from the realm of classical prophecy with its solid historical foundation into the sphere of vision, allegory, and sym-

---

[5] This verse is one of "the emendations of the Scribes" noted by the Masoretes; KJV and RSV both contain the Masoretic reading which removes the affront of God condescending to man.

[6] Gottwald, *op. cit.*, chap. 5.

bolic action on an unprecedented scale. Ezekiel is the first thorough-going visionary in the Bible, but on that account his relevance to his time cannot be discounted. Into the make-up of the prophet went a baffling blend of the ecstatic and the practical. It was he more than any other who set the direction of postexilic Judaism.

Ezekiel's writings present a forbidding exterior. The main difficulty lies in the bizarre visionary complexion of the prophet's mind. His fluctuations from vision to reality and vice versa are seldom noted by the prophet or his editors; for the prophet the visionary was intensely real and therefore determinative of mundane existence. The allegories, more numerous than in any other book of the Bible, are abstruse and labored. Furthermore, the prose style of the majority of the book is woefully dull and repetitive. It is hard to believe that an original and forceful mind could have been so awkward in expression. Many critics are convinced that subsequent editing by far less able men has produced the turgid and prolix style. At any rate the problem of the reader is to interpret what tradition has left him.

PALESTINIAN OR BABYLONIAN MINISTRY?

Ezekiel was a priest deported to Babylon with the exiles of 598, where he carried on a ministry sharply divided by the catastrophic fall of Jerusalem in 587. So closely is he connected with Palestine and so relentlessly is his message directed against Jerusalem, that many interpreters feel constrained to assume a Palestinian ministry, at least for the period before 587. The problem is intimately tied up with the ecstatic temperament of Ezekiel, for in chapters 8–11 he recounts his transport "in the spirit" from Babylon to Jerusalem where he beholds the syncretistic cults that have invaded the very temple precincts. In the most controversial detail of the vision Ezekiel beholds the death of Pelatiah, one of the hostile elders (11:1,13). The prophet might easily have remembered the pagan religious intrusions into the temple from his own experience before deportation, but how could he see the death of Pelatiah when he was hundreds of miles away? If there is an answer it must belong in that debatable sphere of parapsychic phenomena. Ezekiel was gifted with second sight or clairvoyance so that he could see events beforehand and at a distance, yet he himself was convinced that he had seen Pelatiah's death in person. In the light of the personality revealed in the book and the unquestioned fact that unusual psychic powers have been clinically observed, the best account of the mysterious "trip" to Jerusalem is that it was an experience of levitation and clairvoyance.

The gift of clairvoyance is not otherwise evidenced in the prophet. He was not a superhuman seer of any and all future events and he did not employ his psychic gifts to awe or intimidate people into believing him. While there are many psychological quirks about the prophet, his inspiration was not qualitatively different from the other prophets. He too oriented his life around the divine word and called his people to a covenant response. Unlike the distraught Saul, Ezekiel was accepted by his peers and made immense social and religious contributions to his people, which they quickly recognized. This is possible for an eccentric but not for a madman or psychological misfit.

Since the scene of Ezekiel's ministry is complicated by his personality and the style and sequence of the book, a spectrum of views has developed.[7] A *fictitious double ministry* was brilliantly but arbitrarily argued by C. C. Torrey, who insisted that there never was a prophet Ezekiel. Rather, a pseudepigraphon written in 230 B.C. and dated to the time of Manasseh (in order to give it a setting in a period of gross apostasy) was revised in 200 B.C. and transferred to an exilic locale and provided finally with the prophet-priest Pseudo-Ezekiel as its hero. An *exclusively Palestinian ministry* has been advanced, on the theory that an editor has shifted the career of Ezekiel wholly to Babylon to strengthen the impression that the positive factors in later Judaism arose in the Exile. While John Smith assumed a seventh-century ministry in northern Israel and N. Messel a career about 400 B.C. when Nehemiah's reforms were in decline, the majority of this camp of interpretation favor the traditional sixth-century date for the real Ezekiel. The editor who transferred him from Jerusalem to Babylon is dated variously: Herntrich and Harford placed him in 570, I. G. Matthews about 520–500, and G. R. Berry in the third century.

An actual *double ministry* seems the only reasonable solution to A. Bertholet, R. H. Pfeiffer, W. Irwin, H. W. Robinson, and H. G. May. But such divergence in the very agreement! Bertholet believes that Ezekiel fled Jerusalem and spent some time in a nearby city before going to Babylon. Pfeiffer and Robinson depreciate the para-

---

[7] For fuller discussion and bibliography cf. H. G. May, *Introduction and Exegesis of Ezekiel* (IB, vol. 6), Abingdon, 1956, pp. 41–56; and O. Eissfeldt, "The Prophetic Literature," *The Old Testament and Modern Study* (ed. H. H. Rowley), Oxford University Press, 1951, pp. 153–158.

psychic phenomena. Irwin leaves to the prophet 251 poetic verses, no more than one fifth of the book. May holds that at least half of the contents of Ezekiel's book have been worked over by an editor. The traditional view of an *exclusively Babylonian ministry* is retained by many scholars, some without orthodox views on other aspects of the book. G. Hoelscher, for example, cut the authentic work of the prophet down to 170 verses of poetry. A conservative reply to Hoelscher by W. Kessler lambastes the former's critical extremism, but agrees with him on the Babylonian setting. G. A. Cooke finds a substantial unity of authorship though he freely admits editorial expansion. Two students of Albright, C. G. Howie and J. Finegan, have done yeoman's service in careful archaeological and chronological studies of Ezekiel, which show that the author had accurate knowledge of Babylonian life in the first half of the sixth century. O. Eissfeldt has renounced the implication that the strange behavior of Ezekiel is impossible or unworthy of biblical revelation. He asks if we should not take more seriously the possibility "that Ezekiel did live in exile in the body, but in spirit as good as remained in Judah and Jerusalem."[8]

Difficulties beset the traditional view. Pfeiffer, who strongly defends the virtual unity of the prophecy, feels that if the prophet disobeyed the command, "Go, get thee unto the house of Israel" (3:4) by failing to go to Jerusalem then he could not have been faithful to his call.[9] Yet the realistic unity of the Hebrew people wherever they lived, the sense of a common interest in whether the Exile would be short or protracted, the precarious future of Jerusalem, the flood of correspondence that passed back and forth between Palestine and Babylon, make of Ezekiel's determination to preach Jerusalem's fall *to the exiles* altogether understandable. He may have felt that Jerusalem was already well provided with prophetic witness in the person of Jeremiah who most certainly would have been known to him.

Perhaps the single most cogent argument for the traditional Babylonian ministry is the fragmentation and wide disagreement of alternative theories. Once we allow the range of supernormal experience typical of this prophet (and increasingly documented in parapsychic studies), there is no insuperable difficulty in the prima facie evidence. The acceptance of a Babylonian ministry does not, however, imply that the book is without problems. The authorship of certain passages

[8] *Ibid.*, p. 157.
[9] R. H. Pfeiffer, *Introduction to the Old Testament*, Harper, 1941, p. 536.

and the interpretation of many others is not solved by blanket approval or rejection of tradition. Certainly there has been a tendency to evade the problems in Ezekiel research by assuming excision or radical rewriting of sources; so far such attempts have created more problems than they have solved. To accede to the book's setting for the prophet and its witness to his queer behavior is to take a long stride toward understanding the man and his message.

THE COMPOSITION AND CHRONOLOGY OF THE BOOK

The major arguments *for* the unity of the book are its consistent historical background of the early Exile, the uniform style, and the almost encyclopedic range of the prophet's interests as prophet, ritualist, pastor, and apocalyptic. The main arguments *against* unity are the abruptness of transitions, the disordered thought, and the objection that such heterogeneous elements could hardly be included in a single person. The book's subsections are as follows:

Call Vision(s)	Chaps. 1–3
Oracles, Symbolic Actions, and Allegories against Judah	4–24
Oracles and Allegories against Foreign Nations	25–32
Fall of Jerusalem	33
Mixed Oracles and Visions of the New Israel	34–39
Vision of the New Temple and Restored Community	40–48

This structure is held together by the semblance of chronological exactitude. Ezekiel is the first prophet who dates any of his experiences with precision. The form of the notations is to state the year, month, and day of the Exile, reckoned from the deportation of 598. In two cases the months are lacking (26:1 and 32:17, restored from LXX). The ambiguous Jewish dating system makes it difficult to transpose the thirteen dates into absolute chronology.[10]

Inaugural Vision (1:2)	July 21, 592
Vision in the Temple (8:1)	Sept. 7, 591
Inquiry of the Elders (20:1)	Sept. 1, 590
Beginning of the Siege (24:1)	Jan. 15, 588
Oracle against Tyre (26:1)	586, 585?

[10] The absolute dates above are based on the assumption that the Jews were still beginning the year in the autumn (Sept.–Oct.) rather than following the Babylonian system of a spring New Year (March–April), as they did after the Exile. The computations were made by H. G. May, *op. cit.*, p. 59, from tables in R. A. Parker and W. H. Dubberstein, *Babylonian Chronology 626* B.C.–A.D. *45,* Chicago University Press, 1942.

*Oracles against Pharaoh (29:1)	Jan. 6, 587
*Nebuchadnezzar's Conquest of Egypt (29:17)	April 16, 570
Oracle against Pharaoh (30:20)	April 19, 586
Oracle against Pharaoh (31:1)	June 11, 586
*Lament over Pharaoh (32:1)	March 3, 585
*Lament over Egypt (32:17)	April 16, 585
News of Jerusalem's Fall (33:21)	Jan. 8, 585
Vision of the Restored Temple (40:1)	April 17, 572

The four breaches of order that do occur (marked with asterisks) are in the foreign oracles and are explained largely by the editor's desire to keep together all the words of the prophet dealing with Egypt, thereby leaving the vision of the new temple for the climax. In other words, the chronological principle bows to the topical.

While Ezekiel's chronology is remarkably full and orderly in contrast to preceding prophetic books, the value of the chronology is strictly limited. For one thing we cannot be sure that the date refers to any more than the incident or oracle to which it is directly attached. July 21, 592 is not the date of all the units in chapters 1–7; for example, 3:16b–21 with its image of the prophet as a watchman belongs to the time of the city's fall (cf. chap. 18). Also 11:22–25, which tells of the departure of the glory of God from Jerusalem implies a time just before the siege and fall of the city and thus cannot be easily associated with Sept. 7, 591. The siege of the city is momentarily impending in chapter 21 and thus the date Sept. 1, 590 is somewhat early for the oracle.

Further chronological confusion is seen in the superscription with i's double dating, including the erratic notation "in the thirtieth year" equated with "the fifth year of the exile of King Jehoiachin." Does it give the age of the prophet at the time of his call? Is it the thirtieth year of the Deuteronomic Reform, i.e., 592? Is it based on an unknown Babylonian scheme? Is it Ezekiel's allusion to the date of the completion of the written edition of his oracles, 30 years after his call, in 562? The dual superscription (vs. 1 in the first person and vss. 2–3 in the third person) gives a hint of the complex editing that the book has undergone.

As a working hypothesis we may regard Ezekiel as the author of a large part of the book ascribed to him. He dated some of his important experiences (visions, the city's siege and fall, etc.). The primary compiler was probably a disciple of the prophet who arranged the dated material in chronological order (exceptions noted above), but had no clear guide for the remaining portions that he inserted as he saw fit. Ezekiel was by no means a highly gifted prose stylist (though he is credited with some superb poetry, such as the Lament over Tyre, chap. 27), but the redundancy and obfuscation of parts of the book are properly charged to the bungling of the editor and the poor transmission of the text. In some cases the editor had doublets of speeches and events that he worked into the book rather clumsily (cf. 3:16b–21 and 33:7–9; 10:8–17 and chap. 1; 18:21–25 and 33:10–20; 43:1–12 and 44:1–8). Many of the foreign oracles may be credited to Ezekiel, although there are additions, as in the expansions of the Lament over Tyre. The Gog of Magog passage is more doubtful (chaps. 38–39). The stylistic features are close to the P Code and the cosmic scope of the disaster contemplated, as well as the incarnation of all evil in Gog, point toward later authorship. The kernel of the vision of the new temple is Ezekiel's, but it has been elaborated extensively. The first edition (in the thirtieth year, 562?) probably lacked the Gog of Magog apocalypse that was added, along with enlargements on the temple vision, in a second and postexilic edition.

Prophetic Visions, Allegories, and Symbolic Acts

The enigma of Ezekiel is his strangely abnormal powers of perception and modes of behavior. He has been dubbed ecstatic, visionary, neurotic, psychotic, schizophrenic—none of which do much more than put a label on his abnormality without getting at any real understanding of it. He was susceptible to visions, trances, muteness, levitation, and possibly cataleptic fits. Studies that simply reduce his experiences and insight to biochemical abnormalities are philosophically too biased to appreciate the culture he lived in or the religious dynamics of the prophetic revelation. Others who look for parallels, as among the Moslem mystics, can supply a richer cultural background but also may overlook the peculiar self-understanding of a prophet. At any rate, "abnormal" in this context does not mean socially unrelated; it simply means beyond the range of usual experience (even for his own day). Apparently Ezekiel passed back and forth between the mundane and the ecstatic with a facility unequaled by most mystics, for how else can we explain the great influence that he had upon his contemporaries?

The inaugural vision of Ezekiel beside the canal Chebar in Babylonia is dated 592/3. This most exalted of prophetic visions is occasioned by a violent electrical storm. As Ezekiel's eye is fixed upon a mountainous summer storm cloud in which lightning is flashing, Yahweh becomes suddenly manifest. Not in a photographic disclosure but in his holy remoteness Yahweh lets himself be dimly seen, surrounded by his throne guardians and yet lifted above them in a veil of light. Let no labored literalism obscure the bold pageantry, the ponderous yet graceful massiveness of the vision. Four living creatures, compounded of human and animal features (the essential form of throne guardians: winged bulls in Assyria and winged lions in Canaan), each with the four faces of a man, lion, ox, and eagle (expressing elemental qualities of divine power) and four wings apiece (two for flight and two to shield their nakedness), swell out of the cloud, moving in concert, sheathed in blazing light, their genesis in the agitated fire that moves like torches in their midst. Wheels appear beside them, then wheels in the wheels and eyes in the wheels—all in constant movement and proceeding in any or all directions. The mechanism is the throne chariot of deity (the Merkabah of later Jewish mysticism) and all the weird symbolism hymns with mighty voice the omnipotence and omnipresence of God, his mobility and incorporeality, his swift purposiveness and dispatch, his greatness *in* all and *over* all. There is something uncannily effortless about the movement of chariot and beasts as "bovine stolidity is joined to the airiness of wings."[11] The very elements in the vision that initially repel us as grotesque and obscure are its great strength. Once we have mastered them the vision becomes an organic whole, a living body of symbolisms, an anthropomorphism to stagger the mind and to bring it in obeisance before the mighty God of Israel.

But the throne and its guardians are only half of the vision! Above the chariot the firmament of transparent crystal supports the throne, iridescent with the gorgeous blue of lapis lazuli. The beating of the wings gives forth the roar of the cosmic ocean, "the sound of many waters" tamed by the King of the universe. The animated mechanism comes abruptly to a halt and the creatures "when they stood still, let down their wings"; in the awesome hush of those descending wings the world stands silent before its Lord. And then Ezekiel perceives a form like that of a man, wrapped in light "as gleaming bronze, . . . like the bow in the cloud on the day of rain." But the divine face is

[11] *Bulletin of the School of Theology,* Acadia University, vol. 4, no. 3 (1957), p. 1.

lost in the fire above. Ezekiel calls this "the likeness of the glory of Yahweh." Having exhausted all the resources of language at his disposal, the prophet confesses that at best he has seen and described God twice removed. No vision of the divine so replete with imagery was ever so antianthropomorphic; no symbolism of the Godhead ever so palpably insufficient. It is no wonder that all the attempts to picture the vision in art have been miserable failures. The work is already an incomparable surrealist vision; it is useless to copy one work of art from another. Yet mystics such as Dante, William Blake, and W. B. Yeats have paralleled it in their own ways.

The result of what he sees establishes in Ezekiel's mind the unalterable realization of the immense distance between God and man. The prophet is henceforth "son of man," or "mere mortal, frail human" (so called some forty times). Israel is thereafter "rebellious house" and God's work among men is to demonstrate beyond a shadow of doubt that He alone is Lord, for "they (you) shall know that I am Yahweh." The cold, almost icy, and certainly inexorable discharge of his ministry is for Ezekiel necessitated by the mammoth being, the vast import and purpose of Israel's God. "And whether they hear or refuse to hear they will know that there has been a prophet among them" (2:5). If he borders on the reduction of men to automata before deity, it is because he has been so overcome by the divine transcendence that the margin of human merit and range of human freedom are small indeed. But never obliterated! No Jew could quite remove the free response of man without altering the ancient covenant faith beyond recognition, and in Ezekiel's later pastoral ministry the sphere of human responsibility was significantly reasserted and even enlarged.

On analysis this phenomenal vision is seen to be composed of countless elements from Babylonian mythology and art and from the royal enthronement traditions of Israel. In its full development the vision is similar to the grandiose visions of the glory of God in the P source (Exod. 40:34–38) but the imagery sprouts from a preëxilic seedbed. Psalm 29 and Isaiah 6 associate the enthroned Lord with the revelation of his glory. Psalms 18 and 29 also link the revelation of the regnant Yahweh with storm phenomena. Exodus 24:9–11 in the J source envisions the sapphire firmament over which Yahweh reigns. It is probable that the ideology of Yahweh the King is derived from the enthronement cult where the earthly king *represented* (not in-

carnated) the divine king and helped to frame an imagery that could
be enlarged to state Yahweh's lordship over the world and the nations. How much of the vision is a symbolic creation of the prophet
and how much of it a transcript of what he beheld in his mind's eye
we can never know, if only for the reason that the distinction is not
easily drawn in creative intuition. To a rare degree Ezekiel combines
imaginative, numinous experience and a love of detail and didactic
exactness. The dangers of theosophy and occultism led rabbinic Judaism to exclude this chapter from synagogue reading and to forbid
even private reading by anyone under thirty years of age.

The other great vision of the book is the justly famous Valley of Dry
Bones. It is less abstruse than the call vision and has a plainer purport.
Yet the same qualities of Ezekiel's mind show through the symbolism:
a fierce concentration, a grotesque baroque distortion of reality, a
stripping away of nonessentials, a stark coming to grips with the uncompromisingly true. We feel the otherworldly realism that peers from
an El Greco painting or soars through a Franck symphony. Men do
not hesitate long before Ezekiel: either they are repelled by his austerity and oddity or else they grasp at once how grandly he encompassed the supreme realities. Not accidentally have Negro spirituals
chosen as their subjects the visions of the prophet: " 'Zekiel saw de
wheels, way up in de middle ob de air!" and " 'Dem bones, dem
bones, dem dry bones!" They exert a fascination upon the folk mind.
The essential idea of national restoration Ezekiel shared with Isaiah
and Jeremiah but he had to express it in his peculiar way. What more
telling means of picturing the prostrate hopes of Israel in exile than
a desert landscape of parched bones, and "they were very dry"! What
more thrilling manner for expressing the doubt and hesitation of even
the finest leaders of Israel than the repartee of Yahweh, "Son of man,
can these bones live?" and the reply of Ezekiel, "O, Lord God thou
knowest"! Prophesying to the bones, he sees them reconnected before
his eyes and clothed with sinews—but still they do not live. Then he
prophesies to the four winds and the breath (or wind) falls upon the
corpses and they live and stand as a great army. "Son of man, these
bones are the whole house of Israel." Only a divine tour de force
could bring Israel out of the grave of exile and Ezekiel knew it. The
aesthetic shock of Ezekiel's bold and jabbing style, like gobs of pig-
ment smeared on canvas, suits the uproar of his time and the sharp
simplicities that could alone console a mind like his.

Further evidence of Ezekiel's strange personality is provided in the great number of allegories. Although supplied with interpretations, they are generally extremely forced and it is hard to resist the suspicion that some of the "explanations" misrepresent the intent of the prophet. In most of the allegories the principal objects are plants or animals personifying national groups and rulers, so that they are almost fables: the Wild Vine (15), the Two Eagles (17), the Lioness and Her Whelps (19:2–9), the Uprooted Vine (19:10–14), the Rusty Caldron (24:3–14), the Ship Tyre (27), the Egyptian Crocodile (29:2–5; 32:2–8), and the Cedar (31). The one allegorical motif employing human subjects is that of Israel as an orphan harlot thanklessly rescued by Yahweh. This is the traditional image of Hosea, but greatly embroidered into two of the prophet's longest and most repulsive allegories (chaps. 16 and 23): one of Jerusalem, the ingrate harlot of bastard origin, and the other of the sisters Samaria and Jerusalem. He draws out his vulgar comparisons with little sense of delicacy or discretion; it is a deliberate use of the shock method.

The exact delimitation of the symbolic acts is clouded by the possibility that some may be visions or allegories. The siege of the city is mimed on a large tile with a sketch of Jerusalem's walls, while around the tile models of battering rams are drawn up against the ramparts (4:1–3; 9–15). Ezekiel shaves his head to indicate the fall of the city and by different means of disposing of the cuttings declares the fate of the inhabitants (5:1–4). He lies on one side for 390 days (LXX 190) to mark the exile of Israel and on the other 40 days to signify the exile of Judah. Aside from the numbers, which make little sense as they stand, the physical possibility of such a prolonged period of immobility has been questioned. Some regard it as a vision. Probably, however, the prophet spent only some part of each day in the posture indicated (4:4–6,8,13), but that still leaves unresolved the tangled question of how the lengths of the two exiles have been computed. With his personal effects strapped to his back, Ezekiel was to simulate the conditions of an exile leaving the city. He was to dig through the wall, perhaps in the ruins of which he was supposed to be trapped, or possibly to make a night escape from the city (12:3–7). He ate bread and water, staple fare of exiles (12:17–20). He danced menacingly with a sword, indicating that weapons of war were shortly to come against Jerusalem (21:11–17). He dramatically marked the crossroads at which Nebuchadnezzar would decide whether to prose-

cute his plans first against Jerusalem or against Rabbah of the Ammonites. "He shakes the arrows, consults the teraphim, looks at the
liver. Into his right hand comes the lot for Jerusalem." The prophet
may have acted out the role of the king, even to the detail of casting
the lot (21:18–20).

When his wife died, Ezekiel was instructed not to weep or outwardly mourn her passing, for by his demeanor he was to signify to
the exiles that shortly there would be carnage at the fall of the city
(24:15–27). This action is unlike the others in that the prophet did
not initiate it (there is no evidence that in addition to his eccentricities
he was a wife killer!) but made use of what happened independently
to convey a point. The symbolism of joining two sticks on which are
written respectively "for Judah" and "for Joseph" may be simply a
literary imitation of symbolic action (37:15–17). Ezekiel 37, with its
stress on the new David, is incidentally one of the few places outside of
Isaiah where one finds a pronounced messianism in the preëxilic and
exilic prophets.

THE DIVINE HONOR

The weight of Ezekiel's teaching had to do with the honor and glory
of Yahweh. Like the Christian theologian John Calvin, he regarded
the vindication of the divine greatness as the ultimate motivation of
God's action and the chief concern of man. God acts for his own sake.
Ezekiel insists with Deuteronomy (but unlike all the other prophets
who preceded him) that Israel had been faithless and rebellious from
the beginning. The redemption of Israel from the Exile will not be
because of merit, for actually the people have done nothing but bring
dishonor and ill repute upon Yahweh. But he cannot destroy his people for then the nations would reproach him. Thus the logic of the
divine power and greatness impels God to redeem Israel. Such is the
force of the refrain which occurs over fifty times: "and you (they)
shall know that I am Yahweh."

More than merely external or formal recognition is involved since
Ezekiel grants man's need to have his "stony heart" replaced by "a
fleshy heart," i.e., one responsive to the divine will. Nevertheless the
cast of his mind and his mode of expression verge dangerously near
to fostering the concept of a divine tyrant whose chief attributes are
vanity and self-love. It is one thing for the Pentateuchal stories of
Moses to play with legendary wonderment upon the good name of

Yahweh which must be protected against the Egyptians (Exod. 32:11–14). It is another matter for a major prophet so to state the divine-human drama as to imply that God's main interest is in striking back at the personal insults dealt him by men. Ezekiel's vision at this point, like Deuteronomy's grasp of the retribution theory, has much to be said for it. We can imagine how it would catch short those Israelites who assumed that God had nothing better to do than look after them, solely because he was *their* God. But there are serious flaws in his presentation and they lie glaringly exposed when the husband-wife imagery of Hosea is stripped of its aura of intimacy and personal commitment. Ezekiel's intent was enviable: Israel had better stop taking God for granted; her restoration was to be sheerly of grace! But he too easily succeeds in implying an inverted masochism, the barely formed image of God as the unfeeling trafficker in human life, the bully of the nations, delighting in human pain—in short, the God against whom Job rose in outrage.

INDIVIDUAL RESPONSIBILITY

Most momentous of the prophet's teachings was his conviction about individual responsibility. Its classic formulation is in chapter 18 where his deliberations are built around the same popular proverb quoted by Jeremiah: "The fathers have eaten sour grapes and the children's teeth are set on edge" (18:2; Jer. 31:29). The exiles who framed their mood in that pungent adage were deeply despondent and bitterly resentful of God's moral mismanagement of the world. The younger generation, born in exile or mere infants when deported, felt no responsibility for happenings in the homeland; they asked sharply: Why should we suffer for the sins of our fathers?

In contrast to his inflexibility of mind on some matters, Ezekiel adjusted readily to this situation of despair. He struck boldly at the corporate thinking of Israel, not to sweep it aside altogether (for much of his prophecy presupposes its validity) but to qualify it drastically. He gives to men a new responsibility, a new dignity, a new motivation. With typical Hebraic concreteness, the prophet illustrates his viewpoint with three hypothetical generations of men: a righteous father, an iniquitous son, and a righteous grandson. The righteousness and wickedness of the men respectively are not transferable from one to the other. Each makes his own record and is rewarded or punished accordingly. In quasi-propositional form, chapter 18 affirms four notions: (1) *each man receives his own reward,* verses 5–9, 14–17; (2) *each man receives his own punishment,* verses 10–13; (3) *a past life of sin may be canceled by present repentance,* verses 21–23; (4) *a past life of faithfulness may be canceled by present sin,* verse 24. In an introduction the basic principle of individual responsibility is affirmed, verses 1–4; in verses 19–20 the *first* two notions are recapitulated and in verses 25–29 the *last* two are reiterated. The section closes with a direct call to repentance, verses 30–32.

The immediate practical effect of this pastoral advice upon the exilic community must have been renewed hope for flagging spirits. Life once again was worth living, for what men thought and did in the present mattered. It is easy to pick weaknesses in the point of view, especially with the heavy-handed, black and white fashion in which the prophet presents it. (Could Ezekiel have presented it in any other way?) As a moral philosophy applicable to all times and places it is an inadequate and even positively misleading theory. What it does is state boldly the obligation of man for his own destiny, "The soul that sins shall die" (18:4) and *only* that soul! But that is not to deny the heavy weight of the past that we never wholly escape. Even Ezekiel did not rescind the relevance of Israel's past sins as a basis for the Exile. He made it necessary, however, for Jews to work out in their own thought and action the relation between their responsibilities as a people and as individuals. It is not a relationship that any theory can easily comprehend; the data of experience are fundamental. It was Ezekiel's merit that he stated the individual facet with such sharpness.

It was for another exilic prophet to stress the spiritually basic fact that we may not only suffer the consequences of collective wrong but may also reap the good of those who bear wrong in our behalf. We may also cavil at Ezekiel's extreme atomism of character, according to which a present sin negates a past life of good. But he was no superficial moralist. What he refers to is not an unthinking lapse but deliberate presuming on forgiveness: "Though I say to the righteous that he shall surely live, yet if he trusts in his righteousness and commits iniquity, none of his righteous deeds shall be remembered; but in the iniquity that he has committed he shall die" (33:13). It was as much a matter of attitude as of acts, and as a moralist—in the best sense of the word—Ezekiel was seeking to touch the mainsprings of character. He knew that he could not decide for men, nor did he pro-

pose to legislate them into virtue. His favorite self-image is of the
watchman who discerns the movements of the times, reads their meanings, and declares the issues. Once warned the exiles must work out
their own destiny (3:17–21; 14:12–23; 18:1–32; 33:1–20), and the
prophet is all for their ethical triumph: "Say to them, As I live, says
the Lord GOD, I have no pleasure in the death of the wicked, . . .
turn back, turn back from your evil ways; for why will you die, O
house of Israel?" (33:11).

The shift in the direction and stress of Ezekiel's message, from categoric punishment for the people en masse to redemption for upright
and responsible individuals has seemed too great for some interpreters
to tolerate. But if there is any catalytic force in new historical circumstance, then in Hebrew history the fall of Jerusalem was certainly
the traumatic event to reorient any but the most rigid mind. When
we ponder the change of climate that has affected thinking men following the World Wars of this century, it does not seem unusual
that a prophet would be similarly influenced by the new complexion
of things following the dissolution of the Jewish state. And if inconsistencies mottle his thinking it is no more than one should expect in
a man who stood with a foot in each of the eras.

To tell the truth, the former era was the one in which Ezekiel
felt most uncomfortable, for he was "a man untimely born." Vividly
conscious that Jerusalem's fall was a settled matter, he none the less
had to share in its slow agonized death. He chafed to advance into
the new age that Jeremiah had charted; yet for eight years he had to
live in suspended animation, dolefully picturing the doom that he
never doubted and that his listeners never really believed. In this respect the muteness that fell upon him when he first heard of the siege
and that sealed his lips for three full years was lifted with the word
of the city's fall (24:25–27; 33:21–22).[12] Now the prophet, no
longer dumb, was free to lead the groping exiles into a new life. Their
roles were reversed: *they* formerly blithe and hopeful, now crushed
and dejected; *he* previously dour and tense, now buoyant and reas-
suring. It was as though all those previous years were wasted, the
merest marking of time, the sad prelude to the task for which he was

---

[12] The divine injunction of muteness in 3:22–26 cannot be understood as dating
from the call vision, since there are many oracles and conversations prior to the city's
fall recorded in chapters 1–24; probably the injunction to muteness came in 588 during a recurrence of the vision of God's glory and was collected by the editor and
placed topically next to the original vision of chapter 1.

really called: the inculcation of belief in Yahweh as a way of life for individual Jews.

APOCALYPTIC AND THE NEW TEMPLE

Ezekiel has sometimes been called the Father of Apocalyptic. It is true that his bizarre visions, allegories, and symbolic acts carry us into the realm of the fantastic beyond anything encountered in prophecy before. One of the indisputable marks of apocalyptic is the exploitation of fantasy and extravagant symbolism. But in chapters 1–37, however weird the forms of expression, Ezekiel always has reference to the historical experience of Israel. Apocalyptic properly exists only where the end of history is in view and the transformation of this world into another is expected. The otherworldly plane is approached only in the last chapters of the book, in the Gog of Magog passage (38–39) and in some of the elaborations of the vision of the new temple. Gog himself is a great tyrant (perhaps Gyges of Lydia in Asia Minor) who is evil personified, the quintessence of pagan opposition to God. He is slain in a great battle from which Israel emerges victorious. It is a myth of the end as Genesis 1–11 are myths of the beginning. Apocalyptic is essentially the portrayal of the end of history in symbolic garb. Another of the themes of apocalyptic, the transformation of nature, is seen in the artesian fountain of fresh water that bursts forth from the base of the restored temple and, cascading through the wilderness to the Dead Sea, fructifies the lifeless soil and purifies the sea of salt (47:1–12).

In chapters 40–48 Ezekiel describes the restored Palestinian community: the ground plan of the temple, its officials and regulations of worship, the location of the restored tribes, the rebuilt city of Jerusalem, and the domains of the civil ruler or prince. Most scholars believe that the basic temple layout was prepared by Ezekiel,[13] which shows that the prophet not only worked as a pastor among the exiles, but labored in anticipation of the return to Palestine. He pondered the problem of securing unimpeachable loyalty to the God whose profanation had led to the disaster of Jerusalem's capture and the harrowing Exile. Motivating the stipulations for the new community is the basic intent of safeguarding the holiness of God against any possible defilement.

[13] G. A. Cooke, *The Book of Ezekiel* (ICC), Clark, 1936, pp. 425 f. regards chapters 40–42; 43–44 (in part); 46:19–24; 47:1–12 as Ezekiel's; May, *op. cit.,* pp. 53–56 differs only in finding no sign of the prophet's hand in chapter 44.

At this point Ezekiel's delight in ritual indulged itself, for he placed moral sins and ritual sins on the same level of gravity. Like the Deuteronomists, he tried to insure an order of life that would keep

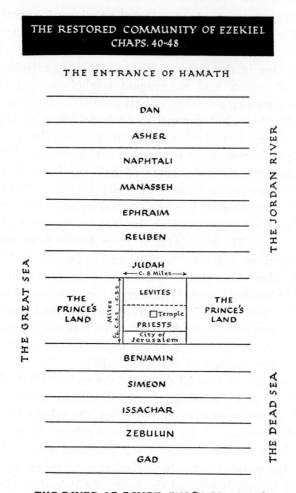

THE RESTORED COMMUNITY OF EZEKIEL
CHAPS. 40-48

THE ENTRANCE OF HAMATH

DAN

ASHER

NAPHTALI

MANASSEH

EPHRAIM

REUBEN

JUDAH

LEVITES

PRIESTS

City of Jerusalem

THE PRINCE'S LAND

THE PRINCE'S LAND

Temple

BENJAMIN

SIMEON

ISSACHAR

ZEBULUN

GAD

THE GREAT SEA

THE JORDAN RIVER

THE DEAD SEA

THE RIVER OF EGYPT (WADI EL-ARISH)

The restored community in Palestine as Ezekiel imagined it. Central to the whole conception is the rebuilt temple. Jerusalem proper occupies an odd-shaped area to the south of the temple, and the civil ruler has holdings on the east and west of the sacred precincts.

Israel faithful. Accordingly, the temple was to be exalted on a mountain, no foreigners permitted within it, only Zadokite priests allowed to serve (the P source favors the Aaronite priesthood instead), and the entire temple compound set apart in a buffer zone. In fact, holiness is treated as an infectious quality, not to be mixed with the profane. Man must not expose himself to too high a dosage of holiness. Analogies to a nuclear plant with its precautionary measures to avoid radiation are apt. The worship of Israel's God is taken with the utmost seriousness, but the attendant risks of depersonalization of the relationship and the oversimplification of the religious life in ceremonial terms are not squarely faced by the prophet.

Of special note is the sharp restriction upon the role of the civil ruler. Israel had learned that kings must be held strictly responsible to the religious norms of the community. No malicious Manasseh or Jehoiakim and no vacillating Zedekiah were to be allowed to choke off the first allegiance of the people. Thus the prince of the restored community was to own lands on either side of the large ecclesiastical holdings of the priests and Levites, but his task was mainly the maintenance of peace and order. The temple was all in all! While ritual thus returns with a vengeance that seems inconsonant with the spirit of preëxilic prophecy, it must be realized that Ezekiel at the same time espouses the highest moral demands. Priest, prince, and common Israelite are to model their lives on the covenant obligations. This concept was of tremendous influence on postexilic Judaism.

The importance of the prophet's temple vision should not, however, be overemphasized. The precise temple Ezekiel foresaw was never built; its monumental size and its symmetrical setting were unrealistic, ignoring as they did the topography of Palestine and the economic limitations of the repatriates. By contrast the temple settled on by the returnees was small and disappointing. But beyond that, it was not many centuries until even the temple ceased to be the center of Jewish life and was replaced—though gradually—by the synagogue. Ezekiel's uniqueness lay less in the utopian terms of his vision than in his adherence to Judaism as *a way of life* that involved lofty morality and precise governance of ritual—both on a par. We cannot see this concept in any of the preceding prophets, for many of them were sublimely disdainful of ritual. At the same time we can see the deep convictions of the preëxilic prophets as a major factor in Ezekiel's thought. He forced a massive synthesis into which prophecy poured its vital power and priestly religion its ardor for order and ceremony. Decisive in the end was the mind of Ezekiel, with its curi-

ous acerbity and monolithic bluntness. No man of subtlety, he was the
person temperamentally suited to set the pace for the minority existence of Judaism. But one wonders how different things might have
been if Jeremiah had been the guide.

THE RISE OF PERSIA, 550–538 B.C.

At the death of Nebuchadnezzar the Chaldean dynasty was visibly
shaken. His son Awel-Marduk ruled two years (562–560) but was
assassinated by a brother-in-law Neriglissar (560–555), whose youthful son Labashi-Marduk (555) was displaced by the usurper Nabonidus.

Nabonidus made a name for himself as the first archaeologist in
recorded history. He had a penchant for the antiquarian, like Ashurbanipal; but, whereas the Assyrian was content to collect literary
works, the Chaldean ranged over his empire excavating public buildings in search of data about the builders. His interest in religion was
likewise guided by historical curiosity and a collector's mania. Instead
of boosting the state cult of Marduk, Nabonidus gathered the images
of gods from all over his realm and put them on display in Babylon.
Unfortunately this did not earn him favor with the Marduk priests
or with the outlying districts whose temples he raided. For political
and religious expansion and opportunism he seems to have had little
time or inclination.

In the Iranian interior the eventual conqueror of Neo-Babylonia
began to stir about five years after Nabonidus came to power. He was
Cyrus of Anshan, one of the petty princes of the Medes, who revolted
against Astyages of Media in 550. He should have been trounced by
the superior forces of the king, but they mutinied and deserted to the
insurgent at a crucial moment; instantly Cyrus had become lord of
Media. Within three years he attacked Croesus of Lydia (western portion of Asia Minor) and in disregard of the etiquette of warfare followed Croesus into his winter retreat and defeated his surprised
troops. Cyrus, now master of the whole region north and east of the
Crescent, began to turn longing eyes on the Neo-Babylonian domain.
His kingdom was known as Persian, from Pasargadae, one of the
tribes of Anshan.

During the rapid rise of Cyrus, Nabonidus was engaged in desultory
military campaigns against the Arabs. He had his headquarters permanently at the oasis of Tema in north Arabia where he remained

with some interruption until 540. With no king to play the leading role, the lavish New Year's Festival was interrupted on several occasions. Dissatisfaction with the Chaldean dynasty was rampant not only among the subject peoples but also among the Babylonian populace, the Marduk priests, and high government officials.

When Cyrus launched a swift attack on Babylonia in 539, after several years of campaigning on the eastern borders of the new empire, there were many in the land who looked upon him as a deliverer. Gobryas, governor of one of the major provinces, sided with Cyrus and became commander in chief of the invading army. The old wall of Nebuchadnezzar north of the city was speedily breached. Under normal conditions there should have been a protracted siege of the city, dragging on for months and years. Babylon's position, abutting on the Euphrates and ringed on the other sides by a double wall, was virtually impregnable. But the city fell without a struggle. Although the sources do not say so, it is presumed that the priests controlling the gates threw them open to the Persians. The Marduk functionaries had every reason to detest Nabonidus and Cyrus' profuse adulation of Marduk probably indicates his gratitude for priestly aid. Herodotus alone reports that Cyrus diverted the flow of the river so that his troops could enter the city through the dried up canal beds, but such an enormous engineering feat could hardly be accomplished in ancient times and certainly not on such short order.

Cyrus proved to be a remarkably tolerant and progressive ruler who sought to develop local autonomy and indigenous cultural life. He was the most humane leader the ancient Near East had ever known. After the cruelties of Assyria and Neo-Babylonia he was a welcome master. His decision to permit the Jews to return to Palestine was consonant with his general outlook and policy.

DEUTERO-ISAIAH

The impact of the Exile on Israelite faith was brilliantly evidenced in Jeremiah's letter to the exiled community and his hope in the new covenant, as well as in Ezekiel's provision for individual religious destiny and his vision of the new community. But the deeper and more spacious responses are found in the work of the anonymous prophet who penned the exhilarating poetry of Isaiah 40–55. His grasp of the divine control over history, of the power of righteous suffering, of the salvation of the nations is stated with a literary magnificence not equaled since the Yahwist. If not the greatest prophet, he is at any rate the climax of Old Testament prophecy, the one who comprehended and epitomized the whole prophetic tradition. He and the likewise anonymous author of Job were the two greatest minds of ancient Israel. Centuries in advance he sketched the mission of Christianity, not by spot predictions but by a fundamental grasp of its spiritual principles as the modes of God's action in his world.

THE COMPOSITION OF ISAIAH 40–66

It is one of the assured results of modern biblical science that chapters 40–66 were not written by the prophet Isaiah of Jerusalem in whose book they now appear. The arguments are clear-cut and leave no reasonable doubt for anyone who admits the validity of historical study of the Old Testament. Since Doederlein first drew the distinctions in 1782, they have been upheld in substance by generations of scholars, barring only traditionalists for whom religious dogma prevents acceptance.

As *literature* the prophecies of Isaiah of Jerusalem are separate vignettes of the prophetic oracular type intended for deliverance to specific audiences. They are written in elegant poetry with a crisp but limited vocabulary. The poetry of chapters 40–66 is more sustained in mood, lyrical and impassioned, as well as more uniform and vast in conception. The vocabulary is more varied and technical. In short, Isaiah of Jerusalem devised isolated oracles in classical prophetic poetry; the poet of 40–66 conceived something nearer to an ode or cycle of poems in a style less restrained and highly rhetorical.

As to *theological* content, the early Isaiah preached mainly a word of doom, with a morally conditioned teaching about the remnant. In chapters 40–66 the new age of redemption is at hand; punishment, once indispensable, is now past. In some ways the real force of this argument is historical, for it shows the entirely different situations faced by the two prophets. Isaiah's vision of the lordship of Yahweh over the nations was focused upon Assyria; in the later chapters by contrast the foe is Babylon and the poet expresses a more articulate philosophy of the unity of nature and history under the one God. The particularity of Isaiah's concern is broadened and deepened in chapters 40–66. Whereas the eschatology of the former involved a remnant and a Davidic ruler, the hope of 40–66 is in a redeeming Servant of Yahweh who himself is a sufferer. The similarities between the two portions (e.g., the name Holy One of Israel for deity) are pronounced enough to explain why these latter chapters were regarded as Isaianic tradition, but there are parallels aplenty with Jeremiah and Ezekiel also.

The clinching criterion is *historical.* The exile of Judah predicted by preceding prophets is the unquestioned backdrop of 40–66. The poet relentlessly speaks of the meaning of God's action in punishing his people and the tremendous miracle of his revival of unworthy Israel. The psychological milieu of his teaching would have been absolutely meaningless to the eighth century. There simply is no analogy in Hebrew prophecy for a man who projects himself two centuries into the future and discourses to an imagined audience on the assumption that some day his words will be understood. More than this, the imminent fall of Babylon is predicted and the agent of its capture, Cyrus, is explicitly named. Those who doggedly retain Isaianic authorship for 40–66 have on their hands a situation as strange as if a writer in the days of the eighteenth-century French and Indian Wars had predicted that another nation, not yet created as a viable international power, would challenge Britain's dream of empire and had actually named Kaiser Wilhelm or Adolf Hitler! To complete the analogy, it would need to be not a brief stab into the future but a sustained presentation in which he wrote as though addressing the Englishmen who rallied behind David Lloyd George or Winston Churchill. To believe such requires a fantastic and irrelevant view of divine revelation.

A secondary separation of chapters 40–55 and 56–66 has been generally accepted since Duhm called attention to pronounced differences.[14] In the final chapters there is a revival of cult, and a clear indication that the poems were written in Palestine after 538 (and in some cases after the rebuilding of the temple in 520–516). There is a stronger note of condemnation than in 40–55, presumably because the blandishments of syncretism were beginning to appeal anew to the Palestinian Jews. On the whole there is a less universalistic climate, yet the similarity of style throughout 40–66 has caused some scholars to insist on the unity of the work.[15] A more acceptable solution is to regard 56–66 as the product of poets influenced by Deutero-Isaiah, some

[14] Bernhard Duhm, *Das Buch Jesaia,* Vandenhoeck & Ruprecht, 1892, pp. xvii–xix, 262 f., 390 f.

[15] See especially C. C. Torrey, *The Second Isaiah; a New Interpretation,* T. & T. Clark, 1928.

written in Babylon (63:15–19; 64:8–12) and some possibly preserving the work of the master poet of 40–55 (60–61:3; 62:10–12).

LITERARY FORMS

Deutero-Isaiah is the greatest poet among the prophets of Israel. Isolated Psalms may rival or excel his average but only the book of Job presents so consistently elevated a style. He was a lyricist, gifted with capacities for stirring and expressing the deepest emotions of his people. No small part of the spell he casts over the minds of men is his rare union of beauty and truth, the soaring phrase that lifts the torpid soul. At the same time he addresses himself realistically to the plight of the exiles and the frustration of Jewish religion. His poetry is rhetorically ornamental, but its object is this earth and God's triumph through Israel to all the world.

From his pen pours a flood of imagery, a surging tide of emotion unparalleled in the Old Testament; his intensity and ecstasy never flag. His imagery displays a special fondness for human emotions, as he carries anthropomorphism to its Old Testament pinnacle. Yahweh is conceived as a travailing woman (42:14), a solicitous mother (49:14–15); Israel is God's servant, recalcitrant and yet his one hope for the world (42:18–25; 43:8–10). The style is punctuated with all the arts of Hebrew literature: the rhetorical question, the heaping up of verbs, the short direct quotation, repetition of key words, profusion of imperatives, participial hymn style. He lays claim to the rich variety of types of speech, some drawn from the prophetic tradition: vision and audition narratives (40:3–5,6–8), oracles of salvation (40:1–2; 43:1–7), invectives (48:1–11), admonitions (51:1–8), theophanies of self-affirmation (43:11–13). Others are gathered from wider poetic usage, some cultic in nature: laments (53:1–9), mocking songs (47), and hymns (40:12–26); judicial proceedings or lawsuits (41:1,21–22); and heraldic messages (40:9–11).[16]

The limits of the strophes and the nature of the types are nebulous, mainly because the prophet transmuted everything he appropriated and combined the forms with sovereign independence. His creative genius breaks and fuses the forms in strange configurations shaped by the torrent of his message. Form criticism is mainly helpful in showing some of the sources of his literary material, but these sources no

---

[16] For fuller analysis of the literary features consult J. Muilenburg, *Introduction and Exegesis of Isaiah 40–66* (IB, vol. 5), Abingdon, 1953, pp. 386–393.

more account for Deutero-Isaiah's artistry than the separate legends of Genesis explain the Yahwist's skill.

The rhetorical intensity of the work corresponds to the scope of the prophet's theme. Unlike any prophet before him, Deutero-Isaiah takes the whole of God's action in history as his province ("the former things . . . and the new thing(s)," 43:18; 46:9; 48:6). His historical sweep encompasses the nations and the special tradition of Israel from Noah to the Exile. He knew JE uncommonly well. The prophetic convictions have been thoroughly mastered: sin and redemption, covenant and grace—to which he adds his own themes of witness and praise, sacrifice and redemption through suffering. One meets the substance of Amos and Hosea, Jeremiah and Ezekiel on every page, even to their images and vocabulary. When one encounters such monumental cohesiveness in a Hebrew prophet the temptation is to look for the structure or plan of his work. Many have insisted that the only coherence is the ecstatic style, that actually the work is an assemblage of poetic fragments. Pfeiffer speaks of "an incoherent succession of ecstatic shouts,"[17] Koehler of the pouring out of "a whirlpool of thoughts, a deluge of declarations."[18] More recent interpreters have stressed the organic unity of chapters 40–55 and have even traced the development of the basic themes from the announcement of comfort for the restored city of Jerusalem to the revelation that the victory of God among the nations is to be achieved by Israel's suffering.[19] Wisdom resides in both positions. The unity that exists is at best circuitous. The major themes have a vast sprawling, cyclical character. They appear and reappear in ever-shifting contexts. The musical compositions that come to mind when reading Second Isaiah are the fugue and the cyclical symphony in which themes recur at random, often transfigured. The book does not have the thread of plot to hold the epic poetry together and yet it is vaster in conception than the fleeting moods of lyric poetry. The orderliness of the thinker struggles to hold the caprice of the poet in check. If, as many believe, the work was prepared as synagogue addresses to the exiles and then released as fly sheets or pamphlets, we must not overdo its unity. In short, it is doubtful that Deutero-Isaiah set out to write a single poetic composition now embraced by 40–55. On the other hand, his separate poems or poetic addresses were edited

[17] Pfeiffer, *op. cit.,* p. 465.
[18] L. Koehler, *Deuterojesaja stilkritisch untersucht,* Töpelmann, 1923, p. 119.
[19] See especially James Muilenburg, *op. cit.*

by himself or followers in order to give some evidence of progression of thought and development of theme (e.g., the movement from Cyrus in 40–48 to the Servant in 49–55).

THE BABYLONIAN STIMULUS

The immediate occasion for the prophetic message of chapters 40–55 was the rise of Cyrus on the ancient Near Eastern scene. This would date the oracles around 545 B.C., after the defeat of Croesus of Lydia (547) and before the fall of Babylon (538). This was a crucial moment, marking the passing of the Semitic Age. Yet it was the very age when the Semitic world became the cradle for a religion that would outlast political decay and go on, in its daughter faith, to determine the ethos of the West. It was not the struggle for empire that was to be the Near East's great gift to mankind, but rather the faith of an absurdly small and weak people. Overshadowing everything else about the brilliant poet of Isaiah 40–55 is the fact that he saw the universal character of Jewish religion in a day when few Gentiles were interested in acknowledging it and few Jews were prepared to share it. He was a man before his time, the one Old Testament thinker who most plainly adumbrated Christianity. Still, he was no mere idealist, for he envisioned the necessity of continuing the community of faithful Jews and to do this successfully he insisted upon the return to the homeland where "the waste places will be rebuilt." He is thus paradoxically *prophet of the return* and *prophet of the nations*.

Illustrative of the prophet's sensitivity to the intellectual climate of Babylon is his familiarity with the Babylonian New Year liturgy, which he more or less intentionally imitated. At Babylon an annual twelve-day festival was held to inaugurate the new year. Described by later historians, such as Herodotus the Greek and Berosus the Babylonian, the liturgy for five of the days still survives.[20] The elements of the festival in their probable order were: *ritual humiliation* of the king before the god Bel-Marduk; *arrival of the gods* Nebo, Enlil, Anu, etc., from their respective sanctuaries to do homage before Marduk, the great patron deity of Babylon; *fixing of the destinies* for the coming year by means of ominous or auspicious oracles about the prospects for agricultural fertility and political stability; *sacred marriage* of Mar-

---

[20] The extant ritual is translated in Pritchard, ANET, pp. 331–334; the elements and significance of the festival are thoroughly discussed in S. Pallis, *The Babylonian Akitu Festival*, Host, 1926.

duk and Ishtar, acted by king and priestess; *procession of the gods* from the major sanctuary of Esagila to the Akitu shrine outside the wall, during which the king "took the hand of Marduk," i.e., was assured of his favor; *recitation of the creation epic* (Enuma Elish), which tells of Marduk's conquest of Tiamat and the creation of the world; *death and resurrection of Marduk,* perhaps also mimed.

The Ishtar processional gate in Nebuchadnezzar's Babylon. The façade was emblazoned with colorful mythological creatures.

The festival would have been at the height of its magnificence and pageantry during the Exile, for Nebuchadnezzar had built lavishly in Babylon. The processional street and Akitu gate were faced with gorgeous tiles on which were emblazoned mythological animal designs of dragons, bulls, and lions. That the Jewish exiles were fascinated, perhaps insidiously swayed, by the colorful religious spectacle is apparent in the poems of the prophet. He mocks and derides the idols, scoffing at the impending fate of the motionless deities, Marduk included! The prophet seems obligated to preëmpt the functions of Babylonian religion for Yahweh.

New Year festival motifs are detectable at several points in chaps. 40–55. Yahweh marches with his people over the processional highway to Palestine (40:3; 42:16; 43:19; 49:11). Creation emerges as a major phase of Yahweh's action (40:12,26; 42:5; 44:24). The destinies are in Yahweh's counsels:

> I form light and create darkness,
>> I make weal and create woe,
>> I am Yahweh, who do all these things (45:7).

The fertility of the earth is promised (41:17–19; 43:20; 44:3–4; 51:3), and the titanic struggle with chaos (analogous to Marduk against Tiamat) is celebrated in the dim recollection of Yahweh's destruction of Rahab the monster (42:13; 51:9). The imagery of suffering applied to Yahweh's Servant may draw for some of its detail on the notion of the suffering king (50:6; 52:13–53:12).

Many of the supposed festival motifs are rooted also in Israelite tradition. The processional way is related to the exodus of Israel from Egypt and the blossoming of the desert looks back to the wilderness wanderings. The battle with chaos may be traced to the primitive theology of Yahweh as man of war in the songs of Exodus 15 and Judges 5. The monster is identified with historical enemies such as Egypt. Creation was a motif of the Yahwist and fertility had been claimed by the prophets Elijah and Hosea as one of the good gifts of Yahweh. The portrait of the Suffering Servant has manifold prototypes in the traditions of Moses' suffering, in the travails of prophets such as Jeremiah, and likely also in the ritual of royal humiliation in the Israelite cult.

That precisely these features should spring forth at the point of intersection between Babylonian mythology and Israelite religion is, however, no accident. The spirit that overmasters all else in Deutero-Isaiah is an Israelite spirit, but the form of expression is born of time and place. Confrontation with the scintillating and alluring religion of Babylon has forced a largeness of scope upon the work of the prophet.

Expansion of the prophetic vision is also evident in that Isaiah was the first Israelite to emphasize a doctrine of full monotheism. Ceaselessly, in conjunction with denigration of idols and men, the divine self-predication trumpets forth: "I am Yahweh; I am He and there is none other." This is the *explicit monotheism* that we have waited for since Moses. As a theoretical statement it seems somewhat anticlimactic and pale. We do not feel that the mere declaration is especially novel; as such it does not say anything that Jeremiah or Ezekiel could not have said—although they did not choose to state it in just those terms. But it is no theoretical statement; it is religiously determined: a watchword, a rallying cry, a defiant shout into the teeth of idolatry and despair. Deutero-Isaiah is not novel because with him Judaism finally gets around to framing a properly phrased formula of monotheism. He is novel because he stands on the ruins of the old world and scans the horizons in all directions and finds that the God of puny Israel is the Lord who fills the earth with his fullness, determines the destinies of the nations, gives breath to all men, and is the ultimate source of all power. There can be no other allegiance—not only for Israel (Moses and all the prophets had said that) but also for the nations! If the nations will not worship Yahweh they have no gods to worship because those gods simply do not exist. Yahweh is lord of space and time, the initiator and interpreter of events through his revealing word, who discloses his will not to titillate curiosity but to elicit trust in his people. Deutero-Isaiah daringly glimpses the day when all the peoples of the earth will share that faith.

Driven to the foundations of his faith and forced to restate the Israelite conception of God, Deutero-Isaiah opened vistas unimagined in any previous prophet. As the Yahwist could not have written without Canaanite religion or Paul without the Greco-Roman world, Deutero-Isaiah is inconceivable without mighty Babylon and her religio-cultural challenge to the Jews.

THE REDEEMING GOD

The prophet staggers the imagination with his theology of history. Yahweh is God alone, Creator ("to create" is reserved solely for the act of God in contrast to common Hebrew words "to make" or "to do" or "to mold") and Redeemer ("to redeem" has a wide range of meaning: to avenge blood, protect, secure the rights of someone). He will protect his just interests and it is solely for his own sake that he now works to glorify his name through a redeemed Israel. In this point Deutero-Isaiah and Ezekiel join hands, though the poet's grasp of the profundity and implications of the notion exceeds the priest's:

Comfort, comfort my people,
    says your God.
Speak tenderly to Jerusalem,
    and cry to her
that her warfare is ended,
    that her iniquity is pardoned,

that she has received from Yahweh's hand
   double for all her sins (40:1–2).

I, I am He
   who blots out your transgressions for my own sake,
   and I will not remember your sins (43:25).

For this is like the days of Noah to me:
   as I swore that the waters of Noah
   should no more go over the earth,
so I have sworn that I will not be angry with you
   and will not rebuke you.
For the mountains may depart
   and the hills be removed,
but my steadfast love shall not depart from you,
   and my covenant of peace shall not be removed,
   says Yahweh, who has compassion on you (54:9–10).

The paradoxical wonder that eludes Ezekiel is conveyed movingly by
Deutero-Isaiah: God loves those who deserve no love. "For my own
sake" does not imply a streak of egotistical vanity but rather God's unambiguous fidelity to his own nature, to his love for Israel. Deutero-
Isaiah succeeds in holding together the severe transcendence of Amos
and Ezekiel and the compassion of Hosea and Jeremiah. In this he was
forerunner of Jesus of Nazareth.

Liberation is assured the exiles because Israel's God is Creator and
Redeemer, Lord of nature and humanity. He is God before whom "the
nations are as nothing" and Israel is small indeed, crushed in lassitude
of spirit, still the obstinate servant (42:18–20). Beside Israel's Lord
what are the idols of Babylon but mute and lifeless shells? The prophet
never wearies of lampooning them in mock lawsuits where they are
summoned to testify, to say something—anything at all. But Yahweh
alone oversees "the former things," the saving acts of Israel's past, and
"the new thing(s)," or Second Exodus.

God's redemptive break-through is at hand. Of special significance
is the theme of the herald of good tidings. The word in Hebrew is
humble and undistinguished, with a usually secular imputation: "herald, messenger, bringer of news," ordinarily favorable tidings but not
always so. In the opening poem, the city of Jerusalem is personified as
a runner who bears the announcement of the return of the exiles to the
other Judean cities:

Get you up to a high mountain,
   O Zion, herald of good tidings;
lift up your voice with strength,
   O Jerusalem, herald of good tidings,
   lift it up, fear not;
say to the cities of Judah,
   "Behold your God!" (40:9).

In two other contexts, however, the herald speaks *to* Jerusalem:

I first have declared it to Zion,
   and I give to Jerusalem a herald of good tidings.
                               (41:27; first line defective Hebrew.)

How beautiful upon the mountains
   are the feet of him who brings good tidings,
who publishes peace, who brings good tidings of good,
   who publishes salvation,
   who says to Zion, "Your God reigns" (52:7).

In the Septuagint of Isaiah the Hebrew term "herald of good tidings" is translated by the Greek word which in the New Testament comes to mean "gospel." On the pages of the New Testament "gospel" is the good news about the salvation of mankind in Jesus Christ, as it is also used for the message Jesus proclaimed, and for the literary form of the first four books of the New Testament collection, the Gospels. While there are other Old Testament passages which the LXX translates with a religious use of the Greek root "to bring or announce good news" (e.g., Pss. 40:9; 96:2), and while the coloration of the word may have been derived from the cultic shout at the king's enthronement, Deutero-Isaiah first imbued the term with that evangelical character which illumines the faith of the early church: God has redeemed his people! Much of the Old Testament yearns toward a time of full redemption, and Deutero-Isaiah revels in its actuality. It is, therefore, of particular relevance that the Synoptic Gospels cite the opening words of Deutero-Isaiah about the preparation of a way in the desert (Isa. 40:3) as fulfilled in the preparatory ministry of John the Baptist. The wonderful deliverance that Deutero-Isaiah anticipated, not merely freedom from foreign bondage but rescue from the tyranny of sin and defeatism into the historical purposes of God, had now transpired in Jesus Christ. The present tense in the gospel message was introduced by the great prophet of the Exile.

What form of redemption did the prophet expect? He saw Cyrus as the conqueror of Babylon and the liberator of the Jews who would rebuild Jerusalem. The profuse praise of Cyrus has impressed some interpreters as unwarranted and misguided, and they have dismissed the prophet's lyrical rapture at the impending release as "so much enthusiastic nonsense."[21] After all, Cyrus never was a Yahweh-worshiper and the restoration of a few thousand Jews to Palestine was a minor operation against the backdrop of movements in the Persian Empire. They argue that Deutero-Isaiah's ecstatic contemplation of the grandeur of Jerusalem restored and the gathering in of the nations was beside the point. But we must consider that the prophet writes poetry, the genre of literature in which reality is most drastically transfigured while it is disclosed. Furthermore, Deutero-Isaiah does not imply that it is in his capacity as a Yahweh convert that Cyrus will free the Jews. Cyrus will topple the Babylonian power and release Israel by virtue of the vast designs of the Creator-Redeemer God who controls world history, "though you [Cyrus] do not know me" (45:4–5).

And if we should set out to test the validity of the great religious leaders by a simple pragmatic test, then who of them could stand? Almost without exception they contemplated truths and realities that for the mass of mankind have never yet seemed realistic. The test for Jewish and Christian leaders is of course uncommonly difficult since both make claims about God's action in history. Deutero-Isaiah's vision of the world worshiping one God was abortive for his age, but it was not absurd for that reason. With a vision of such fundamental importance he cannot be mocked because his timing was wrong. What he states is not a method or a program of world redemption but rather the ultimate aim of Yahwism, a theology of the world mission of Judaism. He grounds method in the nature of God. In his poetic flights he discloses not the irrelevance of his insight but the tremendous demands upon the mind and heart that such a view of Israel's mission entails. One could as readily say that Jesus and Paul were absurd figures in their attempt to call Israel to its ancient prophetic mission to the nations.

THE NATIONS

Deutero-Isaiah is ambivalent in his attitude toward the nations. Naturally his thinking is determined in large measure by Israel's relation

---

[21] Ulrich Simon, *A Theology of Salvation; a Commentary on Isaiah 40–66*, SPCK, 1953, p. 16.

to them: the relation of conquered and conqueror. Babylon has oppressed Israel and, like Assyria before her, has gloated in her world dominion; thus one of the firm notes of the prophecy is retribution upon Babylon, the harlot city (chap. 47). It is precisely this context of Israelite fear before the vanquisher in which the words of the prophet must be read:

All the nations are as nothing before him,
    they are accounted by him as less than nothing and
        emptiness (40:17).

The issue is not divine love but divine power; against Yahweh they are nothing—just as Israel is nothing. Likewise, the prophet castigates the idolatrous worship of the nations. Behind their aesthetic allure, the pomp of their worship, and the frenzy of their devotees, there is absolutely nothing. The impotence of the idols is shown up by satire, for if necessary the prophet will defeat them with jeers of laughter. He pictures the man who cuts down a tree, skillfully fashions an idol from part of it, and with the remainder builds a fire (this is the only section in the prophecy that does not read like poetry): "No one considers, nor is there knowledge or discernment to say, Half of it I burned in the fire, I also baked bread on its coals, I roasted flesh and have eaten; and shall I make the residue of it an abomination? Shall I fall down before a block of wood?" (44:19).

It has been observed that, in the numerous vociferous Israelite condemnations of idolatry, there is never any indication that the Jews really understood the pagan ideology. The myths, rituals, and prayers of Babylonian religion, for example, make it abundantly clear that the gods were thought of as heavenly beings; the idols were simply their earthly representations. This doubtless demonstrates that the Jews had been so long divorced from idolatry that they completely missed its nuances. The Baalism that they knew best was more a religion of fetishism and amulets.

But that is only one side of the story. The ancient world did not readily distinguish between symbol and thing symbolized. While Marduk might be in the heavens, he was also in his house at Babylon and in his image. Furthermore, suppose the Jews had grasped the niceties of pagan polytheism, would they have been one whit more tolerant of idolatry? It is hard to conceive it. What reform could ever have made images of divine beings palatable to them? For the Jews were certainly right in connecting naturalistic polytheism and idolatry as virtual inseparables. They realized that merely to designate Marduk as the one God, still idolized and surrounded with his myth and ritual, and to equate him with the Jewish Yahweh was no true conversion. Deutero-Isaiah was not the least bit interested in a syncretistic monotheism. The conversion of the nations he anticipated was to the aniconic God of Jewish tradition.

With all his firm attitude toward the oppressing and idolatrous nations the prophet has profound concern for them. He does not write them off as lost or consign them to apocalyptic destruction (as in the Gog of Magog apocalypse of Ezekiel 38–39). He is conscious that all men derive their life from the one God Yahweh. This Stoic-like theme revives and expands the incipient universalism of the Yahwist and Amos. By turns this faith in God as Creator is employed to strengthen the minority Jews:

> Have you not known? Have you not heard?
> Yahweh is the everlasting God,
>   the Creator of the ends of the earth.
> He does not faint or grow weary,
>   his understanding is unsearchable (40:28).

and to spur Israel on to its missionary calling:

> Thus says God, Yahweh,
>   who created the heavens and stretched them out,
>   who spread forth the earth and what comes from it,
> who gives breath to the people upon it
>   and spirit to those who walk in it:
> "I am Yahweh, I have called you in righteousness,
>   I have taken you by the hand and kept you;
> I have given you as a covenant to the people,
>   a light to the nations . . ." (42:5–6).

The invitation is broadcast clarionlike to the nations:

> Turn to me and be saved,
>   all the ends of the earth!
>   For I am God, and there is no other (45:22).

In one of the most emphatic verses in the book the prophet rises to a supernational plane that few have ever reached:

> It is too light a thing that you should be my Servant
>   to raise up the tribes of Jacob
>   and to restore the preserved of Israel:

I will give you as a light to the nations,
　that my salvation may reach to the end of the earth (49:6).

His words bring to mind the retort of John the Baptist to his critics, "I tell you, God is able from these stones to raise up children to Abraham" (Matt. 3:9).

Accompanying this generous attitude toward the nations are a number of passages that show them as the subjects, nursemaids, and servants of the restored community of Jews. Some critics take these passages as decisive and treat the universalism lightly. Others, such as Torrey, lay these excrescences of nationalism to Oriental poetics and find some interesting parallels in Arabic verse.[22] Certainly we cannot minimize the fact that the same prophet who called Israel to win the nations also had to encourage the fainting spirits of his people suffering from the spiritual insult of exile. We might try to imagine a group of political exiles from the Soviet satellites being encouraged to convert their captors at the same time they were being steeled against succumbing to the physical and ideological pressures of their overlords. Deutero-Isaiah was not free to compose a balanced treatise or epic; he had a pastoral task quite as necessary as Ezekiel's. The plenitude and scope of his work are therefore all the more impressive. If we must leave unresolved how he could employ imagery that depreciated the nations whom he summoned Israel to convert, then it is no more strange than our contemporary habit of villifying political or social enemies whom our religion commands us to love.

THE SERVANT OF YAHWEH

We have reserved for last the most startling aspect of Deutero-Isaiah, for which alone he must be ranked among the major thinkers of Israel: the portrait of the Suffering Servant of Yahweh. Four classic passages have been isolated as Servant Songs (42:1–4; 49:1–6; 50:4–9; 52:13–53:12), although there are several supplemental poems that speak of the Servant or servants (e.g., 41:8–10; 43:8–13; 44:1–8, 21–22, 24–28; 45:1–8). The significant difference is that in the four songs proper the Servant is highly individualized and supremely and knowingly committed to his task, whereas in the latter contexts Israel is the servant (or Israelites are servants) who has been faithless and blind to his mission. Because of this discrepancy in the portraiture

---

[22] Torrey, *op. cit.,* chap. VII.

and variations in style, Duhm separated the songs as the work of another poet. But that does not dispose of the problem.

Some interpreters try to do justice to the similarity and difference by
regarding Deutero-Isaiah as the poet who penned the songs apart from
the rest of his work and added them later. Thus the two pictures of the
Servant—in the songs and in the context—represent variant phases in
the prophet's thought. Yahweh addresses Cyrus, "his anointed"; some
profess to see a gradual disillusionment of the prophet with Cyrus as
the Servant so that he transferred the honorific title to the newly conceived figure of the songs. If it is maintained that the entire work was
editorially constructed out of a number of separate addresses and poems, then the Servant Songs are no different than other parts of the
book. Written over several years, we may expect to find in them maturation of thought and, especially in poetry, "contradictions" of the
sort that could be turned up in almost any comparable work of the
imagination.

The Songs of the Servant may be characterized according to major
speaker, literary type, and content:

1. *42:1–4, (5–9)*[23]
   Yahweh speaks
   Call or Initiation Oracle
   The Servant as dispenser of *torah* to the nations

2. *49:1–6, (7–9a)*
   The Servant speaks
   Individual Thanksgiving Song
   The Servant's preparation, despair, and universal task

3. *50:4–9, (10–11)*
   The Servant speaks
   Individual Lament
   The Servant persecuted; his trust in God

4. *52:13–53:12*
   Yahweh and the nations (or Jews) speak
   Collective Lament
   The Servant's death and vindication

The portrait unfolds with cumulative power. Whatever the songs'
origin, they have been placed in psychologically convincing order, ad-

[23] Parenthetical numbers denote verses included in the Servant Songs by a minority
of critics.

vancing with steady progression from the Servant's call to his death
and deliverance.

In the first song the subject is announced by Yahweh as "my Servant," endowed with the divine Spirit (cf. 61:1). His prime function is
to "bring forth," i.e., accomplish or make effective, *mishpat* among the
nations. *Mishpat* is basically justice (as in Amos) but its many nuances
permit several meanings, especially since it is in parallelism with *torah*,
"teaching, instruction, revelation." It is not too paraphrastic to render
mishpat, "right" or "truth" and *torah*, "the true religion." The image
of the bruised reed and dimly burning wick is obscure (perhaps some
unknown legal or ritual practice), but its gist is a litotes (an affirmative expressed by the negative of its opposite) describing the pacifistic
mode of the Servant's action. He works quietly and without physical
force. Features of a New David and a New Moses are prominent, yet
with the enlarging factor of a mission to the nations.

The second song, addressed to the nations, includes a meditation of
the Servant and a commission of Yahweh. The Servant is deeply conscious of his predestined calling "from the womb." For a period he
was hidden away like an arrow in a quiver, incognito. When the moment of his mission arrived he experienced only frustration and despair. The Servant feels that his work has been "for nothing . . . I
have labored in vain." But his resolute trust is in the justice of God
who will rightly recompense him.

The Servant's identity is both eased and complicated in this song. He
is named explicitly:

> And he said to me, "You are my servant,
>   Israel, in whom I will be glorified" (49:3).

Two verses later, however, the Servant is given a mission *to* Israel:

> And now Yahweh says,
>   who formed me from the womb to be his servant,
> to bring Jacob back to him,
>   and that Israel might be gathered to him, (49:5)

The song closes with the grandest statement of universalism since
Amos, but whereas Amos leaves Yahweh's relation to the nations un-
articulated, the Servant Song envisions Yahweh's message carried to
the nations and their worship of him on the same terms as Israel. Indeed, Israel's choice can never be exhausted or justified by the salva-

tion of a small group of Jews; Israel exists rather for the world. What a test to put to any religious society, especially a minority!

The third song has sometimes been called "the Gethsemane of the Servant." In a whispered soliloquy the Servant tells of his teaching ministry and of the divine word that first had to strengthen him before he could strengthen others; being teachable he could teach. The measure of his strength is but a daily one, "morning by morning . . ." Above all he has learned not to be rebellious but to accept adversity patiently (cf. Lam. 3:25–33). Since God is his ever-present helper he can bear the suffering. Though he is reviled and physically abused he does not surrender his mission, for his purpose will endure when his tormenters are vanished. Again the figure of Jeremiah comes to mind, except that a patience and restraint toward the foe is displayed which that prophet never evinced. The song expresses in a most effective manner the mixture of strength and weakness in the Servant. His almost superhuman task of teaching with constancy while he is being rejected, is accomplished only because he stays so close to God his Teacher and Vindicator. The tenacious but unassuming spiritual stamina of the Servant prepares for the culminating song.

The final Servant poem is a monumentally constructed hymn of triumph enclosing a lament. It is a tragedy that its artistic and religious integrity is defaced by those who fail to read the first part of the song in chapter 52, without which the reader misses the import of chapter 53. With a technique not unlike the flashback device of movies and novels, the poet rounds out his portrait by setting the tragic end of the Servant in the context of its divine significance. The exaltation of the Servant is achieved not through divine intervention that spares him but through patient endurance of wrong unto death. The strange and baffling paradox that God brings his grace and power to bear through suffering rightly borne is presented with overwhelming effect. Like counter melodies that seem to fight against one another and yet resolve into the totality of the orchestra's performance, the trumpets of transfiguration frame the composition as introduction and conclusion, overture and coda:

> Behold, my servant shall prosper,
>   he shall be exalted and lifted up,
>   and shall be very high (52:13).

. . . .

Therefore I will divide him a portion with the great,
    and he shall divide the spoil with the strong;
because he poured out his soul to death,
    and was numbered with the transgressors;
yet he bore the sin of many,
    and made intercession for the transgressors (53:12).

in bold contrast to the meditative woodwinds and strings:

Who has believed what we have heard?
    And to whom has the arm of Yahweh been revealed?
For he [the Servant] grew up before him [Yahweh] like a
    young plant,
    and like a root out of dry ground;
he had no form or comeliness . . . no beauty. . . .
He was despised and rejected by men;
    a man of sorrows, and acquainted with grief;
    . . . .
    . . . and we esteemed him not.

Surely *he* has borne *our* griefs
    and carried *our* sorrows;
yet *we* esteemed *him* stricken,
    smitten by God, and afflicted.
But *he* was wounded for *our* transgressions,
    he was bruised for *our* iniquities;
upon *him* was the chastisement that made *us* whole,
    and with *his* stripes *we* are healed (53:1–5).

The plaintive lament pulses to its convulsive end in the death and burial of the Servant who is recognized too late by his executioners as the instrument of Yahweh's love toward them.

The poet, who to this point has kept carefully out of view, can no longer restrain himself and he seizes as it were the full force of the orchestra to affirm the truth about the Servant and the nations:

Yet it was the will of Yahweh to bruise him;
    he has put him to grief;
when he makes himself an offering for sin,
    he shall see his offspring, he shall prolong his days;
the will of Yahweh shall prosper in his hand;
    he shall see the fruit of the travail of his soul and
        be satisfied; (53:10, 11*a*).

Suffering appears for the first time in Jewish tradition as a positive good. It is not always the result of wrong; the sufferer need not be a sinner. In truth, individual or national suffering, if borne as a mission from God, may be the means of untold blessing to others. The Servant is disfigured by the abuse heaped upon him, none of which is due to his own wrongdoing. The onlookers who have slain him are the penitents who now confess in awe that he bore their sins. It is hard to convey in English the tremendous effect of the Hebrew with the reiteration of the pronouns *he* and *his* (Hebrew *hu*) and *we* and *our* (Hebrew *nu*) creating an onomatopoetic dirge of mournful and awe-struck regret. What an astonishing disproportion between *his* suffering and *our* abuse of him, *his* innocence and *our* guilt, *his* patience and *our* callous mockery!

The work is poetry and the legion of questions that rises in our minds concerning this revolutionary concept are not easily answered. Has the Servant already suffered his fate or does the final poem anticipate the end prophetically? Who are the onlookers who confess their guilt and salvation? Are they the rulers of the nations or fellow Jews, since the kings according to the introduction are too astounded to speak? If the Servant is an individual, does the poem contemplate his resurrection from the dead, and, if so, is it not early in Israelite religious history for such a concept? One and all, these queries are aspects of the conundrum of conundrums in Old Testament study: *who is the Servant?* On retrospect many of the proposals for explaining the Servant seem fantastic and fruitless, yet it was needful that they be pursued so that no theory would be brushed aside merely because at first glance it seemed unpromising. Even the nontechnical student of Deutero-Isaiah requires an appreciation of the range and variety of solutions advanced, in order that he be chary of snap answers and assure his own viewpoint a sounder basis than mere personal preference.

The theories fall into the categories of individual and collective identifications, with some recent intriguing attempts to combine the best features of each.[24]

1. *The Servant as an Individual*

A. A HISTORICAL PERSON. The history of Israel prior to Deutero-Isaiah has been ransacked in search of the most probable candidate

---

[24] Fuller discussion and bibliography in J. Muilenburg, *op. cit.*, pp. 406–414 and C. R. North, *The Suffering Servant in Deutero-Isaiah*, Oxford University Press, rev. ed., 1956.

for the office of Servant. Among the more common identifications have been Moses, Jeremiah, and Cyrus. The Servant has been equated with Uzziah, Hezekiah, Josiah, and Zerubbabel among royal figures; Isaiah of Jerusalem and Ezekiel among the prophets; and Job and Eleazar (a Maccabean martyr) among the pious. Prior to the work of Duhm around the turn of the century, little impulse was felt to see the same individual in all the songs so that frequently a scholar would claim to find two or more historical Servants in the poems.

Failure of the adherents of a historical Servant to reach any sort of agreement is a serious blow to the theory. Tenuous parallels are drawn in equating the poetic descriptions of the Servant with the sickness, persecution, or martyrdom of the known figures; an overliteralizing of the songs results. There is the obvious inadequacy of any known person to do justice to the terms of the description, not only in the extent of the suffering but in the scope of the Servant's task and his almost superhuman adherence to duty. But the truth in the theory is that elements in the poetic imagery of the Servant are drawn from past leaders. Especially evident are terms reminiscent of Moses the lawgiver and Jeremiah the rejected prophet.

B. AN ANONYMOUS CONTEMPORARY. Bernard Duhm, whose scholarship was always provocative and germinal even when he was perversely wrong, advanced the view that the Servant was a leprous teacher of the law. Since he denied Deutero-Isaianic authorship of the songs he located the torah-teacher, a virtual rabbinic prototype, in fifth-century Palestine. In his death by horrible disease the teacher's disciples beheld God's redemptive love. But the theory does not depend upon any particular notion of authorship, for others have seen in the Servant an exilic martyr or pious sufferer known to the prophet and his contemporaries but not otherwise recorded in history. Most of the objections to the historical identification apply to this position and, in addition, there is the anonymity of the individual that seems to serve more as a smoke screen than as a clarification. How could the Servant have been so influential if he has otherwise completely dropped out of Israel's memory?

C. THE PROPHET HIMSELF. This is the theory of which we have the earliest clear report, for the Ethiopian eunuch in Acts 8:34 asks the apostle Philip, with reference to Isaiah 53, "Of whom does the prophet speak? Himself or another?" While the theory that Deutero-Isaiah pictured himself in the Servant Songs was toyed with through the centuries, being advanced especially by Jews who wished to rebut the Christian interpretation, only with the full statement of the position by Mowinckel in 1921 did it become common. He insisted that the only way to understand the deep inwardness and essential anonymity of the Servant was to realize that the prophet was projecting his own deepest experiences of rejection and commission. Mowinckel was followed in his identification by a number of younger German scholars, though with manifold variations. M. Haller, for example, believed that the prophet turned from his original idea of Cyrus as the servant to the autobiographical view. Sellin, Elliger, and Volz, in order to remove the difficulty that the prophet writes of his own death, transferred the fourth song to disciples.

The great strength of the theory is that it accounts for the fragmentary, esoteric nature of the Servant Songs, analogous to the subjectivity of Jeremiah's Confessions. Certainly no matter whom the prophet recognizes as the Servant, the poetic and spiritual vision would be meaningless except as he shared its tremendous conviction. It is the prophet's conception and in that sense thoroughly autobiographical. There is no good reason for denying that he suffered reversals and saw analogies in his plight to that of the Servant. But it is extremely doubtful that a prophet would write in such immoderate praise of himself, with so little attention to the imperfections of the Servant, and even to the point of penning his own death. Inasmuch as the four poems belong together, to attribute the last poem to disciples seems to cut the heart out of the autobiographical theory. Mowinckel renounced his own theory but has returned to it in a modified and more tentative form. He now suggests that the Servant was an unknown prophet other than Deutero-Isaiah, who may have written the second and third songs himself. The four songs were prepared by a poet-disciple who recognized that his master's rejection and death had saving significance. Both Servant and disciple were in the Deutero-Isaianic circle.[25]

D. MYTHOLOGICAL FIGURE. A minority of scholars, especially those who have dealt extensively with the religions of Israel's neighbors, have identified the Servant as one of the vegetation deities believed to die and rise from the dead periodically. This Tammuz-Adonis figure was domesticated to Israelite religion and finally rose to the surface in the thinking of the great exilic prophet. Ivan Engnell has reopened the theory through his minute comparative studies be-

[25] Sigmund Mowinckel, *He That Cometh,* Abingdon, 1956, pp. 246–255.

tween the fourth song and the extant Babylonian Tammuz liturgies. Some who have been quick to criticize Engnell have failed to note his emphatic warning that he does not believe the Servant figure to be Tammuz but rather the Israelite king described as a sufferer in terms drawn from the liturgies. This shifts the ground of the discussion from the original mythological view of Gressmann, Jeremias, and Zimmern.

Deutero-Isaiah, who had intimate contact with Babylonian cults, could have drawn upon the vocabulary of ritual suffering. While a large percentage of Engnell's parallels are entirely unconvincing, he does make a case for the Tammuz cult origin of some of the images of affliction, death, and resurrection. But the indebtedness is loose enough to be explained by any intelligent Babylonian's knowledge of the ritual. There is no evidence that the prophet copied Babylonian texts or that he conceived the Servant figure as one of the dying and rising nature deities. Such a notion would ill accord with the thoroughly Hebraic texture of the Songs and the repeated emphasis that the Servant is the instrument of Yahweh.

E. THE MESSIAH. The essential feature of this theory, whether in its Jewish or Christian form, is that the Servant is the individual ideal ruler, "the anointed one." The few Jews who have interpreted the songs in this way have been faced with the embarrassment of the Servant's suffering, since Judaism does not normally admit suffering to the role of the messiah. The Targum of Isaiah, however, accomplishes the astounding feat of applying all the suffering of the fourth song not to the Servant but to the observing nations! Some medieval Jews held that there were two messiahs: ben Joseph the suffering messiah would precede ben David the triumphant messiah, and the former was sometimes equated with the Servant. The orthodox Christian theory, still regnant in Roman Catholic and Protestant fundamentalist circles, regards the Servant as Jesus of Nazareth, the Christ. However, the theory has had constant reservations attending it, since it has often been recognized that certain details of the Servant portrait have no analogy in Jesus' ministry (e.g., Jesus was not buried in a dishonored grave, nor did he have children, nor was he restored to normal existence in this world).

It is possible that the Servant is a messiah yet to come from the standpoint of the prophet, but not explicitly Jesus. C. R. North, who has written the most thorough and valuable study on the history of the interpretation of the Servant conception, stresses however that the ideal messianic view does not involve a political mission since "the Servant is a soteriological and not a political figure."[26] But in adopting this position he has greatly changed the proper sense of the term "messianic." The Servant is for him some future saving person whom he identifies with Jesus Christ but who was not known as such to the consciousness of the prophet.

In this camp there are inescapable subtleties involved in the elusive designation "messianic," and the imaginative language of poetry. Two theories are actually in question: the strictly messianic view and the symbolically messianic. The former is out of the question because, while certain of the royal psalms picture the king as suffering (Psalms 18; 89; 118), there is no convincing evidence that the Servant is a king, apart from the gratuitous assumption that any sufferer of communal stature must have been a ruler. The alternative Christian reinterpretation of "messiah" so deprives the term of its Jewish political character as to be really another theory. It is certainly clear to Christian and non-Christian alike that if any individual has come close to characterizing the spirit and destiny of the Servant it was Jesus of Nazareth. But that does not justify the orthodox view that the prophet specifically described Jesus of Nazareth, for such a notion is built on a flat verbal view of inspiration. It ignores the basic principle that every prophetic utterance must have relevance for its own time. To the degree that Jesus fulfills the Servant portrait in principle we are dealing with another category of interpretation.

2. *The Servant as a Group*

All the collective theories agree in recognizing Israel or some significant portion of Israel as the Servant. They take as their basic proof the explicit statement of the text that Israel is the Servant, both in the songs themselves (49:3) and in the context (42:19; 43:10). The collectivists have the manifest advantage of not needing to force the evidence to fit some particular individual; they have the disadvantage of doing little justice to the pronounced individualizing portrait of the Servant. The collectivists, like the individualists, follow divergent paths.

A. THE EMPIRICAL ISRAEL. The great majority of Jewish scholars insist that the exiled Jews constitute the Servant. The ignominies and

[26] C. R. North, *op. cit.,* p. 218.

sufferings of the Exile were redemptively construed; the popularity of this view among Jews is related to the long Jewish experience of exile and the sometimes inarticulate feeling that Jewry's history of suffering has been for the benefit of the nations. Israel as the witnessing, martyred people of God has deep rootage in the Jewish consciousness.

Johann Peter Spaeth, a seventeenth-century convert to Judaism, tells of the event that turned him into a Jew. It happened that a crucifix once dropped from his pocket and was picked up by a Jew who said: "It is Israel, the man of sorrow!" Spaeth comments: "From those words I understood the 53rd chapter of Isaiah: the Jews bore the sins of the heathen, while they were daily persecuted by them. From time immemorial they had been treated in a shameful manner. As the whole history of the Passion tended to render the Jews odious, so the same sort of thing happens nowadays. For instance, the Jews are said to have murdered a child, and to have distributed the blood in quills for the use of their women in childbirth. I have discovered this outrageous fraud in time: and, therefore, I abandon Christianity, which permits such things."[27] Not only Jewish but many Christian exegetes believe that the prophet's image is national. Some try to give full weight to the individual characterization by the assumption that the poems are allegories (J. Lindblom). Others lay stress upon the total historical range of Yahweh's call to Israel: the Servant figure is the quintessence of her summons to bear the divine word self-sacrificially (J. Muilenburg).

B. IDEAL ISRAEL. A number of critics are sensitive to the disparity between the rigorous spiritual demands upon the Servant and the rather casual and indifferent attitude of many of the exiles. To meet the difficulty they assume that the prophet summons his compatriots to a vocation of suffering that ought ideally to be theirs but in fact was not for they had shirked it. The problem is that the suffering remains visionary or hypothetical while the impact of the songs is in the tremendous power of redemptive suffering that has been undergone. The "ideal Israel" variation looks like an attempt to circumvent problems in the "empirical Israel" theme but lacks anything to commend it on its own.

C. A MINORITY IN ISRAEL. In an effort to remove the same difficulty, namely, the spiritual obtuseness of the people vis-à-vis the fidelity of the Servant, others have narrowed the collective theory down

---

[27] *The Jewish Encyclopedia,* Funk and Wagnalls, 1905–1909, vol. 11, p. 484.

to the remnant or order of prophets. A select minority in Israel acts on its behalf. This is more acceptable than the "ideal Israel" theory but it seems to offer no solution that is not as well supplied by an individual portrait. If the minority is the order of prophets, why not select the most likely prophet, Jeremiah?

Both the "ideal" and "minority" theories have been without much support in recent discussion, for as North observes they are more attempts to evade problems in the collective view than they are constructive solutions.

If the poems are taken as integral to the work of Deutero-Isaiah, then the specific reference to Israel as the Servant outside the songs would be determinative for a collective interpretation. But the evidence to that effect is counterbalanced by the sharply focused individual portrait and by the uncontested fact that the Servant is given a mission to Israel. One of the attractive features of the collective theory is that it draws into the interpretation of the Servant the grandeur and richness of Israel's agelong salvation history. Surely no interpretation of the Servant can be accepted that rips him out of the context of Israel's mission to the world, the covenant history from Moses to Deutero-Isaiah. But there are disturbing questions about the collective approach: Did the nation in fact ever take on suffering voluntarily as the Servant does? Did Israel suffer innocently?[28] Did the exiles, whose lot in Babylon was apparently not too onerous from an economic and physical standpoint, ever suffer to the extent pictured by the fourth song?

3. *The Servant as Individual and Group.*

With the delineations balanced between individual and collective features it was inevitable that interpreters would seek to combine the two in a synthesis. In the seventeenth century Solomon de Morini saw three elements in the Servant: Israel, any righteous Israelite, and the Messiah. Franz Delitzsch advanced his famous pyramid theory in which actual Israel was the base, ideal Israel the converging sides of the triangle, and the Messiah the apex. C. C. Torrey suggested that the reference of the Servant, although primarily to the nation, shifts to Abraham and the restorer of Israel, the messiah. The notion of "corporate personality," by which a group is conceived as a single organism with individual consciousness, has been applied to the problem with

---

[28] The suggestion that when the prophet mentions Jerusalem having suffered "double for all her sins" he refers to meritorious excess of suffering that could be applied to the nations seems oversubtle, if not actually nonhebraic.

positive results. H. W. Robinson and Otto Eissfeldt have independently advanced quite similar conceptions, based on socioanthropological notions of "the primitive unconscious" as developed by Durkheim and Lévy-Bruhl. Israel is both an aggregation of persons and a personality with a character of its own, born of the distinctive experience of the community and its greatest leaders. By a process of "oscillation" the Servant image moves between the group and its individual representation. In Robinson's view the individuality to which it contracts is the faithful prophet himself and his loyal followers. For Eissfeldt the individualizing point of contraction is less clear: apparently an ancestral image approaching the "ideal Israel" category. H. S. Nyberg argues for the Servant as a superindividual mythic figure, neither individual nor collective, that has its roots in Tammuz mythology, ritual kingship, and the corporate ancestral figure. Yet his theory is a tour de force, trying to include so much that it does not clarify anything. The Servant has become all things Israelite.

Sifting the preceding expositions of the Servant theories, the following conclusions emerge. The Servant is a theological concept meaningless apart from the salvation history of Israel. But the tendency of Israel's mission to fall upon key individuals, the contraction of understanding and courage to the faithful few (as in the prophets) is striking indeed. Deutero-Isaiah's appeal to his people is evidence of that. He was a prophetic aristocrat who understood that the masses need an object and a dramatic focus for their faith. But the Servant image was shaped by actual experience. Since the prophet's struggle to be heard had caused him suffering, he became sensitive to the rejection previous Israelites such as Jeremiah had experienced. The Servant, while not to be equated with the writer or any one person, must not be vaporized into the ideal. Redemption by suffering is a great reality to the prophet, the motive power for the unification of the nations in the worship of Yahweh. This is the essence of Israel's mission: failing politically she is to succeed spiritually, triumphing in her greatest defeat. Israel is teacher of the nations.

While the collective and individual syntheses probably come closest to grasping the paradox, the poems are after all works of high artistic and religious genius. Were the poet himself in our presence, he might be no more articulate in advancing a precise theory than we are. But the central point he has not left in doubt: Yahweh's love and power are to be made manifest to the nations through Israel, and through some person or persons within Israel who participate in the love of Yahweh to the extent of self-obliteration. Supreme power is in love rather than in coercion.

It is small wonder that Christianity has always seen the Suffering Servant as the summit of the Old Testament. Deutero-Isaiah's insight was not immediately taken up. Judaism was too engrossed in survival in a hostile world to care much about converting the heathen. But the idea did not die; it erupted in the early church. Jesus was deeply influenced by his reading of Isaiah 40–66. The universal salvation promised in Deutero-Isaiah finally came to birth in Christianity.

In what sense then may we speak of Jesus Christ fulfilling the Servant prophecy? He fulfilled it by recognizing himself, his purpose and method in the Servant figure. There was a spiritual affinity between himself and the unknown poet-prophet of the Exile. Is it not prophecy enough that the Servant image should have preceded him, been preserved by his people, and lain at hand for his nourishment? Which is the greater wonder: that Deutero-Isaiah should have foreseen Jesus of Nazareth five centuries in advance or that Jesus should have singled out of his heritage the Servant ideal as the one he was to make his own? "It is Israel, the man of sorrow!" They are different wonders, to be sure, but the latter seems best to accord with historical study and a valid theory of revelation.

Isaiah 40–55 is the literary and religious crown of the Hebrew Bible. His hour in history awakened the prophet to a unitary conception of Israel's mission, rivaled only by the earlier but theologically more adolescent Yahwist. Shorn of the trappings of preëxilic nationalism and thrust beyond an unventurous henotheism, he conceived the transcendent power of the mighty Creator of all who expresses himself through a dedicated people in the patience, the fidelity, and unswerving hope of the Servant. He saw the upsetting truth that God has taken the despised things of this world in order to confound the mighty (I Cor. 1:22–30). Here was the foundation for Christianity.

✤ 12 ✤

RECONSTRUCTION UNDER THE PERSIANS

Behold, I do a new thing . . .
Isa. 43:19

The Persian conquest of Babylon in 538 signaled the return of the Jews to Palestine, yet only a fraction of the Babylonian exiles responded to the opportunity for repatriation. In addition, large numbers of the dispossessed Jews were living in Egypt, Asia Minor, and elsewhere in the Mediterranean world. Henceforth in biblical times Judaism was to be a religion with a double focus: the homeland and temple cultus, on the one hand; the dispersion and synagogue, on the other. As the population in exile increased, the latter became the more important development. But the temple remained a rallying point and the homeland a symbol of God's goodness and Israel's blessing—even for those Jews who never saw Palestine in their lifetime. The great postexilic period from 538 B.C. to the decisive extinction of temple worship in A.D. 70 was a transitional era for Judaism. Far from being a time of spiritual paralysis, Judaism was very much alive and expressed the faith of the prophets in a wealth of ways.

Unfortunately the historical documentation for the postexilic period is less satisfactory than for the preëxilic monarchy. The only well-accounted-for phase is the Maccabean age when a burst of independence awakened national pride and with it the desire to record events. Otherwise, the subservience of the Jews to the world empires did not encourage historiography. Although Josephus treats the pre-Maccabean period, his sources are sketchy and of dubious accuracy. Generally where he goes beyond the biblical data his information is

427

grossly legendary. Our information derives mainly from the prophetic writings of Haggai and Zechariah and the books of Ezra and Nehemiah. Aramaic letters from a Jewish military colony in upper Egypt (Elephantine papyri, *ca.* 450–400) and traditions about the Greek translation of the Old Testament in Alexandria (the Septuagint, *ca.* 250–75 B.C.) serve to fill in but meagerly the gaps in our knowledge of dispersion Judaism.

THE RESTORED COMMUNITY, 538–333 B.C.

The main source of information on Judaism in the Persian period is the Chronicler, author of I and II Chronicles, Ezra, and Nehemiah. The larger part of his work recapitulates the history of Israel from Adam to the Exile; the canonical Kings are quoted extensively. His sources for the postexilic age are uneven, but it is usually conceded that he had trustworthy data in the form of Aramaic letters and official documents. The problem is in his use of the data, for he shared with the Deuteronomists a strong predilection to theologize. The account of the return of Babylonian Jews to Jerusalem must be read in the light of the Chronicler's tendency to exalt the cult. That this is not merely a figment of the critic's imagination is proved in the untouched portrait of the times provided by the prophets Haggai and Zechariah. Without disdaining the many values of the Chronicler's work (his account is after all the only connected one we possess for the age, even if it carries us only down to *ca.* 400), we must nevertheless use him with great caution. In keeping with a general conservative trend in Old Testament studies, the Chronicler's work is presently valued more highly than in the nineteenth century. But that is no carte blanche for sweeping claims of infallibility.

The return to Jerusalem was permitted by the edict of Cyrus. Ezra 1:1–4 understands Cyrus' action as an endorsement of Yahwism, but it was really a part of the conqueror's program of calculated leniency toward local autonomy and culture, religion included. The Cyrus cylinder reports the monarch's restoration of captured deities at a command of Marduk-Bel: "May all the gods whom I have resettled in their sacred cities ask daily Bel and Nebo for a long life for me. . . . "[1] It is possible that in his proclamation to the subject Jews Cyrus named Yahweh and professed his praise of him. But if

---

[1] Pritchard, ANET, p. 316; see Appendix 11, pp. 594–595, for the complete translation.

so, it meant nothing more than politically shrewd flattery of one of the many deities under the hegemony of Marduk-Bel.

The Chronicler reports that 42,360 Jews plus servants returned under Zerubbabel as prince and Joshua as high priest (Ezra 2:64; Neh. 7:66). The figure does not agree with the reports of Haggai and Zechariah, who imply a weak and struggling community. The number may be the total population of the restored community, counting those who had remained in Jerusalem and vicinity. The two-

The audience hall of Persian kings at Persepolis. The palace of Darius is in the background.

fold leadership of Zerubbabel[2] and Joshua was an arrangement acceptable both to the Jews and the Persians. For the Jews it secured a separation of powers that left the high priest free to perform his duties without state interference; it also meant that the prince would accept the wise counsel of his people's religion and rule with a fidelity unknown to most of the preëxilic leaders. To the Persians it assured a division of authority that would prevent a concentration of power in any single leader. Furthermore, until the coming of Nehemiah the

[2] Zerubbabel is elsewhere called Sheshbazzar (Ezra 1:8, 11; 5:16), but they probably are not the same person since both names are Babylonian.

prince was answerable to the governor of the province of Samaria, as well as to the head of the Fifth Satrapy, "Beyond the River."

Moved by a passion for the religion of his people, the Chronicler reports that the rebuilding of the temple was begun at once by the returnees. The prophets who wrote at the time do not agree. Rather they show that a period of eighteen years elapsed before the people laid the foundation of the new temple, and this was done only at the instigation of the prophets. It is obvious that the Chronicler has over-estimated the religious enthusiasm of the repatriated Jews, or at least he has overlooked the desperate economic struggle disclosed by the contemporary prophets. People did not have the means or the will to erect the temple at once. Sacrifice continued on the sacred rock where the gutted temple still stood (e.g., Jer. 41:4–5). The people were content to worship on that basis, with the hope that when a surplus of wealth allowed it a sumptuous temple could be built. Haggai and Zechariah argued in the opposite fashion: that only in an act of faith and loyalty, by putting the requirements of Yahweh worship first, could the people hope to prosper economically. In the period 520–516 the Second or Zerubbabel Temple was erected. It was not as large nor magnificent as Solomon's and it did not follow the grandiose designs of Ezekiel, but it was a triumph for the preaching of Haggai and Zechariah and a focal point for hopes of a revived Judaism.

Ideal as the appointment of Zerubbabel the prince may have seemed to Persia, there is rather substantial evidence that he plotted to reëstablish the Davidic dynasty of which he was in fact a legitimate descendant. In 522, at the death of Cyrus' son Cambyses, the empire was thrown into turmoil and open rebellion. The succession of power was insecure, and an impersonator of Cambyses' brother ruled for several months. In Zech. 6:9–14 a ceremony of coronation is described, presumably in visionary form. While Joshua is called "the Branch" (vs. 12), he is elsewhere sharply distinguished from "my servant the Branch" (3:8) and, in the coronation command, is said to stand "beside his [the Branch's] throne" (6:13). It is practically conclusive that the name of Joshua has been substituted for Zerubbabel; the probable motive was to suppress memory of an abortive messianic uprising. The Persians apparently executed or deported him, for we hear no more of Zerubbabel; but hopes of a renascent Jewish kingdom lingered on.

The half-century from Zerubbabel to Nehemiah is a virtual blank. The little community of transplanted exiles seems to have developed a rather defensive attitude toward fellow-Jews in the north, whom they regarded as less faithful to the law of Moses. Although these northerners (known by postexilic times as Samaritans) had attempted to

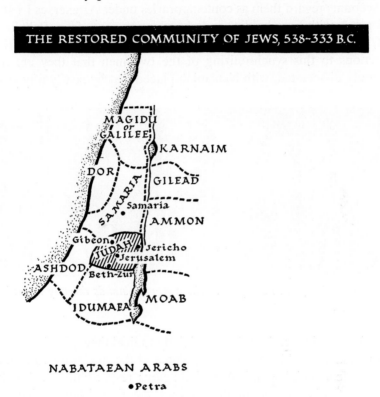

THE RESTORED COMMUNITY OF JEWS, 538-333 B.C.

MAGIDU or GALILEE

KARNAIM

DOR

GILEAD

Samaria

AMMON

Gibeon

JUDAH

Jericho

Jerusalem

ASHDOD

Beth-Zur

MOAB

IDUMAEA

NABATAEAN ARABS

•Petra

////// THE DISTRICT (PROVINCE) OF JUDAH
---- OTHER PALESTINIAN PROVINCES OF
THE FIFTH PERSIAN SATRAPY

participate in the rebuilding of the temple they were sharply rebuffed. They in turn responded with animosity and obstructed the efforts of the returnees to establish themselves. In a sense this was a projection of the older struggle between the northern and southern kingdoms, under altered circumstances that shifted the animus mainly from political to religious matters. The economic distress of the Jerusalem community was a natural result of Judah's depleted soil and her isolation from the major trade routes. How unlike the poetic exuberance of Deutero-Isaiah were the hard realities of life in the holy land!

Into this situation of partial restoration but general economic and spiritual lethargy came the reformers Nehemiah and Ezra. The biblical accounts regard them as contemporaries under Artaxerxes I (464–423 B.C.), with Ezra holding a slight edge (he came from Babylon in 458, whereas Nehemiah arrived in 444). But there are such serious objections to this synchronizing of the two men that they are now generally dissociated, with Nehemiah placed first by nearly fifty years.

Relief of Darius from Persepolis. Prince Xerxes stands directly behind the seated king.

What is the evidence for this superficially radical theory? It is doubtful that two men would have been appointed at the same time to care for the identical social, political, and religious responsibilities. The two pay no attention to one another and are mentioned only incidentally in the other's narratives. Nehemiah prepares a census and in his enumeration includes Zerubbabel's returnees but not Ezra's. Nehemiah finds the city sparsely populated and the defenses laid waste, but Ezra discovers Jerusalem active and thriving with the wall restored. Nehemiah is the contemporary of the high priest Eliashib, while Ezra lives in the time of his grandson Jehohanan. The solution to this puzzle has been to place Nehemiah in the reign of Artaxerxes I as indicated, but Ezra later, in the reign of Artaxerxes II (404–358 B.C.). In this way the biblical dates may be retained at the same time the proper sequence of the two men is restored. That the Chronicler could have made such a grievous error in chronology is not without parallel among ancient writers. The whole Persian period was a dark age in Jewish history; no sources have delineated it with exactitude or fullness. In historiography there is always a tendency to compress little-known periods and to conflate similar personalities.

The work of Nehemiah, accomplished in two visits in 444 and 432, was aimed at strengthening Judaism through the upbuilding of Jerusalem and the enforcement of high religious standards. With Persian approval he established Judah as a district apart from Samaria and he himself served as governor. In a phenomenal burst of energy the segments of the wall still leveled from the Exile were reconstructed in 52 days. Sabbath observance and tithing were enjoined upon the lax populace. Friction between the repatriated Jews and those who had not experienced exile was furthered by Nehemiah, who expelled Tobiah, a pro-Samaritan Ammonite, from the chamber he had occupied in the temple area. Particularly crucial was the prohibition of marriages with "the people of the land," i.e., anybody outside the Jerusalem community. Nehemiah was convinced that only those who had suffered exile were purged of sin and thus faithful to the religion of Moses and the prophets. To fraternize and intermarry with the inhabitants of the land would be to compromise a dearly won purity. The exiles were, in Jeremiah's terms, "a basket of good figs" (Jer. 24). This was not primarily a racial matter, for the majority of "the people of the land" could boast Jewish parentage. It was an issue of religious purity and Nehemiah seized upon the unambiguous procedure of erecting bulwarks between the pure and the impure. It would of course be difficult to separate this frame of mind from a sense of racial superiority, and the Judeans justified their feeling in part by pointing out that the Samaritan populace was a mixture of Jews and Assyrian deportees of 722 B.C. Jeremiah and Deutero-Isaiah would hardly have subscribed to such a simplification of the problem of religious purity. Still, it is conceivable that without Nehemiah's stalwart stand the Yahwism of the postexilic community would have slowly disappeared in curious syncretistic forms.

Ezra, who came to Jerusalem in 398 B.C., further solidified the community. In some respects he had to repeat Nehemiah's labors, especially in restricting marriage to members of the exilic community. It is always precarious to regulate love! His promulgation of *torah* (Neh. 8) was apparently the first step since Josiah's Deuteronomic Reform toward founding the community on the written word. *Torah* was read to the assembled people and interpreted or translated by the Levites from Hebrew to the tongue of the people, Aramaic. Whether the *torah* read on that occasion was the whole Pentateuch, the P Code, or some portion thereof, is much disputed.[3] It does seem, however, that this promulgation of the Law was a key step in the canonization of the first part of the Hebrew Scripture. Ezra's role in the exaltation of Law

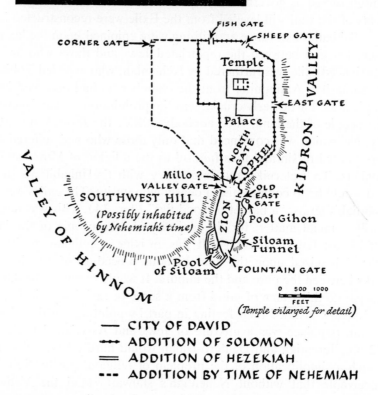

OLD TESTAMENT JERUSALEM

may have been somewhat exaggerated by the Chronicler, and we may leave open the question of the extent of Ezra's *torah;* but we must assume some such moving personality behind the postexilic ratification of Law as the basis of Jewish life. On the other hand, the development of *torah* had been rapidly accelerated by the Exile and Ezra was as much a symptom as a cause.

[3] Raymond A. Bowman, *Introduction and Exegesis of Ezra and Nehemiah* (IB, vol. 3), Abingdon, 1954, p. 733.

During Ezra's reforming career, relations with the Samaritans steadily worsened. Sanballat, governor of Samaria, and Tobiah the Ammonite (who had been expelled from Jerusalem by Nehemiah) opposed the further revival of Jerusalem as a strong Palestinian center. They lodged complaint with the Persians and whispered rumors of insurrection. Sometime after Ezra, the Samaritans made the decisive break with Jerusalem by worshiping exclusively at their own temple on Mt. Gerizim. While this has been called the Samaritan Schism, there was really little choice left to them since they were so adamantly excluded from Jerusalem. They took with them only the Law as Scripture and through the subsequent centuries, as Judaism sloughed off temple worship and turned to the synagogue and rabbinic reinterpretation of the Law, the Samaritans clung to their ancestral worship and renounced everything not found strictly in the books of Moses. The final break came between 400 and 200 B.C.; we cannot be more precise. While the Jerusalem community was seemingly the more rigid it is interesting that it developed far more broadly and deeply than did the schismatic Samaritan group. Unattractive as the exclusivism of Nehemiah and Ezra may seem to us, in the prevailing circumstances their policies were vindicated to the extent that the biblical faith did not die out in Jerusalem but remained virile and creative. But there is still the risk of unfairness to the Samaritans who in their own day could make out a convincing case against the arrogance and narrowness of their southern neighbors.

It should not be forgotten that a majority of Jews continued to live outside of the Jerusalem community. A cache of Aramaic documents from the last half of the fifth century discloses the life of a Jewish military colony at Yeb (modern Elephantine), on an island in the upper Nile. The men were mercenaries in the service of the Persians. Intermarriage with Egyptians seems to have been practiced. A form of Passover was observed and a temple to Yaho (Yahweh) built. One of the letters petitions the authorities to permit rebuilding following an anti-Semitic outburst that had resulted in the temple's destruction. The most surprising feature of the Papyri is the allusions to other deities, Ishumbethel and Anathbethel (the latter presumably a goddess), who were worshiped alongside Yaho.[4] At least this colony of dispersion Jews was considerably laxer than the Jerusalem community.

In the main the Persian period was an era of international peace and

---

[4] Pritchard, ANET, p. 491.

of consolidation for Judaism. History informs us of only one rebellion in the Syro-Palestinian provinces and that was an uprising of Phoenician cities in 351. There is no evidence that the Jews participated. With the exception of the aspirations of Zerubbabel, which appear to have been promptly quelled, Jewish attention throughout the Persian age was devoted to internal affairs. The isolation of the Jerusalem community as the bearer of a purified Judaism was by all odds the major development of the period. The Law won an undisputed place as the cornerstone of that community. The solidity and depth of this reformed Judaism was eventually to be tested by the impact of Hellenism.

POSTEXILIC PROPHECY

Prophecy in the restored Jerusalem community was set off from earlier prophecy by a deliberate and self-evident gulf. The climate of Jewish thought was as decisively changed by the fall of Jerusalem and the Exile as the climate of the modern world was transformed by the First World War. For the preëxilic prophets the salvation history of Israel involved basically the Exodus and the Conquest of the land, sometimes expanded to include the patriarchs. But for the postexilic prophets the holy history had an added chapter: the fall, the Exile, and the return. It became customary to speak of "the former prophets" (Zech. 1:4; 7:7,12). Zechariah climaxes a summary of the more recent phase of salvation history with the pointed promise of Yahweh: "As I purposed to do evil to you, when your fathers provoked me to wrath, and I did not relent, . . . so again have I purposed in these days to do good to Jerusalem and to the house of Judah; fear not" (8:14–15). The tension between the word of doom and the word of hope apparent in Jeremiah's call "to pluck up and break down, . . . to build and to plant" and the same admixture of threat and promise in Ezekiel now gives way to a primary emphasis upon the good that God will do among the people. But this by no means forbade sharp and severe words when obtuseness of heart or waywardness of life demanded them.

Basically postexilic prophecy gave itself to the task of providing a religious structure to replace the crumbled political order. It was intensely concerned with the temple. Some of the prophets were propagandists on behalf of its restoration; others fulminated against its neglect and subsidiary role in the community. These prophets, far from being antagonistic toward institutional reforms, seem to have either prepared for or reinforced the reforming zeal of Nehemiah and Ezra. In their great concern to separate the whole community from evil, the reformers and prophets were enormously influenced by Ezekiel. Through ritual fidelity and avoidance of undue intermingling with apostates the faith could be preserved; precisely as with Ezekiel, the moral requisites of faith in Israel's God were accepted without question by postexilic prophecy. While Malachi's main concern is proper ritual, his book is interspersed with declarations worthy of any of the great prophets: affirmations of the universal worship of Yahweh (1:11), the equality of fellow-Israelites (2:10), and the abhorrence of social injustice (3:5). The teaching of earlier prophets had become axiomatic, although unquestioned acceptance began to erode their radical claims. While these postexilic prophets cannot fairly be charged with neglecting the weightier matters of the law, the whole drift of Judaism was to by-pass the high call of Deutero-Isaiah to win the nations.

Most of all we are impressed by a slackening in the vitality and originality of the prophetic movement. The prophets are less distinctive and impressive persons. Their experiences of God are less dynamic and disruptive (the visions are no longer inaugural upheavals but formal devices). The cutting edge of preëxilic prophecy and the exalted consolation of exilic prophecy vanish in the face of a more pedantic and didactic concept of mission. Why this decline of prophecy? Historical and sociological reasons could be advanced. It is common to say that the law replaced prophecy, and the scribe the prophet. But this was not due to the imposition of legal apparatus that forcibly suppressed prophecy. Prophecy was slowly playing itself out; it showed signs of disintegration for a century before the work of Ezra. Actually, two processes were simultaneous: prophecy faltered and law advanced. It would be just as true to say that legalism rose to fill the void left by prophecy as to say that legalism choked off prophecy. Something in the character of the time, the defensive retreat of Judaism in a last effort at self-preservation, simultaneously stifled the voice of the prophet and strengthened the hand of the lawgiver. There is a residual mystery in this shift from prophetism to legalism, from vitality to form. Why could Greece produce only so many high quality artists and philosophers followed by centuries of imitation? The spiritual aridity of fifth-century Jerusalem is no more strange than the intellectual deprivation of third-century Athens. In each there had been moments of high promise that were not sustained. Is it because when the prophets were successful, when the Exile vindicated their insight, their message became common coin? Did men then over-simplify the prophetic solution and assume that the punishment of exile was sufficient to redress the wrong and secure an enduring di-vine-human rapport? With Ezekiel did the priest triumph over the prophet?

HAGGAI

Haggai, like his contemporary Zechariah, was chiefly remembered for the role he played in securing the temple's reconstruction. The two prophets are mentioned in historical notations in Ezra (5:1; 6:14). Haggai's book consists of four addresses dated in a span of four months during the year 520 B.C. The practice of dating oracles by year, month, and day is evidently imitative of Ezekiel, whose priestly concerns are also visible in Haggai. The superscription describes Haggai as the instrument or medium of the word of Yahweh to Zerub-babel and Joshua. This wording of the prophet's function accents the fact that Haggai was the first of the canonical prophets to secure his immediate aim from the Jewish authorities. We might protest that Haggai's aim was not high enough—the mere erection of a temple—but we should also point out that postexilic Jewish leaders were more ready to listen to a prophet who warned of the dire consequences of the neglect of Yahweh's will.

The four addresses of Haggai are not in proper sequence. Some critics have assumed that there were five addresses and that 2:15–19 is a separate oracle that should be attached to the introductory dating formula of 1:15a, "on the twenty-fourth day of the month, in the sixth month." When this modest transposition is made, the chrono-logical structure is restored:

1. Call to Rebuild the Temple   1:1–14;15b
2. Economic Bounty to Follow Rebuilding   1:15a; 2:15–19
3. The Latter and Former Temples   2:1–9
4. The Adverse Effect of Postponement   2:10–14
   of Rebuilding
5. Zerubbabel as the Messiah   2:20–23

In the first two oracles Haggai stresses the connection between the depleted economy of Jerusalem and the disregard of Yahweh worship.

The meager harvests are no excuse for failing to build the temple, for the economy will never advance until the people in an act of faith put the temple at the center of their life and give God the priority. The appeal to poverty and prosperity as sanctions is used without apology: "Consider how you have fared!" (1:5,7; cf. 2:18). The third address is intended to deal with the psychological impediment of building a temple less magnificent than the one destroyed. Older members of the restored community could remember the Solomonic temple and, looking back across 67 years, their imagination easily enhanced the lavishness of its appointments. The precious metals and fine woods of the preëxilic sanctuary could hardly be repeated. Irked by such nostalgia, the prophet vaults into the realm of imagination and describes the day when all nations would bring their treasures to glorify the house of Yahweh. We are reminded of the same expectation in Isaiah 56–66. There is no clue as to whether Haggai anticipates the Gentiles' voluntary acknowledgment of Yahweh or whether it will be accomplished through apocalyptic upheaval or wars of conquest. Whatever the means, he is certain that "the latter splendor of this house shall be greater than the former."

The fourth address is cryptic. If taken literally it declares that sacrifice offered without a temple is unclean. The whole nation is thereby defiled. Others have regarded the oracle as a symbolic reference to mixing with the Samaritans; the contact of holy and unholy does not lead to the sanctification of the baser but rather to the pollution of the higher. Evil company corrupts! Since the Samaritans are not named, however, it is better to interpret the oracle as a parable impressing upon the restored community the fact that it is easier to pass on evil than good, and especially so in the matter of intentions. It thus teaches the adverse effect of postponement. Putting off the rebuilding of the temple sours the whole religious life of the nation; the resolve to rebuild, on the other hand, is of no significance until it is carried out in action. Each of these interpretations involves a considerable element of subjectivity, but the latter seems most appropriate to the context.

The final address is an open endorsement of Zerubbabel as the reviver of the dynasty of David. Though the title "messiah" is not employed and he is called simply "governor of Judah," the prophet expects a cosmic catastrophe to break heathen kingdoms and thereby to remove all opposition to Zerubbabel whom Yahweh will "make like a signet ring." This allusion is to Jeremiah 22:24 where the rejected

Jehoiachin is likened to a signet ring on Yahweh's hand which he tears off and throws into the hand of Nebuchadnezzar. Haggai announces that Yahweh is to give back the ring, i.e., the foreign powers will surrender the hostage people of Israel who will rule as the sole world power. The part that Haggai (and Zechariah) may have played in agitating for the messianic kingdom is unknown. If there was a revolt the Chronicler is silent about it; from the prophetic books it is not clear that human instrumentality was anticipated. It may be that Haggai and Zechariah frowned upon military action, but that Zerubbabel, infatuated by the prophetic promises, took matters into his own hands. At any rate Haggai's position in Jewish religion is securer as the prophet of the Second Temple than as a messianist.

ZECHARIAH

Three dates in the book (1:1,7; 7:1) locate the ministry of Zechariah in the period 520–518 B.C. While he shared Haggai's cultic concerns the weight of his message is elsewhere than on the rebuilding of the temple. Presumably Haggai had carried on so vigorous a campaign that the foundation had been laid and work was going on apace; Zechariah could assume that the restoration of the cult center would be carried through. Like Ezekiel, what engaged his attention was a passion for the purification of the community. Ritual and moral uncleanness must be extirpated. Zechariah sees this purgation of the Jews as associated with world-wide destruction of evil.

Vision is the chief vehicle of Zechariah's prophecy. The bulk of his book is given over to eight night visions that employ formal and material elements from preëxilic prophecy, especially Amos, but are stamped with the baroque weirdness and unnaturalness of Ezekiel's mind. Zechariah is the first prophet for whom the vision is incontestably a literary vehicle. The inner fire of Ezekiel's inspiration is quenched and in its place appears the strictly didactic use of the vision. We are thus on the boundary between prophecy and apocalyptic. The strange symbolisms are deciphered for the prophet by an interpreting angel, and the unearthiness of the action often points to God's violent disruption of history rather than his working in history. But the distinction is only relative, as in Ezekiel, and there is a clear difference between the work of Zechariah in chapters 1–8 and the universal apocalyptic perspectives of chapters 9–14, even though the latter chapters are not as symbolic. The situation presupposed by Deutero-Zechariah (chaps. 9–14) is the later Macedonian period.

An editor has prefaced the visions with a strong appeal to the people to hear the word of Yahweh, which is mightier than the sinful forefathers and mightier even than the obedient prophets. The participants in the holy history of old have passed away, but the same divine word impinges on the present and must be heeded. The visions are introduced by flexible use of the Amos-like formula, "What do you see?" asked by the angelic guide, followed by the prophet's comment, "I lifted my eyes and saw and behold . . . !" There are eight visions in all:

1. Four Horsemen   1:7–17
2. Four Horns and Smiths   1:18–21
3. Measuring Line   2:1–5
4. Joshua and the Satan   3:1–10
5. Two Olive Trees and Lampstand   4:1–5,10b–14
6. Flying Scroll   5:1–4
7. Woman in the Bushel   5:5–11
8. Four Chariots   6:1–7

There is a certain logic to the order. The opening and closing visions of the four horsemen and chariots as harbingers of world destruction form a frame for the other visions. The middle two feature the communal leaders Joshua and Zerubbabel. The sixth and seventh are lurid symbols of the extreme measures needed to expel sin from the community. Whether Zechariah or an editor was responsible for the sequence is uncertain.

Among the arresting features of the sequence is the inversion of Amos' vision of the plumbline. The city of Jerusalem is to be so heavily populated and will so expand beyond the present limits that a man about to survey for the rebuilding of the walls is advised to desist: "Jerusalem shall be inhabited as villages without walls, . . . For I will be to her a wall of fire round about, says Yahweh, and I will be the glory within her." The appearance of *the* Satan (not a proper name but a functional term meaning "the accuser") is probably the first in Jewish literature, depending upon the date of Job. He appears as the archaccuser against Joshua whom he claims to be defiled, but Yahweh intervenes and abolishes the sin of the old priesthood (or the land itself) and the righteousness of God is substituted. Against this action of God, the Satan is impotent. The Satan is at this point in Jewish thought not the supreme originator of evil but one of the angelic beings whose task it is to search for evil and bring it to God's attention. At this stage he is not even a tempter to evil (thus, for example, there is no basis for

regarding the serpent of the J fall story as the Satan). Yet once introduced into the tradition, the Satan was to grow more malignant and to
assume a central place in speculations about the origin of evil.

A solemn pronouncement in 4:6–10a that Zerubbabel will complete
the temple in spite of serious obstacles is widely conceded to interrupt
the vision of the lampstand and the olive trees. When removed, the
vision is more compact and its main point clear: Zerubbabel and
Joshua are to have prominent places in the dispatch of Yahweh's will
and are to be obeyed. The details of the vision are nevertheless obscure.
Is the lampstand the community of Jews or the symbol of God's all-
seeing presence? (Its seven branches are called "the eyes of Yahweh"
in vs. 10.)

Tacked onto the visions is the promise that Zerubbabel the Branch
(the Davidic shoot from the preëxilic stump) would rule in perfect
accord with Joshua the priest. Zechariah, like Haggai, connects rebuilding the temple with the full rule of the messiah who will enlist not
only the consent of the nations but their active participation. The
eschatology of this prophet is hopeful in the extreme.

Zechariah closes with a long discourse built around an inquiry
about the continuation of the fast days in the fifth and seventh months
(7:1–3; also fourth and tenth months in 8:18) at which the inhabitants of Palestine had annually celebrated the city's tragic fall. The
prophet's reply bears close study. He believes that the fasts should be
discontinued but he does not call for unrestrained festivity in their
place. The promise of God's imminent action is inextricably connected with the repentance and new life of the community. The wonderful love of God toward sinful Jerusalem should awaken the resolve
and power to live by the moral precepts of the former prophets. There
is no cult activity, whether of sacrifice or festival, that can be meaningful without change of heart. The old fasts "shall be to the house of
Judah seasons of joy and gladness, and cheerful feasts; therefore love
truth and peace" (8:19). The discourse comes to a resounding
climax as Zechariah foresees the conversion of the nations. It is his belief that the restored temple will be the lodestone attracting the peoples
of the earth to Yahweh: "In those days ten men from the nations of
every tongue shall take hold of the robe of a Jew, saying, 'Let us go
with you, for we have heard that God is with you.' " So these postexilic prophets were able to embrace ritual and moral demands, particular and universal hopes without trace of contradiction.

MALACHI

Although placed at the close of the Twelve Prophets, and in the English versions at the end of the Old Testament, Malachi is not the last Old Testament writing. It dates after the restoration of the temple and probably before the reforms of Ezra, since he denounces the mixed marriages that Ezra put an end to. The prophet's name is probably a sobriquet, for it means simply "my messenger." The work may be deliberately anonymous. The term *massa'* ("burden" or "oracle") not only introduces this book but appears in Zechariah 9:1 and 12:1. It has been suggested with plausibility that Zechariah 9–11, 12–14, and Malachi were three anonymous documents assembled at the close of the Twelve, the first two becoming associated by editorial accident with Zechariah while the latter retained its independence.

Of the eleven oracles in the book, six are dialogues (marked below with asterisks): a statement of Yahweh is followed by the rejoinder of the people that leads to further argumentation by Yahweh:

*1. Against Edom	1:2–5
*2. Against Imperfect Sacrifices	1:6–14
3. Against Infidelity of the Priests	2:1–9
4. Against Infidelity in Marriage (?)	2:10–12
*5. Against Divorce	2:13–16
*6. Against Injustice	2:17
7. The Promised Messenger of Purgation	3:1–5
*8. Tithing	3:6–12
*9. Against Practical Atheism	3:13–15
10. Book of Remembrance	3:16–18
11. Day of the Lord and Elijah Returned	4:1–5

In a general way the earlier oracles (Nos. 1–6) have to do with current communal practice and the later ones (Nos. 7–11) with eschatology. Some of the oracles are vaguely phrased and their point imprecise (esp. 3 and 4). The book permits brief insight into the attitudes and practices of the fifth-century Jerusalem community. The dislike of the Judeans for their enemies, in this case Edomites, is strongly voiced; in fact, Malachi couples the assurance of God's love for Jacob with his hatred of Esau. (The prophetic book of Obadiah, a bitter oracle of doom on Edom, comes no doubt from the same milieu as Malachi.)

The prophet chides the priests who offer blemished animals and act faithlessly against Yahweh's "covenant with Levi," and he berates the laity who withhold their tithes. His concern for Judah extends, however, to issues not strictly cultic. Marriage is lightly regarded by those who dismiss their wives on a pretext. Justice is ignored by those who ask mockingly, "Where is the God of justice?" Dissatisfaction with the working out of the promised rewards and punishments has led many to say, "It is vain to serve God." Overstress on the visible rewards of faith was having its repercussions; Job was simply the most thoughtful and searching of innumerable protests against a view of religion that was a virtual divine-human barter system offering man's service in return for God's favor.

Malachi develops the eschatological theme of a messenger who is to precede the coming of Yahweh. The "messenger of the covenant" brings judgment and perfects the purgative self-offering of Judah. The wicked are cut off, for God makes a clear distinction between righteous and wicked. The next to last oracle speaks of "the sun of righteousness" who is probably no person at all but simply the personification of God's righteous blessing upon those who pass through the oven fires of judgment. Elijah is announced as the harbinger of the Day of the Lord who seeks the reconciliation of Israelites before the curse of punishment strikes them. Whether "messenger of the covenant" and "Elijah the prophet" are the same person is problematic; but it has been customary, in keeping with New Testament practice, for Christians to apply both images of a forerunner to John the Baptist (Mark 1:2; 9:12; Matt. 11:10; 17:10–13; Luke 1:17). Malachi also contains the first explicit reference to the heavenly Book of Life, later to become a prominent motif in apocalyptic writing.

Isaiah 56–66

"Trito-Isaiah" is the term with which some scholars have dignified this loose collection of poetic oracles. What sets them off from the work of Deutero-Isaiah is the difference in historical setting and religious tenor permeating a majority of the poems. In general the same high literary quality of chapters 40–55 continues to the end of Isaiah, although some of the poems are disappointingly insipid.

The changed situation is the return to Palestine. A large number of the poems presuppose the rebuilt temple and the reinstitution of sacrifice. The sanctuary is described as "a house of prayer for all peoples" (56:7). Foreigners and eunuchs who hold fast to the worship of Yahweh are highly praised (56:1–8). Fast days in the holy city are described (58:1–12), and there is a manifest concern with Sabbath observance (58:13–14). Such cultic scrupulosity is a far cry from Deutero-Isaiah who never mentions the temple and speaks only incidentally of ritual.

Former sins are beginning to creep in once more. There is a stinging rebuke of the types of syncretism that had perverted Yahwism before the city's fall and were again resurgent (chap. 58). Social injustice and sheer callousness toward the covenant are assailed (chap. 59). Even the leadership of the restored community is not without fault; the culpable are described under the cryptic figures of "beasts," "dumb dogs," and "shepherds" (56:9–12). It is apparent that the ecstatic hope that had stirred Deutero-Isaiah was considerably deflated by the actuality of return to Palestine.

Some of the authentic poems of Deutero-Isaiah may have been preserved in the miscellany of Isaiah 56–66. The section 57:14–20 and the greater part of chapters 60–62 seem to belong appropriately to the situation and style of the exilic prophet. Similar agitation of style, the announcement of the return, the gathering of the nations, and even a Servant Song (61:1–4), favor the hypothesis. At least one poem (63:1–9) implies that the Exile is still in effect but it has a lamenting appeal to God not elsewhere paralleled in chapters 40–66. There is no better example in the Old Testament of the haphazard editing of materials than these chapters where the poems of the "school" of Deutero-Isaiah have been gathered at random.

True fasting is the subject of one of the most provocative poems:

Is not this the fast that I choose:
  to loose the bonds of wickedness,
  to undo the thongs of the yoke,
to let the oppressed go free,
  and to break every yoke?
Is it not to share your bread with the hungry,
  and to bring the homeless poor into your house;
When you see the naked, to cover him,
  and not to hide yourself from your own flesh? (58:6–7).

Several poems emphasize the self-vindicating action of God, both in restoring his people to their land and in punishing the wicked among them and among the nations. Yahweh alone is righteous and efficacious (note especially 59:15*b*–20, which has influenced Eph. 6:10–17, and Isa. 63: 1–9). In two passages God is addressed as the

Father of Israelites (63:16; 64:8). The vision of a new heaven and new earth has influenced the New Testament book of Revelation (chapters. 65–66); apocalyptic thought with its hideous symbols and bizarre ideas prevails at the close of the book.

The earliest poems in the collection come from the latter part of the Exile; the latest decry the lax morality and worship of the restored community and depict the new heaven and the new earth. The compilation could have been completed at most any time between 516, when the temple was rebuilt, and 444, when Nehemiah corrected many of the religious abuses lamented in the poems.

JOEL

The prophet Joel, son of Pethuel, was a citizen of Jerusalem during a catastrophic locust plague of the sort Amos had once seen (7:1). Joel pictures the swarms of locusts as an invading army devastating the countryside. The description is enlivened by the use of at least seven action words to depict the locusts (e.g., "cutters," "hoppers," "swarmers," "destroyers," etc.). The plague assumes the role of a divine instrument of punishment upon the people and priests of Jerusalem. In oracles whose prophetic brilliance carry us back to preëxilic idiom, Joel calls upon leaders and worshipers to mourn and repent. Faced with the stripping of vegetation so that there were no cereal or drink offerings to bring to the temple, the prophet calls for repentance and promises the mercy of God:

> "Yet even now," says Yahweh,
>   "return to me with all your heart,
> with fasting, with weeping, and with mourning;
>   and rend your hearts and not your garments" (2:12).

In Joel's mind the locust swarm coalesces with the Day of Yahweh. This may be partially poetic exuberance, but it seems to prepare for the last part of the book, which is cosmic in scope and wherein the Day is a violent judgment on the nations. Scholars are divided as to whether the same prophet wrote 1:1–2:27 and 2:28–3:21. There is an evident difference in temper and perspective, although the career of one man might have been broad enough to encompass both. In the apocalyptic appendix universal ecstasy is expected as the endowment of God's spirit on humankind. The nations are held in disdain and the wonderful promise of peace in Isaiah 2 and Micah 4 is actually reversed:

> Beat your plowshares into swords,
>> and your pruning hooks into spears;
>> let the weak say, "I am a warrior" (3:10).

A battle with the heathen nations is expected in the Valley of Jehoshaphat ("God judges") where they will be destroyed, as in the case of Gog of Magog (Ezekiel 38–39).

Joel's career probably fell between Nehemiah and the middle of the next century (450–350 B.C.). The Exile is presupposed and only Judah and Jerusalem are mentioned (no northern tribes). No kings are named or alluded to. The walls have been rebuilt. Some have placed Joel among the earliest prophets (ninth or eighth century) because of the location of his book second among the Twelve. Recently a Scandinavian scholar has dated the prophet about 600, contemporary with Jeremiah.[5] Yet the weight of the evidence points to the postexilic age, in spite of some scholars having treated the locust prophecy of Joel as preëxilic and the apocalyptic section as a postexilic anonymous writing.

Joel is distinguished as an able poet-prophet, but his message is not noteworthy beyond certain common prophetic themes that he enunciated with earnestness and poetic flashes reminiscent of the eighth-century giants.

In all the postexilic prophets there is a tenacious holding onto the central prophetic conviction that the whole people must live under the will of God. There is a tendency for this claim to be implemented institutionally and for the universal perspective to be sacrificed to more limited interests. There is a formality and an atmosphere of historical stagnation impeding the further action of God. Haggai, Zechariah, Malachi, and the poets of Isaiah 56–66 were prophets who had in a sense outlived prophecy. They may be more aptly understood as preaching and teaching priests, constructors of a new order, more concerned with building than with tearing down. At the same time all of them, especially Zechariah and Joel, point strongly in the direction of apocalyptic. In the conscience of all is lodged the indelible memory

[5] A. S. Kapelrud, *Joel Studies,* Almquist & Wiksells, 1948, pp. 191 f.

of the high covenant demands that even the "purified" community dare not flout. And in the soul of each is the scar of judgment.

THE PRIESTLY CODE

The last stratum of the Pentateuch to be completed was the so-called Priestly or P source. Early nineteenth-century critics often called it G since it formed the groundplan or framework of the Pentateuch (German *Grundschrift*). It was only when Karl Graf correctly discerned that this framework was written last—and not earliest—that the Documentary Hypothesis fell into place. Wellhausen preferred to call it Q (for Latin *quattuor*, "four") since in his opinion the basic theme of the document was the four covenants with Adam, Noah, Abraham, and Moses. More recently Bentzen has suggested A for "the Aaronitic laws" rather than P, for he notes a measure of priestly interest in J and E and still more in D. But the symbol P for Priestly source seems firmly entrenched.

The Characteristics and Purpose of P

Since three earlier accounts of Israel's beginnings had already been prepared (J, E, and D), why was a fourth written? The earlier sources arose in times of political independence and even the extensive legislation of Deuteronomy had features, such as holy war, that were inapplicable to the postexilic community. There was a keenly felt need for an aetiology of the ritual practice of Judaism. Yet the code was no ad hoc fabrication, for much of the vast collection of tradition was rooted in the preëxilic period. It contained elements of varying age but when finally published its intent was to provide the postexilic Judean community with a distinctively Jewish way of life. The fundamental ritual practices of Judaism were traced to their inception in the Mosaic covenant, and in some cases to the early covenants with Abraham and Noah, and even with Adam.

Of the three Pentateuchal sources that tell the story of Israel from pre-Mosaic times onward (D is thus exempted), P is shortest on narrative and longest on legal praxis. The bony structure that holds the work together is the genealogical scheme, which only occasionally is broadened out to include narration. Where stories are incorporated they have passed the muster of genealogical, ritual, or institutional import. In the Abraham traditions, for example, P focuses upon the establishment of circumcision (Genesis 17) and the purchase of the Cave of Machpelah as a burial place for Sarah (Genesis 23). In Genesis the "generations" formula marks off the several divisions of the stratum: "these are the generations of" (2:4; 5:1; 6:9; 10:1; 11:10,27; 25:12,19; 36:1,9; 37:2). The whole work is articulated around three covenants: the first with Noah, sealed by the rainbow; the second with Abraham, enjoining circumcision; and the third with Moses, introducing the Law. Although not explicitly described in Genesis 1, a fourth covenant, contracted with Adam and stipulating Sabbath observance, is likely. The articulation of parts in the P source made a convenient framework for the final editors of the Pentateuch. It is generally agreed that the Priestly writers prepared a separate history of the beginnings, even though they were well acquainted with JE (probably combined by the Exile) and with D as well. The Priestly writers make too many distinctive emphases and at points are too antagonistic to the other sources (e.g., they favor the Aaronite priesthood instead of the Zadokite) to have been satisfied with merely enlarging or touching them up. The final editors chose to sandwich sections of JE into the outline of P, thus creating the present Genesis–Numbers.

The date of P is arrived at only through approximation. The preexilic era shows no sign of P legislation in operation. In Judges and Samuel laymen offer sacrifice at "unconsecrated" spots and the arrangements for the ark are far simpler than those given in Exodus 35–40 and Numbers 3–4. Many of the distinctive features of P are not mentioned at all in the preëxilic history: Day of Atonement, year of Jubilee, Levitical cities. In fact, a much simpler cultic ethos is apparent, a "different *tone of feeling*, . . . both the actors and the narrators in Judges [and] Samuel move in an atmosphere into which the spirit of P has not penetrated."[6] Likewise, Deuteronomy knows nothing of P either by direct reference, quotation, or allusion. It is strange that two major legal corpora should have influenced one another so little. The first affinities with P appear in Ezekiel, who gave impetus to the Priestly movement. The religious conceptions of the Priestly writers point to the Exile and later: the revelatory form of the glory of Yahweh, the suppression of anthropomorphisms, Yahweh as Creator,

[6] S. R. Driver, *Introduction to the Literature of the Old Testament*, T. & T. Clark, new rev. ed., 1910, p. 137.

the conception of holiness, and distance between God and man. The Priestly theological interests and the modes of expression find their closest parallels in Ezekiel and Deutero-Isaiah. Thus, while it contains ancient traditional data (note for example the traditions underlying the creation and flood stories, and the primitive ordeal for determining a wife's faithfulness by giving her bitter water, Num. 5), in its present form the P source must be regarded as a postexilic creation.

A preponderance of legal over narrative data, a tendency accelerated in each successive Pentateuchal stratum, is at its ultimate in P:

1. *The Traditions of the Beginnings: Genesis 1–11*

The Creation Story (Sabbath)	1:1–2:4a
Genealogy from Adam to Noah	5:1–28,30–32
The Flood	6:9–22
	7:6,11,13–16a,18–21
	8:1–2a,3b–5,13a,14–19
The Covenant with Noah (Rainbow)	9:1–17, 28–29
Sons of Shem, Ham, and Japheth (The Table of the Nations)	10:1–7,20,22–23,31–32
Genealogy from Shem to Abram	11:10–27

2. *The Traditions of the Patriarchs: Genesis 12–50*

Terah Journeys from Ur to Haran	11:31–32
Abram Journeys from Haran to Canaan	12:4b–5
Lot Chooses the Cities of the Valley	13:6,11b,12a (. . . in the cities of the valley)
Hagar Bears Ishmael	16:1a,3,15–16
Covenant with Abraham (Circumcision)	17:1–27
Lot Rescued from the Cities	19:29
Birth of Isaac	21:2b–5 (at the time . . .)
Death and Burial of Sarah at Hebron	23:1–20
Death and Burial of Abraham	25:7–11a
Sons of Ishmael	25:12–17
Birth of Esau and Jacob	25:19–20,26b
Esau's Wives	26:34
Jacob Seeks a Wife in Paddan-aram	27:46–28:9
Jacob's Return to Canaan	31:18b; 33:18a

Dinah and the Shechemites	34:1–2a,4,8–10,13–18,20–24, 27–29
Jacob Becomes Israel	35:9–13,15
Sons of Jacob	35:22b–26
Death and Burial of Isaac	35:27–29
Descendants of Esau	36
Preface to History of Jacob's Family	37:1–2a
Joseph in Pharaoh's Service	41:46
Genealogy of Jacob's Descendants	46:8–27
Jacob Settled in Egypt	47:5–6a (. . . best of the land), 7–11,27b–28
Jacob Blesses Joseph's Sons	48:3–7
Death and Burial of Jacob in Hebron	49:29–33; 50:12–13

3. *The Traditions of the Exodus: Exodus 1–15*

Egyptian Oppression of Jacob's Sons	1:1–5,7,13–14
God Remembers His People	2:23b–25
Call of Moses and Aaron to Deliver Israel	6:2–7:13
The Plagues	
Nile Turned to Blood	7:19–20a,21b–22
Frogs	8:5–7
Gnats	8:16–19
Boils	9:8–12
Summary	11:9–10
The Passover	12:1–20,28; 13:1–2
The Journey from Ramses to the Sea	12:37,40–51; 13:20; 14:1–4
The Deliverance at the Sea	14:8–9, 15–18, 21ac (omit J: "and Yahweh drove the sea" through "made the sea dry land"), 22–23,26–27a,28–29; 15:19

4. *The Wilderness and Covenant Traditions (Sinai): Exodus 16–Numbers 35*

| Quail and Manna in the Wilderness of Sin | 16:1–3,6–24,31–36 |
| From Sin to Sinai | 17:1a; 19:1–2a |

Appointed Offerings	28–29
Vows	30
Defeat of the Midianites	31
Itinerary of the Israelites from Egypt to Moab	33
Boundaries of Canaan	34
Cities of Refuge	35

Confusions in the P traditions are especially evident in Leviticus and Numbers. It is apparent, for example, that Leviticus 17–26 (Holiness Code) was at one time a separate entity and has been included without notation. The compact section on offerings in Leviticus 1–7 (often called Sacrificial *Torah*) was probably separate and the writer-editor did not attempt to combine with it the other provisions for sacrifice as reported in Numbers 7, 15, and 28–29. Although P closes his account with a careful itinerary of the wilderness wanderings, practically none of the locations are known; throughout the source the migrations of the Israelite tribes are subordinated to an elaboration of ritual prescriptions. In fact, the way the source now stands, the *Torah* prescriptions are spread out over the whole trip from Sinai to the plains of Moab, contrary to JE where all the legislation is given at the mountain. It is this mass of legal data, disorganized and disparate, that leads critics to presuppose a number of writers or at least a complex editing in the Priestly source. The stratum is a conflate, with greater homogeneity in Genesis–Exodus than in Leviticus–Numbers. Apparently several priestly recensions of the Law and attached codicils or riders were compiled without concern for topical or chronological order.

From a thoughtful perusal of the Priestly source the student concludes that the goal of Yahweh's relation with Israel was the founding of the theocracy in which the Mosaic cultus would be faithfully guarded and administered by a pure priesthood. Salvation history required the possession of the land and the formation of the Davidic kingdom (Gen. 17:6,8); but these never rivaled the Mosaic Law, for it was by the Sabbath, circumcision, festivals, and sacrificial system that the postexilic follower of Yahweh identified himself. The experiment with royalty and power politics had been an unhappy interlude in the genuine history of Israel. Of supreme moment was loyalty to the hallmarks of Judaism that could be enforced apart from place or political circumstance. So thoroughly was this conviction ingrained

that even though one of the major aspects of the P ritual, the temple
and its sacrifices, gradually diminished in importance and eventually
disappeared, the others were able to absorb the shock and to provide
a common body of practice. P stands with Ezekiel as the ardent propo-
nent of the reconstituted community of the Jews: in effect, a church of
politically disinherited who bear a common religious identity through
individual consent to duty. It is no wonder that the political and
broadly historical aspects of the source are negligible.

The reader is quickly aware of the inflated and labored style of the
P source with its wearisome repetitions. Nevertheless in some passages,
such as the Creation story, it attains a marvelous sonority. Pedantic
minds are behind the composition and, even if they had been stylistically gifted, juridical items are difficult to spice up. The limit of tedium
is reached when the exact directions for making the ark, tabernacle,
and priestly appointments are followed by a detailed account of the finished products, corresponding verbatim with the original directives!
This is a fine example of "the epic law of repetition," commonly illustrated in ancient Near Eastern documents, and perfectly suited to the
priestly love of detail. For the same reason some Bible readers never
get beyond the last chapters of Exodus. Among the familiar terms of P
are: "to be fruitful and multiply," "after their families," "throughout
your generations," "he was gathered to his fathers," "this selfsame
day," "establish a covenant" (rather than "cut" as in JE), "this is the
thing which Yahweh has commanded," *nephesh* in the sense of "person," *gulgoleth,* "skull" or "head" with reference to enumerations of
people (as when we say, "so many 'head' of cattle"), *matteh* for "tribe"
(JE *shebet*), Kiriath-arba for Hebron, and Paddan-aram for Aram-
naharaim (homeland of Laban).

P AS THEOLOGIAN

Yet it would be a mistake to minimize the genuine theological dimensions of the P source. It reflects a stanch monotheism and a sense
of divine holiness and transcendence similar to Ezekiel and Deutero-
Isaiah. There is a keen appreciation of Israel's creation and sustenance
by the sheer mystery of divine revelation and grace. The finished tabernacle receives the *kabodh* of Yahweh, the abiding presence of God
with his people. Whereas for JE the pillar of cloud and fire was a temporary guide through the desert, for P the *kabodh* Yahweh is his enduring presence in the cult. The whole apparatus of worship and sacri-

fice is a gift of grace, a channel for unclean man to approach a holy God. Atonement is a divine provision. Motivating and suffusing the legal stipulations is a spirit of the numinous. The Holy One condescends to reveal an order of life by which his people may approach him. Anglo-Catholic scholars have been able expositors of this long-neglected aspect of Old Testament religion.[7]

The early chapters of Genesis have a broad-visioned conception of the cosmos under one God. P sees all men beneath the aegis of Israel's Lord (note the Table of Nations in Genesis 10), yet Yahweh has selected a special people for the sake of his glory, to manifest his holiness. Like Calvin in later centuries, P assumes a rather stark doctrine of the election of the faithful (there is no predestination of the damned as in Calvin). Of course J had previously brought the universal and Israelite strains together in one epic. The difference between J and P is the difference between the tenth and fifth centuries. The Priestly writer's position is more settled and polemical; it has been arrived at by much challenge and doubt, refined during centuries when the election of Israel was often under attack. The Exile was a critical testing period: In the light of Israel's political decline, could Israel really be the people of the one God or indeed of any effective God at all? Did not her fate belie her faith? The Jewish contacts with Babylonian and Persian culture and religion would inevitably force Israel to consider on what basis she could make her claim to special election. In short, the world seemed very large and bewildering in its many claims to truth. Was Yahweh of old operative in this new situation and was Israel still his own? The Priestly source gives the assured answer of post-exilic Judaism to the threat of religious meaninglessness. In this sense the work is not only a quasi-historical and legal document but an apology for Judaism.

CREATION IN BABYLON AND ISRAEL

The Priestly story of creation, although written much later than the Yahwist's story of the beginnings, has been introduced as a grand exordium to the Pentateuch. In the tremendous scope and pristine beauty of the account, the symmetry and magnitude of the creative acts, the editors saw a fitting way to introduce the wonderful works of

[7] A. G. Hebert, *The Authority of the Old Testament,* Faber & Faber, 1947, especially pp. 148–158; W. J. Phythian-Adams, *The People and the Presence,* Oxford University Press, 1942.

Israel's God. The order and number of the acts of creation differ in the early Yahwist and the late Priestly versions:

J		P (numbered by days)	
waterless waste	2:4*b*–6	watery chaos	1:2
man	2:7–8	1. light	1:3–5
plants	2:9	2. firmament	1:6–8
animals	2:18–20	3. dry land and seas	1:9–10
woman	2:21–24	vegetation	1:11–13
		4. heavenly bodies	1:14–19
		5. marine life and birds	1:20–23
		6. land animals	1:24–25
		man (male and female)	1:26–29

While the P account reads with measured dignity, here and there are telltale evidences that the narrative is composite. For one thing, eight creative acts are compressed into six days, with two occurring on the third and sixth days. An originally untimed story appears to have been accommodated to the conception of a six-day divine work week, culminating in Sabbath observance. The obligation of Sabbath worship upon universal man is both naïve and profound! All men must rest on the Sabbath because God himself rested on the seventh day. The stipulation confers on man the privilege of repeating the divine rhythm of work and rest, of participating with God in the sequence of creation and contemplation, of activity and passivity. Another indication of an underlying source that has been reworked by the Priestly writers is the contrast between creation by *fiat* ("And God said, 'Let there be . . .' and there was . . ." on the first and third days) and by *works* ("And God made or created . . ." on the other days). Furthermore, light already exists before the fashioning of the heavenly bodies, but that may be simply a feature of ancient cosmogony—on the theory that the heavenly bodies exist mainly to govern the festivals and seasons rather than give light, which exists independently.

The world envisioned by the writer is the Babylonian cosmos, the universe of flat earth and arched firmament, with waters below and above. This conception of the universe underlies the whole Old Testament. The closest parallels to the orderly survey of Genesis 1 are the speech of Yahweh in Job 38 and the nature hymn of Psalm 104.

Babylonian mythology regarded Marduk-Bel as the creator in the sense that it was he, with the assistance of the younger gods like Ea, who overthrew the rule of the older deities and their chosen combatant Tiamat. Her carcass cut asunder became the earth and the firmament of the extant world. Out of malignant chaos the order of nature and society was wrought by Marduk who is Lord of the seasonal rhythm of nature and the structures of civilization. The forces of chaos are not totally subdued, however; they threaten to return in drought or storm or military catastrophe. The annual New Year's Festival had as one of its prime aims the reëstablishment of cosmic order through the recita-

THE HEBREW CONCEPTION OF THE UNIVERSE

The Hebrew conception of the universe assumed a flat earth supported over a watery abyss. A solid firmament held back the waters above the earth and to it were attached the heavenly bodies. At the outermost limits of the earth a circular range of mountains supported the firmament.

tion of the victory of Marduk over Tiamat. A comparison of the Priestly account of creation with the Babylonian *Enuma Elish* shows startling similarities and more startling differences.[8]

In positing the existence of watery chaos that must be overcome and controlled, the two versions agree. Strictly speaking, there is no *creatio ex nihilo,* "creation out of nothing," in either account, for the potential material of creation is present and partially resistant. The Priestly term *tehom,* "the deep," is linguistically related to Babylonian

[8] See Appendix 1, pp. 565–575.

Tiamat, goddess of the chaotic deep. In some respects the notion is close to Platonic nonbeing or matter, the undifferentiated substance out of which individual earthly realities are formed. But the abyss or deep in Semitic thought does not have an ideational meaning imposed on it; there are no equivalents to Plato's realm of ideas or forms. The deity who acts upon the unformed substance represents dynamism and volition. Also, the abyss itself has a personal, rebellious character that is more than personification. It is not merely "nonbeing." It is "antibeing," struggling against the creative will that would subdue and remold it. It is crucial that when Jewish thought began to speculate about the origin of evil it was not satisfied with the recalcitrance or lag of the material of creation but preferred the explanation of personal and rebellious will in the form of fallen angels.

In the Priestly rendition, however, the primeval chaos or *tehom* recedes into virtual impotence before the absolute and sovereign Lord. The writer does not deal with philosophical questions such as whether anything existed before God began to create. But the relatively minor role given to chaos (in the Babylonian myth there had to be a titanic struggle before it was subdued) and the sublime freedom of the Creator evince a conception of God and creation that a more philosophical mind would describe by *creatio ex nihilo*. Later apocalyptic thought asserted the same control of God over the chaos at the end of time. But already in prophetic and Priestly thought Yahweh God is supreme Lord of the chaos. The consequence is that man need fear nothing in his experience, since all is God's. But at the same time he has an ultimate reckoning with the One who controls all. These aspects of the conquest of chaos are never touched in Babylonian thought for there is no monotheism, no prophetic interpretation, and no eschatology in Mesopotamian myth.

Both accounts show similar basic stages in the fashioning of the cosmos. The identical creative acts are involved, although sometimes in different order, which may be due to the gaps in the Babylonian text. Especially noticeable is the initial act establishing the condition for all the following works of the gods: the separation and containment of the waters by means of the solid earth below and the solid firmament above. In both we find light existing apart from the heavenly bodies whose significance lies in the fixing of the calendar. (The Babylonians named the signs of the zodiac and made considerable strides

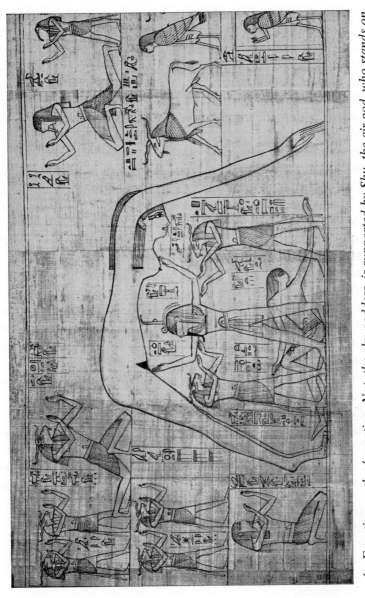

An Egyptian myth of creation. Nut, the sky goddess, is supported by Shu, the air god, who stands on Geb, the earth god.

in the rudiments of astronomy.) There can be little doubt about the common source of both cosmogonies in a similar conception of the structure of the world.

But the broad similarities in the stages do not cloak the fact that the divinities in the Babylonian story are themselves part and parcel of the creation. The gods have evolved ultimately out of Apsu and Tiamat, who are personified fresh water and salt water. Although Marduk's alignment against Tiamat gives a dramatic picture of the opposition of creation and chaos, it is apparent that no monotheistic conception gives absolute power or centrality to the work of Marduk. The theogony so distributes and diffuses authority that Marduk's lordship is really an imperialistic extension of the supremacy of Babylon, of which he was the patron deity. By contrast we have noted the absence of any trace of theogony in either the J or P accounts. Yahweh is underived. The only hints of polytheism are the references to *tehom* and the divine consultation, "Let *us* make . . . ," but to the author the original connotations of both have been lost. *Tehom* is for him merely the Creator's material. The plural "us" is a metaphorical allusion to the divine cortege, the king of the universe addressing his attendants. Monotheism in the sense of denying the existence of any divine beings but One has never existed in human history. Jews, Christians, and Moslems all insist on the role of subordinate beings whose power and freedom are derived from the single Lord. Finally, it should be noted that the male and female principle by which the gods and goddesses of the *Enuma Elish* are spawned is totally excluded in the Hebrew account.

The *Enuma Elish* and Genesis 1 agree in regarding the creation of man through divine consultation as the climax of creation. The conferring of Marduk and Ea has its counterpart in the "Let us make man" of Genesis 1:26. But there the similarities end. The Babylonian view of man's origin and status is a surprisingly dismal and pessimistic one:

> They [the gods] bound him [Kingu] and held him before Ea;
> Punishment they inflicted upon him by cutting
>   (the arteries of) his blood
> With his blood they created mankind;
> He imposed the services of gods (upon them) and
>   set the gods free.[9]

[9] Tablet VI, 31–34; see Appendix 1, p. 574.

Man's creation was chiefly to free the gods from menial activities, and the method of creation was to seize and bleed the unwilling Kingu. While man thus comes at the end of the creative series, he is hardly the pinnacle of creation. Man's position is intentionally servile; in a real sense he is an afterthought, an appendage to creation that otherwise stands complete. Man's position in the world is that of an alien and an outcast. He was in fact born of a punitive act.

How different the Priestly concept of man "in the image of God." The sequence of Creation moves inexorably toward man as the lord of the cosmos. Man's status is less than God's but greater than all other creatures. J expressed human affinity with the natural world through the modeling of man out of the ground. P expresses man's participation in nature through the procreative qualities that he shares with all living things. But as man, according to J, transcended the animal world through "the breath of life," so P sees man stamped with "the image," i.e., the likeness, resemblance, or copy of God.

According to context the image of God means primarily man's appointment to dominion over creation. The divine image is man's power to subdue the earth, his technological conquest of nature. The word "image" means generally a physical likeness and in a later genealogy, P speaks of Adam as the father of Seth, "after his image" (Gen. 5:3). Psychophysical parallelism, the inseparable participation of the body in the life of mind and spirit, was integral to Hebrew thought. While P was far beyond the idea of God as a "big man," he unquestionably regarded God as having form and structure reflected in the total organism of man. The whole ethos of Hebrew thought argues that "image" here means man in his totality as a body-soul unity, as a socially and environmentally related being. In fact, some commentators have contended that the expression "Let *us* make . . . in *our* image" was purposely employed to guard against gross anthropomorphism, i.e., man made in the image of *divinity* rather than *God*.[10] Like the mythical images of the J story of the Garden and the Fall, the notion of man in God's image is a multifaceted truth, capable of unfolding many new meanings. Yet the common affirmation of both the tenth-century J and the fifth-century P myths of creation is emphatic: man shares many of the natural limitations of creaturehood, yet he is free in that he rises *above* creation, but responsible in that he stands *beneath* his Creator. He is himself creature and creator. Thus man's place in the

[10] John Skinner, *The Book of Genesis* (ICC), Scribner's, rev. ed., 1925, p. 31.

world is much more positively and meaningfully conceived in the Genesis story than in the Babylonian account.

As to content the Old Testament accounts of creation are ultimately drawn from a Mesopotamian source, but the spirit is distinctively Hebraic. The Babylonian cosmogony taken over by Israel becomes the occasion for the highest affirmations about God and man. The stuff of the narratives, like man himself, is of the earth earthy, but like the man of God's designing it becomes a living being filled with the unique ethos of Israelite faith. Neither J nor P consulted Babylonian sources as they wrote. The Babylonian elements have been mediated rather through a devious culture and lengthy history and slowly naturalized by the recipients. The recollections of *Enuma Elish* may have been brought by Hebrew ancestors in the migration from Ur to Canaan, or they may have been contributed through the Canaanites after the conquest. Priestly writers had renewed contact in Babylon with old myths and saw the great need for a more grandly conceived statement of Yahweh's lordship than the J account provided.

A word is in order concerning the reconciliation of Genesis and modern science. While the hysteria over this subject has abated somewhat since the days of the Scopes trial, it is still a central issue. In the interests of harmonizing the scientific view of nature and the biblical account some interpreters have assumed a catastrophe after the creation of Genesis 1:1, "In the beginning God created the heavens and the earth." Into this interstice they place vast geological periods, ice ages, dinosaurs, etc. Then God began anew in Genesis 1:2, "The earth was without form and void, and darkness. . . ." Others, less radically, would allegorize "day" into an age or eon on the view that "with the Lord one day is as a thousand years" (II Pet. 3:8). Some would equate the evolutionary stages with the creative acts. The former rigidity of those who would not even concede the great age of the earth seems to be rapidly diminishing. It is of interest, for example, that the Roman Catholic church now interprets the biblical view of man's origins with sufficient flexibility to allow for various forms of biological evolution. No one is prepared to say, as did some hardpressed obscurants in the nineteenth century, that God put the fossils in the rocks to confound the scientists!

All attempts to harmonize Genesis 1 and modern science that proceed on the assumption that the biblical account is a literal transcript, precisely accurate in some verifiable sense as far as it goes, are in vain.

Many of the simplest and most basic elements of modern scientific understanding find no room in the biblical scheme. We are told by the scientists that the simplest forms of animal life and vegetation appeared simultaneously, that birds came long after fishes, and that the sun was simultaneous with or prior to the appearance of the earth. There is no way of defending the literal accuracy of the biblical account that does not at the same time distort and demean it.

But there is another kind of reconciliation or harmonization in the thought of man as he considers the realms of scientific and religious-philosophical discourse. The two realms cannot meet in method or conclusion; but they meet in the mind of man who not only studies human origins but also seeks the meaning of human life. They both refer to human life; they have the same object and subject: man studying himself. The scientist cannot pretend that the "whole response" of man as to his origin and destiny is unimportant. The theologian and philosopher can no longer dismiss or spurn scientific data. While the two methods do not meet and cannot be brought into one-to-one ratio nor made to concur, since they are on essentially different planes, the future of mankind may well depend upon how successful we are in holding these two kinds of truth in fruitful relation, so that *scientia* does not starve the soul of man nor *religio* enslave his mind. S. R. Driver was basically right: "The Cosmogony of Genesis is treated in popular estimation as an integral element of the Christian faith. It cannot be too earnestly represented that this is not the case. . . . it teaches *what science as such cannot discover* (for it is not its province to do so), *the relation in which they* [the secondary causes] *stand to God. . . .* it neither comes into collision with science, nor needs reconciliation with it."[11]

WISDOM LITERATURE

Israelite wisdom literature includes Job, Proverbs, Ecclesiastes, Song of Songs, and a number of sayings, riddles, fables, and psalms scattered through the Old Testament. Unlike prophecy, the wisdom movement of the ancient Near East had a great antiquity and a full-scale development outside of Israel. In a sense wisdom was a purely adventitious growth on the main stock of Judaism and yet its Jewish mutations were of significance. A large body of parallel literature enables us to estimate the way in which Israelite sages made use of a

[11] S. R. Driver, *The Book of Genesis* (WC), Methuen, 12th ed., 1926, pp. 32 f.

genre that had reached definitive form long before Israel had become a nation.

Wisdom as an international movement flourished in the court life of Egypt and Babylon. Its typical originator and bearer was the scribe, whose caste pride was unmatched in antiquity and whose role was indispensable to the recording of public events and the training of courtiers. Here was an official class with leisure to write and with the responsibility of training the nobility. Wisdom in such circumstances was largely of a prudential and utilitarian character, a brand of ancient "how to win friends and influence people." Egyptian literature preserves several examples of a wisdom genre known as Instructions and cast in the form of advice by a prince or prime minister to his son and successor. The Instructions of Hor-Dedef, though poorly preserved, come from the twenty-seventh century B.C., and the bulk of the Instructions date from the Old Kingdom. While there is an occasional dash of lofty idealism in this literature, the great majority of the injunctions inculcate a rather pedestrian ethic of obedience to superiors and assumed manners for the purpose of rapid promotion and smooth relations with people. There is shockingly little concern with truth and goodness for their own sakes or obedience to the gods per se. But the Instructions have a modern ring for Westerners whose outlook on life has often been similarly cheapened by a utilitarian and hedonistic point of view.

Wisdom had other facets. Crass prudence in ethics always leads to its opposite, disillusion and despair. When the neat equities, the nice proportions between virtue and reward are upset, men readily forsake the conduct they have adopted for ulterior purposes or imitated merely out of social habit. And so the wisdom movement created a body of reflective and pessimistic literature. One of the best specimens is the "Babylonian Job" in which a worshiper passes from naïve trust through doubt and dejection to a chastened and humble faith. But some of the surviving examples have no note of faith to lighten the somber doubts. At times they wistfully dwell upon the annihilation of death, as in two pre-Mosaic Egyptian texts: the Song of the Harper and the Dispute over Suicide. The latter contains a poignant poem by one who welcomes death.

> Death is before me today
>> Like the recovery of a sick man,
>> Like going out into the open after a confinement.

Death is before me today
  Like the odor of myrrh,
  Like sitting under an awning on a breezy day.

Death is before me today
  Like the passing away of rain,
  Like the return of men to their houses from an expedition.

Death is before me today
  Like the longing of a man to see his house again,
  After he has spent many years held in captivity.[12]

It is thus apparent that wisdom in the ancient Near East was no philosophy but a craftsman's skill and the articulation of the moods of social conformity or of world-weariness. A rudimentary interest in the true foundations of the ethical life is noted here and there, but it was the Jewish sages who plumbed these questions with profundity and brilliance. In spite of its age-long history, the wisdom movement had not turned into a significant religious or philosophical development. Naturalistic polytheism choked off any potentialities in this regard. Entering rather late upon the scene, the Israelites took over the wisdom genre and both in form and content brought the hoary tradition to maturity.

Wisdom in the Old Testament means as many things as in non-Israelite culture: (1) It is sometimes merely the prudential, hedonistic guide to social and political attainment: this do and you shall prosper! But generally the grossly mechanical character of the appeal is modified by the personal God of Israel who sanctions the sages' teachings. Still the utilitarian tang is pronounced enough to show that Israel did not wholly slough off that aspect of ancient Near Eastern wisdom. Indeed, the strong thisworldliness of Judaism, with its more or less fixed adherence to the Deuteronomic philosophy of history, found a certain affinity with wisdom hedonism. (2) Wisdom is also "skill" or "capacity," whether of craftsman, soldier, or statesman. (3) More basically, however, wisdom is the knowledge of the true values of life on which a man should base his thoughts and actions irrespective of personal gain. The immediately dazzling is not the ultimately satisfying. Here there is a genuine interest in the enduring life, an inchoate philosophical ethics which would have made the sages at home with Platonists,

[12] This translation is mainly from Pritchard, ANET, p. 407 but the first line of each stanza follows James Breasted's rendering in *Development of Religion and Thought in Ancient Egypt*, Scribner's, 1912, p. 195; see also Thomas, DOTT, p. 165.

though the Jews and Greeks would not have readily understood one another's categories. (4) Wisdom in Israel also soared in the sphere of speculation about the moral government of the world and man's place in it, a speculation that was more a protest and an avowal than it was dispassionate reflection. A strong practical bent dominated even the most far-ranging considerations about creation, reward and punishment, and providence. (5) Finally, the Israelite domestication of wisdom becomes most evident in the identification of wisdom with the will and purpose of God for man. "The fear of the Lord is the beginning of knowledge (wisdom)" (Prov. 1:7; 9:10)—that is the touchstone for the sages of Israel. The peak of the process is reached when Wisdom is equated with Law as the perfect embodiment of the divine will.

The extensive transformation needed to overcome the prudential element in wisdom and the danger of inordinate pessimism may seem to have made the risk of the Israelite venture into wisdom greater than the possible returns. But there was one thing that wisdom could provide Israel and that was the framework for fuller thought about the ultimates of religion: issues of origin and destiny, of human desert and divine providence—issues that were implicit in the faith of Israel but had not been extensively explored prior to the Exile. Wisdom thus had a broadening and disturbing effect upon Jewish thought that could not be hidden by the dull and unimaginative prudentialists among the sages.

When may the entrance of wisdom into Israel be dated? Tradition assigns Proverbs, Ecclesiastes, and Song of Songs to Solomon, and the attributions are to be taken as loosely as the claims of Mosaic authorship of Israelite law and Davidic authorship of the Psalms. It may mean nothing more than that Solomon promoted the first cosmopolitan court in Israel and under his patronage a scribal penchant for the collecting of wisdom was encouraged. A distinction must be made between the collecting of proverbs and the creation of finished books. Wisdom in short aphorisms would have to be developed for some time before anyone could create the homogeneous splendor of a book like Job. The other Jewish wisdom books are admittedly less unitary; Proverbs, for example, is a compound of many subcollections and would not be likely to develop short of decades and centuries of collection. Further support of a preëxilic date for Israelite wisdom is the attribution of a segment of Proverbs to Hezekiah (25:1). Then too the wise man is mentioned in Jeremiah 18:18 as one of three classes of communal leaders, the others being prophet and priest. A parallel passage in Ezekiel 7:26 substitutes elder for wise man, indicative that a source of wisdom additional to court life was the circle of elders who governed the tribes and administered local justice. This would help explain why some Israelite wisdom is not only lacking in urban and royal sophistication but is at times actually hostile to it. Solomon received notoriety for a development that had some of its most creative phases entirely outside his court. A reasonable hypothesis is that the collection of proverbs began in preëxilic times, probably as early as Solomon's reign, but the extant wisdom books of the Old Testament are all products of the Exile and after.

The most pervasive and fundamental literary unit in the wisdom literature is the proverb (*mashal*), analogous to the single legend or law in the Pentateuch and the oracle in prophecy. The term is loosely used to designate a taunt or mocking song (Isa. 14:4; Mic. 2:4), and an allegory or similitude (Ezek. 17:2; 24:3); but its most frequent usage is for the *pithy aphoristic saying* that presents a complete, concrete, and memorable thought. Sayings so labeled appear in the historical and prophetic books: "Out of the wicked comes forth wickedness" (I Sam. 24:13), "The days grow long, and every vision comes to naught" (Ezek. 12:22), "Like mother, like daughter" (Ezek. 16:44), and the most noted of all, "The fathers have eaten sour grapes, and the children's teeth are set on edge" (Ezek. 18:2). Each proverb is brief and quasi-rhythmical, often retaining parallelism of members. The book of Proverbs is an anthology of single proverbs, although in parts whole stanzas have been devised by the poet-sage to express a single thought. Another wisdom type was the *riddle* of which there is only one clear Old Testament example, the riddle of Samson (Judg. 14:12–14). That it was a common and much appreciated type is apparent from references elsewhere (Prov. 1:6; Ps. 49:4; Dan. 5:12). The *fable* is also infrequently employed (Judg. 9:7–15 and II Kings 14:9). Thus the mainstay of wisdom literature is the proverb which through compilation and elaboration could be developed into words of the scope and power of Job. The poet of Job has achieved a remarkable cohesion of argument and mood although formally his work consists of strings of proverbs constructed into speeches and the speeches into cycles.

As to the situation in life, we have already noted the scribal provenance of ancient Near Eastern wisdom and the Solomonic tradition in Israel. To this is added the role of the elder who taught in the gates (Prov. 1:20–21; 8:1–3). There may also have been peripatetic teachers on the order of the Greek Sophists. The settled teaching of the sages in schools is first mentioned about 180 B.C. in the work of Ben Sira (Ecclus. 51:23). The wise man was apparently less established in his function than the priest but not so freewheeling as the prophet. In any age or circumstance the sage might also be scribe, judge or elder, soothsayer or diviner. The work of prophet, priest, and wise man was certainly not carried on in isolation. A dramatic instance of the common interests of the three is seen in the prohibition against removing a neighbor's landmark, which appears in prophecy (Hos. 5:10), law (Deut. 19:14), and wisdom (Prov. 22:28).

PROVERBS

There are six divisions to the book of Proverbs and each has a more or less distinct character. Five are marked in the Hebrew by editorial headings and the sixth is supplied with a superscription in the Septuagint. The divisions are actually separate collections of proverbs, generally strung together with little consistent attention to subject matter, but sometimes constructed in "a miniature essay-form."[13] The dates of these subcollections can be determined only in a very general way, but some notion of priority can be hazarded.

1. The ancient nucleus of the book, 10:1–22:16 (see 3 below), is entitled "Proverbs of Solomon." The collection consists of proverbs marked by poetic parallelism. Occasional single lines and tristichs interrupt the prevailing distich pattern. A secondary division within the section is seen in the mainly antithetic parallelisms of chapters 10–15 and the chiefly synonymous or comparative parallelisms of 16:1–22:16. The careless manner of editing is shown by the curious repetitions of proverbs even within the same subsection (e.g., 10:1 and 15:20; 16:2 and 21:2; 19:5 and 19:9). The Solomonic tradition argues for preëxilic origin and is supported by the simple literary form and by the conditions of life presupposed (note especially the reference to the king, 16:10,12–15; 20:8,26,28; 21:1; 22:11). The major obstacle to regarding Solomon as author is the discrepancy between the modest life the proverbs enjoin and the ostentation of his

---

[13] W. O. E. Oesterley, *The Book of Proverbs* (WC), Methuen, 2nd ed., 1929, p. xiii.

manner of living. They may, however, have derived from Solomonic times.

2. The section chapters 25–29 has an even more precise notation, "these also are proverbs of Solomon, which the men of Hezekiah king of Judah copied out." There is no reason to doubt its reliability, for it affords evidence that kings other than Solomon were promoters of wisdom and that under their auspices men of letters preserved the legacy of the past. It demonstrates also how a monarch's name could be attached to wisdom literature that he did not write. The emphatic "also" probably indicates that the editor was familiar with the preceding collection. This section has the simple proverb form and in content suggests a preëxilic origin (note kings and rulers in 25:2–3; 28:15–16; 29:4,14). Chapters 28–29 in their greater religious and legal interest show signs of belonging originally to another collection.

3. The corpus of proverbs in 22:17–24:34 is without editorial introduction in the Hebrew, but the Greek translation supplies a heading "words of the wise," grammatically detached from 22:17, which then reads: "Incline your ear, and hear my words." There are strikingly close parallels between this section of Proverbs and the Egyptian Teaching of Amen-em-Opet, which dates roughly in the period 1000–600 B.C. Direct borrowing from the Egyptian prototype is likely. It should be noted that the literary structure is somewhat more complex, the thought units often being built up with two distichs (tetrastichs), and even some longer units as in the supplement of 24:23–34 (note the preface, "these also are the sayings of the wise"). Not only do the affinities with Amen-em-Opet suggest a preëxilic date but the references to kings strengthen the probability (e.g., 22:29; 24:21).

4. Chapter 30 is introduced with the claim that it contains "the words of Agur son of Jakeh of Massa." This may be a determined linking of the chapter with Arabian wisdom, for Massa is listed as one of the sons of Ishmael in Genesis 25:14. But *massa'* also means simply "oracle" and the superscription may be rendered, "the words of Agur son of Jakeh, an oracle." Also, the Greek reads otherwise: "Be in awe of my words my son and, receiving them, repent." The more elaborate, rhetorical forms suggest a postexilic date, with the proviso that such forms occur earlier (rhetorical question series and the graduated numbers device in Amos) and that the zoological subject matter (leech, ant, eagle) corresponds with the preëxilic wisdom credited to Solomon in I Kings 4:33.

5. Chapter 31 is designated "the word of Lemuel, king of Massa, which his mother taught him." This note is as obscure as the foregoing. The Greek omits the proper name Lemuel. The bulk of the chapter is an acrostic praise of the good wife. The wife as manager of the household and keeper of finances is probably a postexilic ideal.

6. Chapters 1–9 are introduced with the full-dress heading, "Proverbs of Solomon the Son of David, King of Israel." This superscription was intended as a capstone to the entire work. The introduction of 1:1–6 sets forth the rich and varied vocabulary of the wisdom schools; it contains seven terms for wisdom and understanding, as well as four for fools and simpletons. The atomized proverbial form of most of the other sections is overcome by a greater unity of thought sustained through whole stanzas or poems. The notion of wisdom is imbued with a more distinctively Hebraic flavor. It is given some of the dynamic power of prophecy and is infused with moral and religious urgency. Especially effective is the personification of wisdom as a female figure whose attractions more than offset the crude appeals of the sensual woman.

In fact the high-water mark of the book of Proverbs is the personification of wisdom in chapter 8. Her almost evangelical appeal as she stands beside the crossroads of life (8:1–21) leads to a reflection on Lady Wisdom as the attendant of God at creation (8:22–31). She is represented as the first created, thus preceding the existent world. While God fashions the cosmos she revels in its beauty and orderliness. A more precise idea of what is meant is obscured by the Hebrew word in verse 30 which some render as "master workman" or "architect" but others read as "darling child" or "nursling." In the former sense, the passage regards wisdom as an associate who actively assists God in framing the universe. If the latter is more accurate, then wisdom has a less active role and is rather a spectator who sports like a child at the inexpressible joy of creation. Yet in either event the passage affirms in mythopoeic form the role of wisdom as the rational principle of the cosmos.

Wisdom as cosmic order has been compared with the speculations of Stoic philosophy (the Logos) or with the Persian Amesha Spentas (the personified virtues, especially Asha, the rule of right), but it has nearer parallels in the poetic habits of the ancient Near East where any attribute or quality was likely to be invested with personal identity and given a name and character all its own.[14] Of course the major distinction is that the habit flourished always on the foundation of polytheism, where one more deity was no problem. When Proverbs employs the personifying device it is without compromise of monotheism, since wisdom is clearly but an attendant of the Creator and is in fact nothing more than God himself in action. The point of the image translated into less mythic terms would be simply this: in his wisdom God made the world and its every aspect displays the rightness of the creative design. Another possible motive in the feminine personification may have been a counterattack on the mystery religions with their appealing goddesses. Lady Wisdom of Proverbs 8 has even been regarded as "Ishtar purified and converted to Judaism."[15] And the "foreign woman" of chapters 1–8 may be the foreign cult symbolized as a temptress of Jewish youth, rather than a common streetwalker.

Proverbs 8 belongs to a legitimate inner-Israelite development. It fits into a sequence of passages beginning with Job 28 and continuing with Wisdom of Solomon 7 and Ecclesiasticus 24. In the Job passage wisdom is objectified and glorified but not yet personified. By the time of the intertestamental writings she has become "fashioner of all things" (Wisd. Sol. 7:22) and identified with the Law (Ecclus. 24:9). The growing transcendence of God, the development of angelology, the appeal of Greek philosophy with its demand for mediation between the ideal and the actual worlds—all these contributed to the personification and finally the hypostatization of Wisdom. Contact with Persian religion also played its part. And yet this movement toward personification of divine functions or attributes always remained poetically fluid so that it could not be charged with polytheistic error.

The tendency to allow wisdom an independent status, though subordinate to God, became of the first importance for early Christianity. In an attempt to conceptualize the relation of Jesus Christ to God the Father the pathway broken by the wisdom theorists was hastily exploited. The prologue of John's Gospel, for example, is even more readily understood against the backdrop of Old Testament

[14] Helmer Ringgren, *Word and Wisdom, Studies in the Hypostatization of Divine Qualities and Functions in the Ancient Near East,* Ohlason, 1947.

[15] O. S. Rankin, *Israel's Wisdom Literature,* T. & T. Clark, 1936, p. 263.

wisdom literature than of Stoic philosophy. Since Law had become the one supreme medium for knowing God and had been equated with Wisdom, it was easy for Christians to conceive their Saviour as this supremely revealing Wisdom, the Logos or Word, the enlightening and redeeming action of God among men. While a good many significant religious and philosophical streams converge in the Fourth Gospel, certainly not the least of these was the Wisdom movement of Israel.

In spite of recent claims that Ugaritic influences have operated on the personification of wisdom,[16] the finished form of chapters 1–9 is postexilic and the majority of scholars adhere to a date between 400–250 B.C. for the final compilation of Proverbs.

As the book of Proverbs now appears it is a potpourri of sayings and short poems, generally mediocre as literature, tedious as ethics, banal as religion. The first chapters are incomparably the finest and have been suffused with an uplifting and energizing quality that proves at least some of the sages to have been heirs of the prophets, able to do more than mouth platitudes and inculcate "safe" social actions in clever turns of phrase. The sages of chapters 1–9 had at least begun to deal with the deeper motivations for a good life. But in the main the conservative catechetical interest of wisdom reminds us of certain passages of the New Testament that teach a Christian morality too easily misunderstood as a "slave ethic." The book of Proverbs only goes a little way toward alleviating the insidious peril of all "proper" religio-ethical principles: in their obviousness the principles render God necessary only as the Guardian of the system. The atmosphere was precisely the sort in which Job and Ecclesiastes raised their honest protests.

JOB

The book of Job is a rare and ingenious achievement. Its anonymous creator has fashioned a work so unique that it does not fall into any of the literary genre of antiquity or modernity. Though it partakes of the motifs and imagery of wisdom literature, it is infinitely more engaging and personal in its impact than anything written in the ancient Near East. As literature it is neither epic, drama, lyric, or

---

[16] W. F. Albright, "Some Canaanite-Phoenician Sources of Hebrew Wisdom," *Wisdom in Israel and the Ancient Near East,* Brill, 1955, pp. 1–15.

didactic poetry; and yet it partakes of something of each. As religion it is unrivaled in its proclamation of "faith in spite of." The obstacles to trust in God are presented ruthlessly and incisively, and the final triumph of faith is as rugged and convincing as the hero's most savage protests.

The Structure of the Book

Unlike many of the amorphous Old Testament writings, Job has sharply defined divisions:

Prologue	Chaps. 1–2
Curse of Job's Birth	3
First Cycle of Speeches	4–14
Second Cycle of Speeches	15–21
Third Cycle of Speeches	22–28
Job's Summary Argument	29–31
Elihu Speeches	32–37
Whirlwind Speeches of God	38–42:6
Epilogue	42:7–17

But that is not to gainsay the critical difficulties that appear even in this symmetrical form. There is a prose prologue and a prose epilogue. In between all is poetry, beginning with a curse of the day of his birth by the hero, followed by three cycles of speeches in which the friends Eliphaz, Bildad, and Zophar speak respectively and each time are answered by Job. In the third cycle there is textual disturbance. The expected Zophar speech is omitted, and to add to the difficulty the introductory formula "and Job again took up his discourse and said" appears twice when no other speaker has intervened (27:1; 29:1). Furthermore, the sentiment of 27:7–23 on the lips of Job is entirely out of place for he simply echoes the comforters. No psychological explanation can be given for this abrupt reversal of argument; in the following chapters Job as before steadfastly disagrees with the friends. The probable solution of the third cycle's disarray is that an original speech of Zophar has been attributed to Job, although scholars differ as to its extent. Whether the confusion was accidental or willful orthodox editing cannot be ascertained.

The Poem on Wisdom in chapter 28, a finely wrought encomium of wisdom in its secret power and remoteness from acquisitive humanity, is a composition worthy of the author of Job. As it stands, however, it is out of keeping with the spirit and form of the dialogue between

Job and his friends and in no sense advances the argument. It is a poem better suited to inclusion in the Psalms.

The block of speeches by Elihu is almost universally regarded as an insertion to provide the solution that some later sage was unable to find either in the friends or in Job. The arguments against the speeches are straightforward and compelling. Elihu is not mentioned among the comforters of Job either before or after chapters 32–37. No one responds to his speeches in accord with the dialogue pattern of the preceding chapters. He does not add anything substantial to the discussion, although he elaborates the arguments of the friends and anticipates the speech of God from the whirlwind with great effectiveness. Elihu interrupts the dramatic connection between Job's final challenge (chap. 31) and the appearance of Yahweh (chap. 38). The vocabulary and style of the speeches have several striking variations from the rest of the poetic work, although in themselves they would not compel separate authorship. Even a Roman Catholic commentator is led to assume that the Elihu speeches were not in the first edition of the book but were added by the author to the revised edition, for he finds it "difficult to avoid the conclusion that Elihu presents substantially the same view as the three friends . . . the whole section is an afterthought."[17] The major objection is therefore the aesthetic breach, the psychological infelicity that results from the presence of the speeches. They belong to an editorial revision *not* made by the original poet. But this should not blind us to the eloquence of the speeches and their magnificent portraiture of God's ways with man. They should not be dismissed as inferior or trivial, as has often been the habit of commentators. Elihu's lofty conception of God's grace is unfortunately weakened by his blatant self-confidence and arrogance toward Job and the friends.

The speeches of Yahweh from the whirlwind, which cap the present form of the book, have been excluded or questioned by a number of critics. The basic difficulty is that they seem so oblivious of the terms on which Job had demanded a hearing. Instead of justifying himself God reveals the panorama of his universal dominion. Those who are offended by the irrelevance of the divine reply cannot believe that the poet ever intended such a conclusion to his work. They would rather leave Job railing at deity than prostrate before a God who has given him no satisfaction on his plea of innocence. But that is to prejudge

[17] Edward J. Kissane, *The Book of Job,* Browne & Nolan, 1939, p. xxxix.

the poet's work and to rob him of the right to surprise. It is just the disproportion between Job's problem and God's answer that comprises one of the central insights of the poet. To take this from him is to leave his work mutilated, shorn of its overpowering denouement —a *deus ex machina* unparalleled in world literature. It is probable that the whirlwind speech has invited embroidery, such as the descriptions of behemoth (the hippopotamus) and leviathan (the crocodile) in 40:15–41:34, but these deletions leave untouched the mounting tide of rhetorical questions that form the heart of the speech.

No allusion in the book of Job aids us in dating it accurately. It is a work of literary maturity, but Israel had attained maturity in epic by the time of the Yahwist and in prophecy by the time of Deutero-Isaiah. The brooding reflection upon man's plight argues for an age of social breakup and widening horizons. The pronounced similarity between Job's curse of his birth (chap. 3) and Jeremiah's curse (20:14–18) makes dependence one way or the other almost certain. Careful linguistic analysis suggests that Jeremiah's is the more spontaneous and original poem. The many parallels between Job and Deutero-Isaiah, especially in their majestic descriptions of nature, do not provide any clear evidence of priority; and the connections between Job and laments in the Psalter and the book of Lamentations are also in doubt owing to uncertainty as to date and relative sequence. Thus the book of Job may be placed in the broad period 600–200 B.C., and while the trend of nineteenth-century criticism was to locate it in the fourth or third century there is presently a shift toward an earlier date, perhaps in the Exile itself.

The Poet's Purpose and Sources

The author is anonymous like those other Hebrew literary giants, the Yahwist and Deutero-Isaiah. While he did not choose to divulge his name, the poet did not hide behind a pseudonym. He let his work win its own way and without apology. That decision fits the fearlessness of mind evident in his writing. He was widely traveled and urbane, acquainted with foreign culture, notably Egyptian. His vocabulary teems with uncommon and otherwise unknown Hebrew words. In this he was like Shakespeare, for his fertile imagination and grasp of language led him into the evocation of emotion and the unraveling of thought through novel usages and the outright coining of expressions. There is no Old Testament parallel to the distinction and grandeur of his poetry, unless it be in Deutero-Isaiah. Both have a sweeping and exalted eloquence, but whereas the prophet is ornate and visionary, the sage's style is savagely chaste and psychologically penetrating. The poet sustains his gifts through three cycles of speeches and into the whirlwind speech without abatement.

Forcefulness of thought accounts primarily for the writer's impact. In a relentless pursuit of argument through the contention of personalities, he forges a style perfectly suited to his aim. By putting the words directly in the mouths of the participants and by allowing them unmitigated expression of emotion, a quality of realism is achieved that transcends the clichés of lament and suffering from which the poet does not wholly escape. It is really this titanic eruption of intellectual power, this bold delineation of divine-human encounter at the frontier of meaningful existence, that makes the work appealing. Here are men not merely talking about religion, or playing at it, but testing the strength and relevance of the roots of moral and religious conviction. The author has more in mind than puncturing common theories about punishment and reward; he has a concept of man vis-à-vis God that must be heard in its own right.

What were the resources at the poet's disposal? There was a long tradition of Egyptian and Babylonian theodicy, of inquiry into the ways of the gods with men. We have already alluded to the Babylonian Job, probably the closest parallel to the Hebrew book. A suffering pious man describes his hideous afflictions, the injustice of the gods, and his eventual reconciliation with them. In one particularly impressive passage the sufferer speaks of the fickleness of the gods and the instability of men.

> O that I only knew that these things [religious duties] are well pleasing to a god!
> What is good in one's sight is evil for a god.
> What is bad in one's own mind is good for his god.
> Who can understand the counsel of the gods in the midst of heaven?
> The plan of a god is deep waters, who can comprehend it?
> Where has befuddled mankind ever learned what a god's conduct is?
> He who was living yesterday has died today:
> Instantly he is made gloomy, suddenly is he crushed.
> One moment he sings a happy song,
> And in an instant he will moan like a mourner.
> Like day and night their mood changes.

When they are hungry they resemble corpses,
When they are sated they rival their god;
In good luck they speak of ascending to heaven,
When they are afflicted they grumble about going down to the under·
world.[18]

Whether he knew precisely this work or not, the author of Job had
imbibed a spirit that sensed the essentially irrational and inexplicable
ways of the divine. Yet how immeasurably surer was his development of the theme! There is no parallel to the scope of his work, and
the monotheistic base of his thinking is never for a moment qualified,
even by the figure of the Satan who derives all his power from divine
permission.

Job, the legendary patriarch of unexampled piety and suffering,
seems to have exerted a fascination over the mind of the poet analogous to Hamlet's spell over Shakespeare or Faust's bewitchment of
Goethe. The Job of legend is known from the prophet Ezekiel who,
seeking to press home his pleas for individual responsibility, averred:
" . . . even if these three men, Noah, Daniel, and Job, were in it
[the land] they would deliver but their own lives by their righteousness" (14:14; cf. vs. 20). The Daniel mentioned is hardly the
young man of exilic fame, the hero of the biblical book. He is rather
the ancient Daniel, righteous judge in the *Aqhat* text from Ras esh-
Shamra. Noah is of course the survivor of the flood. Similarly the Job
of the prologue is an ancient prototype of righteousness.

The disparity between the prose prologue and epilogue and the
poetic dialogue is not merely a matter of literary form but of more
fundamental considerations. In the *prologue* Job is a nomad of blame-
less character. His piety is epitomized in sacrifice, his suffering is a
testing engendered by the Satan's doubts of his fidelity, and he sub-
mits utterly to the divine chastisement. In the *poetic dialogue*, however, Job lives a settled existence; admits to some measure of sin
(though never adequate to account for his plight); of sacrifice we
hear nothing nor does the Satan or the notion of suffering as testing
appear; and rather than acquiesce, Job rebels and rails bitterly against
God. To this may be added the more frequent use of the name Yahweh
for the deity in the prologue as against Elohim in the poetry. The
prose also has a "fresco-like" quality, reminiscent of the patriarchal

[18] Pritchard, ANET, p. 435.

legends in Genesis; whereas the poetry is imbued with psychological introspection.

Some of these discrepancies are not insurmountable (e.g., Job was probably a seminomad who lived in a house for part of the year and wandered with his flocks for the remainder); but the cumulative effect of the many factors suggests that the prologue and epilogue are traditional material, to some degree already fixed, which the poet took as the starting place for his own work. The theory that the prose was added to the poetry falls to the ground because the poetry is senseless without the sort of introduction that the prologue provides. In an effort to remove the stigma of manifold reward from the poet, some critics have treated the epilogue as a later addition. Whether the Job legend was in written or oral form when the poet received it is uncertain. The problem of bringing into accord the prose and poetry is ultimately insoluble. Probably the popular tale about Job was so well known to his public that the poet told it as everyone knew it and then went on to develop his own interpretation and analysis of the great sufferer.

The Ways of God with Man

Including the Elihu speeches, it appears that the views of at least three men concerning theodicy and the divine-human relation are preserved in the book. All are anonymous and the prose viewpoint is deeply imbedded in the folklore of the people. Yet the book is not a mere agglomeration of tradition, for the poet of chapters 3–31, 38–42:6 has incorporated the prose forerunner and has elaborated the motifs of suffering and providence with tremendous ardor and intellectual energy. Although composite, Job has an architectural symmetry and variety that have led to its comparison to a great cathedral built over the centuries.[19]

1. PROLOGUE. The prose legend indulges in superlatives. Job is an instance of extreme piety, extreme catastrophe, and extreme faith. The hero displays a righteousness and faith unmoved by circumstance. In reply to Satan's cynical question: "Does Job fear God for nought?" he offers his classic retorts (actually addressed to his wife who becomes the devil's advocate): "Naked I came from my mother's womb, and naked shall I return; Yahweh gave, and Yahweh has taken away;

[19] E. Kraeling, *The Book of the Ways of God*, SPCK, 1938.

blessed be the name of Yahweh" (1:21), and "Shall we receive good at the hand of God and shall we not receive evil?" (2:10). While this unquestioning submission is not maintained by the Job of the poet, he probably retained the portrait of the prologue because of its salient point: faith is true faith only when it has God alone as its object and not the advantages of piety. The second striking feature of the prologue is its view of suffering as a test of faith. The evidential value of suffering that uncovers a latent faith or confirms a faith already existing has been underscored by H. W. Robinson: "We often speak of trusting God; is there not often a neglected truth in the thought that God is trusting us?"[20]

Job as the vindicator of God against the crass-minded Satan is a tantalizing subject for thought. But how seriously should it be taken? Can the notion be generalized or is Job the outstanding exception? Moreover, the Satan is a flagrantly symbolic figure whose ontological significance cannot be pressed. The poet certainly does not do anything with the notion, and even in the prologue the permitted power of the Satan is in the hands of God. Finally it is a view of suffering that cannot easily be applied, for men do not overhear the divine counsels. Even Job was oblivious of the true situation and when the poet discloses Yahweh in the whirlwind not a word is said about the evidential value of suffering.

2. POETIC DIALOGUE. In the first round of speeches the friends are courteous and pastoral, but in the second cycle they grow increasingly impatient at the rebellious and intractable spirit of Job. They insist upon the moral coherence of life in spite of temporary upsets and seeming contradictions. Men get their due in time. Yahweh's transcendence and inscrutability are such as to remove him from question, yet his dependability as Rewarder and Punisher cannot be doubted. In his replies to the friends, Job vacillates between despair of life because of the divine disregard of his personal righteousness and vigorous accusation and defiance toward the deity. His protests presuppose the loss of property, death of children, social ostracism, and personal illness as set forth in the prologue.

Now and then Job's prevailing antagonism and malaise are broken by the remembrance of God's former goodness and by the prospect

[20] H. W. Robinson, "The Cross of Job," *The Cross in the Old Testament,* Westminster, 1955, p. 47.

that God will acquit him of guilt and release him from punishment. Such is the import of a number of passages which in details are open to a wide range of interpretation.

> For he is not a man, as I am, that I might answer him,
>   that we should come to trial together.
> There is no umpire between us,
>   who might lay his hand upon us both.
> Let him take his rod away from me,
>   and let not dread of him terrify me (9:32–34).

While his spirit is still defiant, Job hopes for a bridge across the widening gulf between God and man. The word rendered "umpire" must not of course be thought of merely in sports parlance, but in the broader sense of "go-between, negotiator, arbiter."

> If a man die, shall he live again?
>   All the days of my service I would wait,
>   till my release should come.
> Thou wouldest call, and I would answer thee;
>   thou wouldest long for the work of thy hands (14:14–15).

The thought of future life is always in Job the merest fancy, a fabulous improbability, but it is allowed to flicker momentarily in the hero's mind because God's love and righteousness are so emphatic that it seems incredible for death to put a man beyond their reach. Yet this "hope of man" for the ultimate vindication of the right is eroded by the savage torrents of the divine onslaught; the first cycle ends in despair.

But the hope mounts ever afresh:

> O earth, cover not my blood,
>   and let my cry find no resting place.
> Even now, behold, my witness is in heaven,
>   and he that vouches for me is on high (16:18–19).

The fevered mind of Job appeals to God against God, God the vindicator against God the sadist. Some interpreters prefer to regard "the witness" who will exonerate Job's righteousness as one of the angels or some dimly grasped prefigurement of the Incarnate Christ.[21] But in whatever form, the meaning of the passage is Job's assurance that divine righteousness will not overlook him, even in death.

[21] Samuel Terrien, *Exegesis of Job* (IB, vol. 3), Abingdon, 1954, p. 1026.

Oh that my words were written!
   Oh that they were inscribed in a book!
Oh that with an iron pen and lead
   they were graven in the rock forever!
For I know that my Redeemer lives,
   and at last he will stand upon the earth;
and after my skin has been thus destroyed,
   then without my flesh I shall see God,
whom I shall see on my side,
   and my eyes shall behold, and not another (19:23–27).

This passage is a signal instance of a poorly transmitted text, and also of one so Christianized through its use in song and preaching that it is hard to penetrate to the thought of the original poet. The text is fundamentally insecure in verse 26; we cannot be certain whether Job expects resurrection of his body or anticipates vindication apart from any bodily organ, for the verse reads literally: "afterwards my skin they have stricken off (or surrounded) this." Every translator must emend the Hebrew in order to make sense. Certain points are salient: Job is to receive vindication and restitution from God. The translation "Redeemer" is excellent if one realizes that Job does not expect salvation from confessed sin but exoneration from the implication that he has sinned. Whatever his faith—and it is great indeed—Job is a proud and self-convinced man. He expects his reward at the very extremity of life, perhaps in death itself. Though he is about to pass into the silence of Sheol, his unheeded and unrewarded righteousness will be recognized by God and given its due. The discussion as to whether there is an explicit doctrine of resurrection in the passage is beside the main point: even death constitutes no impassable barrier for a conviction of righteousness as stern as Job's.

The third cycle of speeches is in a somewhat different key. The friends are more savage and frontal in their attack. They openly accuse Job of adding presumption to his previous sin. Job in turn answers with a counterblast that not only defends his own position but generalizes about the unjust suffering in the world. For the first time the indictment of the moral government of the world is drawn on the grand scale. Job contends that his position, while admittedly extreme, is by no means isolated; there is a vast weight of suffering that cannot be made to support the casual moralism of the friends. His description of the oppressed and forgotten of society is a jarring protest against the friends and the God in whose righteousness he still believes in spite of evidence to the contrary:

Why are not times of judgment kept by the Almighty,
    and why do those who know him never see his days?
. . . .
They [the wicked] thrust the poor off the road;
    the poor of the earth all hide themselves.
Behold, like wild asses in the desert
    they go forth to their toil,
seeking prey in the wilderness
    as food for their children.
They gather their fodder in the field
    and they glean the vineyard of the wicked man.
They lie all night naked, without clothing,
    and have no covering in the cold.
They are wet with the rain of the mountains,
    and cling to the rock for want of shelter.
. . . .
They go about naked, without clothing;
    hungry, they carry the sheaves;
among the olive rows of the wicked they make oil;
    they tread the wine presses, but suffer thirst.
From out of the city the dying groan,
    and the soul of the wounded cries for help;
    yet God pays no attention to their prayer (24:1,4–8,10–12).

The enlargement of the area of argument, plus the undoubted disruption of speeches, has led some critics to delete the third cycle in whole or part as an addition to the work of the original poet.[22] The criteria for exclusion are much too subjective, for the more virulent attack of the friends and Job's reflection on injustice in the large are both psychologically understandable and serve to intensify the dramatic climax of Job's finale. In the heat of debate the participants are driven beyond their original positions. Besides, if one omits the third cycle there is no effective preparation for the whirlwind speech.

The final discourse of Job is a masterly summary of his case; the original poet holds forth with his characteristic excellence. The speech is articulated in three sections: (1) a recital of Job's former joy as a respected member of society, chapter 29; (2) his present rejection by

[22] F. Baumgärtel, *Der Hiobdialog*, Kohlhammer, 1933, pp. 151–165, and E. G. Kraeling, *op. cit.*, pp. 92–100, 103–122.

relatives, friends, community, and God, chapter 30; (3) an extended oath of clearance by which he avows his innocence of sin, inward and outward, and closes with a challenge to God that he be given a fair hearing, chapter 31. The oath of clearance, in which he invokes repeated curses upon himself should he be lying, is modeled on protestations of guiltlessness drawn from legal practice but also employed in religious texts in the ancient Near East. The inventory of sins that he disavows is remarkable in its scope and inwardness. Job declares himself free from falsehood, adultery, mistreatment of slaves, hardness toward the poor, confidence in wealth, pagan worship, pleasure in the enemy's hardship, hypocrisy, and business malpractice. Sins of thought as well as overt action are embraced, and commentators have repeatedly noted the correspondence between Job's ethics and those of the Sermon on the Mount. A record like this deserves divine acknowledgment! Job strides into God's presence like a prince, confident that when his indictment is publicized it will be in fact an acquittal worthy to be worn as a crown.

What is the issue of this long and vehement exchange between Job and the friends? Undeserved suffering is the point at which the author takes up his story, for the hero is a man whose scale of values and estimate of God's ways with man have undergone a tremendous shock. Job sets out to find why it is that the innocent suffer not in order to solve an intellectual problem but in order to get his deserts. Instead he finds a basis for knowing God that transcends moralism and tangible reward. The theme of the poetry is actually the ultimacy of man's relation with God, laid bare at the point of its maximum testing —in the abysmal reversal of fortune when a man's body is touched with malignancy.

Climaxing the poetic debate is the speech of Yahweh from the whirlwind. God will not be questioned but rather discloses himself only as the Questioner. The magnificent array of rhetorical questions encompasses the whole of the created world: earth, sea, day and night, space and time, light and darkness, the elements, stars and constellations, lion and raven, mountain goat, wild ass, wild ox, ostrich (absent in LXX), hawk and eagle, humankind. The effect of this survey is curiously exalting and abasing; a shift in the frame of reference is achieved. Job is drawn out of himself to behold the wonder of God's world. It must not be supposed that he is merely advised to look around at the beauties of nature and be edified and soothed.

Rather the speech must be understood as Job's grasp of the ineffable wonder and mystery of reality. It is not so much a teleology in the philosophical sense, i.e., the recognition of the rational articulation of the parts of nature, but a tribute to mystery, the wondrous way in which the central and personal power of the universe shows through the veil of nature. The poet plays upon the irrationality of the spheres of nature unrelated directly to man and his systems of meaning, especially the world of wild creatures incommensurate with and useless to man. The whirlwind speech is vibrant with an awakened sense of incongruity, of disproportion resplendent with awe, the shuddering akin to William Blake's when he cried:

> Tyger! Tyger! burning bright,
> In the forests of the night;
> What immortal hand or eye
> Could frame thy fearful symmetry?
> . . . .
> Did He, who made the Lamb, make thee!

The manifold marvel of the world overwhelms Job. He is entranced, enthralled, nourished, humbled, and inwardly restored by the vision of God as the unquestioned Questioner, the unfathomed Creator, by what Otto calls "the sheer absolute wondrousness that transcends thought."[23] Ishmael in commenting on the whiteness of Moby Dick says, "Though in many of its aspects this visible world seems formed in love, the invisible spheres were formed in fright."[24] So too Job might have said, until beholding similar wonders, he saw in them not dumb nothingness but a frightening love.

How does the interpreter estimate so personal a statement of faith? The poet has poured his inmost apprehensions into the denouement. To him there is but one answer to the rationally insoluble riddle of man's existence, and that is an awareness of holy love. In the very form of the book he is saying that human dialogue (Job and the friends) and monologue (Job with himself) must give way to divine-human dialogue (God and Job). Job must meet God for himself; he does not know divinity or the meaning of his afflictions except in the luminous moment of faith. It is really not surprising that the whirl-wind speech makes some of the points insisted on by the friends:

[23] R. Otto, *The Idea of the Holy,* Oxford University Press, 1950, p. 79.
[24] Herman Melville, *Moby Dick,* Signet, 1955, p. 196.

God's omnipotence and inscrutability. The issue is that there are realities that can never be true until a man knows them for himself— not as points scored in a theological argument. There is in fact no truth *about God,* but only the truth of GOD. The deep inward satisfaction of Job, his sense of personal relatedness to deity is firmly underscored in his response:

> I had heard of thee by the hearing of the ear,
>   but now my eye sees thee;
> therefore I despise myself,
>   and repent in dust and ashes (42:5–6).

It is personal holiness and love before which he bows, for a man does not "despise himself" or "repent" in the presence of brute force. The poem of Job ends on a central biblical truth: if God is to be known he must make himself known and no amount of talking about him can replace the reality of his presence or the void of his absence.

If the solaces of friends and the niceties of religious apologetics cannot invoke God, neither can glib morality that boasts and insists on its due. Morality is in fact transcended without being negated. It is crucial that Job is never rebuked for his righteousness per se. The whirlwind speech in its very ambiguity on this issue is itself a revelation. The poet tells us that both Job and the friends have been victimized by a theory, a concept of God shackled to moralism. The friends have had no real communication with Job, for all their devotion to him. (And we must not undersell them! Would we be as patient with an obstreperous disputant?) Job can only rail against God and magnify his innocence. Rather than question the concept, which would be tantamount to examining their self-righteousness, the friends villify Job and Job villifies God. The end of religious moralism is hardness of heart and pride for the devotee, despair and darkness for the disenchanted. The good life is never to be despised but it cannot be the primary basis of trust in God.

A work of such superb artistry will always convey manifold meanings. As for the purpose of suffering, the book of Job offers several suggestions but no dogma. Suffering may be retribution, testing, discipline, or it may in the end be largely inexplicable. What matters is the purity of one's relation with God, unadulterated by the circumstances of success or failure. Some would go so far as to say that it teaches justification by faith. The book of Job insists that God is to be worshiped and adored solely because he is God and that faith is given in no other way than with the ineffable divine presence.

ECCLESIASTES

The Hebrew title of the book is *Qoheleth,* a feminine participle of *qahal,* "to assemble, gather," which could mean "one who assembles or collects" maxims or wisdom literature, or "one who speaks in the assembly," such as a preacher or synagogue speaker. The latter is preferred by the English versions, which uniformly translate *Qoheleth* as Preacher. Ecclesiastes is the Greek translation of the term and has the meaning of "member of the assembly" or "an ecclesiastic" (a leader of the community?).

Solomon is intended as the Preacher, although he is not named (cf. 1:1,12). Chapter 2 speaks of building enterprises, wealth, and wisdom. Any Jew would have immediately recognized Solomon; to name him would have been superfluous. Yet the book does not maintain the guise consistently. Many passages speak of a man of moderate means, without royal authority himself (it is doubtful that the trenchant criticism of kings in 4:13 and 10:5 was written by any monarch, much less the self-important Solomon). It is also unlikely that Solomon would have spoken of "those who were before me in Jerusalem" (1:16; 2:7,9) since only David preceded him as a Hebrew and the Canaanite kings would hardly have counted. Solomon was chosen by the author in keeping with the longstanding tradition of his wisdom. The author also had a desire to impersonate a leading figure who had "been around." It is intrinsic to the argument of the book that its hero was a cosmopolite who had tasted fully of the world and known its satiation and weariness.

Strong Aramaic and even Greek influence on the language of Ecclesiastes points to the postexilic age. The sense of despair and world-weariness in itself is not decisive since that mood was struck in Egypt and Babylon in ancient times, but in Israel it would certainly be most authentic in postexilic times when the earlier exuberance of Yahwism had receded under the economic and political disenchantment of the restored community. The work was finished by 180 B.C. when Ben Sira wrote but probably not before the era of Alexander and the intermingling of Greek and Hebrew culture, which brought a universal perspective and a sharp contesting of values. After the Maccabean age the book would have been inconceivable since it does not take a militant attitude toward the Greeks; furthermore, the fragment of the work from Qumran precludes a date much after 200 for the original. A date of about 250–200 B.C. is likely.

The unity of Ecclesiastes has been hotly disputed. Misplaced passages have been supposed, including the nonsensical hypothesis that the binding of the original pages broke and they were replaced in the wrong order. Multiple authorship has been proposed. The most influential form of the theory has been Carl Siegfried's, who argued for five authors, an epilogist, and two editors. The substratum of the work is by Q1 (the first Qoheleth), a pessimistic Hebrew. Q2 was a Sadducee influenced by Epicureanism; Q3 a *hakham* (wise man) who inserted strings of proverbs; Q4 a *hasidh* (pious one) made the work orthodox by references to divine judgment; and Q5 served as a collective symbol for several glossators.[25] English commentaries by McNeile and Barton accepted the idea of an original pessimistic author with additions by a wise man and a pious exponent of orthodoxy.

Many prefer to see Ecclesiastes as mainly the work of one man. Galling has suggested that it is a collection of independent aphorisms and observations written at various times and published as a journal or diary might be released, but without notations of date and circumstance. Several critics regard almost all but the twelfth chapter as coming from the Preacher (Hertzberg, Volz, and Rankin), while at least a few defend the entire book (most recently Gordis). The issue is how much disjointedness and vacillation in viewpoint can be allowed to one man. It is possible to demand too much consistency from an author swept by various moods. On the other hand a work of the shocking honesty of Ecclesiastes would hardly survive in Jewish circles without some palliation of its pessimism. The somber piety of its author would never be acceptable to the majority of people in any age.

Attempts to define the precise cultural and philosophical influences on the author have proved futile. There are strains of malaise and disillusion with the world in almost every civilization. The counsel of limited contentment in a hostile existence is not solely the advice of Greek Epicureanism, which some have insisted on finding in the

[25] Carl Siegfried, *Prediger und Hoheslied,* Vandenhoeck & Ruprecht, 1898, pp. 2–12.

Preacher's work. The Gilgamesh epic of ancient Babylon, penned long before there was any Athenian civilization, was shot through with the same emphasis:

> Gilgamesh, whither runnest thou?
> The life which thou seekest thou wilt not find;
> (For) when the gods created mankind,
> They allotted death to mankind,
> (But) life they retained in their keeping.
> Thou, O Gilgamesh, let thy belly be full;
> Day and night be thou merry;
> Make every day (a day of) rejoicing.
> Day and night do thou dance and play.
> Let thy raiment be clean,
> Thy head be washed, (and) thyself be bathed in water.
> Cherish the little one holding thy hand,
> (And) let the wife rejoice in thy bosom.
> This is the lot of (mankind . . .).[26]

It is apparent that there is nothing specifically Greek, or for that matter Hebraic, about the advice of the Preacher. In fact one scholar claims Buddhist influence on Ecclesiastes! The Preacher was profoundly influenced by a characteristic mood when culture is in decline, disorder is rampant, contrary ideas and values are sharply opposed, and the majority of men simply vegetate. The most likely time in Jewish circles would have been the Hellenistic age, but there is no distinctive philosophical terminology or ideological tenet that betrays the precise source of the influence.

The Preacher's sentiments are presented with no mincing of words. Life for him has no genuine or inherent meaning. It is "breath, vapour" and thus "nothingness, emptiness," or, as one commentator puts it, life's efforts add up to "zero."[27] This is the term translated "vanity" by the English versions, not in the sense of pride, but of fruitlessness, ineffectuality, the unavailing character of human existence. In man's "toil" or "sorrow" there is no sure reward, no "surplus" or "gain." Life lacks any quality of newness; there is nothing novel "under the sun" (used twenty-five times to express the closed and oppressively repetitious cycle of human life). There is no resting place,

[26] Tablet X, col. 3; translation of A. Heidel, *The Gilgamesh Epic and Old Testament Parallels,* Univ. of Chicago Press, 1946, p. 70.
[27] H. L. Ginsberg, "Studies in Koheleth," *Texts and Studies of the Jewish Theological Seminary of America,* 1950, vol. 17, pp. 1–3.

no point of satisfaction and repose, for all is "striving, desiring, feeding upon wind." All human effort is futile because of the incessant dialectical movement of opposites that crush out every semblance of freedom and novelty.

To complete the sad spectacle, man has no assurance that he will live beyond death; he may be only a beast and even his gifts to posterity may be unappreciated and wasted by the fool. The old Hebraic joy of many children seems but a jest to the Preacher, for he knows how thankless and prodigal children can be. But the work is not sheer capitulation to despair; it takes on the character of contest with deity. It becomes Promethean. The Preacher is no atheist; the closed circle of human existence is broken to the extent that this man rises up to take issue with his Creator. The Preacher is resentful of the animal-like monotony of man's life. He is unhappy but he is enough aware of his sad plight that he can cry out for something better. So his bitter indictment against God becomes a grotesque affirmation of life's meaning. He lodges a stinging complaint that life should hold so much promise but deliver so little satisfaction: "I have seen the business that God has given to the sons of men to be busy with. He has made everything beautiful in its time; also he has put eternity into man's mind, yet so that he cannot find out what God has done from the beginning to the end" (3:10–11).

The difficulty is that, in spite of his suspicions, man is not and can never be an animal. He is disturbed by a relation with God that cannot be shaken off. It is the clash between the high promise of the thoughts of greatness that haunt him and the trivial monotony of his existence that constitutes the mainspring of the Preacher's message. Among the things that shock him most is the stupidity of the simple punishment-reward theory, as it also affronted the author of Job and the writers of several of the psalms. Against that kind of naïve assertion of divine intervention in life, the Preacher sounded his most stunning denials: God, that kind of mathematical God, does not control the world. Rather it is chance, "happenstance" that reigns in its weirdly capricious way. Wealth may be lost suddenly. Men may have health snatched away just as they are about to enjoy the wealth and honor they have amassed. Justice is often perverted by the greater power of the wrongdoer. The nihilism of this claim if logically pursued would lead to atheism, but the Preacher denies only the orthodox God of the pious who seem to have no trouble apprehending the ways of the divine. The sage asserts an agnosticism, a limit upon human knowing, which is nevertheless a thoroughly religious conviction. He is reaching for the God behind the God of orthodoxy.

Positively, what may one derive from life? The Preacher calls man to immediate enjoyment of eating and drinking (2:24; 3:12–13; 5:18; 8:15; 9:7–8), companionship (4:9–12), love and marriage (9:9, note the monogamous ideal), and reserved worship (5:1–2). Above all, relish youth while it is yours! This is eudaemonism, a concern for happiness and well-being; but it is not hedonism, not pleasure for pleasure's sake. He believes in qualities of pleasure, not to be sought blindly but in full awareness of life's fleeting character. Toward morality and religion he has no hostility but rather a wistfulness and sad regret that they do not have more reality in this kind of world. Ecclesiastes has the perennial appeal of a chastened and sober affirmation of limited meaning. It is an ancient example of the existentialist darkness and the "leap of faith," the grasping of meaning that seems to be slipping away on every side, "the courage to be." The Preacher may dismiss life as a farce—especially when he meets those who contentedly see nothing in it but a lark—but he loves the play as dearly as any of the cast.

What does it mean that such a nihilistic work appears in the Old Testament? The God of the Preacher is impersonal and incommunicative. The wisdom movement seems to have run into bankruptcy; Hebrew humanism has reached a dead end. The Preacher accents the meaninglessness of life without strong purpose and above all without a Purposer. He poses the alternative to personal theism. Yet the book also cautions us that our purpose and faith in the Purposer cannot be merely a projection of our hope for something better, a mirror of our cultural values. So the Preacher voices our feelings and also warns us that gods made in man's image to protect us from the dark night of the soul are no gods at all. Better the lonely trek of the Preacher than the closed and stifling world of the petty orthodox. It may seem like strained logic to regard this most negative of Jewish books as a preparation for the New Testament, but the work has a ring of modernity and it sets us starkly before our situation as humans, into which Christ descended not to fashion more gods and theories of gods, of which the world had plenty already, but to lay hold of the toil and the emptiness of the world and in overcoming them to offer man a way of victory.

SONG OF SONGS

The title "Song of Solomon" has been supplied in English versions. The Hebrew text of the book has the more ambiguous editorial heading, "The Song of Songs (to, of, for?) Solomon," which leaves open the question of authorship. It may simply mean "the Song dedicated to Solomon" or "in the style of Solomon." At any rate, by the time of the meeting of rabbis at Jamnia it was the ostensible Solomonic authorship that rescued the Song for the canon. Many, then and now, would have preferred to let it die. A devoted few, notably Rabbi Akiba, championed the Song when the majority of rabbis decried its secularism and portrayal of sex bordering on immodesty and vulgarity.

The work is an unabashed commentary on the sentiment of Proverbs 30:18–19, "three things are too wonderful for me, four I do not understand . . . the way of a man with a maid." There is no mystery about the book in its essential outlines. It is a series of poems describing the delights of human love and written with Oriental sensuousness. While it is characterized by a frank portrayal of the human body and the emotions evoked by the bodily contact of lovers, such as to put it out of good taste in some societies, the only obscenity or vulgarity is that brought to it by the mind of the reader. The poems exalt the psychophysical union of men and women, albeit with a trace of romanticism that is at times airily adolescent. Yet it expresses throughout a fundamental Hebraic feeling about the unalloyed wonder and the essential rightness of the man-woman relationship.

But before it could find acceptance in the Jewish canon, the work had to be interpreted allegorically of God and Israel. The way was open for this line of interpretation ever since Hosea had set forth the union of Yahweh and his people under the marriage symbol. At Jamnia Akiba argued the allegorical theory uncompromisingly and was so unrestrained as to declare that "no day outweighed in glory the one on which Israel received the Song of Solomon." In the Christian Church, it has been common practice to replace Israel with the Church as the Bride of Christ. Mystics such as Bernard of Clairvaux regarded the allegory as bodying forth the relation of Christ and the individual believer. It must be insisted unequivocally, however, that there is no ground whatsoever for an allegorical interpretation. The result of such mitigation of the plain meaning of the poems is a sickly religious eroticism far more objectionable than the healthy emotion expressed by the poet.

The traditional alternative to the allegorical dodge has been the dramatic interpretation, which assumes that the work is a dramatic integrity, its parts consisting of the speeches of the three principal characters: Solomon, a shepherd, and a maiden. The plot traced through the speeches is the story of a "triangle" in which Solomon tries to win the rustic lass from her lover, but true love triumphs over the attractions of wealth and station as the maiden returns to her shepherd lover. It is a variation of a simple and universal love motif, but the progress of the dramatic action is doubtful. One suspects rather that the poems are the voicing of several moods and situations. There is no sustained dialogue and not even as much evidence of staging as in the case of Job, where the dramatic interpretation is also fallacious. Furthermore, Solomon would thereby be cast in an unfavorable light as the "villain"; such a role for the venerated sage and king would hardly have won backing for the book.

The view that the Song is an anthology of lyric poems has, until very recently, held the virtually uncontested lead in modern criticism. Form criticism when applied to the work reveals from twenty-five to thirty separate poems linked together by the common theme of human love. A popular form of the theory was encouraged by the anthropological research of Wetzstein in modern Syria. He found songs of the same sort being used at the marriage festivals. The Song of Songs could be explained similarly as poems to be sung at the ceremonies and festivities of a Jewish wedding. It is interesting that the rather detailed descriptions of physical beauty characteristic of the Song were also found in the Syrian compositions. The chief difficulty with the theory, however, is that a majority of the poems refer explicitly to love *before* marriage. The likely view is that Song of Songs is an anthology of lyrics, some being used in wedding ceremonies, and all adopting the mores and clichés of love prevalent in ancient Semitic society.[28]

In recent scholarship the cult-mythical theory of the Song of Songs has been advanced with much ingenuity. Basically its advocates claim that the work does not refer to human love at all but to the sacred marriage of a god and goddess as celebrated in many of the Near Eastern cults, notably Tammuz worship. Later the songs were spirit-

[28] For similar songs from ancient Egypt see Appendix 5, pp. 584–585.

ualized for monotheistic consumption by replacing the goddess with the figure of Israel, the Bride of Yahweh. Thus, the later allegorizing of the Jews was a kind of surreptitious support of the fertility origin of the Song. The use of the poems liturgically at the Passover festival in later times is also treated as an extension of their primal cultic use. But the straining of scholars for cultic terminology in the Song is grossly overdone, and the insurmountable problem remains: how could a work with such an explicit polytheistic origin ever have found acceptance among the Jews? If, on the other hand, it is argued that the "secular" love songs were influenced by idioms drawn from the fertility cult, then we really have a variant of the lyric theory. When held uncompromisingly, the cult-mythical theory turns out to be only a somewhat more sophisticated form of the allegorical interpretation.

The Song is as near to Romanticism as the Old Testament gets. In fact, here alone is nature considered as a phenomenon in its own right, a world evocative to the senses, aesthetically delightful, mirroring and echoing the lovers' raptures. It is a folk literature, sprung from the peasant heart of Israel, redolent with the native earth of Palestine. The summons of the lover at the coming of springtime never fails to stir the one who chances to overhear those words meant only for the beloved:

> Arise, my love, my fair one,
>> and come away;
> for lo, the winter is past,
>> the rain is over and gone.
>
> . . . .
> Arise, my love, my fair one,
>> and come away.
> O my dove, in the clefts of the rock,
>> in the covert of the cliff,
> let me see your face,
>> let me hear your voice,
> for your voice is sweet,
>> and your face is comely (2:10–11,13b–14).

And at the harvesting of the fruits:

> Come, my beloved,
>> let us go forth into the fields,
>> and lodge in the villages;
> let us go out early to the vineyards,

and see whether the vines have budded,
whether the grape blossoms have opened
and the pomegranates are in bloom.
There I will give you my love.
The mandrakes give forth fragrance,
and over our doors are all choice fruits,
new as well as old,
which I have laid up for you, O my beloved (7:11–13).

The bucolic playfulness of Theocritus, the breathless ecstasy of Keats and the Brownings, need no apology when they appear in the Old Testament. The Song of Songs serves as a welcome reminder that the Hebrews were men like ourselves, that their quest for God and God's choice of them did not nullify their passionate love of life and their simple rejoicing in the sexuality of the race.

RECONSTRUCTION UNDER THE HELLENISTS

The saints of the Most High shall receive the kingdom . . .
Dan. 7:18

THE ENCROACHMENT OF HELLENISM, 333–63 B.C.

When Alexander the Great crossed the Hellespont and launched his conquest of Asia a new epoch in world affairs was opened. Now for the first time East and West met in a significant way; far more important than the clash of arms was the clash of two traditions: the Occidental and the Oriental. To describe the many facets of their interaction is a whole history in itself, and in a real sense the admixture of cultural elements from the ancient Near East and from the classical world is still in process. Each generation is the product of previous combinations and the initiator of new compounds. Alexander, beyond his dreams of military conquest, was the first person in world history to espouse cosmopolitanism. Thus he holds an endless attraction for modernity, since cosmopolitanism has become the crucial issue of our time. But to the postexilic community of Jews it was a major shock to be faced with the prospect of a militant Gentile universalism. Judaism as a way of life, as a body of procedures and customs, could not calmly contemplate cultural assimilation with its inevitable outcome: religious annihilation. The tide of Hellenism unleashed by Alexander in the Orient had the effect of confirming Judaism in its main features through a frontal challenge, but also the more subtle effect of broadening the spirit of Judaism, rendering it flexible through a vigorous sectarian life and preparing it for the emergence of its most creative phase: Jewish Christianity, which so soon became a world church.

495

Alexander built upon the initial successes of his father Philip of Macedon; in 336 he resolved to invade Persia as the Orientals had once invaded Greece. At Granicus in Asia Minor in 334 and a year later at Issus in north Syria, the Persians were defeated. Rather than move directly toward the heart of the empire, Alexander advanced down the Syro-Palestinian corridor and entered Egypt where he founded the city of Alexandria. He established Greek cities as islands of culture in the Oriental sea. Replete with the architectural, cultural, and political accouterments of a Greek city-state, these centers remained the most enduring monuments to the invader. While their influence has sometimes been exaggerated, so that historians have needed to emphasize that large tracts of Asia and Egypt were untouched by them, these centers of culture were potent exponents of Hellenism. Alexander awarded local autonomy whenever possible, partly out of conviction, partly out of sheer inability to administer thoroughly a vast empire conquered in the twinkling of an eye. The tyranny of his successors was born of a strange brew of Hellenistic sophistication and Oriental absolutism. In terms of political institutions the Orient conquered Hellenism rather than the reverse. In 331 at Gaugamela on the northern Tigris the Persian army was decisively defeated and the further exploits of Alexander as far as the Indus River were limited only by the physical ability and loyalty of his troops, both of which were eventually taxed beyond endurance.

Alexander's premature death in 323 left no single powerful leader. That was the dominant factor in the succeeding two centuries of Asian political history. The devastating and cruel internecine struggles among his generals make some of the most trivial and dreary reading in ancient history. There is little high-mindedness of the sort to which Alexander at least occasionally aspired to lighten the sordid tale of ambition and treachery. After two decades of conflict, the empire was split four ways. Cassander held Macedon and Lysimachus ruled in Asia Minor. For Jewish history the more important successors of Alexander were the *Ptolemies in Egypt* and the *Seleucids in Syria*. Ptolemy Lagi had seized Egypt, for he shrewdly recognized it as the most defensible portion of the empire. Ptolemaic sovereignty over Palestine was supreme until 198 B.C. and was replaced in Egypt only by the Romans in 30 B.C. The most important ruler of the dynasty was Ptolemy II Philadelphus (285–246), who beautified Alexandria with imposing buildings and encouraged the Hellenizing of Egypt. It was in his rule that the Septuagint translation of the Hebrew Scriptures was begun. The fourth and largest division of Alexander's realm fell to Seleucus Nicator, who ruled in Syria and Mesopotamia and theoretically throughout Persia and Bactria, as far as Alexander's troops had gone. His capital city and area of greatest influence were in Syria, where his dynasty held sway until the Romans introduced colonial rule in 63 B.C. His kingdom was sharply reduced by the Parthians, who triumphed east of the Euphrates from 129 B.C., but on the west the Seleucids gained territory through the assimilation of the domain of Lysimachus. By 275 B.C. there were only three Hellenistic empires. The Macedonian line ended by 168 and the region became a Roman province in 146.

The small Judean community was now what it had often been in preëxilic days, the no man's land between larger powers. Under the Ptolemies there seems to have been no serious repression of Jewish habits or faith. Taxes were onerous and the cultural suasion of Hellenism welcomed by the libertarian Jews was resented by the stricter adherents of the Law. After a century of Ptolemaic rule over the Jews, the Seleucids led by Antiochus III the Great won a victory at Paneas in 198 that gave Palestine into the hands of the Syrians. From the start the Seleucid goal and method were more steadfastly those of the integration of culture. The larger centers were provided with city-state organization and especially that mark of Greek democracy—the assembly, for the Hellenistic emperors loved the show of democratic institutions even though their own dispositions were tyrannical. The ideal of the beautiful body was fostered through the gymnasium with its organized sports; Greek dress became the rage. Jerusalem experienced this mounting pressure toward Hellenistic conformity in the form of a split between Hellenizing and orthodox Jews.

At this point Antiochus IV Epiphanes ("god revealed," dubbed Epimanes, "madman" by his subjects) occupied the throne. With no tact or foresight he set out to extirpate Judaism, since its mode of life and thought were a menace to the cultural uniformity of his empire. For his part it was solely a political program; bred as he was on the easy-going religious tolerance of the Hellenistic world, he could hardly have guessed at the intense conviction of the Jewish people with regard to their belief. Antiochus sold the office of high priest to the highest bidder and two sycophants rose to the occasion, Menelaus finally outbidding Jason. Increasingly Antiochus committed himself to backing the Hellenizing party in Jerusalem. Yet it passed beyond a Jewish civil war between liberal and orthodox when the Seleucid power intervened in an act that shook Judaism to its moorings. Antiochus in 168 desecrated the temple by sacrificing a pig on the altar (called "the abomination of desolation" in Dan. 9:27; 12:11) and prohibiting henceforth any Jewish sacrifices. The Law was proscribed and those caught with a copy in their possession were executed. The Sabbath could not be observed nor circumcision practiced. To enforce these severe measures a garrison of troops was stationed in an especially constructed section of Jerusalem—actually a self-sustaining city within the city—known as the Akra. Obviously if the policies of Antiochus had been carried out it would have meant the end of Judaism.

There were those, however, who would rather die than capitulate to the proscription of Judaism—and there were some who would rather resist with arms. Such was Mattathias, a priest from the Shephelah town of Modin, whose four outstanding sons carried on the battle he launched. Dramatically Mattathias struck down both the Syrian officer who had come to enforce Hellenistic sacrifice on the villagers and the apostate Jew who first stepped forward to comply with the edict. Fleeing to the hills, the family of Mattathias (known as Hasmoneans, after the priest's great-grandfather; or as Maccabees, a nickname for the oldest son Judas, probably meaning "the Hammerer") carried on a guerrilla-type campaign of constant harassment of the enemy. The apocryphal books of Maccabees describe the maneuvers in detail. Three years after the desecration of the temple, in December of 165, the Feast of the Dedication was celebrated and has been observed by Jews ever since as Hanukkah or the Feast of Lights. The Syrians, who had their hands full with internal division after the death of Antiochus Epiphanes, were willing to grant Jewish religious freedom, thus writing off the whole attempt to suppress Judaism as more costly than it was worth. A party of pious defenders of the Law, known as the Hasidim (derived from Hebrew *hesedh*, "covenant faithfulness"), who had supported the Maccabees while the issue was the life or death of Judaism, now favored acceptance of the Seleucid terms of settlement. But the Maccabees' blood was up and they went on to fight for political freedom.

When Judas Maccabaeus fell in battle, his brother Jonathan succeeded him, directing a "government in exile" from headquarters at

Michmash while the Hellenizers occupied Jerusalem. The political freedom eventually achieved was won mainly by Jonathan cannily throwing his influence first to one side and then the other in the intense struggle of aspirants for the Seleucid throne. At one point he even supplied several thousand Jewish mercenaries who joined in a sack of Antioch! Jonathan was made high priest in 152 and in 142 Judah was granted immunity from tribute. The high point of the drive for Jewish independence was reached in 140 when Simon, who came to power after the treacherous execution of his brother, was declared high priest, commander of the army, and civil ruler (messiah) forever. At the same time the hated Akra was removed from Jerusalem. A year later Simon was striking coins in his own name.

Although the gains of the Maccabees were seriously threatened when Simon was assassinated by his brother-in-law, the successor John Hyrcanus reëstablished them and his long reign from 134 to 104 raised Judah to the rank of a Hellenistic princedom. Judah was in fact the strongest military power in Syria, with troops composed of native levies and mercenaries in considerable number. Alexander Jannaeus (103–76) carried on wars of aggrandizement in the style of Hyrcanus. Judah controlled the coast, Samaria, Idumea (Latin form of Edom, i.e., the portion of the Negeb in which Edomites had settled during the Exile), and Trans-Jordan. The dominating goal throughout this period was the restoration of the kingdom of David. The rulers, actually priest-kings, were generally regarded by their subjects and thought of themselves as the messiah-deliverers of Israel.

Not everyone shared the enthusiasm. The Hasids had by this time come to be known as Pharisees (probably meaning "the separated ones," i.e., those who renounce evil or evil company); they resolutely opposed the worldly conquests and coarse living of the Hasmonean kings. Though they normally resorted to moral suasion, at one point they appealed to the Seleucid Demetrius III to relieve them of the intolerable vanity and depravity of Jannaeus. The plot was on the brink of success when the rank and file Jews were suddenly won back to the king by the prospect of a foreigner reoccupying Jerusalem and erasing the hard-earned freedoms. In retaliation Jannaeus ordered the crucifixion of eight hundred of the Pharisees while he mockingly feasted with harlots. Some scholars believe that the Teacher of Righteousness mentioned in the Dead Sea Scrolls was one of the Pharisees martyred at this time and that the priest-king Jannaeus was the Wicked Priest, persecutor, and murderer of the Teacher.[1] While they suffered horrible defeat, the Pharisees did not have long to wait for relief.

When Salome Alexandra came to power (76–67) she made her son Hyrcanus II high priest and offered immediate overtures of peace to-

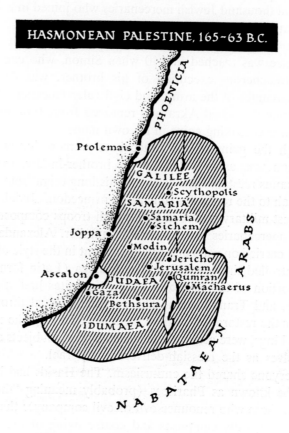

HASMONEAN PALESTINE, 165~63 B.C.

//// THE HASMONEAN KINGDOM
AT ITS ZENITH UNDER
ALEXANDER JANNAEUS
103~76 BC.

ward the Pharisees, some of whom were admitted to membership in the ruling body of Judaism, the Sanhedrin. In the period 67–63, Hyrcanus II and Aristobulus feuded furiously for the Hasmonean throne,

[1] E.g., A. Dupont-Sommer, *The Jewish Sect of Qumran and the Essenes*, Vallentine, Mitchell, 2nd ed., 1955, especially chaps. 2, 3, 4.

the former being supported by Antipater the Idumean (father of Herod the Great) and Arab allies. Both parties offered money to Pompey, who was in Damascus in 63 B.C., but the people of Judah by this time had come to share the disgust of the Pharisees. Actually they saw no valid choice between the two opportunists, and thus the decision of Pompey to take over Palestine as Roman territory was hailed by the Pharisees and many others as preferable to the venal rule of native princes. Hyrcanus was retained as high priest with sharply restricted powers. The dream of the neo-Davidic empire and of the era of righteousness and peace had ended abruptly.

Herod's Temple at Samaria-Sebaste, dedicated to Augustus Caesar.

The intricacies of the Maccabean era fall into three major phases: (1) the struggle for religious liberty, 168–165 B.C.; (2) the struggle for political freedom, 165–140 B.C.; (3) the period of political expansion and decay, 140–63 B.C. The revolt began as a religious protest almost instinctive in nature, a fight for survival. It continued, however, as an attempt to resurrect the ancient Jewish kingdom and dissipated itself in effete and depraved leadership. On the one hand, it assured the continuation of Judaism by congealing the loyal believers in pointed opposition to Hellenism; on the other, it sought a religio-political goal

Chart 7. The Hasmonean or Maccabean Line, 168–35 B.C.

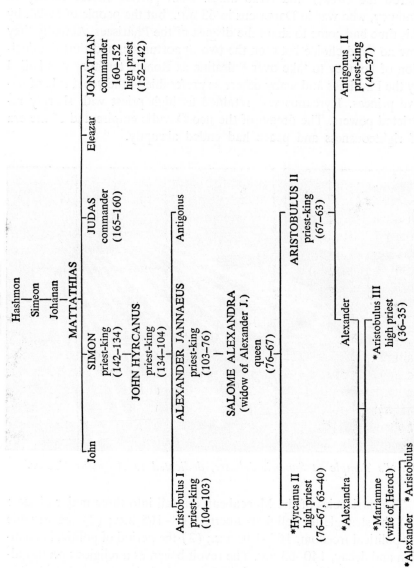

* The murder of these six by Herod marked the extinction of the Hasmonean line.

of Jewish world dominion through increasingly dubious and finally perverse means. At the end large numbers of Jews were unsympathetic or openly resentful of the corruption of the messiah ideal. Ironically, the base decay of Hellenism typified in the morally wretched Seleucids had infected the Hasmonean line, for its kings from Jonathan on were men who became increasingly like the enemy they deplored.

But those who renounced the Hasmoneans and their works did not resort to a merely "spiritual" notion of messiah. He was yet to be the effecter of political-historical rejuvenation, but he was to have the covenant qualities of righteousness, justice, and peace-making so abysmally lacking in the Hasmoneans. The Psalms of Solomon (esp. chap. 17), written by Pharisees shortly after the coup of Pompey, rail against the Jewish priest-kings as "a worldly monarchy" that "laid waste the throne of David in tumultuous arrogance," regard Rome as an agent of divine punishment, and continue to hope for the raising up of the true king, son of David, who would exterminate all the wicked in Israel and among the nations. Judaism, in spite of the bitter experience of the former century, was still a world-affirming, group-centered, historically minded religion.

THE PSALMS

The only Old Testament book well known to many Christians and faithfully read by them is Psalms. This moving devotional poetry seems to make a minimum of demands upon the critical understanding and speaks with an undoubted directness to the deepest stirrings of the human heart. Many who feel that in reading the Pentateuch or the prophets they are "looking through a glass darkly" claim to find communion with God "face to face" in the Psalms. But the universal and unbridled praise of the collection may be somewhat wiser as a result of more careful and critical examination.

A Poetic Anthology

The book is an anthology of 150 poems. In some cases it is obvious that a single composition has been split in two without justification (Psalms 9–10 form a single alphabetic poem and 42–43 are united by a refrain). The fluidity in delimiting the poems is shown in the variant numbering of the Septuagint, which rightly combines 9 and 10 but illogically treats 114 and 115 as a single poem. It also divides 116 and 147 into two poems each and numbers them accordingly. The result is that the Greek-Latin and Hebrew-English enumerations vary, although each tradition has the same number of Psalms. Most translations of Greek or Latin give the Hebrew order in parentheses, e.g., Psalm 88 (89).

Closer scrutiny reveals a fivefold division to the anthology. After each of the first four segments a benediction is appended: Psalms 1–41; 42–72; 73–89; 90–106. The last psalm is a doxology, probably appended to the collection as a grand finale. Since the divisions do not correspond with authorship, literary type, or subject matter, they are best understood as arbitrary imitations of the fivefold division of the Pentateuch. Another interesting distinction is the so-called Elohist psalter of 42–83 in which the occurrence of the divine name Elohim far outnumbers that of Yahweh. This is in sharp contrast to the other psalms. The student may make his own comparison by reading Psalms 14 and 53, which are practically identical except for the divine name.

Superscriptions to most of the Psalms supply information about author, circumstance of origin, and musical execution. The historical value of the notations is decidedly limited. They are of little use in determining the origin of the individual works. What they do show is the existence of subcollections in the postexilic period and the manifest interest of the editors in providing full program notes. In effect the superscriptions indicate how the Psalms were interpreted and used in the Second Temple, although even this benefit is sharply qualified by the enigmatic character of the references, especially the musical directions. Little is known about Hebrew instruments and less about compositions and styles of vocal and instrumental rendition. The spectrum of terms suggests that there was a developed choral and instrumental practice in the Second Temple (this is also supported by the great interest of the Chronicler in temple worship), but most of the details are unintelligible to modern interpreters. For instance, the term Selah, which occurs seventy-one times in the Psalter, has been interpreted variously as a stanza divider, an emphatic similar to Amen, a refrain or benediction marker, crescendo sign, indication of change of voices, pause, repeat—and many more besides! It is possible, as several scholars now argue, that the superscriptions reflect preëxilic cultic practice, but the form of the Psalter is decidedly postexilic.

Analysis of the subcollections according to the superscriptions shows several items of interest:

Although the majority of the David psalms are in the first half of the Psalter and 72:20 declares "the prayers of David, the son of Jesse are ended," seventeen later psalms are associated with him (86, 101, 103, 108–110, 122, 124, 131, 138–145). The notation of 72:20 makes sense only if at one time it concluded a subsection of the present Psalter, i.e., before Psalms 73–150 were included. Yet the nature of

Egyptian musicians and dancers from a Theban tomb painting (ca. 1550–1350 B.C.). The instruments are, left to right, harp, lute, double pipe, lyre.

the Davidic attribution is open to debate. In some cases the superscription is sufficiently detailed to show that the editor regarded David as the author or at least the speaker of the psalm (3, 7, 18, 34, 51, 52, 54, 56, 57, 59, 60, 63, 142 are connected with incidents in the life of David). But the Hebrew preposition in the phrase "psalm *of* David" is flexible in meaning—"of, by, to, for" are all possible renderings depending on context. Many of the superscriptions probably mean no more than "in David's style" or "dedicated to the king." The heading to Psalm 30 is historically impossible, for David was not living at the time of the dedication of the temple; what it means is "royal psalm" and the rededication referred to is either that of Zerubbabel in 516 or Judas Maccabaeus in 165. The fact is that David as the archetypal psalmist, "the sweet singer of Israel," has become the traditional sponsor and architect of the Psalter—even though individual psalms are attributed to others.

Among the other composers of Psalms are Korah and Asaph, identified by Chronicles as heads of guilds of temple singers. It is doubtful that the editor regards those musicians and choirmasters as the poets. The likely meaning is that they were the collectors, that the psalms so titled formed a part of the repertoire of their guilds. Solomon is credited with two psalms (72 and 127) and Moses with one (90). The last subcollection denoted by superscription is that of "the songs of ascents," commonly taken as a group of pilgrim songs for those ascending to Jerusalem, perhaps sung at various stages of the journey. While some are eminently suited to that purpose in that they voice the feelings of joy in the prospective worshiper, others have so inward and meditative a quality as to be inappropriate for processional use. It has been suggested that the "ascents" refer to the steps going up to the altar in the temple yard, on which the priests recited the songs, but the same objection applies. Also, the "ascents" have been referred to the literary device of staircase parallelism or anadiplosis (i.e., the habit of repeating a key word or phrase from the end of one line at the beginning of the next; note especially Psalm 121).

Another significant division of the psalter is the cluster of Hallel or Praise Psalms in 111–118 for use at Passover. One or more of these psalms were sung by Jesus and his disciples at the Last Supper. There are many other divisions that could be designated: acrostic poems employing alphabetic sequence, imprecatory psalms that call down curses on the psalmists' enemies, and wisdom psalms that inculcate piety and praise the Jewish Law.

LITERARY TYPES

The most productive of all the breakdowns of the psalter has been that of Gunkel whose study of types (*Gattungen*) was one of the significant forward steps in twentieth-century biblical science. The five major types that he found in the Psalter were hymns, communal laments, royal psalms, individual laments, and individual thanksgiving songs.[2] Categories of lesser importance he designated as songs of pilgrimage, communal songs of thanksgiving, wisdom poetry, liturgies, and mixed poems.[3] Although there are many reasonable doubts about the aptness of these categories in detail, and many differences of opinion as to how each psalm is to be allocated, the attention that Gunkel focused upon the formal features of the Psalms has been of inestimable worth. What he attempted to show was that far from being purely a collection of independently styled poems, the Psalms drew upon a fund of technical terminology and style that had a great antiquity in Israel. His exhaustive lists of recurrent words and phrases drive home the certainty of a Psalm idiom. Each of the types had a prehistory and an inherent structure and was used in certain ways in the life of the people: the hymns for praise of God at the sanctuary, the laments to appeal for aid on an individual or communal basis, the songs of thanksgiving to express gratitude for divine aid granted, the royal psalms to celebrate monarchic events of importance such as battles, weddings, and coronations. Thus the roots of the Psalter were ritualistic in the broadest sense, intertwined with the fixed habits of private and public life.

Gunkel insisted paradoxically that the writers of the biblical psalms were free agents in that they "democratized" or "individualized" the traditional material. He had a liberal Protestant's pathological dislike of the cult, however, and wherever the Psalms express a particularly deep piety he was inclined to feel that the poems had been detached from sacrificial or ritual practice. He nevertheless conceded that by the time the Psalter was collected during the Second Temple, the poems were again being used in worship situations. In the liturgical use of the temple he saw a tendency for the earlier types to disintegrate into mixed forms. Thus the movement in the psalms was from community ritual through individual prophetic religion to use in the temple worship, and from "pure" or unmixed types to complex hybrid forms.[4]

A second epochal phase of modern study of the Psalter was the work of Mowinckel,[5] who accepted Gunkel's categories in the main

[2] Hermann Gunkel, *Einleitung in die Psalmen*, Vandenhoeck & Ruprecht, 1933, pp. 1–292; Gunkel's views are clearly explained, illustrated, and evaluated by A. R. Johnson, "The Psalms," *The Old Testament and Modern Study* (ed. H. H. Rowley), 1950, pp. 162–181.

[3] Hermann Gunkel, *op. cit.*, pp. 293–415.

[4] *Ibid.*, pp. 415–458.

[5] S. Mowinckel, *Psalmenstudien I–V*, Kristiania, 1922–24; see also A. R. Johnson, *op. cit.*, pp. 189–197.

but came to some radically different conclusions about the use of the psalms and the history of their development. Basically the difference between the two is that Mowinckel has a high regard for the constructive role of the cult and tends to see its function as more pervasive. Gunkel had given the preëxilic monarch a place in the cult, but it was Mowinckel who stressed the king's role as Yahweh's representative in the annual enthronement festival. Whereas Gunkel regarded nine psalms as royal, Mowinckel found over forty in the coronation genre. When the kingdom was destroyed in 587 B.C. and the festival ceased, Mowinckel believes that the hopes of Yahweh's world dominion expressed in the enthronement psalms were projected into the distant future and given a supermundane quality. Thus he regards eschatology as derivative from the frustration of Israelite hopes celebrated in the cult. Whereas Gunkel had stressed the creative role of the prophets as anticultic, Mowinckel saw no such rift but freely regarded the prophets as cult personnel. Mowinckel has a wide following but there are many scholars who resist the large and creative role that he attributes to the royal cult of Israel; this resistance is found among many who acknowledge the existence of the festival but regard it as peripheral to the covenant faith.

So the ground has shifted greatly from the nineteenth-century view that the Psalter was strictly a product of the Second Temple with great numbers of the psalms coming from the Greek and Maccabean periods. Gunkel and Mowinckel, extremely dissimilar in many ways, agree in granting more psalms to the preëxilic period than did their predecessors. They both allow to the cult a greater role in shaping the idiom and ideology of the psalms, although Gunkel's disposition begrudges him the admission and he interprets "cult" as the whole complex of communal habit, while Mowinckel seems to overstate the role of the enthronement festival. They both supply a greatly enriched conception of the psalm literature in spite of the inevitable subjectivity of their conclusions because of the scarcity of controllable evidence.

With such paucity of historical allusion in the Psalms we shall probably never have a clear history of the development of the Psalter. Instead we see a balancing of factors, some supporting the *preëxilic* origin of psalms: the royal cult and the parallel Ras esh-Shamra literature with its stylistic affinities to Psalms 18, 29, 68, etc.; others supporting the *postexilic* origin of many psalms: the reference to national exile and the development of the law-piety as evidenced in the monumental 119th Psalm. Engnell, who maintains that he can find no more than one psalm that is definitely postexilic (137),[6] and Pfeiffer, who finds only two preëxilic psalms (24:7–10; 45), have adopted extreme positions that not many scholars would be willing to defend.[7] Psalms such as 2 and 110 that refer to the anointed, previously thought to be Maccabean, are now frequently assigned to the preëxilic cult. It should be stressed, however, that psalms originating in the earlier cult would naturally have been used in celebrating the revived messianic line of Hasmoneans. And it is easy to believe that the poems would have been reshaped in the process; the garbled text of Psalm 110 may be due to just such frequency of use.

REPRESENTATIVE PSALMS

In the ensuing discussion of individual Psalms, an effort has been made to comment on representative literary types and religious themes, but the author would be the first to admit that preference in such matters is highly personal.

Psalm 1 is a fitting proem to the Psalter, for its teaching of the two ways (the way of the wicked and the way of the righteous) strikes a note common to scores of the Psalms. The image of the righteous student of the law who looks for retribution in this life is a perfect model of the postexilic sage and pious man, but theories that have equated the righteous and wicked with particular social classes or sects in Judaism are too subjective to be proved one way or the other.

Psalm 8 is a hymn in "envelope" style, i.e., the opening and closing lines are synonymous. The poem sets forth a theological humanism according to which God delegated man to lordship over the natural world. All commentators have noted the close connection between this psalm and Genesis 1, although there is no question of direct influence. Man's glory is not an inherent quality but a gift; his glory and honor are expressed in purest form when he exercises his dominion over creation.

Psalm 22 is an individual lament by a forsaken sufferer who promises to witness to God's goodness once he is delivered. The opening line was quoted by Jesus from the cross, "My God, my God, why hast thou forsaken me?" Next to the Suffering Servant of Deutero-Isaiah there is

[6] Ivan Engnell, *Studies in Divine Kingship in the Ancient Near East,* Almquist, 1943, p. 176.
[7] R. H. Pfeiffer, *Introduction to the Old Testament,* Harper, 1941, p. 629.

no portrait in the Old Testament so prefiguring the physical and spiritual abasement and triumph of Christ. Although rejected by men, the sufferer feels most keenly his abandonment by God and the loss of spiritual rapport that had been his consolation from birth. In his prayer for release, there is no trace of vengeance (how unlike Jeremiah and most of the psalms!). He vows to praise God in the congregation, and as a result of his confession the nations will worship Yahweh and future generations will adore him. A typical feature of the lament psalm is here illustrated: the sufferer feels so intensely the surety of God's deliverance that he begins to describe it as accomplished. With similar confidence the prophets sometimes described the future judgment or restoration as though it were contemporary.

Psalm 24 is a liturgy of entrance to the temple in which the pilgrim asks, "Who shall ascend the hill of Yahweh?" The priest gives answer in terms of ethical requirements. To this has been prefaced a tetrastich praising God's act as Creator, and rounding out the psalm is an ark liturgy of antiphonal questions and acclamations used in connection with a procession of the priests into the temple or of the army through the city gates. Since after the building of the temple the ark was apparently kept in perpetual darkness in the holy of holies, many scholars believe that this must be a fragment of the liturgy used in the time of David and possibly written by the king himself.

Psalm 29 is a description of a Mediterranean storm striking the mainland, crossing the Lebanon mountains, and dissipating in the desert—all under the figure of thunder and lightning as "the voice of Yahweh." The work is climaxed by the shout of "Glory!" in the temple; the categories of nature and ritual are fused in the worship of God who is Lord over the chaos and Lord of the covenant.

Psalm 46 is a three-strophe hymn on the stability and security of trust in God. Though catastrophes shake the earth

> Yahweh of hosts is with us;
>   the God of Jacob is our refuge.

This refrain at the end of the last two strophes has probably fallen out of the text after the first stanza. The famous line, "Be still, and know that I am God" is one of the most frequently misinterpreted verses in the Bible. It does not appeal for introspective meditation or study of nature's loveliness. It asks rather that men desist from their frenzied activities in order to see God at work among the nations, making wars to cease. The idea of the city's impregnability when trusting God resembles the legendary account of Isaiah in 701 during Sennacherib's siege (Isa. 36–39), but there is no sound basis for regarding Isaiah as the psalmist.

Psalm 51, technically an individual lament, is in fact a confession of the purest sort. The psalmist asks for no boons or deliverance except cleansing from his desperate wickedness of thought or motive (rather than overt deed; "bloodguiltiness" in vs. 14 should probably be read, "silence"). This penitential psalm has been connected by tradition with the archsinner David, but the depth of contrition, the radical apprehension of divine cleansing (the word "create" stresses the divine initiative and sovereignty in fashioning a new heart for the sinner), and the spiritualization of sacrifice argue against Davidic authorship. With few exceptions scholars regard the last two verses as a post-exilic addition intended to mitigate the original psalmist's indifference toward sacrifice.

Psalm 73 ranks with Job as a deep-felt expression of the love of God for God's sake. The poet's lament at first ranges over the typical affronts to faith: the sorry lot of the righteous and the affluence of the wicked. He reaches the point of the renunciation of his faith:

> All in vain have I kept my heart clean
> and washed my hands in innocence.

Yet he is held back from open impiety by the thought of its adverse effect upon those who would come after him. On further reflection in the temple he comes to realize how short-lived is the prosperity of the evil who have no real substance but are "like a dream when one awakes." The lament then passes over into a psalm of trust with the poet proclaiming the companionship of God as superior to all possible earthly rewards. He even ventures near to the affirmation that death will not destroy his intimate relation with God, for "afterward thou wilt receive me to glory." The psalm exhibits an amazing spiritualization of the notions of reward and punishment both in this life and the next. God alone is the reward of the righteous man; nearness to him is life, separation from him is death. The intrinsic goodness of life with God and the inherent evil of life without him erase all thought of compensation imposed from without: "For lo, those who are far from thee shall perish . . . But for me it is good to be near God."

Psalm 90 is a collective lament that sets frail man in the context of the eternal God. Man's mortality weighs heavily upon the poet whose people have of late known only the unremitting anger of God. Against the backdrop of Israel's bitterly pessimistic experience in exile, the poet asks for a measure of sober wisdom for his people and some sign of God's continued favor. With gripping pathos he entreats:

> Make us glad as many days as thou hast afflicted us,
>   and as many years as we have seen evil.

The lament closes with the inveterately Hebraic hope that God would establish the work of his people and make their labors once again worthwhile. In spite of an undertow of despair, the psalm expresses a tenacious hope in God and the dependability of his future for Israel.

Psalm 99 is a splendid example of the enthronement psalm genre. Yahweh is praised as king upon the throne of the universe. His justice, righteousness, and holiness are effective among men. All the nations are to honor him. The crux in interpreting psalms of this type (in contrast to 2 and 110 where the earthly monarch is mentioned) is simply this: does the psalm imply that the Hebrew king represents Yahweh in the annual festival? If so, as Mowinckel insists, then these compositions are preëxilic and their sentiments of God's universal reign preceded Deutero-Isaiah and were an influence upon his thought and all later eschatology. If not, then as Gunkel claimed, they are postexilic poems, symbolizing God's lordship over the universe in royal terms and have been shaped in imitation of Deutero-Isaiah. The question is not easily answered, although the preëxilic theory seems to have the edge.

Psalm 114 is a disarming recollection of the Exodus. In its quatrain form and ingenuous address to the objects of nature it has that quality of purposeful naïveté that William Blake and Emily Dickinson used with such effect in their poetry.

Psalm 130 is a shattering cry *De Profundis* from a sinner who asks only for the divine forgiveness, since

> If thou, O Yahweh, shouldst mark iniquities,
>   Lord, who could stand?

The stress upon quietistic waiting for God, apparent also in Psalm 131, is an authentic note of postexilic Judaism.

Psalm 137, with the exception of the Shepherd's Psalm, may be the most famous in the Psalter. It tells of the exiles' deep longing for the city of Jerusalem and the social alienation of captives in a far country. It was men who could say

> If I forget you, O Jerusalem,
>   let my right hand wither!
> Let my tongue cleave to the roof of my mouth,
>   if I do not remember you,
> if I do not set Jerusalem
>   above my highest joy!

who through many decades cherished hopes of restoration and were among the first to respond to the edict of Cyrus.

The imprecatory close of the psalm is a savage blast at the Babylonian captors and the Edomite tormentors; it is typical of a number of the psalms in which hatred of enemies, personal and collective, is aired without inhibition. There are many ways in which it can be assessed. We must not forget the intense and hyperbolic character of Semitic rhetoric (even Jesus said that we must "hate" our own families!). Then too the psalmists were not models of patience; their exasperated exhaustion, like that of Jeremiah, must have driven them to violent words. We can of course never know how much of merely personal pique and how much of "righteous indignation" is involved (any more than we can assess those factors in ourselves with surety). Instead of evoking pious tush-tushes from the comfortably situated reader of today such sentiments might better turn his thoughts to the great cost of love. Love hardly comes by fiat, by deleting unpleasant statements, by stoical elimination of hatred, by never getting excited enough to hate. The great love of prophets and apostles and of Jesus Christ take on real meaning against the background of the free expression of hatred and vengeance. Biblical love must be vigorous enough to embrace and absorb the vehemence of biblical hatred. It is not merely in avoiding unpleasant words and thoughts that religion has its major task; rather it is in reaching into the wellsprings of the human heart to establish a whole new dynamism. Hebrew hatred and Hebrew love touch the viscera as well as the brain.

Psalm 139:1–18 (vss. 19–24 are generally treated as an intrusion) dwells upon the mystery of the divine omniscience, omnipresence, and foreknowledge in profoundly personal terms. The poet glories in the knowledge of God who encompasses his life in its daily routine and penetrates into the recesses of his mind where the words of his mouth are framed. From God's Spirit there is no flight in space or time, and even the darkness is as light to him. When he was as yet unborn, God foresaw his life, beheld his "unformed substance." How great and noble a God, the psalmist's consolation and delight! The spirituality of his faith is unexcelled in either Testament.

Although the analysis of types according to form and function has been extremely valuable, the Psalms resist reduction to any simple scheme or formula. In truth they offer a wealth of variations upon almost every theme in the history of Israel's religion. Among the dominant motifs, the spirit of devotion in the style of Jeremiah's confessions and the note of praise in the manner of Deutero-Isaiah's hymnal idiom might be singled out for emphasis. These are mainly communities of style, the "subjective" and the "objective," and not identifications of authorship or priority of influence. It was once assumed that the Psalter, being mainly postexilic, received its major impetus from the respective pieties and idioms of the prophets. Today it is as logically arguable that Jeremiah and Deutero-Isaiah drew upon already existing literary genres, confessional and hymnal, which they developed to a consummate degree.

In a sense the prime contribution of the Psalms to the student of the faith of Israel is the manner in which these poems vividly illustrate the amazing range of Israel's piety and its living developmental character. Coming to its final shape in the very period when the Law was gaining status among the Jews, the Psalter helps offset the impression of Yahweh as an arbitrary despot and of his requirements as consisting solely of scrupulous obedience to externals. Always in these psalms Yahweh is high and holy, but he is also personal and approachable. Law receives its due attention, but it is a delight and not a burden; and many of the psalms speak of a relation with God quite apart from legal stipulations, inasmuch as he searches the heart and receives the contrite. The poetry of the Psalms embraces all the antinomies of Israel's faith: nature and history, grace and obedience, the believer and the community, God as remote and God as present, God as King and God as Father.

RELIGIOUS FICTION

The postexilic period produced at least three canonical short stories. Two of them, Ruth and Esther, have sufficient cultural and historical verisimilitude to be classed as historical fiction. The other, Jonah, makes only the faintest attempt to pass as factual. It is doubtful that any Jew would have taken it too literally, for it teems with improbabilities and has a sharply drawn lesson. Beside being splendid specimens of the art of story construction, these tales have at least two things in common.

First, they are very *difficult to date*. The only concrete reference in the stories is to King Ahasuerus (Xerxes I, 485–465 B.C.), proof that Esther is postexilic. The authors of the others, however, have adopted preëxilic situations. Ruth is set in the time of the judges and Jonah is probably to be equated with the prophet of the reign of Jeroboam II (cf. II Kings 14:25). While preëxilic versions of both may have existed, their finished forms may be as late as the third century, and Esther's as late as Maccabean times.

Of more importance is the manner in which the stories reflect pressures and tensions in *the attitude of the Jewish community toward outsiders*. Esther shows the more exclusive and negative policy, while Ruth and Jonah are measurably more favorable and inclusive. Since we do not know the dates or circles of thought in which the stories arose, they do not illumine the inner history of the community in any exact way. We must rest content with the fascination of the books as well-told stories and the reflection they give of the distinctiveness of the Jewish community and its self-scrutiny as to standards of membership and attitudes toward the heathen.

ESTHER

The tale of the Jewess who became queen and saved her people from a horrible pogrom is set in fifth-century Susa, capital of the Persian empire. Not only is it full of strange and symmetrically contrived coincidences, such as could hardly occur in real life, but there are a great number of historical improbabilities which suggest that the book was not written by a contemporary (of which not the least is the fact that Mordecai, Esther's cousin, carried off in the exile of 598, was living under Xerxes over 120 years later!). Yet there is sufficient knowledge of Persian court life and palace layout to show that the author made use of traditional material to fill in his story.

Esther is a historical romance intended to explain the origin of the Jewish festival of Purim. In the course of contriving his story, the author has made use of his knowledge of Persian court life and of the traditional motif of the success of Jewish foreign servants. The theme of the Jew at court is illustrated as early as the Joseph cycle in the J and E sources and is paralleled in the late canonical Daniel. There are also the subthemes of the king who displays his beautiful wife, the court maidens who vie for royal favor, and the monarch who is won to patronage of the Jewish religion. Probably the most original element of the story is the hatred of Haman for Mordecai and the poetic justice by which Haman is hanged on the gallows he prepared for Mordecai.

The artful dialogue and delightfully dovetailed turns of fortune must not blind us to the story's function as an aetiology: it explains the feast of Purim (interpreted as a derivative of Persian *pur* or "lot," the device by which Haman selected the day for the proposed massacre of Jews, 3:7). The retaliatory massacre of the enemies of the Jews— in sum 75,000—took place on the 13th (and in Susa also on the 14th) day of Adar. Thus the next day, the 14th (and in some regions the 15th), was observed as Purim, the celebration of the deliverance of the Jews from destruction and of vengeance on their enemies. Many scholars have regarded 9:20–32 as an appendix to the original since it seems to ignore the distinction in observance between the two days. Yet it may have been one of the purposes of the book to explain a variant procedure already existing and to legitimize either date—or actually to encourage both ("that without fail they would keep these two days," i.e., 14th and 15th of Adar, 9:27).

Nothing is known of the origin of the Feast of Purim. Other festivals arose in the time of the Maccabees: the Feast of Lights or Dedication of the Temple, known as Hanukkah in recollection of the reconsecration of the temple in 165, and the Feast of Nicanor in honor of a major victory during the war. In fact II Maccabees 15:36 supplies the first mention of the feast, where in conjunction with the Day of Nicanor, Purim is called the Day of Mordecai and is specified as the 14th of Adar. The fiercely vindictive spirit of the book toward the enemies of the Jews strongly indicates Maccabean origin. Nevertheless a plausible case can be made for the origin of the festival and the book in the eastern dispersion in the fourth or third century. The major obstacle to the latter, however, is that there is no evidence of pogroms against the Jews before the second century. The aggressive wars against the heathen prosecuted by John Hyrcanus provide the most likely milieu. Placing the action in Persian times was a deliberate archaizing device, similar to the practice of the author of Daniel in choosing an exilic hero for his Maccabean tales. It may be of some significance for dating that the only Old Testament book not represented at Qumran is Esther.

When Esther is employed for teaching purposes the model behavior of the queen in putting her people's welfare before her own safety is generally lauded. It may be pointed out that her commendable courage is somewhat sullied by deceit (she hides her Jewishness, 2:10), self-consideration (she hesitates at first to approach the king on behalf of her people, 4:11), and callous misrepresentation (she refuses to correct the king's impression that Haman has attacked her when in truth he was only pleading for consideration, 7:8). To be sure Esther comes off as well as anyone in the book. All the characters are stereotypes whose applicability in current character education is virtually nil, except by way of warning.

By all odds the most disturbing thing about Esther is the hateful revenge of the Jews upon their tormentors. It is futile to dismiss it as mere self-defense; there is no denying that the "punch" of the climax is the aroused glee of the avengers. The slaughter of the Gentiles is plotted and described, not in the heat of emotion, but with a detached calculation that exudes the poison of vengefulness. The exegete who tries to explain that away has a fruitless and morally unworthy task. But to see the book in its time and place, as a liturgical catharsis of a people who had undergone so much ill treatment, is at least to better understand both the people and the book. If part of the climate of postexilic Judaism was hatred and misunderstanding between Jew and Gentile, then the book's justification in the canon is plain enough. Only if the inspiration of Scripture means the morally ennobling character of the literature need we blanch at its being included in the canon. Only if men no longer are set against one another in loathing and venom of spirit can the attitude of the book be dismissed as beneath the interest or concern of believers today. Since it touches such sensitive emotions, the book is fraught with dangers. It is not easy to use it without approving its spirit or without looking down with superiority upon those who found it an outlet for pent-up resentment against their oppressors. As Pfeiffer has rightly commented, "Christians have written far too much in this viciously bellicose vein to be the first to 'cast a stone' at Esther."[8]

---

[8] *Ibid.*, p. 747.

RUTH

Ruth is a lovely idyll whose characters are as uniformly enviable as those of Esther are repugnant. Ruth, the Moabite daughter-in-law of the Israelitess Naomi, devotedly remains with her husband's people at his death. For her faithfulness, Ruth is befriended and wedded by Naomi's wealthy kinsman Boaz. The setting for the events is the era of the judges and, however late the present form, the representation of ancient Israelite customs is largely authentic and unusually revealing. Among the instructive aspects of ancient life is the revelry accompanying the harvest (3:6–7), the gleaning of grain by the poor (2:2–3), the obligation to retain land within the family (4:1–4), and the levirate marriage (from Latin *levir,* "brother-in-law"), according to which a man was duty-bound to marry his brother's widow or the widow of his next of kin if the deceased had left no sons (3:10–13; 4:4–5). All these elements of preëxilic social life are attested elsewhere in Judges or the law codes, including the shoe ceremony by which the kinsman renounces his duty of levirate marriage (4:7; cf. Deut. 25:9).

The notation in 4:7, which interprets the shoe ceremony as the confirmation of a business transaction, appears to be a much later rationalization and has consequently been a factor in dating the book in postexilic times. In Deuteronomy 25:9 the practice is confined to the renunciation of the levirate duty and has a definite social stigma. Some recent students of the book are convinced that the Ruth account of the levirate practice predates Deuteronomy. Assessing the whole atmosphere of the work, the latter is hardly permissible. In truth, confused sociological data should warn exegetes against overpressing the text (e.g., Naomi's plot of ground appears abruptly in 4:2 unintegrated with the preceding story. If Naomi had such a plot, why was Ruth gleaning in Boaz' field?). In general it seems that the nature of ancient storytelling, including variant versions edited as one, is more responsible for the present form than social development.

Closely related to the social atmosphere of the book is the question of its purpose. Ruth may have attempted to revive or preserve the ancient custom of levirate marriage. If so, the tale ought to be clearer in its depiction of the practice. Commonly it is considered an indirect criticism of the reforming policy of Nehemiah and Ezra in forbidding marriage with foreigners. On such a theory the main point is established effectively by showing the original contact with the Moabites as a matter of necessity (Naomi's family went to Moab because of famine), whereas the Moabitess goes to Israel willingly and displays a rare spirit of self-sacrifice and devotion to her newly accepted heritage. Proselytism is encouraged through a hospitable reception of foreigners, but there is no suggestion that the Jews should actively seek the conversion of foreigners. The blessing upon those who join themselves to Israel is verbalized by Boaz, "Yahweh recompense you for what you have done, and a full reward be given you by Yahweh, the God of Israel, under whose wings you have come to take refuge!" (2:12).

That the story was told merely for entertainment ought not to be summarily dismissed. It is certainly better to accept it as a warm-hearted folk story than to strain after occult meanings. Yet it is legitimately objected that stories were seldom written down in antiquity without a purpose. The tendency to think of the work as a glorification of friendship and love has a rather modern romantic basis. (How often has "Entreat me not to leave you . . ." been used in marriage ceremonies, when in fact it is Ruth's word to her mother-in-law!) Still it is not to be denied that the Jew reading the story would be impressed by the commendably loyal attitude and practice of Ruth, but the strength of the loyalty would be in her dedication to the continuity of the family and not in sentimental affection for Naomi or romantic love for Boaz (in fact it is apparent that Boaz is an older and less attractive "catch" than Ruth might normally have hoped for, 3:10). The genealogical appendix in 4:18–21 connecting David with the line of Boaz is not integral to the story. It overlooks the fact that the first male child, Obed, would not be reckoned to Boaz at all but to Ruth's deceased husband Mahlon (cf. Deut. 25:6). Practically identical with I Chronicles 2:3–13, which also is somewhat out of place, the appendix was possibly deemed suitable for Ruth because of the mention of Perez (cf. 4:12,18). There is no way of checking on the Moabite ancestry of David (sending his parents to asylum in Moab, I Sam. 22:3–4, is insufficient evidence).

In conclusion, there are probably two purposes in the book. As it stood originally Ruth praised the strong family ties of Israelite society. The main characters are all loyal family folk who are willing to sacrifice personal pleasure and gain for the preservation of domestic ties. It probably circulated *orally* in monarchic times. In the later telling of the story, the heroine's Moabitic ancestry came to be emphasized and Jews tended to draw from the book the lesson of kindness and receptivity toward proselytes, especially as the preëxilic conditions of life vanished. One reader could not resist the impulse to attach to the book a tradition that even the great David had Moabite blood in his veins. The probable time of *writing* was the fifth or fourth century. The high level on which the instinct to preserve the family is expressed (in contrast to the wiles of Noah's daughters and Tamar in the J account, Gen. 19:30–38; 38), as Bentzen has stressed, is strong presumption for a postexilic date. The apparent fogging of some of the ancient customs also supports this general impression.

JONAH

Unique among the minor prophets is the story of Jonah who fled God's command to go to Nineveh and who, when finally forced to comply, was unwilling to accept the repentance of the Assyrians and the divine forgiveness toward them. The style is similar to the biographical portions of the great prophets. Jonah, son of Amittai, is mentioned in II Kings 14:25 as a prophet who heralded the expansion of the kingdom of Jeroboam II. Budde has proposed that what is now the book of Jonah once stood in the text of II Kings where the prophet is named and that it was an edifying midrash of the sort concerning Elijah and Elisha.[9] This is gratuitous, since it is just as possible that the name Amittai has slipped into the text of Jonah 1:1 in harmonization with II Kings.

How is the book to be understood? Does it relate actual events in the ministry of the prophet? There are too many objections: the lack of specific names or dates; the absence in other prophets of any such mission to preach to a foreign people in their land; the fortuitous and improbable dovetailing of events: the abrupt beginning and ending of the storm, the three days in the stomach of the fish, the sudden and wholesale conversion of Nineveh otherwise unrecorded, the miraculous growth of the gourd and the devouring worm; the inaccuracies in the description of Assyria: the monarch is called "King of Nineveh," as egregious an error as to title our chief executive "President of Washington, D.C.," and the fantastic size of the city, "three days' journey" in diameter.

Anyone who is not tied to the defense of the work as literal happen-

---

[9] Karl Budde, "Vermutungen zum Midrasch des Buches der Könige," *Zeitschrift für die Alttestamentliche Wissenschaft,* (1892), pp. 37 ff.

ing is easily convinced on the strength of the data that the genre of the story is that of didactic fiction. It is futile to attempt to prove the factuality of Jonah by showing that Jesus referred to the prophet's preaching as a warning for his own generation and to Jonah's experience in the fish as a sign of his resurrection (Luke 11:29–32; Matt. 12:39–41). To do so is to assume that Jesus had full knowledge of historical matters, which in fact he did not pretend to have. The fictitious Jonah could have been quite as suitable a sign for Jesus as was the equally fictitious prodigal son suitable for his teaching.

But what sort of didactic purpose did the author have in mind? Has he written an allegory? One can and has been constructed out of it: Jonah is Israel (the name means "dove" and "beloved") with a mission to Nineveh, the nations at large. The storm is her oppressors, the fish is the Babylonian exile, and the disgorgement the return to Palestine. Some have even understood the vine as Zerubbabel ("the Branch"). The problem of course is that no allegorical clue is provided and the reconstruction grows appallingly arbitrary in the search for veiled references to Israel's historical experience. One noticeable flaw is that the fish is not a punitive device but a beneficent one. The storm has punished Jonah; it is the fish that rescues and casts him upon the shore.

Or is the story more in the nature of a parable? Certainly not in the usual sense of the term. It does not set forth moral or religious truth through a matter-of-fact narrative. The book of Jonah is already an explicitly religious document but it shares with the parable an emphasis upon one or two major themes or "points," which it illuminates with great force. Indeed, as Bentzen comments, "The truth of the allegorical [and we could add the parabolic] interpretation is that the story aims at instruction."[10] The patently fictitious character of the story would be evident to the average Jew. He would see at once a didactic device, full of entertainment as well as admonition, avoiding the dullness and arbitrariness of allegory and the morass of difficulties inherent in historical literalism. James Smart offers the appealing suggestion that the story is also parabolic in the sense that, like some of the best biblical parables (II Sam. 12:1–6 and Luke 7:41–43), it leads men to judge themselves. The very extremity of the caricature brings the reader to behold himself in the ludicrous posture of Jonah, and

[10] Bentzen, *Introduction to the Old Testament*, Gad, rev. ed., 1952, vol. 2, p. 147.

thus to scrutinize his own attitude toward his calling and especially toward the non-Jew.[11]

The unity of the book is mainly challenged by the position and character of the psalm that Jonah sings in the fish's belly (2:2–9). The mood and descriptive terms of the psalm seem to make it inappropriate to the situation that the author has provided. He can hardly have composed it himself or it would be more apposite, and if he has chosen it from tradition his sensitivity was equally faulty. We expect a lament rather than a thanksgiving song. In the psalm there is no specific mention of fish or the details of Jonah's plight. The cosmic waters of verse 5 have no relation to the Mediterranean Sea and, as Wellhausen tersely remarked, "weeds do not grow in a whale!"[12] The penitence that the psalm professes is not apparent in Jonah once he has gone to Nineveh. The psalm would have been more logically placed after 2:10 instead of 2:1, namely, after he had been vomited out by the fish. Like others placed in the mouths of biblical personages (cf. Song of Hannah in I Sam. 2:1–10 and Hezekiah's Prayer in Isa. 38:10–20), the psalm actually is a general composition applied arbitrarily to the situation at hand. The true "life situation" of Jonah's psalm is that of a former worshiper at the temple who, rescued from the grip of death, vows to sacrifice once again at the shrine. It is doubtful that the writer of the short story would supply so incongruous a psalm; it is probably from an editor who wished to vivify and enlarge on Jonah's experience in the fish's belly.

Similar inconsistencies in the composition have prompted questions. Two reports of the proclamation of a fast by the Ninevites appear in 3:5 and 3:6–9. Jonah is aware of Yahweh's change of mind toward Nineveh according to 4:1–4, but in 4:5 he sits outside the city waiting incredulously. Though apparently protected by a booth he has constructed (4:5), Jonah is shaded by a gourd plant which God causes to come up overnight (4:6). There may be interpolations in the text or possible transpositions. A few scholars have claimed the presence of two interwoven sources (the divine name criterion is used in part; note the conflate Yahweh Elohim in 4:6). It is best, however, to lay the discrepancies for the most part to the redundancies and illogicalities of an Oriental storyteller, with the possibility of a gloss here and there.

Jonah provides vivid commentary on at least three themes: the in-

---

[11] J. D. Smart, *Introduction to Jonah* (IB, vol. 6), Abingdon, 1956, pp. 871–873.
[12] Cited in Bentzen, *op. cit.,* p. 145, footnote 4.

escapability of God, the purity of the prophetic motives, and the universal love of God with the attendant universal obligation of Israel.

Hoping to evade his summons to Nineveh, the prophet took ship in the opposite direction toward the Phoenician colony of Tarshish (Spain). Yahweh, however, proves to be Lord of the great deep and sovereign of a shipful of heathen seamen. Jonah's experience reads like an illustration of Psalm 139:

> Whither shall I go from thy Spirit?
>   Or whither shall I flee from thy presence?
> . . . .
> If I take the wings of the morning
>   and dwell in the uttermost parts of the sea,
> even there thy hand shall lead me,
>   and thy right hand shall hold me (7,9–10).

The man who has been given a mission by God will find all the events and forces of life conspiring to thrust that mission upon him should he at first deny it.

With respect to the motives of the renegade prophet, there is a distinct affinity with Jeremiah's confessions. The prophet relishes the punishment of those to whom he has ostensibly preached repentance. His motives are corrupted by the exercise of power; he has fallen into the fatal sin of resenting rather than loving those to whom he preaches. Having declared their doom he is compelled to save face by gaining their punishment at any cost. This danger in the prophetic messenger, which Jeremiah saw clearly, is expressed with savagery by the hateful and petulant retort of the rebellious prophet: "I pray thee, Lord, is not this what I said when I was yet in my country? That is why I made haste to flee to Tarshish; for I knew that thou art a gracious God and merciful, slow to anger, and abounding in steadfast love, and repentest of evil" (4:2). Jonah's outburst ends in a peevish plea for death. With penetrating awareness of its double aspect, the author has cast Jonah in the role of the prophet, not only as the medium for the word of judgment and grace to others, but also as one greatly in need of being ministered to by that same word. The instrument of God may be recalcitrant and, through hardness of heart, less responsive to God's will than those outside the pale. If the author intended the Jew to see himself in the person of Jonah, a timely warning is thus addressed to the covenant people not to forsake their obedient sensitivity to God's will nor through entrenched dislike of the heathen nations to miss opportunities for their conversion.

The supranational love of God is pointedly declared in the great concern of Israel's Lord for Nineveh, which has obviously been chosen as a byword of wickedness. The author clearly does not share the hopes of Ezekiel 38–39, Joel 3, Obadiah, and Esther that the heathen nations will be slaughtered. He has a positive and open-hearted attitude toward them. He appears to anticipate and invite their belief in and worship of Yahweh. The fictitious garb of the book leaves the reader wondering just what form this concern for the nations took. It would be easy to think of its author as a leading promoter of the proselyte movement that flourished in Hellenistic and early Roman times. The mass conversion of the Ninevites is probably no more than an effective dramatic device, but it is hard to avoid the impression that this Jew favored going to the Gentiles and actively seeking their conversion.

Here was a man who drank deeply at the springs of prophecy, who saw the covenant bond as demanding responsible and continued enlargement so as to include, not merely stragglers from the nations, but many—if not all—the heathen. Deutero-Isaiah's hope for universal conversion seems to have won at least one sympathetic follower in the postexilic period.

APOCALYPTIC

In the prophetic books of Isaiah, Ezekiel, Zechariah, and Joel there are frequent apocalyptic traits. It is only in the book of Daniel, however, that apocalyptic as a form becomes explicit and unmistakable. Apocalyptic is both an idiom and a way of thinking. The main reason for Bible readers being perplexed by apocalyptic is their insistence either on taking it with absolute literalness or, in despair, resorting to purely subjective interpretations in order to wrest some sense from the text. In order to understand apocalyptic it is necessary to consider the biblical examples (including the book of Revelation in the New Testament) in conjunction with the score or more of noncanonical apocalypses that are represented in the Pseudepigrapha: Enoch, Baruch, Ezra, the Assumption of Moses, the Ascension of Isaiah, etc. These are basically Jewish works but a number have been interpolated or edited by Christians and many of them, repudiated by the Jews after the fall of Jerusalem in A.D. 70, were preserved in the Christian Septuagint. While there are many details of apocalyptic symbolism that remain meaningless, the general features are clear enough to suggest some basic principles of procedure for the interpreter.

Apocalyptic is earmarked by a bizarre and grotesque mode of expression. The visions of prophecy are generally of objects of nature that serve as vehicles for the divine directive. The visions of apocalyptic are, however, unnatural combinations of known realities (almost surrealist in nature) but grouped together for didactic purpose. Thus the ideal of all interpreters is to "crack" the symbolic code. Among the common symbols are animals as world empires, the horn as the powerful individual leader, and the sea as the realm of evil. There is a fondness for numbers and their cryptic meanings. In many of the apocalypses the writer provides an interpreting angel to expound the baffling symbolism. World history is divided into stated periods, generally dominated by world empires, the successive phases worsening and hastening toward the divinely appointed end. Most of the apocalypses are fictitiously attributed to ancient personages. Favorite eras for securing pseudonyms are the primeval period (Adam, Enoch, Noah, Abraham) and the time of Exile and restoration (Baruch, Daniel, Ezra). Apocalyptic is thus connected with an archaistic attachment to the normative periods of Israel's faith: ancient sages predict and prepare men for the end of history. Although apocalyptic looks to the future, it sees that future as a return of the halcyon days of old. An incipient philosophy of history lies close to the surface of apocalyptic.

What is this curious and grotesque literary form seeking to express? Essentially it adapts prophecy to the historically new situation. Prophecy assumed the freedom of men to frame a new course, to act decisively in response to the will of Yahweh. How different was the postexilic period in which the Jewish community had little opportunity to shape outer history. The affairs of the world were in the hands of Persians and Greeks and the initiative was not with the Jews. Apocalyptic is the dramatization of the transcendent meaning of existence, of God's control of the world, of the near presence of his reign. It contains an exceedingly practical admonition for Jews to remain faithful and to bear their minority, for "the Most High God rules the kingdom of men and sets over it whom he will"; at the time of his choosing the oppressors shall be shattered and the rule of his saints established.

Apocalyptic is a mythology of the end, as Genesis 1–11 is a mythology of the beginning. As surely as the origins of the world were in the hands of God, so are its destinies. The first and last acts of the human drama are alike his to dispose. As in most philosophies of history there is a tendency to overlook the dimensions of freedom. The great panorama is foreordained of God and men puppetlike carry out his will. The art forms in which apocalyptic decks itself contribute to that impression. Yet it would appear that the authors were not recluses but active participants in the affairs of their day. To be sure, they saw their own acts of fealty to Israel's God in a rather restricted and somber light. This was not only because of the narrowed sphere of Jewish freedom, but also because of their vivid awareness of the near end of history.

The Greco-Roman world found men on many fronts awake to dim forebodings and prophetic forerunners of the new age. The Jewish response was to perceive the imminent inrush of the kingdom of God, and apocalyptic was the symbolic expression of that faith. It did not rest upon the precise date of the end (although some apocalyptic writers were bold enough to state a time), but upon the apprehension of the conditioned character of all human history under the rule of God. For the apocalyptic mind the end is not merely something at the termination of a sequence, but it is the transience of the historical world within the larger will of its Maker and Disposer. "The proper and paradoxical subject of the late apocalyptic [writer] is a future that is no longer time and he anticipates this subject so that for him all that may yet come in history no longer has a historical character. Man cannot achieve this future, but he also has nothing more to achieve."[13] For this reason apocalyptic is open to the charge of ethical irrelevance, as it is worthy of high praise for its unifying faith in God beyond history.

Apocalyptic is the extension of prophecy and also its metamorphosis. The central themes of God's rule over history and his will to establish a people for himself persist throughout both. But in apocalyptic the end is final and not a point for the renewal of historical activity. The New Creation is God's work alone. Man's role within it is a gift. Yet it is a role in which he participates by the character of his response to the divine will here and now—when it is hard to be obedient and easy to consent to the efficacy of worldly power. In their insist-

[13] Martin Buber, "Prophecy, Apocalyptic, and the Historical Hour," *Union Seminary Quarterly Review,* vol. 12, no. 3 (1957), p. 18.

ence on the relevance of divine truth for historical existence, prophecy and apocalyptic maintain an unbroken affinity of spirit. Their differences are understandable to any believing man who has hoped to accomplish a major relocation of reality by his own free decision, and yet who has also known what it is to face the ineluctable and virtually determined future with courage. If we can once understand that difference of mood, apocalyptic need not be minimized or excised as a foreign growth in the body of Judaism. Its excesses and perversions (especially in the mind of the curious and imbalanced) may seem to make it a regrettable development, but if the prophet as such could not survive in the new age, it was well that the seer spoke his ancient truth. Placid eras will always find apocalyptic baffling and repellent, but in times of turbulence its lurid idiom speaks with phenomenal power.

DANIEL

The book of Daniel is an apocalypse (an "unveiling" of the future) and an apocryphon (a book allegedly written by an ancient, in this case a pious youth in the Exile, and stored up until publication at the end of history). Daniel, one of the Babylonian exiles, is cast in the role of predictor of the course of history from the Exile to the Maccabean age. The sudden appearance of the book in the second century B.C. is accounted for by the fact that its author kept it hidden until that time. But if historical science is allowed to work at all upon the book its true origin becomes immediately apparent. The language, including a large section of Aramaic in 2:4–7:28, is postexilic. The earliest of the many noncanonical apocalypses was hardly written before 200 B.C. There are a number of inaccuracies concerning Babylonian history that would hardly have been possible for an exilic author. The knowledge of the Persian and Greek periods is extremely hazy but the closer the "prediction" comes to the Maccabean period the fuller is the account and the more accurate the detail. Finally, it is certain that the work was written after the desecration of the temple by Antiochus Epiphanes (168 B.C.) but before the rededication (165 B.C.). The evidence is plain and only those who must defend a preëstablished view of inspiration of Scripture refuse to see the literary guise that the author has adopted, a guise wholly accepted and appropriate in his cultural setting.

Daniel is a tract for the times, with something of the avowed intent of arousing public sentiment that we find in works such as Thomas Paine's *Common Sense* or Harriet Beecher Stowe's *Uncle Tom's Cabin*. The work follows the typical apocalyptic pattern of discounting the world empires that are "to have their little day" but are marked for judgment and extinction. It achieves its purpose by two avenues: first by *legends* about the fearlessness of the Babylonian exiles under testing and, second, by *visions* of the end. Its obvious encouragement to the struggling supporters of the Maccabees should not, however, obscure the fact that the work is no simple piece of party propaganda. The seer specifically rules out human instrumentality in the establishment of God's kingdom. The immense image of the world empires with its metallic parts is dashed to pieces by "a stone cut out by no human hand" (2:34). Apparently the author was a pious Hasid who only reluctantly favored fighting, if at all. His models are willing to be martyrs and do not defend themselves. It is possible, however, that resistance by arms was deliberately excluded from Daniel lest the book fall into Seleucid hands. The reply of the three young men to Nebuchadnezzar is only a thin disguise of the retort all faithful Jews are advised to give to Antiochus and his minions: "If it be so, our God whom we serve is able to deliver us from the burning fiery furnace; and he will deliver us out of your hand, O king. But if not, be it known to you, O king, that we will not serve your gods or worship the golden image which you have set up!" (3:17–18). Concerning the role of armed action in the coming of the kingdom, the book of Daniel expresses that uncertainty and ambiguity felt by many pious Jews.

Chapters 1–6 are mainly a series of legends about Daniel (renamed Belteshazzar by the Babylonians) and his three companions Hananiah (Shadrach), Mishael (Meshach) and Azariah (Abednego) who were among the exiles of 598.[14] The youths rose rapidly in government service; in fact the interest in the faithfulness of Jews tested by foreign success and their skill in dream interpretations remind the reader of the E account of Joseph. The connection here may also be an intended linking of the two termini of Israel's history: the people of God begin in Egyptian bondage and end in Babylonian bondage. As lesser officials under Nebuchadnezzar these young Jews demonstrate their su-

---

[14] A Qumran fragment from Cave 4, entitled "Prayer of Nabonidus," recounts a tale similar to that of Daniel 4 and appears to give a more primitive form of the legend; see Frank Cross, *The Ancient Library of Qumran and Modern Biblical Studies*, Doubleday, 1958, pp. 123 f.

periority as leaders in spite of their strange religious practices and aloofness from Babylonian ways.

Uniting the legends and the visions is the theme of God's control of the world empires. It is he who grants dreams to the ruler and interpretations to Daniel, for ". . . there is a God in heaven who reveals mysteries" (2:28). Over against the transience of the kingdoms and the frailty of a monarch whose insanity turns him into a beast of the field (this is the meaning of Nebuchadnezzar's eating grass), is the eternality of God's reign:

How great are his signs,
    how mighty his wonders!
His kingdom is an everlasting kingdom,
    and his dominion is from generation to generation (4:3).

In his exuberance the author has the foreign rulers Nebuchadnezzar and Darius praise the God of Daniel.

The types of testing that the young men face all concern the peculiarities of Jewish practice, the distinctives which infuriated Antiochus because they marked off the Jews as unassimilable and therefore unbendable to political purpose. Dietary exclusiveness, rejection of idolatry, fidelity in daily prayer toward Jerusalem are the three counts with which the youths are charged. In the first case, by a ten-day test they prove their diet more nutritious than the rich food of their masters. In the other two instances they are brought to punishment, the three companions in the fiery furnace and Daniel in the lion's den. The legendary element in each case is heightened to a frightening extent by the heating of the furnace so that even the attendants who cast the young men into the furnace are consumed by the licking flames, and by the false accusers of Daniel when thrown into the den being voraciously devoured in mid-air by the lions that had been docile toward Daniel! From first to last these stories magnify the unshaken rule of God and nerve the man of faith to act worthily in the face of regnant wrong, inasmuch as he who does so participates already in that eternal rule of God which is and is yet to come.

Chapters 7–12 contain five visions granted to Daniel in exile. They are not successive or complementary in any certain sense, but rather serve as independent illuminations of the same compelling conviction that the end is near, stressing various facets of the hope which this divine certainty holds out for the beleaguered Jews.

The vision of the Four Beasts and the Son of Man (chap. 7) is the most significant from the point of view of later apocalyptic development. The four beasts are world powers, climaxed with the fourteen horns (representing kings and pretenders of the Seleucid dynasty, the last of whom is Antiochus Epiphanes). God, described as "the Ancient of Days," is set forth in the lavish imagery of the mythology of creation and chaos. His essential feature is that of world ruler and judge over the ripening harvest of evil in his realm. Suddenly the fourth beast is slain and "one like a son of man" is delegated with authority to establish the divine kingdom. This figure is interpreted as follows: "the saints of the Most High shall receive the kingdom, and possess the kingdom for ever, for ever and ever."

Now the Son of Man is a transcendent person, and in this respect the very opposite of "son of man" in Ezekiel, where the term is an epithet for the frail prophet. In addition, the expression here is a surrogate for the "saints of the Most High." "Son of man" is really quintessential man, redeemed humanity, the aggregate of the pious ones who receive the rule of God. As a collective symbol of this sort, all thought of a divine-human intermediary is ruled out. Many interpreters point out, however, that the beasts contrasted with the Son of Man are not only collective designations for the world empires, they are also the kings who incarnate the kingdoms they represent. Perhaps then there is a collective-individual polarity in the concept Son of Man, similar to that in the image of the Suffering Servant. Something of the sort seems likely since, purely as a symbolism of the pious ones, it is hard to see why the Son of Man comes "with the clouds of heaven," unless the pious dead are so envisioned (but there is no indication of resurrection in this vision). Whatever the view of the author of Daniel, in the somewhat later apocalyptic book of Enoch the Son of Man is a definite individual who descends from above, bringing the kingdom among men. Jesus preferred this title for himself and generally his use of the term is closer to Daniel and Enoch than to Ezekiel. Thus a study of Jesus' thought about himself must inevitably embrace the debatable Danielic Son of Man.

The vision of the Ram and He-Goat (chap. 8) pictures the ram (Media-Persia) destroyed by the he-goat (Macedonia, with Alexander as the great horn and the successors as "the four conspicuous horns"). Antiochus as the little horn invades and desecrates the sanctuary with his self-imposed worship. Then Daniel overhears an angelic conversation in which the burning question is asked, "For how long is the vision concerning the continual burnt offering, the transgression that makes desolate, and the giving over of the sanctuary and host to be trampled under foot?" The answer is framed numerically: 1,150 days, or about three years. As it was, exactly three years elapsed between Antiochus' desecration of the temple and Judas' rededication (Dec. 168–165). The interpreting angel Gabriel is the first angel in the Old Testament to be given a name; thereafter the practice of naming the divine messengers and interpreters became common in intertestamental literature.

The third vision is built around Jeremiah's prophecy of a 70-year exile (chap. 9). In meditating on the words of Jer. 25:11–12 the seer suddenly breaks into a prayer (which may be interpolated since it stresses sin and grace as nowhere else in the book). It shows how radically some postexilic Jews took the problem of human sin and God's gift of forgiveness, "for we do not present our supplications before thee on the ground of our righteousness, but on the ground of thy great mercy." While praying, Daniel is visited by Gabriel with a reinterpretation of the 70 years, now to be understood as "seventy weeks of years," i.e., 490 years which are broken down into three eras of seven, 62, and one respectively (divided into half weeks). When decoded, the chronology is approximately as follows:

7 weeks	=	49 years	(587–538 B.C.)
62 weeks	=	434 years	(538–171)
1 week	=	7 years	(171–165)
[½ week	=	3½ years	(168–165)]

The error of 66 years in computing the time from the restoration to the murder of Onias ("an anointed one shall be cut off," vs. 26) in 171 B.C. is not particularly surprising. The Persian and Greek periods were a virtual dark age in Jewish history and all chronological data dealing with the period, biblical and extrabiblical, suffer from confusion. Actually the author of Daniel has come closer in his estimate than most authorities, including Josephus, who had the habit of compressing the period, since so little was known about developments.

The vision of the Angel and the Resurrection (chaps. 10–11) has as its purpose the unfolding of subsequent history down to the end. The Persian and Macedonian phases are quickly summarized and then the relations of the Ptolemies ("kings of the south") and the

Seleucids ("kings of the north") are set forth in more detail. A careful interpreter can discern in the marriages, assassinations, and wars the faint outlines of otherwise familiar history in the period from Alexander to Antiochus, whose "abomination that makes desolate," perpetrated upon the Jerusalem sanctuary, is grimly described. The wide-ranging victories of Antiochus and his irresistibility are recounted, and the summary comment is tersely delivered, "yet he shall come to his end, with none to help him." Then Michael, prince of angels, previously mentioned as a participant in the heavenly warfare of which the struggles on earth are only a mime (10:13), will arise and herald the resurrection of "some to everlasting life, and some to shame and everlasting contempt" (12:2). This is the first biblical reference to resurrection that includes the wicked (Isa. 26:19 speaks only of the raising of the righteous). The teaching was of tremendous significance to the Maccabean martyrs who, on the basis of the promised resurrection, could hope to share in the kingdom of God.

This last vision puts great emphasis upon written truth (chap. 12). The destinies of humankind are "inscribed in the book of truth" from which the angel reads but a chapter or two to Daniel. The seer is instructed to "shut up the words, and seal the book, until the time of the end." The *apocalyptic* notion of the book of destinies and the *legalistic* notion of the book of binding teaching (Deuteronomy, Priestly Code, etc.) strengthened the idea of written revelation. Apocalyptic contributed not only to a fixed view of divine-human operations through its deterministic schema, but it also contributed to a fixed view of divine revelation in which the words themselves become important. In both Deuteronomy and Daniel the Hebrew-Jewish faith is asserted in the face of serious challenge and with that assertion goes a self-consciousness about revelation and authority.

It is apparent from this brief analysis of the book that it offers no help to those who would like to plot the course of events in the modern world. Our future is "apocalyptic" enough in its own right without trying the ludicrous equation of the events of Daniel (and Revelation) with contemporary happenings. That does not mean that Daniel is without significance for us. It stresses the unique importance of the final act of history, conceived of course symbolically—as indeed all thought of absolute beginnings and endings must be. To be sure, the apocalyptist's sense of the nearness of the end characteristically betrays him into setting times. In this he is invariably wrong (it should be noted how assiduously Jesus avoided the setting of times). On the other hand the responsibility of living with the assurance of the world's relativity and tenuousness before God is a salutary religious experience. Furthermore, apocalyptic sounds a clear belief in the justice of God over all of history. The New Creation is to have continuity in the righteous purpose of God. Once the symbolism is acknowledged as such, then the central teaching of apocalyptic stands or falls, as does the whole faith of the Bible, on the conviction that God is sovereign over history and active within it.

INTERTESTAMENTAL JUDAISM

Since the writings finally deemed canonical were all written before the Maccabean wars (with the exception of Daniel and possibly Esther and a few Psalms), the intertestamental era is generally defined as the period ca. 168 B.C.–A.D. 70. It is demarcated on either side by Jewish wars of independence, the first successful against the Seleucids, the second unsuccessful against the Romans. While there was a gap of about two hundred years between the last Old Testament writing and the first New Testament writing, Judaism was not at a literary or religious standstill. In fact there was never so productive a period in Jewish literary history. Some of the vast quantity of literature has been included in the Apocrypha and Pseudepigrapha. The finds from the Qumran caves have given an inkling of the large output. Religiously, Judaism was feeling its way in a world politically and ideologically hostile. Some attempts were made to cross the gulf between Israel and the Gentile world (as in the philosopher Philo and the energetic proselyte movement). In the main, however, the key developments were internal, with a vigorous partisan or sectarian life as proof of the vitality of Judaism.

The familiar breakdown of the Jewish parties is that of Josephus who explained them to his Roman readers as "philosophies." He distinguished four: Pharisees, Sadducees, Zealots, and Essenes. The *Pharisees* were the party that determined the destiny of Judaism. They insisted on supplementing the written Torah with an oral tradition to keep it contemporary, although they believed that the oral tradition was derived from Moses. The Pharisaic rabbis formulated and interpreted the oral tradition which finally was codified in the Talmud (Mishnah plus Gemara) in the period A.D. 200–600. Among their distinctive tenets was a belief in bodily resurrection. The Pharisees were largely men of the middle class, who supported their families with a trade and spent long hours of study following the day's work. It is they who largely influenced the piety and practice of the synagogues. While they are severely criticized in the New Testament (so much so that the word has become a synonym for hypocrite), they were for the most part not malicious or insincere. The self-righteousness implicit in their type of faith is a universal danger and has often found expression among Christians.

The *Sadducees* were the party of the aristocratic priesthood. They were the wealthy landowners. On excellent terms with the Romans, they supported the *status quo* of foreign occupation in return for Roman permission to operate the temple with financial profit. They were reactionary in their refusal to accept any Scriptural authority beyond the five books of Moses. The oral tradition of the Pharisees was anathema to them; they opposed resurrection and angelology because they could not find them in the Pentateuch. Considering the emoluments involved, the Sadducees undoubtedly produced a fairly high incidence of venal and unworthy priests. Their collaboration with Rome certainly made them unpopular with the masses, but there were many high-minded priests among them and their compromise with wealth and power was certainly no greater than that of many a Christian prelate.

The *Zealots* were the revolutionaries who favored revolt against Rome and actually forced the rebellion of A.D. 66–70. They sought to repeat the victories of the Maccabees, but Rome was not to be decoyed or divided like the Seleucids. Other than their intensely nationalistic and destructive policies, we do not know of any distinctive Zealot beliefs. They were probably men who on other counts would have seen eye to eye with the Pharisees. There is no evidence, however, that even their leaders such as John of Gischala were priests or rabbis. They appear to have been especially strong in Galilee; this explains some of the expectations about Jesus of Nazareth whom many regarded as another potential Zealot leader.

The *Essenes* are described as a party of ascetics living in communal centers, some in the countryside and others in the towns. They held goods in common. In general they seem not to have married, but were replenished by a constant flow of novitiates. A strict regimen of worship, study, and work was enforced. Seekers were on probation until they proved their stability and earnestness. Of all the parties in Judaism, perhaps they alone should be called a "sect" since they withdrew from the mass of men and thought of themselves as the saving remnant. The community at Qumran where the famed scrolls were discovered appears to have been an Essene center.

Students of the intertestamental period have, however, long been uneasy about the "four philosophies" of Josephus. Our knowledge of the internal conditions of Judaism in the intertestamental era is sur-

View of the ruins of Qumran from the northwest tower. The long room on the left is the scriptorium where the sect's manuscripts were copied. The rooms on the right were probably study cells.

prisingly meager. Aside from the books of Maccabees we are dependent mainly on Josephus and Philo of Alexandria. Heated party strife sometimes erupted in violence, as between Jannaeus and the Pharisees. Josephus was writing for non-Jews and saw no reason to go into any great detail in describing inner-Jewish differences. He omitted altogether anything that might have proved offensive to Gentiles (e.g., the messianic idea so soon after the revolt of A.D. 66). Josephus had every excuse for being overly schematic. There were doubtless many more religious groups than those he mentions. The historian has probably blandly lumped related but disparate parties under the four major headings. Epiphanias, a later Christian writer, lists seven Judean and four Samaritan sects. Most important, the sense of membership in these parties, while clear-cut in some cases, must have been vague in the case of other Jews. Quite apart from the great mass known as "the people of the land" (Jesus was classed as one of them), there were many educated Jews who did not strictly fit into any of the parties. Then too the parties were not opposed on all issues, and as we move away from the hard core membership of each, the degree of eclecticism of thought must have been considerable. Lacking doctrinal fixation and as yet a final canonical consensus, this kind of flux would be inevitable. Qumran underscores the point, for while the sectarians who wrote the scrolls are most closely related to those called "Essenes" by Josephus and Philo, the multiple interests at Qumran of a "Pharisaic" and "Sadducean" nature show how flexible Judaism was in this age.

Behind each of the major groups was a long history and the farther back one probes into the first two pre-Christian centuries, the more the party terms become fragmented and lost in the haze of origins. This leads to a principle of importance: the relative fixity of the sects in the middle of the first Christian century is only of limited value when applied to the earlier period. Support of this is seen in the fact that every one of the party names is general and lacks distinctiveness. A Pharisee is a "separatist" or "exegete." A Sadducee is a "follower of Zadok, a Zadokite" (but which Zadok?), "a priest," "a righteous one." A Zealot is "one full of zeal," "a rebel." An Essene (the most doubtful etymology of all) is "a pious one," "a modest one," "a healer," "a wonder worker." This suggests another caution in the study of intertestamental Judaism: the force of the party names is more adjectival than nominal, specifying types of piety and practice rather than well-defined groups.

The apocryphal literature sensitizes us to the vigor with which Judaism was seeking to find its pathway into the future. It was not a time of stagnation but of creative exploration of alternatives. From among the competing possibilities, normative Judaism eventually chose the course of the Torah and the Talmud. Jewish Christianity chose the way of the new covenant with its insistence upon the actualization of the messianic hope in Jesus of Nazareth. Yet the discoveries at Qumran have vividly disclosed a party that also claimed the divine grace and salvation, the new covenant, and the messianic hope. This is not to find any simple or direct lines of connection between the Qumran covenanters and the early Christians. The notions of the messiah, of the new covenant, and salvation through suffering are rudimentary at Qumran compared with their explosive development in early Christianity. But the possibility cannot be ruled out that Qumran, and other communities like it, contributed many of the first Christian converts as well as formative elements of thought and organization to the church at Jerusalem.

The faith of the Old Testament was far from dead, although its possibilities of political implementation were sharply restricted by Roman imperialism. The deeply implanted hope that God would bring his kingdom was still alive and the confidence in a messiah who would bring peace and righteousness into effective operation in the world was running high. The great quantity of apocalyptic and messianic literature shows that Jews were more keenly aware of some impending great act of God than they had been at any time in their history. "The fullness of time" was at hand.

Chart 8. Kings of the Divided Monarchy, 922–587 B.C.

Kings of Judah		Kings of Israel	
REHOBOAM	922–915	JEROBOAM I	922–901
Abijah (Abijam)	915–913		
Asa	913–873	Nadab	901–900
		Baasha	900–877
		Elah	877–876
		Zimri	876
Jehoshaphat	873–849	OMRI	876–869
		AHAB	869–850
Jehoram (Joram)	849–842	Ahaziah	850–849
Ahaziah	842	Jehoram (Joram)	849–842
Athaliah	842–837	JEHU	842–815
Joash (Jehoash)	837–800	Jehoahaz (Joahaz)	815–801
Amaziah	800–783	Joash (Jehoash)	801–786
UZZIAH (Azariah)	783–742	JEROBOAM II	786–746
		Zechariah	746–745
		Shallum	745
Jotham	742–735	Menahem	745–738
		Pekahiah	738–737
AHAZ (Jehoahaz I)	735–715	Pekah	737–732
		Hoshea	732–724
HEZEKIAH	715–687		
Manasseh	687–642		
Amon	642–640		
JOSIAH	640–609		
Jehoahaz II (Shallum)	609		
JEHOIAKIM (Eliakim)	609–598		
Jehoiachin			
(Coniah, Jeconiah)	598		
ZEDEKIAH (Mattaniah)	598–587		

NOTE: The dates are derived from W. F. Albright, "The Chronology of the Divided Monarchy of Israel," *Bulletin of the American Schools of Oriental Research* 100 (1945), 16–22. Kings of political and religious importance are capitalized. For explanation of the alternate names of kings see the Preface.

GLOSSARY

Etymologies are given in parentheses; words with asterisks are cross references; terms italicized are unrelated in meaning but easily confused because of similarity in sound.

Ab, Ninth of. Jewish fast day commemorating the fall of Jerusalem to the Neo-Babylonians in 587 B.C.

Achaemenids. Persian rulers, 538–331 B.C.

Adonai. Generic OT name for deity, translated Lord in RSV.

Aetiology. (Gr. "study of cause.") Legendary explanation of the origins of peoples, customs, places of worship, natural features, etc.

Akh-en-Aton. (Egy. "he who is serviceable to the Aton.") Name adopted by Pharaoh Amen-hotep IV (1380–1363 B.C.) when he initiated the solar monotheism of the Aton.*

Akiba. Prominent Pharisee who fixed the consonantal text of the Hebrew OT, *ca.* A.D. 100. *Aqabah; Aquila; Arabah.*

Akkad. (Also **Accad, Agade.**) Capital city of the Akkadian Empire, located in Babylonia, apparently on the Tigris River.

Akkadian. (1) Semitic Empire of Sargon and Naram-Sin, *ca.* 2400–2200 B.C. (2) Language and script that became the diplomatic and commercial medium of the Near East for centuries. See Cuneiform.*

Akra. (Gr. "citadel, fortress.") A heavily fortified section of Jerusalem built by the Seleucids* during the Maccabean War; it was populated with Hellenizing Jews and defended by Seleucid troops.

Amalekites. Nomadic people, similar to the Midianites, who ranged over the Negeb* and Sinai Peninsula; early foes of Israel, they disappeared by monarchic times.

Amorites. (Heb. "highlanders"; Bab. "Westerners.") (1) Branch of Semites who entered the Fertile Crescent 2200–1800 B.C., established the Old Babylonian dynasties of Zimri-Lim and Hammurabi, and populated Syria-Palestine with groups later to be known as Canaanites, Ammonites, Moabites, and Edomites. (2) As employed in OT it normally refers either to the Canaanites in general or to one of their subdivisions.

Amphictyony. (Gr. "they that dwell around.") The league or confederacy of Israelite tribes bound by worship of Yahweh at the central sanctuaries of Shechem in the north and Hebron in the south.

Anatolia. Asia Minor, seat of the Hittite Empire.

Anthropomorphism. (Gr. "human form.") The representation of deity in the physical or psychic likeness of man.

Apiru. Egyptian equivalent of Habiru* and cognate of Hebrew.*

Apocalypse. (Gr. "unveiling, revelation.") A book written in the symbolic idiom of apocalyptic thought, e.g., the book of Daniel. *Apocrypha.*

Apocalyptic. A type of thought and style of expression in postexilic Judaism presenting views about the end of history. See Eschatology.*

Apocrypha. (Gr. "hidden things.") (1) *Cap.* A group of intertestamental writings included in the Roman Catholic and Eastern Orthodox OT, but excluded altogether by Jews and relegated to a separate and inferior status by Protestants. (2) Books claiming to be written by ancient personages and "hidden" until some later unveiling, e.g., Daniel. See Pseudepigrapha (2).* (3) Loosely applied to noncanonical books in general, including the Pseudepigrapha (1).* Often carries the stigma of spuriousness or untrustworthiness, especially as an adjective "apocryphal." *Apocalypse.*

Aqabah, Gulf of. Arm of the Red Sea forming the southern continuation of the Jordan Rift; on its east were Midian and Arabia and on its west, the Sinai Peninsula. *Aquila; Akiba; Arabah.*

Aquila. Translator of a second century A.D. Greek Old Testament that replaced the Septuagint among Jews. *Aqabah; Akiba; Arabah.*

Arabah. (Heb. "desert, dry place.") The Jordan Rift; strictly speaking the region from the Dead Sea to the Gulf of Aqabah, but by extension it applies also to the area from the Sea of Galilee to the Dead Sea (known also by the Arabic term, the Ghor). *Akibah; Aqabah; Aquila.*

Aramaic. Language of the Arameans;* from about 1000 B.C. replaced Akkadian as the international language of diplomacy and commerce and after the Exile succeeded Hebrew as the common tongue of the Jews; portions of Ezra and Daniel are in Aramaic. See Targum.*

Arameans. Semites who entered the Fertile Crescent 1500–1000 B.C., established kingdoms of Aram-Damascus, Aram-Zobah, Aram-Hamath in Syria, and became the commercial middlemen of the Near East. See Aramaic.*

Ark. (1) The ship built by Noah to withstand the great flood, Gen. 6–9. (2) The cult object built at the command of Moses; an imageless throne and palladium symbolizing the presence of Yahweh, later established in the innermost temple chamber.

Asher, Ben. A Masorete* of the Tiberian School of Palestine whose manuscripts are regarded as the purest form of the Masoretic tradition; they form the basis of the RSV.

Asherah. (1) Hebrew-Canaanite name for the chief Canaanite goddess, regarded as wife or sister of Baal. Known to the Babylonians as Ishtar and to the Greeks as Astarte. Sometimes called Ashtoreth in OT. (2) The cult object of the goddess, probably a wooden pole that stood beside the stone pillar of Baal at Canaanite high places.

Assyria. (1) A region on the northern Tigris River, site of the Assyrian capital cities of Ashur and Nineveh, and center of Assyrian power. (2) Semitic Empire that dominated the Fertile Crescent, 1100–612 B.C. *Syria.*

Aton. The sun disk, regarded by Pharaoh Akh-en-Aton* as the sole deity.

Baal. (Heb. "owner, master, lord"; pl. **Baalim** or **Baals**.) Canaanite male deity with many local manifestations, husband or brother of Asherah.*

Babylon. (Bab. "gate of god.") City on the middle Euphrates River; capital of the Old Babylonian Empire of Hammurabi and of the Neo-Babylonian or Chaldean Empire of Nebuchadnezzar.

Babylonia. (1) The middle portion of Mesopotamia, sometimes broadened to include the southern region. (2) The Semitic Empires first of Hammurabi, 1830–1550 B.C., and later of Nebuchadnezzar, 612–538 B.C.

Booths, Feast of. See Tabernacles, Feast of.

Canaan. Palestine west of the Jordan River.

Canaanite. The inhabitants of Canaan, Amorite in origin, ethnically related but culturally superior to the Hebrews. See Phoenicia.*

Canon. (Gr. "reed, measure, standard.") A collection of writings officially recognized as authoritative; the OT canon was settled at the Rabbinic Assembly at Jamnia in A.D. 90.

Chaldeans. (1) A mountain people who settled at the head of the Persian Gulf and founded the Neo-Babylonian Empire, 612–538 B.C. (2) Astrologers or soothsayers so called because of the expertness of Chaldean priests in astronomy.

Charismatic. (Gr. "gift.") A community leader endowed by the spirit with physical strength and military acumen, and spontaneously recognized rather than chosen by heredity or election; specifically, a judge* of Israel.

Chayyim, Ben. Editor of the Bomberg Bible in A.D. 1524–1525, which became the Hebrew Old Testament Textus Receptus;* it was used as the basis of subsequent Hebrew printed texts and translations until Kittel's *Biblia Hebraica* and RSV.

Chemosh. National God of Moab.

Cherethites. The elite army corps and bodyguard of David drawn from Philistia; the term is probably a form of "Cretan." See Pelethites.*

Cherubim. (pl. of **Cherub.**) Winged mythological creatures, half-animal and half-human; they are generally pictured as throne attendants of deity; probably same as Seraphim.

Chronicler, The. Anonymous author of the biblical books of Chronicles, Ezra, and Nehemiah.

Codex. (Lat. "book.") Manuscript form developed by early Christians but replacing the earlier scroll form among Jews as well; it consisted of folded sheets sewn together.

Covenant. (Heb. "binding"?) (1) A social, political, military, or economic agreement between individuals or groups. (2) An agreement or compact between God and men, especially the covenant at Sinai following the Exodus; covenant involves a mutual promise and pledge of loyalty; see Testament.*

Crescent. See Fertile Crescent.

Cult. (Or **Cultus;** Lat. "care, worship.") A system of religious worship, esp. referring to public rites and ceremonies.

Cuneiform. (Lat. "wedge-form.") A type of script, written on clay tablets with a wedge-shaped stylus; it was developed in the Sumerian language but was adapted for Akkadian (2),* Assyrian, Hittite, Persian, etc.

D. Symbol of the anonymous author(s) of the source of the Pentateuch* that became the basis of the Deuteronomic Reformation* in 621 B.C.; abbreviation derived from Deuteronomy, the book in which the source is most fully represented; see Documentary Hypothesis.*

Dead Sea Scrolls. Several hundred biblical and nonbiblical manuscripts in whole or part found since 1947 in caves overlooking the Dead Sea; they formed the library of a Jewish sect whose communal center was at nearby Qumran.*

Decalogue. (Gr. "ten word[s].") The Ten Commandments, appearing in three variants: Exod. 20; 34; Deut. 5.

Descent, The. The emigration of Jacob and his sons from Palestine to Egypt, Gen. 46–47.

Deutero-Isaiah. The anonymous poet of the Exile who wrote Isaiah 40–55; "The Second Isaiah" in contrast to Isaiah of Jerusalem who wrote much of chaps. 1–31.

Deuteronomic Reformation. The centralization of worship at Jerusalem and the suppression of pagan religions advocated in the book of Deuteronomy and implemented by Josiah, king of Judah, in 621 B.C.

Diadochi. (Gr. "successors.") The Hellenistic political successors of Alexander the Great among whom his empire was divided, including the Ptolemies* and the Seleucids.*

Diaspora. (Gr. "scattering.") The body of Jews living outside Palestine from the time of the Babylonian captivity; same as Dispersion;* see Exile, The.*

Dispersion. The scattering of the Jews outside of Palestine; see Diaspora.*

Distich. (Gr. "two lines.") The basic sense unit in Hebrew poetry, consisting of two stichs* in parallelism.*

Documentary Hypothesis. Theory of the authorship of the Pentateuch* that assumes at least four anonymous authors or groups of writers and a number of editors or redactors. See J,* E,* D,* P.*

E. Symbol of the anonymous author of the early northern source of the Pentateuch (950–850 B.C.) according to the Documentary Hypothesis;* abbreviation for the source's preference for Elohim* as the name of God.

Egypt, River of. *Not* the Nile, but rather the Wadi el-Arish, 60 miles SW of Beersheba.

El Shaddai. Occasional Old Testament name for deity, translated God Almighty by RSV.

Elder. (1) In the preëxilic period, a clan or tribal leader who by virtue of wisdom and experience administered justice. (2) After the Exile, a ruler of the synagogue.

Elohim. Generic OT name for deity, translated God in RSV; typical of the E* source of the Pentateuch.

Elohist. Coined term for the anonymous author of the E* source of the Pentateuch; so called because of his preference for the divine name Elohim.*

Enuma Elish. (Bab. "When on high.") Ancient Babylonian creation story, telling of Marduk's slaying of Tiamat, the formation of the cosmos and human civilization; it takes its name from the opening words.

Ephod. (1) The outer garment of a priest in which the sacred lots (see Urim and Thummim*) were carried. (2) In some OT passages a cult object, probably an idol.

Ephraim. (1) One of two sons of Joseph and eponym* of the tribe of Ephraim. (2) Chief tribe of the north and poetic equivalent of the political entity, Israel.

Eponym. (1) A person, real or legendary, from whom a tribe, place, institution, etc., takes its name; applied in biblical study especially to the patriarchs, e.g., Jacob-Israel is the eponym of the Israelite people.

(2) Any Assyrian official whose name was used to designate his year of office.

Eschatology. (Gr. "study of the end.") (1) Strictly, the branch of theological study dealing with final things, i.e., with events and realities at the end of history; in this sense Israelite eschatology was postexilic. (2) By extension, any teaching about the future, including God's relation to man within history; in this sense Israelite eschatology was preëxilic.

Essenes. A late Jewish sect of communal ascetics probably represented by the Qumran* community.

Exile, The. (1) The Babylonian deportation and captivity in 598 and 587 by Nebuchadnezzar, lasting until 538 B.C. (2) The centuries-long alienation of Jews from Palestine, following the revolts against Rome in A.D. 66–70 and 135. See Diaspora.*

Exodus, The. (Gr. "a going out.") The deliverance and departure of Israel from Egyptian bondage under the leadership of Moses; probably to be dated in thirteenth century B.C.

Feast. See specific feasts: Hanukkah,* Passover,* Tabernacles,* Weeks.*

Fertile Crescent. Semicircle of arable Near Eastern land between the mountains and desert, extending from the Persian Gulf to the Nile Delta; term coined by James Breasted.

Gemara. (Aramaic, "completion," i.e., "supplementary learning") Commentary on the Mishnah* or Oral Law of late Judaism; Mishnah and Gemara form the Talmud.*

Geniza. (Heb. "storehouse.") A synagogue room for collecting worn-out or defective copies of Scripture, from which they were later removed for burial.

Gospel. (Anglo-Saxon, "God's tale.") Early Christian term used variously for the message of salvation in Christ, the message Jesus himself preached, and the literary form of the four lives of Jesus; the Christian connotation of the Greek word "herald of good tidings" roots in the Septuagint* of Deutero-Isaiah.*

Habiru. Semitic seminomadic freebooters and mercenaries, active in the Fertile Crescent in the second millenium; the term is cognate with Hebrew;* see also Apiru.*

Hanukkah, Feast of. (Heb. "dedication.") Jewish festival celebrating the rededication of the temple in December of 165 B.C. by Judas Maccabaeus; also known as Feast of Lights.

Hasids. (also **Hasidim;** Heb. "pious ones.") Jewish party of strict Law observers who supported the Maccabees in the war for religious survival; probable forerunners of the Pharisees.*

Hasmoneans. An independent Jewish dynasty of the Maccabees,* named after Hashmon, great-grandfather of Mattathias; ruled 140–62 B.C.

Hebraism. The preëxilic faith of Israel, in contrast to postexilic Judaism.*

Hebrew. (Heb. "one who crosses over, an immigrant, a transient.") (1) A Semitic descendant of Eber, including Israelites, Arabs, Edomites, Moabites, and Ammonites. (2) The people of Israel in the preëxilic period, in contrast to postexilic Jew.* (3) Semitic language in which the OT is largely written; Canaanite in origin, it was replaced by Aramaic* as the spoken tongue of the Jews after the Exile.

Henotheism. (Gr. "belief in one god.") Worship of one particular deity among others conceded to exist; characteristic of Hebrew religion until the prophets; see Monolatry,* Monotheism.*

Hexapla. (Gr. "six columns.") Origen's critical edition of the OT, including the Hebrew and several Greek texts.

Hexateuch. (Gr. "six scrolls.") The first six books of the OT, Genesis through Joshua.

Israel. (1) The third patriarch, Jacob. (2) The northern kingdom, in contrast to the southern kingdom, Judah.* (3) An all-embracing term for the people of God, including preëxilic Hebrew* and postexilic Jew.*

J. Symbol of the anonymous author of the early southern source of the Pentateuch* (950–850 B.C.) according to the Documentary Hypothesis;* represents the source's preference for Yahweh* (German: Jahveh) as the name of God.

Jamnia. Site of the Rabbinic Assembly that in A.D. 90 determined the limits of the OT canon.*

Jebusites. Pre-Israelitic inhabitants of Jerusalem.

Jehovah. A hybrid English word used in ERV and ASV to translate Hebrew Yahweh.*

Jew. Contraction of Judah;* term used after the Exile to designate a Hebrew* or Israelite.

Judah. (1) Son of Jacob and Leah and eponym* of the tribe of Judah. (2) The southern kingdom, in contrast to the northern kingdom, Israel.* (3) The southern highlands around Jerusalem; in postexilic times a Persian province.

Judaism. The religion of postexilic Israelites, so named after the tribe Judah; by extension it is sometimes applied to the religion of Israel from the time of Abraham or Moses.

Judea. (also **Judaea.**) Greco-Roman equivalent of Judah.*

Judge. Religiously endowed military leaders of one or more Israelite tribes during the settlement of the land; see Charismatic.*

Kenites. The Midianite clan of Jethro, father-in-law of Moses.

Kenite Hypothesis. Theory that Moses received his religious conceptions and practices from the Kenite clan.

Khirbet Qumran. The ruins of Qumran.*

Koine. (Gr. "common.") The Hellenistic dialect of classical Greek that became the common tongue of the Roman Empire in which the Septuagint and New Testament were written.

LXX. (Lat. "seventy.") Symbol for the Septuagint.*

Legend. (Lat. "something to be read.") An unverifiable tradition, generally handed down orally.

Levirate. (Lat. "brother-in-law.") Hebrew custom requiring that a man marry the widow of his brother or nearest of kin, if the deceased had left no sons. *Levites.*

Levites. (1) The tribe descended from Levi and forming the landless priesthood of Israel. (2) After the Deuteronomic Reformation,* the term was increasingly applied to the priests of second rank who assisted the Jerusalemite priesthood of Zadok. *Levirate.*

Lights, Feast of. See Hanukkah, Feast of.

Maccabee. (Heb. "the hammerer"?) (1) An epithet for the five sons of Mattathias, the priest of Modin, who led a successful Jewish revolt against the Seleucids, 168–165 B.C.: John, Simon, Judas, Eleazar, and Jonathan. (2) By extension, to the Hasmonean* dynasty that ruled from 140 to 63 B.C. and included two of the original Maccabees: Simon and Jonathan.

Manasseh. (1) Son of Joseph and eponym* of the tribe of Manasseh. (2) Northern tribe located on either side of the Jordan River. (3) King of Judah in the seventh century.

Masorah. (Heb. also **Massorah;** "tradition.") The biblical textual annotations of the Masoretes,* copied at first on manuscript margins and later in separate tracts.

Masoretes. (also **Massoretes.**) Early medieval Jewish scholars who copied, annotated, and supplied vowel pointing in the OT texts.

Megilloth. (Heb. "scrolls.") The five OT writings read at annual feasts: Song of Songs, Ruth, Lamentations, Ecclesiastes, and Esther.

Mesopotamia. (Gr. "between the rivers.") The Tigris-Euphrates Valley, embracing the ancient Near Eastern regions of Sumeria,* Babylonia (1),* and Assyria (1).*

Messiah. (Heb. "anointed.") (1) Any especially delegated person, as indicated by anointing with oil, e.g., priests, kings. (2) A royal deliverer of the Davidic dynasty who would come to establish Jewish world dominion and rule with peace and righteousness.

Millo. (Heb. "filling.") Part of the defense works of Jerusalem, perhaps a fortress, built by David and strengthened by Solomon and Hezekiah.

Mishnah. (Heb. "repetition, study.") The Oral Law of Judaism put in writing A.D. 180–220, and forming the basis of the Talmud.*

Molech. The national deity of Ammon, sometimes worshiped by the fiery sacrifice of the first-born son.

Monolatry. (Gr. "worship of one.") Worship of one god, though others are conceded to exist; equivalent to henotheism.*

Monotheism. (Gr. "belief in one God.") Belief in the existence of only one God; in Israel it was first fully advanced by the prophet Deutero-Isaiah.*

Myth. (Gr. "speech, story.") (1) A story with a god or demigod as subject, e.g., Gen. 6:1–4. (2) A story about origins and first principles cast in symbolic form, e.g., Gen. 1–11.

Nabataeans. Arabs whose kingdom controlled large sections of the Sinai Peninsula, the Negeb,* and Trans-Jordan* in the period 200 B.C.–A.D. 100.

Naphtali, Ben. Masorete of the Tiberian School of Palestine whose manuscripts formed the basis of ben Chayyim's* printed Bible and of the Textus Receptus* of subsequent English versions.

Nazirite. (Heb. "one separated or dedicated.") A person specially consecrated to God by virtue of a vow, e.g., Samson and Samuel. Not to be confused with *Nazarene,* a resident of the town of Nazareth.

Negeb. (Heb. "parched land, south.") A barren region of Palestine south of Judah, extending roughly from Beersheba to Kadesh-Barnea.

Neo-Babylonia. The Chaldean* Empire of 612–538 B.C., in contrast to the Old Babylonian Kingdom of Hammurabi.

Omrids. The dynasty of Omri, ninth-century ruler of Israel; it also included Ahab, Ahaziah, and Jehoram.

Ophel. (Heb. "swelling.") The SE hill of Jerusalem on which the city of David was located; apparently equivalent to Zion (1).*

Oracle. (1) A prophetic declaration, not necessarily predictive. (2) A literary unit of prophecy, generally brief and pointed.

P. Symbol of the anonymous author(s) of the late southern source of the Pentateuch* (550–450 B.C.) according to the Documentary Hypothesis;* abbreviation for the Priestly Source.

Palestine. Roman name for southern Syria, formerly known as Canaan;* the term is a Latinization of Philistine.*

Papyrus. A reedlike plant whose pith was used as material for writing.

Parallelism of Members. The fundamental formal feature of Hebrew poetry: the correspondence of thought and phraseology in successive half lines or stichs.*

Parchment. The skin of sheep or goat prepared for use as writing material; replaced papyrus for more valuable documents.

Passover, Feast of. Jewish festival commemorating the deliverance of Israel from Egyptian bondage; refers to the destroyer who "passed over" Israel to strike the first-born of Egypt.

Patriarchs. (Gr. "heads of families.") The eponyms* of Genesis regarded as the fathers of the human race and of Israel, specifically: Abraham, Isaac, and Jacob.

Pelethites. Probably a form of Philistine;* see Cherethites.*

Pentateuch. (Gr. "five scrolls.") The first five books of the OT, Genesis through Deuteronomy; see Torah (2).*

Peshitta. (Syr. common.") The Syriac translation of the OT.

Pharisees. (Heb. "separated ones.") Late Jewish party that interpreted the Law with strictness; an outgrowth of the Hasids,* they became the dominant influence in later Judaism, and compiled the Talmud.*

Philistines. Non-Semitic sea people who migrated from the Aegean Islands and settled on the Palestinian coast about 1100 B.C.

Phoenicia. The coastal region of Canaan* from Tyre north to Arvad, whose Canaanite inhabitants from 1500 B.C. turned increasingly toward maritime commerce and colonization; land of Hiram and Jezebel.

Postexilic. One of the two major eras of OT history: the period after the restoration of the Jews to Palestine in 538 B.C.

Preëxilic. One of the two major eras of OT history: the period prior to the Babylonian Exile of 587 B.C.

Prophets, The. The second division of the Hebrew canon,* consisting of Former Prophets (Joshua–Kings) and Latter Prophets (Isaiah, Jeremiah, Ezekiel, and the Twelve*).

Pseudepigrapha. (Gr. "false writings.") (1) *Cap.* A group of intertestamental writings included in some of the Eastern Orthodox canons, but excluded altogether by Jews, Roman Catholics, and Protestant Christians. (2) Books fictitiously claiming an ancient sage as author.

Ptolemies. Hellenistic rulers of Egypt, 323–30 B.C., named after Ptolemy Lagi, one of Alexander's successors.

Purim, Feast of. (Heb. "lots.") Festival celebrating the deliverance of Jews from the plot of Haman by the intercession of Esther.

Qumran. Site of the communal headquarters of a Jewish sect, probably Essene,* on the NW shores of the Dead Sea; it flourished *ca.* 100–30 B.C. and A.D. 6–66.

Rechabites. Descendants of Jonadab, son of Rechab, who formed a primitivist Yahweh party opposing the civilized life of Canaan.

Reformation, Deuteronomic. See Deuteronomic Reformation.

Sadducees. (Heb. "those of Zadok.") Aristocratic high priestly party who controlled the temple in intertestamental times and opposed the Pharisaic interpretations of the Law.

Samaria. (1) Capital of the northern kingdom built by Omri. (2) The middle portion of the Western Highlands of Palestine, between Galilee on the north and Judah on the south; formed a province under Assyria and Persia; see Samaritans.* *Sumeria*.

Samaritans. (1) Inhabitants of the city or region of Samaria. (2) Usually of the schismatic Jews who separated from the restored religious community at Jerusalem and set up their own temple at Mt. Gerizim, 400–200 B.C.

Sanhedrin. (Gr. "council, assembly, session.") The chief ecclesiastical and judicial body of postexilic Judaism, consisting of 71 members.

Satan. (Heb. "adversary.") Mythological Jewish figure of superhuman status, at first the investigator of human evil, then a tempter, and finally the rebellious fallen angel and source of human evil.

Scribe. (1) Professional court secretary who formed a distinct class in ancient society. (2) A copyist and interpreter of the Jewish Law in the postexilic era; see Sopherim.*

Seleucids. Hellenistic rulers of Syria, 312–63 B.C., named after Seleucus Nicator, one of the successors of Alexander.

Semites. (1) Sons of Shem in the Table of Nations in Gen. 10. (2) A group of Near Eastern peoples with linguistic unity, in contrast to the Indo-Europeans to the north and east and the Hamites to the west and south.

Septuagint. (Lat. "seventy.") Greek version of the OT translated in 250–75 B.C. at Alexandria, according to tradition by 70 (72) elders sent from Jerusalem; see LXX.*

Shema. (Heb. "Hear!") A Jewish liturgical confession of faith consisting of readings from the Torah, beginning with Deut. 6:4–9.

Sheol. (1) The grave. (2) The realm of the dead conceived as a subterranean land of gloom; similar to Greek notion of Hades, yet without any idea of reward and punishment.

Shephelah. (Heb. "lowlands.") The foothills and valleys of Judah between the highlands and the Philistine Plain.

Son of Man. (1) In Ezekiel a term for the prophet that expresses his frailty and mortality. (2) In Daniel a personification of the saints, the true humanity who inherit the kingdom of God; in Enoch it is more highly individualized.

Sopherim. (Heb. "bookmen.") Copyists, guardians, and interpreters of the Law in the period 400 B.C.–A.D. 600; see Scribe (2).*

Stich. (Gr. "row, line.") The basic unit of Hebrew poetic composition, two of which normally create a parallelism.* See Distich.*

Suffering Servant. The personification of Israel as an obedient and sacrificial servant of God, pictured in four poems of Isaiah 40–55.

Sukkoth. Hebrew for Tabernacles, Feast of.*

Sumeria. Lower portion of the Tigris-Euphrates Valley at the head of the Persian Gulf. *Samaria.*

Sumerians. First inhabitants of the Tigris-Euphrates Valley in historical times, *ca.* 2800–2000 B.C.

Superscription. An introductory note to a biblical book, source, or poem, particularly the brief prefaces to prophetic books and psalms.

Symmachus. Second-century Greek translator of the OT.

Synagogue. (Gr. "a gathering, congregation.") A postexilic gathering of Jews for the purpose of worship and study; replaced the temple* after A.D. 70.

Syria. (1) The region of the Fertile Crescent extending from the Upper Euphrates down the Mediterranean littoral, sometimes including Palestine but normally ending at the Litani River. (2) The Aramean kingdom with its capital at Damascus. *Assyria.*

Tabernacle. The portable sanctuary for housing the ark (2)* during the wilderness wanderings; so called in P* source, but "Tent of Meeting" in E* source.

Tabernacles, Feast of. Jewish autumn festival celebrating the grape vintage and the wandering of the Israelites in the wilderness when they lived in tabernacles or booths.

Talmud. (Heb. "study, instruction.") The codification of the late Jewish Oral Law or Mishnah* along with its commentary, the Gemara.*

Targum. (Aramaic, "interpretation.") An Aramaic paraphrase of the Hebrew OT developed orally in postexilic times and committed to writing in the early Christian period.

Temple, The. (1) Temple of Solomon at Jerusalem (965–587 B.C.) which after the Deuteronomic Reformation* became the sole legitimate Jewish sanctuary; destroyed by Neo-Babylonians. (2) Temple of Zerubbabel (516–20 B.C.) or Second Temple. (3) Temple of Herod (20 B.C.– A.D. 70) destroyed by Romans.

Testament. (Lat. "a will.") Latin equivalent of covenant;* it eventually passed into English as the name for the two parts of the Christian canon: Old and New Testaments.

Textus Receptus. The Received Text of late medieval times, based on ben Naphtali* masoretic manuscripts; it became the basis for the English versions until the twentieth century.

Theodicy. (Gr. "justification of God.") A vindication of God's ways with man, especially of his justice.

Theodotion. Second-century Greek translator of the OT.

Theophany. (Gr. "appearance of God.") A manifestation or appearance of God to man, auditory or visual.

Torah. (Heb. "revelation, instruction, law.") Basically, the revealed will of God in its several senses: (1) An instruction concerning religious practice or ethical conduct given by priests, prophets, kings, or sages. (2) *Cap.* The five books of Moses or Pentateuch;* this usage is post-exilic. (3) *Cap.* The entire Jewish scripture, including OT and the Talmud;* this usage arose in the early Christian centuries.

Trans-Jordan. The region of Palestine east of the Jordan River from Bashan in the north to Edom in the south.

Trisagion. (Gr. "threefold holy.") The threefold adoration of the divine holiness voiced by the seraphim in Isaiah's vision, "Holy, holy, holy."

Twelve, the Book of the. A collection of twelve prophetic books (Hosea–Malachi); equivalent to the so-called "Minor Prophets."

Ugarit. Ancient city in northern Syria where Canaanite religious texts, including the Baal and Anath epics, were discovered.

Urim and Thummin. (Heb. "lights and perfections.") The sacred lots of Israel, in the custody of priests; as interpreters of the divine will they were replaced by prophets.

Vulgate. (Lat. "common.") The Latin version of the Bible translated by Jerome, *ca.* A.D. 400.

Weeks, Feast of. Jewish festival in late spring, celebrating the grain harvest and in later Judaism, the giving of the Law; observed seven weeks after Passover; same as Pentecost.

Writings, The. The third division of the Hebrew canon.

Yahweh. Distinctive OT name for the God of Israel, translated LORD in the RSV and Jehovah in ERV and ASV; typical of the J* source of the Pentateuch.*

Yahwism. The religion of the ancient Hebrews, worship of the national deity Yahweh.

Yahwist. Coined term for the anonymous author of the J* source of the Pentateuch.*

Zealots. Fanatical patriotic party in intertestamental Judaism favoring open revolt against Rome.

Ziggurat. Sumerian and Babylonian temple built as a staged tower.

Zion. (Heb. "fortress, stronghold"?) (1) Apparently originally identical with the Jebusite city of Jerusalem or Ophel.* (2) The whole eastern ridge, including the temple, and poetically of the city as graced by God's presence. (3) Eventually applied to the entire city, including the western hill.

RECOMMENDED FURTHER READING

CHAP. I   ANGLE OF VISION

Among the better introductory works to the Old Testament are: B. W. Anderson, *Understanding the Old Testament,* Prentice-Hall, 1957 (an excellent interweaving of literary, historical, and theological approaches); Aage Bentzen, *Introduction to the Old Testament,* Gad, 1950, 2 vols. (strong on oral tradition and literary types); J. A. Bewer, *The Literature of the Old Testament in its Historical Development,* Columbia University Press, rev. ed., 1933 (constructed as a literary history); S. R. Driver, *An Introduction to the Literature of the Old Testament,* Scribner's, new rev. ed., 1910 (the best compendium of 19th-century research in English); Fleming James, *Personalities of the Old Testament,* Scribner's, 1939 (well-written biographies with brief critical introductions); R. H. Pfeiffer, *Introduction to the Old Testament,* Harper, rev. ed., 1948 (the fullest Introduction in English; it features literary criticism).

The best one-volume Bible dictionary is M. S. Miller and J. L. Miller, *Harper's Bible Dictionary,* 1952. Archaeologically and historically up-to-date but theologically rigid is *Unger's Bible Dictionary,* Moody, 1957. Less satisfactory than either is *The Westminster Dictionary of the Bible,* 1944. Revision of the one-volume J. Hastings, *Dictionary of the Bible,* 1909, is in process, and a multivolume *Interpreter's Dictionary of the Bible* is in preparation. Of the larger works, James Hastings, *A Dictionary of the Bible,* 1898–1904, 5 vols., is somewhat more even in quality and coverage than T. K. Cheyne and J. S. Black, *Encyclopedia Biblica,* 1899–1903, 4 vols., but both are badly outdated.

Vol. 1 of *The Interpreter's Bible,* Abingdon, 1952–1957, contains valuable general articles on the Bible and Old Testament. Three works prepared by members of the British Society for Old Testament Study present the results of 20th-century inquiry into the Old Testament in balance and depth: A. S. Peake, ed., *The People and the Book,* 1925; H. W. Robinson, ed., *Record and Revelation,* 1938; H. H. Rowley, ed., *The Old Testament and Modern Study,* 1951.

As to the history of Old Testament interpretation, Emil Kraeling, *The Old Testament Since the Reformation,* Harper, 1956, analyzes Christian attitudes toward the Old Testament, and Herbert Hahn, *The Old Testament in Modern Research,* Muhlenberg, 1954, focuses on types of critical study of the Old Testament in the last two centuries.

The Old Testament as literature is treated in several classic studies: Mary Ellen Chase, *The Bible and the Common Reader,* Macmillan, 1944; Charles A. Dinsmore, *The English Bible as Literature,* Houghton Mifflin, 1931; Richard G. Moulton, *A Literary Study of the Bible,* Heath, 2nd ed., 1899; Laura Wild, *A Literary Guide to the Bible,* Harper, 1922.

The cultural influence of the Hebrew Bible is treated briefly but ably in Harold H. Watts, *The Modern Reader's Guide to the Bible,* Harper, rev. ed., 1959, and in William Irwin, *The Old Testament: Keystone of Human Culture,* Schumann, 1952. Fuller treatises are given by Ernst von Dobschütz, *The Influence of the Bible on Civilization,* Scribner's, 1914, and Edwyn R. Bevan and Charles Singer, eds., *The Legacy of Israel,* Oxford University Press: Clarendon, 1927 (includes essays on Old Testament influence on Western jurisprudence, Puritanism, European languages, and modern literature).

Among the handbooks that present the Old Testament as inerrant Scripture are John Steinmueller, *A Companion to Scripture Studies,* Wagner, 1941–1943, 3 vols. from the Roman Catholic point of view; and Merrill F. Unger, *Introductory Guide to the Old Testament,* Zondervan, 1951, and Edward J. Young, *An Introduction to the Old Testament,* Eerdmans, 1949, from the Protestant perspective.

An older critical classic is Julius Wellhausen, *Prolegomena to the History of Israel,* 1885 (reprinted by Meridian Books, 1957). More recent cultural and anthropological emphases will be found in Johannes Pedersen, *Israel, Its Life and Culture,* Oxford University Press, Vol. 1–2, 1926; Vol. 3–4, 1940.

The 20th-century revival of Old Testament theology is apparent in a wealth of titles. *Studies in Biblical Theology,* Student Christian Movement Press, is a series that publishes specific studies on both Testaments for a modest price. Manuals that elucidate key Old Testament terms and ideas are Norman Snaith, *The Distinctive Ideas of the Old Testament,* Epworth, 1944 (unexcelled in English); Alan Richardson, *A Theological Word Book to the Bible,* SCM, 1950; and J.-J. von Allmen, *A Companion to the Bible,* Oxford University Press, 1958.

Considering the recent translations of foreign works, the English student now has a rich supply of Old Testament theologies: A. B. Davidson, *The Theology of the Old Testament,* Scribner's, 1904 (old but superb in parts); Walter Eichrodt, *Theology of the Old Testament,* Westminster, in press (the standard work in its field; uses covenant as the key theological category); Edmund Jacob, *The Theology of the Old Testament,* Harper, 1958 (French Protestant); Ludwig Köhler, *Old Testament Theology,* Lutterworth, 1957 (develops the sovereignty of God as the basic Old Testament motif); H. W. Robinson, *Inspiration and Revelation in the Old Testament,* Oxford University Press, 1946 (prolegomena to a theology; the finest all-around theological study of the Old Testament originating in English); Th. Vriezen, *An Outline of Old Testament Theology,* Blackwell's, 1958.

CHAP. II   THE ANCESTRY OF THE OLD TESTAMENT

Excellent translations of nonbiblical texts are available in James B. Pritchard, ed., *The Ancient Near East: an Anthology,* Princeton University Press, 1958. This is a selection of texts and pictures that appear separately in the large volumes: *Ancient Near Eastern Texts Relating to the Old Testament,* 2nd rev. ed., 1955, and *The Ancient Near East in Pictures,* 1955. Fuller notes accompany the translations in D. Winton Thomas, ed., *Documents from Old Testament Times,* Nelson, 1958. J. Finegan, *Light from the Ancient Past,* Princeton University Press, 1946 places many of the literary products in their historical and cultural settings.

The standard full-scale treatment of the Old Testament canon remains that of H. E. Ryle, *The Canon of the Old Testament,* rev. ed., 1909. Ryle and G. Wildeboer, *The Origin of the Canon of the Old Testament,* Luzac, 1895, though seriously outdated, are indispensable. The best recent discussion is by Arthur Jeffery in Vol. 1 of IB.

On the text there are superb works of recent vintage: B. J. Roberts, *The Old Testament Text and Versions,* Univ. of Wales, 1951, and Ernst Würthwein, *The Text of the Old Testament,* Macmillan, 1957. Paul Kahle, *The Cairo Geniza,* Brit. Acad., 1947, elucidates recent trends in textual studies. Jeffery's article in Vol. 1 of IB is unexcelled considering its brevity.

With the publication of the RSV Apocrypha (1957) there is renewed interest in the intertestamental literature. Bruce Metzger, *An Introduction to the Apocrypha,* Oxford University Press, 1957, traces the history of the Apocrypha in the church, sketches its influence in literature and the arts, and introduces the individual books. R. H. Pfeiffer, *History of New Testament Times with an Introduction to the Apocrypha,* Harper, 1949, is really two books in one. His introductions to the books of the Apocrypha are full and authoritative. R. H. Charles, ed., *The Apocrypha and Pseudepigrapha of the Old Testament,* Oxford University Press, 1913, 2 vols., is the standard critical edition of the writings, and includes introductions and notes.

Three books that survey the history of the Bible translations, with special emphasis on the English versions, are: Frederic Kenyon, *Our Bible and the Ancient Manuscripts,* Harper, 5th ed. rev., 1958; Ira Price, *The Ancestry of Our English Bible,* Harper, 3rd rev. ed. by William Irwin and Allen Wikgren, 1956; and H. W. Robinson, *The Bible in its Ancient and English Versions,* Oxford University Press, 1954 (appendix added).

CHAP. III   THE OLD TESTAMENT WORLD

There are now three excellent Bible atlases in English, each with its peculiar virtues. G. E. Wright and F. V. Filson, *The Westminster Historical Atlas to the Bible,* Westminster, rev. ed., 1956, has the finest set of maps in terms of contrast and detail, and the texts and maps are well correlated. The Roman Catholic work of L. H. Grollenberg, *Atlas of the Bible,* Nelson, 1956, has the most vibrant collection of photographs on biblical lands ever assembled in one volume. By symbols and legends the maps are made to tell the history. Emil G. Kraeling, *Rand McNally Bible Atlas,* 1956 discusses at length many of the tangled geographical and historical problems of Scripture. Although some of the maps possess greater detail, in format they are not the equal of those in the preceding atlases.

Greatly outmoded in many of its details, G. A. Smith, *Historical Geography of the Holy Land,* Harper, 25th ed., 1931, is still a classic. It is admirably supplemented by Denis Baly, *The Geography of the Bible,* Harper, 1957.

CHAP. IV   THE FATHERS OF ISRAEL

Hebrew beginnings are ably treated in W. F. Albright, *From the Stone Age to Christianity,* Doubleday, 2nd ed., 1957; G. A. Barton, *Semitic and Hamitic Origins,* Univ. of Pennsylvania Press, 1934; and T. J. Meek, *Hebrew Origins,* Harper, rev. ed., 1950.

CHAP. V   THE PEOPLE OF THE COVENANT

The knotty questions of Pentateuchal authorship are clearly dealt with by D. C. Simpson, *Pentateuchal Criticism,* Hodder & Stoughton, 1944. The fullest English analysis of the Documentary Hypothesis is J. E. Carpenter and G. Harford, eds., *The Composition of the Hexateuch,* Longmans, Green, 1902 (replete with charts and tables). More concise digests are available in S. R. Driver, *Introduction to the Literature of the Old Testament,* Scribner's, new rev. ed., 1910. Twentieth-century objections to and modifications of the Documentary Hypothesis are expounded lucidly by C. R. North, "Pentateuchal Criticism," *The Old Testament and Modern Study,* ed. H. H. Rowley, Oxford University Press, 1951.

James A. Breasted's works on Egypt are still epochal: *A History of Egypt from the Earliest Times to the Persian Conquest,* 2nd ed., Scribner's, 1905 and *Development of Religion and Thought in Ancient Egypt,* Scribner's, 1912. Historical supplement is supplied by G. Steindorff and K. C. Seele, *When Egypt Ruled the East,* Univ. of Chicago Press, 2nd ed., 1957. An analysis of Egyptian religion in sharp contrast to Breasted's evolutionary approach is H. Frankfort, *Ancient Egyptian Religion,* Columbia University Press, 1948.

There is a great gap in English literature on the history of Israel's religion. Apart from Martin Buber, *Moses,* East & West Library, 1946, the student must turn to the theologies of the Old Testament (see above under Chap. I) for profound and detailed analysis of the work of Moses, and especially of his notion of covenant; see also G. E. Mendenhall, *Law and Covenant in Israel and the Ancient Near East* (reprinted from *The Biblical Archaeologist*), 1955.

CHAP. VI THE SETTLEMENT OF THE LAND

As for general histories of Israel, for many years the standard English work has been T. H. Robinson and W. O. E. Oesterley, *A History of Israel,* Oxford University Press: Clarendon, 1932, 2 vols. A. T. Olmstead, *History of Palestine and Syria,* Scribner's, 1931, subordinates Palestinian history to the larger history of Syria, with often illuminating results. Martin Noth, *A History of Israel,* Harper, 1958, is fuller than Robinson and Oesterley on political and cultural aspects. He makes wide use of the latest archaeological and historical data, and gives the most detailed exposition in English of the view that the Israelite tribal confederacy of the Conquest was the source of the normative traditions of the prophets and later Judaism. G. Ricciotti, *The History of Israel,* Bruce, 1955, 2 vols., is the English translation of a Roman Catholic work that appeared in Italian some fifteen years ago.

Two volumes of merit treat the Old Testament attitude toward history: C. R. North, *The Old Testament Interpretation of History,* Epworth, 1946, and C. R. Dentan, ed., *The Idea of History in the Ancient Near East,* Yale University Press, 1955.

The Canaanites, their civilization, and impact on the Hebrews are well described in W. C. Graham and H. G. May, *Culture and Conscience,* Univ. of Chicago Press, 1936, and in G. Ernest Wright, *Biblical Archaeology,* Westminster, 1957, which incidentally provides a superb running archaeological commentary on Bible history.

In addition to the standard histories of Israel, there are several interesting attempts to work out the tangled problems of the Exodus and Settlement of Canaan. Yehezkel Kaufmann, *The Biblical Account of the Conquest of Palestine,* Heb. University Press, 1953, is a hard-hitting criticism of the Alt school. A more temperate evaluation is John Bright, *Early Israel in Recent History Writing* (SBT, 19), 1956. Three of the finest constructive solutions are: C. F. Burney, *Israel's Settlement in Canaan,* British Academy, 2nd ed., 1917; H. H. Rowley, *From Joseph to Joshua,* British Academy, 1948; and T. J. Meek, *Hebrew Origins,* Harper, rev. ed., 1950.

Hebrew poetry is clearly and concisely explained and illustrated by T. H. Robinson, *The Poetry of the Old Testament,* Duckworth, 1947. Parallelism and meter are discussed in greater detail by G. B. Gray, *The Forms of Hebrew Poetry,* Hodder and Stoughton, 1915.

CHAP. VII THE GREAT KINGDOM

The fullest description of the Philistines is given in R. A. S. Macalister, *The Philistines, Their History and Civilization,* British Academy, 1914. The ideology of kingship is discussed in sharply contrasting manner by H. Frankfort, *Kingship and the Gods,* University of Chicago Press, 1948, who finds Israel at odds with other Near Easterners, and S. H. Hooke, ed., *Myth and Ritual,* Oxford University Press, 1933, and *The Labyrinth,* Macmillan, 1935, who emphasizes the prevalence of Near Eastern myth among the Hebrews. Hooke's most recent volume, *Myth, Ritual, and Kingship,* Oxford University Press, 1958, considerably qualifies the earlier two.

B. Davie Napier, *From Faith to Faith,* Harper, 1955, expounds the position of von Rad with respect to the Yahwist. This should be compared with H. Gunkel, *The Legends of Genesis,* Open Court, 1901.

CHAP. VIII THE KINGDOM DISRUPTED

The Deuteronomic theology of history as illustrated in Kings is brilliantly elucidated by Gerhard von Rad, *Studies in Deuteronomy* (SBT, 9), 1953.

The chronology of the monarchy followed in this book is that of W. F. Albright. A simple statement of the principles and results will be found in G. A. Barrois' article in Vol. 1 of IB (it includes extremely useful charts and tables of the Jewish calendar and festivals, linear measures, dry and liquid measures of capacity, weights, and coins). Because the data are meager and capable of various interpretations there is no universally agreed-upon chronology. Edwin R. Thiele, *The Mysterious Numbers of the Hebrew Kings,* University of Chicago Press, 1951, offers the most thorough study in English. His conclusions depart considerably from those of Albright. Thiele is followed by P. van der Meer, *The Chronology of Ancient Western Asia and Egypt,* Brill, 2nd rev. ed., 1955. Van der Meer's synchronistic table is especially helpful to students.

A comparison between ancient Near Eastern prophecy and the Hebrew phenomenon is interestingly worked out by A. Guillaume, *Prophecy and Divination among the Hebrews and Other Semites,* Harper, 1938, who comes to the currently dominant conclusion that there were no psychological criteria for distinguishing biblical from nonbiblical or "false" prophecy.

CHAP. IX   THE COLLAPSE OF ISRAEL

Standard for Assyrian history is A. T. Olmstead, *History of Assyria,* Scribner's, 1923. G. Contenau, *Everyday Life in Babylonia and Assyria,* St. Martin's, 1954, is a well-illustrated account emphasizing social and religious life. Valuable also is André Parrot, *Nineveh and the Old Testament* (Studies in Biblical Archaeology, No. 3), SCM, 1955.

There are many good studies on Hebrew prophecy. R. B. Y. Scott, *The Relevance of the Prophets,* Macmillan, 1944, and J. P. Hyatt, *Prophetic Religion,* Abingdon, 1947, organize their introductions to prophecy topically. Martin Buber, *The Prophetic Faith,* Macmillan, 1949, expounds the prophets theologically in their historical order. Adolphe Lods, *The Prophets and the Rise of Judaism,* Dutton, 1937, and J. M. P. Smith and W. A. Irwin, *The Prophets and Their Times,* University of Chicago Press, 2nd ed., 1941, are rich in historical emphasis. W. C. Graham, *The Prophets and Israel's Culture,* University of Chicago Press, 1934, approaches the prophets through their sociological and cultural function. Sigmund Mowinckel, *Prophecy and Tradition,* Dybwad, 1946 illustrates the Scandinavian stress on oral tradition and prophetic schools.

CHAP. X   THE DECLINE OF JUDAH

L. W. King, *History of Babylon,* Chatto & Windus, 1919, is a readable and still generally accurate history. The stirring events surrounding the fall of Assyria are correctly described in C. J. Gadd, *The Fall of Assyria,* British Academy, 1923. Contenau, *Everyday Life in Babylonia and Assyria,* St. Martin's, 1954, vivifies the ancient history by recreating the ancient culture.

CHAP. XI   THE PEOPLE IN EXILE

The religious impact of the Exile on the Jewish prophets is discussed in detail by C. F. Whitley, *The Exilic Age,* Longmans, 1957. J. Finegan has dramatized the world-wide ferment of the sixth century B.C. in his novel *Wanderer upon Earth,* Harper, 1956 (this was the traditional century of Zoroaster, Buddha, and Confucius).

CHAP. XII   RECONSTRUCTION UNDER THE PERSIANS

The history of the Jews in the Persian, Greek, and early Roman periods is tersely presented in Norman Snaith, *The Jews from Cyrus to Herod,* the Religious Education Press, 1949. The standard history of the Persians is A. T. Olmstead, *History of the Persian Empire,* University of Chicago Press, 1948.

Religious developments are dealt with by Adam Welch, *Post-exilic Judaism,* Blackwood, 1935. C. C. Torrey, *Ezra Studies,* University of Chicago Press, 1910 contains much of value but is marred by special pleading for the author's theory that the Exile and restoration were fictions of the Chronicler. Torrey is well balanced at this point by Adam Welch, *The Work of the Chronicler,* British Academy, 1939.

A cautious comparison of the Babylonian and Hebrew creation accounts is undertaken by Alexander Heidel, *The Babylonian Genesis,* University of Chicago Press, 2nd ed., 1951. The role of creation in Israelite thought, as contrasted with the ancient Near Eastern mythologies, is discussed in Eric C. Rust, *Nature and Man in Biblical Thought,* Lutterworth, 1953.

The wisdom writings are introduced by Harry Ranston, *The Old Testament Wisdom Books and Their Teaching,* Epworth, 1930. Of greater interest theologically and philosophically are O. S. Rankin, *Israel's Wisdom Literature, its Bearing on Theology and the History of Religion,* T. & T. Clark, 1936 (deals with notions of reward and punishment, providence, and future life) and J. C. Rylaarsdam, *Revelation in Jewish Wisdom Literature,* University of Chicago Press, 1946 (treats the problems of natural and special revelation as they appear in the wisdom movement, with special reference to the New Testament).

CHAP. XIII   RECONSTRUCTION UNDER THE HELLENISTS

Concise and instructive are G. H. Box, *Judaism in the Greek Period,* Oxford University Press: Clarendon, 1932, and W. O. E. Oesterley, *The Jews and Judaism in the Greek Period,* SPCK, 1941. Fuller treatment of historical questions will be found in the studies of Edwyn R. Bevan, *The Ptolemaic Dynasty,* Arnold, 1927; *The House of Seleucus,* Arnold, 1902, 2 vols.; and *Jerusalem under the High Priests,* Arnold, 1904.

Jewish apocalyptic thought is explained, illustrated, and its relevance assessed by Stanley Frost, *Old Testament Apocalyptic, its Origin and Growth,* Epworth, 1952, and H. H. Rowley, *The Relevance of Apocalyptic,* Lutterworth, 1944. Basic as sourcebooks on messianism are Joseph Klausner, *The Messianic Idea in Israel,* Macmillan, 1955 (includes messianism in the Apocrypha, Pseudepigrapha, and Talmud) and Sigmund Mowinckel, *He That Cometh,* Abingdon, 1956 (he carries the discussion into later Judaism and briefly into the New Testament).

For the intertestamental history R. H. Pfeiffer, *The History of New Testament Times and Introduction to the Apocrypha,* Harper, 1949, is superb. R. H. Charles, *Religious Development between the Old and New Testaments,* Holt, 1914, is still of great value, although every publication in this field prior to the discovery of the Dead Sea scrolls is in need of revision.

On the scrolls, A. Dupont-Sommer, *The Jewish Sect of Qumran and the Essenes,* Macmillan, 1955, and John Allegro, *The Dead Sea Scrolls,* Penguin, 1956 are excitingly written but somewhat extreme in conclusion. More temperate and trustworthy for the beginner are Millar Burrows, *The Dead Sea Scrolls,* Viking, 1955; *More Light on the Dead Sea Scrolls,* Viking, 1958; and Frank M. Cross, *The Ancient Library of Qumran and Modern Biblical Studies,* Doubleday, 1958. Many of the nonbiblical Dead Sea texts are translated with notes in Theodor H. Gaster, *The Dead Sea Scriptures,* Doubleday, 1956.

The fundamental study on Judaism in this period is George F. Moore, *Judaism in the First Centuries of the Christian Era,* Harvard University Press, 1927–1930, 3 vols. Louis Finkelstein, *The Pharisees, the Sociological Background of their Faith,* JPS, 1938, 2 vols., is filled with basic information, although its sociological typing of the party is highly debatable. The core of the Talmud is available in a one-volume translation with notes: Herbert Danby, ed., *The Mishnah,* Oxford University Press, 1938.

COMMENTARIES AND SPECIAL STUDIES
ON INDIVIDUAL BOOKS

Genesis
  S. R. Driver, (WC), 15th ed., 1948
  John Skinner, (ICC), rev. ed., 1925
Exodus
  A. H. McNeile, (WC), 1908
  J. C. Rylaarsdam, (IB, vol. 1), 1952
Leviticus
  G. B. Gray, *Sacrifice in the Old Testament,* Oxford University Press, 1925
  A. R. S. Kennedy, (NCB), n. d.
  N. Micklem, (IB, vol. 2), 1953
Numbers
  G. B. Gray, (ICC), 1903
  John Marsh, (IB, vol. 2), 1953
Deuteronomy
  S. R. Driver, (ICC), 1895
  G. A. Smith, (CB), 1918
  Gerhard von Rad, *Studies in Deuteronomy* (SBT, 3), 1953
  G. E. Wright, (IB, vol. 2), 1953
Joshua
  John Bright, (IB, vol. 2), 1953
  G. A. Cooke, (CB), 1918

Y. Kaufmann, *The Biblical Account of the Conquest of Palestine,* Hebrew University Press, 1955

Judges

C. F. Burney, *The Book of Judges,* Rivingtons, 1918

G. F. Moore, (ICC), 1895

J. M. Myers, (IB, vol. 2), 1953

Ruth

G. A. Cooke, (CB), 1913

Samuel

G. B. Caird, (IB, vol. 2), 1953

A. R. S. Kennedy, (NCB), n.d.

H. P. Smith, (ICC), 1899

Kings

J. A. Montgomery, (ICC), 1952

John Skinner, (NCB), 1904

N. H. Snaith, (IB, vol. 3), 1954

Chronicles

E. L. Curtis and A. A. Madsen, (ICC), 1910

W. A. L. Elmslie, (IB, vol. 3), 1954

C. C. Torrey, *Ezra Studies,* University of Chicago Press, 1910.

Ezra-Nehemiah

L. W. Batten, (ICC), 1913

R. A. Bowman, (IB, vol. 3), 1954

Esther

B. W. Anderson, (IB, vol. 3), 1954

L. B. Paton, (ICC), 1908

Job

S. R. Driver and G. B. Gray, (ICC), 1921

E. G. Kraeling, *The Book of the Ways of God,* Scribner's, 1938

A. S. Peake, (NCB), 1905

James Strahan, *The Book of Job,* T. & T. Clark, 1914

Samuel Terrien, (IB, vol. 3), 1954

Psalms

Fleming James, *Thirty Psalmists,* Putnam, 1938

A. F. Kirkpatrick, (CB), 1912

E. A. Leslie, *The Psalms,* Abingdon, 1949

W. O. E. Oesterley, *The Psalms,* Macmillan, 1940

Proverbs

W. O. E. Oesterley, (WC), 2nd ed., 1929

C. H. Toy, (ICC), 1899

Ecclesiastes

G. A. Barton, (ICC), 1908

Robert Gordis, *Koheleth, the Man and His World,* Bloch, 1955
O. S. Rankin, (IB, vol. 5), 1956
Song of Songs
Robert Gordis, *The Song of Songs,* Jewish Theological Seminary, 1954
T. J. Meek, (IB, vol. 5), 1956
H. H. Rowley, "The Interpretation of the Song of Songs," *The Servant of the Lord and Other Essays,* Lutterworth, 1952
Isaiah
G. B. Gray, *Chaps. 1–27* (ICC), 1912
Curt Lindhagen, *The Servant Motif in the Old Testament,* Lundequistska, 1950
James Muilenburg, *Chaps. 40–66* (IB, vol. 5), 1956
C. R. North, *The Suffering Servant in Deutero-Isaiah,* Oxford University Press, 2nd ed., 1956
R. B. Y. Scott, *Chaps. 1–39* (IB, vol. 5), 1956
Ulrich Simon, *A Theology of Salvation,* SPCK, 1953
John Skinner, (CB), 1915–1917
G. A. Smith, *The Book of Isaiah,* Harper, rev. ed., 1928
C. C. Torrey, *The Second Isaiah,* Scribner's, 1928
Jeremiah
J. P. Hyatt, (IB, vol. 5), 1956
A. S. Peake, (NCB), 1910–1911
John Skinner, *Prophecy and Religion,* Cambridge University Press, 1922
G. A. Smith, *Jeremiah,* Harper, 1923
A. C. Welch, *Jeremiah,* Macmillan, 1928
Lamentations
N. K. Gottwald, *Studies in the Book of Lamentations* (SBT, 14), 1954
A. S. Peake, (NCB, bound with Jeremiah), 1910–1911
Ezekiel
G. A. Cooke, (ICC), 1937
J. B. Harford, *Studies in the Book of Ezekiel,* Cambridge University Press, 1935
C. G. Howie, *The Date and Composition of Ezekiel,* 1950
H. G. May, (IB, vol. 6), 1956
I. G. Matthews, *Ezekiel,* American Baptist Pub. Soc., 1939
Daniel
R. H. Charles, *A Critical and Exegetical Commentary on the Book of Daniel,* Oxford University Press: Clarendon, 1929
Arthur Jeffery, (IB, vol. 6), 1956
J. A. Montgomery, (ICC), 1927
Amos and Hosea
S. L. Brown, Hosea, (WC), 1932

R. S. Cripps, *A Critical and Exegetical Commentary on the Book of Amos,* SPCK, 2nd ed., 1955

S. R. Driver, *Joel and Amos,* (CB), rev. ed., 1915

W. R. Harper, *Amos and Hosea,* (ICC), 1905

J. Morgenstern, *Amos Studies,* Hebrew Union College, 1941

H. W. Robinson, *The Cross of Hosea,* Westminster, 1949

Norman Snaith, *Mercy and Sacrifice,* SCM, 1953

The Remainder of the Twelve

R. C. Dentan, *Zechariah 9–14 and Malachi* (IB, vol. 6), 1956

H. T. G. Mitchell, J. M. P. Smith, and J. A. Bewer, *Haggai, Zechariah, Malachi, and Jonah* (ICC), 1912

Arvid Kapelrud, *Joel Studies,* Alquist & Wicksells, 1948

James D. Smart, *Jonah* (IB, vol. 6), 1956

J. M. P. Smith, W. H. Ward, and J. A. Bewer, *Micah, Zephaniah, Nahum, Habakkuk, Obadiah, and Joel* (ICC), 1911

D. Winton Thomas, *Haggai and Zechariah 1–8* (IB, vol. 6), 1956

APPENDIX: NEAR EASTERN TEXTS RELATED TO THE OLD TESTAMENT

In the following translations parentheses enclose words that have no equivalent in the original but have been added for fluency or intelligibility. Words in brackets are restorations. (?) is added to words of uncertain meaning. Ellipses due to breaks in the original or due to the unintelligibility of the text are marked. . . . Words in italics are transliterations from the original language.

1. THE BABYLONIAN CREATION STORY[1]

When above the heaven had not (yet) been named,
(And) below the earth had not (yet) been called by a name;
(When) Apsu primeval, their begetter,
Mummu, (and) Tiamat, she who gave birth to them all,
(Still) mingled their waters together,
And no pasture land had been formed (and) not (even) a reed marsh
    was to be seen;
When none of the (other) gods had been brought into being,
(When) they had not (yet) been called by (their) name(s, and their)
    destinies had not (yet) been fixed,
(At that time) were the gods created within them.
Lahmu and Lahamu came into being; they were called by (their) names.
Even before they had grown up (and) become tall,
Anshar and Kishar were created; they surpassed them (in stature).

[1] Translation from Alexander Heidel, *The Babylonian Genesis,* University of Chicago Press, 2nd ed., 1951. Tablet I, 1–92; II, 1–37, 88–129; IV, 1–140; VI, 1–65.

They lived many days, adding years (to days).
Anu was their heir presumptive, the rival of his fathers;
Yea, Anu, his first-born, equaled Anshar.
And Anu begot Nudimmud, his likeness.
Nudimmud, the master of his fathers was he;
He was broad of understanding, wise, mighty in strength,
Much stronger than his grandfather, Anshar;
He had no rival among the gods his brothers.
The divine brothers gathered together.
They disturbed Tiamat and assaulted(?) their keeper;
Yea, they disturbed the inner parts of Tiamat,
Moving (and) running about in the divine abode(?).
Apsu could not diminish their clamor,
And Tiamat was silent in regard to their [behavior].
Yet, their doing was painful [to them].
Their way was not good . . . .
Then Apsu, the begetter of the great gods,
Called Mummu, his vizier, and said to him:
"Mummu, my vizier, who gladdenest my heart,
Come, let us [go] to Tiamat!"
They went and reposed before Tiamat;
They took counsel about the matter concerning the gods, their first-born.
Apsu opened his mouth
And said to Tiamat in a loud voice:
"Their way has become painful to me,
By day I cannot rest, by night I cannot sleep;
I will destroy (them) and put an end to their way,
That silence may be established, and then let us sleep!"
When Tiamat heard this,
She was wroth and cried out to her husband;
She cried out and raged furiously, she alone.
She pondered the evil in her heart (and said):
"Why should we destroy that which we ourselves have brought forth?
Their way is indeed very painful, but let us take it good-naturedly!"
Mummu spoke up and counseled Apsu;
[. . . .] and unfavorable was the advice of his Mummu:
"Yes, my father, destroy (their) disorderly way;
(Then) verily thou shalt have rest by day (and) sleep by night!"
When Apsu [hear]d it, his face grew bright,
Because of the evil he planned against the gods his children.
Mummu embraced [his] neck,
Sat down on his knee, and kissed him.

Whatever they planned in their assembly
Was communicated to the gods, their first-born.
When the gods heard (it), they hasten(ed) about;
They took to silence, they sat quietly.
The one of supreme understanding, the skilful (and) wise,
Ea, who understands everything, saw through their plan.
He made and established against it a magical circle for all.
He skilfully composed his overpowering, holy incantation.
He recited it and thus caused (it) to be upon the water.
He poured out sleep upon him, (so that) he slept soundly.
When he had put Apsu to sleep, (Apsu) being suffused with sleep,
Mummu, his adviser, ...
He loosened his band (and) tore off [his] tiara;
He carried off his splendor (and) put (it) on himself.
When he had (thus) subdued Apsu, he slew him.
Mummu he shut in (and) barred (the door) against him.
On Apsu he established his dwelling place;
Mummu he seized for himself, holding (him) by his noserope.
After Ea had vanquished (and) subdued his enemies,
Had established his victory over his foes,
(And) had peacefully rested in his abode,
He named it Apsu and appointed (it) for shrines.
In his place he founded his chamber;
(There) Ea (and) Damkina, his wife, dwelt in splendor.
In the Chamber of fates, the abode of destinies,
The wisest of the wise, the wisest of the gods, *the* God was begotten.
Within the Apsu Marduk was born;
Within the holy Apsu [Marduk] was born.
He who begot him was Ea, his father;
Damki[na], his mother, was she who bore him.
He sucked the breasts of goddesses.
The nurse that cared for him filled (him) with awe-inspiring majesty.
Enticing was his figure, flashing the look of his eyes,
Manly was his going-forth, a leader(?) from the beginning.
When E[a], his father that begot (him), saw him,
He rejoiced, he beamed, his heart was filled with joy.
He distinguished(?) him and con[ferred upon him(?)] dou[ble] equal-
    ity with the gods,
(So that) he was highly exalted (and) surpassed them in everything.

After Tiamat had made str[ong] preparations,
She made ready to join battle with the gods her offspring.

To avenge Apsu, Tiamat did (this) evil.

How she got ready for the attack was revealed to Ea.

When Ea heard of this matter,

He became benumbed with f[ea]r and sat in silent gloom.

Af[ter he had] reflected on (the matter) and his wrath had subsided,

He went to Anshar, his (grand)father.

And when he had [co]me into the presence of Anshar, his grandfather,

He communicated to him all that Tiamat had planned.

"My father, Tiamat, our bearer, hates us.

She held a meeting and raged furiously.

All the gods went over to her;

Even those whom ye have created march at her side.

They separated themselves(?) and went over to the side of Tiamat;

They were angry, they plotted, not resting day or night;

They took up the fight, fuming and raging;

They held a meeting and planned the conflict.

Mother Hubur, who fashions all things,

Added (thereto) irresistible weapons, bearing monster serpents

Sharp of tooth and not sparing the fang(?).

With poison instead of blood she filled their bodies.

Ferocious dragons she clothed with terror,

She crowned them with fear-inspiring glory (and) made them like gods,

So that he who would look upon them should perish from terror,

So that their bodies might leap forward and none turn back their breasts.

She set up the viper, the dragon, and the *lahamu,*

The great lion, the mad dog, and the scorpion-man,

Driving storm demons, the dragonfly, and the bison,

Bearing unsparing weapons, unafraid of battle.

Powerful are her decrees, irresistible are they.

Altogether(?) eleven (kinds of monsters) of this sort she brought into
   being.

Of those among the gods, her first-born, who formed her assembly,

She exalted Kingu; in their midst she made him great.

To march at the head of the army, to direct the forces,

To raise the weapons for the engagement, to launch the attack,

The high command of the battle,

[She int]rusted to his hand; she caused him to sit in the assembly, . . ."

All the Anunnaki were assembled at the place.

Their lips were closed, [they sat in] silence.

"No god whatever can go t[o battle]

(And) escape w[ith his life] from the presence of Tiamat."

Lord Anshar, the father of the gods, [arose in] majesty;

His heart [prom]pted (him) [to speak to the Anunnaki]:

"[He] whose [strength] is mighty shall be the avenger of [his] father.

[That one is] the . . . . in battle, the valia[nt] Mar[duk]!"

Ea called [Marduk] to [his] private room;

[He ad]vised (him), telling him the plan of his heart:

"Marduk, consider my idea, hearken to thy father.

Thou art he, my son, who relieves his heart;

Draw nigh [into the presence of] Anshar, (ready) for battle(?);

[Speak and] stand forth; when he sees thee, he will be at rest."

The lord was glad at the word of his father;

He drew nigh and stood before Anshar.

When Anshar saw him, his heart was filled with joy;

He kissed his lips, his fear was removed.

"[Anshar], be not silent, (but) open thy lips;

I will go and accomplish all that is in thy heart!

[Yea, Anshar], be not silent, (but) open thy lips;

[I will g]o and accomplish all that is in thy heart!

What man is it who has brought battle against thee?

[. . . . T]iamat, who is a woman, is coming against thee with arms!

[My father, c]reator, be glad and rejoice;

Soon thou shalt trample upon the neck of Tiamat!

[Yea, my father, c]reator, be glad and rejoice;

Soon thou shalt trample upon [the neck of] Tiamat!"

"My [so]n, who knowest all wisdom,

Quiet [Tiamat] with thy holy incantation.

On the storm [chari]ot(?) quickly pursue (the way)!

[. . . .] . . . . turn (her) back!"

The lord [was glad] at the word of his father;

His heart [ex]ulted, and he said to his father:

"Lord of the gods, destiny of the great gods,

If I am indeed to be your avenger,

To vanquish Tiamat and to keep you alive,

Convene the assembly and proclaim my lot supreme.

When ye are joyfully seated together in the Court of Assembly,

May I through the utterance of my mouth determine the destinies, instead of you.

Whatever I create shall remain unaltered,

The command of my lips shall not return (void), it shall not be changed."

They erected for him a lordly throne-dais,

And he took his place before his fathers to (receive) sovereignty.

"Thou art (the most) important among the great gods;

Thy destiny is unequaled, thy command is (like that of) Anu.
Marduk, thou art (the most) important among the great gods,
Thy destiny is unequaled, thy command is (like that of) Anu.
From this day onward thy command shall not be changed.
To exalt and to abase—this shall be thy power!
Dependable shall be the utterance of thy mouth, thy command shall not prove vain.
None among the gods shall infringe upon thy prerogative.
Maintenance is the requirement of the sanctuaries of the gods;
And so at (each) place of their shrines shall be appointed a place for thee.
Marduk, thou art our avenger;
To thee we have given kingship over the totality of the whole universe,
So that when thou sittest in the assembly, thy word shall be exalted.
May thy weapons not miss, may they smite thy foes.
O lord, preserve the life of him who puts his trust in thee;
But as for the god who has espoused evil, pour out his life!"
Then they placed a garment in their midst;
To Marduk, their first-born, they said:
"Thy destiny, O lord, shall be supreme among the gods.
Command to destroy and to create, (and) they shall be!
By the word of thy mouth, let the garment be destroyed;
Command again, and let the garment be whole!"
He commanded with his mouth, and the garment was destroyed.
He commanded again, and the garment was restored.
When the gods his fathers beheld the power of his word,
They were glad (and) did homage, (saying:) "Marduk is king!"
They bestowed upon him the scepter, the throne, and the royal robe(?);
They gave him an irresistible weapon smiting the enemy, (saying:)
"Go and cut off the life of Tiamat.
May the winds carry her blood to out-of-the-way places."
After the gods his fathers had determined the destiny of Bel,
They set him on the road—the way to success and attainment.
He made a bow and decreed (it) as his weapon;
An arrowhead he put (on the arrow and) fastened the bowstring to it.
He took up the club and grasped (it) in his right hand;
The bow and the quiver he hung at his side.
The lightning he set before him;
With a blazing flame he filled his body.
He made a net to inclose Tiamat within (it),
(And) had the four winds take hold that nothing of her might escape;
The south wind, the north wind, the east wind, (and) the west wind,

The gift of his (grand)father, Anu, he caused to draw nigh to the bor-
der(s) of the net.
He created the *imhullu:* the evil wind, the cyclone, the hurricane,
The fourfold wind, the sevenfold wind, the whirlwind, the wind incom-
parable.
He sent forth the winds which he had created, the seven of them;
To trouble Tiamat within, they arose behind him.
The lord raised the rain flood, his mighty weapon.
He mounted (his) irresistible, terrible storm chariot;
He harnessed for it a team of four and yoked (them) to it,
The Destructive, the Pitiless, the Trampler, the Flier.
They were sharp of tooth, bearing poison;
They knew how to destroy, they had learned to overrun;
[. . . .] they [smo]te, they were frightful in battle;
To the left [. . . .].
He was clad in a terrifying coat of mail;
Terror-inspiring splendor he wore on his head.
The lord took a direct (route) and pursued his way;
Toward the place of raging Tiamat he set his face.
Between his lips he holds [a talisman(?)] of red paste;
An herb to destroy the poison he grasped in his hand.
Then the gods r[un] about him, the gods run about him.
The lord drew nigh to look into the heart of Tiamat,
(And) to see the plan of Kingu, her spouse.
As he gazes, (Kingu) is confused in his plan;
Destroyed is his will and disordered his action.
As for the gods his helpers, who were marching at his side,
When they saw the valiant hero, their vision became blurred.
Tiamat set up a roar(?) without turning her neck,
Upholding with her li[ps] (her) meanness(?) (and) rebellion:
". . . . have the gods risen up to thee?
(Or) have they gathered from their [place] to thy place?"
Then the lord [raised] the rain flood, his mighty weapon.
[As for T]iamat, who was furious, thus he answered her:
"[In arrogance(?)] thou art risen (and) hast highly exalted thyself(?).
[Thou hast caused] thy heart to plot the stirring-up of conflict.
[. . . .] the sons treat their fathers unjustly;
(And) thou, their bearer, dost hate (them) wi[thout cause(?)].
Thou hast exalted Kingu to be [thy] spouse;
Thine illegal [authority] thou hast set up in place of the authority of
Anu.
[Against] Anshar, the king of the gods, thou seekest evil,

And hast proven thy wickedness [against the god]s my fathers.
Let thine army be equipped! Let them be girded with thy weapons!
Come thou forth (alone) and let us, me and thee, do single combat!"
When Tiamat heard this,
She became like one in a frenzy (and) lost her reason.
Tiamat cried out loud (and) furiously,
To the (very) roots her two legs shook back and forth.
She recites an incantation, repeatedly casting her spell;
As for the gods of battle, they sharpen their weapons.
Tiamat (and) Marduk, the wisest of the gods, advanced against one another;
They pressed on to single combat, they approached for battle.
The lord spread out his net and enmeshed her;
The evil wind, following after, he let loose in her face.
When Tiamat opened her mouth to devour him,
He drove in the evil wind, in order that (she should) not (be able) to close her lips.
The raging winds filled her belly;
Her belly became distended, and she opened wide her mouth.
He shot off an arrow, and it tore her interior;
It cut through her inward parts, it split (her) heart.
When he had subdued her, he destroyed her life;
He cast down her carcass (and) stood upon it.
After he had slain Tiamat, the leader,
Her band broke up, her host dispersed.
As for the gods her helpers, who marched at her side,
They trembled for fear (and) faced about.
They tried to break away to save their lives,
(But) they were completely surrounded, (so that) it was impossible to flee.
He imprisoned them and broke their weapons.
In the net they lay and in the snare they were;
They hid in the corners (and) were filled with lamentation;
They bore his wrath, being confined in prison.
As for the eleven (kinds of) creatures which she had laden with terror-inspiring splendor,
The host of demons that marched impetuously before her,
He cast (them) into fetters (and) [tied(?)] their arms [together(?)];
With (all) their resistance, [he tr]ampled (them) underfoot.
As for Kingu, who had become chief among them,
He found him and counted him among the dead gods.

He took from him the tablet of destinies, which was not his rightful pos-
session.
He sealed (it) with (his) seal and fastened (it) on his breast.
After he had vanquished (and) subdued his enemies,
Had overpowered the arrogant foe like a bull(?),
Had fully established Anshar's victory over the enemy,
Had attained the desire of Nudimudd, the valiant Marduk
Strengthened his hold upon the captive gods;
And then he returned to Tiamat, whom he had subdued.
The Lord trod upon the hinder part of Tiamat,
And with his unsparing club he split (her) skull.
He cut the arteries of her blood
And caused the north wind to carry (it) to out-of-the-way places.
When his fathers saw (this), they were glad and rejoiced
(And) sent him dues (and) greeting-gifts.
The lord rested, examining her dead body,
To divide the abortion (and) to create ingenious things (therewith).
He split her open like a mussel(?) into two (parts);
Half of her he set in place and formed the sky (therewith) as a roof.
He fixed the crossbar (and) posted guards;
He commanded them not to let her waters escape.

As [Mar]duk hears the words of the gods,
His heart prompts (him) to create ingenious things.
He conveys his idea to Ea,
Imparting the plan [which] he had conceived in his heart:
"Blood will I form and cause bone to be;
Then will I set up lullu, 'Man' shall be his name!
Yes, I will create lullu: Man!
(Upon him) shall the services of the gods be imposed that they may be
at rest.
Moreover, I will ingeniously arrange the ways of the gods.
They shall be honored alike, but they shall be divided into two
(groups)."
Ea answered him, speaking a word to him,
To make him change his mind concerning the relief of the gods:
"Let a brother of theirs be delivered up;
Let him be destroyed and men be fashioned.
Let the great gods assemble hither,
Let the guilty one be delivered up, and let them be established."
Marduk assembled the great gods,

Ordering (them) kindly (and) giving instructions.

The gods pay attention to his word,

As the king addresses a word to the Anunnaki, (saying:)

"Verily, the former thing which we declared unto you has come true!

(Also now) I speak the truth under an oath(?) by myself.

Who was it that created the strife,

And caused Tiamat to revolt and prepare for battle?

Let him who created the strife be delivered up;

I will make him bear his punishment, be ye at rest."

The Igigi, the great gods, answered him,

The "king of the gods of heaven and earth," the counselor of the gods, their lord:

"Kingu it was who created the strife,

And caused Tiamat to revolt and prepare for battle."

They bound him and held him before Ea;

Punishment they inflicted upon him by cutting (the arteries of) his blood.

With his blood they created mankind;

He imposed the services of the gods (upon them) and set the gods free.

After Ea, the wise, had created mankind,

(And) they had imposed the service of the gods upon them—

That work was not suited to (human) understanding;

In accordance with the ingenious plans of Marduk did Nudimmud create (it)—,

Marduk, the king, divided

The totality of the Anunnaki above and below;

He assigned (them) to Anu, to guard his decrees.

Three hundred he set in the heavens as a guard.

Moreover, the ways of (the gods of) the earth he defined.

In heaven and in earth six hundred he caused to dwell.

After he had issued all the decrees,

(And) to the Anunnaki of heaven and earth had allotted their portions,

The Anunnaki opened their mouth(s)

And said to Marduk, their lord:

"Now, O lord, who hast established our freedom from compulsory service,

What shall be the sign of our gratitude before thee?

Come, let us make (something) whose name shall be called 'Sanctuary.'

It shall be a dwelling for our rest at night; come, let us repose therein!

There let us erect a throne dais, a seat with a back support!

On the day that we arrive, we will repose in it."

When Marduk heard this,

His countenance shone exceedingly, [lik]e the day, (and he said:)
"So(?) shall Babylon be, whose construction ye have desired;
Let its brickwork be fashioned, and call (it) a sanctuary."
The Anunnaki wielded the hoe.
One year they made bricks for it;
When the second year arrived,
They raised the head of Esagila on high, level with the Apsu.
After they had built the lofty stagetower of the Apsu,
They established an abode therein(?) for Marduk, Enlil, (and) Ea.

2. THE BABYLONIAN FLOOD STORY[2]

Gilgamesh said to him, to Utnapishtim the Distant:
"I look upon thee, Utnapishtim,
Thine appearance is not different; thou art like unto me.
Yea, thou art not different; thou art like unto me.
My heart had pictured thee as one perfect for the doing of battle;
[But] thou liest (idly) on (thy) side, (or) on thy back.
[Tell me], how didst thou enter into the company of the gods and obtain life (everlasting)?
Utnapishtim said to him, to Gilgamesh:
"Gilgamesh, I will reveal unto thee a hidden thing,
Namely, a secret of the gods will I tell thee.
Shurippak—a city which thou knowest,
[And which] is situated [on the bank of] the river Euphrates—
That city was (already) old, and the gods were in its midst.
(Now) their heart prompted the great gods [to] bring a deluge.
[There was(?)] Anu, their father;
Warlike Enlil, their counselor;
Ninurta, their representative;
Ennugi, their vizier;
Ninigiku, (that is,) Ea, also sat with them.
Their speech he repeated to a reed hut:
'Reed hut, reed hut! Wall, wall!
Reed hut, hearken! Wall, consider!
Man of Shurippak, son of Ubara-Tutu!
Tear down (thy) house, build a ship!
Abandon (thy) possessions, seek (to save) life!
Disregard (thy) goods, and save (thy) life!

[2] Translation from Alexander Heidel, *The Gilgamesh Epic and Old Testament Parallels,* University of Chicago Press, 1946. Tablet XI, 1–196.

[Cause to] go up into the ship the seed of all living creatures.
The ship which thou shalt build,
Its measurements shall be (accurately) measured;
Its width and its length shall be equal.
Cover it [li]ke the subterranean waters.'
When I understood this, I said to Ea, my lord:
'[Behold], my lord, what thou hast thus commanded,
[I] will honor (and) carry out.
[But what] shall I answer the city, the people, and the elders?'
Ea opened his mouth and said,
Speaking to me, his servant:
'Thus shalt thou say to them:
[I have le]arned that Enlil hates me,
That I may no (longer) dwell in yo[ur ci]ty,
Nor turn my face to the land of Enlil.
[I will therefore g]o down to the *apsu* and dwell with Ea, my [lor]d.
[On] you he will (then) rain down plenty;
[. . . . of b]irds (?), ... of fishes.
[. . . .] harvest-wealth.
[In the evening the leader] of the storm(?)
Will cause a wheat-rain to rain down upon you.'
As soon as [the first shimmer of mor]ning beamed forth,
The land was gathered [about me].

. . . .

The child [brou]ght pitch,
(While) the strong brought [whatever else] was needful.
On the fifth day [I] laid its framework.
One *iku* was its floor space, one hundred and twenty cubits each was
    the height of its walls;
One hundred and twenty cubits measured each side of its deck.
I 'laid the shape' of the outside (and) fashioned it.
Six (lower) decks I built into it,
(Thus) dividing (it) into seven (stories).
Its ground plan I divided into nine (sections).
I drove water-stoppers into it.
I provided punting-poles and stored up a supply.
Six *shar* of pitch I poured into the furnace,
(And) three *shar* of asphalt [I poured] into it.
Three *shar* of oil the basket-carriers brought:
Besides a *shar* of oil which the saturation(?) (of the water-stoppers)
    consumed,
Two *shar* of oil [which] the boatman stowed away.

Bullocks I slaughtered for [the people];
Sheep I killed every day.
Must, red wine, oil, and white wine,
[I gave] the workmen [to drink] as if it were river water,
(So that) they made a feast as on New Year's Day.
I [. . . .] ointment I put my hands.
[. . . .]. . the ship was completed.
Difficult was [the . . . .].
. . . . above and below.
[. . . .]. . its two-thirds.
[Whatever I had I] loaded aboard her.
Whatever I had of silver I loaded aboard her.
Whatever I [had] of gold I loaded aboard her;
Whatever I had of the seed of all living creatures [I loaded] aboard her.
After I had caused all my family and relations to go up into the ship,
I caused the game of the field, the beasts of the field, (and) all the craftsmen to go (into it).
Shamash set for me a definite time:
'When the leader of the sto[rm(?)] causes a destructive rain to rain down in the evening,
Enter the ship and close thy door.'
That definite time arrived:
In the evening the leader of the sto[rm(?)] caused a destructive rain to rain down.
I viewed the appearance of the weather;
The weather was frightful to behold.
I entered the ship and closed my door.
For the navigation(?) of the ship to the boatman Puzur-Amurri
I intrusted the mighty structure with its goods.
As soon as the first shimmer of morning beamed forth,
A black cloud came up from out the horizon.
Adad thunders within it,
While Shullat and Hanish go before,
Coming as heralds over hill and plain;
Irragal pulls out the masts;
Ninurta comes along (and) causes the dikes to give way;
The Anunnaki raised (their) torches,
Lighting up the land with their brightness;
The raging of Adad reached unto heaven
(And) turned into darkness all that was light.
[. . . .] the land he broke(?) like a po[t(?)].

(For) one day the tem[pest blew].

Fast it blew and [. . . .].

Like a battle [it ca]me over the p[eople].

No man could see his fellow.

The people could not be recognized from heaven.

(Even) the gods were terror-stricken at the deluge.

They fled (and) ascended to the heaven of Anu;

The gods cowered like dogs (and) crouched in distress(?).

Ishtar cried out like a woman in travail;

The lovely-voiced Lady of the g[ods] lamented:

'In truth, the olden time has turned to clay,

Because I commanded evil in the assembly of the gods!

How could I command (such) evil in the assembly of the gods!

(How) could I command war to destroy my people,

(For) it is I who bring forth (these) my people!

Like the spawn of fish they (now) fill the sea!'

The Anunnaki-gods wept with her;

The gods sat bowed (and) weeping.

Covered were their lips . . . .

Six days and [six] nights

The wind blew, the downpour, the tempest, (and) the flo[od] overwhelmed the land.

When the seventh day arrived, the tempest, the flood,

Which had fought like an army, subsided in (its) onslaught.

The sea grew quiet, the storm abated, the flood ceased.

I opened a window, and light fell upon my face.

I looked upon the sea, (all) was silence,

And all mankind had turned to clay;

The . . . . was as level as a (flat) roof.

I bowed, sat down, and wept,

My tears running down over my face.

I looked in (all) directions for the boundaries of the sea.

At (a distance of) twelve (double-hours) there emerged a stretch of
land.

On Mount Nisir the ship landed.

Mount Nisir held the ship fast and did not let (it) move.

One day, a second day Mount Nisir held the ship fast and did not let
(it) move.

A third day, a fourth day Mount Nisir held the ship fast and did not
let (it) move.

A fifth day, a sixth day Mount Nisir held the ship fast and did not let
(it) move.

When the seventh day arrived,
I sent forth a dove and let (her) go.
The dove went away and came back to me;
There was no resting-place, and so she returned.
(Then) I sent forth a swallow and let (her) go.
The swallow went away and came back to me;
There was no resting-place, and so she returned.
(Then) I sent forth a raven and let (her) go.
The raven went away, and when she saw that the waters had abated,
She ate, she flew about, she cawed, (and) did not return.
(Then) I sent forth (everything) to the four winds and offered a sacrifice.
I poured out a libation on the peak of the mountain.
Seven and (yet) seven kettles I set up.
Under them I heaped up (sweet) cane, cedar, and myrtle.
The gods smelled the savor,
The gods smelled the sweet savor.
The gods gathered like flies over the sacrificer.
As soon as the great goddess arrived,
She lifted up the great jewels which Anu had made according to her wish:
'O ye gods here present, as surely as I shall not forget the lapis lazuli on my neck,
I shall remember these days and shall not forget (them) ever!
Let the gods come near to the offering;
(But) Enlil shall not come near to the offering,
Because without reflection he brought on the deluge
And consigned my people to destruction!'
As soon as Enlil arrived
And saw the ship, Enlil was wroth;
He was filled with anger against the gods, the Igigi:
'Has any of the mortals escaped? No man was to live through the destruction!'
Ninurta opened his mouth and said, speaking to warrior Enl[il]:
'Who can do things without Ea?
For Ea alone understands every matter.'
Ea opened his mouth and said, speaking to warrior Enlil:
'O warrior, thou wisest among the gods!
How, O how couldst thou without reflection bring on (this) deluge?
On the sinner lay his sin; on the transgressor lay his transgression!
Let loose, that he shall not be cut off; pull tight, that he may not ge[t (too) loose]

Instead of thy sending a deluge, would that a wolf had come and dim[inished] mankind!

(Or) instead of thy sending a deluge, would that a famine had occurred and [destroyed] the land!

(Or) instead of thy sending a deluge, would that Irra had come and smitten mankind!

(Moreover,) it was not I who revealed the secret of the great gods;

(But) to Atrahasis I showed a dream, and so he learned the secret of the gods.

And now take counsel concerning him.'

Then Enlil went up into the ship.

He took my hand and caused me to go aboard.

He caused my wife to go aboard (and) to kneel down at my side.

Standing between us, he touched our foreheads and blessed us:

'Hitherto Utnapishtim has been but a man;

But now Utnapishtim and his wife, shall be like unto us gods.

In the distance, at the mouth of the rivers, Utnapishtim shall dwell!'

So they took me and caused me to dwell in the distance, at the mouth of the rivers.

3. TELL EL-AMARNA LETTERS[3]

286. ABDI-HEBA OF JERUSALEM TO THE KING

[T]o the king, my lord, say. Thus saith Abdi-Heba, thy servant: At the two feet of my lord, the king, seven times and seven times I fall down. What have I done to the king, my lord? They slander me to the king, the lord: "Abdi-Heba has become faithless to the king, his lord." Behold, neither my father nor my mother has put me in this place. The mighty hand of the king has led me into the house of my father. Why should I practise mischief against the king, the lord? As long as the king, my lord, lives I will say to the deputy of the king, [my] lo[rd]: "Why do you love the Habiru, and hate the regents?" But therefore am I slandered before the king, my lord. Because I say: "The lands of the king, my lord are lost," therefore am I slandered to the king, my lord. But let the king, my lord, know (this): After the king, my lord, had appointed a garrison, Eenhamu took i[t] [al]l . . . . [There is n]o garrison here. [So] let the king [c]are for his land. [Let] the king [ca]re for his land. [The land]s of the king, the lord, have all deserted. Ilimilku has devastated the whole land of the king. So let the king, the lord, care for his land. I say: "I will enter into the presence of the king, my lord, and I will see the two eyes of the

---

[3] Translation from Samuel A. B. Mercer, *The Tell El-Amarna Tablets,* The Macmillan Company of Canada, 1939.

king, my lord." But hostility has become mighty against me, and so I cannot come to the king, my lord. So, let it seem right to the king to send a
garrison, and I will enter and see the two e[yes] of the king, my lord.
So long as the king, [my] lor[d] lives, so long as de[puties] go forth, I will
say: "The lands of the king are going to ruin." (But) you do not listen
to me. All regents are lost; there remains not a regent to the king, the lord.
Let the king turn his attention to the archers so that the archers of the
king, my lord, will go forth. No lands of the king remain. The Habiru
plunder all lands of the king. If archers are here this year, then the lands of
the king, the lord, will remain; but if archers are not here, then the lands of
the king, my lord, are lost. [T]o the scribe of the king, my lord, thus saith
Abdi-Heba, thy servant: Bring words, plainly, before the king, my lord:
[A]ll the lands of the king, my lord, are going to ruin.

290. ABDI-HEBA OF JERUSALEM TO THE KING

[To] the king, my lord, say. Thus saith [Abdi]-Heba, thy servant: At the
two feet [of the king], my lord, seven times and seven times I fall down.
[Be]hold, the d[ee]d which Milkilu and Suardatu have committed against
the land of the king, my lord: They have hired soldiers of Gazri, soldiers
of Gimti, and soldiers of Kilti; they have conquered the land of the city
of Rubute. The land of the king has fallen away to the Habiru; and now
in addition to that a city of the land of Jerusalem, whose name is Bit-
Ninib, a city of the king, has gone forth where the people of Kilti are. Let
the king listen to Abdi-Heba, thy servant, and send archers that they may
again restore the land of the king to the king. But if there are no archers the
land of the king will desert to the Habiru. This (will be) the fate of the
la[nd]. [L]et him [smi]te(?) the sons of Milki[lu], [and l]et him sm[it]e(?)
the so[n of Suardat]u . . . . Ginti, and let the king care for [his] land.

4. BAAL AND ANATH[4]

Place corals on her chest as a gift
For the love of Aliyn Baal
   The affection of Pdry, girl of light,
     The devotion of Tly, girl of rain,
      The love of Arsy, girl of Y'bdr.
Like lads and [harbin]gers(?)
At Anath's feet bow and fall
   Prostrate yourselves and honor her.
And say to the Virgin Anath!
   Declare to the Sister-in-Law of Nations:

[4] Translation from Cyrus H. Gordon, *Ugaritic Literature,* Pontifical Biblical Insti-
tute, 1949.

"The message of Aliyn Baal
  The word of Aliy Qrdm:
'Put bread(?) in the earth
  Place mandrakes(?) in the dust
Pour a peace offering in the midst of the fields!
.   .   .   .
To me let thy feet run
  To me let thy legs hasten(?)
For I have a word that I'll tell thee
  A matter that I'll declare to thee
'Tis the word of the tree
  Yea the whisper of the stone
    The murmur of the heavens to the earth
      Of the deeps to the stars.
I understand lightning which the heavens do not know
  A matter that men do not know
    Nor the multitudes of the earth understand.
Come and I shall show it
In the midst of the mountain of me, god of Sapan, in the sanctuary
  In the mountain of mine inheritance, in the good place
    In the hill of Tliyt.' "

We came to the goodness of the land of Dbr
  To the beauty of fields of Shlmmt
We came upon Baal prostrate on the earth.
Dead is Aliyn Baal
  Perished is the Prince, Lord of Earth!
Thereupon Ltpn, God of Mercy,
  Goes down from the throne
    Sits on the footstool
      And from the footstool sits on the earth.
He pours the ashes of grief(?) on his head
  The dust of wallowing on his pate
    For clothing, he is covered with sackcloth(?).
He roams(?) the mountain in mourning(?)
  Yea through the forest in grief(?)
He cuts cheeks and chin
  He lacerates his forearms
He plows the chest like a garden
  Like a vale he lacerates the back.
He lifts his voice
  And shouts:

'Baal is dead!
Woe(?) to the people of Dagan's Son
   Woe(?) to the multitudes of Baal!
I shall go down into the earth.'
Also Anath goes
   And treads every mountain to the midst of the earth
      Every hill to the midst of the fields.
She comes to the good[ness of the land] of Dbr
   The beauty of the fields of [Shl]mmt
She [comes] upon Baal prostra[te on the ea]rth.
   [For clothing] she is covered with sack[cloth](?).

She approaches him
As with the heart of a cow toward her calf
   As with the heart of a ewe toward her lamb
      So is the heart of Anath toward(?) Baal.
She seizes Mo[t] in ripping(?) (his) garment.
   She grabs(?) [him], in tearing (his) clothes.
She lifts her voice
   And [shou]ts:
'Come, Mot, yield my brother!'
And the god Mot replies:
'What dost thou ask, O virgin Anath?
I was going
   And roaming(?)
Every mountain to the midst of the earth
   Every hill to the midst of the fields.
A soul was missing among men
   A soul of the multitudes of the earth.
I arrived at the goodness of the land of Dbr
   The beauty of the fields of Shlmmt.
I meet(?) Aliyn Baal
   I make him like a lamb in my mouth
      Like a kid in my jaws(?) he is crushed(?).'
The Luminary of the God, Sun, glows
   The heavens gleam(?) on account of the god Mot.
A day, two days pass
   From days to months.
The Maiden Anath meets him
As with the heart of a cow toward her calf
   As with the heart of a ewe toward her lamb
      So is the heart of Anath toward(?) Baal.

She seizes the god Mot
With a sword she cleaves him
  With a pitchfork(?) she winnows him
    With fire she burns him
      With millstones she grinds him
        In the fields she plants him
So that the birds do not eat his flesh(?)
  Nor anyone(?) destroy his portion(?)
Flesh(?) calls to flesh(?).

  .   .   .   .

'And if A[liyn Baal] is alive
  And if the Prince, Lor[d of Earth], exists,
In a dream of Ltpn, God of Mercy(?),
  In a vision of the Creator of Creatures
Let the heavens rain oil
  The wadies run with honey
That I may know that Aliyn Baal is alive
  That the Prince, Lord of Earth, exists.'
In a dream of Ltpn, God of Mercy(?),
  In a vision of the Creator of Creatures
The heavens rain oil
  The wadies run with honey.
Ltpn, God of Mercy(?), rejoices.
His feet he sets on the footstool
  He breaks formality(?) and laughs.
He lifts his voice
  And shouts:
'Let me sit and rest
  And let my soul repose in my breast
For Aliyn Baal is alive
  For the Prince, Lord of Earth, exists.'

5. EGYPTIAN LOVE SONGS[5]

The love of my sister is on yonder side
Of the stream in the midst of the fish.
A crocodile stands on the sandbank;
Yet I go down into the water.

[5] Translation from D. Winton Thomas (ed.), *Documents from Old Testament Times,* Thomas Nelson & Sons, New York, 1958.

I venture across the current;
My courage is high upon the waters.
It is thy love which gives me strength;
For thou makest a water-spell for me.
When I see my sister coming,
Then my heart rejoices.
My arms are open wide to embrace her;
My heart is glad in its place

. . . .

When my mistress comes to me

Seven days to yesterday I have not seen my sister,
Sickness has entered into me.
I have become heavy of body,
Forgetful of my own self.
If the greatest physicians come to me,
My heart will not be contented with their remedies,
The lector-priests—there is no way in them;
My sickness will not be discerned.
To say to me, 'She is here', that is what will revive me.
Her name is that which will lift me up,
The coming and going of her messengers is that which will revive my
    heart.
My sister is more beneficial for me than all the medicines;
She is more to me than the collection of medical lore.
My health is her coming in from without.
To see her—then health.
Let her but open her eye—my body is young again.
To speak with her—then I am reinvigorated.
When I embrace her, she drives evil away from me.
[But] she has gone forth from me for seven days.

6. HYMN TO ATON[6]

Thou dost appear beautiful on the horizon of heaven,
    O living Aton, thou who wast the first to live.
When thou hast risen on the eastern horizon,
    Thou hast filled every land with thy beauty.

[6] Translation from D. Winton Thomas (ed.), *Documents of Old Testament Times*,
Thomas Nelson & Sons, New York, 1958.

Thou art fair, great, dazzling, high above every land;
  Thy rays encompass the lands to the very limit of all thou hast
  made.
Being Re, thou dost reach to their limit
  And curb them [for] thy beloved son;
Though thou art distant, thy rays are upon the earth;
  Thou art in their faces, yet thy movements are unknown(?).

When thou dost set on the western horizon,
  The earth is in darkness, resembling death.
Men sleep in the bed-chamber with their heads covered,
  Nor does one eye behold the other.
Were all their goods stolen which are beneath their heads,
  They would not be aware of it.
Every lion has come forth from his den,
  All the snakes bite.
Darkness prevails, and the earth is in silence,
  Since he who made them is resting in his horizon.
At daybreak, when thou dost rise on the horizon,
  Dost shine as Aton by day,
Thou dost dispel the darkness
  And shed thy rays.
The Two Lands are in festive mood,
  Awake, and standing on (their) feet,
For thou has raised them up;
  They cleanse their bodies and take (their) garments;
Their arms are (lifted) in adoration at thine appearing;
  The whole land performs its labour.

All beasts are satisfied with their pasture;
  Trees and plants are verdant.
The birds which fly from their nests, their wings are (spread) in adora-
  tion to thy soul;
  All flocks skip with (their) feet;
All that fly up and alight
  Live when thou hast risen [for] them.
Ships sail upstream and downstream alike,
  For every route is open at thine appearing.
The fish in the river leap before thee,
  For thy rays are in the midst of the sea.

Thou creator of issue in woman, who makest semen into mankind,
  And dost sustain the son in his mother's womb,

Who dost soothe him with that which stills his tears,
 Thou nurse in the very womb, giving breath to sustain all thou dost
  make!
When he issue from the womb to breathe on the day of his birth
 Thou dost open his mouth completely and supply his needs.
When the chick in the egg cheeps inside the shell,
 Thou givest it breath within it to sustain it.
Thou has set it its appointed time in the egg to break it,
 That it may emerge from the egg to cheep at its appointed time;
 That it may walk with its feet when it emerges from it.
How manifold is that which thou hast made, hidden from view!
 Thou sole god, there is no other like thee!
Thou didst create the earth according to thy will, being alone:
 Mankind, cattle, all flocks,
Everything on earth which walks with (its) feet,
 And what are on high, flying with their wings.

The foreign lands of Hurru and Nubia, the land of Egypt—
 Thou dost set each man in his place and supply his needs;
Each one has his food, and his lifetime is reckoned.
 Their tongues are diverse in speech and their natures likewise;
 Their skins are varied, for thou dost vary the foreigners.
Thou dost make the Nile in the underworld,
 And bringest it forth as thou desirest to sustain the people,
As thou dost make them for thyself,
 Lord of them all, who dost weary thyself with them,
Lord of every land, who dost rise for them,
 Thou Aton of the day, great in majesty.

As for all distant foreign lands, thou makest their life,
 For thou hast set a Nile in the sky,
That it may descend for them,
 That it may make waves on the mountains like the sea,
 To water their fields amongst their towns.
How excellent are thy plans, thou lord of eternity!
 The Nile in the sky is for the foreign peoples,
For the flocks of every foreign land that walk with (their) feet,
 While the (true) Nile comes forth from the underworld for Egypt.

Thy rays suckle every field;
 When thou dost rise, they live and thrive for thee.
Thou makest the seasons to nourish all that thou hast made:
 The winter to cool them; the heat that they(?) may taste thee.

Thou didst make the distant sky to rise in it,
  To see all that thou has made.
Being alone, and risen in thy form as the living Aton,
  Whether appearing, shining, distant, or near,
Thou makest millions of forms from thyself alone:
  Cities, towns, fields, road, and river.

Every eye perceives thee level with them,
  When thou art the Aton of the day above the earth(?)
When thou didst go away because all men existed,
  Thou didst create their faces that thou mightest not see [thy]self
  [alone].
  . . . . one . . . . which thou didst make.
Thou art in my heart;
  There is no other that knows thee,
Save thy son Akhenaton,
  For thou has made him skilled in thy plans and thy might.
The earth came into being by thy hand,
  Just as thou didst make them (i.e. mankind).

When thou hast risen, they live;
  When thou dost set, they die.
For thou art lifetime thyself; one lives through thee;
  Eyes are upon (thy) beauty until thou dost set.
All labour is put aside when thou dost set in the west;
  When [thou] risest [thou] makest . . . flourish for the king.
As for all who hasten on foot,
  Ever since thou didst fashion the earth,
Thou dost raise them up for thy son who came forth from thyself,
  The King of Upper and Lower Egypt, Akhenaton.

7. THE ISRAEL OR MERNEPTAH STELA[7]

The sun, dispelling the cloud that was over Egypt,
  Letting To-meri see the rays of the sun disk;
Removing the copper mountain from the neck of the patricians,
  Giving breath to the plebeians who were shut in;
Slaking the desire of Memphis over their foes,
  Making Tjanen rejoice over his adversaries;

[7] Translation from D. Winton Thomas (ed.), *Documents of Old Testament Times*, Thomas Nelson & Sons, New York, 1958.

Opening the doors of Memphis which had been blocked up,
   And letting its temples receive their food(-offerings). . . .

The sole one, restoring the courage of hundreds of thousands,
   For breath enters their nostrils at the sight of him;
Breaking into the land of Temeh in his lifetime;
   Putting eternal terror into the hearts of the Meshwesh;
Making the Libyans, who had trampled Egypt, retreat
   With great dread in their hearts because of To-meri;
Their advanced-troops abandoned their rear,
   Their feet did not stand firm, but ran away;
Their archers cast away their bows,
   The hearts of their running men were faint from travelling;
They loosened their water-skins, which were thrown to the ground,
   Their packs were untied and cast away.

The wretched enemy prince of Libya
   Fled alone in the depth of night;
No feather was on his head, his feet were unshod,
   His wives were seized in his presence;
The grain(?) for his food was taken away,
   He had no water in the water-skin to sustain him.
His brothers' faces were fierce enough to slay him,
   One fought the other amongst his leaders.
Their tents were burned and reduced to ashes;
   All his belongings became food for the soldiers.
When he reached his (own) country, in grief,
   Every survivor in his land was discontented at receiving him. . . .

Great rejoicing has risen in Egypt,
   Jubilation has issued from the towns of To-meri;
They recount the victories
   Which Merneptah wrought in Tehenu:
'How beloved he is, the victorious ruler!
   How exalted is the king among the gods!
How fortunate he is, the master of command!
   Ah, how pleasant it is to sit when one is engaged in chatter'!

One may walk freely on the road,
   Without any fear in the hearts of men.
Fortresses are left to themselves;
   Wells are open, accessible to messengers;

The ramparts of the encircling wall are secure in the sunlight
  Until their watchmen awake.
The Medjay are stretched out in sleep,
  The Tjukten hunt in the fields as they wish. . . .

The princes lie prostrate, saying, 'Salaam'!
  Not one lifts his head among the Nine Bows.
Destruction for Tehenu! Hatti is pacified;
  Canaan is plundered with every evil;
Ashkelon is taken; Gezer is captured;
  Yanoam is made non-existent;
Israel lies desolate; its seed is no more;
  Hurru has become a widow for To-meri;
All the lands in their entirety are at peace,
  Everyone who was a nomad has been curbed by King Merneptah.

8. THE MOABITE STONE[8]

I am Mesha, son of Chemosh- . . . , king of Moab, the Dibonite. My
father was king over Moab thirty years and I became king after my father.
And I made this sanctuary for Chemosh at Qrchh, [a sanctuary of] salvation; for he saved me from all the kings and let me see my desire upon
my adversaries. Omri, king of Israel, he oppressed Moab many days, for
Chemosh was angry with his land. And his son succeeded him and he too
said, 'I will oppress Moab.' In my days he spoke (thus), and I saw my
desire upon him and upon his house, when Israel perished utterly for ever.
And Omri had taken possession of the land of Medeba and [Israel] dwelt
in it his days and half the days of his son, forty years; but Chemosh dwelt
in it in my days. And I built Baal-meon and made in it the reservoir, and I
built Qaryaten. And the men of Gad had long dwelt in the land of Ataroth,
and the king of Israel had built Ataroth for himself. But I fought against
the town and took it and I slew all the people of the town, a spectacle for
Chemosh and Moab. And I brought back from there the altar-hearth of
David and I dragged it before Chemosh at Qeriyoth. And I settled there the
men of Sharon and the men of Mchrt. And Chemosh said to me, 'Go, take
Nebo against Israel.' And I went by night and fought against it from the
break of dawn till noon; and I took it and slew all: seven thousand men,
boys, women, and [girls] and female slaves, for I had consecrated it to
Ashtar-Chemosh. And I took from there the vessels of Yahweh and

[8] Translation from D. Winton Thomas (ed.), *Documents of Old Testament Times*,
Thomas Nelson & Sons, New York, 1958.

dragged them before Chemosh. And the king of Israel had built Jahaz and he dwelt in it while fighting against me. But Chemosh drove him out before me. And I took from Moab two hundred men all of them leaders and led them up against Jahaz and took it to annex it to Dibon. I built Qrchh, the walls of the parks and the walls of the mound; and I built its gates and I built its towers; and I built the king's house; and I made both the reservoirs for water inside the town. And there was no cistern inside the town at Qrchh, so I said to all the people, 'Make yourselves each one a cistern in his house.' And I had ditches dug for Qrchh by prisoners of Israel. I built Aroer and I made the road by the Arnon. I built Beth-bamoth, for it was destroyed; I built Bezer, for it was in ruins, with fifty men of Dibon, for all Dibon is under my authority. And I reigned [over] hundreds of towns which I had annexed to the country. And I built . . . Medeba and Beth-Diblathen and Beth-Baal-Meon, and I led up there the breeders of the sheep of the land. And as for Hauronen, there dwelt in it . . . Chemosh said to me, 'Go down, fight against Hauronon.' And I went down . . . [and there dwelt] in it Chemosh in my days . . . from there . . . and I . . .

9. THE SILOAM INSCRIPTION[9]

(? the completing of) the piercing through. And this is the story of the piercing through. While (the stone-cutters were swinging their) axes, each towards his fellow, and while there were yet three cubits to be pierced through, (there was heard) the voice of a man calling to his fellow, for there was a crevice(?) on the right . . . And on the day of the piercing through, the stone-cutters struck through each to meet his fellow, axe against axe. Then ran the water from the Spring to the Pool for twelve hundred cubits, and a hundred cubits was the height of the rock above the head of the stone-cutters.

10. ASSYRIAN ANNALS[10]

Shalmaneser III: The Battle of Karkar, 853 B.C.
    From the Euphrates I departed, I drew near to Halman (Aleppo). They were afraid to fight with (me), they seized my feet. Silver, gold, as their tribute I received. I offered sacrifices before the god Adad of

[9] Translation from D. Winton Thomas (ed.), *Documents of Old Testament Times,* Thomas Nelson & Sons, New York, 1958.
[10] Translations from D. D. Luckenbill, *Ancient Records of Assyria and Babylonia,* University of Chicago Press, 1926.

Halman. From Halman I departed. To the cities of Irhuleni, the Hama-thite, I drew near. The cities of Adennu, Barga, Argana, his royal cities, I captured. His spoil, his property, the goods of his palaces, I brought out. I set fire to his palaces. From Argana I departed. To Karkar I drew near.

Karkar, his royal city, I destroyed, I devastated, I burned with fire, 1,200 chariots, 1,200 cavalry, 20,000 soldiers, of Hadadezer, of Aram (? Damascus); 700 chariots, 700 cavalry, 10,000 soldiers of Irhuleni of Hamath, 2,000 chariots, 10,000 soldiers of Ahab, the Israelite, 500 sol-diers of the Gueans, 1,000 soldiers of the Musreans, 10 chariots, 10,000 soldiers of the Irkanateans, 200 soldiers of Matinuba'il, the Arvadite, 200 soldiers of the Usanateans, 30 chariots, . . .,000 soldiers of Adunu-ba'il, the Shianean, 1,000 camels of Gindibu, the Arabian, . . .,000 soldiers of Ba'sa, son of Ruhubi, the Ammonite,—these twelve kings he brought to his support; to offer battle and fight, they came against me. (Trusting) in the exalted might which Assur, the lord, had given (me), in the mighty weapons, which Nergal, who goes before me, had presented (to me), I battled with them. From Karkar, as far as the city of Gilzau, I routed them. 14,000 of their warriors I slew with the sword. Like Adad, I rained destruction upon them. I scattered their corpses far and wide, (and) cov-ered (lit., filled) the face of the desolate plain with their widespreading armies. With (my) weapons I made their blood to flow down the val-leys(?) of the land. The plain was too small to let their bodies fall, the wide countryside was used up in burying them. With their bodies I spanned the Arantu (Orontes) as with a bridge(?). In that battle I took from them their chariots, their cavalry, their horses, broken to the yoke.

Shalmaneser III: Tribute of Jehu of Israel, 842 B.C.

Tribute of Iaua (Jehu), son of Omri (*mar Humri*). Silver, gold, a golden bowl, a golden beaker, golden goblets, pitchers of gold, lead, staves for the hand of the king, javelins, I received from him.

Sargon: The Fall of Samaria, 722 B.C.

At the beginning of my rule, in my first year of reign. . . . Sameri-nai (the people of Samaria). . . . of Shamash who causes me to at-tain victory. . . . 27,290 people, who lived therein I carried away; 50 chariots for my royal equipment, I selected from among them. . . . The city I rebuilt, I made it greater than it was before; people of the lands my hand had conquered, I settled therein. My official I placed over them as governor. Tribute, tax, I imposed upon them as upon the As-syrians. . . .

Sennacherib: The Jerusalem Campaign, 701 B.C.

The officials, nobles and people of Ekron, who had thrown Padi, their king, bound by (treaty to) Assyria, into fetters of iron and had given him over to Hezekiah, the Jew (Iaudai),—he kept him in confinement like an enemy,—they became afraid and called upon the Egyptian kings, the bowmen, chariots and horses of the king of Meluhha (Ethiopia), a countless host, and these came to their aid. In the neighborhood of the city of Altaku (Eltekeh), their ranks being drawn up before me, they offered battle. (Trusting) in the aid of Assur, my lord, I fought with them and brought about their defeat. The Egyptian charioteers and princes, together with the charioteers of the Ethiopian king, my hands took alive in the midst of the battle. Altaku (and) Tamna I besieged, I captured and took away their spoil. I drew near to Ekron and slew the governors and nobles who had committed sin and hung their bodies on stakes around the city. The citizens who had sinned and treated (Assyria) lightly, I counted as spoil. The rest of them, who were not guilty of sin and contempt, who were without sin,—I spoke their pardon. Padi, their king, I brought out of Jerusalem, I set him on the royal throne over them and imposed upon him my kingly tribute. As for Hezekiah, the Jew, who did not submit to my yoke, 46 of his strong, walled cities, as well as the small cities in their neighborhood, which were without number,—by escalade and by bringing up siege engines(?), by attacking and storming on foot, by mines, tunnels and breaches(?), I besieged and took (those cities). 200,150 people, great and small, male and female, horses, mules, asses, camels, cattle and sheep, without number, I brought away from them and counted as spoil. Himself, like a caged bird, I shut up in Jerusalem, his royal city. Earthworks I threw up against him,—the one coming out of his city gate I turned back to his misery. The cities of his, which I had despoiled, I cut off from his land and to Mitinti, king of Ashdod, Padi, king of Ekron, and Silli-bel, king of Gaza, I gave them. And (thus) I diminished his land. I added to the former tribute, and laid upon him as their yearly payment, a tax (in the form of) gifts for my majesty. As for Hezekiah, the terrifying splendor of my majesty overcame him, and the Urbi (Arabs) and his mercenary(?) troops which he had brought in to strengthen Jerusalem, his royal city, deserted him. In addition to 30 talents of gold and 800 talents of silver, (there were) gems, antimony, jewels(?), large *sandu*-stones, couches of ivory, house chairs of ivory, elephant's hide, ivory, maple(?), boxwood, all kinds of valuable (heavy) treasures, as well as his daughters, his harem, his male and female musicians, (which) he had (them) bring after me to Nineveh, my royal city. To pay tribute and to accept servitude he dispatched his messengers.

11. THE CYRUS CYLINDER[11]

In all lands everywhere he (i.e. Marduk) searched, he looked through them and sought a righteous prince, after his own heart, whom he took by the hand. Cyrus, king of Anshan, he called by name, to lordship over the whole world he appointed him. The land of Qutu, all the Umman-manda, he cast down at his feet. The black-headed people, whom he gave his hands to conquer, he took them in justice and righteousness. Marduk, the great lord, looked joyously on the caring for his people, on his pious works and his righteous heart. To his city Babylon he caused him to go, he made him take the road to Babylon, going as a friend and companion at his side. His numerous troops, in number unknown, like the waters of a river, marched armed at his side. Without battle and conflict he permitted him to enter Babylon. He spared his city Babylon a calamity. Nabonidus, the king, who did not fear him, he delivered into his hand. All the people of Babylon, of Sumer and Akkad, princes and governors, fell down before him and kissed his feet. They rejoiced in his sovereignty, their faces shone. The lord, who by his power brings the dead to life, who amid destruction(?) and injury(?) had protected them, they blessed him joyously, honoring his name.

I am Cyrus, king of the world, the great king, the powerful king, king of Babylon, king of Sumer and Akkad, king of the four quarters of the world, son of Cambyses, the great king, king of the city of Anshan, grandson of Cyrus, the great king, king of the city of Anshan; great-grandson of Teispes, the great king, king of the city of Anshan; eternal seed of royalty whose rule Bel and Nabu love, whose government they rejoice in in their heart. When I made my triumphal entrance into Babylon with joy and rejoicing I took up my lordly residence in the royal palace, Marduk, the great lord, moved the noble heart of the inhabitants of Babylon to me, while I gave daily care to his worship. My numerous troops marched peacefully into Babylon. In all Sumer and Akkad I permitted no enemy to enter. The needs of Babylon and of all its cities I gladly took heed to. The people of Babylon [and . . .], and the dishonoring yoke was removed from them. Their dwellings, which had fallen, I restored. I cleared out their ruins. Marduk, the great lord, rejoiced in my pious deeds, and graciously blessed me, Cyrus, the king who worships him, and Cambyses, my own son, and all my troops, while we, before him, joyously praised his exalted godhead. All the kings dwelling in palaces, of all the quarters of the earth, from the Upper to the Lower sea dwelling . . . all the kings of the Westland dwelling in tents brought me their heavy tribute, and in Babylon kissed my feet. From

[11] Translation from R. W. Rogers, *Cuneiform Parallels to the Old Testament,* The Abingdon Press, 1926.

. . . to Asshur and Susa, Agade, Eshnunak, Zamban, Meturnu, Deri, with
the territory of the land of Gutium, the cities on the other side of the Tigris,
whose sites were of ancient foundation—the gods, who dwelt in them, I
brought them back to their places, and caused them to dwell in a habitation
for all time. All their inhabitants I collected and restored them to their
dwelling places. And the gods of Shumer and Akkad, whom Nabonidus, to
the anger of the lord of the gods, had brought into Babylon, by command
of Marduk, the great lord, I caused them peacefully to take up their dwelling in habitations that rejoiced the heart. May all the gods, whom I brought
into their cities, pray daily before Bel and Nabu for long life for me, and
may they speak a gracious word for me and say to Marduk, my lord, "May
Cyrus, the king who worships thee, and Cambyses, his son, their . . . I
permitted all to dwell in peace. . . ."

INDEX OF SUBJECTS

INDEX OF AUTHORS

INDEX OF BIBLICAL REFERENCES

The books are listed in their order in the English versions.